Business, Institutions, and Ethics
A Text with Cases and Readings

Business, Institutions, and Ethics
A Text with Cases and Readings

John W. Dienhart
Seattle University

New York   Oxford
OXFORD UNIVERSITY PRESS
2000

Oxford University Press

Oxford   New York
Athens   Auckland   Bangkok   Bogotá   Buenos Aires   Calcutta
Cape Town   Chennai   Dar es Salaam   Delhi   Florence   Hong Kong   Istanbul
Karachi   Kuala Lumpur   Madrid   Melbourne   Mexico City   Mumbai
Nairobi   Paris   São Paulo   Singapore   Taipei   Tokyo   Toronto   Warsaw

and associated companies in
Berlin   Ibadan

Published by Oxford University Press, Inc.,
198 Madison Avenue, New York, New York, 10016
http://www.oup-usa.org
1-800-334-4249

Library of Congress Cataloging-in-Publication Data
Dienhart, John William.
Business, institutions, and ethics : a text with cases and
readings / by John W. Dienhart.
p.   cm.
ISBN 0-19-508080-7 (pbk.)
1. Business ethics.   2. Business ethics—Case studies.   3. Social
responsibility of business—Case studies.   I. Title.
HF5387.D543   1999
174'.4—DC21   99 17556
                                                    CIP

Printing (last digit): 9 8 7 6 5
Printed in the United States of America
on acid-free paper

for Jean

Contents

Part III
Applying the Framework: Cases and Articles

Foreword

There are numerous books on business ethics, and business and society. There are many books on ethics and the law. But until the publication of John Dienhart's *Business, Institutions, and Ethics,* there has been no book that tackled all three subjects, and treated them as integrated concepts in the conduct of business.

Dienhart's groundbreaking work argues that the phenomenon of commerce or business is not merely a collection of economic contracts and exchanges. Ethics, the rule of law, and the relation between business and society are all integral to business, as much a part of business as economics. Dienhart analyzes what he calls the "institutional infrastructures" of ethics, economics, and law in which the conduct of business takes place. These economic, ethical, social, and legal infrastructures work on the macro, mezzo, and individual levels to create markets, organize and run corporations, and execute business decisions.

What is unique about *Business, Institutions, and Ethics* is the way in which Dienhart integrates all these aspects of business in a text that is clearly written, comprehensive, and accessible to students and practitioners. The book is a "must read" for scholars, students, and practitioners.

PATRICIA H. WERHANE
Ruffin Professor of Business Ethics
Darden School of Business
University of Virginia

Preface

I had been teaching business ethics for about five years when I realized that I had no coherent answer to the question, "What is business ethics?" Of course, I knew the *topics* covered by business ethics. What I did not know was what tied these topics together beyond what the term "business ethics" implies: a list of topics resulting from the intersection of business and ethics.

The problem with this definitional approach is that people disagree about what ethics is. Is ethics about individuals or relationships, rights or care? People also disagree about what business is. Is education a business? What about medicine? The definitional approach will work only if we already agree about the antecedent definitions.

As I began to read the business and society literature, which is based in the social sciences, I discovered another question that I could not answer: What is the difference between the disciplines of business and society and business ethics? I knew the traditional answer: business ethics is prescriptive while business and society is descriptive. Unfortunately, the answer did not seem to fit the facts. Business ethics often *describes* how business operates in its attempt to prescribe how it should operate. Business and society may not always be overtly prescriptive, but the point of the discipline is to help managers make *better* decisions. The use of the word "better" presupposes some normative point of view.

To answer these questions, I examined the topics covered by business and society and business ethics to see if I could find patterns of similarities and differences. I soon found that both disciplines discussed many of the same topics. (A distillation of these topics appears below.) While examining this list, however, I noticed that both disciplines often relied on psychology, ethics, economics, and law. I became more confused—it was definitely not a case of "The more the merrier." Then I remembered Benedict Spinoza and his view of neutral monism.

Spinoza was discussing the mind–body problem, and he was especially worried about dualism. Dualists, like Descartes, hold that the mind and body are two completely different things: body is physical and mind is nonphysical. The problem is that it is very difficult to explain how the physical and the nonphysical are connected. Spinoza argued the connection problem could never be solved because the dualistic premise was wrong. He argued, instead, that human beings were made of just *one* kind of substance that had mental and physical *qualities*. This is called "monism" because it posits just one substance; it is called "neutral" because this substance is neither mental nor physical.

Taking Spinoza's lead, I began to think of psychology, ethics, economics, and law as disciplines that studied qualities or aspects. But I still had no answer to the question, "Qualities or aspects of what?" In 1993 I was led to the work of Douglass North and Robert Fogel. They had just won the Nobel Prize for Economics for their work on how social institutions affect economic efficiency. I devoured their writings, especially North's. Although the analogy is far from perfect, I began to think of social institutions as a neutral substance in which business transactions take place. This institutional "substance" has psychological, ethical, economic, and legal qualities.

UNIFYING DIVERSE ISSUES

One advantage of an institutional approach is that it unifies the many topics covered by the disciplines of business ethics and business and society. Consider the following list:

- The effect of GATT on global economic development
- Child labor at home and abroad
- The effect of NAFTA on Mexico's environment
- Truth in advertising
- Plant closings
- Whistleblowing
- Requiring overtime that forces an employee to miss a school conference

These topics arise in *markets* that are embedded in social institutions that guide behavior, involve *organizations* that have internal structures (institutions) that guide behavior, and involve *individuals* making decisions in the context of market and organizational institutions and relationships. Topics that arise at one level of analysis are often connected to topics that arise in the other two levels.[1]

I do not pretend to offer a definitive answer to the questions with which I began: What is business ethics and how does it differ from business and society? The institutional view does, however, provide a useful heuristic for understanding the similarities and differences of these two disciplines.

Business ethics focuses on how we use and should use traditional ethical views to evaluate how institutions orchestrate human behavior. Since institutions use economic and legal incentives that themselves presuppose a view of human psychology, business ethics must include or assume economic, legal, and psychological explanations of how humans behave.

Business and society focuses on how economic and legal incentives intersect with human psychology. Since individuals and (business) groups use ethical concepts to evaluate institutions, make plans, and stake claims, business and society must include or assume ethical analyses.

The institutional approach developed here suggests that business ethics and business and society are inseparable. Yet, it is useful to focus on one or the other, as academics and practitioners have done for some time. It is also useful to examine the individual disciplines on which the two disciplines rely, as long we keep in mind the larger context in which they arise.

BUILDING A MODEL OF THE BUSINESS ENVIRONMENT

One way to understand how psychological, ethical, economic, and legal aspects of institutions fit together is to *build a model of the institutional settings of business.* A model can help us because we have limited, or bounded, rationality, and because the institutional settings of business are complex.

The institutional model we will build is similar to those that meteorologists build to understand and predict the weather. Like business, weather has an enormous number of elements and relationships. Meteorologists choose the most important features of the weather: wind speed and direction, temperature, humidity, dew point, etc. Meteorological models can even take into account the presence of large cities. They do not, however, differentiate between cities of 1 million and 1.1 million, nor do they differentiate between groupings of 40-story buildings and groupings of 30-story buildings, although these features may affect the weather. The model includes only the most important items and relationships, and even these must be simplified. This makes the model workable, but imprecise. There can be many good models of the business environment; this book develops only one.

There are four steps to building a model.

1. Choose the basic elements of the model
2. Choose concepts and principles to interpret and configure the basic elements
3. Test the model
4. Use test results to evaluate the model.

The book opens with a case study, S and R Electronics (A). The officers of S and R must decide whether to move production overseas. They consider market, organizational, and individual variables to make their decision. This case is used to illustrate and integrate the concepts and principles in Parts I and II that are used to construct the model.

Parts I and II of this book are devoted to steps 1 and 2 of model building. Part I presents three articles, each of which is devoted to one element of the model.

- Markets
- Organizations
- Individuals

Part II uses concepts and principles from four disciplines to interpret and configure the relationships between markets, organizations, and individuals.

- Psychology
- Ethics
- Economics
- Law

Part II has a chapter devoted to each discipline. It also includes a seven-step decision-making strategy that shows how principles from these four disciplines can help us make managerial decisions.

Part III contains readings (articles and cases) that cover a wide range of domestic and international issues. These readings are categorized by traditional economic market categories: property, risk–reward relationships, information, and competition. These readings are useful in two ways. First, they provide examples for applying and interpreting the model. Second, they are a way of testing the model; the definitive test, of course, is when the model is used to guide managerial decision making.

The progression from the need for a model to its construction is illustrated in Figure P.1.

Building a model of this complexity may seem too ambitious for one book and one

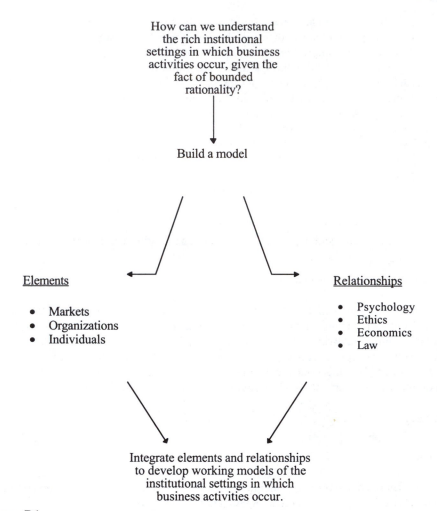

How can we understand
the rich institutional
settings in which business
activities occur, given the
fact of bounded
rationality?

Build a model

<u>Elements</u>   <u>Relationships</u>

- Markets   - Psychology
- Organizations   - Ethics
- Individuals   - Economics
                                            - Law

Integrate elements and relationships
to develop working models of the
institutional settings in which
business activities occur.

Figure P.1

course. The goal is realistic, however, because most people already have a set of beliefs, what social scientists call a "cognitive model," about how markets, organizations, and individuals do and should work together. These cognitive models can be vague, specific, or somewhere in-between. This book is designed to help readers better understand their cognitive models about how business does and should operate, allowing them to adapt more easily to the dynamic world of business. To this end, the book adopts a critical, conversational style.

ACKNOWLEDGMENTS

Many people helped me with this book. First, there is my family, who put up with my evenings and weekends upstairs in my office, and who gave me so much love that I rarely felt alone in those solitary hours. Special thanks go to Patricia Werhane, who encouraged me with the project from the beginning. As a reviewer, she advised me to pay more attention to the individual, organizational, and market levels of analysis. As the reader can see, these levels are now an integral part of this book. Norman Bowie was also very helpful. He pointed out several problems: some needed therapeutic revision whereas others required surgery. I am also grateful to the anonymous reviewers.

R. Edward Freeman, Stefanie Lenway, and Ian Maitland played crucial roles in helping me understand the complex world of business, economics, and society. In 1985 I received a grant from the Bush Foundation to study business at the University of Minnesota's Carlson School of Management. I could not have hoped for a more inspiring and knowledgeable group of people. Their influence bubbles up throughout these pages. Thomas Dunfee made several suggestions that greatly improved the chapter on law. Craig Dunn helped me to understand why it is important for the book to be "incomplete," that is, not following up all arguments and theses to what I take to be their inevitable conclusions. This has at least two benefits: first, it gives readers more opportunities to use the text creatively and usefully, and second, it helps avoid tediousness and redundancy. Readers can decide how well I followed this advice. I also want to thank three people who have inspired and guided me by their research and their scholarly personae: A. R. Gini, Kenneth Goodpaster, and Deborah Vidaver-Cohen.

I owe a special debt of gratitude to Barbara Seefeldt, Matthias Steup, John Bahde, and the rest of the Department of Philosophy at St. Cloud State University for giving me a teaching schedule that made research possible. Dean Michael Connaughton and his successor, Roland Specht-Jarvis, have been exceptionally helpful. My Department and College accorded me every kindness and convenience. St. Cloud State University's support for this project goes back to 1984, when Dennis Nunes, then Assistant Vice President of Academic Affairs, helped me secure the Bush Grant mentioned above. Dave Carr, then Associate Dean of the College of Social Science, also helped by involving me in his three-year FIPSE grant on professional ethics. George Yoos deserves special mention. He took me under his wing when I arrived at St. Cloud in 1979, and taught me how to work and flourish in organizational settings. George arranged for me to teach business ethics courses in our College of Business, which was the beginning of my interest in the subject.

Sandra Foderick was a wonderful research assistant. She also proofread an early draft and helped critique the book from a student point of view. Tammy Sandy worked overtime getting copyright permission for the cases and articles. Christy Eichenberger helped prepare the final manuscript for submission. Carolina Randolph Steup proofread the final versions of the manuscript and made many useful suggestions. I greatly appreciate their persistence, organizational skills, and their willingness to help. Jean Boler read through the final manuscript, giving me many useful suggestions. Wendy Boucher cared for our daughter, Rose, for the six years I worked on this book. A more devoted and loving Nanny could not be found.

Finally, I want to thank Elmer Klemke, a fabulous philosopher and teacher. His joy of philosophy inspires me to this day.

J.W.D.

Note

Richard De George. *Competing with Integrity in International Business.* New York: Oxford University Press, 1993, pp. 97–99.

Business, Institutions, and Ethics
A Text with Cases and Readings

Introduction

The two main pillars of art and science are curiosity and criticism.

—JOHN STEINBECK

That business has an ethical dimension, as well as an economic and a legal dimension, is now widely accepted. There is no consensus, however, about the nature of this ethical dimension. Some argue for a *stockholder* view: managers have an ethical duty to increase the returns to the owners. To meet this duty, managers should act only in accord with the impersonal market forces that demand efficiency and profit. Others argue for a *stakeholder* view: managers have an ethical duty to respect the rights or promote the good of all those affected by the firm. Stakeholders can include "suppliers, customers, employees, stockholders and the local community, as well as management in its role as agent for these groups."[1]

The stockholder and the stakeholder views both hold that managers have ethical duties, but they disagree about what those duties are and to whom they are owed. One way of understanding this disagreement is to note that in the stockholder view ethics and economics intersect primarily at the market level, whereas in the stakeholder view ethics and economics intersect at the market, organizational, and individual levels.

Milton Friedman[2] argues for a stockholder view, asserting that ethics and business intersect primarily at the market level. If managers increase profits and use these profits to increase stockholder value, they respect the property rights of the shareholders and promote the general social good. If managers rely on ethics to make day-to-day business decisions, they violate their duties to the owners and interfere with the market's ability to promote the general welfare.

Philip Cochran[3] argues for a stakeholder theory of the firm based on ownership. He argues that there are more models of ownership than Friedman acknowledges. Owners can be employees, consumers, suppliers, and even the community. With the growth of pension funds and mutual funds, millions of people have joined the ranks of owners.

Ethics intersects with economics at the market, organizational, and individual levels because owners have interests that arise at each level.

R. Edward Freeman[4] also argues that ethics intersects with business at all three levels. Businesses and individuals cannot avoid using ethical standards in their day-to-day decisions because business decisions benefit some stakeholders and harm others. The decision to distribute benefits and harms in one way rather than another is an ethical one. Managers need to respect the rights of all stakeholders because they are human beings with intrinsic value.

Each of these theorists uses ethical, economic, and legal reasons to support their view of the ethical role of management.

Ethical reasons. Friedman cites the property rights of the owners and the tendency of efficient markets to promote group welfare; Cochran cites the way ethical duties follow property rights; Freeman cites the duty of managers to respect the rights of all stakeholders.

Economic reasons. Friedman cites competitive market forces and the need for firms to make a profit; Cochran cites the need for all stakeholders to get a return on their contribution; Freeman cites the need for stakeholders to work together to generate profits.

Legal reasons. Friedman cites the legal status of the corporation and the fiduciary duties of managers; Cochran cites how law creates and enforces the ownership structures of firms; Freeman cites the legal contracts between labor and management and case law that supports the rights of nonowning stakeholders.

To evaluate these competing views we need to understand the institutional infrastructures in which business occurs. According to Douglass North, "Institutions are . . . humanly devised constraints that structure political, economic and social interaction."[5] These infrastructures are normative; they tell us what we should do. This "should" typically has ethical, economic, and legal aspects.

We will begin our examination of the institutional infrastructure of business by examining a case, S and R Electronics (A), in which managers must make a decision in an institutional environment with conflicting values. Parts I and II use the S and R case to explore the ethical, economic, and legal aspects of the institutional frameworks of business. Part III contains cases and articles that elaborate on and test the institutional view of business presented here.

A UNIFYING CASE STUDY: S AND R ELECTRONICS (A)

The CEO and CFO of S and R Electronics need to decide whether to move production facilities overseas. S and R is embedded in multiple institutions that have ethical, economic, and legal features. There is the town in which S and R is located, the relationships with labor and suppliers, case and statutory law that stipulate the relationships between managers and owners, the court system that disgruntled stakeholders can use to influence S and R, and the international trade regimes that set many of the rules on which S and R will rely if they move overseas. The two managers themselves are embedded in multiple institutions that guide their behavior in their jobs, marriages, divorce settlements, parenting, and charitable activities.

PART I: MARKETS, ORGANIZATIONS, AND INDIVIDUALS

Chapter 1: Market Institutions, Organizational Practices, and Individual Decision Making

The first chapter contains three articles that set the stage for the more detailed presentations in Part II. The first article, "Institutions," is by Douglass C. North. According to North,

> Institutions are . . . humanly devised constraints that structure political, economic and social interaction. They consist of both informal constraints (sanctions, taboos, customs, traditions, and codes of conduct), and formal rules (constitutions, laws, property rights). Throughout history, institutions have been devised by human beings to create order and reduce uncertainty in exchange. Together with the standard constraints of economics they define the choice set and therefore determine transaction and production costs and hence the profitability and feasibility of engaging in economic activity.[6]

Institutions, then, are social mechanisms that use ethical, economic, and legal rules and principles to coordinate behavior, as summarized below.

Ethics. Institutions tell us what we should do in particular situations. If we have borrowed money, we should pay it back. If employees have done their job, they should be paid. At a more specific level, institutions specify how houses are bought and how trades are executed on the New York Stock Exchange. These economic institutions are *partly constituted* by ethical rules that require us to tell the truth and keep our promises.

Economics. Institutions "create order and reduce uncertainty in exchange," allowing economic actors to plan for the future. If the future is uncertain, economic actors will not invest in long-term projects. Without long-term projects, business as we know it would not exist.

Institutions also determine how business is organized. In Cuba, for example, citizens cannot form corporations or even hire employees. If a person has a product or service, such as repairing bicycles, and needs more help, the only choice is to bring in people as partners.[7] This contrasts with the United States and most of the rest of world, where the legal status of the corporation makes it the standard way to organize production.

Law. Law is an institution that affects business behavior in many ways. On the institutional view, law is a social institution that reinforces and clarifies other social institutions. For example, much of contract law is based on the institutional practice of promising. We need contract law for at least two reasons. First, it provides the context that makes complex promises possible. Second, it provides an incentive for people to fulfill their contracts when they do not want to.

In the second article, Lynn Sharp Paine argues that organizations are guided by internal institutions[8] that have ethical, economic, and legal features. She describes several companies whose internal institutions encouraged unethical decision making. These decisions resulted in substantial economic loss and legal problems. She goes on to describe three companies that have successfully integrated ethical, economic, and legal princi-ples into their daily work. It is important to note that Paine is not making the old and du-bious claim that "good ethics" has good economic consequences. Instead, she argues that successful organizations are usually proficient in all three areas.

In the third article, David M. Messick and Max H. Bazerman discuss individual de-cision making. They argue that successful decision making requires individuals to have good information about three things: the world, other people, and themselves. Messick and Bazerman discuss the kinds of mistakes we make in these three areas and suggest ways we can avoid them. These mistakes often result from inaccurate perceptions of the institutional infrastructure in which we make decisions.

Taken together, these articles suggest that markets and organizations have ethical, economic, and legal features that individuals need to understand to make sound business decisions. Part II examines these three features in more depth.

PART II: ETHICS, ECONOMICS, AND LAW: AN INSTITUTIONAL APPROACH TO DECISION MAKING

Chapter 2: Ethical Decision Making: Psychological Foundations

Chapter 2 examines some psychological aspects of ethical decision making. The chap-ter begins by discussing the research of two social psychologists: Lawrence Kohl-berg and Carol Gilligan. Kohlberg and Gilligan investigate how individuals learn about and evaluate the ethical aspects of social institutions. This chapter uses their research to help us understand how we perceive the institutions in which business operates.[9]

Although Kohlberg and Gilligan disagree on some major points, they agree on the following:

- Individuals use ethical rules, principles, and concepts in all aspects of their lives. These rules and principles tend to focus on self, personal relationships, groups, and universal responsibilities and principles such as nonviolence and fairness.
- Moral development includes acquiring a better understanding of social institutions and their constituent ethical rules and principles.
- Moral development requires us to critically evaluate institutional rules. Hence, be-coming moral has a rational component.
- Ethical rules and principles serve as information-gathering tools.

The second part of Chapter 2 examines how organizational structure can affect de-cision-making. Linda Trevino, Dennis Gioia, and Irving Janis argue that the internal in-stitutional structure of organizations not only alters how we reason about ethical issues, but also influences what we consider to be ethical issues. The chapter concludes with a seven-step Decision-Making Strategy for Cases.

Chapter 3: Ethical Decision Making: Exploring Alternative Values

In Chapter 2, we saw that we base decisions on self-interest, personal relationships, group welfare, and/or principles such as nonviolence and justice. There is, however, no agreement on what a good self, relationship, or group is. Nor is there agreement about how to interpret nonviolence and justice. To understand these decision-making strategies, Chapter 2 discusses five ethical theories: egoism, care, utilitarianism, intrinsic value theories based on rights and fairness, and pluralism.

Chapter 4: Economics and Ethical Decision Making

Chapter 4 examines the macroinstitutions that form markets and the microinstitutions that form organizations. The first part of the chapter discusses the four conditions of markets: property rights, risk–reward relationships, information, and competition. These economic conditions are partly constituted by the ethical principles and rules discussed in Chapters 2 and 3. Since economic reasoning is partly constituted by ethical principles, and since business decision making has significant economic components, we need ethical concepts to give a *factually* adequate description of business decision making.

The second part of Chapter 4 discusses the goal and contract views of organizations. Each view is connected to broader institutional values. The goal view is associated with the values of loyalty and teamwork, whereas the contract view is associated with the values of autonomy and free agreement. The chapter ends with a discussion of an article by Herbert Simon in which he tries to reformulate the goal view of organizations in view of recent contract theory.

Chapter 5: Law and Ethical Decision Making

The first part of Chapter 5 discusses how law integrates and stabilizes ethical and economic values. On this view, law reinforces and interprets institutional values to provide a predictable social setting for business. Government regulation is discussed in terms of supply and demand. The traditional view of government regulation is that groups demand regulation to pursue a variety of goals. For example, public interest groups may lobby for regulation to promote racial or gender equality, whereas business groups may lobby for government protection from imported products.

Chapter 5 concludes with S and R Electronics (B). The CEO and the CFO receive information about their institutional settings that helps them make an informed decision about relocating their production facilities. They get information about the General Agreement on Tariffs and Trade, the Foreign Corrupt Practices Act, the Federal Sentencing Guidelines for Organizations, and the structure of the semiconductor manufacturing market. This knowledge helps them generate alternatives that can mitigate the harms of the move without sacrificing, and perhaps increasing, the benefits of the move.

In sum, Part II discusses the ethical, economic, and legal–political elements of the social infrastructure in which business operates. The S and R case shows how managers can rely on principles from these three areas to make informed decisions.

PART III: APPLYING THE FRAMEWORK: CASES AND ARTICLES

The Introduction to Part III discusses "A Decision-Making Strategy for Cases" introduced at the end of Chapter 2. Also presented is "A Strategy for Analyzing Articles." Both strategies emphasize the ethical, economic, and legal aspects of the institutional settings of business.

The Introduction to Part III is followed by four chapters of readings (cases and articles) that cover domestic and international issues. The issues are introduced by cases. Each case is a concrete instance in which ethical, economic, and legal institutional values prescribe conflicting behavior. This gives readers an opportunity to use the theoretical material in Parts I and II to clarify issues in the case and to suggest courses of action. It also provides a practical context for the articles that follow the case. The chapters in Part III are based on the four economic conditions of markets: property, risk–reward relationships, information, and competition.

Chapter 6: Property

Chapter 6 focuses on property, with cases on software ownership, domestic and international environmental pollution, and the international trade in human blood. Articles address the stakeholder–stockholder debate, the fiduciary duties of owners, the limits of pollution, and special problems of international trade.

Chapter 7: Risk–Reward Relationships

Chapter 7 focuses on risk–reward relationships, with cases on unethical orders given to an employee, the special risks of women in the workplace, the responsibility of rich multinationals to help the poor in countries in which they do business, and the propriety of bribing foreign officials. Articles address employment at will, employee rights to know about workplace risks, international codes of conduct, and the Foreign Corrupt Practices Act.

Chapter 8: Information

Chapter 8 focuses on information, with cases on deceptive marketing, whistleblowing, and the transfer of dangerous industries to third world countries. Articles address consumer autonomy, employee loyalty, and the plausibility of collective consent.

Chapter 9: Competition

Chapter 9 focuses on competition with cases on using legal loopholes to gain a competitive advantage, moving production to third world countries to save labor costs, and influencing foreign governments to get a competitive advantage. The articles address the ethical consequences of competition and the moral obligations of multinational enterprises to their stakeholders.

A final note. The cases and articles in Part III almost always involve all four economic conditions. I categorized readings to highlight what I believed were their most important issues. You may disagree with my choices, and doing so is in the spirit of the book. The goal is not to argue for a particular categorization of a reading, but to heighten awareness of the ethical, economic, and legal values that constitute the institutional settings of business.

Notes

1. Freeman "A Stakeholder Theory of the Modern Corporation," reprinted in Chapter 6.
2. Friedman, "The Social Responsibility of Business Is to Increase Its Profits," reprinted in Chapter 6.
3. Cochran, "Deriving Ethical Principles from Theories of the Firm," reprinted in Chapter 6.
4. Freeman, "A Stakeholder Theory of the Modern Corporation," reprinted in Chapter 6.
5. North, "Institutions," reprinted in Chapter 1.
6. *Ibid.*
7. Author's field research.
8. This is not the term Paine uses.
9. It should be noted that there are other explanations of moral acquisition, such as the Freudian, behavioral, or social-learning theories. I have argued elsewhere (Dienhart, *A Cognitive Approach to Counseling Psychology*) that the cognitive–developmental theory is, on the whole, more adequate than its competitors, but the reader need not accept this when reading the discussions of cognitive–developmental theory that follow. All the reader needs to accept is that morality has a rational, cognitive component and that rationality is an important part of the story of how we become moral. The extent to which that story needs to be filled in by other psychological principles can be left open.

S and R Electronics (A):
Case Study for Parts I and II

S and R is a small to medium sized business that designs and produces chemical–mechanical planarization (CMP) tools, used for manufacturing semiconductor chips.[1] CMP tools are used by Intel, Motorola, Micron Technology, and Advanced Micro Devices. S and R is located in Frieberg (pronounced FREE-berg), a small town in New England. It is not the largest employer in Frieberg, but it is the most prestigious, and its economic impact on the town is significant. Not only does it supply high-paying jobs, but the professional community that S and R helped spawn has drawn upper middle-class residents from a nearby metropolitan area.

S and R is headed by Anita Jameson. Anita Jameson has been with S and R Electronics for 15 years. Recruited out of a top business school in the East, she spent her first 10 years working her way up to CFO. For the past 5 years she has been CEO. She became CEO in 1991 after engineering a plan that reoriented S and R's business in significant ways.

In 1986, 80% of S and R's output and 60% of its revenue came from the production of electrical components for consumer items such as radios and tape players; 20% of its output and 40% of its revenue came from the production of CMP tools. It acquired its CMP line from a conglomerate that was refocusing its business. In 1988, S and R was under severe price competition from producers outside the United States for their consumer parts. Rather than fight with labor for wage cutbacks and freezes, Jameson suggested S and R eliminate their consumer electronics division and focus instead on CMP tools. She had some preliminary contacts with Sematech, a government-sponsored consortium designed to help the United States regain the lead in semiconductor production. They seemed willing and able to help.

She made her case to the Board of Directors in five ways. First, S and R could not compete with overseas labor costs in the area of consumer electronic components. Second, the semiconductor factor market was relatively stable, since even if the demand for chips went down, the need to retool for the next generation of chips was constant. Third, profit margins for CMP tools were greater than for their consumer electronics parts. Fourth, there was only one other supplier of CMP tools in the United States. Fifth, Sematech's support would give them the edge to succeed. The board was skeptical, but Fred Heslinger, the CEO at that time, and Jameson's mentor, managed to get it through.

Sematech helped S and R secure low-interest loans and a great deal of information about the projected needs of chip manufacturers. They helped Heslinger and Jameson negotiate contracts with Intel and Motorola, who were S and R's first large-scale customers. S and R soon became a major supplier of CMP tools. They used their relationships with Intel and Motorola to create a network to distribute supplies produced by other firms. The growth of the personal computer industry and other industries that depended on chips grew beyond projections, and when the CEO retired in 1991, a majority of the Board voted for Anita Jameson.

S and R now faces a new threat. Although the United States has regained the lead in making high-powered computer chips, overseas producers are starting to focus on dedicated chips that go in everything from cars to toasters. If S and R is going to grow, it needs to supply these overseas producers. However, the high cost of labor and the U.S. location make it difficult for S and R to break into these overseas markets. This problem is not nearly so urgent as the first one Jameson faced, since S and R should remain highly profitable for the next few years, even if they do nothing new. Still, the stock fell 5% when the *Wall Street Journal* did a story on the foreign production of dedicated chips, and mentioned that U.S. producers have a difficult time entering those factor markets. The stock has regained some of its value, but the Board has registered its concerns, as has a pension fund that owns 4% of S and R stock. Further, S and R has a shareholder meeting in 5 months, and shareholders are already complaining about the stock price.

This time Jameson does not see an easy way out. She could try to renegotiate the union contract, but that would take a lot of time, and she believes the chances of success are low. Even if she could lower production costs, that does not address the location problem. Jameson is beginning to think that they should relocate their manufacturing operations overseas, and at this preliminary stage she is thinking of Taiwan. Producing in Taiwan would make it much easier to build ongoing relationships with Asian chip producers. Taiwan has a large number of chip manufacturers, and they have the labor force to support them. Jameson wants to keep their home office in Frieberg. This strategy would have four benefits: first, it would give S and R more access to foreign chip makers; second, it would reduce their labor costs; third, it would send a message to Wall Street that S and R is healthy and growing; and fourth, keeping their office in Frieberg would save some jobs, and allow Frieberg to retain some of its tax base.

The other major decision maker at S and R is the current CFO, John Mamet. In their first formal meeting on this issue, Mamet agreed with Jameson's reasons to relocate. According to his information, labor in Taiwan costs about one-third of U.S. rates. There is no way they could get labor to accept these kinds of cuts. Moving to Taiwan is expensive, but the Taiwanese government has provided other U.S. manufacturers with a package of incentives that has reduced these costs. Both officers believe that S and R could get similar help.

Although Jameson and Mamet are leaning toward relocation, they are not happy with many of its consequences. On a personal level, neither of them relish the travel involved in setting up a new plant. Jameson has a husband and two children. She also is an active member of the community, serving on several charitable boards; she is a deacon at her church. She likes her present life very much, and does not want to spend months away from home. She would have jumped at a chance like this earlier in her life, but now she has other priorities. She is also concerned about her family. Her husband will have a hard time at work if S and R production facilities leave Frieberg. She also fears that her children, high school students, will be harassed and taunted at school.

Mamet also has personal concerns that do not fit with relocation. He is recently divorced and has dual custody of his children. If he were to renegotiate the custody arrangement to fit his travel needs, his wife might get full custody. He does not want to take that chance. Also, he does not like to travel. After his heart attack 2 years ago, he has been exercising regularly and eating a low-fat diet. When he travels on business, it is difficult to maintain the healthy life-style he has fought hard to attain.

Jameson and Mamet are also worried that the union may sue S and R if it tried to relocate. In the summer of 1995, 800 workers received $11.5 million because Maytag breached an implicit contract to keep the plant open. The implicit contract was inferred from management's response to employee concerns about closing the plant. Management stated several times that the jobs in the plant were secure. Because of these promises, many employees purchased homes and other big ticket items such as cars and boats. The trial ended abruptly after 3 days when Maytag rushed to settle the case, fearing an even larger damage award by the jury.[2]

Jameson and Mamet had never explicitly made assurances about keeping their plant going, but when they thought about their statements to the press and in the company newsletter about their "continuing contribution to Frieberg" in the form of jobs, they began to worry. Mamet was especially concerned. His previous company suffered a long and, in his view, irrational strike. The final labor contract did not begin to cover the cost to the strikers. He now believes that labor, or any group standing for "principle," can spend irrational amounts of money and time to pursue their goals.

Suppliers are also an issue. Over the years S and R has depended heavily on two suppliers for specialized components. If S and R tells these suppliers early that they will be leaving, it may not have enough supplies for the last months of production, as these suppliers look for new business and begin retooling. However, if S and R waits until the last minute to notify their suppliers, it puts these suppliers and their employees in jeopardy. Further, Jameson and Mamet are not sure about suppliers in Taiwan yet; they may still need these suppliers after they move.

The two officers are also concerned about the reaction of the local community. Jameson is proud of the relationship she has with the community, and she fears that relocating the plant would violate the trust that underlies that relationship. Mamet is concerned about the possibility of labor unrest, vandalism, and sabotage once they announce plans to move.

Jameson and Mamet have also talked about the benefits to the community where they would relocate. While in college, Mamet spent his junior year in a program that took him and 90 other students on a trip around the Pacific Rim. As a result of that trip, he became convinced of two things: economic development was necessary to ease the poverty he saw and there were opportunities for substantial economic growth in those areas. Although Taiwan is not a poor country, it would provide entry into the entire Asian market, much of which is poor and underdeveloped.

In the past, Jameson and Mamet's decisions tended to promote S and R's interests *and* the well-being of its stakeholders: stockholders, labor, suppliers, community, and themselves. The relocation issue pits these stakeholders against each other. Jameson and Mamet are unsure how to consider these issues since they are so different from each other. In their meeting, Mamet said that the different factors were incommensurate, like apples and oranges. Jameson replied that at least apples and oranges are fruit. This problem, she said, is more like comparing and contrasting pasta, meat, and spices—there seems to be no common standard that applies to them all.

In their second formal meeting on this topic, it became clear to Jameson and Mamet that they could not deal with the economic issues alone. If they were to focus on the concerns of shareholders, and decide to relocate in order to maximize shareholder wealth, they could face suits by labor, suppliers, and perhaps the community itself. The cost of the legal actions and the resulting delays could harm the shareholders more than not relocating. Further, if they are not willing to make personal sacrifices by spending time away from home, the move might fail. Jameson and Mamet know that all of these pieces must fit together, but they do not know what that fit looks like.

Mamet has talked to several companies that have relocated overseas. Many of the companies recommended a consulting agency, the International Consultant Ensemble

(ICE). ICE has the resources to help S and R with all aspects of relocation, including the relocation decision itself. Jameson and Mamet decide to set up a meeting with ICE to discuss the feasibility of relocating. In the meantime, they decide to tell no one of the possibility of relocating, not even their families.

USING THE S AND R CASE

Jameson and Mamet will make their decision in specific market and organizational settings. Part I consists of three articles that explore these settings. The first article discusses markets in terms of social institutions. The second article discusses organizations in terms of their structures and practices, what we will call microinstitutions. The third article discusses individual decision making in market and organizational settings. The four chapters that make up Part II examine ethical, economic, and legal reasoning to help us understand and integrate the diverse issues that arise in the S and R case.

The reader may wonder whether managers ever act like Jameson and Mamet. The answer is yes. We will look at some examples in this book. There are also business decision makers who focus only on shareholders, or themselves, or religious causes, or other issues. Business decision makers, like most people, value all sorts of things. Between them, Jameson and Mamet care about all their constituencies. However, they are not sure they *should* care, given their managerial duties. And if they should care about all of these constituencies, they do not know how to go about it.

Notes

1. The two organizations in this case, S and R and ICE, are fictional, as are all the individuals associated with them. The description of the product and basic market features is based on research. For example, until 1996, CMP tools were made in the United States by two small companies. The advice that ICE gives S and R in Chapter 4 in S and R (B) is based on actual market features. This case presents a business decision-making scenario intended to illustrate and unify the theoretical issues that follow. It is not intended to portray good or bad managerial behavior.
2. P. Kilbourn. "Appliance Maker Agrees to Pay for Moving Away." *New York Times,* Wednesday, Aug. 16, 1995, p. A8, A20.

P A R T

I

Markets, Organizations, and Individuals

CHAPTER 1

Market Institutions, Organizational Practices, and Individual Decision-Making

The officers of S and R will make the relocation decision in a variety of institutional settings. The articles in this chapter discuss these settings, and how individuals make decisions in them.

The first article, "Institutions," is by Douglass C. North. North is a leader in what is sometimes called "New Institutional Economics." He and Robert Fogel won a Nobel prize in 1993 for their contributions to economic theory. We can define institutions as "complexes of norms and behaviors that persist over time by serving collectively valued purposes."[1] Institutions tell us what we should do in a variety of situations. For example, the institution of promise keeping tells us to keep promises even when we do not want to and even though the promisee is a stranger to us.

North argues that social institutions can result in long-term inefficiencies even though efficient methods are readily available. This view departs from neoclassical economics that states that markets will always find the most efficient means to an end. Despite North's rejection of this aspect of neoclassical economics, he accepts many of its assumptions, such as the belief that people are primarily self-interested.

One of the questions North addresses is why England started the seventeenth century much poorer than Spain, but ended the century much richer. Part of the reason is that the social institutions of England allowed self-interest to be channeled in ways that promoted invention, production, and trade. In Spain, the main avenues to well-being were the Church, the courts, and the army, none of which creates wealth.

In the second article, "Managing for Organizational Integrity," Lynn Sharp Paine argues that the rules and principles (microinstitutions) that guide internal organizational relationships affect organizational output. She cites a variety of cases in which companies that promote honest and respectful relationships solve problems better than those that do not. One of the main features of honest and respectful organizations is the efficient transfer of information and use of resources.

In the final article, "Ethical Leadership and the Psychology of Decision Making," David M. Messick and Max H. Bazerman argue that managerial decision making relies on beliefs about the world (for example, how markets and organizations work), beliefs about others (their competence, motives, and ethical beliefs), and beliefs about ourselves (our competence, motives, and ethical beliefs). They discuss several ways our decision making goes wrong in these three areas, and suggest some ways to prevent these mistakes.

Note

1. Norman Uphoff. "Grassroots Organizations and NGO's in Rural Development: Opportunities with Diminishing States and Expanding Markets." *World Development* 21:4 (1993), pp. 607–622.

Douglass C. North

Institutions

Institutions are the humanly devised constraints that structure political, economic and social interaction. They consist of both informal constraints (sanctions, taboos, customs, traditions, and codes of conduct), and formal rules (constitutions, laws, property rights). Throughout history, institutions have been devised by human beings to create order and reduce uncertainty in exchange. Together with the standard constraints of economics they define the choice set and therefore determine transaction and production costs and hence the profitability and feasibility of engaging in economic activity. They evolve incrementally, connecting the past with the present and the future; history in consequence is largely a story of institutional evolution in which the historical performance of economies can only be understood as a part of a sequential story. Institutions provide the incentive structure of an economy; as that structure evolves, it shapes the direction of economic change towards growth, stagnation, or decline. In this essay I intend to elaborate on the role of institutions in the performance of economies and illustrate my analysis from economic history.

What makes it necessary to constrain human interaction with institutions? The issue can be most succinctly summarized in a game theoretic context. Wealth-maximizing individuals will usually find it worthwhile to cooperate with other players when the play is repeated, when they possess complete information about the other player's past performance, and when there are small numbers of players. But turn the game upside down. Cooperation is difficult to sustain when the game is not repeated (or there is an endgame), when information on the other players is lacking, and when there are large numbers of players.

These polar extremes reflect contrasting economic settings in real life. There are many examples of simple exchange institutions that permit low cost transacting under the former conditions. But institutions that permit low cost transacting and producing in a world of specialization and division of labor require solving the problems of human cooperation under the latter conditions.

It takes resources to define and enforce exchange agreements. Even if everyone had the same objective function (like maximizing the firm's profits), transacting would take substantial resources; but in the context of individual wealth-maximizing behavior and asymmetric information about the valuable attributes of what is being exchanged (or the

---

performance of agents), transaction costs are a critical determinant of economic performance. Institutions and the effectiveness of enforcement (together with the technology employed) determine the cost of transacting. Effective institutions raise the benefits of cooperative solutions or the costs of defection, to use game theoretic terms. In transaction cost terms, institutions reduce transaction and production costs per exchange so that the potential gains from trade are realizeable. Both political and economic institutions are essential parts of an effective institutional matrix.

The major focus of the literature on institutions and transaction costs has been on institutions as efficient solutions to problems of organization in a competitive framework (Williamson, 1975; 1985). Thus market exchange, franchising, or vertical integration are conceived in this literature as efficient solutions to the complex problems confronting entrepreneurs under various competitive conditions. Valuable as this work has been, such an approach assumes away the central concern of this essay: to explain the varied performance of economies both over time and in the current world.

How does an economy achieve the efficient, competitive markets assumed in the foregoing approach? The formal economic constraints or property rights are specified and enforced by political institutions, and the literature simply takes those as a given. But economic history is overwhelmingly a story of economies that failed to produce a set of economic rules of the game (with enforcement) that induce sustained economic growth. The central issue of economic history and of economic development is to account for the evolution of political and economic institutions that create an economic environment that induces increasing productivity.

INSTITUTIONS TO CAPTURE THE GAINS FROM TRADE

Many readers will be at least somewhat familiar with the idea of economic history over time as a series of staged stories. The earliest economies are thought of as local exchange within a village (or even within a simple hunting and gathering society). Gradually, trade expands beyond the village: first to the region, perhaps as a bazaar-like economy; then to longer distances, through particular caravan or shipping routes; and eventually to much of the world. At each stage, the economy involves increasing specialization and division of labor and continuously more productive technology. This story of gradual evolution from local autarky to specialization and division of labor was derived from the German historical school. However, there is no implication in this paper that the real historical evolution of economies necessarily paralleled the sequence of stages of exchange described here.[1]

I begin with local exchange within the village or even the simple exchange of hunting and gathering societies (in which women gathered and men hunted). Specialization in this world is rudimentary and self-sufficiency characterizes most individual households. Small-scale village trade exists within a "dense" social network of informal constraints that facilitates local exchange, and the costs of transacting in this context are low. (Although the basic societal costs of tribal and village organization may be high, they will not be reflected in additional costs in the process of transacting.) People have an intimate understanding of each other, and the threat of violence is a continuous force for preserving order because of its implications for other members of society.[2]

As trade expands beyond a single village, however, the possibilities for conflict over the exchange grow. The size of the market grows and transaction costs increase sharply because the dense social network is replaced; hence, more resources must be devoted to measurement and enforcement. In the absence of a state that enforced contracts, religious precepts usually imposed standards of conduct on the players. Needless to say, their effectiveness in lowering the costs of transacting varied widely, depending on the degree to which these precepts were held to be binding.

The development of long-distance trade, perhaps through caravans or lengthy ship voyages, requires a sharp break in the characteristics of an economic structure. It entails substantial specialization in exchange by individuals whose livelihood is confined to trading and the development of trading centers, which may be temporary gathering places (as were the early fairs in Europe) or more permanent towns or cities. Some economies of scale—for example, in plantation agriculture—are characteristic of this world. Geographic specialization begins to emerge as a major characteristic and some occupational specialization is occurring as well.

The growth of long distance trade poses two distinct transaction cost problems. One is a classical problem of agency, which historically was met by use of kin in long-distance trade. That is, a sedentary merchant would send a relative with the cargo to negotiate sale and to obtain a return cargo. The costliness of measuring performance, the strength of kinship ties, and the price of "defection" all determined the outcome of such agreements. As the size and volume of trade grew, agency problems became an increasingly major dilemma.[3] A second problem consisted of contract negotiation and enforcement in alien parts of the world, where there is no easily available way to achieve agreement and enforce contracts. Enforcement means not only such enforcement of agreement but also protection of the goods and services en route from pirates, brigands, and so on.

The problems of enforcement en route were met by armed forces protecting the ship or caravan or by the payment of tolls or protection money to local coercive groups. Negotiation and enforcement in alien parts of the world entailed typically the development of standardized weights and measures, units of account, a medium of exchange, notaries, consuls, merchant law courts, and enclaves of foreign merchants protected by foreign princes in return for revenue. By lowering information costs and providing incentives for contract fulfillment this complex of institutions, organizations, and instruments made possible transacting and engaging in long-distance trade. A mixture of voluntary and semi-coercive bodies, or at least bodies that effectively could cause ostracism of merchants that didn't live up to agreements, enabled long-distance trade to occur.[4]

This expansion of the market entails more specialized producers. Economies of scale result in the beginnings of hierarchical producing organizations, with full-time workers working either in a central place or in a sequential production process. Towns and some central cities are emerging, and occupational distribution of the population now shows, in addition, a substantial increase in the proportion of the labor force engaged in manufacturing and in services, although the traditional preponderance in agriculture continues. These evolving stages also reflect a significant shift towards urbanization of the society.

Such societies need effective, impersonal contract enforcement, because personal ties, voluntaristic constraints, and ostracism are no longer effective as more complex and impersonal forms of exchange emerge. It is not that these personal and social alternatives are unimportant; they are still significant even in today's interdependent world. But in the absence of effective impersonal contracting, the gains from "defection" are great enough to forestall the development of complex exchange. Two illustrations deal with the creation of a capital market and with the interplay between institutions and the technology employed.

A capital market entails security of property rights over time and will simply not evolve where political rulers can arbitrarily seize assets or radically alter their value. Establishing a credible commitment to secure property rights over time requires either a ruler who exercises forebearance and restraint in using coercive force, or the shackling of the ruler's power to prevent arbitrary seizure of assets. The first alternative was seldom successful for very long in the face of the ubiquitous fiscal crises of rulers (largely as a consequence of repeated warfare). The latter entailed a fundamental restructuring of the polity such as occurred in England as a result of the Glorious Revolution of 1688, which resulted in parliamentary supremacy over the crown.[5]

The technology associated with the growth of manufacturing entailed increased fixed capital in plant and equipment, uninterrupted production, a disciplined labor force, and a developed transport network; in short, it required effective factor and product markets. Undergirding such markets are secure property rights, which entail a polity and judicial system to permit low costs contracting, flexible laws permitting a wide latitude of organizational structures, and the creation of complex governance structures to limit the problems of agency in hierarchical organizations.[6]

In the last stage, the one we observe in modern western societies, specialization has increased, agriculture requires a small percentage of the labor force, and markets have become nationwide and worldwide. Economies of scale imply large-scale organization, not only in manufacturing but also in agriculture. Everyone lives by undertaking a specialized function and relying on the vast network of interconnected parts to provide the multitude of goods and services necessary to them. The occupational distribution of the labor force shifts gradually from dominance by manufacturing to dominance, eventually, by what are characterized as services. Society is overwhelmingly urban.

In this final stage, specialization requires increasing percentages of the resources of the society to be engaged in transacting, so that the transaction sector rises to be a large percentage of gross national product. This is so because specialization in trade, finance, banking, insurance, as well as the simple coordination of economic activity, involves an increasing proportion of the labor force.[7] Of necessity; therefore, highly specialized forms of transaction organizations emerge. International specialization and division of labor requires institutions and organizations to safeguard property rights across international boundaries so that capital markets (as well as other kinds of exchange) can take place with credible commitment on the part of the players.

These very schematic stages appear to merge one into another in a smooth story of evolving cooperation. But do they? Does any necessary connection move the players from less complicated to more complicated forms of exchange? At stake in this evolution is not only whether information costs and economies of scale together with the development of improved enforcement of contracts will permit and indeed encourage more complicated forms of exchange, but also whether organizations have the incentive to acquire knowledge and information that will induce them to evolve in more socially productive directions.

In fact, throughout history, there is no necessary reason for this development to occur. Indeed, most of the early forms of organization that I have mentioned in these sections still exist today in parts of the world. There still exist primitive tribal societies; the Suq (bazaar economies engaged in regional trade) still flourishes in many parts of the world; and while the caravan trade has disappeared, its demise (as well as the gradual undermining of the other two forms of "primitive" exchange) has reflected external forces rather than internal evolution. In contrast, the development of European long-distance trade initiated a sequential development of more complex forms of organization.

The remainder of this paper will examine first some seemingly primitive forms of exchange that failed to evolve and then the institutional evolution that occurred in early modern Europe. The concluding section of the paper will attempt to enunciate why some societies and exchange institutions evolve and others do not, and to apply that framework in the context of economic development in the western hemisphere during the 18th and 19th centuries.

WHEN INSTITUTIONS DO NOT EVOLVE

In every system of exchange, economic actors have an incentive to invest their time, resources, and energy in knowledge and skills that will improve their material status. But in some primitive institutional settings, the kind of knowledge and skills that will pay off will not result in institutional evolution towards more productive economies. To illustrate this argument, I consider three primitive types of exchange—tribal society, a regional economy with bazaar trading, and the long-distance caravan trade—that are unlikely to evolve from within.

As noted earlier, exchange in a tribal society relies on a dense social network. Elizabeth Colson (1974, p. 59) describes the network this way:

> The communities in which all these people live were governed by a delicate balance of power, always endangered and never to be taken for granted: each person was constantly involved in securing his own position in situations where he had to show his good intentions. Usages and customs appear to be flexible and fluid given that judgement on whether or not someone has done rightly varies from case to case. . . . But this is because it is the individual who is being judged and not the crime. Under these conditions, a flouting of generally accepted standards is tantamount to a claim to illegitimate power and becomes part of the evidence against one.

The implication of Colson's analysis as well as that of Richard Posner in his account of primitive institutions (1980) is that deviance and innovation are viewed as threats to group survival.

A second form of exchange that has existed for thousands of years, and still exists today in North Africa and the Middle East is that of the Suq, where widespread and relatively impersonal exchange and relatively high costs of transacting exist.[8] The basic characteristics are a multiplicity of small-scale enterprises with as much as 40 to 50 percent of the town's labor force engaged in this exchange process; low fixed costs in terms of rent and machinery; a very finely drawn division of labor; an enormous number of small transactions, each more or less independent of the next; face to face contacts; and goods and services that are not homogeneous.

There are no institutions devoted to assembling and distributing market information; that is, no price quotations, production reports, employment agencies, consumer guides, and so on. Systems of weights and measures are intricate and incompletely standardized. Exchange skills are very elaborately developed, and are the primary determinant of who prospers in the bazaar and who does not. Haggling over terms with respect to any aspect or condition of exchange is pervasive, strenuous, and unremitting. Buying and selling are virtually undifferentiated, essentially a single activity; trading involves a continual search for specific partners, not the mere offers of goods to the general public. Regulation of disputes involves testimony by reliable witnesses to factual matters, not the weighting of competing, juridical principles. Governmental controls over marketplace activity are marginal, decentralized, and mostly rhetorical.

To summarize, the central features of the Suq are (1) high measurement costs; (2) continuous effort at clientization (the development of repeat-exchange relationships with other partners, however imperfect); and (3) intensive bargaining at every margin. In essence, the name of the game is to raise the costs of transacting to the other party to exchange. One makes money by having better information than one's adversary.

It is easy to understand why innovation would be seen to threaten survival in a tribal society but harder to understand why these "inefficient" forms of bargaining would continue in the Suq. One would anticipate, in the societies with which we are familiar, that voluntary organizations would evolve to insure against the hazards and uncertainties of such information asymmetries. But that is precisely the issue. What is missing in the Suq are the fundamental underpinnings of institutions that would make such voluntary organizations viable and profitable. These include an effective legal structure and court system to enforce contracts which in turn depend on the development of political institutions that will create such a framework. In their absence there is no incentive to alter the system.

The third form of exchange, caravan trade, illustrates the informal constraints that made trade possible in a world where protection was essential and no organized state existed. Clifford Geertz (1979, p. 137) provides a description of the caravan trades in Morocco at the turn of the century:

> In the narrow sense, a zettata (from the Berber TAZETTAT, 'a small piece of cloth') is a passage toll, a sum paid to a local power . . . for protection when crossing localities where he is such a power. But in fact it is, or more properly was, rather more than a mere payment. It was part of a whole complex of moral rituals, customs with the force of law and the weight of sanctity—centering around the guest-host, client-patron, petitioner-petitioned, exile-protector, suppliant-divinity relations—all of which are somehow of a package in rural Morocco. Entering the tribal world physically, the outreaching trader (or at least his agents) had also to enter it culturally.

> Despite the vast variety of particular forms through which they manifest themselves, the characteristics of protection in the Berber societies of the High and Middle Atlas are clear and constant. Protection is personal, unqualified, explicit, and conceived of as the dressing of one man in the reputation of another. The reputation may be political, moral, spiritual, or even idiosyncratic, or, often enough, all four at once. But the essential transaction is that a man who counts 'stands up and says' (*quam wa qal,* as the classical tag has it) to those to whom he counts: 'this man is mine; harm him and you insult me; insult me and you will answer for it.' Benediction (the famous *baraka*), hospitality, sanctuary, and safe passage are alike in this: they rest on the perhaps somewhat paradoxical notion that though personal identity is radically individual in both its roots and its expressions, it is not inca-

pable of being stamped onto the self of someone else.

While tribal chieftains found it profitable to protect merchant caravans they had neither the military muscle nor the political structure to extend, develop, and enforce more permanent property rights.

INSTITUTIONAL EVOLUTION IN EARLY MODERN EUROPE

In contrast to many primitive systems of exchange, long distance trade in early modern Europe from the eleventh to the sixteenth centuries was a story of sequentially more complex organization that eventually led to the rise of the western world. Let me first briefly describe the innovations and then explore some of their underlying sources.[9]

Innovations that lowered transaction costs consisted of organizational changes, instruments, and specific techniques and enforcement characteristics that lowered the costs of engaging in exchange over long distances. These innovations occurred at three cost margins: (1) those that increased the mobility of capital, (2) those that lowered information costs, and (3) those that spread risk. Obviously, the categories are overlapping, but they provide a useful way to distinguish cost-reducing features of transacting. All of these innovations had their origins in earlier times; most of them were borrowed from medieval Italian city states or Islam or Byzantium and then elaborated upon.

Among the innovations that enhanced the mobility of capital were the techniques and methods evolved to evade usury laws. The variety of ingenious ways by which interest was disguised in loan contracts ranged from "penalties for late payment," to exchange rate manipulation (Lopez and Raymond, 1955, p. 163), to the early form of the mortgage; but all increased the costs of contracting. The costliness of usury laws was not only that they made the writing of contracts to disguise interests complex and cumbersome, but also that enforceability of such contracts became more problematic. As the demand for capital increased and evasion became more general, usury laws gradually broke down and rates of interest were permitted. In consequence, the costs of writing contracts and the costs of enforcing them declined.

A second innovation that improved the mobility of capital, and the one that has received the most attention, was the evolution of the bill of exchange (a dated order to pay, say 120 days after issuance, conventionally drawn by a seller against a purchaser of goods delivered) and particularly the development of techniques and instruments that allowed for its negotiability as well as for the development of discounting methods. Negotiability and discounting in turn depended on the creation of institutions that would permit their use and the development of centers where such events could occur: first in fairs, such as the Champagne fairs that played such a prominent part in economic exchange in twelfth and thirteenth century Europe; then through banks; and finally through financial houses that could specialize in discounting. These developments were a function not only of specific institutions but also of the scale of economic activity. Increasing volume obviously made such institutional developments possible. In addition to the economies of scale necessary for the development of the bills of exchange, improved enforceability of contracts was critical, and the interrelationship between the development of accounting and auditing methods and their use as evidence in the collection of debts and in the enforcement of contracts was an important part of this process (Yamey; 1949; Watts and Zimmerman, 1983).

Still a third innovation affecting the mobility of capital arose from the problems associated with maintaining control of agents involved in long distance trade. The traditional resolution of this problem in medieval and early modern times was the use of kinship and family ties to bind agents to principals. However, as the size and scope of merchant trading empires grew, the extension of discretionary behavior to others than kin of the principal required the development of more elaborate accounting procedures for monitoring the behavior of agents.

The major developments in the area of information costs were the printing of prices of various commodities, as well as the printing of manuals that provided information on weights, measures, customs, brokerage fees, postal systems, and, particularly, the complex exchange rates between monies in Europe and the trading world. Obviously these developments were primarily a function of the volume of international trade and therefore a consequence of economies of scale.

The final innovation was the transformation of uncertainty into risk. By uncertainty, I mean here a condition wherein one cannot ascertain the probability of an event and therefore cannot arrive at a way of insuring against such an occurrence. Risk, on the other hand, implies the ability to make an actuarial determination of the likelihood of an event and hence insure against such an outcome. In the modern world, insurance and portfolio diversification are methods for converting uncertainty into risks and thereby reducing, through the provision of a hedge against variability, the costs of transacting. In the medieval and early modern world, precisely the same conversion occurred. For example, marine insurance evolved from sporadic individual contracts covering partial payments for losses to contracts issued by specialized firms. As De Roover (1945, p. 198) described:

> By the fifteenth century marine insurance was established on a secure basis. The wording of the policies had already become stereotyped and changed very little during the next three or four hundred years. . . . In the sixteenth century it was already current practice to use printed forms provided with a few blank spaces for the name of the ship, the name of the master, the amount of the insurance, the premium, and a few other items that were apt to change from one contract to another.

Another example of the development of actuarial, ascertainable risk was the business organization that spread risk through either portfolio diversification or institutions that permitted a large number of investors to engage in risky activities. For example, the commenda was a contract employed in long distance trade between a sedentary partner and an active partner who accompanied the goods. It evolved from its Jewish, Byzantine, and Muslim origins (Udovitch, 1962) through its use at the hands of Italians to the English Regulated Company and finally the Joint Stock Company, thus providing an evolutionary story of the institutionalization of risk.

These specific innovations and particular institutional instruments evolved from interplay between two fundamental economic forces: the economies of scale associated with a growing volume of trade, and the development of improved mechanisms to enforce contracts at lower costs. The causation ran both ways. That is, the increasing volume of long distance trade raised the rate of return to merchants of devising effective mechanisms for enforcing contracts. In turn, the development of such mechanisms lowered the costs of contracting and made trade more profitable, thereby increasing its volume.

The process of developing new enforcement mechanisms was a long one. While a variety of courts handled commercial disputes, it is the development of enforcement mechanisms by merchants themselves that is significant. Enforceability appears to have had its beginnings in the development of internal codes of conduct in fraternal orders of guild merchants; those who did not live up to them were threatened with ostracism. A further step was the evolution of mercantile law. Merchants carried with them in long distance trade mercantile codes of conduct, so that Pisan laws passed into the sea codes of Marseilles; Oleron and Lubeck gave laws to the north of Europe, Barcelona to the south of Europe; and from Italy came the legal principle of insurance and bills of exchange (Mitchell, 1969, p. 156).

The development of more sophisticated accounting methods and of notarial records provided evidence for ascertaining facts in disputes. The gradual blending of the volun-taristic structure of enforcement of contracts via internal merchant organizations with enforcement by the state is an important part of the story of increasing the enforceability of contracts. The long evolution of merchant law from its voluntary beginnings and the differences in resolutions that it had with both the common and Roman law are a part of the story.

The state was a major player in this whole process, and there was continuous interplay between the state's fiscal needs and its credibility in its relationships with merchants and the citizenry in general. In particular, the evolution of capital markets was critically influenced by the policies of the state, since to the extent the state was bound by commitments that it would not confiscate assets or use its coercive power to increase uncertainty in exchange, it made possible the evolution of financial institutions and the creation of more efficient capital markets. The shackling of arbitrary behavior of rulers and the development of impersonal rules that successfully bound both the state and voluntary organizations were a key part of this whole process. The development of an institutional process by which government debt could be circulated, become a part of a regular capital market, and be funded by regular sources of taxation was also a key part (Tracy, 1985; North and Weingast, 1989).

It was in the Netherlands, Amsterdam specifically, that these diverse innovations and institutions were combined to create the predecessor of the efficient modern set of markets that make possible the growth of exchange and commerce. An open immigration policy attracted businessmen. Efficient methods of financing long distance trade were developed, as were capital markets and discounting methods in financial houses that lowered the costs of underwriting this trade. The development of techniques for spreading risk and transforming uncertainty into actuarial, ascertainable risks as well as the creation of large scale markets that allowed for lowering the costs of information, and the development of negotiable government indebtedness all were a part of this story (Barbour, 1949).

CONTRASTING STORIES OF
STABILITY AND CHANGE

These contrasting stories of stability and change go to the heart of the puzzle of accounting for changes in the human economic condition. In the former cases, maximizing activity by the actors will not induce increments to knowledge and skills which will modify the institutional framework to induce greater productivity; in the latter case, evolution is a consistent story of incremental change induced by the private gains to be realized by productivity-raising organizational and institutional changes.

What distinguished the institutional context of western Europe from the other illustrations? The traditional answer of economic historians has been competition among the fragmented European political units accentuated by changing military technology which forced rulers to seek more revenue (by making bargains with constituents) in order to survive (North and Thomas, 1973; Jones, 1981; Rosenberg and Birdzell, 1986). That is surely part of the answer; political competition for survival in early modern Europe was certainly more acute than in other parts of the world. But it is only a partial answer. Why the contrasting results within western Europe? Why did Spain, the great power of sixteenth century Europe, decline while the Netherlands and England developed?

To begin to get an answer (and it is only a beginning), we need to dig deeper into two key (and related) parts of the puzzle: the relationship between the basic institutional framework, the consequent organizational structure, and institutional change; and the path dependent nature of economic change that is a consequence of the increasing returns characteristic of an institutional framework.

In the institutional accounts given earlier, the direction and form of economic activity by individuals and organizations reflected the opportunities thrown up by the basic institutional framework of customs, religious precepts, and formal rules (and the effectiveness of enforcement). Whether we examine the organization of trade in the Suq or that in the Champagne Fairs, in each case the trader was constrained by the institutional framework, as well as the traditional constraints common to economic theory.

In each case the trader would invest in acquiring knowledge and skills to increase his wealth. But in the former case, improved knowledge and skills meant getting better information on opportunities and having greater bargaining skills than other traders, since profitable opportunities came from being better informed and being a more skilled bargainer than other traders. Neither activity induced alteration in the basic institutional framework. On the other hand, while a merchant at a medieval European Fair would certainly gain from acquiring such information and skills, he would gain also from devising ways to bond fellow merchants, to establish merchant courts, to induce princes to protect goods from brigandage in return for revenue, to devise ways to discount bills of exchange. His investment in knowledge and skills would gradually and incrementally alter the basic institutional framework.

Note that the institutional evolution entailed not only voluntary organizations that expanded trade and made exchange more productive, but also the development of the state to take over protection and enforcement of property rights as impersonal exchange made contract enforcement increasingly costly for voluntary organizations which lacked effective coercive power. Another essential part of the institutional evolution entails a shackling of the arbitrary behavior of the state over economic activity.

Path dependence is more than the incremental process of institutional evolution in which yesterday's institutional framework provides the opportunity set for today's organizations and individual entrepreneurs (political or economic). The institutional matrix consists of an interdependent web of institutions and consequent political and economic organizations that are characterized by massive increasing returns.[10] That is, the organizations owe their existence to the opportunities provided by the institutional framework. Network externalities arise because of the initial setup costs (like the de novo creation of the U.S. Constitution in 1787), the learning effects described above, coordination effects via contracts with other organizations, and adaptive expectations arising from the prevalence of contracting based on the existing institutions.

When economies do evolve, therefore, nothing about that process assures economic growth. It has commonly been the case that the incentive structure provided by the basic institutional framework creates opportunities for the consequent organizations to evolve, but the direction of their development has not been to promote productivity-raising activities. Rather, private profitability has been enhanced by creating monopolies, by restricting entry and factor mobility, and by political organizations that established property rights that redistributed rather than increased income.

The contrasting histories of the Netherlands and England on the one hand and Spain on the other hand reflected the differing opportunity sets of the actors in each case. To appreciate the pervasive influence of path dependence, let us extend the historical account of Spain and England to the economic history of the New World and the striking contrast in the history of the areas north and south of the Rio Grande River.

In the case of North America, the English colonies were formed in the century when the struggle between Parliament and the Crown was coming to a head. Religious and political diversity in the mother country was paralleled in the colonies. The general development in the direction of local political control and the growth of assemblies was unambiguous. Similarly, the colonist carried over free and common socage tenure of land (fee simple ownership rights) and secure property rights in other factor and product markets.

The French and Indian War from 1755–63 is a familiar breaking point in American history. British efforts to impose a very modest tax on colonial subjects, as well as curb westward migration, produced a violent reaction that led via a series of steps, by individuals and organizations, to the Revolution, the

Declaration of Independence, the Articles of Confederation, the Northwest Ordinance, and the Constitution, a sequence of institutional expressions that formed a consistent evolutionary pattern despite the precariousness of the process. While the American Revolution created the United States, post-revolutionary history is only intelligible in terms of the continuity of informal and formal institutional constraints carried over from before the Revolution and incrementally modified (Hughes, 1989).

Now turn to the Spanish (and Portuguese) case in Latin America. In the case of the Spanish Indies, conquest came at the precise time that the influence of the Castilian Cortes (parliament) was declining and the monarchy of Castile, which was the seat of power of Spain, was firmly establishing centralized bureaucratic control over Spain and the Spanish Indies.[11] The conquerors imposed a uniform religion and a uniform bureaucratic administration on an already existing agricultural society. The bureaucracy detailed every aspect of political and economic policy. There were recurrent crises over the problem of agency. Wealth-maximizing behavior by organizations and entrepreneurs (political and economic) entailed getting control of, or influence over, the bureaucratic machinery. While the nineteenth century Wars of Independence in Latin America turned out to be a struggle for control of the bureaucracy and consequent policy as between local colonial control and imperial control, nevertheless the struggle was imbued with the ideological overtones that stemmed from the American and French revolutions. Independence brought U.S.-inspired constitutions, but the results were radically different. In contrast to those of the United States, Latin American federal schemes and efforts at decentralization had one thing in common after the Revolutions. None worked. The gradual country-by-country reversion to centralized bureaucratic control characterized Latin America in the nineteenth century.[12]

The divergent paths established by England and Spain in the New World have not converged despite the mediating factors of common ideological influences. In the former, an institutional framework has evolved that permits complex impersonal exchange necessary to political stability as well as to capture the potential economic benefits of modern technology. In the latter, "personalistic" relationships are still the key to much of the political and economic exchange. They are the consequence of an evolving institutional framework that has produced erratic economic growth in Latin America, but neither political nor economic stability, nor realization of the potential of modern technology.

The foregoing comparative sketch probably raises more questions than it answers about institutions and the role that they play in the performance of economies. Under what conditions does a path get reversed, like the revival of Spain in modern times? What is it about informal constraints that gives them such a pervasive influence upon the long-run character of economies? What is the relationship between formal and informal constraints? How does an economy develop the informal constraints that make individuals constrain their behavior so that they make political and judicial systems effective forces for third party enforcement? Clearly we have a long way to go for complete answers, but the modern study of institutions offers the promise of dramatic new understanding of economic performance and economic change.

References

ARTHUR, W. BRIAN, "Self-Reinforcing Mechanisms in Economics." In Anderson, Phillip W., Kenneth J. Arrow, and David Pines, eds., *The Economy as an Evolving Complex System.* Reading, MA: Addison-Wesley, 1988.

ARTHUR, W. BRIAN, "Competing Technologies, Increasing Returns, and Lock-In by Historical Events," *Economic Journal,* 1989, *99,* 116–131.

BARBOUR, VIOLET, "Capitalism in Amsterdam in the Seventeenth Century," *Johns Hopkins University Studies in Historical and Political Science,* Volume LXVIII. Baltimore: The Johns Hopkins University Press, 1949.

The Cambridge Economic History. Cambridge: Cambridge University Press, 1966.

CHANDLER, ALFRED, *The Visible Hand.* Cambridge: The Belknap Press, 1977.

COLSON, ELIZABETH, *Tradition and Contract: The Problem of Order.* Chicago: Adeline Publishing, 1974.

CURTIN, PHILIP D., *Cross-Cultural Trade in World History.* Cambridge: Cambridge University Press, 1984.

DAVID, PAUL, "Clio and the Economics of QWERTY," *American Economic Review,* 1985, *75,* 332–37.

DE ROOVER, F. E., "Early Examples of Marine Insurance," *Journal of Economic History,* November 1945, *5,* 172–200.

GEERTZ, C., H. GEERTZ, AND L. ROSEN, *Meaning and Order in Moroccan Society.* Cambridge: Cambridge University Press, 1979.

GLADE, W. P., *The Latin American Economies: A Study of Their Institutional Evolution.* New York: American Book, 1969.

GREIF, AVNER, "Reputation and Economic Institutions in Medieval Trade: Evidences from the Geniza Documents," *Journal of Economic History,* 1989.

HUGHES, J. R. T., "A World Elsewhere: The Importance of Starting English." In Thompson, F. M. L., ed., *Essays in Honor of H. J. Habakkuk.* Oxford: Oxford University Press, 1989.

JONES, E. L., *The European Miracle: Environments, Economies, and Geopolitics in the History of Europe and Asia.* Cambridge: Cambridge University Press, 1981.

KALT, J. P. AND M. A. ZUPAN, "Capture and Ideology in the Economic Theory of Politics," *American Economic Review,* 1984. *74,* 279–300.

LOPEZ, ROBERT S., AND IRVING W. RAYMOND, *Medieval Trade in the Mediterranean World.* New York: Columbia University Press, 1955.

MILGROM, P. R., D. C. NORTH, AND B. R. WEINGAST, "The Role of Institutions in the Revival of Trade: The Medieval Law Merchant," *Economics and Politics,* March 1990, *II.*

MITCHELL, WILLIAM, *An Essay on the Early History of the Law Merchant.* New York: Burt Franklin Press, 1969.

NELSON, DOUGLAS, AND EUGENE SILBERBERG, "Ideology and Legislator Shirking," *Economic Inquiry,* January 1987, *25,* 15–25.

NORTH, DOUGLASS C., "Location Theory and Regional Economic Growth." *Journal of Political Economy,* June 1955. *LXIII,* 243–258.

NORTH, DOUGLASS C., *Structure and Change in Economic History.* New York: Norton, 1981.

NORTH, DOUGLASS C., AND ROBERT THOMAS, *The Rise of the Western World: A New Economic History.* Cambridge: Cambridge University Press, 1973.

NORTH DOUGLASS C., AND BARRY R. WEINGAST, "The Evolution of Institutions Governing Public Choice in 17th Century, England," *Journal of Economic History,* November 1989. *5,* 172–200.

POSNER, RICHARD, "A Theory of Primitive Society, with Special Reference to the Law," *Journal of Law and Economics,* April 1980, *XXIII,* 1–54.

ROSENBERG, NATHAN, AND L. E. BRIDZELL, *How the West Grew Rich: The Economic Transformation of the Industrial World.* New York: Basic Books, 1986.

STIGLITZ, JOSEPH, "Markets, Market Failures, and Development," *American Economic Review,* 1989, *79,* 197–203.

TRACY, JAMES, *A Financial Revolution in the Hapsburg Netherlands: Renters and Renters in the Country of Holland, 1515–1565.* Berkeley: University of California Press, 1985.

TRACY, JAMES, *The Rise of Merchant Empires.* Cambridge: Cambridge University Press, forthcoming.

UDOVITCH, ABRAHAM, "At the Origins of the Western Commenda: Islam, Israel, Byzanteum?" *Speculum,* April 1962, *XXXVII,* 198–207.

VELIZ, C., *The Centralist Tradition of Latin America.* Princeton: Princeton University Press, 1980.

WALLIS, JOHN J., AND DOUGLASS C. NORTH, "Measuring the Transaction Sector in the American Economy, 1870–1970." In Engermann, Stanley, and Robert Gallman, eds., *Income and Wealth: Long-Term Factors in American Economic Growth.* Chicago: University of Chicago Press, 1986.

WATTS, R., AND J. ZIMMERMAN, "Agency Problems, Auditing, and the Theory of the Firm: Some Evidence," *Journal of Law and Economics,* October 1983, *XXVI,* 613–633.

WILLIAMSON, OLIVER E., *Markets and Hierarchies: Analysis and Antitrust Implications.* New York: Free Press, 1975.

WILLIAMSON, OLIVER E., *The Economic Institu-tions of Capitalism.* New York: Free Press, 1985.

YANEY, B. S., "Scientific Bookkeeping and the Rise of Capitalism," *Economic History Review,* Second Series, 1949, *II,* 99–113.

Notes

1. In an article written many years ago (North, 1955), I pointed out that many regional economies evolved from the very beginning as export economies and built their development around the export sector. This is in comparison and in contrast to the old stage theory of history derived from the German historical school, in which the evolution was always from local autarky to gradual evolution of specialization and division of labor. It is this last pattern that is described here, even though it may not characterize the particular evolution that in fact has occurred.

2. For an excellent summary of the anthropological literature dealing with trade in tribal societies, see Elizabeth Colson (1974).

3. Jewish traders in the Mediterranean in the eleventh century "solved" the agency problem as a result of close community relationships amongst themselves that lowered information costs and enabled them to act as a group to ostracize and retaliate against agents who violated their commercial code. See Avner Greif (1989).

4. Philip Curtin's *Cross Cultural Trade in World History* (1984) summarizes a good deal of the literature, but is short on analysis and examination of the mechanisms essential to the structure of such trade. The Cambridge Economic History, Volume III (1966), has more useful details on the organization of such trade.

5. North and Weingast (1989) provide a history and analysis of the political institutions of seventeenth century England leading up to the Revolution of 1688 and of the consequences for the development of the English capital market.

6. See North (1981), particularly chapter 13, and Chandler (1977). Joseph Stiglitz's (1989) essay, "Markets, Market Failures, and Development," details some of the theoretical issues.

7. The transaction sector (that proportion of transaction costs going through the market and therefore measureable) of the U.S. economy was 25 percent of GNP in 1870 and 45 percent of GNP in 1970 (Wallis and North, 1986).

8. There is an extensive literature on the Suq. A sophisticated analysis (on which I have relied) focused on the Suq in Sefrou, Morocco is contained in Geertz, Geertz, and Rosen (1979).

9. For a much more detailed description and analysis of the evolution of European trade see Tracy

(forthcoming), particularly Volume II. For a game theoretic analysis of one aspect of this trade revival see Milgrom, North, and Weingast (1990).

10. The concept of path dependence was developed by Brian Arthur (1988, 1989) and Paul David (1985) to explore the path of technological change. I believe the concept has equal explanatory power in helping us understand institutional change. In both cases increasing returns are the key to path dependence, but in the case of institutional change the process is more complex because of the key role of political organizations in the process.

11. The subsequent history of Spanish rise and decline is summarized in North and Thomas (1973).

12. For a summary account of the Latin American experience, see Veliz (1980) or Glade (1969).

Lynn Sharp Paine

Managing for Organizational Integrity

Many managers think of ethics as a question of personal scruples, a confidential matter between individuals and their consciences. These executives are quick to describe any wrongdoing as an isolated incident, the work of a rogue employee. The thought that the company could bear any responsibility for an individual's misdeeds never enters their minds. Ethics, after all, has nothing to do with management.

In fact, ethics has *everything* to do with management. Rarely do the character flaws of a lone actor fully explain corporate misconduct. More typically, unethical business practice involves the tacit, if not explicit, cooperation of others and reflects the values, attitudes, beliefs, language, and behavioral patterns that define an organization's operating culture. Ethics, then, is as much an organizational as a personal issue. Managers who fail to provide proper leadership and to institute systems that facilitate ethical conduct share responsibility with those who conceive, execute, and knowingly benefit from corporate misdeeds.

Managers must acknowledge their role in shaping organizational ethics and seize this opportunity to create a climate that can strengthen the relationships and reputations on which their companies' success depends. Executives who ignore ethics run the risk of personal and corporate liability in today's increasingly tough legal environment. In addition, they deprive their organizations of the benefits available under new federal guidelines for sentencing organizations convicted of wrongdoing. These sentencing guidelines recognize for the first time the organizational and managerial roots of unlawful conduct and base fines partly on the extent to which companies have taken steps to prevent that misconduct.

Prompted by the prospect of leniency, many companies are rushing to implement compliance-based ethics programs. Designed by corporate counsel, the goal of these programs is to prevent, detect, and punish legal violations. But organizational ethics means more than avoiding illegal practice; and providing employees with a rule book will do little to address the problems underlying unlawful conduct. To foster a climate that encourages exemplary behavior, corporations need a comprehensive approach that goes beyond the often punitive legal compliance stance.

An integrity-based approach to ethics management combines a concern for the law with an emphasis on managerial responsibility for ethical behavior. Though integrity strategies may vary in design and scope, all strive to define companies' guiding values, aspirations, and patterns of thought and conduct. When integrated into the day-to-day operations of an organization, such strategies can help prevent damaging ethical lapses while tapping into powerful human impulses for moral thought and action. Then an ethical framework becomes no longer a burdensome constraint within which companies must operate, but the governing ethos of an organization.

HOW ORGANIZATIONS SHAPE INDIVIDUALS' BEHAVIOR

The once familiar picture of ethics as individualistic, unchanging, and impervious to organizational influences has not stood up to scrutiny in recent years. Sears Auto Centers' and Beech-Nut Nutrition Corporation's experiences illustrate the role organizations play in shaping individuals' behavior-and how even sound moral fiber can fray when stretched too thin.

In 1992, Sears, Roebuck & Company was inundated with complaints about its automotive service business. Consumers and attorneys general in more than 40 states had accused the company of misleading customers and selling them unnecessary parts and services, from brake jobs to front-end alignments. It would be a mistake, however, to see this situation exclusively in terms of any one individual's moral failings. Nor did management set out to defraud Sears customers. Instead, a number of organizational factors contributed to the problematic sales practices.

In the face of declining revenues, shrinking market share, and an increasingly competitive market for undercar services, Sears management attempted to spur the performance of its auto centers by introducing new goals and incentives for employees. The company increased minimum work quotas and introduced productivity incentives for mechanics. The automotive service advisers were given product-specific sales quotas— sell so many springs, shock absorbers, alignments, or brake jobs per shift—and paid a commission based on sales. According to advisers, failure to meet quotas could lead to a

transfer or a reduction in work hours. Some employees spoke of the "pressure, pressure, pressure" to bring in sales.

Under this new set of organizational pressures and incentives, with few options for meeting their sales goals legitimately, some employees' judgment understandably suffered. Management's failure to clarify the line between unnecessary service and legitimate preventive maintenance, coupled with consumer ignorance, left employees to chart their own courses through a vast gray area, subject to a wide range of interpretations. Without active management support for ethical practice and mechanisms to detect and check questionable sales methods and poor work, it is not surprising that some employees may have reacted to contextual forces by resorting to exaggeration, carelessness, or even misrepresentation.

Shortly after the allegations against Sears became public, CEO Edward Brennan acknowledged management's responsibility for putting in place compensation and goal-setting systems that "created an environment in which mistakes did occur." Although the company denied any intent to deceive consumers, senior executives eliminated commissions for service advisers and discontinued sales quotas for specific parts. They also instituted a system of unannounced shopping audits and made plans to expand the internal monitoring of service. In settling the pending lawsuits, Sears offered coupons to customers who had bought certain auto services between 1990 and 1992. The total cost of the settlement, including potential customer refunds, was an estimated $60 million.

Contextual forces can also influence the behavior of top management, as a former CEO of Beech-Nut Nutrition Corporation discovered. In the early 1980s, only two years after joining the company, the CEO found evidence suggesting that the apple juice concentrate, supplied by the company's vendors for use in Beech-Nut's "100% pure" apple juice, contained nothing more than sugar water and chemicals. The CEO could have destroyed the bogus inventory and withdrawn the juice from grocers' shelves, but he was under extraordinary pressure to turn the ailing company around. Eliminating the inventory would have killed any hope of turning even the meager $700,000 profit promised to Beech-Nut's then parent, Nestlé.

A number of people in the corporation, it turned out, had doubted the purity of the juice for several years before the CEO arrived. But the 25% price advantage offered by the supplier of the bogus concentrate allowed the operations head to meet cost-control goals. Furthermore, the company lacked an effective quality control system, and a conclusive lab test for juice purity did not yet exist. When a member of the research department voiced concerns about the juice to operating management, he was accused of not being a team player and of acting like "Chicken Little." His judgment, his supervisor wrote in an annual performance review, was "colored by naïveté and impractical ideals." No one else seemed to have considered the company's obligations to its customers or to have thought about the potential harm of disclosure. No one considered the fact that the sale of adulterated or misbranded juice is a legal offense, putting the company and its top management at risk of criminal liability.

An FDA investigation taught Beech-Nut the hard way. In 1987, the company pleaded guilty to selling adulterated and misbranded juice. Two years and two criminal trials later, the CEO pleaded guilty to ten counts of mislabeling. The total cost to the company—including fines, legal expenses, and lost sales—was an estimated $25 million.

Such errors of judgment rarely reflect an organizational culture and management philosophy that sets out to harm or deceive. More often, they reveal a culture that is insensitive or indifferent to ethical considerations or one that lacks effective organizational systems. By the same token, exemplary conduct usually reflects an organizational culture and philosophy that is infused with a sense of responsibility.

For example, Johnson & Johnson's handling of the Tylenol crisis is sometimes attributed to the singular personality of then-CEO James Burke. However, the decision to do a nationwide recall of Tylenol capsules in

order to avoid further loss of life from product tampering was in reality not one decision but thousands of decisions made by individuals at all levels of the organization. The "Tylenol decision," then, is best understood not as an isolated incident, the achievement of a lone individual, but as the reflection of an organization's culture. Without a shared set of values and guiding principles deeply ingrained throughout the organization, it is doubtful that Johnson & Johnson's response would have been as rapid, cohesive, and ethically sound.

Many people resist acknowledging the influence of organizational factors on individual behavior—especially on misconduct—for fear of diluting people's sense of personal moral responsibility. But this fear is based on a false dichotomy between holding individual transgressors accountable and holding "the system" accountable. Acknowledging the importance of organizational context need not imply exculpating individual wrongdoers. To understand all is not to forgive all.

THE LIMITS OF A LEGAL COMPLIANCE PROGRAM

The consequences of an ethical lapse can be serious and far-reaching. Organizations can quickly become entangled in an all-consuming web of legal proceedings. The risk of litigation and liability has increased in the past decade as lawmakers have legislated new civil and criminal offenses, stepped up penalties, and improved support for law enforcement. Equally—if not more—important is the damage an ethical lapse can do to an organization's reputation and relationships. Both Sears and Beech-Nut, for instance, struggled to regain consumer trust and market share long after legal proceedings had ended.

As more managers have become alerted to the importance of organizational ethics, many have asked their lawyers to develop corporate ethics programs to detect and prevent violations of the law. The 1991 Federal

Sentencing Guidelines offer a compelling rationale. Sanctions such as fines and probation for organizations convicted of wrongdoing can vary dramatically depending both on the degree of management cooperation in reporting and investigating corporate misdeeds and on whether or not the company has implemented a legal compliance program. (See the insert "Corporate Fines Under the Federal Sentencing Guidelines.")

Such programs tend to emphasize the prevention of unlawful conduct, primarily by increasing surveillance and control and by imposing penalties for wrongdoers. While plans vary, the basic framework is outlined in the sentencing guidelines. Managers must establish compliance standards and procedures; designate high-level personnel to oversee compliance; avoid delegating discretionary authority to those likely to act unlawfully; effectively communicate the company's standards and procedures through training or publications; take reasonable steps to achieve compliance through audits, monitoring processes, and a system for employees to report criminal misconduct without fear of retribution; consistently enforce standards through appropriate disciplinary measures; respond appropriately when offenses are detected; and, finally, take reasonable steps to prevent the occurrence of similar offenses in the future.

There is no question of the necessity of a sound, well-articulated strategy for legal compliance in an organization. After all, employees can be frustrated and frightened by the complexity of today's legal environment. And even managers who claim to use the law as a guide to ethical behavior often lack more than a rudimentary understanding of complex legal issues.

Managers would be mistaken, however, to regard legal compliance as an adequate means for addressing the full range of ethical issues that arise every day. "If it's legal, it's ethical," is a frequently heard slogan. But conduct that is lawful may be highly problematic from an ethical point of view. Consider the sale in some countries of hazardous products without appropriate warnings or the purchase of goods from suppliers who operate inhumane sweat-shops in developing countries. Companies engaged in international business often discover that conduct that infringes on recognized standards of human rights and decency is legally permissible in some jurisdictions.

Legal clearance does not certify the absence of ethical problems in the United States either, as a 1991 case at Salomon Brothers illustrates. Four top-level executives failed to take appropriate action when learning of unlawful activities on the government trading desk. Company lawyers found no law obligating the executives to disclose the improprieties. Nevertheless, the executives' delay in disclosing and failure to reveal their prior knowledge prompted a serious crisis of confidence among employees, creditors, shareholders, and customers. The executives were forced to resign, having lost the moral authority to lead. Their ethical lapse compounded the trading desk's legal offenses, and the company ended up suffering losses— including legal costs, increased funding costs, and lost business—estimated at nearly $1 billion.

A compliance approach to ethics also overemphasizes the threat of detection and punishment in order to channel behavior in lawful directions. The underlying model for this approach is deterrence theory, which envisions people as rational maximizers of self-interest, responsive to the personal costs and benefits of their choices, yet indifferent to the moral legitimacy of those choices. But a recent study reported in *Why People Obey the Law* by Tom R. Tyler shows that obedience to the law is strongly influenced by a belief in its legitimacy and its moral correctness. People generally feel that they have a strong obligation to obey the law. Education about the legal standards and a supportive environment may be all that's required to insure compliance.

Discipline is, of course, a necessary part of any ethical system. Justified penalties for the infringement of legitimate norms are fair and appropriate. Some people do need the threat of sanctions. However, an overempha-

CORPORATE FINES UNDER THE FEDERAL SENTENCING GUIDELINES

What size fine is a corporation likely to pay if convicted of a crime? It depends on a number of factors, some of which are beyond a CEO's control, such as the existence of a prior record of similar misconduct. But it also depends on more controllable factors. The most important of these are reporting and accepting responsibility for the crime, cooperating with authorities, and having an effective program in place to prevent and detect unlawful behavior.

The following example, based on a case studied by the United States Sentencing Commission, shows how the 1991 Federal Sentencing Guidelines have affected overall fine levels and how managers' actions influence organizational fines.

Acme Corporation was charged and convicted of mail fraud. The company systematically charged customers who damaged rented automobiles more than the actual cost of repairs. Acme also billed some customers for the cost of repairs to vehicles for which they were not responsible. Prior to the criminal adjudication, Acme paid $13.7 million in restitution to the customers who had been overcharged.

Deciding before the enactment of the sentencing guidelines, the judge in the criminal case imposed a fine of $6.85 million, roughly half the pecuniary loss suffered by Acme's customers. Under the sentencing guidelines, however, the results could have been dramatically different. Acme could have been fined anywhere from 5% to 200% the loss suffered by customers, depending on whether or not it had an effective program to prevent and detect violations of law and on whether or not it reported the crime, cooperated with authorities, and accepted responsibility for the unlawful conduct. If a high ranking official at Acme were found to have been involved, the maximum fine could have been as large as $54,800,000 or four times the loss to Acme customers. The following chart shows a possible range of fines for each situation:

WHAT FINE CAN ACME EXPECT?

	Maximum	Minimum
Program, reporting, cooperation, responsibility	$2,740,000	$685,000
Program only	10,960,000	5,480,000
No program, no reporting no cooperation, no responsibility	27,400,000	13,700,000
No program, no reporting no cooperation, no responsibility, involvement of high-level personnel.	54,800,000	27,400,000

Based on Case No.:88-266, United States Sentencing Commission, *Supplementary Report on Sentencing Guidelines for Organizations.*

sis on potential sanctions can be superfluous and even counter-productive. Employees may rebel against programs that stress penalties, particularly if they are designed and imposed without employee involvement or if the standards are vague or unrealistic. Management may talk of mutual trust when unveiling a compliance plan, but employees often receive the message as a warning from on high. Indeed, the more skeptical among them may view compliance programs as nothing more than liability insurance for senior management. This is not an unreasonable conclusion, considering that compliance programs rarely address the root causes of misconduct.

Even in the best cases, legal compliance is unlikely to unleash much moral imagination or commitment. The law does not generally seek to inspire human excellence or distinction. It is no guide for exemplary behavior—or even good practice. Those managers who define ethics as legal compliance are implicitly endorsing a code of moral mediocrity for their organizations. As Richard Breeden, former chairman of the Securities and Exchange Commission, noted, "It is not an adequate ethical standard to aspire to get through the day without being indicted."

INTEGRITY AS A GOVERNING ETHIC

A strategy based on integrity holds organizations to a more robust standard. While compliance is rooted in avoiding legal sanctions, organizational integrity is based on the concept of self-governance in accordance with a set of guiding principles. From the perspective of integrity, the task of ethics management is to define and give life to an organization's guiding values, to create an environment that supports ethically sound behavior, and to instill a sense of shared accountability among employees. The need to obey the law is viewed as a positive aspect of organizational life, rather than an unwelcome constraint imposed by external authorities.

An integrity strategy is characterized by a conception of ethics as a driving force of an enterprise. Ethical values shape the search for opportunities, the design of organizational systems, and the decision-making process used by individuals and groups. They provide a common frame of reference and serve as a unifying force across different functions, lines of business, and employee groups. Organizational ethics helps define what a company is and what it stands for.

Many integrity initiatives have structural features common to compliance-based initiatives: a code of conduct, training in relevant areas of law, mechanisms for reporting and investigating potential misconduct, and audits and controls to insure that laws and company standards are being met. In addition, if suitably designed, an integrity-based initiative can establish a foundation for seeking the legal benefits that are available under the sentencing guidelines should criminal wrongdoing occur. (See the insert "The Hallmarks of an Effective Integrity Strategy.")

But an integrity strategy is broader, deeper, and more demanding than a legal compliance initiative. Broader in that it seeks to enable responsible conduct. Deeper in that it cuts to the ethos and operating systems of the organization and its members, their guiding values and patterns of thought and action. And more demanding in that it requires an active effort to define the responsibilities and aspirations that constitute an organization's ethical compass. Above all, organizational ethics is seen as the work of management. Corporate counsel may play a role in the design and implementation of integrity strategies, but managers at all levels and across all functions are involved in the process. (See the chart, "Strategies for Ethics Management.")

During the past decade, a number of companies have undertaken integrity initiatives. They vary according to the ethical values focused on and the implementation approaches used. Some companies focus on the core values of integrity that reflect basic social obligations, such as respect for the rights of others, honesty, fair dealing, and obedience to the law. Other companies emphasize aspirations—values that are ethically desirable but not necessarily morally obligatory—such as good service to customers, a commitment to diversity, and involvement in the community.

When it comes to implementation, some companies begin with behavior. Following Aristotle's view that one becomes courageous by acting as a courageous person, such companies develop codes of conduct specifying appropriate behavior, along with a system of incentives, audits, and controls. Other companies focus less on specific actions and more on developing attitudes, decision-making processes, and ways of thinking that reflect their values. The assumption is that personal commitment and appropriate decision processes will lead to right action.

Martin Marietta, NovaCare, and Wetherill Associates have implemented and lived with quite different integrity strategies. In each case, management has found that the

THE HALLMARKS OF AN EFFECTIVE INTEGRITY STRATEGY

There is no one right integrity strategy. Factors such as management personality, company history, culture, lines of business, and industry regulations must be taken into account when shaping an appropriate set of values and designing an implementation program. Still, several features are common to efforts that have achieved some success:

☐ *The guiding values and commitments make sense and are clearly communicated.* They reflect important organizational obligations and widely shared aspirations that appeal to the organization's members. Employees at all levels take them seriously, feel comfortable discussing them, and have a concrete understanding of their practical importance. This does not signal the absence of ambiguity and conflict but a willingness to seek solutions compatible with the framework of values.

☐ *Company leaders are personally committed, credible, and willing to take action on the values they espouse.* They are not mere mouthpieces. They are willing to scrutinize their own decisions. Consistency on the part of leadership is key. Waffling on values will lead to employee cynicism and a rejection of the program. At the same time, managers must assume responsibility for making tough calls when ethical obligations conflict.

☐ *The espoused values are integrated into the normal channels of management decision making and are reflected in the organization's critical activities:* the development of plans, the setting of goals, the search for opportunities, the allocation of resources, the gathering and communication of information, the measurement of performance, and the promotion and advancement of personnel.

☐ *The company's systems and structures support and reinforce its values.* Information systems, for example, are designed to provide timely and accurate information. Reporting relationships are structured to build in checks and balances to promote objective judgment. Performance appraisal is sensitive to means as well as ends.

☐ *Managers throughout the company have the decision-making skills, knowledge, and competencies needed to make ethically sound decisions on a day-to-day basis.* Ethical thinking and awareness must be part of every managers' mental equipment. Ethics education is usually part of the process.

Success in creating a climate for responsible and ethically sound behavior requires continuing effort and a considerable investment of time and resources. A glossy code of conduct, a high-ranking ethics officer, a training program, an annual ethics audit—these trappings of an ethics program do not necessarily add up to a responsible, law-abiding organization whose espoused values match its actions. A formal ethics program can serve as a catalyst and a support system, but organizational integrity depends on the integration of the company's values into its driving systems.

---

initiative has made important and often unexpected contributions to competitiveness, work environment, and key relationships on which the company depends.

MARTIN MARIETTA: EMPHASIZING CORE VALUES

Martin Marietta Corporation, the U.S. aerospace and defense contractor, opted for an integrity-based ethics program in 1985. At the time, the defense industry was under attack for fraud and mismanagement, and Martin Marietta was under investigation for improper travel billings. Managers knew they needed a better form of self-governance but were skeptical that an ethics program could influence behavior. "Back then people asked, 'Do you really need an ethics program to be ethical?'" recalls current President Thomas Young. "Ethics was something personal. Either you had it, or you didn't."

The corporate general counsel played a pivotal role in promoting the program, and

STRATEGIES FOR ETHICS MANAGEMENT

Characteristics of Compliance Strategy

Ethos	conformity with externally imposed standards
Objective	prevent criminal misconduct
Leadership	lawyer driven
Methods	education, reduced discretion, auditing and controls, penalties
Behavioral Assumptions	autonomous beings guided by material self-interest

Characteristics of Integrity Strategy

Ethos	self-governance according to chosen standards
Objective	enable responsible conduct
Leadership	management driven with aid of lawyers, HR, others
Methods	education, leadership, accountability, organizational, systems and decision processes, auditing and controls, penalties
Behavioral Assumptions	social beings guided by material self-interest, values, ideals, peers

Implementation of Compliance Strategy

Standards	criminal and regulatory law
Staffing	lawyers
Activities	develop compliance standards train and communicate handle reports of misconduct conduct investigations oversee compliance audits enforce standards
Education	compliance standards and system

Implementation of Integrity Strategy

Standards	company values and aspirations social obligations, including law
Staffing	executives and managers with lawyers, others
Activities	lead development of company values and standards train and communicate integrate into company systems provide guidance and consultation assess values performance identify and resolve problems oversee compliance activities
Education	decision making and values compliance standards and system

legal compliance was a critical objective. But it was conceived of and implemented from the start as a company-wide management initiative aimed at creating and maintaining a "do-it-right" climate. In its original conception, the program emphasized core values, such as honesty and fair play. Over time, it expanded to encompass quality and environmental responsibility as well.

Today the initiative consists of a code of conduct, an ethics training program, and procedures for reporting and investigating ethical concerns within the company. It also includes a system for disclosing violations of federal procurement law to the government. A corporate ethics office manages the program, and ethics representatives are stationed at major facilities. An ethics steering committee, made up of Martin Marietta's president, senior executives, and two rotating members selected from field operations, oversees the ethics office. The audit and ethics committee of the board of directors oversees the steering committee.

The ethics office is responsible for responding to questions and concerns from the company's employees. Its network of representatives serves as a sounding board, a source of guidance, and a channel for raising a range of issues, from allegations of wrongdoing to complaints about poor management, unfair supervision, and company policies and practices. Martin Marietta's ethics network, which accepts anonymous complaints, logged over 9,000 calls in 1991, when the company had about 60,000 employees. In 1992, it investigated 684 cases. The ethics office also works closely with the human resources, legal, audit, communications, and security functions to respond to employee concerns.

Shortly after establishing the program, the company began its first round of ethics training for the entire workforce, starting with the CEO and senior executives. Now in its third round, training for senior executives focuses on decision making, the challenges of balancing multiple responsibilities, and compliance with laws and regulations critical to the company. The incentive compensation plan for executives makes responsibility for promoting ethical conduct an explicit requirement for reward eligibility and requires that business and personal goals be achieved in accordance with the company's policy on ethics. Ethical conduct and support for the ethics program are also criteria in regular performance reviews.

Today top-level managers say the ethics program has helped the company avoid serious problems and become more responsive to its more than 90,000 employees. The ethics network, which tracks the number and types of cases and complaints, has served as an early warning system for poor management,

quality and safety defects, racial and gender discrimination, environmental concerns, inaccurate and false records, and personnel grievances regarding salaries, promotions, and layoffs. By providing an alternative channel for raising such concerns, Martin Marietta is able to take corrective action more quickly and with a lot less pain. In many cases, potentially embarrassing problems have been identified and dealt with before becoming a management crisis, a lawsuit, or a criminal investigation. Among employees who brought complaints in 1993, 75% were satisfied with the results.

Company executives are also convinced that the program has helped reduce the incidence of misconduct. When allegations of misconduct do surface, the company says it deals with them more openly. On several occasions, for instance, Martin Marietta has voluntarily disclosed and made restitution to the government for misconduct involving potential violations of federal procurement laws. In addition, when an employee alleged that the company had retaliated against him for voicing safety concerns about his plant on CBS news, top management commissioned an investigation by an outside law firm. Although failing to support the allegations, the investigation found that employees at the plant feared retaliation when raising health, safety, or environmental complaints. The company redoubled its efforts to identify and discipline those employees taking retaliatory action and stressed the desirability of an open work environment in its ethics training and company communications.

Although the ethics program helps Martin Marietta avoid certain types of litigation, it has occasionally led to other kinds of legal action. In a few cases, employees dismissed for violating the code of ethics sued Martin Marietta, arguing that the company had violated its own code by imposing unfair and excessive discipline.

Still, the company believes that its attention to ethics has been worth it. The ethics program has led to better relationships with the government, as well as to new business opportunities. Along with prices and technology, Martin Marietta's record of integrity, quality, and reliability of estimates plays a role in the awarding of defense contracts, which account for some 75% of the company's revenues. Executives believe that the reputation they've earned through their ethics program has helped them build trust with government auditors, as well. By opening up communications, the company has reduced the time spent on redundant audits.

The program has also helped change employees' perceptions and priorities. Some managers compare their new ways of thinking about ethics to the way they understand quality. They consider more carefully how situations will be perceived by others, the possible long-term consequences of short-term thinking, and the need for continuous improvement. CEO Norman Augustine notes, "Ten years ago, people would have said that there were no ethical issues in business. Today employees think their number-one objective is to be thought of as decent people doing quality work."

NOVACARE: BUILDING SHARED ASPIRATIONS

NovaCare Inc., one of the largest providers of rehabilitation services to nursing homes and hospitals in the United States, has oriented its ethics effort toward building a common core of shared aspirations. But in 1988, when the company was called InSpeech, the only sentiment shared was mutual mistrust.

Senior executives built the company from a series of aggressive acquisitions over a brief period of time to take advantage of the expanding market for therapeutic services. However, in 1988, the viability of the company was in question. Turnover among its frontline employees—the clinicians and therapists who care for patients in nursing homes and hospitals—escalated to 57% per year. The company's inability to retain therapists caused customers to defect and the stock price to languish in an extended slump.

After months of soul-searching, In-Speech executives realized that the turnover rate was a symptom of a more basic problem: the lack of a common set of values and aspi-

rations. There was, as one executive put it, a "huge disconnect" between the values of the therapists and clinicians and those of the managers who ran the company. The therapists and clinicians evaluated the company's success in terms of its delivery of high-quality health care. InSpeech management, led by executives with financial services and venture capital backgrounds, measured the company's worth exclusively in terms of financial success. Management's single-minded emphasis on increasing hours of reimbursable care turned clinicians off. They took management's performance orientation for indifference to patient care and left the company in droves.

CEO John Foster recognized the need for a common frame of reference and a common language to unify the diverse groups. So he brought in consultants to conduct interviews and focus groups with the company's health care professionals, managers, and customers. Based on the results, an employee task force drafted a proposed vision statement for the company, and another 250 employees suggested revisions. Then Foster and several senior managers developed a succinct statement of the company's guiding purpose and fundamental beliefs that could be used as a framework for making decisions and setting goals, policies, and practices.

Unlike a code of conduct, which articulates specific behavioral standards, the statement of vision, purposes, and beliefs lays out in very simple terms the company's central purpose and core values. The purpose— meeting the rehabilitation needs of patients through clinical leadership—is supported by four key beliefs: respect for the individual, service to the customer, pursuit of excellence, and commitment to personal integrity. Each value is discussed with examples of how it is manifested in the day-to-day activities and policies of the company, such as how to measure the quality of care.

To support the newly defined values, the company changed its name to NovaCare and introduced a number of structural and operational changes. Field managers and clinicians were given greater decision-making authority; clinicians were provided with additional resources to assist in the delivery of effective therapy; and a new management structure integrated the various therapies offered by the company. The hiring of new corporate personnel with health care backgrounds reinforced the company's new clinical focus.

The introduction of the vision, purpose, and beliefs met with varied reactions from employees, ranging from cool skepticism to open enthusiasm. One employee remembered thinking the talk about values "much ado about nothing." Another recalled, "It was really wonderful. It gave us a goal that everyone aspired to, no matter what their place in the company." At first, some were baffled about how the vision, purpose, and beliefs were to be used. But, over time, managers became more adept at explaining and using them as a guide. When a customer tried to hire away a valued employee, for example, managers considered raiding the customer's company for employees. After reviewing the beliefs, the managers abandoned the idea.

NovaCare managers acknowledge and company surveys indicate that there is plenty of room for improvement. While the values are used as a firm reference point for decision making and evaluation in some areas of the company, they are still viewed with reservation in others. Some managers do not "walk the talk," employees complain. And recently acquired companies have yet to be fully integrated into the program. Nevertheless, many NovaCare employees say the values initiative played a critical role in the company's 1990 turnaround.

The values reorientation also helped the company deal with its most serious problem: turnover among health care providers. In 1990, the turnover rate stood at 32%, still above target but a significant improvement over the 1988 rate of 57%. By 1993, turnover had dropped to 27%. Moreover, recruiting new clinicians became easier. Barely able to hire 25 new clinicians each month in 1988, the company added 776 in 1990 and 2,546 in 1993. Indeed, one employee who left during the 1988 turmoil said that her decision to return in 1990 hinged on the company's adoption of the vision, purpose, and beliefs.

WETHERILL ASSOCIATES: DEFINING RIGHT ACTION

Wetherill Associates, Inc.—a small, privately held supplier of electrical parts to the automotive market—has neither a conventional code of conduct nor a statement of values. Instead, WAI has a *Quality Assurance Manual*—a combination of philosophy text, conduct guide, technical manual, and company profile—that describes the company's commitment to honesty and its guiding principle of right action.

WAI doesn't have a corporate ethics officer who reports to top management, because at WAI, the company's corporate ethics officer *is* top management. Marie Bothe, WAI's chief executive officer, sees her main function as keeping the 350-employee company on the path of right action and looking for opportunities to help the community. She delegates the "technical" aspects of the business—marketing, finance, personnel, operations—to other members of the organization.

Right action, the basis for all of WAI's decisions, is a well-developed approach that challenges most conventional management thinking. The company explicitly rejects the usual conceptual boundaries that separate morality and self-interest. Instead, they define right behavior as logically, expediently, and morally right. Managers teach employees to look at the needs of the customers, suppliers, and the community—in addition to those of the company and its employees—when making decisions.

WAI also has a unique approach to competition. One employee explains, "We are not 'in competition' with anybody. We just do what we have to do to serve the customer." Indeed, when occasionally unable to fill orders, WAI salespeople refer customers to competitors. Artificial incentives, such as sales contests, are never used to spur individual performance. Nor are sales results used in determining compensation. Instead, the focus is on teamwork and customer service. Managers tell all new recruits that absolute honesty, mutual courtesy, and respect are standard operating procedure.

Newcomers generally react positively to company philosophy, but not all are prepared for such a radical departure from the practices they have known elsewhere. Recalling her initial interview, one recruit described her response to being told that lying was not allowed, "What do you mean? No lying? I'm a buyer. I lie for a living!" Today she is persuaded that the policy makes sound business sense. WAI is known for informing suppliers of overshipments as well as undershipments and for scrupulous honesty in the sale of parts, even when deception cannot be readily detected.

Since its entry into the distribution business 13 years ago, WAI has seen its revenues climb steadily from just under $1 million to nearly $98 million in 1993, and this in an industry with little growth. Once seen as an upstart beset by naysayers and industry skeptics, WAI is now credited with entering and professionalizing an industry in which kickbacks, bribes, and "gratuities" were commonplace. Employees—equal numbers of men and women ranging in age from 17 to 92—praise the work environment as both productive and supportive.

WAI's approach could be difficult to introduce in a larger, more traditional organization. WAI is a small company founded by 34 people who shared a belief in right action; its ethical values were naturally built into the organization from the start. Those values are so deeply ingrained in the company's culture and operating systems that they have been largely self-sustaining. Still, the company has developed its own training program and takes special care to hire people willing to support right action. Ethics and job skills are considered equally important in determining an individual's competence and suitability for employment. For WAI, the challenge will be to sustain its vision as the company grows and taps into markets overseas.

At WAI, as at Martin Marietta and NovaCare, a management-led commitment to ethical values has contributed to competitiveness, positive work-force morale, as well as solid sustainable relationships with the company's key constituencies. In the end, creating a climate that encourages exemplary conduct may be the best way to discourage damaging misconduct. Only in such an environment do rogues really act alone.

David M. Messick and Max H. Bazerman

Ethical Leadership and the Psychology of Decision Making

Changes in today's business environment pose vexing ethical challenges to executives. We propose that unethical business decisions may stem not from the traditionally assumed trade-off between ethics and profits or from a callous disregard of other people's interests or welfare, but from psychological tendencies that foster poor decision making, both from an ethical and a rational perspective.

Identifying and confronting these tendencies, we suggest, will increase both the ethicality and success of executive decision making.

Executives today work in a moral mine field. At any moment, a seemingly innocuous decision can explode and harm not only the decision maker but also everyone in the neighborhood. We cannot forecast the ethical landscape in coming years, nor do we think that it is our role to provide moral guidance to executives. Rather, we offer advice, based on contemporary research on the psychology of decision making, to help executives identify morally hazardous situations and improve the ethical quality of their decisions.

Psychologists have discovered systematic weaknesses in how people make decisions and process information; these new discoveries and theories are the foundation for this paper. These discoveries involve insights into errors that people make when they estimate risks and likelihoods, as well as biases in the way they seek information to improve their estimates. There are new theories about how easily our preferences can be influenced by the consequences we consider and the manner in which we consider them. Social psychologists have new information about how people divide the world into "us" and "them" that sheds new light on how discrimination operates. Finally, there has been important new research into the dimensions along which people think that they are different from other people, which helps explain why people might engage in practices that they would condemn in others.[1]

We focus on three types of theories that executives use in making decisions—theories about the world, theories about other people, and theories about ourselves. Theories about the world refer to the beliefs we hold about how the world works, the nature of the causal network in which we live, and the ways in which our decisions influence the world. Important aspects of our theories about the world involve our beliefs about the probabilistic (or deterministic) texture of the world and our perceptions of causation.

Theories about other people are our organized beliefs about how "we" are different from "they." Interestingly, "they" may be competitors, employees, regulators, or foreigners, and whoever is "we" today may be "them" tomorrow. Our beliefs about others influence the ways in which we make judgments and decisions about other people, and these influences are often unconscious.

Finally, we all correctly believe that we are unique individuals. However, theories about ourselves lead us to unrealistic beliefs about ourselves that may cause us to underestimate our exposure to risk, take more than our fair share of the credit for success (or too little for failure), or be too confident that our theory of the world is the correct one. If most of the executives in an organization think that they are in the upper 10 percent of the talent distribution, there is the potential for pervasive disappointment.

Our discussion of these three theories focuses on the ways they are likely to be incorrect. Our message, however, is not that executives are poor decision makers. We focus on problem areas because they are the danger zones where errors may arise. They are the places where improvements may be achieved, areas in which executives would like to change their decision making if only they better understood their existing decision processes.

THEORIES ABOUT THE WORLD

Successful executives must have accurate knowledge of their world. If they lack this knowledge, they must know how to obtain it. One typical challenge is how to assess the risk of a proposed strategy or policy, which involves delineating the policy's consequences and assessing the likelihood of various possibilities. If an executive does a poor assessment of a policy's consequences, the policy may backfire and cause financial as well as moral embarrassment to the firm and the decision maker. There are three components to our theories of the world: the consideration of possible consequences, the judgment of risk, and the perception of causes.

The Cascade of Consequences

A principle in ecology that Hardin has called the First Law of Ecology is, simply stated, "You can never do just one thing."[2] Major decisions have a spectrum of consequences, not just one, and especially not just the intended consequence. Everyday experience as well as psychological research suggests that, in making complex choices, people often simplify the decision by ignoring possible outcomes or consequences that would otherwise complicate the choice. In other words, there is a tendency to reduce the set of possible consequences or outcomes to make the decision manageable. In extreme cases, all but one aspect of a decision will be suppressed, and the choice will be made solely on the basis of the one privileged feature. The folly of ignoring a decision's possible consequences should be obvious to experienced decision makers, but there are several less obvious ways in which decision errors can create moral hazards. The tendency to ignore the full set of consequences in decision making leads to the following five biases: ignoring low-probability events, limiting the search for stakeholders, ignoring the possibility that the public will "find out," discounting the future, and undervaluing collective outcomes.

• **Ignoring Low-Probability Events.** If a new product has the potential for great acceptance but a possible draw-back, perhaps for only a few people, there is a tendency to underestimate the importance of the risk. In the case of DES (diethylstilbestrol), a synthetic estrogen prescribed for women with problem pregnancies, there was some early indication that the drug was associated with a higher than normal rate of problems not only in pregnant women but also in their daughters. The importance of this information was insufficiently appreciated. Worrisome risks may be ignored if they threaten to impede large gains.

• **Limiting the Search for Stakeholders.** DES's most disastrous effects did not befall the consumers of the drug, namely, the women who took it; the catastrophe struck their daughters. When there is a tendency to restrict the analysis of a policy's consequences to one or two groups of visible stakeholders, the decision may be blindsided by unanticipated consequences to an altogether different group. A careful analysis of the interests of the stakeholders (those persons or groups whose welfare may be affected by the

decision under consideration) is essential to reasonably anticipating potential problems. A basic tenet of moral theories is to treat people with respect, which can be done only if the interests of all concerned people are honestly considered. Assessing others' interests would have required research, for instance, on the long-term effects of DES.

• **Ignoring the Possibility That the Public Will "Find Out."** The stakeholder who should always be considered is the public in general. Executives should ask, "What would the reaction be if this decision and the reasons for it were made public?" If they fear this reaction, they should reconsider the decision. One reason for the test is to alert executives that if the decision is made, they will have to conceal it to avoid adverse public response. The need to hide the decision, and the risk that the decision and its concealment might be disclosed, become other consequences to face. The outrage provoked by the revelation that a crippling disease, asbestosis, was caused by asbestos exposure was partly due to the fact that Johns Manville had known about and hidden this relationship for years while employees and customers were continuously exposed to this hazard. A decision or policy that must be hidden from public view has the additional risk that the secret might be revealed. Damage to self-respect and institutional respect of those who must implement and maintain the concealment should also be considered a consequence.

• **Discounting the Future.** The consequences that we face tomorrow are more compelling than those we must address next week or next year. The consequences of decisions cascade not only over people and groups, but also over time. Figuring out how to address the entire temporal stream of outcomes is one of the most challenging tasks executives face. Policy A will earn more money this year than Policy B, but a year from now, if we get there, Policy B will probably leave us stronger than Policy A. Theories of the world that fail to cope with the temporal distribution of consequences will not only leave executives puzzled about why they are not doing better; they will also expose executives to accusations that they squandered the future to exploit the present. The tendency to discount the future partly explains the decaying urban infrastructure, the U.S. budget deficit, the collapse of fisheries, global warming, and environmental destruction. While there is much debate about the destructiveness of these issues, in each instance, the key decision makers have clearly underweighed the future in making the appropriate balanced decisions.

• **Undervaluing Collective Outcomes.** Accurate theories of the world must also be sensitive to the collective consequences of decisions. When E.F. Hutton's managers decided to earn money by kiting checks, not only did they put the reputation of their own firm in jeopardy, they also endangered the reputation of the entire securities industry. When a chemical firm decides to discharge waste into a public lake, it pollutes two collective resources, the lake and the reputation of the chemical industry in general. There is a tendency to treat these collective costs as externalities and to ignore them in decision making. To do so, however, is to ignore a broad class of stakeholders whose response could be. "If they voluntarily ignore the collective interests, then it is in the collective interest to regulate their activity."

Ethical decisions must be based on accurate theories about the world. That means, at a minimum, examining the full spectrum of a decision's consequences. Our perspective suggests that a set of biases reduces the effectiveness of the search for all possible consequences. It is interesting to evaluate the infamous Pinto decision from this consequential perspective. Ford executives knew that the car had a fire risk, but the cost they associated with it was small. Their deliberations gave no consideration to their customers' interests. They made no effort to ask car buyers if they were willing to pay an extra $10 to shield the gas tank. The Pinto decision proved a colossal embarrassment to Ford; when the documents were released, the effort to conceal the decision failed, and public opinion, fueled by Ralph Nader's book *Unsafe at Any Speed,* ran

deeply and strongly against Ford.[3] The public felt that there was a collective interest in automobile safety and that Ford and, by association, the other auto manufacturers, were indifferent to that concern. From the public's perspective, it would be stupid to permit unethical firms to police themselves.

Judgment of Risk

Theories of the world will be inaccurate if they systematically fail to account for the full spectrum of consequences associated with decisions. And they will be inaccurate if they systematically err in assessing the probabilities associated with the consequences. Let's first consider these two scenarios:

• A tough-minded executive wants to know if the company's current promotion practices have caused any specific case of demonstrated discrimination against a minority employee. He explains that he is not interested in vague possibilities of discrimination but is concerned that the firm not do anything that "really" causes discrimination.

• Edmund Muskie, a candidate in the 1972 U.S. presidential election, borrowed the words of President Harry Truman when he stated that what this country needed was a "one-armed" economist. When asked why, he responded that he was tired of economists who said "on the one hand . . . , but on the other hand. . . ."

• **Denying Uncertainty.** These decision makers are grasping for certainty in an uncertain world. They want to know what *will* or *did* happen, not what *may* or *might have* happen(ed). They illustrate the general principle that people find it easier to act as if the world were certain and deterministic rather than uncertain and often unpredictable. The executive in the first scenario wants to know about "real" discrimination, not the possibility of discrimination. Muskie expressed frustration with incessantly hearing about "the other hand." What people want to hear is not what *might* happen, but what *will* happen. When executives act as if the world is more certain than it is, they expose themselves to poor outcomes, for both themselves and others. It is simply foolish to ignore risk on one's own behalf, but it is unethical to do so on behalf of others.

There are some good reasons why people underestimate the importance of chance. One is that they misperceive chance events. When the market goes up on five consecutive days, people find a reason or cause that makes the world seem deterministic (for example, a favorable economic report was published). If the market goes up four days and then down on the fifth, people say a "correction" was due. Statistical market analyses suggest that changes in indices such as the Dow Jones index are basically random. Yet each morning, we are offered an "explanation" in the financial pages of why the market went up or down.

One implication of the belief in a deterministic world is the view that evidence should and can be perfect. The fact that there is a strong statistical relationship between smoking and bad health, for instance, is insufficient to convince tobacco company executives that cigarettes are harmful, because the standard of proof they want the evidence to meet is that of perfection. Any deviation from this standard is used strategically as evidence that smoking is not harmful.

We believe in a deterministic world in some cases because we exaggerate the extent to which we can control it. This illusion of control shows up in many contexts, but it seems maximal in complex situations that play out in the future. The tendency appears in experimental contexts in which people prefer to bet on the outcome of a flip of a coin that has not yet been tossed rather than on one that has already been thrown but whose outcome is unknown to the bettor.[4] The illusory sense that a bet may influence the outcome is more acute for future than for past events.

The illusion of control undoubtedly plays a large role in many business decisions. Janis has suggested that President Kennedy's disastrous decision to invade Cuba at the Bay of Pigs was flawed by, among other things, an erroneous belief that the invasion forces, with U.S. support, could control the battle's outcome.[5] Evidently, the Russian military offered similar assurances to support their attack on Grozny.

One common response to the assertion that executives underestimate the importance of random events is that they have learned through experience how to process information about uncertainty. However, experience may not be a good teacher. In situations in which our expectations or predictions were wrong, we often misremember what our expectations, in fact, were. We commonly tend to adjust our memories of what we thought would happen to what we later came to know did happen. This phenomenon, called the "hindsight bias," insulates us from our errors.[6]

We fail to appreciate the role of chance if we assume that every event that occurred was, in principle, predictable. The response "I should have known . . ." implies the belief that some future outcome was inherently knowable, a belief incompatible with the fact that essentially random events determine many outcomes. If every effort has been made to forecast the result of a future event, and the result is very different from predictions, it may be ill-advised to blame ourselves or our employees for the failure. This, of course, assumes that we made every effort to collect and appropriately process all the information relevant to the prediction.

• **Risk Trade-offs.** Uncertainty and risk are facts of executive life. Many risky decisions concern ethical dilemmas involving jobs, safety, environmental risks, and organizational existence. How risky is it to build one more nuclear power plant? How risky is it to expose assembly-line employees to the chemicals for making animal flea collars? At some point, our decisions are reduced to basic questions like: What level of risk is acceptable? How much is safety worth?

One unhelpful answer to the second question is "any price." That answer implies that we should devote all our efforts to highway improvement, cures for cancer, reducing product risks, and so on, to the exclusion of productivity. Throughout our lives, dealing with risk requires trading off benefits and costs; however, this is not a process that people find easy. It is much simpler, but completely unrealistic, to say "any price." The illusion that a riskless world can be created is a myth that is consistent with a theory of the world that minimizes the role of chance.

If we deal irrationally or superficially with risk, costly inconsistencies can occur in the ways we make risk trade-offs. Experts point out that U.S. laws are less tolerant of carcinogens in food than in drinking water or air. In the United Kingdom, 2,500 times more money per life saved is spent on safety measures in the pharmaceutical industry than in agriculture. Similarly, U.S. society spends about $140,000 in highway construction to save one life and $5 million to save a person from death due to radiation exposure.

A special premium seems to get attached to situations in which all risk can be eliminated. Consider the following two scenarios:

Scenario A. There is a 20 percent chance that the chemicals in your company's plant might be causing ten cancer-related illnesses per year. Your company must decide whether to purchase a multimillion-dollar filtration system that would reduce this probability to a 10 percent chance

Scenario B. There is a 10 percent chance that the chemicals in your company's plant might be causing ten cancer-related illnesses per year. Your company must decide whether to purchase a multimillion-dollar filtration system that would entirely eliminate this risk.

Evidence suggests that executives would be more likely to purchase the filtration system in scenario B than in scenario A.[7] It appears to be more valuable to eliminate the entire risk than to make an equivalent reduction from one uncertain level to another. Rationally, all reductions in a risk of 10 percent should have the same value for the decision maker. The "preference for certainty" suggests that a firm might be willing to spend more money to achieve a smaller risk reduction if that smaller reduction totally eliminated the risk. Were this the case, not only

would the firm's decision be wasteful, it would be unethical because it failed to accomplish the greatest good with the budget allocated for it.

Perceptions of risk are often faulty, frequently resulting in public and private decision makers' misdirected risk-reduction efforts. Is it not a breech of ethics if incoherent policies save fewer lives at greater costs than other possible policies? Failure to explicitly deal with risk trade-offs may have created precisely such a situation.

• **Risk Framing.** Whether a glass is half-full or half-empty is a matter of risk framing. When the glass is described as half-full, it appears more attractive than when described as half-empty. Similarly, a medical therapy seems more desirable when described in terms of its cure rate than its failure rate. This finding probably occurs because the cure rate induces people to think of the cure (a good thing), whereas an equivalent description in terms of failures induces people to think of failures (not a good thing).

A less obvious effect has been found with regard to the framing of risks. Consider this example:

• A large car manufacturer has recently been hit with a number of economic difficulties. It appears that it needs to close three plants and lay off 6,000 employees. The vice president of production, who has been exploring alternative ways to avoid the crisis, has developed two plans.

Plan A will save one of the three plants and 2,000 jobs.

Plan B has a one-third probability of saving all three plants and all 6,000 jobs, but has a two-thirds probability of saving no plants and no jobs.

Which plan would you select? There are a number of things to consider in evaluating these options. For example, how will each action affect the union? How will each plan influence the motivation and morale of the retained employees? What is the firm's obligation to its shareholders? While all these questions are important, another important factor influences how executives respond to them. Reconsider the problem, replacing the choices provided above with the following choices.

Plan C will result in the loss of two of the three plants and 4,000 jobs.
Plan D has a two-thirds probability of resulting in the loss of all three plants and all 6,000 jobs, but has a one-third probability of losing no plants and no jobs.

Now which plan would you select? Close examination of the two sets of alternative plans finds the two sets of options to be *objectively* the same. For example, saving one of three plants and 2,000 of 6,000 jobs (plan A) offers the same objective outcome as losing two of three plants and 4,000 of 6,000 jobs (plan C). Likewise, plans B and D are objectively identical. Informal empirical investigation, however, demonstrates that *most* individuals choose plan A in the first set (more than 80 percent) and plan D in the second set (more than 80 percent).[8] While the two sets of choices are objectively the same, changing the description of the outcomes from jobs and plants *saved* to jobs and plants *lost* is sufficient to shift the prototypic choice from risk-averse to risk-seeking behavior.

This shift is consistent with research showing that individuals treat risks concerning perceived gains (e.g., saving jobs and plants—plans A and B) differently from risks concerning perceived losses (e.g., losing jobs and plants—plans C and D). The way in which the problem is "framed"or presented can dramatically change how executives respond. If the problem is framed in terms of losing jobs and plants, executives tend to take the risk to avoid any loss. The negative value placed on the loss of three plants and 6,000 jobs is usually perceived as not being three times as bad as losing one plant and 2,000 jobs. In contrast, if the problem is framed in terms of saving jobs and plants (plans A and B), executives tend to avoid the risk and take the sure "gain." They typically view the gain placed on saving three plants and 6,000 jobs as not being three times as great as saving one plant and 2,000 jobs.

This typical pattern of responses is consistent with a general tendency to be risk averse with gains and risk seeking with losses.[9] This tendency has the potential for creating ethical havoc. When thinking about layoffs, for instance, most employees surely focus on their potential job loss. If executives adopt a risk-prone attitude in such situations—that is, if they are willing to risk all to attempt to avoid any losses—they may be seen as reckless and immoral by the very people whose jobs they are trying to preserve. If different stakeholders have different frames, the potential for moral disagreement is great.

Perception of Causes

The final aspect of executives theories of the world, perhaps the most important, is the beliefs that executives and other people cherish about the causal texture of the world, about *why* things happen or don't happen. Everyone holds beliefs about business successes and failures. As we mentioned earlier, every morning we're given a reason for why the stock market rose, fell, or stayed the same, thus reinforcing the theory that the world is deterministic. Moreover, judging causal responsibility is often a precursor to judging moral accountability and to blaming or praising a person, organization, or policy for an outcome. However, even under the best of circumstances, causation is usually complex, and ambiguity about causation is often at the heart of disputes about responsibility, blame, and punishment.

Consider, for example, the *Herald of Free Enterprise,* a ferry that carried automobiles from the Belgian port of Zeebrugge to Dover, England. Several years ago, it sank in a placid sea a few minutes after leaving Zeebrugge; 180 persons drowned. An investigation determined that the boat sank because the bow doors, through which the cars enter, had been left open, allowing water to pour into the vessel. The assistant bosun, who was responsible for closing the bow doors, had, tragically, taken a nap.

There were no alarm lights to warn the captain that the doors were open. The captain had requested such lights, but the company had denied his request; it felt warning lights were unnecessary because the first mate monitored the closing. On this occasion, the first mate failed to monitor the bow-door closing because he was needed elsewhere on board due to a chronic manpower shortage. Furthermore, the monitoring system was a "negative" check system, which means that signals were sent only if problems were detected. The lack of a signal was construed as an indication that all was well; the captain did not have to wait for a "positive" signal from the boat deck. Finally, there was the question of why water entered the ship since the bow doors are normally several meters above sea level. The answer was that the ship had taken on ballast to enable it to take cars onto the upper car deck. The captain had not pumped out the ballast before departing because he needed to make up twenty minutes to get back on schedule. Thus the ship left harbor at full throttle, creating a bow wave, with the ship's bow unusually low in the water.

What caused the *Herald of Free Enterprise* to capsize? Who is to blame? We have many candidates for blame: the assistant bosun, the first mate, the captain, the person who refused to provide warning lights, the person who instituted the negative check system, and the owners of the line for failing to provide adequate crew for the boat.

- **Focus on People.** A central issue in this case is the tendency of most people to *blame a person*. This principle is at the heart of the slogan of the National Rifle Association, a U.S. lobbying organization for gun manufacturers and users: "Guns don't kill people, people do." "Human error" becomes the cause assigned to many accidents involving complex technologies (such as ferries). We tend to blame people because it is easy to imagine them having done something to "undo" or prevent the accident. If the assistant bosun had not fallen asleep, if the first mate had stayed on the car deck to supervise the bow door closing, if the captain had not left the harbor at full speed before pumping the ballast, and so on.

It is less easy to imagine changing the ship's equipment and procedures, and these appear less salient as a cause of the disaster. The absence of warning lights allowed the ship to depart with the bow doors open. The negative check system invited a nonmessage to be misconstrued as an "all clear" signal. The point is that human "errors" occur within systems that may vary widely in the degree to which they are "error proof." Our theories about the world usually involve people as the causal agents, rather than environments either that influence people for good or bad or that can compensate for human weaknesses such as drowsiness. From an engineering viewpoint, what is easier to change—warning lights or periodic drowsiness?

- **Different Events.** Theories about causes often lead people to disagree, because, as McGill has pointed out, they are explaining different events.[10] When Sears introduced a commission-based sales system at its automotive repair shops, there was an increase in consumer complaints, usually accusing the shop of performing unnecessary, expensive work. Sears acknowledged that there had been some "isolated abuses" but denied that the problem was widespread. In subsequent public discussions, some of the controversy confused two phenomena. The first is why a particular employee would recommend and perform unnecessary work. The question, "Why did Jack do this?" may lead to determining how jack is different from Bill and other employees who did not recommend unnecessary work. These causes answer the question, "Why did Jack do this, while others did not?" Are there changes in Jack's situation that can explain his misconduct? "Why did Jack do this now, when he did not do it earlier?" is another way to construe this question.

The second question is why Sears had more complaints in the new system. The fact that there was a change raises an important issue: different systems may produce different levels of unethical conduct. If we focus only on Jack, or if we never change the system, we fail to see that the system itself can be a cause of problems. In many cases, something like the method of compensation appears in the background. If an employee behaves dishonestly, we tend to contrast him or her with honest workers, rather than ask if there is something encouraging dishonesty. When we change situations, we can sometimes see that an organization's features can have a causal impact on human actions, analogous to what happens when a community is exposed to a carcinogenic agent. The overall cancer rate in the community will increase, but it may be difficult to ever determine whether any specific individual's cancer was caused by the toxin. There may be convincing proof that the agent is a cause of cancer in the community generally, but not of any particular cancer.

• **Sins of Omission.** We have no problem judging that the assistant bosun bears some responsibility for the passenger deaths on the *Herald of Free Enterprise,* even though his contribution to the disaster was a failure to act. In many other situations, in which expectations and duties are not as well defined as they were with the *Herald,* a failure to take an action is used to shield persons from causal and, hence, moral responsibility. Is a public health official who decides not to authorize mandatory vaccinations responsible for the deaths of those who succumb to the disease?[11] Is the executive who fails to disclose his knowledge of a colleague's incompetence responsible for the harm that the colleague causes the firm? Many people would answer these questions in the negative, largely because they perceive that the immediate cause of the deaths or harm is the virus or incompetence. But since the actions of the public health official and the executive could have prevented the harm, their actions are *logically in* the same category as those of the assistant bosun. It is an old adage that evil prevails when good people fail to act, but we rarely hold the "good" people responsible for the evil.

THEORIES ABOUT OTHER PEOPLE

An executive's social world is changing at least as fast as his or her physical world. The

internationalization of manufacturing and marketing exposes executives to very different cultures and people, and they need to be tolerant of different customs, practices, and styles. More women are entering the work force. In the United States, both the African American and Latino populations are growing faster than the Anglo population, a demographic fact reflected in labor markets. Also, the United States, like many other nations, prohibits employment discrimination on the basis of religion, race, gender, age, and other types of social or personal information. This combination of factors—the increasing social diversity of the business world and the inappropriateness of using such social information in making decisions—creates many ethical hazards that executives must avoid. Incorrect theories about social groups— about women, ethnic minorities, or other nationalities—increase executives' danger markedly. In this section, we discuss how executives, like other people, are likely to harbor erroneous theories about other groups.[12]

Ethnocentrism

The characteristics of our nation, group, or culture appear to us to be normal and ordinary, while others appear foreign, strange, and curious. Implicit in this perception is the assumption that what is normal is good and what is foreign, different, and unusual is less good. This perception that "our"way is normal and preferred and that other ways are somehow inferior has been called ethnocentrism. In the ethnocentric view, the world revolves around our group, and our values and beliefs become the standard against which to judge the rest of the world.

Everyone is ethnocentric to some degree. We probably cannot escape the sense that our native tongue is "natural" while other languages are artificial, that our food is normal while others are exotic, or that our religion is the true one while others are misguided. The fact that ethnocentrism is basic and automatic also makes it dangerous. We do not have to harbor hostile views of members of other groups in order to subtly discriminate. We must merely believe that our own group is superior, a belief that is often actively and officially encouraged by the groups in question and that most of us find all too easy to maintain.

The consequences of ethnocentrism are pervasive. We may describe the same actions of "us" and "them" in words that are descriptively equivalent but evaluatively biased. We are loyal, hard-working, and proud: they are clannish, driven, and arrogant. We are fun loving; they are childish.

Furthermore, "we" tend to be like each other and quite different from "them." "We" come in all shapes and sizes, while "they" tend to be all alike. We take pleasure in "our" successes and grieve over "our" failures, while we are relatively uncaring about "their" outcomes. We expect aid and support from others of "us" and are more willing to support "us" than "them." We may not wish "them" harm but would not go out of our way to help "them." What is curious about this phenomenon is that today "we" may be residents of Chicago and "they" may be rural residents of Illinois, and tomorrow "we" may be Americans and "they" may be Europeans, or "we" may be men and "they" may be women.

Ethnocentric thinking exaggerates the differences between "us" and "them" in ways that can expose leaders to the risk of making ethically unsound decisions. Intensely competitive situations, such as military contexts, illustrate this type of distortion. Military strategists have often made different assumptions about how "we" and "they" will react to intensive attack. They seem to believe that the enemy's spirit can be broken by a prolonged artillery or bombing attack and associated deprivations. Their belief does not seem to have been weakened by the evidence of Leningrad, London, Dresden, Vietnam, or, more recently, Sarajevo. In all these cases, civilian populations were subjected to intensive, prolonged attack, the main consequence of which seems to have been to strengthen the afflicted people's resolve to resist the aggressors. U.S. leaders did not share the Japanese belief that a swift and decisive victory over the U.S. Pacific fleet at Pearl Harbor would destroy the American will to wage a Pacific war. These instances reflect the belief that "they" will be more discouraged by extreme hardship than "we" would be. These incorrect theories about "them" turned out to be seriously wrong and immeasurably costly.

It is an error to think that the effects of ethnocentrism are always as momentous or conspicuous as in these examples. Consider the charge of pervasive racial discrimination in mortgage lending. There is evidence that a higher proportion of minority applicants than white applicants are rejected. This difference in rejection rates remains after accounting for the effects of differences in income, employment stability, credit history, and other indicators of creditworthiness. Yet mortgage bankers vigorously deny that they are harder on minority applicants than on white ones.

Much research indicates that the way ethnocentrism often works is not by denigrating "them" but by rendering special aid to "us." This has been called the "in-group favoritism" hypothesis.[13] In mortgage lending, this hypothesis suggests that the difference in approval rates for whites and minorities may not reflect the fact that qualified minority applicants are denied, but that unqualified white applicants are given loans. This difference has important implications for banks that want to understand and correct the disparity. Establishing a review procedure for rejected minority loans would not be an advisable policy if the in-group favouritism hypothesis is correct, because there may be few, if any, qualified minorities who are rejected. Looking only at rejected minority loans would uncover no evidence of racial discrimination. To find where the discriminatory action lies, the bank needs to examine the marginally unqualified applicants. The in-group favoritism hypothesis predicts that, of this group, more white than minority applicants will be approved.

Stereotypes

In addition to the "theory" that "our" group is better than others, we often have specific beliefs about particular groups, which constitute implicit theories about people in these groups. We have stereotypes about different nationalities, sexes, racial groups, and occupations. To the extent that we rely on stereotypes rather than information about individuals, we risk making unfair, incorrect, and possibly illegal judgments. The issue here is not the extent to which stereotypes are accurate; the issue is whether people will be judged and evaluated on the basis of their individual qualities or on the basis of their group membership. The fact that women are generally smaller and weaker than men is irrelevant to the question of whether a particular woman is strong enough to perform a physically demanding job.

Like ethnocentrism, stereotypes are dangerous because we are often unaware of their influence. We tend to think that our beliefs about groups are accurate, and we can often draw on experience to support these beliefs. Experience, however, can be a misleading guide. Think about the people whom you consider to be the most effective leaders in your company. What qualities do they have that make them effective? For a purely historical reason, there is a good chance that the people who come to mind as effective leaders are men. For that reason, many of the qualities you associate with effective leadership may be masculine. Consequently, you may find it difficult to imagine a woman who could be an effective leader.

It is instructive to review the origins of the common belief that business leaders are masculine. First, there is the fact that twenty to thirty years ago, almost all businesspeople were men. Thus *successful* businesspeople today—those who have been in business twenty or thirty years—are also men. If we form our impressions of what it takes to succeed by abstracting the qualities of the successful people we know, a perfectly reasonable process, our impressions will have a distinctly masculine aura. It is not that we have evidence that women do not succeed; rather, we have little evidence about women at all. If you are asked to imagine people in your company who are notorious failures, the people you conjure up would probably also be men. The stereotypical failure is probably also a man.

How can we guard against the dangers of ethnocentric and stereotypical theories? Starting with ethnocentrism, we should question arguments based on the belief that "they" are different from "us." The safest assumption to make, in the absence of contrary evidence, is that "they" are essentially the same as "us" and that if we want to know how "they" will react to a situation, a wise first step is to ask how "we" would react. Historically, far more harm has been incurred by believing that different groups are basically different than by assuming that all people are essentially the same.

Many decisions that executives make involve promotion, hiring, firing, or other types of personnel allocations. These decisions are stereotypical when they use considerations about the group rather than information about the person. "Women can't handle this kind of stress" is a stereotypical statement about women, not an assessment of a particular individual. Executives should be especially alert for inappropriate theories about others when the criteria for evaluation and the qualifications under discussion are vague. Ethnocentric or stereotypical theories are unlikely to have a large impact if rules state that the person with the best sales record will be promoted. The criteria and qualifications are clear and quantified. However, vague criteria such as sociability, leadership skill, or insight make evaluation susceptible to stereotyping.

One of the most effective strategies for combating ethnocentrism and stereotypes is to have explicit corporate policies that discourage them, such as adopting and publishing equal opportunity principles and constantly reminding employees that group-based judgments and comments are unacceptable. Executives must be the ethical leaders of their organizations.

THEORIES ABOUT OURSELVES

Low self-esteem is not generally associated with successful executives. Executives need confidence, intelligence, and moral strength to make difficult, possibly unpopular decisions. However, when these traits are not tempered with modesty, openness, and an accurate appraisal of talents, ethical problems can arise. In other words, if executives' theories about themselves are seriously flawed, they are courting disaster. Research has identified several ways in which peoples' theories of themselves tend to be flawed.[14] We discuss three: the illusion of superiority, self-serving fairness biases, and overconfidence.

Illusion of Superiority

People tend to view themselves positively. When this tendency becomes extreme, it can lead to illusions that, while gratifying, distort reality and bias decision making. Scholars have identified three such illusions: favorability optimism, and control.[15]

• **Illusion of Favorability.** This illusion is based on an unrealistically positive view of the self, in both absolute and relative terms. For instance, people highlight their positive characteristics and discount their negatives. In relative terms, they believe that they are more honest, ethical, capable, intelligent, courteous, insightful, and fair than others. People give themselves more responsibility for their successes and take less responsibility for their failures than they extend to others. People edit and filter information about themselves to maintain a positive image, just as totalitarian governments control information about themselves.

• **Illusion of Optimism.** This illusion suggests that people are unrealistically optimistic about their future relative to others. People overestimate the likelihood that they will experience "good" future events and underestimate the likelihood of "bad" future events. In particular, people believe that they are less susceptible than others to risks ranging from the possibility of divorce or alcoholism to injury in traffic accidents. To the extent that executives believe themselves relatively immune from such risks, they may be willing to expose themselves and their organizations to hazards.

• **Illusion of Control.** The illusion of optimism is supported by the illusion of control that we referred to earlier. One reason we think we are relatively immune to common risks is that we exaggerate the extent to which we can control random events. Experiments have demonstrated the illusion of control with MBA students from some top U.S. business schools, so there is no reason to think that executives who have attended these schools will be immune to them.[16] (Indeed, the belief that one is exempt from these illusions, while others are not, is an excellent illustration of the illusion of optimism.)

These illusions may also characterize peoples' attitudes about the organizations to which they belong. The result is a kind of organizational ethnocentrism, as we discussed earlier. Managers may feel that their company's contributions to society are more important than those of other companies, even when a neutral observer sees comparability. Similarly, executives may feel that the damage their firms cause society is not as harmful as that created by other organizations. Such a pattern of beliefs can create a barrier to societal improvement when each organization underestimates the damages that it causes. Often, however, firms and their executives genuinely believe that they are being fair and just in their positions (and that others are biased, an illustration of the illusion of favorability).

Self-Serving Fairness Biases

Most executives want to act in a just manner and believe they are fair people. Since they are also interested in performance and success, they often face a conflict between fairness and the desired outcome. They may want a spacious office, a large share of a bonus pool, or the lion's share of the market. Furthermore, they may believe that achieving these outcomes is fair because they deserve them. Different parties, when judging a fair allocation among them, will often make different judgments about what is fair, and those judgments will usually serve the party's interest. These judgments often reflect disagreements about deservedness based on contributions to the collective effort. It is likely that if you asked each division in your organization to estimate the percentage of the company's worth that is created by the division, the sum of the estimates would greatly exceed 100 percent. (Research has been shown this to be true with married couples. The researchers who did the study reported that they had to ask the questions carefully because spouses would often be amazed, and then angry, about the estimates that their mates gave to questions like, "What percentage of the time do you clean up the kitchen?"[17])

One important reason for these self-serving views about fairness is that people are more aware of their contributions to collective activities than others are likely to be; they have more information about their own efforts than others have or than they have about others. Executives may recall disproportionately more instances of *their* division helping the corporation, of *their* corporation helping the community, and of *their* industry helping society.

Furthermore, executives, like other people, credit themselves for their efforts, whereas they are more likely to credit others only for their achievements. They also credit themselves for the temptations that they resisted but judge others strictly by their actions, not by their lack of action. An executive who is offered a substantial bonus to misrepresent the financial well-being of her firm may feel proud of her honesty when she declines, but others may either not know of the temptation or, if they do, believe that she merely followed the rules. While she may feel that the firm owes her gratitude, the firm may not share that feeling.

These fairness biases are particularly problematic during negotiations, when costly delays and impasses result. Egocentric interpretations of fairness hinder conflict resolution because each party believes that its own demands are fair and thus is unwilling to agree to what it perceives as inequitable set-tlements. It is not just a matter of different interests, it is a matter of what is fair and proper. The difference in perspectives can lead parties to question each others' ethics and morality. The temptation to view the other side as immoral when they fail to agree with us is especially pronounced in situations in which ethnocentric impulses may be aroused—for instance, international negotiations, labor management negotiations, or negotiations that involve issues of race or gender. For example, Price Waterhouse, a major accounting firm, was surprised when it lost a sexual discrimination suit. The firm's view of its procedures' fairness was at odds with the plaintiff's and judge's views.

Overconfidence

Most people are erroneously confident in their knowledge. In situations in which people are asked factual questions and then asked to judge the probability that their answers are true, the probability judgments far exceed the actual accuracy measures of the proportion of correct answers.[18] For instance, when asked, "Which city is farther north, Rome or New York?," most respondents choose New York and indicate a probability of about 90 percent that it is true. In fact, it is not true; Rome is slightly north of New York. Research has indicated that when people (including executives) respond to a large group of two-option questions for which they claim to be 75 percent certain, their answers tend to be correct only 60 percent of the time.[19] For confidence judgments of 100 percent, it is not uncommon for subjects to be correct only 85 percent of the time. Other research found that subjects who assign odds of 1,000:1 to their answers are correct only 90 to 96 percent of the time.[20] Overconfidence has been identified among members of the armed forces, executives, business students, and C.I.A. agents.[21]

The danger of overconfidence is, of course, that policies based on erroneous information may fail and harm others as well as the executive who established the policy.

Overconfidence, as part of our theories about ourselves, coupled with flawed theories about the world or about other people, poses serious threats to rational and ethical decision making.

To the degree to which people are overconfident in their (conservative) risk assessments—in their beliefs about the availability of scarce resources or the character of people unlike themselves—they will fail to seek additional information to update their knowledge. One cost of overconfidence is a reluctance to learn more about a situation or problem before acting.

Even if people acknowledge the need for additional information, research has shown that their process for gaining that information may be biased to confirm prior beliefs and hypotheses.[22] This tendency was initially demonstrated in a series of studies in which the subjects were given a three-number sequence, 2-4-6. Their task was to discover the numeric rule to which the three numbers conformed. To determine the rule, they were allowed to generate other sets of three numbers that the experimenter would classify as either conforming or not conforming to the rule. At any point, subjects could stop when they thought that they had discovered the rule.

The rule is "any three ascending numbers." Suppose you thought the rule was "the difference between the first two numbers equals the difference between the last two numbers" (a common expectation). Testing confirming sequences, like 1-2-3, 10-15-20, or 122-126-130, will provide positive feedback and increase confidence in the original, but incorrect, hypothesis. To discover how the true rule differs from this rule, you must try sequences that do not conform to the hypothesized rule. You need to ask questions that, if answered positively, would disconfirm your rule. This is a less comfortable mode of acquiring information, partly because it may appear that you are not confident in your belief.

Transpose this idea to an executive questioning an engineer about the safety of a tool grip. The executive wants to and does believe that the grip is safe. If the executive asks questions like, "This really is a safe grip, isn't it?" or "Does this grip meet all the standards that have been set for this type of tool?," he is doing two things that may distort the information that he will receive. First, he is displaying the confirmation bias by asking questions he expects to be answered "yes." Second, he is unconsciously exploiting social politeness, because people are more likely to agree than disagree. So by asking these types of questions, the executive is less likely to learn if the engineer has misgivings about any design features than if he asked questions such as, "What are the advantages and disadvantages of the grip?" or "What are the things we have most to worry about with this design?"

These processes suggest that executives may be favorably biased toward themselves and their firms. Will feedback help to eliminate or reduce these biases? We believe that feedback may provide only limited help because of the tendency to seek and notice confirming information, which forms an additional barrier to learning through experience.

When we consider the combined impact of the three processes described in this section—the illusion of superiority, self-centered perceptions of fairness, and overconfidence—we can see the peril associated with erroneous theories of the self. The major peril is that we will come to see ourselves as people for whom the normal rules, norms, and obligations do not apply. The danger is that an executive, especially a successful executive, will hold himself above conventional ethical principles and subject himself only to self-imposed rules that others might judge to be self-serving. He might justify telling a lie on the ground that it permits him to achieve important benefits for others (such as shareholders or employees) even though the shareholders or employees are being duped. He might feel that inflating an expense account or using company property for personal ends is not "really" wrong because of the value that he contributes to the company. Finally, he may undertake an immoral or illegal act, convinced that he will never be caught. The tendencies to feel superior, to generate self-serving, on-the-spot moral rules, and to be over-confident about beliefs create the potential for moral shallowness and callowness.

IMPROVING ETHICAL DECISION MAKING

Our position is that the causes of poor ethical decisions are often the same as the causes of poor decisions generally; decisions may be based on inaccurate theories about the world, about other people, or about ourselves. We suggest that ethical decision making may be improved in the same way that general decision making is improved. In this final section, we outline three broad criteria that executives can focus on: quality, breadth, and honesty.

Quality

Executives who make higher-quality decisions will tend to avoid ethical mistakes. Improving the quality of decision making means ensuring that all the consequences of actions are considered. It implies having accurate assessments of the risks associated with possible strategies and being attuned to the pitfalls of egocentric biases.

A general principle is that the types of flaws and biases we have discussed are likely to influence decision making more when decisions are intuitive, impulsive, or subjective rather than concrete, systematic, and objective. Stereotypes, for instance, have less influence on personnel decisions or performance appraisals if the evaluation criteria are quantitative rather than subjective and vague. Managers often resist this suggestion because they feel that using quantitative procedures makes their judgment "mechanical" or superfluous. The argument in favor of such procedures is that they reduce, or at least identify, opportunities for inappropriate information to influence decisions. Using a quantitative process allows a manager to identify precisely the source of such inappropriate information. Often, systematic procedures result in the same decision as more subjective ones,

but the results are more acceptable because the process is viewed as objective, fair, and less subject to bias.

Whenever possible, executives should base decisions on data rather than hunches. In uncertain situations, the best guide comes from close attention to the real world (e.g., data), not from memory and intuition. People worry more about death by murder than death by automobile accident, even though the latter is, statistically, a much greater threat than the former. Reasoning by anecdote—for example, "My engineering chief says he is convinced the product is safe, regardless of what the test results say"—not only wastes resources expended to gather the data but also irresponsibly exposes others to avoidable risks. A corollary is that getting high-quality data is obligatory. In business, as in science, passing off poor, unreliable data as good is fraudulent and inexcusable.

Sometimes executives cannot escape making decisions and judgments on subjective, intuitive bases. But they can take steps to prevent some of the biases from distorting judgment. To combat overconfidence, for instance, it is effective to say to yourself, "Stop and think of the ways in which you could be wrong." Similarly, to avoid minimizing risk, you can ask, "What are the relevant things that I don't know?" Often, a devil's advocate, who is given the role of scrutinizing a decision for false assumptions and optimistic projections, can play this role. A major difference between President Kennedy's Bay of Pigs fiasco and his skillful handling of the Cuban missile crisis was his encouragement of dissenting opinions and inclusion of people whose political orientations disagreed with his own.[23]

One threat to rational and ethical decision making that we noted earlier stems from the untrustworthiness of human memory. The first step in managing this threat is to acknowledge it. The second is to compensate for it with improved, detailed record keeping. This recommendation corresponds to a tenet of the total quality management movement—record keeping and benchmarking are central to measuring objectively how well a process is performing. Quality management and ethical management are close companions; what promotes one generally promotes the other. Erroneous theories threaten both.

Breadth

By breadth, we mean assessment of the full range of consequences that policies may entail. An ethical audit of a decision must take into account the outcomes for all stakeholders. The first task is to compile a list of the stakeholders. The second is to evaluate a decision's likely outcomes from the stakeholders' perspective.

One approach to identifying stakeholders is to make the decision process as open as possible and invite input from interested parties. However, different groups may have different access to public information, so this technique risks overlooking important constituencies. A potential solution is to include representatives of the important groups on the decision-making team. Broad consultation, which requires an active search to enlist all affected parties into the decision-making process, is important. Openness itself is often a signal to potential opponents that nothing is being hidden and there is nothing to fear. For example, a few years ago, two relatively similar construction projects in Arizona differed greatly in the care they took to involve the active environmental groups in their communities. The project that worked continually with citizens gained their trust and support for the project, while the one that ignored environmentalists faced expensive legal challenges in court.

Socially responsible executive decision making recognizes that a company is part of a broader community that has an interest in its actions. A full accounting for decisions must include a community-impact assessment. If there is community opposition to a policy, it is far better to address it early on rather than risk being ambushed by it later.

Finally, executives' decisions affect those not only in the present but also in the future. Executives' responsibility is to manage so that the world's social and physical environments are not spoiled for future generations. The continual squandering of nonrenewable resources or overuse of renewable ones gives privileges to the current generation at the expense of later ones. Likewise, postponing the payment for what we enjoy today saddles future generations with paying for current consumption. None of us would intentionally make our own children worse off than we are, and we would not want others to do so either.

Breadth is an important quality of ethical decision making because it is both ethically proper *and* strategically sound. It means doing the right thing and doing the smart thing. Intentional decisions to exclude stakeholders' interests or input may not only violate their rights, which is an ethical infraction, but also invite opposition, resentment, and hostility, which is stupid.

Honesty

In discussing breadth, we urged openness. But executives can rarely divulge all the information involved in a decision. Much information is proprietary, gives competitors an unfair advantage, and is legally confidential. A policy of openness does not require executives to tell all. It is perfectly ethical and appropriate to withhold some types of information. It is inappropriate to withhold information about a project or policy merely because an executive is ashamed to make it public. We propose that, if an executive feels so embarrassed about some aspect of a project that she wants to hide the information, she probably should not undertake the project. Conscience, in short, is a good litmus test for a decision's ethicality. If an idea cannot stand the light of day or the scrutiny of public opinion, then it is probably a bad idea. A variant of this "sunshine test" is to imagine how you would feel if you saw the idea or decision on the front page of the *New York Times*.

As we pointed out earlier, you cannot always trust your reaction to a hypothetical test. It's easy to say, "I wouldn't mind it if my family knew that I misstated the firm's income by $20 million," when this is, in fact, completely untrue. As one scholar points out, we ourselves are the easiest audience that we have to play to and the easiest to fool.[24] Consequently, we should imagine whether our audience would accept the idea or decision. In particular, we should ask whether the people with the most to lose would accept the reasons for our actions. If not, we are probably on moral thin ice.

One risk often overlooked when practicing deceit is the continual need to maintain deception. Not only are original facts hidden, but the fact of hiding must also be hidden. In the notorious Watergate scandal, President Nixon was forced from office not for what occurred in the Watergate complex, but for the efforts the White House made to hide the offense.

While it is important to be honest with others, it is just as important to be honest with yourself. Self-deception—being unaware of the processes that lead us to form our opinions and judgments—is unavoidable. We think we remember things accurately, but careful studies show that we do not. We think we know why we make judgments about other people, but research shows us other reasons.

If we can accept the fact that the human mind has an infinite, creative capacity to trick itself, we can guard against irrational, unethical decisions. To deny this reality is to practice self-deception. We can learn to suspect our naive judgments. We can learn to calibrate ourselves to judge risk. We can examine our motives in judging others; are we using hard, reliable information to evaluate subordinates, or are we using stereotypes?

The topic of executive ethics has been dominated by the assumption that executives are constantly faced with an explicit trade-off between ethics and profits. We argue, in contrast, that unethical behavior in organizations is more commonly affected by psychological tendencies that create undesirable behavior from both ethical and rational perspectives. Identifying and confronting these psychological tendencies will increase the success of executives and organizations.

References

1. For the research on which we based this article, see M.H. BAZERMAN, *Judgment in Managerial Decision Making* (New York: John Wiley, 1994); R.M. DAWES, *Rational Choice in an Uncertain World* (San Diego, California: Harcourt Brace Jovanovich, 1988); T. GILOVICH, *How We Know What Isn't So* (New York: Free Press, 1991); and S. PLOUS, *The Psychology of Judgment and Decision Making* (New York: McGraw Hill, 1993). A forthcoming book will explore these and other topics in greater detail. See D.M. MESSICK AND A. TENBRUNSEL, *Behavioral Research and Business Ethics* (New York: Russell Sage Foundation, forthcoming).
2. G. HARDIN, *Filters Against Folly* (New York: Penguin, 1985).
3. R. NADER, *Unsafe at Any Speed* (New York: Grossmans Publishers, 1965).
4. M. ROTHBART AND M. SNYDER, "Confidence in the Prediction and Post-diction of an Uncertain Outcome," *Canadian Journal of Behavioral Science* 2 (1970): 38–43.
5. I.L. JANIS, *Groupthink: Psychological Studies of Policy Decisions and Fiascoes* (Boston: Houghton Mifflin, 1982).
6. B. FISCHHOFF, "Hindsight: Thinking Backward," *Pyschology Today* 8 (1975): 71–76.
7. D. KAHNEMAN AND A. TVERSKY, "Prospect Theory: An Analysis of Decision under Risk," *Econometrica* 47 (1979): 263–291.
8. BAZERMAN (1994); AND KAHNEMAN AND TVERSKY (1979).
9. KAHNEMAN AND TVERSKY (1979).
10. A.L. McGILL, "Context Effects in the Judgment of Causation." *Journal of Personality and Social Psychology* 57 (1989): 189–200.
11. I. RITOV AND J. BARON, "Reluctance to Vaccinate: Omission Bias and Ambiguity," *Journal of Behavioral Decision Making* 3 (1990): 263–277.
12. For further details on many of these issues, interested readers may consult S. WORCHELAND AND W.G. AUSTIN, *Psychology of Intergroup Relations* (Chicago: Nelson-Hill, 1986).
13. M.B. BREWER, "In-Group Bias in the Minimal Intergroup Situation: A Cognitive-Motivational Analysis," *Psychological Bulletin* 86 (1979): 307–324.
14. For example, see S.E. TAYLOR, *Positive Illusions* (New York: Basic Books, 1989).

15. S.E. TAYLOR AND J.D. BROWN, "Illusion and Well-Being: A Social Psychological Perspective," *Psychological Bulletin* 103 (1988): 193–210.

16. R.M. KRAMER, E. NEWTON, AND P.L. POMMERENKE, "Self-Enhancement Biases and Negotiator Judgment: Effects of Self-Esteem and Mood." *Organizational Behavior and Human Decision Processes* 56 (1993): 110–133.

17. M. ROSS AND F. SICOLY, "Egocentric Biases in Availability and Attribution," *Journal of Personality and Social Psychology* 37 (1979): 322–336.

18. S. LICHTENSTEIN, B. FISCHHOFF, AND L. D. PHILLIPS, "Calibration of Probabilities," in D. Kahneman, P. Slovic, and A. Tversky, eds., *Judgement under Uncertainty: Heuristics and Biases* (Cambridge: Cambridge University Press, 1982), pp. 306–334.

19. B. FISCHOFF, P. SLOVIC, AND S. LICHTENSTEIN, "Knowing with Certainty: The Appropriateness of Extreme Confidence," *Journal of Experimental Psychology: Human Perception and Performance* 3 (1977): 552–564.

20. Ibid.

21. R.M. CAMBRIDGE AND R.C. SHRECKENGOST, "Are You Sure? The Subjective Probability Assessment Test" (Langley, Virginia: Office of Training, Central Intelligence Agency, unpublished manuscript, 1980).

22. P.C. WASON, "On the Failure to Eliminate Hypotheses in a Conceptual Task," *Quarterly Journal of Experimental Psychology* 12 (1960): 129–140.

23. JANIS (1982).

24. S. BOK, *Lying: Moral Choice in Public and Private Life* (New York: Vintage Books, 1989).

P A R T

II

Ethics, Economics, and Law: An Institutional Approach to Decision Making

CHAPTER 2

Ethical Decision Making: Psychological Foundations

ETHICS IN PERSONAL AND BUSINESS SETTINGS

Jameson and Mamet are not sure what criteria they should use to make the relocation decision. They turned first to economic criteria, which favored moving the plant. Moving the plant, however, had legal and ethical aspects that were inseparable from the economic aspects. In this chapter we will discuss different kinds of ethical problems and examine some of the psychological processes we use to resolve them.

The section, "Ethical Conflicts and Their Context," offers working definitions of ethical problems, dilemmas, and false dilemmas. This will give us a clearer idea of the issues facing Jameson and Mamet. Conflicts are interpreted in terms of their "institutional settings." Institutions affect the cost of the move and the projections of future market share and revenues (see North, Chapter 1).

The next two sections, "Understanding Institutions: Kohlberg's Rights-Based Theory of Moral Development" and "Understanding Institutions: Gilligan's Care-Based Theory of Moral Development," discuss cognitive–developmental explanations of ethical reasoning, focusing on Lawrence Kohlberg and Carol Gilligan. Kohlberg and Gilligan argue that there are three levels of moral thought through which human beings progress: a self-oriented level, a group-oriented level, and a reflective level in which we critically examine our own reasoning strategies and group norms. Although some of this research is contentious, Kohlberg and Gilligan have demonstrated that we use ethical categories to understand and guide our behavior in all areas, including business. One implication of their research is that we need ethical concepts for a factually adequate understanding of business decision making. "Three Conditions of a Successful Decision-Making Strategy" distills insights about decision making from the work of Kohlberg and Gilligan that we will use to evaluate business reasoning. "Moral Imagination and Expanding the Domain of Post-Conventional Reasoning" discusses Patricia H. Werhane's argument that a failure of moral imagination is at the heart of many business problems. One way to expand our moral imagination is to understand that ethical views, such as egoism and conventionalism, can have post-conventional underpinnings.

"Ethical Decision Making: Opportunities and Constraints in Organizations" discusses how organizational settings affect ethical reasoning. It relies on Linda Trevino's model of decision making. Trevino, Dennis Gioia, and others have noted that there is no direct link between moral reasoning and behavior. Trevino argues that the reasoning–behavior link is affected by individual and situational moderators.

"Organizing Decision Making" includes a description of a seven-step process for understanding and resolving—not solving—ethical issues in business. The distinction between resolving problems and solving them is crucial. For many people, the word "solve" implies that there is a single right answer to be discovered. This is rarely true with complex business interactions; the use of the word "resolve" tries to capture this complexity. The decision-making strategy shows how ethical, economic, and legal criteria can help managers identify and interpret information necessary for an informed decision.

ETHICAL CONFLICTS AND THEIR CONTEXT

Ethical Conflicts: Problems, Dilemmas, and False Dilemmas

We will consider three kinds of ethical conflicts: problems, dilemmas, and false dilemmas. We have an ethical problem when we do not want to do what we believe is right. For example, suppose that Jameson and Mamet decide that relocating the plant is the right thing to do, but neither of them want to do it for family reasons. As managers, they believe they should not put their own interests of self and family ahead of the firm and its stockholders. In this scenario, Jameson and Mamet do not want to do what they believe is right.

We have an ethical dilemma when every course of action violates important ethical concerns. In the S and R case, Jameson and Mamet believe they face an ethical dilemma. They believe they have important duties to their families, the community, their employees, and their suppliers that suggest not moving. They also believe they have important duties to the owners and to themselves that suggest moving. All courses of actions violate what they perceive to be important ethical concerns.

Sometimes, what appears to be a dilemma is a false dilemma. A false dilemma is a conflict that initially appears as a dilemma, but disappears on further analysis.[1] For example, Jameson and Mamet can acquire new facts or resolve value conflicts in ways that eliminate the dilemma. Suppose S and R hires a consultant that tells them not to move. This new fact removes an important duty to move. Or, suppose Jameson and Mamet decide their duty to the corporation is very strong, but their duties to family, community, employees, and suppliers are weak. This value decision removes an important reason for staying. In this second scenario, Jameson and Mamet have ordinally ranked the duty to move first and the duty to stay second. They have also given the duty to stay a very low cardinal ranking.[2] We can rank ordinally without ranking cardinally, but not conversely.

These two kinds of ranking are important to managerial decision making. To see why, let us continue with the scenario that Jameson and Mamet ordinally rank their duties to shareholders first and their combined duties to others second.

Ordinal Ranking: The duty to shareholders is first, the duty to others is second.

For the purposes of illustration, let us assume that numbers can be assigned to these alternatives using a 1–10 scale, with 10 as the highest. Now consider these two cardinal rankings:

> *Cardinal Ranking A:* The duty to move has a value of 10 and the duty to stay has a value of 9.
>
> *Cardinal Ranking B:* The duty to move has a value of 10 and the duty to stay has a value of 3.

Cardinal rankings A and B have the same ordinal rankings, but could easily result in different decisions. Notice that neither ordinal nor cardinal ranking will give a mechanical answer, but must be applied to the facts of the case. Consider Cardinal Ranking B: if moving the plant resulted in minuscule improvements for owners (0.01 cent per share over 5 years) and massive harm for the community (thousands thrown out of work, bankruptcies, suicides, etc.), this ranking could still result in a decision not to move the plant.

Ethical Conflicts, Great and Small

Some business problems become scandals that reach epic proportions: the chemical leaks in Bhopal that killed thousands; the toxic waste dump at Love canal that has cost hundreds of millions of dollars and may have harmed the health of hundreds, and the savings and loan collapse in the late 1980s that has cost U.S. taxpayers more than a billion dollars. These kinds of dramatic cases, however, are far outnumbered by less dramatic, common ethical issues. Because of this, it can be misleading to focus on sensational cases.

The following six scenarios illustrate some common ethical conflicts. Examining these will help us obtain a sense of how making business decisions fits with the decisions we make in other parts of our lives. The scenarios concern self, family, friends, school, work, and government.

1. You have worked at your present job for 6 months as a research assistant for the Vice President in charge of finance. He is evaluating three bids for a new software program for the accounting department. It is 2 days before the deadline for bids, but only two of three bids have come in. The third bid is coming from a firm whose CEO is a friend of your boss. Your boss hands you the two bids, and tells you to fax them to his friend. Should you fax the bids?[3]

2. You have worked long and hard on getting your MBA. Your parents have lent you money to help with tuition, and you will start paying them back when you get a good job. You are offered an ideal position in a distant city. When you tell your parents the good news, they are devastated. They had expected you to stay in the area. They are getting old, and they are feeling alone and insecure. Should you take the job?

3. It is 5:00 A.M. on a warm summer morning. A long-time friend, whose car is always breaking down, calls you to give him a push start so he can get to work. He pleads with you to help him, explaining that if he is late to his job again, he will be fired. Should you get up and help him?

4. Your finance teacher, who is also the placement director, asks you to do research for a publication she is working on. She says she will pay you for your work and cite you in the publication if you do a good job. You have heard that her student helpers have a hard time getting paid and are rarely cited for the work they do. Should you accept the research job?

5. One of the people you manage in your department, with whom you have socialized a few times outside work, comes to ask you for a favor. He wants to be with his son,

who is going through chemical dependency treatment, but he has used all of his discretionary leave time. Your friend/employee wants to count this as sick leave, and he asks you not to require the mandatory written explanation by a doctor. What should you do?

6. You are pulled over on a very rainy evening for making an illegal left-hand turn at a nearly flooded intersection. You saw the sign prohibiting left-hand turns, but, as you could see no cars, you deliberately disobeyed it to save time. As the officer comes up to the car, you think of telling her the following: "I did not intend to turn, but I started to skid to the left when the car hit the water. So, I continued turning left to avoid going up on the sidewalk." Do you tell this story, or just accept the ticket?

These situations call for ethical reasoning and decisions in a variety of settings. In the first case, your self-interest, interpreted in terms of income and career, is at stake. Also at stake are your self-image, character, and reputation with your boss and peers. If you send the fax and it is discovered by the other bidders, you are afraid you will lose your job. You also worry that your boss may ask you to do other unethical things. If you refuse to fax the bids, are you implying that you are more ethical than your boss? Will he find this insulting? If he does not fire you for your refusal, he could make life so hard for you that you will be forced to quit.

In the second situation, you are evaluating the nature of your obligations to your parents and your obligation to yourself. What you should do will depend in part on the particular nature of the relationship between you and your parents and your opportunities for other jobs.

The third example concerns your friendship with the caller, and how that affects your obligation and your desire to help. If you help him, that is just the kind of thing a friend would do. However, if you do not help him, that may encourage him to take better care of his car, and so not rely on his friends to bail him out all the time. Either way, you are basing your decision on considerations of friendship and self-interest.

In the fourth situation, there are some new concerns. First, do you trust the bad reports that you have received about your finance teacher? Perhaps the disgruntled students were not paid or cited because they did very little work, or because what they did was not helpful. On the other hand, if you believe the reports and help your teacher, are you giving your tacit support to the way she treats students? Perhaps you should encourage the students who were harmed to report it to the chair of the department. Perhaps you decide to do the research because you are interested in getting a good job. All of these choices have ethical aspects, and a successful decision-making strategy needs to account for them.

The fifth situation is more complex. One important part of being a manager is to obey the rules of the company, and not to give special favors to friends. However, since the person asking for the favor needs to be with his son, you might wonder if this employee will be more productive if you grant the request. Your job is also to help your employees be as productive as possible. Your self-interest is also a factor. What risk will you take if you lie, or simply fail to make the proper report (and is the failure to make a report a kind of lie)? You may also wonder whether the previous absences were legitimate, and this may make you skeptical of the present request. Issues of loyalty, honesty, self-interest, obligation, and fairness are involved in your decision. You need some form of reasoning that will recognize and integrate them.

In the last situation, you have broken a traffic law, but you have "a story" that might get you out of the ticket. Is being caught making the illegal turn like being called on a bluff in a poker game? If so, it's time to pay up. But if it is a game, what *part* of the game are you playing? Perhaps talking to the officer is where the bluffing occurs. If so, does the police officer really expect you to tell the truth? Perhaps it is part of the game for you to lie, or better, bluff. If bluffing is normal in this situation, lying to the officer is no more unethical than bluffing in poker. In this case you are making a decision about what you should do based on your view of how you relate to the police officer and to the rules of society. Is the person who lies unethical, or is the person who tells the truth a "chump"? Once again, ethical concepts figure prominently in this decision making, and we need to integrate them.[4]

The S and R relocation problem incorporates dilemmas similar to those discussed above. Although relocating a plant is not the kind of case that executives face regularly, the need to resolve conflicts between self, friends, family, community, and corporate duties is a component of everyday business decision making. We will focus on the nature of these conflicts, how they fit into institutional settings, and how to resolve them.

Ethics in Context: The Institutional Settings of Business

The six conflicts described above arise within institutions. According to Uphoff,

> Institutions are . . . complexes of norms and behaviors that persist over time by serving collectively valued purposes.[5]

Institutions shape markets by influencing what Douglass North calls "choice sets." A choice set is the set of alternatives open to a person or organization. Hence, institutions create the possibility of, and set limits on, choices. Institutions can be practices like the pursuit of self-interest or promising, documents like the Koran or the working constitution of a country, roles like parent or church leader, and organizations like the Supreme Court or General Motors. An important (proper) subset of institutions forms the social infrastructure that makes economic activity possible. North argues:

> Throughout history, *institutions have been devised by human beings to create order and reduce uncertainty in exchange.* Together with the standard constraints of economics they define the choice set and therefore determine transaction and production costs and hence the profitability and feasibility of engaging in economic activity. They evolve incrementally, connecting the past with the present and the present with the future. . . . *Institutions provide the incentive structure of an economy.* (emphasis added)[6]

Institutions consist of the roles, rules, and principles that define relationships between strangers, friends, family members, fellow workers, citizens, and government. These relationships are characterized by mutual expectations. As long as these expectations are fulfilled, the institutions are invisible to us: they form the infrastructure of social life.

Conflicts and Institutions

Conflicts between institutional expectations throw institutional settings into relief.[7] Each of the six cases above involves institutional relationships tested by conflicts. Although it is the conflict that gets our immediate attention, we can understand the conflict only if we understand the institutional setting out of which the conflict arises. Because conflicts highlight particular aspects of institutions, they are valuable diagnostic tools for investigating and evaluating institutional settings.

CONFLICTS AS DIAGNOSTIC TOOLS

Consider the third problem regarding the early morning call for help. This conflict makes sense only against the institution of friendship in terms of which the two people define their relationship. It is the friendship, defined in part by loyalty and self-sacrifice, that gets the sleeping person to consider seriously getting up at 5:00 A.M. The conflict can be an opportunity to think about the institution of friendship in general and how that institution applies to this friendship in particular (though not at 5:00 o'clock in the morning!). To appreciate the importance of this institutional setting, imagine that the caller is someone who stole money from the person called, or someone the person met briefly for the first time a few days ago. In these two cases there would not be much conflict about what to do, or perhaps the conflict would be different: should the person hang up or be polite?

Institutions and Ethics

On the institutional view we are developing, ethical rules and principles are an essential part of the institutions that direct our lives in nonconflict situations, from the most intimate to the most impersonal.[8] The primary function of ethics is not to force us to do something we do not want to do, although we tend to notice ethical rules and principles when they are contrary to our current interests or desires.

Preview of Chapter

In "Understanding Institutions: Kohlberg's Rights-Based Theory of Moral Development" and "Understanding Institutions: Gilligan's Care-Based Theory of Moral Development" we will discuss Lawrence Kohlberg's and Carol Gilligan's cognitive–developmental theories of moral development to see how we come to understand the institutions that guide our professional and personal lives. Their theories are based on extensive longitudinal and cross-sectional studies. There are many disagreements among cognitive–developmental theorists about the details of moral development. Perhaps the most serious split occurs between Kohlberg and Gilligan concerning the relevance of gender. Despite these conflicts there are important areas of agreement. We will focus on the areas of agreement.

In "Three Conditions of a Successful Decision-Making Strategy" we will distill some common elements of successful decision making from the theories of Kohlberg and Gilligan. The next section, "Moral Imagination: Expanding the Domain of Post-Conventional Reasoning," argues that we are not limited to the moral reasoning of the kinds described by Kohlberg and Gilligan.

"Ethical Decision Making: Opportunities and Constraints in Organizations" discusses how moral reasoning can be affected by organizational structure and incentive systems. Although this can result in good people lying and cheating, it can also influence the less scrupulous to act ethically.

The penultimate section, "Organizing Decision Making," presents a seven-step strategy that is based on the psychology of decision making. This seven-step strategy also includes elements of ethics, economics, and law, which are the subjects of Chapters 3, 4, and 5, respectively.

UNDERSTANDING INSTITUTIONS: KOHLBERG'S
RIGHTS-BASED THEORY OF MORAL DEVELOPMENT

Social institutions serve many functions. We will concentrate on the following four:

1. Institutions create opportunities for pursuing self-interest.
2. Institutions create opportunities for developing family relationships and friend-ships.
3. Institutions create opportunities for establishing formal groups and promoting their interests.
4. Institutions create opportunities for pursuing fairness, justice, human rights, and the good of all.[9]

Cognitive–developmental psychologists such as Lawrence Kohlberg and Carol Gilligan have examined how we come to understand and reason about the social insti-tutions that create and direct these opportunities.

In the late 1950s, Lawrence Kohlberg began what turned out to be a worldwide project to examine how we acquire moral beliefs and how we reason about moral issues. Kohlberg based his initial research on an 18-year longitudinal study of 50 American males between the ages of 10 and 28. On the basis of that and many subsequent studies, he argued that we acquire moral beliefs in a rational and predictable way. Shared ethical values arise because we use the same rational methods to select them, not because we blindly copy them from our social environment.

Kohlberg argued that there are three very general ethical reasoning patterns, or lev-els, through which we progress in a serial order; the Preconventional Level, the Con-ventional Level, and the Postconventional Level. Each of these levels is further divided into stages. Let us look at the levels first.

As their names suggest, the three levels of moral reasoning are defined by the way individuals understand the moral rules that make up social institutions.[10] In the Precon-ventional Level, individuals interpret these rules egoistically: parental, school, and gov-ernment rules are arbitrary instruments of the powerful for doing what they want. A Level I person would reason as follows: If the rules benefit me, they are good rules; if they harm me, they are bad rules; if they do not affect me, or if their affect on me is nei-ther good nor bad, then the rules are neither good nor bad. Level I reasoners are typically not capable of reasoning abstractly, and so they cannot understand how institutions or-chestrate group behavior to promote goods and prevent harms that no one person could.

In the Conventional Level, individuals realize that formal and informal institutional rules play a central role in group stability and order. These rules define our rights and du-ties. Punishment is used to maintain group stability. Enforcement is the job of legitimate authority. Legitimacy is understood in terms of institutional roles, such as being a par-ent, a company officer, or a public official. The center of ethical value is the group to which the individual belongs, not the individual.[11] Individuals in the Conventional Level tend to believe in the goodness of their leaders and in the ethical supremacy of the rules of their group.

In the Postconventional Level, the final level of moral development, people still value institutional rules, but they believe that these rules, as well as legitimate leaders, can be morally wrong. Examples of rules that are wrong are the slavery laws in the United States prior to the Civil War. Examples of leaders who made morally wrong decisions are Hitler and other members of the German bureaucracy in the 1930s and 1940s who first oppressed and then slaughtered the Jews. Since groups can act from immoral rules, individuals in the Post-Conventional Level search for universal standards or principles, like fairness and the good of all, that do not depend on group acceptance. These principles are universal because they apply to everyone, not because everyone accepts them.

The center of ethical value in the Postconventional Level is the individual human being, apart from any group affiliation or relationship. Institutions are evaluated in terms of how well they respect the rights of all individuals or in terms of how well they promote the well-being of all individuals. The ability to understand the moral value and limits of social institutions and the ability to distinguish between legitimate and illegitimate acts of legitimate authorities are central features of postconventional moral reasoning.[12]

There is an intimate link between moral and social development. As people progress through these levels, they understand better how complex societies work, or as we put it earlier, they understand better the roles, rules, and principles that constitute the social institutions that guide behavior.

Post-conventional reasoning is best able to represent institutional settings because it is the only type of reasoning that helps us understand how the principles embodied in an institution can be used to evaluate the institution itself as well as other institutions. For example, in Chapters 4 and 5 we will see that the values underlying the institution of private property set limits on the use of private property. We will also see how the values underlying the institution of competition can affect the rules governing private property.

The link between moral and social development illustrates an important way in which cognitive–developmental theory is relevant to problems in business and society: the institutional settings that people come to understand as they move from pre-conventional to conventional to post-conventional reasoning are the institutional settings in which business decisions are made; to understand one is to understand the other.

A Functional View of Ethical Beliefs

According to cognitive–developmental theory, moral beliefs have two major functions:

1. Moral beliefs help us direct our own behavior.
2. Moral beliefs help us understand and evaluate the behavior of others.

If our moral beliefs do not adequately serve these functions, we modify them or seek new ones that will serve these functions better. Since problems occur in institutional settings, we are constantly testing our understanding of those institutions. It is this process of testing and evaluating our moral beliefs—a process similar to testing hypotheses in science—that cognitive–developmental theorists have studied in some detail.

To get a better understanding of this process of hypothesis testing, we will examine the levels and stages in more detail, discuss some general principles of stage progression, and examine why an individual would progress through these levels and stages.

The Levels and Stages of Moral Development

LEVEL I: THE PRE-CONVENTIONAL LEVEL

Individuals have a limited understanding of, and no loyalty to, institutional groups or rules. Groups and rules are valuable only if they promote the interest of oneself. Individuals make moral judgments in terms of concrete consequences to themselves.

Stage 1: The Punishment and Obedience Orientation. Right acts are those that are not punished. Punishment consists of either corporal punishment or the loss of a privilege. Authorities are those with the power to punish.

Stage 2: The Instrumental-Relativist Orientation. Right acts promote one's interest now or in the future. Individuals understand how reciprocity can justify current loss to secure greater rewards later (delay of gratification). However, they will delay gratification only if the later reward is large enough to outweigh the immediate loss as well as the greatest possible immediate reward.

LEVEL II: THE CONVENTIONAL LEVEL

Individuals understand how institutions such as families and governments promulgate rules that bind individuals together in groups. They make moral judgments in terms of rule following and the concrete consequences to their group, and so can justify self-sacrifice. One's group is viewed as morally superior to other groups.

Stage 3: The Interpersonal Concordance of the "Good Boy–Nice Girl" Orientation. Right acts accord with group rules, promote the good of a small group, or are approved by legitimate authorities. Reciprocity is valuable because it holds a group together, not because we as individuals are better off. There is loyalty to the group, its rules, and authorities.

Stage 4: The Law and Order Orientation. Right acts accord with group rules or promote the good of a large group, like a nation, that is a group of groups. There is loyalty to the large group, its laws, and its leaders.

LEVEL III: THE POST-CONVENTIONAL LEVEL

Individuals use universal ethical standards. The partiality of Levels I and II is rejected in favor of impartiality, which views all human beings as equally valuable. The Post-Conventional Level represents the first time individuals consciously interpret and reintegrate institutional values. In the Pre-Conventional and Conventional Levels, individuals see their institutional world as beyond their control: the only options are to conform or not conform. Post-Conventional reasoners view institutions as socially constructed. By relying on the values embodied in institutions, they can adapt institutions to meet new needs and interests. If enough people do this, the institution itself changes.

Stage 5: The Social-Contract Legalistic Orientation. Right acts and policies are those that are fair or promote the well-being of all affected, although these two standards are not clearly distinguished from each other. Institutions of all kinds, from the pursuit of self-interest to family and governmental structures, can be unjust. There is loyalty to rules and groups only insofar as they respect human beings.

Stage 6: The Universal Ethical Principle Orientation. Right acts and policies should respect human dignity. The good of all is rejected as a moral standard. There is loyalty to a universal principle of human dignity, not to laws or to groups.[13]

General Features of Moral Development

In the 30 years since Kohlberg's initial study, an enormous amount of research has been done on men and women in a variety of cultures. On the basis of these studies, Kohlberg and other cognitive–developmental theorists have argued that moral development is not dependent on gender or culture, but is similar throughout the world.

This is an amazing claim. It is common knowledge that cultures differ significantly from each other, and that some of their greatest differences lie in their ethical views. Kohlberg's theory, however, does not deny cultural ethical diversity. Rather, he claims to have found similarities that underlie and, in fact, help explain cultural differences. Kohlberg argues that people from all cultures progress through the same types or structures of moral reasoning, even though these structures may be composed of different moral beliefs or content. The structure–content distinction is a crucial one. It will help us understand cognitive–developmental theory and the problem-solving strategy described at the end of this chapter.

The structure of moral reasoning refers to the way in which moral beliefs are related to each other to form a system. The content of moral reasoning refers to the particular beliefs in the system. It is the structure of moral beliefs that determines how we reason, not the content. For example, in Stages 2 and 3, we value ourselves and our families, but we structure these beliefs differently. In Stage 2 we value ourselves more than our families; in Stage 3 we value our families more than ourselves.

The distinction between structure and content accounts for cultural moral diversity in the following way. In all cultures, people begin their lives reasoning in terms of self-interest. However, the content of self-interest will vary depending on the person, the situation, and the culture. For example, a child in a tribe of hunter–gatherers in the Amazon rainforest and a child on a family farm in Iowa may both structure their beliefs in terms of self-interest, but the content of their moral reasoning will be different. The hunter–gatherer child may value the story telling of the elders while the farm child may value watching a television show.

In the Conventional Level, the structure of moral reasoning is determined by group loyalty. For example, Japanese and French managers may both believe that their companies contribute to their home country's welfare, and so justify company loyalty in terms of national loyalty. The structure of their reasoning is the same since they both appeal to the good of their home country. However, since they have different home countries, the content of their reasoning is different.

The structure of the Post-Conventional Level is determined by the universality of principles. The content is determined by the particular universal ethical principles one adopts. According to Kohlberg, we are limited to a choice between principles of intrinsic value (human dignity, rights, fairness, justice) or a principle of utility (promoting the well-being of all).

The structure–content distinction helps answer two central questions about the development of moral reasoning:

1. Why do we adopt new forms of moral reasoning?
2. When we do progress, what happens to the moral reasoning we leave behind?

We adopt new forms of moral reasoning because of cognitive disequilibrium (CD).[14] CD occurs when our stage of moral reasoning is unable to perform one or both of its functions: to direct our own behavior and to understand and evaluate the behavior of others. Depending on the importance of the situation and the extent of disequilibrium, CD may cause anything from mild annoyance to great anxiety or pain. It is this discomfort, and our desire to remove it, that prompts us to seek better ways to understand our institutional environment.

To see how CD would provide an incentive to search for a new problem-solving strategy, consider Jameson and Mamet's plant relocation dilemma. In the past, they tried to make decisions that benefited S and R and that helped, or at least did not harm, Frieberg. Relocation brings these two strategies in conflict. They have never had to deal with this particular conflict, at least not when the stakes have been this high. Until they come up with a strategy to resolve this conflict, their cognitive disequilibrium will remain.

When cognitive disequilibrium pushes us to change how we think about problems and the institutions in which they arise, we retain much of the content of the earlier stage. Kohlberg refers to this process as hierarchical integration (HI). Although the content of a stage is reintegrated at higher levels, it is important to note that the structures of those previous stages are no longer present. A stage is nothing more than a set of relationships between beliefs; when those relationships change, the old stage disappears and a new one emerges.

To see how content can remain but structure does not, consider an analogous case. A group of contractors buys a nineteenth-century farm with all of its buildings. They plan to build a housing development. The site where the old farmhouse stands is particularly beautiful, wooded and hilly. The contractors decide to keep this site intact, and to build a luxury home on it. The contractors plan to tear down the farmhouse, but to use as much of this material as possible in constructing the new house. The aged wooden slats and beams will be fitted into a new and more functional dwelling. Much of the content remains, but the previous structure is gone. This is like the process of stage progression. When our structure of moral reasoning is no longer useful, we dismantle it, and use what parts we can to build a new structure.

Kohlberg's work suggests that we need to do three things to resolve problems successfully:

1. analyze the problem;
2. analyze the institutional setting in which the problem arose; and
3. evaluate the reasoning we use in 1 and 2.

We are now ready to take a closer look at moral development. We will see how deficiencies in the first two steps and the attendant CD prompt us to do step 3, which in turn prompts us to adopt a new structure of moral reasoning that allows us to do 1 and 2 more successfully.

The main purpose of this discussion is to understand how conflicts can lead us to reevaluate institutional settings as well as our reasoning processes, not to understand Kohlberg's theory in itself. Jameson and Mamet must do be able to do 1, 2, and 3 to resolve the relocation problem. In general, managers must do this when they face novel problems and/or institutional conflicts.

The Rational Process of Moral Development

In this section we will examine how an individual at each stage of moral reasoning would react to the relocation problem in the S and R case. We then will examine the stage's strengths and weakness. The weaknesses lead to CD, whereas the strengths lead to HI.

Each stage can justify moving and not moving. This is because each stage is a set of beliefs about rules and principles that needs to be interpreted and applied to a set of facts. Since we can interpret and apply these rules and principles in a variety of ways, knowing a person's stage does not allow us to predict what decision that person will make. We can predict, however, what factors are important to that person, and how that person is likely to integrate them to produce a solution.[15]

The first three stages are inadequate for analyzing the problem that Jameson and Mamet face. It is not merely that they are ethically inadequate; they are factually inadequate. People who reason in these elementary ways cannot understand the complexities of human motivation, how organizations work, or how organizations are imbedded in larger groups and institutions. It is not until Stage 4, or perhaps 5, that a complete factual account is possible.

LEVEL I: PRE-CONVENTIONAL MORAL REASONING

As we noted above, people who reason in a pre-conventional fashion (Stages 1 and 2) are unable to comprehend fully how rules define and maintain groups. Individuals in the Pre-Conventional Level justify their actions in terms of the concrete consequences to themselves. In most cases, they are unable to appeal to anything but their own interests. Figure 2.1 is a test to determine if a person can recognize groups.

If you ask a person who does not have the concept of a group (this is usually, but not always, a child) how many things are in Figure 2.1, the person will count each of the 18 dots. If you then inform the person that there are also three things present, the person will very likely tell you that you are wrong, and may proceed to count the dots again to show you the error of your ways.

Without the concept of a group, a person cannot understand that there are three groups as well as 18 dots. A person who reasons in this way will have difficulty with issues, including moral ones, that involve groups. Hence, it is not surprising that individuals in Level I have difficulty understanding how rules function in groups. Since moral issues, especially managerial ones, typically involve groups in one way or another, pre-conventional reasoners lack the ability to consider a class of important facts that forms the substance of these problems. This is not to say that pre-conventional reasoners do not act morally, only that they will interpret the problem as one in which individuals are tied to each other by unique bonds. They cannot understand the relationships that individuals have to groups or the way that rules standardize our relationships.[16] Because of these limitations, it is virtually certain that Jameson and Mamet are not at Level I. However, what we are interested in here is how a Level I person would react to their problem.

Stage 1 describes right and wrong primarily in terms of the concrete and immediate consequences to the individual reasoner. The ideal life for Stage 1 reasoners is doing what they want independently of rules and other people. When rules or other people interfere with satisfying one's desires, circumventing those obstacles is wrong only if you are caught and punished. Consider the following Stage 1 responses to Jameson and Mamet's problem.

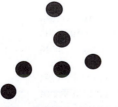

Figure 2.1

1. They should move. They are the bosses, and they can do what they want. No one can hurt them. And once they move they will be out of reach anyway. I really don't see why they have a problem.

2. They should not move. Sounds like they both want to stay because their friends and families will punish them if they leave. They are in charge, and nobody can tell them what to do. I really don't see why they have a problem.

Stage 1 moral reasoning is characterized by the avoidance of punishment to the individual reasoner. The interests or rights of others, even close family members, are not considered. Further, individuals in this stage have a rather crude view of their own interest, which they define in terms of avoiding physical pain. Notice the unrealistic notion of being a boss. Stage 1 views those in charge as beyond the criticism of others. They have no understanding of how organizations work, or of how organizations fit into the larger society. Individuals must progress beyond this primitive reasoning if they are to be successful in organizations.

We leave Stage 1 behind when we begin to see that merely avoiding punishment will not help us get benefits that are possible only through cooperation. CD forces us to look for a reasoning strategy that incorporates cooperative strategies. The major component of Stage 2 reasoning is reciprocity. Once we understand reciprocal relationships, we can begin to see how it characterizes relationships between family members, friends, bosses, and teachers. If you cooperate, others are more likely to cooperate with you. The fact that leaders need the cooperation of others is an important realization, since it is the first step to a more adequate view of groups and organizations.

In the transition to Stage 2, we retain the belief that physical punishment is bad, but we balance punishment against the benefits of cooperation (HI). This is an elementary form of cost–benefit analysis. If the cooperative gains of an action are great and the immediate punishment small, we can justify suffering a small loss now for the future reward. However, if the punishment for a particular act is great, and the cooperative benefits are small, we will judge cooperation to be wrong. Cooperation is not valuable in itself, only as a means to self-interest.

Although understanding reciprocal relationships is an important step forward, it is still limited. To see this, consider the following Stage 2 responses to the S and R case.

1. They should move. Jameson and Mamet are the bosses, but they depend on the shareholders for money and support. The people in Frieberg cannot really do anything to them. If they help the shareholders, the shareholders will help them. If they think about it this way, they will see they should move.

2. They should not move. Sounds like they both want to stay, for family reasons. Families do a lot of things for us that we do not have time to do for ourselves. As far as the company goes, Jameson and Mamet can control the shareholders by deciding what to tell them. If the CEO and CFO say that is it is better not to move, the shareholders do not know enough to argue. When Jameson and Mamet see that they control the information, they will realize they don't have to move.

Families, friends, and others have no value in themselves, but are important only in terms of what they can do for the individual reasoner. We should note that these responses do not indicate that Stage 2 reasoning is as emotionally detached as it may seem. Kohlberg's tests are designed to elicit our reasoning about ethical issues, not our emotional responses to them. The fact that subjects do not mention the importance of emotional connections does not mean that they do not have them.

Like Stage 1, these Stage 2 responses are factually inadequate, which can lead to CD. As we develop emotionally we begin to see that *quid pro quo* reasoning does not capture the relevant facts of relationships based on love and friendship. It is at this point that conventional reasoning becomes attractive because it better represents the social institutions in which we live. As we become able to identify groups and see how rules and leaders make groups possible, we begin to see that the world is composed not only of individuals, but also of groups that tie individuals together in a number of ways.

LEVEL II: CONVENTIONAL MORAL REASONING

Conventional moral reasoning bases moral judgments on the well-being of one's group. We move to conventional reasoning when we develop the capacity to understand groups as abstract entities and to empathize with needs of others.

Typically, the first group with which we identify is our family. We also begin to understand our empathetic feelings toward our friends, and even to characters in movies and books. Our growing emotional capacities change what we think of as rewards and punishments. Stage 2 defines rewards and punishments in terms of physical things: money, candy, and the like. In Stage 3, we can value our personal relationships with family and friends more than our own physical pleasures.

It is important to note that restructuring what gives us pleasure and pain does not result in a new form of egoism. Commentators from Aristotle[17] to Robert Frank[18] have noted that the pleasures and pains we get from our personal relationships are possible only because we already have commitments to people.[19] It is our caring for others that grounds our empathetic pleasures and pains. In Stage 3, the pleasure and pain we feel are only indicators of right and wrong; what defines right and wrong are features of the relationship itself.

As Stage 3 reasoners we do not cease to care about ourselves. If we have to sacrifice our interests, however, our sacrifice should be done in a way that accords with our group's rules and needs as stipulated by recognized institutions. Consider these Stage 3 responses to the S and R case.

1. They should move. A company is like a family, and Jameson and Mamet are like parents. They have a responsibility to look out for the shareholders, who are like an extended family. I feel bad for the employees' families, but each family needs to look out for itself. Besides, the employees' families will find other ways to support themselves, maybe even better ways.

2. They should not move. Both Jameson and Mamet will have family problems if they leave. Also, think about all the families that will be affected by people losing their jobs. The families of the workers will be hurt a lot more than the families of the owners, who are probably rich anyway. As for the families at the relocation site, well, they need to be cared for by people there. They are not Jameson's and Mamet's responsibility.

Family duty and loyalty are at the center of these two responses. To most people, these responses are the first ones that seem like moral responses. They rely heavily on the value of the family and the role of parents as protectors.

The main difference between these two Stage 3 responses is what counts as family. The first response views S and R as the relevant family. The second response focuses on the families of various stakeholders. This is also the stage at which intentions begin to have moral weight. For example, a Stage 3 reasoner could say the first response was right even if the relocation failed, as long as Jameson and Mamet had the intention to benefit the organizational "family."

Although Stage 3 reasoning can help us better understand and resolve problems at the level of small groups, it will run into problems at the level of the larger society. Both Stage 3 responses showed very little understanding of how business organizations work in complex institutional environments, and neither was able to consider adequately the international aspects of the case. The first response mistakenly viewed the corporation as a family. The second response ignored, among other things, the role of suppliers and the present community. These kinds of problems tend to cause CD. Typically, CD will arise for Stage 3 when it needs to coordinate the interests of the family with groups outside the family.

Stage 4 defines morality in terms of adherence to the laws and loyalty to the leaders of one's country. These laws, and the leaders who enforce them, provide a framework of rules that enable individuals and groups to work together to achieve their common and separate goals. The importance of intentions that emerged in Stage 3 is integrated into a legal system that uses intentions to classify, and assign penalties for, crimes and torts.

Stage 4 reasoners could respond to the S and R case as follows.

1. They should move. The laws of the country give managers the right and the duty to maximize the wealth of shareholders. The more that managers do this, the better off the country will be.

2. They should not move. The country needs these jobs. Moving violates a fundamental duty to the country. Using our country's resources to build up a company and then shipping it and its benefits overseas is like stealing. The people in these other countries have no right to these jobs.

Both of these responses cite the social obligations of corporations. They disagree about what the social obligation is. The importance of families is not necessarily diminished, but the interpretation of that value has changed. Now family well-being is important because it promotes national stability.

Although Stage 4 can represent the facts of broad social problems better than Stage 3, CD can arise for a number of reasons. First, people using Stage 4 reasoning will have difficulty understanding and resolving problems that include people and groups that come from other cultures. They will also have trouble understanding how moral considerations, such as fairness and the good of all, can play a role in changing the laws of a nation, especially their own. Finally, they will have difficulty determining what the national interest is. In the United States, for example, the President, the Congress, and the courts can disagree over policy. There are also conflicts between states and the federal government, and between communities within states. The complex network of federal, state, and local government makes it impossible to believe that one's country is always right. At any given time, there can be as many official and conflicting views about a problem as there are governmental levels and branches involved.

These problems with Stage 4 reasoning are especially acute in the global business environment. International business requires us to understand different cultures and to resolve cultural conflicts. Taking the position that one's own country is always right is not likely to lead to long-term international business success. We need a way to recognize the value of all cultures without giving any one of them veto power.

LEVEL III: POST-CONVENTIONAL MORAL REASONING

One way to handle problems with Stage 4 is to base our problem solving on universal principles, such as fairness or the good of all. When we do this, we stop identifying morality solely in terms of our group.

Stage 5, the first stage of autonomous moral reasoning, holds that the institutions and laws of our country are not necessarily right. Political and business leaders, like the rest of us, can make good and bad moral decisions. The Post-Conventional Level adopts an egalitarian approach to moral reasoning and judgment. The egalitarian approach assumes that all individuals have the right to make their own moral decisions.

This egalitarian approach may look like a kind of moral relativism, but it is not. The egalitarian attitude is grounded on the inalienable right of individuals to make their own moral judgments. Stage 5 reasoners would reject any institution or act that is incompatible with this right, such as slavery or genocide, no matter how much an individual or culture believes those practices are morally justified. Our own moral freedom does not allow us to interfere with the moral freedom of others.

Consider the following Stage 5 responses to the S and R case.

1. They should move. The laws of the country give managers the right and the duty to maximize the wealth of shareholders. The more that managers do this, the better off the country will be. Further, they will be strengthening economic and political connections to other countries, which should be good for everyone. They need to be careful, however, not to exploit the workers in those other countries. Those workers have the same rights to protection as any other human being.

2. They should not move. The country needs these jobs, and so does Frieberg. S and R used the country's resources to build up the company, and moving it and its benefits overseas is unfair. If they move, they should compensate Frieberg for the losses; but if they do that the move is no longer economically feasible. If the company were going bankrupt, things would be different, but in this case it is a matter of the company and its owners doing a little bit better, and that is not enough to override the other considerations.

These responses exhibit a good understanding of the relationships between business, government, and society. They also have a good grasp on the international aspects of the case. Compare these answers with people using Stage 1, or even Stage 4 reasoning, and it is clear that a person using Stage 5 reasoning is better able to understand and weigh the facts of this case.

Individuals in Stage 5 can clearly distinguish between legal and moral issues, using the moral to evaluate the legal. For example, if there were a law that prevented S and R from relocating, the first respondent could argue that such a law is morally wrong. On the other hand, since there is no law to make S and R compensate for the benefits it received free of charge, the second respondent could argue that morality requires us to have such a law.

Two Problems with Kohlberg's Theory

The first problem concerns Stage 6. Kohlberg once argued that a small, but significant number of people advanced to Stage 6. However, further research led him to revise his view. In the late-1970s he argued that Stage 6 reasoning was virtually nonexistent in the general population.[20] We will not discuss Stage 6 here, although we will examine Kant in Chapter 3, whom Kohlberg characterized as Stage 6.

The second problem concerns gender. Carol Gilligan, a former colleague of Kohlberg's, argues that many women use a form of moral reasoning that is very different from the rules and rights reasoning that Kohlberg identifies. We now turn to her theory of moral development.

UNDERSTANDING INSTITUTIONS: GILLIGAN'S CARE-BASED THEORY OF MORAL DEVELOPMENT

Carol Gilligan argues that Kohlberg's theory of moral development fails to describe how women make moral decisions. In one study, Gilligan found that approximately one-third of women make moral judgments based on care and compassion.[21] The care perspective interprets morality in terms of personal relationships, responsibility, and care. She contrasts this with Kohlberg's rights perspective, which interprets morality in terms of individuality, rules, and rights.

Care reasoners and rights reasoners notice different aspects of institutions and the conflicts that arise within them. Care reasoners focus on the dynamic contexts of relationships and believe that no rule can cover all situations; rights reasoners focus on rules that apply to many different kinds of situations.

The vase–face illustration illustrates the difference between care and rights (Figure 2.2). To see the faces, we take the white area as the background and the black area as the figure; to see the vase, we reverse background and figure. Most of us can switch between seeing the faces and vase. But suppose you had two people, one who could see only the faces and one who could see only the vase. How could they decide what the figure really is? The most they could do, it seems, is agree that they see it differently. Neither

Figure 2.2

would understand why the other sees it differently. Now consider what would happen if these two people had to work together to create a picture. To do this they must agree on what is background and what is figure, but this is precisely where their perceptions differ. Gilligan argues that care and rights reasoners disagree about ethical judgments just as the two people described disagree about visual judgments. It will be very difficult for care reasoners and rights reasoners to resolve conflicts with each other.

Although the relationship between gender and moral reasoning is an important and interesting issue, we will not focus on it here. Instead we will examine how care reasoning can contribute to understanding moral reasoning in general. Focusing on moral reasoning is in keeping with Gilligan's own intention as she expressed it in the introduction to *In a Different Voice,* in which she says that the correlation of voice to gender is "not absolute," and that

> the contrast between male and female voices are presented . . . to highlight a distinction between two modes of thought and to focus on a problem of interpretation rather than to represent a generalization about either sex.[22]

Many researchers, including Gilligan,[23] believe that both genders can use both kinds of reasoning, and so we need to understand both to understand how men and women reason morally.

Caring and Cognition

Gilligan began her research interviewing women about issues that had special meaning to women, such as abortion. She chose these topics because she believed that they were most likely to draw out the feminine moral voice if it existed. Gilligan found three levels of moral reasoning based on care that are structurally similar to Kohlberg's three levels of moral reasoning.[24] She did not attempt to divide these levels into stages, as Kohlberg did. In comparing and contrasting Gilligan's and Kohlberg's theories, we will talk only in terms of levels.

In the first level of care, women rely on their own needs to determine the right course of action. They focus on how their relationships with friends and family affect their own happiness. They are less concerned with how their decision will affect the well-being of others.

Gilligan's Level I and Kohlberg's Level I are both self-interested, but they interpret self-interest differently. In Kohlberg's Level I, institutions and rules allow people to promote their interests by punishing and benefiting from others. In Gilligan's Level I, intimate relationships help us avoid loneliness and get the pleasure of friendship.

If we apply Level I care reasoning to the S and R case, we find many of the same limitations that we found with Kohlberg's Level I.[25] It is not that someone in this stage would give the wrong answer. The problem is that Level I care reasoners would not be able to identify or understand important facts of the case. Without this understanding it unlikely that even the best answer could be successfully implemented. Consider the following responses.

1. **S and R should move.** If they don't move and S and R goes bankrupt, then Jameson and Mamet will lose their friends and maybe their families, too. At least by moving they will be able to maintain their relationships in Frieberg, since their home office will still be there. They will have some trouble, but their good friends should be on their side.

2. They should not move. If they move, they will get nothing but grief from their families. They have good friends in Frieberg, and it will be hard to replace them. Jameson and Mamet have no special ties to the shareholders. Besides, the shareholders can be fooled, since they don't know what is really going on.

Both decisions are based solely on the personal well-being of Jameson and Mamet. Well-being is understood in terms of maintaining important personal relationships. There is no understanding of the fiduciary duties that Jameson and Mamet have to shareholders or how organizations work. There is no recognition of the needs of suppliers and the community. There is no mention of legal issues, and no understanding of the international dimensions of the case.

In the second level of care reasoning, women reasoned in terms of their conventional responsibilities to friends and family. Conventional care reasoners tend to have very traditional views about the role of women. Women in this level of reasoning believed that they had to take care of others, especially children, at large costs to themselves, and even when others were available to help. These responsibilities are not viewed by conventional care reasoners as external constraints. Rather, women at this level internalize these responsibilities, making them their own. These responsibilities are grounded on empathy and caring for others.

The most obvious similarity between Gilligan's Level II and Kohlberg's Level II is that both look to social institutions to define right and wrong. The difference lies in what aspects of institutions are emphasized. Care reasoners emphasize how institutions structure our relationships; rights reasoners emphasize how institutions structure our rights and duties.

This difference in emphasis results in different views of what we should do. Rights reasoners tend to think that as long as they do not violate important duties, they can do as they please. This is because duties are usually expressed in negative terms, as with laws that prohibit us from harming others, but rarely require us to help others. Morality is a constraint on behavior. As long as one acts within these constraints, one can do as one wants. Donaldson and Dunfee refer to the area within these moral constraints as "moral free space."[26]

Care reasoners do not tend to make such a sharp distinction between what they are forbidden to do and free to do. This is because relationships between friends and family are defined by responsibilities of care, not by rules that restrict behavior. For example, parents have a responsibility to nurture their children into adulthood, which requires more than simply not harming them. For care reasoners, then, there is less "moral free space." Consider the following responses to the S and R care using conventional care reasoning.

1. S and R should move. There are so many people involved that it is going to be impossible to please all of them, but that is Jameson and Mamet's job. It will be hard on their two families, but they should be fine, once everyone adapts. It will be better for everyone if they move, especially the shareholders. People depend on pension funds for retirement; S and R can't ignore that. If they stay and go bankrupt, then everyone will suffer.

2. They should not move. According to the case, there was no guarantee that moving would help anyone, but we do know that moving would tear personal relationships apart. Jameson and Mamet need to help the families that depend on them. The families that would be helped in their new location are important, but not as important as the families with whom S and R already has relationships.

These responses show a much better understanding of how business works than the first level. Still, they evaluate decisions solely in terms of pleasing people and maintaining personal relationships. There is no mention of rules and laws that are good for the group even though they might not help all of the stakeholders. The international dimensions of the case are not well understood. To understand these international dimensions requires going to the third level of care.

In the third level of care reasoning, women integrate their concern for themselves with their concern for others, relying on the intrinsic value of people and relationships. The women in Gilligan's study progressed to this third level when their selfless conventional reasoning resulted in their neglecting their own interests to such an extent that they could no longer help others.

The third level of care reasoning views relationships not in terms of who serves whom, but in terms of mutual care, at least when participants in the relationship are equals. When participants have different abilities and roles, as in the parent–child relationship, the responsibilities are different, since the parent needs to nurture the child. In both cases, however, there is a responsibility to promote healthy relationships.

1. S and R should move. This is the best way to promote the health of all the relationships affected, including those in the new location. If they go bankrupt, or are bought out by some other firm, then Frieberg could lose the home office as well as the production facilities. Moving will mean some problems for the families and friends of Jameson and Mamet, but sometimes we have to make these kinds of sacrifices to do the right thing:

2. They should not move. Moving would cause great hardship to Frieberg, the workers, and the suppliers. The gains to the shareholders and those in the new location are small or unknowable. Even if the most important relationship is between management and the stockholders, their small benefit does not outweigh the great harm to the personal lives of many others (see the previous discussion of ordinal and cardinal ranking).

These responses show an understanding of how organizations work, how they fit into communities, the importance of large organizations to small communities, and international issues.

The third level of care reasoning shares some central features with Kohlberg's Level III. Most importantly, both care and rights reasoners critically evaluate institutional rules and expectations in terms of intrinsic value, though in neither case are these institutions rejected entirely. Rather, this level of reasoning seeks the values embedded in institutions. These embedded values are used to make decisions in institutional settings.

Gilligan's third level differs from Kohlberg's because it takes nonviolence and compassion as universal standards, whereas Kohlberg takes fairness, rights, justice, and the good of all as universal standards. Further, Gilligan and Kohlberg argue that these universal standards are applied differently. A care reasoner's universal concern for nonviolence and nurturing is tempered by the realization that relationships are complex and culturally bound. Because responsibility within relationships is context sensitive, mature care reasoners are very reluctant to judge others. Rights reasoners, argues Gilligan, tend to be less reluctant to make moral judgments. Because rights reasoners abstract from personal relationships when making a decision, they need less detailed information to make a judgment.

Mature care reasoners may see themselves as connected not only to friends and family, but to humans everywhere. As a result of this perceived connection to all people, they can feel responsible to help the poor and oppressed on the other side of the globe. According to Gilligan, a rights Level III reasoner, on the other hand, tends to sharpen the distinction between what the rules prohibit and what we are free to do. As long as no rule requires us to help others, we have no obligation to do so. Helping others is a good thing to do from the rights perspective, but helping is above and beyond the call of duty. This is why Kohlberg sees moral development as culminating in autonomy. Not only do we make our own moral decisions, but the way we make our decisions gives us a large area of moral free space.

For a care reasoner, helping others constitutes good relationships. Hence, as we develop within the care perspective, we become more connected to others, not less. Still, mature care reasoning does embody an important sense of autonomy. Mature care reasoners realize that they are responsible for their own decisions, even when they follow the wishes of others.

The differences between care reasoning and rights reasoning lead Gilligan to argue that the two forms of reasoning are incompatible: care reasoning focuses on partial relationships and rights reasoning focuses on impartial relationships. For a mature care reasoner, primary responsibility is determined by the particular relationships that form the institutional setting of the problem. For the mature rights reasoner, primary responsibility is determined by the universal features that form the institutional setting of the problem. Since one cannot be partial and impartial at the same time, care and rights reasoning are incompatible.

Despite their differences, there are significant similarities between Gilligan and Kohlberg. Both assert that the first level of moral reasoning focuses on oneself, the second level focuses on the institutions of one's group, and the third level focuses on universal standards to evaluate one's own reasoning strategies and the roles, rules, and principles that make up social institutions. They both agree that we get a better understanding of our social institutions as we progress through these levels. Further, the mechanics of moral development are the same for care and rights reasoners; both are pushed by CD to adopt new reasoning strategies to understand conflicts and their institutional settings. Like rights reasoners, care reasoners retain their successful beliefs and strategies as they develop new levels of moral reasoning.

THREE CONDITIONS OF A SUCCESSFUL DECISION-MAKING STRATEGY

The work of Kohlberg and Gilligan suggests that a successful decision-making strategy should help us do three things:

A. Identify the major features of the problem.

B. Understand and evaluate the institutional settings of the problem.

C. Understand and evaluate the reasoning strategies we use in steps A and B.

If we cannot do A and B, CD will set in. If we cannot do C, we will not be able to adequately modify our reasoning strategies to do A and B better. Before proceeding, we should note that no decision-making strategy will mechanically churn out an answer. Mechanical strategies do not exist for any important problems in business, whether they are in finance, management, or ethics. The most we can do is consider the information that is reasonably accessible, and evaluate it in defensible ways.

Condition A

A problem resolution strategy should help us identify the major features of the problem. We saw that Kohlberg's and Gilligan's first two levels of moral reasoning did not have the conceptual resources to represent several issues in the S and R case. In the egoistic level of moral reasoning, we were not able to represent how groups, organizations, and communities worked. In the conventional level, we relied too heavily on the actual rules and expectations of those involved, were unable to see how rules and expectations need to adapt to new problems, and could not fully understand international issues.

Post-conventional reasoners understand how and why institutions need to be modified to resolve new problems. They also have a much deeper understanding of universal responsibilities and principles like care, fairness, and rights. A post-conventional reasoner can view these universal principles as effective, stabilizing decision-making strategies.

Although these remarks seem to endorse the theories of Kohlberg and Gilligan, they need not be taken this way. Instead, these remarks distill some insights about moral reasoning from their theories that, once stated, can stand apart from their specific theories. For example, in the S and R case we saw that we need to understand and evaluate self-interest, relationships between friends and family, the dynamics and interests of formal groups, and principles such as fairness, justice, and rights. We need to understand these different issues because they are part of the institutional settings in which Jameson and Mamet will make their decision. Since these values can conflict with each other, we need a way to integrate them. In Kohlberg's and Gilligan's theories, only people in the highest, or post-conventional, level of reasoning could reason in these integrative, comprehensive ways. No matter what we call this multifaceted form of reasoning, we need something like it to resolve the complex social problems managers often face.

Condition B

A decision-making strategy should help us describe and evaluate the institutional setting of the problem.[27] The second condition is closely connected to the first. Problems do not arise in a vacuum. Rather, they result from conflicts between values and in relationships that are imbedded in institutional settings. These conflicts can arise for at least two reasons. First, individuals may develop false expectations because they misinterpret their relationships or the institutional values guiding those relationships. When this happens, we need to have the resources to evaluate the source of the misinterpretation. For example, if Jameson and Mamet are going to respond adequately to labor and the community, they need to understand the way these groups use rights and fairness to support their claims.

A second source of conflict arises when relationships and institutions have internal conflicts, and so problems arise even when everyone acts in accordance with accepted values.[28] This also is part of the problem that Jameson and Mamet face. S and R has reached institutional status in Frieberg because it is a sound business that generates job and tax revenues. Yet, S and R wants to move precisely because it is a sound business. In other words, the same strategy/institution set that integrated the interests of Jameson, Mamet, S and R, labor, suppliers, and Frieberg is now separating those interests. To understand this new conflict, we need to understand how institutions define and integrate the pursuit of self-interest, care, group interest, and justice.

Condition C

A decision-making strategy should help us understand and evaluate our decision-making strategies. This condition concerns the problem-solving strategy itself. There are at least two kinds of situations in which we need to evaluate our problem-solving strategies. First, some situations may not be appropriate to our preferred strategy. The S and R case stated that Mamet had usually relied on financial considerations to solve business problems. However, this strategy was not rich enough to include many of the issues involved in relocation. For example, when Mamet tried to factor in the cost of the community and labor fighting the move, he could not calculate those costs without having some idea of how far they would go to press their case. In general, Mamet believed that when it is cheaper to back down than to continue fighting, people back down. However, his experience with a strike in his former company led him to believe that if the community and labor believe relocating is an issue of fairness and self-respect, these groups might fight long and hard, sacrificing a great deal of time and money to preserve those values.

A second kind of situation in which we need to evaluate our reasoning strategies is when the strategy is appropriate, but we have trouble applying it. For example, Jameson had been successful promoting the good of herself, her family, S and R, labor, suppliers, and Frieberg. She still wants to use this strategy, but because of the need to relocate, she either has to give up this strategy or find a new way to formulate it. She prefers to do the latter, but she will need to examine her reasoning strategy to do this.

It is difficult to evaluate our reasoning strategies. We need to adopt some reasoning strategy as our base, and use that to evaluate the other reasoning strategies we use. Which reasoning strategy we should use as our base is a difficult question, but it is a question we cannot avoid. We will discuss this more fully in Chapter 3.

MORAL IMAGINATION AND EXPANDING THE DOMAIN OF POST-CONVENTIONAL REASONING

We do not always associate imagination with morality. However, Mark Johnson[29] and Patricia Werhane[30] are changing that. They argue that to resolve complex problems of business, we need a rich moral imagination based on sophisticated cognitive skills. Werhane has argued that some of the most publicized business scandals occur because the participants do not have a good grasp of the problem, of the institutional setting, or of their own reasoning strategies.[31]

To develop a rich moral imagination we need to do two things that post-conventional reasoners can do: evaluate institutional values and evaluate reasoning strategies.[32] To do these two things, however, we do not need to adopt the rights or the care perspectives that Kohlberg and Gilligan use to describe post-conventional reasoning.

In Chapter 3, we will see that there are other forms of post-conventional reasoning. Epicurus and Ayn Rand argue for post-conventional ethical theories based on self-interest, whereas Hume argues for a post-conventional ethical theory based on preserving social institutions. At first, it may appear that the views of Epicurus and Rand, who are egoists, and Hume, who is a conventionalist, cannot be true post-conventional views. However, we will see that the reasoning they use to support egoism and conventionalism is universal, and it is this reasoning that makes their theories post-conventional. Giving these views post-conventional status will greatly increase our understanding of social institutions and enrich our moral imagination.

Trying to develop a defensible ethical view is a daunting task, since it is a search for values to guide our lives, to understand and evaluate others, and to evaluate the social institutions in which we and others live and work. The task may also seem presumptuous: Who are we to say what is the best ethical explanation? Yet, we all have some ethical view that we use to direct our behavior and explain and evaluate the behavior of others. Even ignoring moral concerns is an ethical view of sorts.[33]

Kohlberg and Gilligan examined moral reasoning in the context of social institutions that define family, friendship, and citizenship. There is much evidence that moral reasoning in organizations is affected by incentive systems, the behavior of corporate leaders, peer evaluation, and other organizational factors. We now turn to a discussion of how moral reasoning, as described by Kohlberg and Gilligan, can be affected by organizations.

ETHICAL DECISION MAKING: OPPORTUNITIES AND CONSTRAINTS IN ORGANIZATIONS

To make effective decisions, we need to understand the institutional settings in which they are made and implemented. To understand decision making within organizations, we need to consider their unique institutional frameworks.[34]

From Judgment to Behavior

Linda Trevino argues that how we act in organizations depends on our stage of moral reasoning, individual characteristics, and the organizational structure. The relationships between these elements is displayed in Figure 2.3.[35] Her work integrates the insights of Paine (Chapter 1), who focused on organizational structure, and Messick and Bazerman (Chapter 1), who focused on shared individual characteristics. The efficacy of individual characteristics and organizational structure is good news and bad news. The good news is that organizational structure can promote ethical decision making even for those who care little about ethics. The bad news is that people with high levels of moral reasoning can fail to behave ethically in an unsupportive organizational context.

INDIVIDUAL MODERATORS

Ego strength refers to the ability to carry out actions a person believes are right. People with a low level of moral reasoning and little ego strength can be influenced to act ethically if there are strong organizational incentives to do so. Those with a high level of ethical reasoning and little ego strength may not act in accord with their beliefs in the face of strong organizational incentives to act unethically.[37]

Field dependence refers to how we react to information about how others want us to act. Field-dependent individuals are more likely to act in ways that others want them to act; field-independent individuals are more likely to follow their own judgments. People with a low level of moral reasoning who are highly field dependent may act ethically if their organizational colleagues frown on unethical behavior. People with a high level of moral reasoning who are highly field dependent may not act in accord with their beliefs if their organizational colleagues frown on ethical behavior.[38]

Locus of control refers to how individuals perceive themselves as controlling their lives. People who believe they control their own destinies are referred to as "internals."

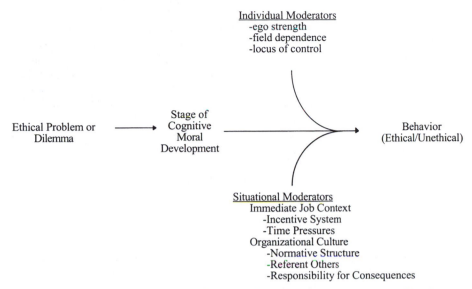

Figure 2.3   An adaptation of Trevino's interactionist model of ethical decision making in organizations.
(Used with the permission of the Academy of Management Review.*)*

Internals believe the locus of control is within them. People who do not believe they control their own destinies are referred to as "externals." Externals believe the locus of control is outside of them. Externals with a high level of moral reasoning may not act in accord with their ethical beliefs because they do not believe they can affect the outcome.[39]

Since ego strength, field dependence, and locus of control are individual characteristics, management cannot control them directly. Still, organizational structure and training programs can help employees and managers develop ego strength, evaluate field inputs, and develop a realistic sense of control.[40]

SITUATIONAL MODERATORS

In the Immediate Job Context, Trevino lists two features that affect our use of moral reasoning in organizations. The first, organizational incentive systems, refers to the rewards and punishments associated with behavior in an organization. People with low levels of moral reasoning may act ethically if there are strong incentives to do so. People with high levels of moral reasoning may not act ethically if there are strong incentives to do so. Paine (Chapter 1) makes a similar point in her analysis of the Sears case, in which auto repair personnel were selling unneeded parts and repairs to motorists. These fraudulent sales occurred after a new incentive system was put into place that included quotas for how many brakes, mufflers, and other repairs employees were expected to sell.

The second feature of the Immediate Job Context is time pressure. Acting ethically sometimes requires information that is hard to acquire. If people are pushed to make decisions without having time to get important information, those with a high level of moral reasoning may act in ways that are contrary to their beliefs. Below, we will see how time pressures affected Dennis Gioia, who was recall coordinator for Ford during the Pinto crisis.

Under Organizational Culture, there are three factors that can influence moral behavior: normative structure, referent others, and responsibility for consequences. The first, normative structure, refers to the way an organization defines right and wrong behavior. Organizational normative structures can be weak or strong. Strong normative structures have clear and enforceable rules; weak ones have vague rules that are difficult to enforce. Even people with little concern for ethics may act well in a strong normative environment that encourages ethical behavior. On the other hand, people with high levels of moral reasoning may not act in their preferred ways in a strong normative culture that disregards ethical issues. In the Beech-Nut case (Paine, Chapter 1) the CEO was so focused on making a profit for a particular year that he disregarded information about problems with their apple juice. Beech-Nut was caught selling substandard juice, and incurred losses much greater than they would have if they had replaced the juice. This is the kind of case in which ethical action could have saved the firm a great deal of money. Why did no one act? We do not know enough about the case to answer this question with certainty, but the normative environment that stressed profits may have screened out those who would have spoken up.[41]

The second element, referent others, refers to how recognized leaders in an organization affect the behavior of others. Ethical behavior by recognized leaders promotes ethical behavior in others. Even people with little concern for ethics may act well in an environment in which recognized leaders act ethically. Similarly, unethical behavior by recognized leaders, such as the CEO of Beech-Nut, promotes unethical behavior in others.[42]

The third element is responsibility for consequences. If we do not know about the consequences of our actions, or if we believe we are not responsible for these consequences, we may act in ways that do not accord with our ethical beliefs. As Trevino has argued, organizations, by their very nature, diffuse responsibility. People with high levels of moral reasoning may not act ethically if they do not believe they are responsible for the outcome.[43]

Ethical Reasoning and Situational Moderators in the Ford Pinto Case

Dennis Gioia uses several of these situational moderators to understand his own behavior as the recall coordinator for Ford Motor Company. Gioia, who is now a professor of management at Pennsylvania State University, has written and spoken extensively of his experiences. A thorough account occurs in his "Pinto Fires and Personal Ethics: A Script Analysis of Missed Opportunities."[44]

Gioia's personal ethical system was strong and independent at the time he joined Ford in the early 1970s. He was so critical of big business that many of his classmates in the MBA program asked him why he was studying business at all. Gioia received his MBA in 1972 (his undergraduate degree was in engineering) and joined Ford Motor Company that same year. He gives two reasons for his choice of Ford: he wanted to make big business more socially responsible and he liked cars.[45] One year later he became Ford's Recall Coordinator.

Gioia writes

I found myself on the fast track at Ford, participating in a "tournament" type of socialization (Van Masnen, 1978), engaged in a competition for recognition with other MBA's who had recently joined the company. The company itself was dynamic; the environment of business, especially the auto industry, was intriguing; the job was challenging and the pay was great. The psychic rewards of working and succeeding in a major corporation proved unexpectedly seductive. I really became involved in the job.[46]

Ford's normative structure was based on the goals of pay, prestige, and power in the service of revenues and profits. Despite internal competition for these goods, those at Ford felt unified. It was "we against them," "them" being other car manufacturers, government, and anyone else who challenged Ford.[47] (See Messick and Bazerman, Chapter 1, for more on how the "we–them" phenomenon affects decision making.)

The recall coordinator position had immense time and psychic pressures. When Gioia took over, there were over 100 recall campaigns in progress, and many other open files that required analysis and judgment. When he first saw reports of Pinto's "lighting up," he did not become concerned because the explosions did not meet the two criteria he used for his initial screening of recall cases: high frequency of occurrence or directly traceable causes [to design or manufacturing].[48]

A large part of the reason that Gioia did not see "directly traceable causes" was that Ford had concealed Pinto's crash test data from the recall office. Gioia did not know that in tests of rear end collisions, 8 of 11 Pintos experienced "potentially catastrophic gas tank ruptures" and that the three cars that survived had been changed to protect the gas tank.[49]

It would have cost $11 dollars per vehicle to fix the exploding gas tank problem, yet Ford did not do it. Gioia gives five reasons. First, the 1968 Federal Standards that would have declared the car unsafe did not go into effect until 1976. At the time the Pinto was tested, it met all legal safety standards. Second, redesigning the car was costly, and the profit margins set for the Pinto were already very small. Third, there was the belief that small cars were dangerous anyway. Fourth, Ford believed that safety did not sell. Fifth, Ford did a cost–benefit analysis of fixing the Pinto that Gioia describes as follows.

Costs of fixing the Pinto: $137,000,000

[Estimated as the costs of a production fix to all similarly designed cars and trucks with the gas tanks aft of the axle (12,500,000 vehicles × $11/vehicle)]

Benefits of fixing the Pinto: $49,530,000

[Estimated as the savings from preventing (180 projected deaths × $200,000/death) + (180 projected burn injuries × $67,000 for each injury) + (2100 burned cars × $700/car)]

The cost–benefit decision was then construed as straightforward. No production fix would be undertaken. The philosophical and ethical implications of assigning a financial value for human life or disfigurement do not seem to have been a major consideration in reaching this decision.[50]

Although Gioia did not know about the rear end crash tests when he began as recall coordinator, why didn't the reports and pictures of accidents that he saw, with their occupants burned beyond recognition, move him to act? Gioia explains his inaction in several ways. First, the time pressures of the job were immense. He had to perform a kind of auto-triage to determine which cases he should examine. The Pinto, as we saw, did not pass this initial test. Second, although he was at first overwhelmed by the fact that his job dealt with human suffering, he soon took the facts of his job—burns, injury, and death—as routine. There was no other way to do the job. Pictures of burn victims from Pinto crashes did move him to evaluate the case again, but he and his staff still decided not to issue a recall.

Finally, Gioia and his staff learned about the internal crash test data. They met and discussed this new data, but did not recall the Pinto. The main reason rested on comparing the Pinto to other small cars. As Gioia states, "the Pinto was merely the worst of a bad lot."

Looking back on these events, Gioia asks two questions:

> First, how could my value-system apparently have flip-flopped in the relatively short space of 1–2 years? Second, how could I have failed to take action on a retrospectively obvious safety problem when I was in the perfect position to do so?[51]

As we have seen, he cites many of the factors Trevino lists as Situational Moderators. He also says:

> My own schematized (scripted) knowledge influenced me to perceive recall issues in terms of the prevailing decision environment and to unconsciously overlook key features of the Pinto case, mainly because they did not fit an existing script. Although the outcomes of the case carry retrospectively obvious ethical overtones, *the schemas driving my perceptions and actions precluded consideration of the issues in ethical terms because the scripts did not include ethical dimensions.*[52] [emphasis changed]

Schemas, Scripts, and the Recognition of Ethical Issues

James Rest argues that there are four steps leading to ethical behavior.

1. Recognition that a problem is an ethical problem.
2. Moral reasoning that yields a judgment about the problem.
3. An intention to act on one's moral judgment.
4. Behavior that incorporates the moral judgment.[53]

Kohlberg and Gilligan focused on the second step, judgment. Trevino focused on how the third step can be shaped by individual and organizational moderators. Gioia uses schemas and scripts to focus on step 1.

Gioia states that he never recognized the recall of the Pinto as an ethical issue because the schemas and scripts that guided his organizational perception and behavior did not include ethical elements. Since he did not perceive the case as ethical, step 1 never occurred, and so step 2, his ethical value system, never came into play.

Gioia defines a schema as follows:

> A schema is a cognitive framework that people use to impose structure upon information, situations, and expectations to facilitate understanding (Gioia and Poole, 1984; Taylor and Crocker, 1981). Schemas . . . once formed, preclude the necessity for further active cognition. As a consequence, such structured knowledge allows virtually effortless interpretation of information and events (cf., Canter and Mischel, 1979).[54]

A schema is a set of beliefs that is invoked by appropriate cues. We have schemas for all parts of our lives—being a family member, being a manager, even being a grocery shopper. Each of these roles and tasks requires us to gather and interpret different kinds of information because the goals, relationships, and institutional settings are different. A successful family schema will not help us understand the layout of a grocery store or recall defective cars.

Gioia defines a script as follows:

> A script is a specialized type of schema that retains knowledge of actions appropriate for specific situations and contexts (Abelson, 1976, 1981). One of the most important characteristics of scripts is that they simultaneously provide a cognitive framework for understanding events as well as a guide to appropriate behavior to deal with the situation faced. They thus serve as linkages between cognition and action (Manz, 1985).[55]

Scripts are subsets of schemas. For example, we have a grocery store schema, but we have scripts of particular grocery stores. We have a schema regarding business meetings, but scripts for particular kinds of business meetings.

Schemas and scripts are essential for social and organizational life. We do not have the time, information, or rational powers to assess every situation anew. Schemas and scripts allow us to quickly identify situations so that we can spend our time attending to the special characteristics of the situation—what we are shopping for, the point of the meeting, the evaluation of crash data (see the discussion of bounded rationality in Chapter 4 for more on this). Scripts become more important with time pressure. When Gioia became recall coordinator he was deluged with information.

A script analysis can explain why the Pinto did not get further consideration before the crash test data were known. It seems more difficult to use scripts to explain why Gioia and his staff did not issue a recall after they discovered the crash data.

To understand the organizational dynamics of this more context-sensitive decision, we need to combine the schema and script analyses with the normative culture of Ford as it emerged in the Recall Office. The screening criteria were purely technical. There was no mention of human death or injury. There was also a directive from Ford's legal department never to use the word "problem," since it suggested that Ford was at fault—the preferred term was "condition."

So, while the Pinto problem passed into a higher stage of analysis once the crash test data became known to Gioia and his staff, it passed through a script filter that blocked out considerations of human life and well-being. To use a different analogy, Gioia's scripts acted as a kind of "cookie-cutter" that gave the problem a technical shape. Faced with this technical issue, Gioia and his staff acted reasonably—they looked at the safety of small cars from other manufacturers, found that the Pinto was very close to them, and did not issue a recall.

Figure 2.4 shows how we can fit the schema/script analysis into Trevino's model. Schemas and scripts are individual moderators, but we use them to act efficiently in organizational environments. Gioia points out that gains in efficiency result in a loss of information.

Gioia does not argue that Ford intentionally created a system that made it difficult to identify ethical problems. The operant scripts and schemas resulted from a complex interaction between Ford, its institutional settings, and standard psychological features of human beings.

Schemas and scripts are necessary for social and organizational life. Since we cannot eliminate them, the most we can do is manage them. Managing schemas and scripts is difficult because they work automatically, which accounts for their usefulness. Gioia suggests that "job descriptions, management development, mentoring, etc." should be revised to include ethical considerations. This will embed ethical issues in organizational scripts, increasing the probability that individuals will recognize ethical issues when they arise.

Another approach would be to teach managers and employees about the scripting process itself. Not all scripts are equally automatic, as illustrated in Figure 2.5.[56]

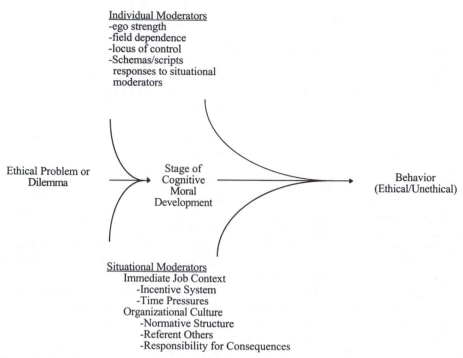

Individual Moderators
-ego strength
-field dependence
-locus of control
-Schemas/scripts
 responses to situational
 moderators

Ethical Problem or
Dilemma

Stage of
Cognitive
Moral
Development

Behavior
(Ethical/Unethical)

Situational Moderators
Immediate Job Context
-Incentive System
-Time Pressures
Organizational Culture
-Normative Structure
-Referent Others
-Responsibility for Consequences

Figure 2.4 Trevino's interactionist model of ethical decision making in organizations with a schema/script analysis.
(Used with the permission of the Academy of Management Review.*)*

According to Figure 2.5, we act without thinking only in the most routine situations, such as saying hello, or waiting for a red light. As we move to the left, we are more likely to actively process information, weigh alternatives, and decide on courses of action. These cognitive elements allow us to intervene in our scripts.

In his classic article, "Groupthink," Irving Janis also talks about ways to avoid pitfalls in organizational decision making. Although Janis focuses on government, his suggestions are relevant to the individual and situational moderators identified by Trevino and Gioia. Not all of Janis's suggestions can or should be used in all situations. Further, they must be tailored to the specific organizational contexts in which they will be used.

1. The group leader should encourage all members to critically evaluate group proposals and processes. The leader must accept criticism for the encouragement to be effective.

2. When leaders assign tasks, they should not state their own beliefs about the usefulness of the task or the outcomes they expect.

3. Different groups should work on the same question. When possible, use groups outside the organization.

4. Group members should regularly discuss the group's deliberations with people in their functional units and report these reactions to the group.

5. The group should invite one or more outside experts to their meetings and encourage them to challenge the group's views.

6. Before reaching a consensus, at least one member should play devil's advocate.

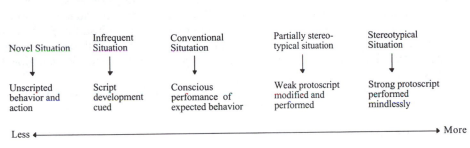

Figure 2.5 Gioia and Poole's continuum of script development showing the differences of conscious cognitive processing when following scripts.
(Used with the permission of the Academy of Management Review.)

7. When the issue involves other organizations, the group should survey those organizations to look for complements and conflicts. The group should also develop alternative scenarios of what other organizations might do.

8. Groups should divide into two or more subgroups to meet separately and then come back together to discuss their conclusions and the way they reached them.

9. If a consensus is reached, the group should hold a "second-chance" meeting in which members express any reservations they have.[57]

Each of these suggestions would inhibit the routine following of schemas and scripts. Suggestion 1 would allow doubts about scripted interpretations and behavior to be aired. In Figure 2.5, we saw that scripts can be more or less conscious. It is unlikely that all members of a group will be at the same level of script enactment. If those in the middle of the awareness scale challenge a script, this can force those at the right to evaluate the script as well. The goal is not to eliminate the script, but to make sure it is appropriate.

Suggestion 2 addresses the way scripts are learned. Gioia distinguishes indirect (vicarious) learning from direct learning.[58] Direct learning arises when we participate in a scripted process, such as a meeting or an interview. Indirect learning arises when we are told what appropriate behaviors are. Assigning tasks in an impartial way should reduce the likelihood that specific expectations will be communicated, thus reducing indirect learning.

Suggestions 3, 4, 5, 7, and 8 increase the likelihood that groups will consider incompatible scripts together. When this happens it is impossible to follow them mindlessly. Suggestion 4 has the added feature that the competing scripts will come from different functional units. This can reveal the extent to which scripts have purposes relevant to the well-being of the organization. Suggestions 5 and 7 have the added feature of bringing in information from outside the organization that can move members to challenge scripts. Suggestions 6 and 9 reinforce suggestion 1.

ORGANIZING DECISION MAKING

In the discussion of moral development, we saw that moral stage progression results from an inability to understand and act within the roles, rules, and principles of our institutional settings. Coming to understand these institutional settings allows us to make more informed decisions. The first three steps of the following decision-making strategy isolate central features of institutional settings. The fourth step asks you to choose the values you will use to evaluate the problem as you have described it so far. These values will guide you in the fifth step, identifying alternatives, and the sixth step, choosing an alternative. The final step concerns a monitoring plan appropriate to the institutional settings.

This strategy will not in itself result in good decision making. How we interpret and use this strategy will be a function of the relevant

- Social institutions (North, Chapter 1)
- Organizational structure (Paine, Chapter 1; Trevino; Gioia; Janis)
- Individual psychological characteristics (Messick and Bazerman, Chapter 1; Trevino; Gioia)

The most we can do is take steps to ameliorate the factors that distort our judgment. Messick and Bazerman, Gioia, and Janis suggested some ways to do this. Some of their suggestions are incorporated into the decision-making strategy. This strategy is best thought of as the beginning of a conversation, with oneself and others, about how to resolve conflicts.

A Decision-Making Strategy for Cases

1. Identify stakeholders (people, groups, organizations who have a stake in the problem and its resolution) who are central to the conflict. When possible, work with others to do this step, but take steps to avoid "groupthink."

2. **a.** Describe the relationships that connect the stakeholders.

   b. Identify the institutions that create and/or regulate these relationships.

   c. Identify the ethical, economic, and legal–political values that underlie these institutions.

   When possible, seek help from the stakeholders identified in Step 1. This will increase the amount and diversity of information you have. In an organization, acquire information from different functional areas.

3. Show how the problem arose as the stakeholders shaped their relationships by the values identified in Step 2. (Doing this step may suggest changes to your first two responses.)

   Be wary of vagueness and ambiguity. For example, do the stakeholders have a well-defined sense of self-interest, and do they distinguish it from selfishness? Do they have similar views of the institutions and relationships that bring them together, and are their views correct? The comments under Step 2 are relevant here.

4. Identify the most important ethical, economic, and legal–political values of the relevant institutions. Use these values to evaluate the problem and its institutional settings.

5. Identify alternatives that will solve the problem and can be implemented in the institutional setting. Make sure these alternatives account for the ethical, economic, and legal–political values you discussed in Step 4.

Separate the process of finding alternatives from the process of choosing the best one. Brainstorming, without critical evaluation, can be an effective way to generate creative alternatives.

Role play: what alternatives would different stakeholders suggest. When possible, get the information directly from stakeholders, rather than imagining what they would say. Make sure you account for broad social institutions, specific organizational institutions, and standard psychological characteristics when choosing alternatives.

6. Choose the alternative that best resolves the current problem and that will prevent such problems in the future.

As you evaluate alternatives, state clearly which institutional values they support and which values they subordinate. Ask yourself: Is this the set of values I want to guide my behavior in the future?

Determine whether the alternatives require restructuring the institutions and relationships that tie stakeholders together? If so, does the problem warrant such extreme action?

7. Develop and implement a plan to monitor results.

As with the first six steps, work with a diverse set of people to develop and implement a plan of action. This plan does not have to "stand alone." Ideally, it should be incorporated into the ongoing mechanisms that already exist to guide and monitor organizational behavior.

To use this decision-making strategy effectively, we need a deeper understanding of ethics, economics, and law. Chapter 3 examines how ethical values underlie institutions and guide individual decisions. Chapter 4 examines how economic factors influence the institutions and organizations in which we make business decisions. Chapter 5 examines how law reinforces the ethical and economic aspects of institutions.

SUMMARY AND TRANSITION TO CHAPTER 3

In this chapter we focused on the nature of ethical conflicts and on the process of ethical decision making. Some key points are as follows:

- An ethical conflict can be categorized as a problem, dilemma, or false dilemma.
- We use ethical rules and principles to resolve conflicts in all aspects of lives, including business.
- Our moral beliefs result from a rational evaluation of our social institutions. Moral development helps us understand how social institutions work.
- We can classify ethical rules and principles in terms of four categories: self-interest, personal relationships, group well-being, and universal ethical principles.
- These four categories of values represent the four major purposes of social institutions. This is why we need to understand ethical rules and principles to understand the institutional settings of business.
- Rights reasoning and care reasoning illuminate different aspects of institutions. We need both to understand institutional settings.
- The highest levels of rights and care reasoning enable us to (A) evaluate problems,

(B) evaluate the institutional setting of the problems, and (C) evaluate the standards we use to do A and B. It is these three abilities that make a Post-Conventional Level of moral reasoning useful.

• We develop schemas and scripts to understand and act efficiently in organizations. These scripts are necessary, but they can harm us, personal relationships, groups, and violate universal principles.

• The seven-step decision-making strategy is an aid to decision making, not a substitute for decision making. It can help us identify important elements of conflicts and the institutions and relationships out of which conflicts arise.

• In the next chapter we will look more closely at the four categories of ethical principles and concepts we use to understand social institutions. Each of these categories admits of more diversity than either Kohlberg or Gilligan acknowledge. We need to understand this diversity to use our decision-making abilities to their fullest.

Notes

1. Richard De George argues that many of the conflicts facing multinational corporations are false dilemmas (see "Ethical Dilemmas for Multinational Enterprises: A Philosophical Overview," in Chapter 6).
2. See discussion of Kant, Chapter 3: he assigns infinite value to human beings because they can make free decisions and finite value to objects (everything that cannot make free choices).
3. See the Kate Simpson case, Part III.
4. For more on this, see section on "Truth Telling" in Tom Donaldson and Patricia Werhane, eds. *Ethical Issues in Business,* 5th ed. Upper Saddle River, NJ: Prentice Hall, 1997; and the section on "Gathering, Concealing, and Gilding Information" in Tom Beauchamp and Norman Bowie, eds. *Ethical Theory and Business,* 5th ed. Upper Saddle River, NJ: Prentice Hall, 1997.
5. Norman Uphoff. "Grassroots Organizations and NGO's in Rural Development: Opportunities with Diminishing States and Expanding Markets." *World Development* 21:4 (1993), p. 614
6. Douglass North. "Institutions." *Journal of Economic Perspectives* 5:1 (1991), p. 98.
7. Deborah Vidaver-Cohen. "Moral Imagination in Organizational Problem Solving: An Institutional Perspective." *Business Ethics Quarterly* 7:4 (1997).
8. *Ibid.*
9. Institutions also give us the opportunities to subvert these values and goals.
10. Kohlberg focuses on rules, not institutions. We will apply his theory to institutional rules.
11. Deborah Vidaver-Cohen. "Moral Imagination in Organizational Problem Solving."
12. In our discussion of moral development, we will assume that cognitive and affective development proceed together. For example, we will assume that when people understand why groups and individuals are valuable, they also care about them. Although this relationship does not always hold, our assumption will make presenting the theory much easier.
13. Based on Kohlberg's descriptions of the levels and stages. See John W. Dienhart. *A Cognitive Approach to the Ethics of Counseling Psychology.* Lanham, MD: University Press of America, 1982, pp. 48–51. In that same volume, I argue that Kohlberg's descriptions of Stages 5 and 6 are not logically coherent (pp. 70–78). This incoherence, however, is not necessarily a problem, since these stages and levels are supposed to describe how people reason. If Kohlberg is right about his findings, this means only that we sometimes rely on principles that do not cohere with each other.
14. In general the terminology of cognitive–developmental theory, though cumbersome, is designed to describe the kind of phenomena being named. For example, both of the words in this phrase have Latin roots, which, if translated literally, would mean something like "thinking unbalanced."
15. The responses to the S and R problem are hypothetical, but are based on the research of Kohlberg and others. As such they represent typical reactions of people in each stage. There is a small group of individuals who advance cognitively but not morally—typically sociopaths and psychopaths— who would not give the kind of answers suggested here in Stages 3, 4, and 5.
16. The concept of a group is a necessary condition for seeing the family as a group with moral worth. It is not a sufficient condition. One could be an advanced formal reasoner and be immoral or amoral.

17. See Aristotle. "Nicomachean Ethics." *The Basic Works of Aristotle.* Ed. Richard McKeon. New York: Random House, 1941, pp. 935–1112, especially Book X.
18. Robert Frank. *Passions Within Reason: The Strategic Role of the Emotions.* New York: Norton, 1988, especially Chapters 1, 2, and 10.
19. See William Alston. "Moral Attitudes and Moral Judgments." *Nous* 2:1 (1968). He argues that a "bad conscience" could not be the reason an individual judges an act or intention to be wrong. In order to have a bad conscience, one must already believe that the act or intention is wrong.
20. Lawrence Kohlberg, "Revisions in the Theory and Practice of Moral Development." *Moral Development,* no. 2. Ed. William Damon. San Francisco: Jossey-Bass, 1978, p. 86.
21. Carol Gilligan. "Moral Orientation and Moral Development." *Women and Moral Theory.* Eds. Eva Kittay and Diana Meyers. Savage, MD: Rowman and Littlefield, 1987, p. 26.
22. Carol Gilligan. *In a Different Voice.* Cambridge: Harvard University Press, 1982, p. 2
23. *Ibid.,* pp. 166–172. Gilligan argues that women can use rights reasoning and men can use care reasoning, but that women will view rights in terms of care and that men will view care in terms of rights.
24. *Ibid.,* pp. 84–91. Gilligan does not refer to these different forms of reasoning as levels. I use the terminology of levels for convenience of reference and to facilitate comparison with Kohlberg's theory.
25. These responses to the S and R problem are hypothetical, but are based on the research of Gilligan and others. As such they represent typical reactions of people in each level. There is a small group of individuals who advance cognitively but not morally—typically sociopaths and psychopaths— who would not give the kind of answers suggested here.
26. Thomas Donaldson and Thomas Dunfee. "Toward a Unified Conception of Business Ethics: Integrative Social Contracts Theory." *Academy of Management Review* 19:2 (1994), pp. 252–284.
27. Vidaver-Cohen. "Moral Imagination in Organizational Problem Solving."
28. *Ibid.*
29. Mark Johnson. *Moral Imagination: Implications of Cognitive Science for Ethics.* Chicago: The University of Chicago Press, 1993.
30. Patricia H. Werhane. "Moral Imagination and the Search for Ethical Decision Making in Management." Ruffin Lectures, 1994.
31. *Ibid.*
32. Vidaver-Cohen. "Moral Imagination in Organizational Problem Solving."
33. If this "no ethics" point of view leads to the pursuit of one's immediate pleasure regardless of others, that is suspiciously like the crude self-interest we saw in Kohlberg's Stages 1 and 2.
34. Vidaver-Cohen. "Moral Imagination in Organizational Problem Solving."
35. For an introduction to this approach, see Linda Trevino and Karen Nelson. *Managing Business Ethics: Straight Talk About How to Do It Right.* New York: Wiley, 1995.
36. Linda Trevino. "Ethical Decision Making in Organizations: A Person-Situation Interactionist Model." *Academy of Management Review* 11:3 (1986), p. 603.
37. *Ibid.,* p. 609; also see Trevino. "Moral Reasoning and Business Ethics." *Journal of Business Ethics* 11 (1992), pp. 445–459.
38. *Ibid.,* p. 610.
39. *Ibid.,* p. 610.
40. *Ibid.,* pp. 601–617.
41. *Ibid.,* p. 612.
42. *Ibid.,* p. 612.
43. *Ibid.,* p. 613.
44. Dennis Gioia. "Pinto Fires and Personal Ethics: A Script Analysis of Missed Opportunities." *Journal of Business Ethics* 11 (1992), pp. 379–380. (Quotes used with kind permission of the author and Kluwer Academic Publishers.)
45. *Ibid.,* pp. 379–380.
46. *Ibid.,* p. 380.
47. *Ibid.,* p. 380.
48. *Ibid.,* p. 381.
49. *Ibid.,* p. 381.
50. *Ibid.,* p. 381.
51. *Ibid.,* p. 385.
52. *Ibid.,* p. 385.
53. James Rest. *Moral Development: Advances in Research and Theory.* New York: Praeger, 1986.
54. *Ibid.,* p. 385.
55. *Ibid.,* p. 385.

56. Dennis Gioia and Peter Poole. "Scripts in Organizational Behavior." *Academy of Management Review* 9:1 (1984), p. 454.
57. Adapted from Irving Janis. "Groupthink." *A Diagnostic Approach to Organizational Behavior.* Boston: Allyn and Bacon, 1983, p. 326.
58. Gioia and Poole, p. 451. Also see Dennis Gioia and Charles Manz. "Linking Cognition and Behavior: A Script Processing Interpretation of Vicarious Learning." *Academy of Management Review* 10:3 (1985), pp. 528, 531–534.

CHAPTER 3

Ethical Decision Making: Exploring Alternative Values

ETHICAL RULES AND PRINCIPLES: THE NEED FOR INTERPRETATION

Jameson and Mamet face a problem that concerns themselves, their families, the community of Frieberg, S and R, its suppliers, and its labor force. These stakeholders can use various combinations of self-interest, care, group welfare, and justice to support their decisions. These are the same ethical categories that Kohlberg and Gilligan found in their empirical studies of moral reasoning. In this chapter we will examine some of the ways these ethical categories can be interpreted. For example, ambitious entrepreneurs who spend all their time at work and rarely see their families can justify their behavior in terms of self-interest (their career) and care (their families need the money). These entrepreneurs can go on to use the same values to justify quitting and taking a part-time job: self-interest (they want to do other things) and care (their family needs to see more of them).

The ambiguity of values shows that the question of institutional purpose is more complicated than it originally appeared. These purposes are as follows:

1. Institutions create opportunities for pursuing self-interest.
2. Institutions create opportunities for developing family relationships and friendships.
3. Institutions create opportunities for establishing formal groups and promoting their interests.
4. Institutions create opportunities for pursuing fairness, justice, and human rights.

To understand the different ways these values can be interpreted by individuals and expressed in institutions, we will examine ethical theory, focusing on the way ethical theories identify a preferred interpretation of these values and how these values can be used to evaluate behavior and institutions.

From Moral Psychology to Ethical Theory

The major difference between moral psychology and ethical theory is that the former attempts to *describe* how we reason about ethical issues, whereas the latter attempts to *prescribe* how we should reason about ethical issues. Despite this difference, moral psychology and ethical theory share two fundamental features.

- **Function.** Moral psychology and ethical theory both concern how we interpret social institutions, direct and evaluate our own behavior, and explain and evaluate the behavior of others.
- **Content.** Moral psychology and ethical theory both work with the same values: self-interest, care, group welfare, and the intrinsic value of human beings (dignity, fairness, justice, rights).

Ethical theory tends to be more rigorous than ordinary moral reasoning, but that is because ethicists have more time for research and reflection. They are not better people, nor do they have special moral insight.

Ethical Relativism and the Universality of Ethical Values

Before we turn to ethical theory, we must briefly discuss the issue of ethical relativism. Ethical relativists argue that it does not matter which ethical theory we choose because moral truth is relative. *Individual relativists* argue that moral truth is dependent on the beliefs of the person making the decision; *cultural relativists* argue that moral truth is dependent on cultural institutions.

One of the most common reasons given for relativism is the striking ethical diversity we see throughout the world. Marriage customs, child rearing, and truth telling are viewed differently in different cultures. Cultures also have different attitudes on business practices such as gift-giving, bribery, subsidies, and nepotism, to name only a few. It seems that any attempt to say what is universally right or wrong amid this diversity is doomed.

There is a way to argue for universal moral values and still account for moral diversity. Kohlberg and Gilligan argue that the structure of moral reasoning is universal, although the specific beliefs are not. People in every culture begin life egoistically, and most move on to a conventional level. If they move beyond the conventional level, they adopt moral principles to explain and critically evaluate social institutions in terms of care, rights, fairness, or the good of all.

Also, cultural diversity may not be as pronounced as it sometimes seems. Consider bribery, a practice that most agree is viewed differently in different cultures. In 1976, Lockheed spent $9 million to bribe Japanese officials to secure $1.3 billion in airplane contracts.[1] When the bribe became public, the CEO of Lockheed argued that this was standard business practice in Japan, and so he had done nothing wrong. He further argued he was promoting the good of Lockheed, as was his managerial duty.[2] To cultural relativists, this looks like a good explanation.

If we look more closely, we may come to a different conclusion. The Prime Minister of Japan was forced to resign. There was also a huge outcry in the United States, and the CEO and other top officers of Lockheed were forced to step down. This scandal was a major reason that the United States passed the Foreign Corrupt Practices Act (FCPA) (Chapter 5), which makes it illegal for representatives of U.S. companies to bribe foreign officials. While bribery occurs, it is not accepted in Japan or the United States.

There is also a movement toward a global condemnation of bribery as international business increases. The General Agreement on Tariffs and Trade (Chapter 5) strongly supports free trade and competition, which are incompatible with bribery. This makes sense, since economic systems that exclude bribery should be more efficient than those that allow it (Chapter 4). In 1997, the members of the Organization for Economic Co-operation and Development, composed of 29 countries, including the United States, Germany, Japan, South Korea, and Mexico, signed an agreement to outlaw the bribery of foreign officials.[3] The agreement calls for all member states to pass laws similar to the FCPA by the end of 1998.[4] Norman Bowie (Chapter 9) argues that as business inter-actions become more global, we may see more international agreement on standard business practices and the values that underlie them.

Ethical Theory and Human Nature

Ethical theories tacitly or explicitly presuppose a view of human nature. Since ethics is about what we should do, it must account for what we can and are likely to do. This is why we examined the psychology of ethical reasoning in Chapter 2. In this chapter we will see, for example, that egoistic theories tend to assume that we are naturally self-in-terested, whereas group-oriented theories tend to assume that we are or can be loyal to our groups. In each of the ethical theories we examine, we will note its psychological assumptions.

The Use and Limits of Ethical Theory

Ethical theories are sets of principles that specify the good and the right. They try to show one or both of the following:

A. That decision *procedures* should promote, or be consistent with, self-interest, care, group interest, intrinsic value, or human excellence.

B. That the *outcomes* of our decisions should promote, or be consistent with, self-inter-est, care, group interest, intrinsic value, or human excellence.

Ethical theory cannot *in itself* produce A or B.[5] This is not a defect, however, since no theory can produce practical effects unless it is used, and used well. Compare ethical theory to a recipe. We do not object to a recipe for a delicate, delicious soufflé because it alone cannot produce the desired result. Neither do we object to the recipe if a person with no knowledge of cooking cannot produce the soufflé. Like recipes, ethical theories help us identify and work with ingredients to produce a result. Although this increases our chances of success, we must be realistic: for even the most practiced, plans fail, souf-flés fall.

The ethical theories discussed here are not presented as final products that should be completely accepted or rejected. Instead, use them as starting points to help you think about your own moral system of beliefs and the institutions and relationships of which you are a part.

Developing Your Own Moral Point of View

Developing your own moral point of view may seem like too large a task for one book and one course. It would be if you did not already have a moral point of view. Almost everyone reading this book believes they have obligations to themselves; to their families and friends; to the various groups to which they belong, including school, work, and their home nation; and beliefs about fairness and justice. One of the goals of this book is to help readers systematize and critically evaluate their ethical beliefs so that they can make sound managerial decisions.

Preview of Chapter

The first four sections discuss four major ethical theories: self-interest, care, utilitarianism, and intrinsic value theory (human dignity, rights, and fairness). Each section discusses at least two major figures that have argued for the theory being discussed. In the fifth section, "Ethical Pluralism and Decision Making," it is argued that it is possible to treat the first four theories as *principles* that, taken together, can form a more complete ethical theory.

SELF-INTEREST AND DECISION MAKING: EPICURUS AND AYN RAND

How we understand self-interest in the S and R case depends on whose interests we consider. Stockholders, employees, suppliers, and others stand to gain and lose. The employees, for example, have built their lives around their wages. For many, losing even 5% of their income can force them to move to smaller homes, sell boats, cancel vacations, and a host of other undesirable things.

Jameson and Mamet are both concerned with their own interests. They have worked hard to attain their present positions, and they do not want to jeopardize their careers. They have good compensation packages, and enjoy the advantages that money and security bring.

If Jameson and Mamet are going to use self-interest to solve their problem, they need to examine self-interest more closely. Egoism has been discussed for the four thousand years of recorded history. We will look at Epicurus, who lived in Ancient Greece, and Ayn Rand, who lived in our own century.

Egoism states that the ultimate good is the good of oneself, and that right actions are those that best promote one's good. It is schematically very simple (Figure 3.1).

Egoism seems well suited to business, or at least to popular conceptions of business. We assume that people go in to business to get money or power. We also assume that business institutions are designed so people can pursue self-interest. Self-interest is at the foundation of many economic and legal theories (Chapters 3 and 4).

Epicurus (341–270 BCE) and Ayn Rand (1905–1982) both believe that we are born self-interested, but that we are *not* born knowing what our interest are. They argue that we must work hard to discover our interests, and then discipline ourselves to promote them. If we do not do this hard work, and instead follow our most immediate or most compelling desires, we will harm, or even destroy, ourselves. In contemporary language, Epicurus and Rand argue for "enlightened self-interest."

Goal   (self-interest)

↑

Right Actions/Good Character Traits

Figure 3.1

Epicurus and Rand argue for the moral superiority of the interests of the *self,* not themselves. Their theories are universal, that is, they are supposed to apply to everyone.

Epicurus

SELF-INTEREST, NOT SELFISHNESS

Epicurus argues that knowledge of self, others, society, and the physical environment is necessary to promote self-interest.[6] A truly self-interested person should be honest and fair, have a few good friends, and be careful to live in a way that promotes physical and mental well-being. Trustworthiness is important to secure the help of others and to prevent them from interfering with our interests. Living a life of self-interest requires discipline and, at times, sacrifice.

It is especially important to obey the laws of our community. Justice is a contract in which each person agrees not to harm others. We agree to this contract because it is in our interest to live in a peaceful, orderly society. Epicurus argues that his brand of ethical egoism will lead to social harmony. If we live according to his theory, we will not harm each other in our pursuit of self-interest; in fact, we are likely to help each other.

Epicurus' brand of egoism is quite different from egoism as we normally think of it. In everyday life we use the terms "egoist" and "egotist" to refer to selfish and opportunistic people. Epicurus argues that selfish, opportunistic people are mistaken about what their true interests are. Further, selfishness is a character trait, not an ethical theory. An ethical theory is an attempt to understand and organize our most basic ethical beliefs. A character trait is a unified pattern of behavior.

To appreciate the distinction between selfishness and self-interest, consider for a moment the people we describe as selfish. Selfish people take more than their share of cake or pizza or profits; they abandon luncheon dates if a better offer comes along; they rip pages out of library books to save money copying the material or to secure an advantage on a test. Epicurus would reject all of these actions since they are not likely to be in one's long-term self-interest. Robert Frank, an economist at Cornell, agrees. He cites research that suggests that honest people may do better in the long run, even though they pass up some opportunities in which deception would give them extra material benefits.[7]

Jameson and Mamet are self-interested, not selfish. They rose to their present positions by cooperating with others, keeping their word, and being loyal to their mentors. They often had to compete with others for projects and jobs, and sometimes those battles got nasty. They think of themselves as lucky, though, because they never had to compromise their most basic beliefs. However, their previous jobs were with growing, vibrant companies. They never had to lay off workers or close a plant.

PSYCHOLOGICAL EGOISM

Epicurus was not only an ethical egoist, but a *psychological egoist.* He argued that we are psychologically disposed to pursue our own interest at all times. This presents a problem for his ethical thesis, since it seems odd to recommend that we *should* do what we *must* do. It is a little like urging someone to head toward the ground once they have parachuted out of a plane. However, just as there are more and less comfortable ways to position your body in free-fall and better and worse ways to land, there are better and worse ways of understanding and pursuing our interests.

Epicurus believes that although we are born with a desire to pursue our own interest, we are not born knowing what our interest is, or how to promote it. In the past, Jameson and Mamet felt they knew what their interests were and how to promote them. The relocation issue, however, has shaken their confidence.

HEDONISM

Although we are not born knowing what our interest is, we have some compelling clues. Epicurus notes that we are naturally inclined to pursue our own pleasure and avoid our own pain. Using this as a starting point, he argues that pleasure is in our interest and we should pursue it, whereas pain is contrary to our interest and we should avoid it.

This seemingly simple doctrine is complicated by the fact that there are two kinds of pleasure. One kind, which Epicurus called *kinetic pleasure,* is what we think of as pleasant sensations. These are the kind of pleasures we get from food, alcohol, sex, and so-called recreational drugs. Kinetic pleasures, like all pleasures, are good in themselves, but unfortunately they can lead to pain later, resulting in a low net pleasure in comparison with other acts. Our desires for kinetic pleasures can get out of control because they have no natural limit. The more we get, the more we want, until we are consumed with desires we cannot possibly fulfill. A paradigm case of this is drug or alcohol addiction, but Epicurus seemed to believe that we could have a similar problem with power. Those who pursue these kinetic pleasures are not bad people; they are simply making a factual mistake about what is good for them.

Another kind of pleasure, *static pleasure,* is contentment. It is the absence of pain in the body and absence of fear in the mind. Static pleasure is its own limit, so to speak—once we have achieved it fully, there is no more to attain, although we must be careful to maintain our state of health and contentment. We achieve static pleasure through living frugally and carefully, reducing our desires to those that are necessary for life, avoiding stressful civic and personal relationships, obeying the law, and by learning about the physical world. Learning about the physical world helps us manipulate it better. It also makes us less susceptible to superstition and its attendant fears.

Jameson and Mamet exemplify part of Epicurus' theory. They have been honest, loyal, and truthful as a general rule. They violated these institutional values in only two types of cases. First, they would misrepresent their bottom line in negotiation situations with labor and suppliers. Second, they sometimes lied to people who were clearly lying to them. Since most people approve of not telling the truth in these cases, this did not damage their reputation. On the contrary, their behavior has earned them a reputation as honest business people who cannot be tricked or otherwise manipulated. However, because business is so competitive, even the best people will run into stressful and trying problems. Epicurus would advise Jameson and Mamet to settle the relocation problem in a way that causes the least problems for themselves, and then find a way to live that does not involve so many conflicts.

Ayn Rand

Ayn Rand's ethical egoism[8] is different from Epicurus'. On her view, there is no conflict between business and ethics, since it is our ethical duty to promote our self-interest. Successful business people are paragons of ethical virtue, and a free and unencumbered capitalism that promotes business is the only justifiable social arrangement. Business ethics, far from being an oxymoron, expresses a *necessary truth.*

Rand argues that our only moral obligation is to be selfish. She uses the word "selfish" because it contrasts so well with altruism, a view she wants to refute. Rand also opposes what she calls "brutish" egoism. Brutish egoism defines our interest in terms of kinetic or felt pleasure and power over others. The kinds of issues she raises, when compared and contrasted with Epicurus, show the depth and the complexity of ethical egoism. Being an ethical egoist, as opposed to blindly pursuing whims, can be intellectually and emotionally demanding.

We will begin with Rand's rejection of altruism and see how that leads her to egoism. We will then examine her egoistic theory, and how she distinguishes it from hedonic and power-oriented egoism.

THE FAILURE OF ALTRUISM

According to Rand, altruism requires us to treat the good of others as the sole ethical goal. She argues that altruism cannot perform the two crucial functions of ethical theory: to give sensible evaluations of the behavior of others and to direct one's own behavior. (Note the similarity between Rand's view of the function of ethics and Kohlberg and Gilligan's view of the function of ethics.) To illustrate the first kind of problem, she compares a wealthy business person and a wealthy gangster. Rand argues that from an altruistic point of view, they are both equally immoral, and for the same reason: they have enriched themselves, and have not devoted their lives to serving others. Since altruism implies that the business person and the gangster are morally equivalent, altruism must be false. She also considers the case of a dictator who uses repressive acts for the good of others, but does not try to enrich himself. According to altruism, the dictator is virtuous. Once again, Rand argues that this is an outrageous conclusion. Altruism must be rejected.

Rand also thinks that altruism is inconsistent, since it implies that it is morally justified for us to receive something, but not morally justified to get the very same thing for ourselves. Again, Rand finds this result absurd. If it is good to have something, its value is not reduced if you work for it. Further, an altruistic social and political system would have to be a dictatorship to make people serve each other.

Lastly, Rand argues that we are born self-interested, not altruistic. Hence, if we subscribe to altruism we have two undesirable choices: we can ignore our natural desires and live an unnatural and unfulfilling life or we can pursue our own interest by pretending to be altruistic. Both consequences are bad for us and we should avoid them.

Jameson and Mamet are not worried about being altruistic; they are worried about harming people. They fear that employees and their families will be devastated by the plant closing. Rand would advise them not to worry about the employees. They are adults and can take of themselves. If they are good workers, and willing to move, they can find other, perhaps better employment. To worry about the employees' interests is to treat them like children.

HUMAN NATURE AND SELF-INTEREST

To find out what our interests are, Rand begins by contrasting human beings with animals. Nonhuman animals live by instinct; human beings live by choices. As humans, we have two related capacities that enable us to make choices: rationality and self-awareness.[9]

Rationality and self-awareness are promoted by "productive work." Productive work can be studying physics, being an investment banker, or digging ditches, as long as we do it because it serves our interests and it does not interfere with others legitimately pursuing their interests. Productive work often requires us to endure pain and forego pleasure. Our ability to assess rationally our interests and goals over the span of our lives enables us to see why such sacrifices are necessary. If we choose productive work that fits our talents, we will live well.

When we use our rational and reflective capacities to pursue our talents through productive work, we feel the pleasure of legitimate pride. This pleasure is a good thing, but it is *not* the standard by which we should judge our behavior. Rather, pleasure is the result of acting in accord with our talents. Happiness, though good, is also not the standard by which we should evaluate our acts or our overall life.[10] Pleasure and happiness are *signs* or indications that we are acting and living well. This is not to say that we cannot use pleasure or happiness as our standards; we certainly can. However, if we do, we will not develop our essential nature as rational, self-aware beings. Paradoxically, developing these two natural capacities will give us more pleasure and happiness than seeking pleasure or happiness directly.

Rand would applaud Jameson's and Mamet's business careers. They have worked hard and deserve their material benefits and the pleasure of rising through the ranks. Equally important, they have developed as rational, reflective human beings. They are successful because they have good problem-solving skills and clear ideas of who they are and what they want.

The relocation decision puts all of Jameson's and Mamet's gains at risk. Rand would urge them not to look out for others. If they examine their true motives, they will see that they are more worried about the negative reactions of others and the battles they will have to fight. This is nothing more than a concern for their own comfort. Seeking comfort is a weak and undisciplined form of self-interest. They should have the courage to choose the best path for themselves, even if others do not like it.

THE LIMITS OF SELFISHNESS

Like Epicurus, Rand argues that egoism is incompatible with acts of lawlessness, free-riding, and pleasure seeking. These acts and motivations do not help us develop our rational and reflective capacities. She also argues that it is wrong to coerce others to serve us. She claims that each person is intrinsically valuable, an "end in itself," and that our intrinsic value forbids us from serving others and from coercing others to serve us. We can, of course, choose to work for others for adequate compensation.

RAND'S SOCIAL VIEWS

Like Epicurus, Rand believes that social harmony will result from people looking after themselves. However, unlike Epicurus, she argues that social harmony results from people engaging in "productive work" to satisfy their desires, not from a reduction of desires. If all people engage in productive work, no one has the need to live off others or to coerce others. Pure capitalism, in which government is limited to protecting property and enforcing contracts, is the social system most conductive to promoting productive work, since people can pursue their projects as they see fit and can keep the rewards of their endeavors. As business people in a capitalist environment, Jameson and Mamet should promote the goals of S and R, reap the benefits, and let others take care of themselves.

An Institutional Analysis of Egoism

Epicurus and Rand argue that most social institutions do not allow for the free pursuit of self-interest. Because they have different views of self-interest, they differ about what is wrong with these institutions and what we should do about them. For Epicurus, we should not try to change the prevailing institutions. We should retire from society and join with others who share our views. This will result in a new community with institutions that promote self-interest. For Rand, we need to be forceful agents of change, as she perceived herself to be. Our self-interest is intrinsically tied to the institutions of capitalism, and so it is in our interest to reshape these institutions to promote self-interest.

If Jameson and Mamet followed Epicurus, who defined self-interest in terms of contentment and the avoidance of conflict, they would solve the problem as painlessly as possible, and then find a less stressful way to live. If they followed Rand, who defined self-interest as the pursuit of rational excellence and self-awareness, they would pursue their careers and not worry about the interests of others.

There are many contemporary examples that illustrate (but do not prove) Epicurus' and Rand's views. We will mention just two. From an Epicurean point of view, the trading scandals on Wall Street in the late 1980s resulted from faulty views of self-interest.[11] Michael Milken and Ivan Boesky seem to have defined their interests in terms of money and power. They achieved these, but in their quest for more, they broke security laws and went to jail. Milken kept much of his money, but not his power. Moreover, he never had peace of mind. The fact that Milken never recanted, as did Boesky, would be of little concern to Epicurus. Epicurus would argue that Milken is so confused about his interests that he, much like the alcoholic or drug addict, cannot see what a good life is or how to achieve it.

If we relied on Rand, we would applaud Bill Gates and his company, Microsoft. She would not object to Gates' wealth, which at the time of this writing tops 80 billion dollars. He earned it within the rules by productive work. Those who want to redistribute Gate's wealth to others are severely misguided. This will not help Gates, and it will not help those who get his money.

One way to evaluate Epicurus' and Rand's theories is to ask if they are right about human nature. It is possible that Epicurus has correctly described some people, Rand has correctly described others, and that there are other kinds of people, too. Jameson and Mamet, for example, seem to care about themselves, their families, the groups and organizations to which they belong, and fairness. It is very unlikely that they would opt for Epicurus' or Rand's extreme egoistic positions.

One reason Jameson and Mamet could reject egoism, oddly enough, is that it is not in their interest. If they were to follow the egoistic advice discussed above, they would violate their fundamental beliefs of who they are. They cannot imagine, for example, betraying their friends, family, or country to pursue their own interest. These considerations about their characters suggest that they need a way to think about their interests in terms of their careers, their personal relationships with friends and family, their relationships to their community, and their beliefs about what is fair and just. These are the topics of the next three sections.

CARING AND DECISION MAKING: MARY MIDGLEY, NEL NODDINGS, AND MARILYN FRIEDMAN

Friends and family are important to Jameson and Mamet. If they base their decision about moving S and R on how these relationships would be affected, they probably would not move. The standard analysis of business requires officers to act as agents for the owners, not for themselves or their families. On this view, Jameson and Mamet would be *morally wrong* to base their relocation decision on their own personal interests. Their primary ethical obligation is to promote the interest of the shareholders.

These ethical judgments are based on the values that underlie the social institutions that govern decision making within organizations. Still, even on the standard analysis, family concerns can legitimately affect some business decisions, such as whether to resign, or in different circumstances, whether to accept a promotion or move to a different site.

Even if Jameson and Mamet do not base their official decision on personal relationships, they want to make sure that their decision will not harm their families or their relationships with their families. The care ethic focuses on close, personal relationships. According to care theorists, we cannot live well if our important personal relationships are troubled.

We begin by discussing Mary Midgley's evolutionary account of how our natural affections form the basis of morality. Next, we will discuss Nel Nodding's care ethic. We will then look at the work of Marilyn Friedman, who argues that we need to combine rights and care.

Mary Midgley: Natural Affections and the Origin of Morality

Mary Midgley, a contemporary British philosopher, argues that morality begins with our natural affections for family and friends. She quotes Darwin as a proponent of this view: natural affections, he said, "supply the raw material of the moral life—the general motivations which . . . give it its rough direction—while still needing the work of intelligence . . . to contribute to its form."[12] Using rational thought, we develop reasoning strategies to understand and shape our emotions and our personal relationships. As the human species developed, successful strategies, such as obeying the rules of the group and doing what your parents say, were passed on to future generations. On this evolutionary view, *morality is a set of conflict resolution strategies that preserves relationships* and so promotes the survival of the species. This view of ethics is very similar to the functional view of Kohlberg and Gilligan.

If Midgley is right, an account of morality must include some reference to our natural affections. Natural affections for friends and family did not play a central role in the egoistic theories of Epicurus or Rand. These issues are very important for Jameson and Mamet, however. According to care theorists, people and relationships are valuable in themselves. When we care for people, we value them in themselves, not because they will benefit us.

When we value others in themselves, we get satisfaction from helping them to promote their interests, and we feel bad about their misfortunes. If we do not care about others, we get no pleasure from helping them. Consider lending your car to a friend, and the pleasure you get from helping someone you like. Later, you discover that the person stole $500 from another friend of yours, and used your car to go the airport. You no longer feel pleasure, but anger. This example illustrates that the pleasure we get from helping others depends on how we view them. Jameson and Mamet care about the individuals and groups involved, and this is why they have a hard time with the decision. Care theorists such as Nel Noddings would urge them to focus on their most intimate relationships.

Nel Noddings: An Ethic of Care

Caring, says Nel Noddings, is helping others pursue their own projects.[13] We do this by listening carefully to others, taking their concerns seriously, and giving them support.

Caring is not making people live the way we think is best. Noddings' view of care leaves a great deal of room for people to decide their own moral values, but it is not a relativistic doctrine. The care ethic rejects hatred and violence.

Noddings argues that caring can be tough.[14] Sometimes we must refuse to help people if helping makes them too dependent on us or others. We can also interfere with the projects of others if they are destructive to themselves or others. At other times, we may need to care for ourselves first, and help others second. Consider the set of instructions about oxygen masks given to us by airline flight attendants when we fly. Flight attendants tell us that if we are traveling with a small child, we should put our oxygen masks on first, and then put on the child's mask. This is because the adult needs oxygen to help the child.

Airlines tell us this because most of us would help our children first. We would not rationally calculate what is best for us or the child in an emergency. Our caring instinct would take over. However, it is better to reject this impulse and act in a way that is more likely to help the child *and* ourselves. In fact, in this situation there is no conflict between our interests and the child's interests. This example illustrates two points.

First, morality is underlain by an instinctual caring response. We are moved to help others when their needs are great and the means of helping them are clear. Second, morality is more than just following our instincts. Acting morally involves a *choice* about what we are going to do. As passengers with small children listen to these instructions, they recognize how the advice helps them to care for their child. In recognizing this, they make a conscious decision to act in a caring fashion by putting their mask on first if an emergency arises. It is this conscious decision that carries the ethical weight.

Noddings argues that even the most caring people are not going to care for others all the time. When our natural caring response is not forthcoming, Noddings argues, we must force ourselves to act in a caring fashion. To do this, we need to commit ourselves to a caring life. Nodding does not denigrate caring when it is easy and chosen; caring in these circumstances produces some of the best times of our lives. When times are hard, however, our caring selves are tested. It is also when we can fail to care.

When we fail to care, or to care appropriately, we must decide how to deal with our failure. Let us go back to our airline example. A parent hears the instructions about the oxygen masks. In flight, the cargo doors blow off, the cabin becomes depressurized, and the oxygen masks fall from the ceiling. In terror, the parent reaches for the mask and instinctively tries to put it on the child. Just as the mask is almost in place, the plane lurches, and the mask is knocked off the child's face as the parent passes out. A fellow passenger is able to share a mask with the parent, but cannot reach the child, who dies.

How should the parent deal with this tragedy? In cases such as these, our caring selves are put to a dramatic test because we must continue to care for ourselves, despite the feelings of worthlessness that almost certainly will follow. Caring about ourselves will be tough, and it will not happen right away. However, it must happen if the parent is to continue to care for others.

According to Noddings, Jameson and Mamet are right to care for the various groups involved. They are also right to be confused and troubled. Much is at stake for many people. Following Noddings, we could argue that Jameson and Mamet need to pay attention to their families first. This does not mean that they should make their relocation decision on this basis, but it could mean that they should resign.

There are more options than resigning, however. As we saw in Chapter 1, conflicts are a window into our institutions and relationships. Jameson and Mamet could use this opportunity to establish better and closer relationships with their families. If they can talk about the ramifications of the relocation based on their care for others and themselves, they may emerge with stronger and better families. These kinds of discussions sometimes reveal surprising things. Jameson may discover that her children would love to move to Taiwan for the few months it will take to relocate. Mamet may find out his wife wants to go law school, and she would not mind if he took their child overseas, as long as they could agree on a nanny.

Noddings is not an idealist. She knows that people can be mean, petty, jealous, hateful, and a host of other undesirable things. Jameson and Mamet could be setting themselves up for real trouble if they initiate the kinds of conversations we just discussed. How Jameson and Mamet ought to approach this issue with their families depends on may contextual details. They may be able to make reliable judgments about what they should do, but there are no certainties.

Marilyn Friedman: Integrating Justice and Care

In "Beyond Caring: The De-Moralization of Gender," Marilyn Friedman argues that the care ethic needs to be supplemented with justice.[15] She argues for three points: that both men and women use a care ethic, that care and justice overlap, and that although care and justice overlap, they are still different notions.

GENDER AND MORAL VOICE

Friedman cites various studies that suggest that men and women use care and rights reasoning equally. However, Friedman also cites studies that show that both sexes tend to *believe* that most women use care reasoning and that most men use justice reasoning. Taken together, these two sets of studies imply that we are mistaken about how we actually reason about moral issues.

Friedman explains our misperception by arguing that morality "is fragmented into a division of labor," with each gender being assigned certain tasks and duties. Women are expected to take care of relationships with family and friends, whereas men have been assigned the more public duties regarding government and business. This division of moral labor suggests that "genders are moralized," which means that we expect different moral behavior from each gender, and, because of this, we tolerate different moral shortcomings from each gender.

For example, we expect women to be more sensitive than men to crying children. Because of this expectation, it is a deep moral failure for a woman to ignore a crying child, but a man with the same reaction would not be as harshly criticized. Similarly, we expect men to fight in battle and have the courage to sacrifice their lives if necessary. A man who is afraid to go to the front of battle is thought to be deeply morally flawed, whereas a woman who behaves in the same way would not be as harshly criticized.

Our perceptions about how we reason are inaccurate because our expectations about how women and men should behave override our perceptions. Since we expect women to reason empathetically, we focus on confirming instances and tend to ignore or reinterpret disconfirming instances. We do the same thing with men. Further, individuals of both sexes have a stake in acting within their gender roles. This means that we do not merely expect others to reason in ways consistent with social gender expectations, we expect *ourselves* to reason in gender-appropriate ways.

Friedman would applaud the way Jameson and Mamet are approaching this problem. They are wrestling with the conflict between caring for their family and respecting the rights of the shareholders to a fair return on their investment. What they need is a way to combine their concerns for care and justice.

THE COMPATIBILITY OF CARE AND JUSTICE

If the structure of social institutions is strong enough to make us believe that men and women reason differently, why can't it actually get women and men to reason differently? Friedman's answer is intriguing. She thinks society cannot restrict care reasoning to women and justice reasoning to men because the pure concepts of care and justice are too limited to solve the variety of practical issues we encounter. We need care in situations in which justice is a major concern, and justice in situations in which care is a major concern. It is the latter issue on which Friedman spends the most time. Her comments about integrating justice into care can help us understand how to integrate care into justice.

Friedman argues that there are "*special* duties of justice" that arise in personal relationships. These special duties, which are grounded on affection and kinship, can take three forms: distributive justice, corrective justice, and a third type of justice that she does not name, but that we will call "institutional justice." Distributive justice concerns how wealth, rights, and duties are distributed. Friedman argues that personal relationships can be unjust in the distributive sense if one of the parties has the responsibility for doing most of the work to maintain the relationship. Friedman cites Marilyn Frye who argues that women suffer this kind of distributive injustice in all cultures and classes.

Corrective justice concerns how rule breaking is redressed. Personal relationships can be unjust in the corrective sense when there is no compensation or rectification for harms done. Friedman notes that we are much more vulnerable in personal relationships than in our impersonal relationships. She does not speculate what rectificatory justice would look like in personal relationships, but certainly one of the stumbling blocks in devising rules for rectification in personal relationships is that the ideal case of rectification would seem to require that the transgressor truly regret the transgression. This regret includes the desire to rectify the harm, and perhaps the desire to modify character traits that led to the harm. In personal relationships, more than behavior is needed; sometimes what is required is a change of heart, and no rule can do this.

Institutional justice deals with the integration of care, distributive justice, and corrective justice to promote healthy, flourishing relationships. Friedman writes:

> Personal relationships may also be regarded in the context of their various *institutional* settings, such as marriage and the family. Here justice emerges again as a relevant ideal, its role being to define appropriate institutions to structure interactions among family members, other household co-habitants, and intimates in general. The family, for example, is a miniature society, exhibiting all the major facets of large-scale social life: decision-making affecting the whole unit; executive action; judgments of guilt and innocence; reward and punishment; allocation of responsibilities and privileges, of burdens and benefits; and monumental influences on the life chances of both its maturing and its matured members.[16] (emphasis added)

For a family to be just in this third sense, it must be structured to nurture children into competent adults. To do this, it must be just in the distributive and corrective senses, but it must be more than this, too. Social groups such as The Rotary Club may be just in the distributive and corrective senses, but no one would think that such groups would excel at bringing up children. What makes a family just in this third sense is the affection and sacrifice that has as its goal helping all its members, from the most vulnerable to the most independent, live the best life possible.

To eliminate the notion of justice from personal relationships is dangerous, according to Friedman, since this fails "to acknowledge the potential for *violence and harm* in human relationships and human communities."[17] Groups are institutionally just insofar as they help all members of the group develop to their full potential. Groups help their members develop in three distinct but related ways: first, by providing an environment that is just in distributive and corrective senses; second, by nurturing the development of deep, caring relationships; and third, by helping the members learn the skills they need to live well in the contemporary world. Each of these three goals requires the other two.

Institutional justice would explain Jameson's and Mamet's concerns about their families. They are not merely worried they will make their families feel bad or uncomfortable, although these are important considerations. Their concern is based on their responsibility to promote an institutionally just and caring family. They are not likely to do this if they unilaterally decide to uproot or abandon their families. However, the shareholders have rights that need to be respected, too. From Friedman's point of view, *Jameson and Mamet need to resolve this conflict without abandoning either value.*

Just as justice applies to private relationships, so care applies to justice in the public arena:

> care in the public realm would show itself, perhaps in foreign aid, welfare programs, famine or disaster relief, or other social programs designed to relieve suffering and attend to human needs.[18]

The Family and Medical Leave Act[19] and the movement to reform health care are driven, in part, by concerns of care. Yet, if care is not applied in accord with the standards of justice, we could end up helping only a few, ignoring those whose needs are as great or greater. Friedman cites the late Mayor Daley of Chicago, who was loyal to friends and family by giving them city jobs and contracts, but who ignored the needs of others in the city. His was a care ethic without justice.

The S and R case supports Friedman's view that we need to integrate rights and care. The fact that Jameson and Mamet do not know how to do this does not show that they are deficient. Their inability to integrate care and justice only reflects the fact that social institutions do not integrate these values well. In Ethical Pluralism and Decision Making: Adam Smith and Aristotle, we will look at one way to integrate these two values.

TENSIONS BETWEEN CARE AND JUSTICE

Although justice and care need each other, Friedman argues that the care and the justice perspectives have very different "primary moral commitments." The care perspective takes "particular persons" as its primary focus. With care,

> the key issue is the sensitivity and responsiveness to another person's emotional states [and] . . . differences. The 'care' orientation focuses on whole persons and de-emphasizes adherence to moral rules.[20]

The justice orientation, on the other hand, "involves a focus on general and abstract rules, values, or principles."[21] It does not pay attention to the particular circumstances of people. It is the essence of justice that these rules be applied impartially. Respect for others from this perspective is based on their humanity, a property all people have equally.

The care ethic's commitment to context is incompatible with the right's commitment to ignore context. For example, we cannot resolve a conflict with a friend using both forms of reasoning. To view the friend as a friend, we will view the person as a unique individual in the context of our special relationship. We cannot *at the same time* abstract from that unique friendship and rely on impersonal rules of justice. We can switch between these two views, like seeing the vase or the faces (Chapter 1), but we cannot inhabit the two views at the same time.

Although we cannot use the care perspective and the justice perspective at the same time, this does not prevent us from integrating information from each perspective. Many situations, such as the one facing Jameson and Mamet, call for both kinds of reasoning.

An Institutional Analysis of Care

Noddings and Friedman would probably agree that the U.S. institutional framework undervalues family and friendship. Many parents need to work long hours at one or more jobs to make ends meet, severely limiting the amount of time they can spend with their children. The Family and Medical Leave Act was supposed to ameliorate these problems, at least in times of crisis.

Noddings and Friedman would probably disagree about how to change institutions. Noddings would want to ensure that business and government make family and friends the first priority. As I understand Friedman, she would be suspicious of government playing too much of a role in family relationships. She would look for a way to integrate care and justice that would increase the institutional respect for families without damaging the infrastructure that enables business to act efficiently.

There are many contemporary examples of the care ethic. At the policy level, we have already mentioned the Family and Medical Leave Act. There is a growing number of people leaving lucrative, high-stress jobs for a simpler life-style. This movement is called "Voluntary Simplicity, Downshifting [or] Simple Living."[22] In a 1996 poll, 28% of a cross section of U.S. citizens said they had voluntarily cut back on their jobs to pursue other interests. Many did so to spend more time with family and friends.[23]

Turning to the S and R case, Noddings would argue that Jameson's and Mamet's primary moral obligations are to improve or at least maintain their personal relationships. This could require them to stay in Frieberg. This does not mean that S and R should stay in Frieberg, however. If it is clear that S and R should move, Jameson and Mamet will have to find a way not to spend months overseas. Perhaps they could delegate the traveling to others. If they did this, they would have to take into account the personal relationships of these new individuals. Noddings makes it clear that we cannot harm people for the sole purpose of helping others. If Jameson and Mamet cannot delegate the traveling, they may have to resign. As we have just seen, this path is chosen by more than a few people.

On Friedman's analysis, the S and R case is good example of why the care ethic by itself is not sufficient. A full analysis of the case requires us to consider the abstract but compelling relationships between the officers of S and R and its many stakeholders. To understand and evaluate these more abstract and legal relationships we need to rely on ethical theories that value groups, as do utilitarian theories, or on theories that value the rules and principles that guide interactions within and between individuals and groups, as do theories of justice and rights. Once we understand these abstract duties better, we will have to integrate these abstract obligations with our personal obligations.

GROUP WELL-BEING AND DECISION MAKING: DAVID HUME AND JOHN STUART MILL

Jameson and Mamet want to promote the good of S and R's shareholders, employees, suppliers, Frieberg, and the community where they might move. As citizens, they want to promote their country's welfare, or at least not harm it. Utilitarianism asserts that their first obligation is to promote the good of those affected by their decision, and so it fits with the way Jameson and Mamet are already thinking. We can characterize the structure of utilitarianism as shown in Figure 3.2.

Individual well-being is affected by the groups to which individuals belong. Jameson and Mamet cannot decide which group is most important: owners, employees, suppliers, and Frieberg are some of the groups they are considering. The British philosophers David Hume (1711–1776) and John Stuart Mill (1806–1873) assumed that the nation-state is the most important group because it provides the social and physical infrastructure that makes subgroups, such as S and R and its owners, possible.

Once we decide the scope of utilitarian reasoning, we need to define group welfare. Hume and Mill both define group well-being in terms of happiness, but they do not define happiness in the same way. Hume emphasizes security and predictability, whereas Mill emphasizes "higher human pleasures." These goals seem too abstract to help Jameson and Mamet with their relocation problem. Luckily, both Hume and Mill show how we can promote these goals in our everyday lives.

David Hume's Utilitarianism: Stability and Predictability

Hume argues that the most important social problem is *scarcity,* since it breeds competition. Competition without rules leads to anarchy, which makes us all suffer. To control competition for scarce resources, societies develop and enforce rules of *property.*[24]

The rules of property help the group, but they do not always help particular individuals, such as when we have to pay back debts. Hume argues that we morally approve of rules that can sometimes harm us, such as property, because these rules are good for the group as a whole. This approval is based on *sympathy.* Sympathy, which he defines as the ability to understand and care about others, is the foundation of morality[25] (see Midgley and Noddings in the previous section for a similar view).

Hume believes that private property handles the scarcity problem better than communal property because it better integrates our need to promote our personal interests (ourselves, families, and friends) with the need to promote group welfare. Private property does this by providing incentives for people to create wealth for themselves. The

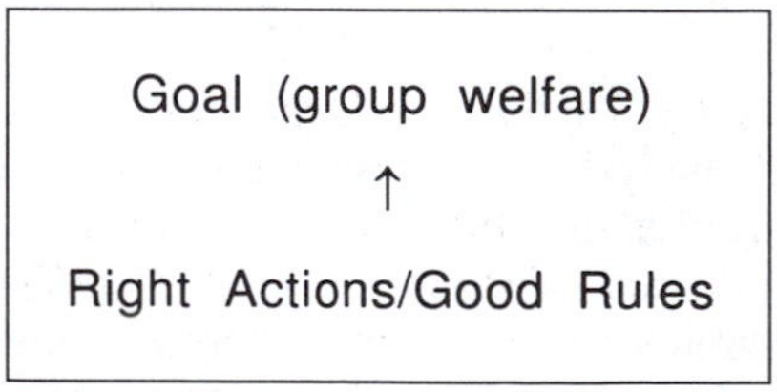

Goal (group welfare)

↑

Right Actions/Good Rules

Figure 3.2

more people do this, the more wealthy their group becomes. Hume warns against redistributing property according to moral principles such as equality and fairness, since this would inhibit business and require repressive government policies. (See Ayn Rand for a similar account.)

SYMPATHY: THE FUNDAMENTAL MORAL EMOTION

Sympathy is the foundation of morality. To see how this works, consider how you would react if two of your friends had been cheated by their business partner who is now living comfortably in the Cayman Islands. The harm to your friends triggers your capacity for sympathy, and you feel a pain that is similar to, but less intense than, the pain of your friends. Now consider what you feel when you read about strangers who are cheated in a similar way. Your sympathetic feeling is less intense than with your friends, but is still strong enough to condemn the cheating. Now consider a work of fiction, say a film, where you boo the villain and cheer for the hero. You feel sympathy even in this fictional case. In all these cases you are not the initial subject of harm. Still, you feel as if you were harmed, and that in itself is a kind of harm.

A problem with using sympathy as the basis of moral judgment is that our sympathy varies with how much we like or know about people. In the S and R case, Jameson is more familiar with the people of Frieberg, and tends to be more sympathetic to them. Mamet is impressed by the poverty he saw in his travels, and his close encounters with impoverished Asians left him very sympathetic to their interests. According to Hume, though, moral judgments should be *impartial,* that is, we should judge all people in the same way. When we take an impartial perspective, we make the same moral decision whether the person is a friend, enemy, or stranger.

Hume argues that sympathy can be impartial if we apply it from an objective point of view, much as a judge should do in court. We rely on rules and procedures, but we do not favor any side for personal reasons. If Jameson and Mamet were to follow this advice, Jameson would ignore her special feelings for the people in Frieberg and Mamet would ignore his special feelings for the poor he saw along the Pacific Rim. If Jameson and Mamet subtract these personal relationships and experiences from their evaluations, and if they agree on the facts of the case, they should come to similar moral judgments.

Although Hume bases moral *judgment* on sympathy, he recognizes that self-interest is often a stronger force in guiding *behavior.* In fact, he takes it as a strength of his theory that it can explain the "extensive sympathy"[26] on which morality is based and the "limited generosity" that seems to characterize our actions. For example, it would not surprise Hume if Jameson and Mamet believe that their moral duty is to relocate, but that they stay in Frieberg for family or self-interested reasons.

NATURAL VIRTUES, ARTIFICIAL VIRTUES, AND CONSTITUTIVE RULES

One of Hume's most important contributions to understanding the rules and practices of groups is his discussion of natural and artificial virtues. *Natural virtues,* like kindness and generosity, can occur without rules. For example, if we see someone on crutches who needs help opening a door, we do not need any rules to help that person. *Artificial virtues,* such as justice and politeness, are based on rules created by the group. Basic property rules are *constitutive* because they constitute or create an infrastructure that makes certain kinds of actions possible. For example, Jameson and Mamet work in a corporation that could not exist as it does without the incorporation laws that define it.

Sympathy is the basis for the moral nature of natural and artificial virtues, but in different ways. For the natural virtues, sympathy approves of each *act,* such as helping a person in need. When we see a parent taking extra time to help a distraught child, we sympathetically approve of the act in itself. Our sympathetic approval for the artificial virtues, however, is based on the beneficial effect that the constitutive *rules* have on the group. Property rules, the most important of the constitutive rules, are necessary not only for law and order, but for production and commerce; they create the very possibility of business behavior. *The function of constitutive law is to create new types of behavior, not to prevent behavior.* This point is the foundation of the economic and legal theories discussed in the next two chapters.

We can approve of constitutive rules even when they harm individuals in specific cases. For example, Hume believes that we should make loan payments even when doing so means less food on the table for our family. If we were to examine this particular act out of context, the harm to ourselves and our family may be greater than the benefit the lender gets by timely repayment. However, without the rule that demands timely loan repayment, no one would lend money, or would do so only at much higher interest rates. This would interfere with the capital markets that finance the production of food, shelter, and clothing, making everyone worse off.

The goods made possible by property rules are constitutive goods, because we could not have them without the rules of property that make their financing, production, and distribution possible. The harms made possible by property rules are constitutive harms, because we could not have these without the rules of property, either. Hume recognizes this, but argues that property's constitutive goods far outweigh its constitutive harms. If Hume were alive today he could point to Somalia, Bosnia, and the problems of the former Russian republics to support his view.

Applying Hume's theory to S and R, Jameson and Mamet should look at the constitutive rules that govern their jobs as managers. Legal rules and social practice suggest that officers should promote the welfare of the owners. Hume would argue that these rules and practices promote the good of all. However, if Jameson and Mamet have made implicit promises to keep the plant in Frieberg, they need to decide whether to keep their promises to labor or promote the good of shareholders. Hume would probably say that the responsibility to shareholders is more important, since that is more strongly and consistently enforced by society.

JUSTICE: THE CHIEF CONSTITUTIVE VIRTUE OF INDIVIDUALS AND INSTITUTIONS

Hume argues that justice, by which he means following the constitutive rules of property, is created and maintained for the overall good. To show the importance of property to the good of all, Hume considers two situations in which property would not exist.[27] The first situation is one in which supply greatly exceeds demand, such as in the story of the Garden of Eden. There would be no need for the "jealous virtue of justice,"[28] since there would be no need to claim an object as our own. It is costly to create and enforce property rules. We would not devote our time and other resources to creating and maintaining property unless there were clear benefits.

The second situation is one in which there is not enough for all to live, as in an extreme famine. In this case, the instinct for survival would overcome all rules of property, and people would take what they needed to survive. Since property exists only if there are stable rules to guide our expectations and behavior, and there are no such rules in conditions of extreme scarcity, there is no property.

Most societies are between extreme abundance and extreme scarcity. Through the creation and enforcement of property rights, groups can produce a great wealth of goods, reducing scarcity even further. Property rules provide incentives for production. They also protect our goods from others. Our moral approval of property, and the business practices that property makes possible, is based on our sympathetic approval of how property and business benefit all.

Hume argues that private property, in which owners keep the rewards of production and bear the costs of failure, is best. Hume considers the possibility of distributing property according to religious virtue or other forms of merit, but he argues that such a system would soon result in chaos because of individual self-interest and conceit. Most of us would believe that we were superior to others, and so each would demand more goods than others (see Messick and Bazerman in Part I). Nor would it be possible to distribute property equally. Since we all have different talents and levels of motivation, an equal distribution of goods would soon result in an unequal distribution.

These remarks on property suggest that Jameson and Mamet should follow the values that underlie the institutions of business: maximize shareholder wealth. Hume would argue that if we start adjusting these rules to fit particular cases we will create an unpredictable business environment that reduces investment, thus making everyone worse off. However, if S and R were in a country that required corporations to account for the harms and benefits to their communities when making relocation decisions, Hume would urge S and R to follow that rule.

Hume is concerned with preserving the rules that guide everyday interactions. Despite this, Hume is not a relativist. Rather, he has a universal utilitarian moral standard that allows for a great deal of cultural diversity. The right thing to do is to follow the rules of the socioeconomic system in which you are doing business, because that leads to the stability and predictability necessary for human well-being.

John Stuart Mill's Utilitarianism: Promoting Happiness

John Stuart Mill believes we should shape social policy to bring the greatest good to the greatest number of people.[29] Unlike Hume, Mill is concerned with *distributive justice*. Distributive justice concerns the political and economic institutions that distribute rights and duties, benefits and burdens. If political and economic institutions do not promote the good of all, Mill is ready to change them, as long as we are careful to maintain a stable and predictable environment. Mill was an influential economist, philosopher, and member of the British Parliament. Following his utilitarian views, he fought for women's rights to educational, economic, and political opportunity. His argument for women's rights was simple: women are half the labor force, and society should not waste such an abundance of talent.[30]

THE GREATEST HAPPINESS PRINCIPLE

Like Hume, Mill believes that most people are sympathetic, and that this psychological capacity is the beginning of morality. Mill states his version of the utilitarian principle as follows:

> The Greatest Happiness Principle [GHP] holds that actions are right in proportion as they tend to promote happiness, wrong as they tend to produce the reverse of happiness.[31]

Mill identifies happiness with pleasure, but argues that there are better and worse pleasures. Our best and highest pleasures come from doing things that are uniquely human, such as thinking and acting *rationally*. The physical pleasures are of lesser value. (See Ayn Rand for a similar view of human nature.)

Mill gives us a test to distinguish higher from lower pleasures. We simply ask those who have experienced both. For example, he thinks that those who have experienced both intellectual and physical pleasures will consistently rank the intellectual pleasures higher. Compare the pleasure of successfully managing a complex company with the physical pleasure of being a bicycle courier (assume you love biking). For those who have done both, the strategy and complexity of management make it more pleasurable than the bicycling. Although these complex activities leave more room for frustration and lack of fulfillment, those who do them would not trade them for lesser activities that are more easily fulfilled (see Epicurus for a different view).

Mill considers several objections to using the GHP as a problem-solving strategy. The first objection is that the GHP is not a realistic goal, since not all people can be happy. Mill replies that the GHP can still be effective because it points us in the right direction. The closer we get to the goal, the better.

The second objection is that the GHP can justify lying and fraud when these acts lead to the overall good. Mill replies that lying and fraud are very unlikely to promote the overall good. First, lying and fraud are almost always done to benefit those who lie and defraud, not the group. Further, lying and fraud are often discovered. The result is a general lack of trust, which is harmful to all (see the discussion of Lockheed in the introduction to this chapter). Still, there are exceptions to truthtelling: we should not tell murderers and rapists where their intended victims are. When we need to violate commonly accepted rules such as truthtelling, we should do so only when the gains to the general happiness are very large and the risks to the general happiness are low. Calculating these gains and risks must include the likelihood that our breaking the accepted rules will damage rule-following in the future.

The third objection is that there is not enough time or knowledge to apply the Greatest Happiness Principle. We cannot evaluate each situation, imagine various alternatives, calculate and compare their contributions to the general happiness, and then choose the best one.[32] Mill replies that the GHP requires nothing of the sort. He argues that cultures have "secondary rules," such as "tell the truth," "pay back your debts," and "be loyal to friends and country," that tend to promote the good of all and simplify the application of the GHP. Government officials should, of course, consider the GHP directly when they make public policy.

Although general rules require truthtelling and honesty, their application is guided by particular relationships. For example, if Jameson and Mamet decide to relocate, their responsibility to tell their families, employees, suppliers, the community, and the shareholders are all different. Suppose Jameson's husband reads about the decision to relocate in the morning paper. Since the secondary rules in families usually require that important information about family life be shared, he may decide he has been deceived. Employees, who are feeling secure in their jobs because of assurances by management, are also likely to believe they have been deceived if they read about it in the paper. Community business leaders with no personal or fiduciary connections to Jameson or Mamet who read about the move in the newspaper are not deceived, since there are no secondary rules that require that they be informed ahead of time.

There are many important secondary rules that Jameson and Mamet must consider to use a utilitarian decision-making process. These include statute, case, and regulatory laws, as well as standard financial and economic practices. They will need to turn to specialists to get much of this information. *There are also facts they should ignore.* Hume and Mill would both say that Jameson's and Mamet's self-interest and family interests have nothing to do with the relocation decision. These personal considerations are important to whether they will resign, and to their ability to implement the relocation, but they are irrelevant to the relocation decision itself.

Justice: A Utilitarian Explanation and Justification

The GHP justifies the rule of law because security is essential to our social and personal well-being. Since security is essential to attain all other goods, our feelings about justice are much stronger than our feelings about charity and kindness. Unlike Hume, Mill argues that justice is not confined to current legal rules. Justice also includes *moral rights*.[33] If legal rules violate significant moral rights, it can be wrong to follow them. However, our rights are less important than the Greatest Happiness Principle. For example, Mill says that the GHP can override our moral right to fair treatment before the law. He believed that the cases in which moral rights can be overridden by the GHP were becoming increasingly rare. Slavery and serfdom, he notes, were once socially expedient; they are now viewed as tyrannical. Soon, Mill argued, distinctions based on "colour, race, and sex" will become uneconomical and will be abandoned.[34]

An Institutional Analysis of Utilitarianism

Hume and Mill, though both utilitarians, have different views on how social institutions promote the good of the nation-state. Hume is the more conservative of the two, urging us to follow institutional rules and practices in almost all circumstances. Only by doing so can we preserve an economic environment in which scarcity is not only controlled, but reduced.

Mill was more amenable to changing institutional rules because he believed that rules could become ineffective as technology and social systems changed. Given that rules need to be changed over time, he concentrated on how best to change them. The surest method of coming up with a good result is to follow the secondary rules that typically promote group welfare.

Neither theorist would suggest that Jameson and Mamet violate rules simply because they believe it would promote the good of all. If the rules required Jameson and Mamet to consider only shareholders, that is what they should do. Mill would also urge Jameson and Mamet to try to change the rule favoring shareholders if they thought that their efforts would promote the good of all. Hume would urge them to attend to the business of S and R.

Although Hume and Mill can be of some help, Jameson and Mamet still have no way of identifying the groups they need to consider or of sorting out the conflicts between those groups. Both Hume and Mill believed that the nation–state is the most important group, but this does not help Jameson and Mamet. U.S. institutions are not clear about the problems Jameson and Mamet face; in fact, these institutions are changing. As Patricia Werhane argues in Chapter 7, the employment at will doctrine is being eroded at the case, statute, and regulatory levels. This erosion gives employees and communities a greater standing in affecting business decisions such as the one facing Jameson and Mamet.

The importance of groups external to the firm is reflected in the following statements by three corporate leaders. The CEO of Monsanto argues that environmentalism is important because a sustainable environment is "for the good of all people in developed and less-developed nations."[35] Part of his concern stems from the realization that organizational well-being is dependent on the institutions of society. This dependency is also reflected by Jerry Martin, Dow's Vice President of Environmental Affairs, who said "If we don't have public acceptance, the chemical industry won't be here twenty years from now."[36] There is also a realization that the distinction between those internal and external to the firm sometimes breaks down. Joan Bavaria, President of Franklin Research and Development, said "Understand that the people inside companies are people—they care, they live on the earth, they breathe the air, they drink the water, and they are responsive to [environmental] issues."[37]

These comments illustrate how organizations are dependent on social institutions and stakeholders. These executives do not offer plans to implement their concerns. This is not a criticism. As we saw in the S and R case, the institutions are changing that guide our decisions in these kinds of cases. Since institutions guide our decision making, we would expect uncertainty and ambiguity. In the next section we will look at theories of human dignity, property, and justice to see if they can help us understand the changing institutional setting of business.

INTRINSIC VALUE AND DECISION MAKING: IMMANUEL KANT, ROBERT NOZICK, AND JOHN RAWLS

Jameson and Mamet have always thought of themselves as tough but fair individuals. When competing with others they have adopted a game-among-equals model: they viewed their opponents as equals who, like them, were taking risks to achieve objectives. Winning and losing is fair as long as everyone obeys the basic rules of the game. The relocation issue has aspects that do not fit this model. The community, employees, and suppliers have little, if any, say in the decision, yet they stand to lose a great deal.

Jameson and Mamet tend to believe that they have a duty of some kind to the stakeholders, but they do not know exactly what it is. In this section we will see how ethical theories based on the intrinsic value of human beings can help us understand their vaguely felt duties. Human intrinsic value prohibits us from using people, including ourselves, as tools to promote egoistic or utilitarian ends. This does not mean that it is wrong to promote self-interest or the interest of groups. It means only that we must always respect human intrinsic value when we promote these goals.

Each theorist in this section focuses on a different aspect of intrinsic value. Immanuel Kant (1724–1804) argues that our intrinsic value resides in our ability to make *rational decisions*. This gives us a duty to respect all human beings and the choices and agreements they make. To respect the choices of others does not mean that we agree with them. It may mean, however, that we need to include others when we make decisions that affect them in important ways (see Freeman, Chapter 6). On this view, Jameson and Mamet will have to find some way to consider the interests of the community, employees, and suppliers.

Robert Nozick argues that our intrinsic value resides in our fundamental rights to life, liberty, and property. He focuses on property because we need it to secure life and liberty. Society cannot take away our fundamental rights, although it may disregard or violate them. Government is justified by a social contract. We evaluate the social contract by how well it protects our rights. This is a *rights*-based social contract theory that focuses on *property* rights. Jameson and Mamet should follow the rules governing property, which would tend to favor the interests of S and R's shareholders.

John Rawls argues that our intrinsic value is best expressed in our free agreement to the rules that guide and limit our behavior. Like Nozick, he argues that government is justified by a social contract. However, Rawls develops a *fairness*-based social contract theory. He evaluates the social contract by the fairness of the decision procedure that creates the contract. Like Kant, Rawls' theory suggests that Jameson and Mamet should find a way to consider the interests of S and R's stakeholders.

Kant: A Theory of Duty

Immanuel Kant argues that we have a duty to act ethically no matter what we or others might want or need.[38] He incorporates two widely held beliefs in his ethical theory.

Belief 1. Moral rules are *impartial,* that is, they apply to everyone equally. It is wrong to lie, cheat, or harm others whether they are rich or poor, powerful or weak, friend or foe.

Belief 2. Morality concerns our *intentions.* The morality of an action depends on what we *intend* to do, not the consequences of what we do. Good swimmers who try to save drowning victims are doing the right thing even if they fail.

THE CATEGORICAL IMPERATIVE

Kant says that we act from "imperatives," which are commands that we give ourselves. There are two kinds of imperatives: hypothetical and categorical. A *hypothetical imperative* tells us what we should do to achieve a goal. For example, "If I want to borrow money, I need to establish a good credit history" is a hypothetical imperative, since it is grounded on the desire for credit. Without the desire for credit, the imperative will not move us to act. The imperatives of egoism and utilitarianism are hypothetical, since they are based on goals that we can accept or reject.

A *categorical imperative* gives us a duty to act no matter what we want, and no matter what our circumstances. Kant argues that moral commands, such as the command to tell the truth, are categorical imperatives. There are several formulations of the categorical imperative, which, Kant argues, are equivalent to each other. We will look at two of them.[39] The first one asks us to see ourselves as rule makers, which is a central task of managers.

Categorical Imperative: Version 1: An action is moral only if you can make your reason for acting into a rule that everyone can follow.

To see how the categorical imperative works, suppose you are tempted to lie to secure a loan. The rule you would make is: Lie to secure loans. If everyone follows this rule, no one would lend money, since no one would trust borrowers to pay back their loans. Since no one would lend money, no one could borrow money. *Following this rule destroys the possibility of following the rule.* Another example is the person who wants to "butt in front of the line to get better tickets." If everyone follows this rule, everyone would try to get in front of the line, destroying the line. Without lines, we cannot force our way to the front of them.

In the S and R case, the reason for relocating is to maximize profits and increase market share. Rules that command us to pursue these goals are legitimate using the categorical imperative. However, to pursue them we must do many other things. We must deal with labor, suppliers, community leaders, and other stakeholders. All of these subsidiary actions must also meet the standard of the categorical imperative. This will be a problem if there was an implicit promise to the employees to stay. Jameson and Mamet also have an agreement with shareholders to increase share value. It is not clear how Kant would handle these conflicting responsibilities, although the 11.5 million dollar Maytag settlement [see S and R Electronics (A)] points to a possible course of action. Assuming there is a promise to S and R's employees not to move the plant, the shareholders are responsible because their agents, the managers, made these promises. The responsibility of shareholders to take a loss here is similar to their responsibility to suffer the consequences of a high-interest loan that was badly negotiated by Jameson and Mamet.

Here is another version of the categorical imperative.

> **Categorical Imperative: Version 2:**   Never use people simply as a means to an end; always treat yourself and others as beings with infinite value.

Anticipating current economic theory, Kant argues that price expresses the value of things for which *substitutions* are available. If no substitutions are possible for something, it has a dignity that makes it priceless, or of infinite value. Kant argues that people are unique in a way that makes substitutions impossible. Consider: If a child or friend dies, we may have other children or other friends, but we cannot replace the particular lost child or friend. If we participate as traders in a system of slavery, the money that we take in no way reflects the *value* of those whose dignity we violate. Things and services have prices (substitutions); people have intrinsic value (no substitutions are possible).

Kant is not saying that we cannot use others as means to an end, only that when we do so we must also treat them as intrinsically valuable. Jameson and Mamet need to ask themselves if they are treating all stakeholders as beings with infinite value, or whether they are using them as mere means. For example, suppose Jameson and Mamet do not tell suppliers or labor about the move until the last minute to prevent those two groups from defecting. In this scenario Jameson and Mamet are using these groups as *mere means* to promote their own interests and/or corporate welfare.

To treat stakeholders as beings with infinite value, Jameson and Mamet will have to give them enough information to make rational decisions, and to include them in the decision making as much as possible. Treating stakeholders in this way does not mean that everyone will like the decision. For example, if employees lose their jobs they will not like the relocation decision, but that does not mean that S and R should stay. Similarly, if Jameson and Mamet have to resign to make relocation possible, they may not like that decision. But, again, the likes and dislikes of employees, management, or anyone are not relevant to Kantian ethics.

Rights-Based Social Contract Theories: Robert Nozick

John Locke argued that people have a natural right to life, liberty, and property.[40] We have the first two rights simply by being human. We can acquire the right to property in three ways: by *mixing* our labor with something that is unowned, by voluntary exchange, or by accepting a gift.

Locke thought that we once lived without government in a "state of nature" that had extended families working the land. These families owned the land because they mixed their labor with it through cultivation. Unfortunately, some people did not respect the life, liberty, and property of others, and so people in the state of nature formed a government to protect themselves. This government is the result of a *social contract,* by which people transfer some of their rights to the state. In exchange, the state promises to protect their rights. If the state violates individual rights in a ubiquitous and systematic manner, citizens can remove the offending government and create a new one through a new social contract. Government is purely instrumental, and has no value in itself.

Nozick agrees that we have rights to life, liberty, and property, and that a government can be evaluated by how well it respects those rights.[41] Nozick focuses on property rights because they are essential for us to have any meaningful rights to life and liberty. A government should interfere with our liberty only to protect the fundamental rights of others.

The state gets its rights from individuals who freely transfer some of their natural rights to the state. Since this is the only source of state rights, the state can have no more rights than an individual has. In a state of nature we have the right to protect the life, liberty, and property of ourselves and others, and so the state can do this, too. But in a state of nature we do not have the right to force other adults to live better lives, nor do we have the right to take property from some people to help others. Because we do not have these rights in the state of nature, the state does not have them, either.[42]

NOZICK: THE NATURE AND LIMITS OF PROPERTY RIGHTS

Nozick wants to explain how we can justifiably

1. Acquire property from an unowned state (a state of nature)
2. Transfer property
3. Rectify violations of the first two principles.

Nozick's theory is historical or backward looking, because it looks to the origin of property rights. He rejects utilitarianism, which is forward looking, because it considers only how property will affect group welfare in the future. This means that the work we put into a product is not the crucial factor in deciding whether we can keep the product. This violates our right to property, and because property is necessary for life and liberty, these latter rights are also violated.

The S and R case concerns the property rights of stockholders. Up to this point, Jameson and Mamet have been able to make community and owner interests coincide, but now they conflict. The officers will violate the property rights of the owners if they promote the interests of other stakeholders at the owners' expense.

ACQUIRING PROPERTY FROM AN UNOWNED STATE (A STATE OF NATURE)

Nozick accepts Locke's view that we acquire property from an unowned state by "mixing our labor" with it. However, he suggests several problems in applying this principle. For example, if one cultivates unowned land, does one own the mineral rights as well? If a space traveler lands on a planet (or a sixteenth-century explorer lands on an island or continent), and claims ownership of that land, how much of the planet (island, continent) is owned? Finally, what if we acquire property in something that is necessary for life, such as water, and there are no other sources of water in the area? Do we have the right to let others die of thirst because we do not want to sell or give away our water?

Locke argues that when we acquire property from an unowned state, there must be "enough and as good left in common for others."[43] This Proviso, as it is known, is intended to prevent us from harming others when we acquire property. Unfortunately, it is very broad. As it stands, it invalidates all private property, since any acquisition restricts what others can do, and so does not leave "enough and as good" for others. Nozick argues that the Proviso can be made to work if we interpret it correctly.[44]

First, the Proviso applies only to cases in which life and important liberties and property are at stake. It clearly prevents us from killing others by hoarding water. For the same reason, the owner of an island does not have the right to prevent castaways from landing. However, if we develop a new drug that can save people's lives, the Proviso does not require us to give the drug to those who need it to live. The process of discovery is owned by the people who put up the capital. Sick people have no right to this drug simply because they need it. However, the Proviso would prevent us from hoarding the *ingredients* of the drug. The Proviso is intended to make sure that we all have the opportunity to *pursue* our welfare, it does not give us the duty to make sure others *succeed* in pursuing their welfare.

Second, the proviso allows private property because private property makes others better off: it promotes efficiency, and so tends to conserve resources for future generations. It also promotes experimentation in the creation and production of goods. It is these productive aspects of private property that explain why acquisitions do not make others worse off. Although we pay an opportunity cost when others acquire property, our other opportunities increase and tend to outweigh this cost.[45]

Making a point that we will rely on in Chapters 3 and 4, Nozick states that property rights are not *overridden* by the Proviso. Rather, *the Proviso is part of the definition of property;* acts that violate the proviso can never result in property acquisition of any kind.

The Proviso would seem to play no role in the S and R case. S and R is not hoarding materials necessary for life. The employees are free to move if there are no jobs in Frieberg. Jameson and Mamet should be able to move to promote shareholder wealth without worrying about the wealth or jobs of other stakeholders.

TRANSFERRING PROPERTY: EXCHANGES AND GIFTS

Legitimate transfers of property occur as long as the giver freely gives and the recipient freely receives. Anything that we own can be freely given and received as long as it does not violate our rights to life, liberty, and property. The one restriction on free trade is the Proviso. It is not permissible to purchase all the water resources and charge prices that would cause others to die of thirst. If a monopoly of necessary resources occurs unintentionally by a set of transfers, some of those transfers are invalid.

The Proviso will justify state action in the market only in emergency conditions, such as water and food shortages. In general, individuals will be able to do what they want with their products, no matter how much others may need them. We may give others what they need if we wish, and that would usually be a good, charitable thing to do. Also, we have the negative duty not to harm others or their property, which is why we cannot hoard water or other goods essential for life. It is also why we cannot pollute the environment in ways that impinge on the basic rights of others.

As far as we know, the property arrangements and transfers that created and maintain S and R are legitimate. To penalize the shareholders for the sake of others would be an illicit redistribution of goods, unless those other stakeholders themselves have property rights that need to be protected. It is hard to say with certainty how Nozick would interpret Jameson's and Mamet's statements about S and R's continuing contribution of jobs and taxes to Frieberg. Most likely, those statements would have weight only if they were stated in a context in which it was clear to all that promises were being made, and that they were not publication relations hype or puffery.

RECTIFYING VIOLATIONS OF THE FIRST TWO PRINCIPLES

When our property rights are violated, we need a principle of rectification to help us restore justice. A principle of rectification that makes violators return ill-gotten goods or otherwise compensate victims is *not* property redistribution. People who steal have no property rights to the things they take, so making them give them back is not redistribution of property. A special problem arises when injustice travels through generations. How do we repair an injustice done to those in the past that is affecting their descendants? Nozick does not answer this question, but he believes that in theory such wrongs should be corrected.

As far as we know there are no property violations and no broken contracts in the S and R case. Relying on Nozick, the officers should act as agents for the owners. They should ignore their own interests, the interests of employees, suppliers, and the community (unless some of these stakeholders are owners, too).

A Fairness-Based Social Contract Theory: John Rawls

FAIRNESS AND PROCEDURAL JUSTICE

John Rawls uses fairness to develop a conception of just rules and practices.[46] Rather than focusing on the rules themselves, he focuses on the *procedure* for choosing the rules. If the decision procedure is fair, so are the rules. Consider the following case. Suppose two people inherit an antique car, and they cannot agree to sell it and split the money. They could agree to use a random procedure, like flipping a coin, to settle who gets the car. As long as the flip is not rigged and they *freely* agree to this procedure, the outcome is fair, even if the person who loses needs or wants the item more than the person who wins. The outcome "inherits" the fairness of the procedure, as depicted in Figure 3.3.

THE ORIGINAL POSITION

Rawls tries to design a fair procedure to generate and justify principles of justice. These principles of justice, in turn, are used to evaluate the basic institutions that distribute political rights and duties and economic benefits and burdens. These basic rules guide the interactions between business and society. This structure of inherited justification is depicted in Figure 3.4.

As we can see, if we start with a fair procedure, fairness is inherited by each subse-

```
+-----------------------------+
|                             |
|      Fair  Result           |
|                             |
|           ↑                 |
|                             |
|      Fair  Procedure        |
|                             |
+-----------------------------+
```

Figure 3.3

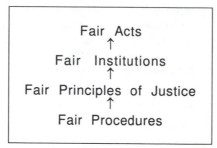

Figure 3.4

quent step. Unlike the antique car case, defining political and economic institutions is too complex and too important to be decided by a coin flip. What, then, would be a fair procedure? Rawls' answer is the Original Position. The Original Position is a hypothetical state of affairs in which we choose the basic principles to guide our civic lives. These principles will apply only to the most important goods, what Rawls calls "primary goods." Primary goods are "rights and liberties, powers and opportunities, income and wealth"[47] These are goods that every rational agent wants because without them, no one could pursue a "rational plan of life."[48]

For the Original Position to be fair, all participants must be equally rational and have the same information. (See Chapter 4 to see why these assumptions are important in economics.) The decision must also be unanimous; this ensures that no one can be coerced by the majority. Since we choose our own limits, we remain free.

THE VEIL OF IGNORANCE

Although we are equally rational and knowledgeable, Rawls is still worried that we might find ways to rig the process in unfair ways. To prevent this, he puts us behind a "veil of ignorance." This veil keeps us from knowing our place in society, our gender, whether we are rich or poor, and whether we have family or friends. We do not even know our physical, intellectual, or individual psychological characteristics. All we know are general facts about human nature, and that we are choosing principles to guide us when we go back to our positions in society, whatever they are. The veil of ignorance ensures fairness: we cannot rig the principles to serve our special needs or interests since we do not know what our special needs and interests are.

Rawls argues that we would demand perfect equality in the Original Position. We would not agree to principles that give more to others than to ourselves; similarly, we would not propose principles that give less to ourselves than to others. We know that we are all equally rational, and so we know that all other people will think the same way.

We will modify our demand for perfect equality if inequalities can make us all better off, including the least advantaged. (Remember, when we go back to society, we may be the most disadvantaged.) For example, we might agree to pay people more to join difficult and socially useful professions, such as medicine and engineering, so that people will invest in the training necessary to pursue these careers. This kind of inequality can make us all better off. This is not a utilitarian condition, since this inequality in wealth is not justified by increasing the sum or average of group welfare.

THE TWO PRINCIPLES OF JUSTICE

Rawls argues that people in the Original Position will choose the following two principles to evaluate their social and political institutions that distribute primary goods. The first principle is more important than the second principle.

1. Each person is to have an equal right to the most extensive basic [political] liberty compatible with a similar liberty for others.
2. Social and economic inequalities are to be arranged so that they are *both*
   a. reasonably expected to help those least well off
   b. attached to positions open to all.[49]

The first principle ensures that all individuals will be politically equal. Everyone will have the right to pursue public office, to vote, to associate with others, etc. The second principle stipulates that an unequal distribution of social and economic goods is legitimate only if the least advantaged do better than they would in a perfect state of equality. Further, the well-paid jobs and positions must be open to all. The first principle is more important because we cannot have enduring economic freedom without political freedom. Political freedom provides the security necessary for us to pursue economic interest.

Rawls believes that these two principles will secure *social cooperation* from those on the low end of the social and economic ladder better than utilitarian principles, since the two principles of justice protect their interests better than utilitarian principles. Things such as genocide and slavery, which could be justified from a utilitarian view, cannot be justified using these principles.

We can apply Rawls' theory to the S and R case in at least two ways. The first way is to examine the United States and the host country's laws that govern relocation to see if they accord with the two principles of justice. This is often not helpful in a case such as this, since there is usually no way to change laws to affect decisions that need to be made in the near future. However, challenging home country laws, the United States in this case, can be useful if they could be suspended by court injunction. Or, if a host country required the use of slave labor or the abuse of a minority, it would be unjust to move there unless the move was likely to end the country's abusive policies.

The second way is to focus on *procedure*. Jameson and Mamet are trying to decide which *outcome* would be fair and just. Rawls would say that this is a hopeless task, and that instead they should focus on a fair *procedure* for settling the issue. If the procedure is fair, the outcome will be fair. They need to find a way to bring the relevant stakeholders into the decision-making process (see Freeman, Chapter 7). Unfortunately, different stakeholders have different kinds of claims. The shareholders have legal claims against Jameson and Mamet in a way that the other stakeholders do not. At the very least, Jameson and Mamet must get as much information as they can so their decision incorporates the legitimate needs of stakeholders. Craig Dunn and F. Neil Brady distinguish managing stakeholders and managing *on behalf of* stakeholders. Managing stakeholders is figuring out how to manipulate them to achieve goals they may or may not share. Managing on behalf of stakeholders is taking stakeholder interests as important in themselves in order to devise policies that respect the value of everyone involved.[50] Rawls would argue that Jameson and Mamet must make their decision on *behalf* of stakeholders.

Addendum to Intrinsic Value Theory: Clarifying Rights

The language of rights has become common across the globe. There are numerous U.N. charters that deal with human rights, and human rights are discussed in many government documents.[51] Unfortunately, there is no agreement on what these rights are. We need to find a way to distinguish real from spurious rights.

Traditionally, people have distinguished between negative and positive rights. *Neg-*

ative rights are rights to be free from interference. Nozick claims that the right to life, liberty, and property are negative rights. For example, people have a duty not to kill us, but no duty to keep us alive by feeding us or giving us medicine. *Positive rights* are rights to something that others have a *duty* to supply. If we have positive rights to life, liberty, and property, which Nozick denies, then others have a duty to give us the means to life, liberty, and property. Nozick rejects Rawls, in part, because he believes that Rawls' system will create false positive rights to things such as education and medical care that will interfere with the property rights of those who will be forced to pay for these services.

Henry Shue argues that there is no clean separation between negative and positive rights because some negative rights presuppose positive rights.[52] For example, if people have a negative right to life, then they have a positive right to the *enforcement* of this negative right, such as police protection. But if this negative right to life implies that people have a positive right to police protection, this negative right may also imply positive rights to education, housing, and medical care, insofar as they reduce crime.

Thomas Donaldson and Thomas Dunfee argue for what they call "hypernorms." Hypernorms are rights and duties that are so basic to human life that no society could exist without them.[53] For example, every society protects the physical integrity of at least most of its members; the relative hypernorm could be formulated as follows: people have a right to be free from arbitrary physical harm. Societies are free to arrange their own property systems as long as they respect hypernorms. There is broad agreement on fundamental negative rights across the globe. Disagreement exists, however, over how these negative rights are interpreted. For example, does the right not to be harmed mean that we should have court-appointed attorneys if we cannot afford them? Does it mean that we have a right to basic medical treatment? There are no clear answers to these questions. This makes rights theory difficult to apply.

Kant and Rawls avoid this problem with rights. They argue that rights are based on our intrinsic value. For Kant, we have a right to be treated only in those ways that everyone can be treated. We cannot be deprived of primary goods because of unique characteristics such as gender, race, and religion. Rawls comes to the same conclusion using the decision procedure in Original Position. Political systems, whether national or organizational, must be derivable from fair procedures.

We can use Kant and Rawls to argue that rights vary between different social groups because there can be many different ways of *expressing* and *respecting* human dignity. For example, in some hunter–gatherer societies, old but healthy individuals are sometimes left to die. This seems harsh by the ethical standards of wealthy societies, but in a small band of nomads with limited resources, this may be the only way that the young, and therefore the group, can survive. The fact that people can have different rights in different societies does not mean that rights are relative. If the nomadic society becomes settled and wealthy, for example, leaving the old but healthy to die is no longer justified.

An Institutional Analysis of Intrinsic Value

An institutional analysis from a Kantian perspective would examine the extent to which institutions respect human dignity. As we suggested, the institutions governing corporate management appear to do this, since they conform to the categorical imperative. This test rules out, for example, using self-interest or family interest to make the relocation decision. If officers made corporate decisions on these bases, and everyone knew it, no one would invest in them, and no corporations would exist. Jameson and Mamet must be careful how they apply their institutional powers. In achieving shareholder wealth they need to be truthful and honest, while still respecting S and R's proprietary information. This is part of their problem. If they announce they are thinking of moving, then labor, suppliers, and Frieberg may take actions that will interfere with the move. Because of this, even the announcement that they may move may be seen as a violation of their duties to shareholders. Not announcing the possibility of moving seems to violate other duties.

An institutional analysis from a Nozickian perspective would examine the extent to which institutions respect property rights. The institutions governing management require Jameson and Mamet to promote shareholder wealth. The property rights approach, however, would not allow Jameson and Mamet to violate valid contracts or the property rights of other stakeholders to promote shareholder interests. If S and R had signed long-term agreements that required them to stay in Frieberg, they should stay or renegotiate those contracts.

An institutional analysis from a Rawlsian perspective would examine the extent to which the relocation decision is the result of fair procedures. Jameson's and Mamet's legal roles prohibit them from giving up their decision-making power to outside parties, but they can get input from employees, shareholders, suppliers, and the community. They will need to develop a procedure that shows the stakeholders that their views are considered seriously, even though they do not have the legal right to make the decision. As Dunn and Brady have argued, Jameson and Mamet need to manage on behalf of stakeholders. Rawls argues that this approach is more likely to lead to harmony. If people agree to the procedures that generate the outcome, or if they see that they would have agreed if they could have participated, they are more likely to act in accord with the outcome.

Do business people ever act from these kinds of considerations? Sometimes they do. Aaron M. Feuerstein owns Malden Mills Industries, which manufactures Polartec, a high-tech fabric used in sporting apparel. In December 1995 the nineteenth-century building in which Polartec was produced burned to the ground. Feuerstein could have relocated to a place that did not have the high labor, land, and utility costs of Lawrence, Massachusetts, but he stayed.[54]

He built a factory, at extra expense, that has architectural features similar to the one that burned down. He even paid the 1380 workers their full salary for up to 90 days until he could get a temporary plant going. He did this for two reasons, he said. One was an obligation to his workers, who developed Polartec at a time when the falling demand for the company's main products, real and fake fur, forced it into bankruptcy. If it were not for their ingenuity, the company would not exist. The other reason for paying the workers was to get manufacturing going as quickly as possible. Paying the workers ensured a qualified workforce when production began again.

Manufacturing Polartec requires highly trained and dedicated employees. Small changes in humidity and temperature can alter the product. Operators of the basic machines must constantly evaluate the output, being ready to shut it down as soon as trouble appears. "I give to catching imperfections the same importance that I would give if this were my own business," said one of the workers, a single mother who makes $11 an hour after 2 years.[55] This is 10% more than she would receive for similar jobs in the surrounding area.

Malden Mills has about $425 million in annual sales and 30 million in net income. Rebuilding the plant and paying laid off workers is costing over $300 million. As of June 1996, only $70 million had been collected. Feuerstein expects insurance and growth to cover the extra costs, but he could lose the company if insurance payments or growth

fall short. His wife said, "Here is Aaron, as a national spokesman for worker loyalty, trying to save jobs, and what if he loses the company? That would be a terrible thing."[56]

Mr. Feuerstein is not a standard case of business decision making. A Rawlsian
analysis could even say he went too far. His actions, however, show how the values of
fairness and duty can influence business decisions.

ETHICAL PLURALISM AND DECISION MAKING:
ADAM SMITH AND ARISTOTLE

Integrating Self-interest, Care, Group Interest, and Intrinsic Value

The ethical principles we have examined so far focus on different aspects of institutions,
and so highlight different kinds of information. Self-interest focuses on how the move
would affect Jameson and Mamet; care highlights issues with families and friends; utilitarianism focuses on the groups that constitute and supply S and R, the community of
Frieberg, and the communities at the relocation site; intrinsic value theory focuses on
how the relocation affects the dignity, property, and autonomy of the stakeholders.

If Jameson and Mamet adopt one of these four theories, they will subordinate or reject the other three. This strategy can have at least two undesirable effects. First, if any
principles are rejected entirely, the information associated with these principles might
become more difficult to identify and evaluate. At worst, information may be ignored
altogether.

Second, choosing one principle can alienate stakeholders who have used the rejected or subordinated principles to support their views. The "losers" may suspect they
are being arbitrarily sacrificed to the interests of others. If this happened at S and R,
Jameson and Mamet might find themselves being sued by labor or the community.

Ethical pluralism tries to integrate the ethical principles that ground these four ethical theories in a way that mitigates these two problems. David Messick cites several
cases in which conflicts were successfully resolved by adopting a plurality of principles.

Do It Several Ways

The framers of our government were faced with the conflict between the populous states
and the smaller states over the interpretation of equality. Should political representation
be based on the equality of people or the equality of states? As we all know, the decision was made to do it both ways, to establish two houses of the Congress, with each
body reflecting one of these principles. *Deciding to do it both ways avoids the problem
of having to choose, but creates the corollary problem of figuring out how to integrate
the two bodies.* This latter problem, I suggest, is generally a less difficult problem than
choosing one interpretation of equality over the other. Why might this be so?

If forced to choose one principle over the other, there would have been one winning side
and one losing side, and the bitterness, moral outrage, and resistance of the losing side
would have been profound. Efforts may have been made to sabotage the implementation of a solution that involved choosing in favor of the larger states or the smaller. Gaining support from both the winners and the losers would have been a challenge.

It is not just that one side would have lost in the deliberations; more importantly, a reasonable moral principle, as both principles are, would have been rejected. For the losers, this rejection of their moral principle may have taken on the appearance of immorality and illegitimacy on the part of the winners. The losers would experience not

only the frustration of losing but also the perception that an injustice had been done (Shklar, 1990) and its accompanying moral outrage.

Doing it both ways legitimizes both principles and eliminates winners and losers. Neither principle is elevated at the expense of the other, so that neither side has cause to feel that its interests were unjustly handled. Moral outrage and its potentially destructive consequences are avoided. Moreover, both sides remain participants in the dialog about how to combine the principles and both sides have a stake in finding solutions. Rather than empowering one side and disempowering the other, both sides of the dispute have an incentive to work together on the details of coordinating the work of the two bodies.

Solving a conflict by trying to do it several (or all) ways is an approach that can be applied in many contexts. . . .

Combine the Different Solutions

The trick with this approach is to find a reasonable way to combine the solutions offered by the different principles, interpretations, or positions. . . . The solution for the bicameral congress of the United States involved the complicated assignment of duties and prerogatives to each of the houses of the congress, while maintaining equality by requiring both houses to approve a bill in order for it to become a federal law. . . .

The case of the Montecito Water District allocation scheme [during a drought] represents a different approach for combining conflicting principles into a single system. [T]he problem here was whether equality should be interpreted as equal amounts of water per household, per acre of land, or per unit of water previously used. Reasonable arguments can be made for each of these interpretations. Rather than choosing from among them, the Montecito Water Board combined them into a mixed allocation system. For residential customers, each household received 144 units (a unit is 100 cubic feet) or an equal share of 25% of the total residential supply, whichever was larger. The 144 units was selected on the assumption that a person's minimal need is 36 units per year and that the average household contains four persons. Thus this first component was allocated according to the principle of equality per household.

The remainder of the total was divided into two components. The first of these two components, 65% of the remainder, was allocated on the basis of the gross acreage of the lot (up to a maximum). This component reflected the second principle: equal amounts per acre. The remaining 35% of the water . . . was allocated proportionally to the previous allocation. This component was based approximately on past use. The allocation system that was finally adopted thus incorporated all three of the conflicting concepts of equality. Most water consumers in Montecito would probably have preferred combination weights somewhat more in the direction that would favor themselves, but disagreeing about weights is much less acrimonious than disagreeing about principles. . . .

The more abstract rule that is reflected here is that the principles are not necessarily mutually exclusive . . . it makes more sense to discuss how these principles should be combined than to fight about which should be chosen.[57]

Although Messick addresses how to handle conflicting interpretations of one principle, equality, his arguments suggest that pluralism can be a good way to handle the different ethical principles we have been discussing. There has been a recent spate of literature supporting ethical pluralism. Cavenaugh, Moberg, and Velasquez[58] argue that an ethical view that combines care, group good, justice, and rights will be more effective than a theory that is based on fewer of these concerns. Patricia Werhane[59] and Mark Johnson[60] argue that using different ethical approaches can help us gather information and creatively resolve problems (Chapter 2). These authors make a compelling case for pluralism.

For pluralism to be a viable theory, however, it needs to answer two questions.

- What principles should we include in a pluralistic theory?
- How should we resolve conflicts between the principles?

If we can develop a viable, if not complete, pluralism, this will help us see how Jameson and Mamet can combine the conflicting institutional values they face. We will examine the pluralistic ethical theories of Adam Smith and Aristotle.

Identifying Adam Smith as a pluralist may seem surprising, since some passages from his *Wealth of Nations* suggest that he is a utilitarian. Patricia Werhane has argued that these passages have been taken out of context. To understand Smith, she argues, we have to look at *The Theory of the Moral Sentiments,* his lectures on jurisprudence, and other relevant passages from *The Wealth of Nations.* These three sources reveal that although Smith valued utility, he also valued justice, relationships with family and friends, and prudence (self-interest based on self-respect). He did not try to show, as Hume did, that these last three considerations were valuable because they promoted group good. Smith thought these considerations had value in themselves. In our examination of Smith, we will follow Patricia Werhane's analysis in *Adam Smith and His Legacy for Modern Capitalism.*[61]

Ethical Pluralism: Adam Smith

Adam Smith's *The Wealth of Nations* (WN), which appeared in 1776, is widely regarded as the beginning of modern economics. The Nobel laureate, George Stigler, wrote in 1976 that Smith's explanation of the determination of prices "is to this day the center of the economists' theory of value."[62] Stigler relies on the common interpretation that Smith has an egoistic theory of human nature and a utilitarian theory of ethics. The free market works, as if by an "invisible hand," to coordinate our self-interested behavior so that it benefits everyone. As business people pursue profit for themselves, they supply products to consumers, jobs to citizens, and taxes to government.

The Theory of Moral Sentiments (TMS) was published 17 years before WN. It went through six editions, the last of which was published after WN. In TMS Smith argues that we have three kinds of passions: *self-regarding passions,* such as the desire for pleasure and wealth, which need not be selfish;[63] *social passions,* such as the desire for family and friendship; and *unsocial passions,* such as envy and hatred.[64] These passions, though not good or bad in themselves, can have good and bad effects on ourselves and others depending on how we use them. Our self-regarding passions can lead us to a life of productive work or a life of drugs. Our social passions can lead us to help our country or to band together with others to exploit our country. Our unsocial passions can lead us to destroy ourselves and others or, if directed against dangerous enemies, preserve ourselves and others.

According to Werhane, Smith holds that prudence, benevolence, and justice are all equally moral, and none is derivable from the others.[65] If Werhane is right, Smith presents a pluralistic ethical view in TMS. The question is how to integrate these values. Werhane thinks the answer to this question lies in WN. In WN, Werhane argues, Smith believes that the overall group welfare will result from people acting from prudence in a market system that is fundamentally just.[66]

To support Werhane's interpretation of Smith, we begin with two of the most well-known quotations from WN that seem to be incompatible with it.

> It is not from the benevolence of the butcher, the brewer, or the baker, that we expect our dinner, but from their regard to their own interest. We address ourselves, not to their humanity but to their self-love, and never talk to them of our necessities, but of their advantages.[67]

and

> [a business person] intends only his . . . own gain, and he is in this, as in many other cases, led by an *invisible hand* to promote an end [the good of society] which is not part of his intention. . . . By pursuing his own interest he frequently promotes that of the society more effectually than when he really intends to promote it.[68] (emphasis added)

In the first quotation, the crucial issue is self-love. According to Werhane, Smith distinguishes between self-interest and self-love (see the discussion of egoism in this chapter for another approach to this issue). Self-interest can be used to explain why people cheat and why they get a good education. Smith is not arguing we appeal to the baker's desire to cheat us. Self-love is a narrower term, and it refers to carefully taking care of oneself by doing such things as eating in a healthy fashion, getting a good education, and running a fair, competitive business. To appeal to the self-love of the baker is to appeal to the care he has for himself, and assuming a standard set of social passions, to the care he has for his family and friends.[69]

In the second quotation, the crucial issue is how markets coordinate our different needs and interests in a way that benefits the group. Werhane agrees that competition plays an important role in getting this utilitarian result, but that competition is not enough. For Smith, self-love will promote group welfare only if competition occurs in a system that respects our *natural* and *conventional rights*.[70] As the names imply, natural rights are based on our human nature, and so are the same in all cultures. We have natural rights to be free from harm and injury, and to live as we want as long as we respect the rights of others. Conventional rights are based on the rules of social systems and so vary between societies.

Smith did not believe that all conventional systems are equally good. In fact, one of the reasons he wrote WN was to show why a system with free trade is superior to state-controlled systems of trade. He also argued that a conventional economic system that is fair will be better than one that is not. By fairness, Smith did not mean equality of outcomes. Smith believed that productive societies would have great disparities in wealth, and that it would be dangerous to try to fix this by taking resources from some and giving them to others (see Hume for a similar point). Instead, the society should focus on procedural fairness (Rawls is appropriate here) so that all people can be free to *compete* for scarce resources. Property rules must be well defined and enforced if the system is to work at all. Monopolies should be restricted, since they will use their power to control supply and prices. People must be able to enter and exit markets at will, so they can make the best use of their resources. In a fair market system in which people act from self-love, market mechanisms will coordinate our interests to promote group good. However, if the market is not fair or if people are selfish, the market will fail. In Chapter 4 we will see that contemporary economists make many of these same points.

Smith would understand that Jameson and Mamet's social passions would lead them to consider the well-being of family, friends, suppliers, employees, Frieberg, etc.

They should also realize, Smith might point out, that they are working in a market system that requires them to act in ways that sometimes do not promote the well-being of each person or group. We can speculate that Smith, like Hume, would urge Jameson and Mamet to focus on their jobs as managers, and let the market take care of the rest of the stakeholders. By relying on the market, they would still be relying on their social passions, since the market should produce social good.

We saw earlier that Smith believed markets would have good consequences only if they are just and only if economic agents act from self-love, not from selfishness. If the markets in which Jameson and Mamet operate do not have these two features, which they surely do not, what should Jameson and Mamet do? Smith can not help us with this problem. Smith seems to offer what is known as a "perfect compliance theory": he describes what will happen when everyone follows the rules. What we need is a partial compliance theory, that tells us what to do in a variety of imperfect conditions. For example, how unjust does a system have to be before we should not follow the rules?[71]

Werhane notes that Smith was planning to write a treatise on law that when joined with his ethical theory and his economic theory would provide an integrated theory of what we now call business and society.[72] Unfortunately, he never finished it and, on his orders, all his unpublished papers were burned when he died. In the next section we will examine Aristotle's theory, which gives us a way to complete Smith's project.

Ethical Pluralism: Using Aristotle to Integrate Different Ethical Principles

Aristotle argues that the goal of life is to be socially and intellectually excellent. We will focus on social excellence. The best way to become socially excellent is by making decisions using the four types of ethical principles we looked at earlier. Aristotle treats these ethical principles as *problem-solving strategies*. He develops a theory of human nature that explains why we need to fit these principles together to live well.

Most of the ethical theorists we have discussed view the individual as independent of, and in competition with, others in the social environment. Aristotle has a different view of the individual. He argues that we are partly constituted by our social habits. If we are honest and trustworthy, that is part of our identity. If we are dishonest and untrustworthy, that is part of our identity too. Since these habits are social—they involve other people—we are partly social. Because we are partly social, the extreme antagonism between self and others is not a central problem for Aristotle. Conflicts occur, of course, but they arise as value conflicts in institutional settings, not from a basic tension between individuals.[73]

For Aristotle and his fellow Greeks, the best life is one in which an individual's desires harmonize with each other, and do so in a way that promotes individual excellence and group well-being. In the past 10 years there has been a resurgence of interest in Aristotle. Robert Solomon[74] and Edwin Hartman[75] are two proponents of an Aristotelian point of view.

THE ROLE OF ETHICAL THEORY

According to Aristotle, the function of ethical theory is to integrate ethical principles. We must not emphasize conflicts between principles too much. Conflicts only provide a window into the institutions that guide our personal and social lives (Chapter 2). Aristotle argues that the four types of ethical principles we discussed earlier—self-interest, care, group welfare, and justice—aim at goals that make up or *constitute* the good life. He means this literally: the good life is one in which we develop our talents, have sufficient material goods, have good relationships with friends and family, are good citizens of a good state, and are fair and just. Ethics helps us interpret and integrate these goals.

Although no one of these ethical principles is intrinsically more important than the others, one of them may be more important in a particular situation. Situations can be so different from each other, in fact, that we cannot predict in advance which principle will be the most important. Studying cases, real and hypothetical, can help us understand how these four types of ethical reasoning fit together, but the *particular* reasoning used in one case cannot be easily transferred to other cases. Even very similar cases can be different in important ways. Understanding how to apply ethical principles while paying attention to contextual details is an important part of learning how to think and act effectively. We will use the S and R case to explain many of Aristotle's points, but this is no more than an illustration. We would need to use this theory in a variety of cases to see how it works. (The articles and cases in Part III provide some opportunity for application to different issues.)

In the 2300 years since Aristotle, we have had many discussions about egoism, care, utilitarianism, and intrinsic value. We will use Aristotle's theory as a framework to integrate some of these insights. This new theory, that we will call simply "pluralism," is different from Aristotle's ethical theory in many ways. It will, however, reflect Aristotle's views on at least three things: the relationship between human nature and ethics, the methodology of ethics, and the purpose of the ethical project. Let us look at these in order.

HUMAN NATURE AND ETHICS

Aristotle argues that human beings are essentially *rational* and *social,* and that ethics is the study of how to promote the excellence of these two related capacities.[76] As individuals, we promote these capacities through learning and self-control.[77] Communities should promote these capacities in two ways: first, they should educate the young to help them discover and develop their fundamental human capacities, and second, they should provide a participatory political structure that allows individuals to exercise their social and rational capacities.[78]

METHODOLOGY

Aristotle argued that we must do three things to discover and achieve human excellence: observe and evaluate how good people lead their lives, examine and evaluate the most compelling accounts of the good life, and test these insights by living by them. Due to the nature of these sources, the study of ethics is imprecise, and our conclusions will always be open to revision.[79]

Aristotle's focus on how people actually live is like the case method used in business, law, and medicine. Cases are used to illustrate principles and strategy, not as models to be mechanically copied. Since people, relationships, and communities change, principles and strategies need to be constantly readjusted. We can and should group together similar cases to understand the social environment, but these judgments are always open to revision (see Gioia on scripts and schemas, Chapter 2).

Imprecision is not a defect of ethics, just as it is not a defect of business, law, or medicine. Imprecision is a necessary feature of any discipline that studies changeable objects with changeable relationships. We should not expect it to be like mathematics, which deals with unchanging numbers and relationships. It is the mark of wisdom, Aristotle observed, to expect only as much precision as the subject matter allows.[80]

The imprecision of ethics is mitigated by the public and the practical nature of its methodology. The *public* aspect of ethical thinking is brought in by discussing what other thoughtful commentators say about these matters. Examining their views, as we are doing in this text, gives us access to how people and communities think about these issues.[81] We carry on this ethical conversation today in many different arenas: schools, television, newspapers, legislatures, boardrooms, as well as with friends and neighbors. We do not have to agree with what we hear to learn from it.

An ethical theory must also be put to *the practical test of living*. If an ethical theory does not help us promote individual and group excellence, we must modify or reject it. The success or failure of our strategies should be part of the public conversation we just mentioned. Of course, these public and practical tests do not preclude error, they simply make it a little less likely, and show us how to deal with the mistakes we do make.

Applying this to S and R, we can say that Jameson and Mamet should take three steps. Step 1: Because this is a decision that affects the well-being of many individuals and groups, they should turn to public institutions to guide them. These institutions give some guidance, but they do not give clear answers for two reasons. First, institutional values are broad: this allows them to cover a variety of cases, but prevents them from giving unambiguous direction. Second, institutional values can conflict with each other. This leads to Step 2: Jameson and Mamet should use these conflicts to test and investigate the institutions that constitute their social environment. Step 3: They should take the information they gain from the first two steps to evaluate their own reasoning strategies.[82]

The possibility of error should not tempt us to abandon the ethical project. We all must choose our actions in some way or other. Even if we act without thinking, there is a sense in which we choose, or allow ourselves, to act spontaneously. As Kant might say, our rule would be "Act without thinking." Since we cannot escape the ethical project, it makes sense to investigate its strengths and limitations.

THE NATURE OF THE ETHICAL PROJECT

Aristotle assumes that we can, without too much difficulty, identify the most important ethical principles. We use these ethical principles to construct an ethical view that refines, explains, and integrates them. For those who accept the importance of ethics, Aristotle is like all other ethical theorists: he wants to convince them that his view is best. However, Aristotle does not try to convince those who reject ethics all together. If people do not value themselves, their friends, their groups, and justice, they are not ready to study ethics.[83]

This treatment of ethical skepticism may seem dogmatic on Aristotle's part. There are two responses to this. First, if it is dogmatic, it is no more dogmatic than the way many skeptics treat ethics. Second, there is good reason to think it is not dogmatic. To see this, compare the ethical skeptic with a mathematical skeptic who claims that the plus function and the identity function in mathematics really are the same, because an individual can *decide* to treat them as the same. No matter what theory is proposed, the skeptic can always "decide" to reject it. The fact that no mathematical theory is immune from these skeptical responses does not show that there is some deep flaw in mathematics.

In what follows, we will discuss Aristotle's view that self-interest, personal relationships, group welfare, and justice all play essential roles in forming healthy individuals and communities. The theories that we looked at earlier dealt with these principles in some detail. We will not duplicate those efforts here. Our present goal is to show how these different ethical concerns can fit together.

ACTIONS AND VALUES

Our everyday behavior is part of a system of values and goals. We walk to school to get an education to get a job to get a career to buy a house to live comfortably to. . . . The list goes on. We all have our own lists. Although our lists are different, they are similar, too. Almost all of us want basic goods such as food, shelter, some form of companionship, and opportunities to discover and develop our talents (see Rawls on primary goods).

Aristotle argues that we all have the same ultimate goal, happiness, which is based on universal aspects of human nature.[84] Asserting that there is a universal human goal seems to fly in the face of cultural diversity. As we will see, pluralism can avoid this problem because it characterizes happiness in a way that leaves a great deal of room for individual and cultural differences.

To understand happiness, we need to understand what a good human life is. "Good" is a term that we apply when something performs its function well. For example, a good knife is sharp and well balanced enabling us to cut well; good flute players have good breathing and coordination enabling them to play well.[85] Aristotle argues that the function of human beings is to live with others and think about practical and theoretical matters. To perform these functions well we must develop our *social* and *rational capacities*. Although we do not choose our capacities, we do choose how to develop and use them. Happiness consists of being excellent in these two ways.[86]

Although happiness is defined in terms of our social and rational nature, we should not forget our physiological nature. We cannot be happy if we are sick or constantly tired. The happy person is physiologically, socially, and intellectually *virtuous. Arete,* the Greek word we translate as virtue, can also be translated as *excellence.* Using this translation, we can say that happiness consists of being in excellent physical shape, having fulfilling social relationships, and mastering rational thought and decision making. Happiness also includes the pleasure, satisfaction, and the enjoyment we get when we live well. We also need two other things to be happy: a bit of luck (or not too much bad luck) and a social environment that values these human virtues.

Happiness is not something different from physical, moral, and rational excellence—it is made up of them just as a house is made up of timbers, plumbing, etc.[87] There is no house over and above its parts, and there is no happiness over and above its parts.

This view of happiness can help us understand why Jameson and Mamet are concerned about so many different aspects of the relocation problem. Their families, community, and other stakeholders form a large part of their personal well-being. If Jameson and Mamet make a decision that injures these groups or their relationships with these groups, they too will suffer. Further, Jameson and Mamet have developed their talents at S and R. They have learned how to be better managers, and they have enjoyed the complex rational-social problems they have faced. *The social systems in which they have achieved these things are part of who they are.* This is not disguised self-interest, Aristotle would argue, but the realization that our happiness lies in developing our social and rational capacities in a community of human beings.

Aristotle argues that we benefit as *individuals* if our social behavior is guided by habits such as honesty, loyalty, and truthfulness. These habits promote stable, fulfilling social relationships; they also make us reliable, especially in difficult situations. We lend money to those who make payments when it is hard to do, not just when it is easy to do. Honest people understand how dishonest behavior can be financially advantageous to them, but they are not excessively tempted. They can ignore their financial interests for the same reason that soldiers can make themselves go to the front, or athletes can push themselves to do painful and difficult things: training, habit, and a belief in the importance of the activity.

Having social virtues, then, makes life easier. People trust us, and so we have fewer social conflicts. Honest people enjoy being honest, which minimizes their internal conflicts between what they want to do and what they think they should do.[88] A *community* of morally virtuous people will be the most harmonious and successful kind of community. Not only will there be the positive aspects of shared purposes and goodwill, but the social cost of lying, theft, and dishonesty will be minimized.[89]

Moral Virtue Coordinates Self and Social Interests

Moral virtue coordinates self-interest and public good. Because morally virtuous behavior is good for the individual and the community, there is no necessary "trade-off" between ourselves and others. Of course, Aristotle realized that individuals and communities would not be perfectly harmonious. What he does assert, though, is that individuals are not naturally opposed to society. Conflicts between self and society are due to the improper education of individuals, institutional arrangements that pit individuals and groups against each other, or both.[90]

Vices are character traits that interfere with our health, social relationships, or rationality, and so constitute *unhappiness*.[91] Unhappiness is not pain or displeasure, but the abuse of our bodies and our capacities. Pain results from this abuse, but it is only a symptom of our unhappiness, not the unhappiness itself. If vices make us unhappy and cause us pain, why do we develop them? This is a complex issue that we cannot cover fully here. The short answer is that we are fooled by the immediate pleasure we get from certain activities. We take a drink, have fun, and forget our troubles. In moderation this is fine, but if we use this as a strategy to deal with discomfort, we will soon destroy our health, our social relationships, and our rational capacities. In our job we may get what we want by intimidating someone, but if we use this as a general strategy, we will alienate others, which will interfere with getting what we want. Since we can be fooled by immediate pleasure, we need to use our imagination and our rationality to think about future consequences to ourselves and our relationships.[92]

Aristotle says that the moral virtues represent a "Golden Mean" between two extremes. According to the principle of the Golden Mean, our character is destroyed by excess and strengthened by moderation.[93] We cannot develop courage, for example, if we flee in fear from even small dangers, and, if we are already courageous, such behavior will soon destroy our courageousness. Similarly, we do not develop courage by being afraid of nothing; taking all risks is simply foolish. We become courageous by facing danger when there is good reason to do so, such as defending our friends and family.

Our emotions have a mean between excess and deficiency, too. For example, courageous people feel fear, but not so much that they cannot overcome it, and not so little that they will be foolish.[94] Although we cannot control how we feel in any given instance, *we can train our passions over time*. This is why we are responsible for even our most passionate actions.

Discovering the Golden Mean is difficult.[95] We can learn from others, but we cannot simply copy them since we have different needs, desires, and fears. For example, some people can drink alcohol in moderation, but have trouble controlling their eating; some are just the opposite; and some have no trouble with either. Hence, we cannot specify in advance what the mean is for eating food and drinking alcohol, since what is acceptable for one person may be disastrous for another. We can be sure, however, that doing something once tends to make it easier to do the next time. This is why we need to be careful when we act. We are not just acting in a particular situation, we are also forming our character. As we get better and better at seeking the mean, we find pleasure in hitting it; this pleasure helps us maintain the virtue.

Being virtuous is necessary for living well. However, as Bernard Williams argues, just because being virtuous is to our overall benefit does not mean that virtuous behavior is *motivated* by self-interest.[96] Quite the contrary is true. As we saw above, a virtuous action must be done for the right reason. For example, honest people pay their debts because they have promised to do so, not to secure another loan in the future. Acting from the first reason is virtuous, acting from the second reason is not. Those who act in the first way are more reliable, since they will repay debts even if there is no coercion. Consider the following true story. Bill, we will call him, read in the paper that his dentist died, and he was very upset. Why was he upset? Because he paid his dental bill the day before. Bill is not honest, but pays his bill to avoid punishment and to secure future services. Aristotle thinks it is obvious that we would rather do business with honest people, and so honesty is in our self-interest. However, for honesty to be in our interest, our *motive* cannot be self-interest; our motive must be the love of honesty itself or, perhaps, the love of our relationships that honesty makes possible.

Jameson and Mamet value themselves, their personal relationships, their formal relationships, and fairness. How can pluralism help them? First, it will help them discover how their personal well-being is dependent on their relationships to the many stakeholders involved. This dependency is based on *instrumental* and *intrinsic* values imbedded in social institutions. Instrumentally, these stakeholders do a great deal for Jameson, Mamet, and S and R. Jameson and Mamet also seem to believe that these stakeholders have intrinsic value that they want to respect, so they need to focus on the needs and interests of others, as loyalty and honesty would prescribe. This kind of reasoning will generally give them better and more complete information than will focusing on their own narrow career needs. Since their interests are intimately related to those of the stakeholders, this will give them information about their own interests, too.

Like most of us, Jameson and Mamet have vices as well as virtues. Vices can make it difficult to consider stakeholders as intrinsically valuable. If these two officers are only a little overconcerned with their public image, for example, they may be able to overcome this easily. If they obsessively think about their careers, they will have a much harder time valuing the interests of others. Overcoming their vices in this instance will make it easier to overcome them in the future. Succumbing to their vices will make it harder to overcome them in the future. Robert Prout, a criminologist who does ethics training for police officers, makes a similar point. When we first begin to do unethical things, we feel as if we are putting on a mask that we can take off whenever we want. Eventually, we find that the mask has fused to our face, and that it is painful to take it off. If we fail to take it off, the mask *becomes* our face, and there is no turning back.[97]

Aristotle would agree with Prout, but he would add that the same is true of acting virtuously. When we begin to act virtuously, it may feel like a mask. It is uncomfortable and we can take it off at will. However, the longer we wear the mask, the more indistinguishable we become from it.

Aristotle endorses traditional virtues and vices, but their moral value derives from how they promote individual and group excellence, not from social approval. It is the notion of human excellence that carries the ethical weight.

JUSTICE

Aristotle argues that we tend to act in those ways that please us. Communities need to structure their institutions so that individuals get pleasure from acting virtuously. We need the rule of law to do this, because only the law has the power to shape the young who do not yet know how to lead their lives.[98] Law is also needed to control adults who cannot control themselves.

Aristotle was one of the first to distinguish between *distributive* and *corrective* justice.[99] Distributive justice refers to the way that goods and opportunities are divided among citizens. Corrective justice concerns compensating victims and punishing wrongdoers. (See Marilyn Friedman for more on this.)

Aristotle argues that a distributively just social system allows people to get what they merit. Determining merit is difficult. We have seen various attempts in this chapter. Nozick argued that merit should be determined by property rights. Hume thought that merit should be defined by the rules of the group. Rawls argued that merit should be determined by a fair social–economic system. Aristotle discusses variants of these theories, but argues that justice should promote individual excellence and group well-being. The best way to do this is to base distributive justice on private property because it provides incentives for people to use goods and opportunities in ways that benefit themselves and others. (See Smith and Hume for similar arguments.)

Corrective justice takes two forms: compensating for transactional losses by fraud, and compensating for nontransactional losses, such as theft, murder, and slander. In both cases, people act unjustly to get more than their due, and society must rectify this and discourage others from doing the same. People who are just and fair seek only what they are due. They take pleasure in getting what they merit, but do not like getting *less* or *more*. Corrective justice concerns only the rectification of the harm done, not the character of the people involved. It makes no difference, Aristotle says, whether a good person harms a bad person or a bad person harms a good one.[100] In each case, we should compensate for the loss and punish the violator.

Aristotle's view of justice has some implications for the S and R case. The property rights of owners would forbid Jameson and Mamet taking resources away from shareholders to increase the welfare of others unless the shareholders agreed to this. However, the community also has a value in itself to which Jameson and Mamet should feel committed. Community needs can outweigh individual rights. Aristotle would caution that Jameson and Mamet should not look for certainty. Social institutions allow room for individual differences. They are also complex, and so it is difficult to predict the outcomes of our actions. Finally, they are subject to change; even subtle changes can affect outcomes in significant ways.

FRIENDSHIP

Aristotle argues that friendship is necessary for the good life. The best kind of friendship provides the context in which we develop our social excellences and learn to value others as we value ourselves.

Friendship can be based on the usefulness, pleasure, or character of the friend. In the first two kinds of friendship we focus on ourselves: people are useful to us or they entertain us. In the third kind of friendship we admire the person's character. This type of friendship, noble friendship, is the most valuable and stable. It can exist only between those who have developed the moral virtues, such as honesty and loyalty, because these values are part of the character that we respect.[101]

Noble friendship is not based on reciprocity. We help our friends because we *care* about them. Reciprocity is, however, a critical component of a good friendship. For example, if you always help a friend who never helps you in return, that is a sign that the person does not view the friendship in the same way. The fact that the person never helps may end the friendship, but not merely because the person failed to reciprocate. The failure to reciprocate is *information* that the other person is not viewing the relationship in the same way, and it is this mismatch that ends the relationship.

Selfish people can have only the first two kinds of friendship. If we are selfish, we are concerned with always getting the larger share of material goods, pleasure, or recognition. These character traits make it impossible for us to care for other. Self-love is concerned with being virtuous; it promotes the excellence of our unique human capacities, and one of these is the capacity to care for others in themselves. We love ourselves, and part of what we love is how we care for others. The best kind of friendship is between those who love themselves in this way. Selfish self-love, on the other hand, diminishes ourselves and others.

Problems can arise in business relationships if we develop noble friendships with competitors. Friends are supposed to look after each other's interests, but as commercial rivals they are supposed to maximize their individual interests. There is no mechanical procedure to determine how to direct this relationship. Still, the decision is important: it will affect our friendship and our character.

We are social animals, which means that we need to live with each other.[102] Virtuous friends are viewed as good in themselves, but we must not think that this excludes them from being useful and pleasurable. (See Kant for a similar point.) In fact, friends in the best sense are the *most* useful and the *most* pleasurable because they are trustworthy and caring companions.

Relocating seemed good for S and R and a few other groups, but Jameson also believes that it might betray her friends. Aristotle would argue that this is an important issue because friendship is a kind of proving ground for the moral virtues and for our other relationships. Jameson and Mamet need to find some way to act on behalf of S and R without betraying their friends. This will not be easy to do. It may be impossible to do. Pluralism does not guarantee that all issues are nicely resolvable. However, when good things need to be sacrificed, we should do it in a way that best promotes the twofold goal of individual and communal excellence. If this is our standard and stakeholders know this, then the losers will know they are losing to a principle that helped build their community in first place. They will not like it, but they may endorse it.

PLEASURE AND HAPPINESS

Pleasure is part of happiness. We get the most pleasure when we act excellently in accord with our social and rational capacities, just as the well-conditioned athlete enjoys exercise and the accomplished violinist enjoys playing the violin. Life itself is an activity that can be accompanied by pleasure. There is a sense in which the good person does aim at a life of pleasure. But the pleasure aimed at by the good person is the enjoyment of unique human activities. Some of these pleasures are sensual, but many of them are not.[103]

Happiness is a goal given to us by our nature. We do not choose it, but we do choose the means to achieve it. In our current institutional setting, happiness consists of five things:

- Living a physically healthy life with standard human abilities
- Having friends, family, and a good civic life, which for most involves some kind of career
- Thinking well about abstract issues
- Enjoying the exercise of these three activities
- Luck.

Happiness, although intensely personal, is not completely in our control. Misfortune, disease, and tragedy for ourselves and those we love can interfere with or destroy our happiness. We also have little control over the society in which we live. To be happy, we need to live in a society that respects physical, moral, and intellectual virtues.[104] Individuals can achieve excellence in adverse conditions, of course, but society should promote excellence, not hinder it. In the next section, we will see how governance systems can encourage and discourage individual human excellence.

GROUP RELATIONSHIPS AND GOVERNANCE SYSTEMS

Jameson and Mamet are concerned about the relationship S and R has with Frieberg and its citizens. They are also concerned with the employee's union and the suppliers who have dedicated R&D and production capacity to S and R.

These stakeholders operate in a structure of institutional relationships that has ethical, economic, legal, and political dimensions. City, state, and national governments create laws that define and enforce many of these relationships. These different levels of government are made up of organizations with their own needs and interests. The relationships that obtain between private and governmental organization in large nations such as the United States are incredibly complex. However, if Jameson and Mamet are going to resolve the relocation question successfully, they need to understand these relationships.

Aristotle argues that a state needs a shared vision of human and communal good to coordinate the activities of its constituent groups.[105] This vision should include promoting physical, social, and intellectual excellence. We need these higher values to prepare us for the sacrifices we must sometimes make to preserve the state.

Jameson and Mamet have no control over the overall structure of the United States or of Frieberg, but they can make decisions that promote the physical, social, and intellectual excellence of many people. They have power to do this within S and R. As managers they should set up incentive systems that encourage successful social interaction and rational decision making for all members.[106] This does not mean that no one should have power. Power in social systems is inevitable; the question is how it should be conceived and distributed. Aristotle argued that the best form of governance system will depend on the group's function. A governance system that works for S and R may fail miserably for the employee's union. This is not because the people are different, but because the purposes of the organizations, and the skill and incentives necessary to achieve those purposes, are different.

Of course, not every organization can help employees achieve physical, social, and intellectual excellence. An organization may be more suited to promote one type of excellence than another. The responsibility of the organization is to promote whatever kinds of excellence it can, and not to discourage or prevent members from seeking excellence in other ways.

One of our most fundamental goods is our ability to plan our own lives and to carry out those plans. Although this is a personal activity, we do it in institutional settings. Aristotle argues that a social system based on private property and participatory government is the best way to promote this self-direction. Private property encourages long-term planning and individual responsibility. Participatory government, at the level of voting and office holding, gives us the ability to shape the social structures that create opportunities and restrictions.[107]

This endorsement of participatory government does not necessarily apply to organizations. When participation will promote organizational goals, it should be used. When it does not, it should not be used. An organization does not need to be, nor can it be, all things to all people. This is the function of the society as a whole. A society is a group of groups that together presents us with opportunities to pursue physical, social, and intellectual excellence.

Jameson and Mamet do not have the power to change society, nor would most of us want them to have that power, as Milton Friedman has pointed out.[108] Yet they do have the power to bring employees into the relocation decision. Whether they should do so depends on, among other things, their current and past relationships with the employees and their union. If the situation is antagonistic, there may be no way to include employees. That does not mean that Jameson and Mamet should give up the goal of participatory management, only that a great deal of groundwork may need to be done if they are going to achieve it in the future.

An Institutional Analysis of Ethical Pluralism

According to pluralism institutions are social devices that integrate our individual and social needs. As such, all four institutional purposes are equally important.

1. Institutions create opportunities for pursuing self-interest.
2. Institutions create opportunities for developing family relationships and friendships.
3. Institutions create opportunities for establishing formal groups and promoting their interests.
4. Institutions create opportunities for pursuing fairness, justice, and human rights.

No one of these purposes is intrinsically more important that the others, but some may dominate in a particular situation. The Aristotelian-based pluralism described above uses the standards of individual and group excellence to explain why these four values are important, and to guide our decision making when they conflict.

Institutions provide the stability and predictability we need for economic development and well-being (Hume), but they are open to interpretation as relationships and technology evolve (Mill, Rawls). It is this *interpretational openness* that gives individuals and organizations the autonomy to shape themselves, their relationships, and their behavior. According to pluralism, each individual, organization, and social group puts together its own interpretational set of the four basic ethical values.

These interpretations have limits. The theorists we examined generally agreed on what these limits are. They tended to value the working institutional structure to some degree. They also shared a belief in the importance of moral values such as honesty, loyalty, care, and justice, although they had different reasons for supporting them.

For pluralism, the values that guide and limit the interpretations of institutions come from within the institutions themselves. To discover what these values are, and to interpret them in reasonable and defensible ways, we need to examine economic and legal institutions. These are the topics of the next two chapters.

SUMMARY AND TRANSITION TO CHAPTER 4

In this chapter we have seen that egoism, care, utilitarianism, and intrinsic value can take many forms. Most of the authors we examined argued for one ethical value or principle. Marilyn Friedman, however, argued that we need care and justice together. Pluralism, as advanced by Adam Smith and Aristotle, argues that we need all four values.

If our goal is to understand business decision making in institutional contexts, pluralism can be more helpful than the other theories we examined. By giving all four values equal status, at least initially, pluralism can help us explore social institutions with fewer preconceptions about their ultimate or best purpose(s). This is the approach we will use in the rest of the book. Those who are committed to a different ethical point of view can treat this pluralistic approach as a heuristic device for examining different aspects of the business environment. Those who are not yet committed to an ethical point of view can use this approach to help them develop a more refined and usable set of moral beliefs.

Some of the key points in the chapter are as follows:

- Ethical principles help us seek, understand, and evaluate information.
- *Egoism* requires hard work, since we may have to give up present pleasures for future good. It also requires a clear view of self, since our view of our self is the standard we use to evaluate decisions.
- *Care* can be tough, since it can require us to ignore the requests of others that are harmful to themselves or others.
- *Utilitarianism* can be used at the small group, national and universal levels, and everything in-between. How we define the good of these groups is crucial. The goals of pleasure, happiness, and financial return will yield different standards of behavior.
- *Intrinsic value* can be expressed in terms of duty, rights, and procedural fairness.
- *Ethical pluralism* gives us a way to understand the diversity of basic human values and institutions.
- Institutions consist of constitutive and regulative rules that help determine what goals and actions are good and bad, right and wrong. (These issues will be discussed further in Chapters 4 and 5.)

In Chapter 4 we will use our psychological and normative discussions of ethics to examine how economic institutions guide individual behavior in organizations and markets.

Notes

1. M. Velasquez. *Business Ethics: Concepts and Cases,* 3rd ed. Englewood Cliffs, NJ: Prentice Hall, 1992, pp. 207–209.
2. *Ibid*
3. David E Sanger. "29 Nations Agree to a Bribery Ban." *New York Times,* National edition May 24, 1997, pp. 1, 34.
4. *Ibid.*
5. When ethical theories do try to answer these questions, they rely on empirical claims about human nature and social institutions.
6. See selections on Epicurus in W.T. Jones et al., eds. *Approaches to Ethics,* 3rd ed. New York: Mc-Graw-Hill, 1977.
7. Robert Frank. *Passions Within Reason: The Strategic Role of the Emotions.* New York: Norton Press, 1988. See the Preface and Ch. 2.
8. For a short introduction to her views, see Ayn Rand. "The Objectivist Ethics" in *The Virtue of Selfishness.* New York: Signet, 1964.
9. Rand uses the word "consciousness." However, "self-aware" seems to fit her meaning better.
10. For more on the distinction between pleasure and happiness, see the discussion of Aristotle at the end of this chapter.
11. For an account of this scandal, see James B. Stewart. *Den of Thieves.* New York: Simon & Schuster, 1992.
12. Mary Midgley. "The Origin of Ethics." *A Companion to Ethics.* Ed. Peter Singer. Cambridge: Basil Blackwell, 1991, p. 9.
13. Nel Noddings. *Caring: A Feminine Approach to Ethics and Moral Education.* Berkeley: University of California Press, 1984, p. 81.
14. *Ibid.,* p. 98.
15. Marilyn Friedman. "Beyond Caring: The De-Moralization of Gender." *Canadian Journal of Philosophy* 13 (1987), pp. 87–110.
16. *Ibid.,* p. 102.
17. *Ibid.,* p. 104.
18. *Ibid.,* p. 103.
19. Barbara Noble. "Making Family Leave a Reality; Benefits Exceeded Burdens in Law's First Year, the Labor Department Says." *The New York Times,* National edition, July 31, 1994, F19.
20. Marilyn Friedman, *op. cit.,* p. 106.
21. *Ibid.,* p. 105.
22. Carey Goldberg. "The Simple Life Lures Refugees from Stress." *The New York Times,* National edition, September 21, 1995, B1, C1.
23. *Ibid.*
24. See selections on David Hume in W.T. Jones, *op. cit.,* pp. 198–218.
25. *Ibid.*
26. *Ibid.,* p. 211.
27. He actually considers three situations; we will discuss only two of them.
28. *Ibid.,* p. 214.
29. John Stuart Mill. "Utilitarianism." *Ethical Theory: Classical and Contemporary Readings.* Ed. Louis P. Pojman. Belmont, CA: Wadsworth, 1989, pp. 161–180.
30. *Ibid.,* pp. 163–170. There is much more to his argument. I encourage the reader to read the primary source.
31. *Ibid.,* p. 164.
32. In this argument, Mill foreshadows Herbert Simon's work on satisficing. See Herbert Simon. *Administrative Behavior,* 3rd ed. New York: The Free Press, 1976, pp. xxviii–xxxi, 38–41, 80–81, 240–244, 272.
33. *Ibid.,* p. 174.
34. *Ibid.,* p. 180.
35. Craig Cox and Sally Power. "Executives of the World, Unite!" *Business Ethics* Sept./Oct. (1992).
36. *Ibid.*
37. *Ibid.*
38. See Chapters 1 and 2 of Immanuel Kant. *The Groundwork of the Metaphysic of Morals.* Ed. and trans. H. J. Paton. New York: Harper Torchbook, 1964.
39. I have interpreted Kant's statements to make them more accessible to contemporary readers.
40. See "An Essay Concerning the True Original, Extent and End of Civil Government" (often called

the "Second Treatise on Government"). Ed. E. Burtt. *The English Philosophers from Bacon to Mill.* New York: Modern Library, 1939, Ch. 2, pp. 404–409.

41. See "A Libertarian Theory of Justice" in Louis P. Pojman, *op cit.,* pp. 562–576.
42. This implies that state-imposed welfare programs are not justified. However, Nozick is not merely opposed to welfare programs to help the poor and uneducated. He would also oppose all aid to business, whether these came in the form of tax breaks, tariffs, subsidies, price guarantees, monopoly rights, or the many other ways in which businesses enlist the aid of government. In fairness to Nozick, he does not think that his theory is heartless, but ennobling, since it respects individuals, and allows them to keep all the fruits of their labor except for the small amount of taxes the state needs to protect them. Nozick, and libertarians generally, believe that such a system would create such economic prosperity that the problems of the poor and homeless would virtually disappear. For those who were truly unable to provide for themselves, there would be enough private charity to cover their needs. And for those who could provide for themselves but choose not to, the state would have the responsibility to leave them alone, for that is the way to respect them as free, choosing human beings.
43. John Locke, *op. cit.,* Sec. 27, p. 414.
44. Louis P. Pojman, *op. cit.,* pp. 572–575.
45. This seems to be a hidden utilitarian principle. In the preproperty state, reducing the opportunities for others is justified by the benefits they get. There is no need to get their consent for this trade-off, and it does not matter whether those who lose are the same individuals who benefit.
46. See Louis P. Pojman, *op. cit.,* pp. 576–589.
47. *Ibid.,* p. 583.
48. *Ibid.,* p. 583.
49. *Ibid.,* p. 582. I have changed some of the wording.
50. Craig Dunn and F. Neil Brady. "From Rules to Relationships: A Review of the Search for an Ethical Justification of Stakeholder Interests." *Proceedings of the International Association for Business and Society,* 1995, p. 47.
51. See Ian Browline, *Basic Documents on Human Rights.* Oxford: Oxford University Press, 1975. Also see John Nickle. *Making Sense of Human Rights: Philosophical Reflections on the Universal Declaration of Human Rights.* Berkeley: University of California Press, 1987.
52. See H. Shue. *Basic Rights.* Princeton: Princeton University Press, 1980 pp. 35–64.
53. Thomas Donaldson and Thomas Dunfee. "Toward a Unified Conception of Business Ethics: Integrative Social Contracts Theory." *Academy of Management Review* 19:2 (1994), pp. 252–284.
54. L. Uchitelle. "The Risks of Keeping a Promise; In Becoming an Icon, Mill Owner Imperils His Company." *New York Times,* National edition, July 4, 1996, C1, C3.
55. *Ibid..*
56. *Ibid.*
57. David Messick. "Equality, Fairness, and Social Conflict." *Social Justice Research* 8:2 (1995), pp. 165–171.
58. G.F. Cavenaugh, D.J. Moberg, and M. Velasquez. "The Ethics of Organizational Politics." *Academy of Management Review* 6 (1981), pp. 363–374; G.F. Cavenaugh, D.J. Moberg, and M. Velasquez. "Making Business Ethics Practical." *Business Ethics Quarterly* 5:3 (1995), pp. 399–418.
59. Patricia H. Werhane. "Moral Imagination and the Search for Ethical Decision Making in Management." Ruffin Lectures, 1994.
60. Mark Johnson. *Moral Imagination: Implications of Cognitive Science for Ethics.* Chicago: The University of Chicago Press, 1993.
61. Patricia H. Werhane. *Adam Smith and His Legacy for Modern Capitalism.* New York: Oxford University Press, 1991.
62. Adam Smith. *An Inquiry into the Nature and Causes of the Wealth of Nations.* Ed. Edwin Cannan. Chicago: University of Chicago Press, 1976, p. xii.
63. Patricia H. Werhane, *op. cit.,* p. 26.
64. *Ibid.,* p. 26.
65. *Ibid.,* pp. 27, 41–45.
66. *Ibid.,* pp. 88, 105–108.
67. Adam Smith, *op. cit.,* p. 18.
68. *Ibid.,* p. 477.
69. *Ibid.,* pp. 28–30.
70. *Ibid.,* pp. 57–59, 105–108.
71. See Rawls. *A Theory of Justice.* Cambridge: Harvard University Press, 1971, pp. 8, 142–150, 243–251, 350–391.

72. Patricia H. Werhane, *op. cit.,* pp. 55–56.
73. Compare with Freud, who argues that individual drives and the needs of society are fundamentally opposed. See "Civilization and Its Discontents" in *The Complete Works of Sigmund Freud.* Ed. and trans. James Strachey. London: Hogarth Press, 1961.
74. R. Solomon. *Ethics and Excellence: Cooperation and Integrity in Business.* New York: Oxford University Press, 1992.
75. E. Hartman. *Organizational Ethics and the Good Life.* New York: Oxford University Press, 1996.
76. Aristotle, "Nicomachean Ethics" in *The Basic Works of Aristotle.* Ed. Richard McKeon. New York: Random House, 1941. Book I, Chs. 7 and 13. I will use Books and Chapters to identity references so passages can be located in other editions.
77. *Ibid.,* Book II, Chs. 1–7.
78. Aristotle. "Politics" in McKeon, *op. cit.,* Book VII (IV), Chs. 13–17.
79. Aristotle. "Nicomachean Ethics," *op. cit.,* Book I, Ch. 3.
80. *Ibid.*
81. *Ibid.,* Book X, Ch. 8.
82. Note the similarity with these three steps and the elements of reasoning strategy distilled from Kohlberg and Gilligan in Chapter 1.
83. Aristotle. "Nicomachean Ethics," *op. cit.,* Book I, Ch. 3.
84. *Ibid.,* Book I, Chs. 4–7.
85. *Ibid.,* Book I, Chs. 1–2.
86. *Ibid.,* Book I, Ch. 13.
87. I am relying on the exoteric interpretation of happiness.
88. Aristotle. "Nicomachean Ethics," *op. cit.,* Book II, Ch. 1–Book III, Ch. 5.
89. Francis Fukuyama. *Trust: The Social Virtues and the Creation of Prosperity.* New York: The Free Press, 1995. The entire book deals with this subject, but see Chapter 1 for an overview.
90. It may be that human communities are so complex that there is no institutional order that eliminates conflicts. For Aristotle, this is a good reason to make ethics the center of our education, since it deals with the healthy resolution of these conflicts.
91. Aristotle. "Nicomachean Ethics," *op. cit.,* Book II, Ch. 2.
92. *Ibid.,* Book II, Ch. 3.
93. *Ibid.,* Book II, Chs. 5–9.
94. *Ibid.,* Book II, Ch. 6.
95. *Ibid.,* Book II, Ch. 9.
96. Bernard William. *Ethics and the Limits of Philosophy.* Cambridge: Harvard University Press, 1985, pp. 49–53.
97. Personal conversation with the author.
98. This is a major rationale for public education in the United States and elsewhere. Public education tries to ensure that all citizens have a common conception of how to live together.
99. Aristotle. "Nicomachean Ethics," *op. cit.,* Book IV, Chs. 3–4.
100. Ibid., Book IV, Ch. 4.
101. *Ibid.,* Book VIII, Ch. 3.
102. *Ibid.,* Book IX, Ch. 9, and "Politics," Book III, Ch. 6.
103. Aristotle. "Nicomachean Ethics," I, Book X, Chs. 4–5.
104. *Ibid.,* Book X, Chs. 6–9.
105. Aristotle. "Politics," *op. cit.,* Book III, Ch. 6.
106. See Edwin Hartman, *op. cit.* This is a theme of the entire book, but Chapters 3, 5, and 7 are especially relevant.
107. Aristotle argued for rule by the elite, who would move in and out of political office. We can apply this insight to constitutional democracies, for which he gave some support. See "Politics," Book III, Chs. 6 and 7. I believe that the Aristotelian arguments on which I rely work equally well in a constitutional representative democracy, although Aristotle does not think so. There is not time to argue for this here.
108. See Milton Friedman, Chapter 6.

CHAPTER 4

Economics and Ethical Decision Making

FROM ETHICS TO ECONOMICS: MARKETS AS ETHICAL ENGINES

Jameson and Mamet work in an economic organization guided by the ethical, economic, and legal principles of its institutional settings. In Chapters 2 and 3 we discussed how decision making incorporates ethical principles. In this chapter we will discuss how economic principles are related to ethical principles, and how both serve as standards for decision making.

Let us begin by discussing the four ways we can understand institutions.

1. Institutions create opportunities for defining and pursuing self-interest.
2. Institutions create opportunities for shaping and developing family relationships and friendships.
3. Institutions create opportunities for establishing formal groups and promoting their interests.
4. Institutions create opportunities for interpreting and pursuing fairness, justice, and human rights.

It has long been acknowledged that *economic institutions* create *opportunities* to pursue self-interest and group interest. As we saw in Chapter 3, however, self-interest and group interest have different interpretations. Hence, our ethical views directly influence our economic views about markets, organizations, and how individuals should work within them.

Before we discuss ethical aspects of economic markets, we must first address the widespread belief that ethics has little or nothing to do with markets. This belief seems to rest on three assumptions:

1. Market principles and rules determine organizational and individual behavior.

2. These principles and rules are economic.

3. Economic principles are incompatible with ethical principles.

Let us accept the first two assumptions for the moment. We can question the third assumption in at least two ways. In Part I, North and Paine argued that markets and organizations are guided by a number of ethical principles. In Chapters 2 and 3 we identified four general categories of ethical principles: self-interest, care (personal relationships), group welfare, and intrinsic value. Since we use these ethical principles to make decisions with economic consequences, there has to be some connection between ethics and economics. Second, economists themselves connect ethics and economics. Adam Smith argued that markets incorporate positive and negative versions of these four ethical values (Chapter 3). Milton Friedman argues that free markets are more likely than government-controlled markets to promote individual freedom and group well-being (Chapter 6).

Markets as Ethical Engines

According to Adam Smith, Milton Friedman, and the institutional view, markets are *ethical engines:* they coordinate our decisions in ways that affect ourselves, our relationships, and our communities. We can take an *external* or an *internal* approach to the relationship between ethics and economics.

THE EXTERNAL APPROACH

On the external approach, ethical principles are completely separate from economic principles. To continue the engine metaphor, economic engines help us *get to* ethical or unethical places, but have no ethical features themselves. Milton Friedman relies on the external view. The external view has at least three problems:

1. If economic and ethical principles are so different, it is difficult to explain how they work together in decision making.

2. There seems to be no conclusive way to show that one ethical principle or set of principles is superior to others. So, while economic decisions have ethical consequences, we cannot justify using ethical principles or consequences to guide our decision making.

3. Even if we could show that one ethical principle or set of principles is superior to others, business people will usually choose economic concerns over ethical concerns, so ethics has little practical value.

THE INTERNAL APPROACH

On the internal approach, ethical principles are a *part of* economic engines. Ethical principles serve the same kind of functions as fuel and timing systems do in engings: impetus and coordination. Ethical principles interpret, integrate, and rank self-interest, care, group interest, and intrinsic value. Philip Cochran and R. Edward Freeman (both in Chapter 6) rely on an internal view. The internal view avoids the three problems just discussed.

1. Economic and ethical principles can work together in decision making because they both rely on the same set of values—self-interest, care, group welfare, and/or intrinsic value.

2. The ethical principles we should use are (at least) those that already guide economic institutions. Focusing on these working ethical principles can lead us to consider other ethical principles and other interpretations of those working ethical principles.

3. Since economic institutions affect behavior, and since ethical principles partially constitute these institutions, ethics has practical value.

Preview of Chapter

The first section following the Introduction, "Economic Institutions," examines descriptive and normative economics, and shows some links between the two. There is also a brief discussion of how the ethical values that underlie institutions can affect productive behavior.

The second section, "Institutions and Market Conditions: Property, Risk–Reward Relationships, Information, and Competition," examines how ethical values shape these conditions. As North argued in Chapter 1, market conditions set the basic rules for organizational and individual behavior. The third section, "Individuals in Organizations: Goals or Contracts?," examines how the ethical values imbedded in the four market conditions are inherited by organizations and individuals.

The final section, "Making Decisions within Economic Institutions," summarizes the various ways we can combine and interpret the values that underlie economic institutions.

ECONOMIC INSTITUTIONS

Economics

It will be helpful to begin with a definition of economics. Samuelson and Nordhaus offer the following:

> Economics is the study of how people and society *choose* to employ scarce resources that could have alternative uses to *produce* various commodities and to *distribute* them for consumption, now or in the future, among various groups [and individuals] in society.[1] (emphasis added.)

Economists examine the connections between choice, production, and distribution at the macro- and the microlevels. Macroeconomics examines the economy as whole, studying, for example, the relationship between output, productivity, and prices at a national level. Microeconomics deals with specific issues in firms and in particular markets.

Economists examine economic relationships from descriptive and prescriptive perspectives. *Descriptive economics* tries to explain and predict economic behavior. Samuelson and Nordhaus's definition, above, is a definition of descriptive economics. *Normative economics* identifies an economic goal or set of goals we should promote, and is based on ethical principles and values. Traditionally, descriptive economics has been viewed as free of values, since it attempts to say only what *is* the case, not what *should* be the case. However, there are reasons to believe that descriptive economics incorporates ethical values.

Descriptive and Normative Economics: Some Connections

Let us begin with the following question: Why do we value efficiency? Most economists would reply that an efficient economic system conserves scarce resources and has prices that reflect marginal cost. But why do we care about preserving scarce resources and marginal cost pricing? The traditional answer is that conserving scarce resources and marginal cost pricing help an economic system satisfy *demand,* now and in the future.

So, efficiency is valuable because it helps us meet demand. Why is satisfying demand valuable? Satisfying demand is valuable because people are valuable, and this is where the ethical buck appears to stop: the value of human beings. In sum, efficiency is valuable because it helps us meet demand, and demand is valuable because of the value of those who make demands.

This discussion shows that efficiency is a "two-placed predicate." A two-placed predicate denotes a *relationship* between two things. Other two-place predicates are "is a partner of" and "has a larger market share than." When we say "X is efficient," this is a shorthand way of saying "X is efficient for Y." Hence, the concept of efficiency is necessarily linked to some goal. Only if we value the goal will we value the efficient means to that goal.

For example, if we are shoe manufacturers, we will value efficient shoe-making machines. Society also values such machines, since the machines conserve scarce resources while producing needed goods. However, terrorists can also be efficient, but since we abhor the goal, we abhor the means to the goal. In fact, the more efficient the terrorist, the worse the situation is. In short, efficiency inherits the value of its goal.

There is another way that the concept of efficiency incorporates ethical values. Economists usually assume that an efficient economic system is reached by a series of *voluntary* trades or choices, as Samuelson and Nordhaus put it. The discussion of advertising in Chapter 8 relies heavily on determining the nature of voluntary choice.

A system that coerces people to make transactions is unlikely to meet demand. The Italian economist, Vilfredo Pareto, formulated a view of efficiency that takes voluntary trades as central (see Appendix to this chapter). Pareto or allocative efficiency relies on individuals making free and uncoerced choices about their preferences. Freedom and coercion are normative, and so descriptive economics relies, in part, on normative concepts. The economist Frank Knight made this point in the following way:

> Scrutiny of any typical case of unfree behavior reveals that the coercive quality rests on an *ethical* condemnation, rather than the ethical condemnation [resting] on a factually established unfreedom.[2] (emphasis added)

> We say that the victim of a highwayman is coerced, not because . . . his choice . . . is different from other choice[s], but because we think the robber does "wrong" in making the [victim's] alternatives what they are.[3] (emphasis added)

In this passage, Knight argues that coercion does not result from the lack of choice itself. The victim *can* decide to die. The coercion lies in the way the victim is forced into these two alternatives. These same considerations can be used to understand market exchanges. Consider two separate scenarios that could occur in the S and R case.

Scenario 1. Suppose Frieberg's mayor makes it clear that if S and R moves, the town will condemn its unused property, forcing them to tear down buildings and restore the sites at great cost. Or, to avoid these costs, S and R can sell the property to Frieberg for $1, allowing the city to resell it for millions of dollars.

Scenario 2. Suppose S and R makes it clear that it is going to move its production facilities no matter what, and that if it does not get lower taxes and improved sewers and roads, they will move their main office, too.

On Knight's view, both of these scenarios could result in nonvoluntary trades, since one player is forcing another to choose between two very unpleasant alternatives. Frieberg stands to gain in Scenario 1 and S and R stands to gain in Scenario 2. In both scenarios, however, other stakeholders will lose: resources are spent to minimize the harm of coerced alternatives instead of improving product quality or distribution.

These two scenarios illustrate a problem that permeates many issues in business society: what is good for an economic entity is not always good for the economic system in which the entity operates. This is especially true of monopolistic behavior, discussed later in this chapter. This problem is discussed in Velasquez's article in Chapter 6 and in De George's article in Chapter 8 and is addressed in all the readings in Chapter 9.

The Impact of Economic Institutions on Wealth

Institutions affect qualitative and quantitative economic output. In Part I, North argued that in the seventeenth century, England's economy grew faster than Spain's because its economic institutions were more conducive to development than Spain's.

- England had a social system in which individualism figured prominently; Spain had a social system based on deference to authority.
- England's political structure was less centralized than Spain's. In England, Parliament helped establish stable property rights and a monetary system. In Spain, the monarchy could confiscate property and change the monetary system at will.
- In England, the legal system aimed at impartial resolution of disputes. In Spain, the courts deferred to political power.
- In England, there were entrepreneurial routes to wealth. In Spain, the best way to become wealthy was through the army, the Church, or the courts.[4]

England's system of secure private property, a reliable monetary system, and relatively impartial court system allowed people to seek wealth and security through trade and production. Trade and production generated the wealth that funded the English monarchy that, in turn, gave the monarchy incentives to promote more business activity.[5]

Institutions also affect the distribution of wealth in an economic system. The English system allowed more people access to wealth than the Spanish system because it had an entrepreneurial road to wealth as well as political and filial road. This does not mean that England in the eighteenth century was a land of opportunity. Far from it. For example, both Hume and Smith acknowledged that Britain's economic system was unjust, but argued that political and economic stability would be threatened if the state tried to correct for this.

Constitutive and Regulative Aspects of Institutions

Institutions consist of rules and principles that tell us what we should do. These rules and principles are of two kinds: constitutive and regulative. *Constitutive rules and principles* are essential to the existence of an institution. The rules and principles that specify the four conditions of markets—property, risk–reward relationships, information, and competition—constitute the infrastructure in which market transactions occur. For example, we could not buy a house or a car unless there were constitutive rules that establish private property. *Regulative rules and principles* govern how we act in institutional settings, but are not necessary for the existence of an institution. For example, there are many regulative rules regarding the purchase of houses and cars, such as buying insurance, that are not necessary for the institution of private property. We use constitutive and regulative rules and principles to guide and evaluate our own behavior, and to help us explain, predict, and evaluate the behavior of others.[6]

We will examine the constitutive and regulative aspects of the four market conditions later in this chapter. For now, let us look at the constitutive and regulative aspects of promising to see how ethics promotes economic coordination. The willingness of most people to keep promises is a *constitutive* part of the institution of promising. If no one ever followed the rule about keeping promises, the institution of promising would not exist (Kant, Chapter 2). Not complaining about fulfilling a promise is a *regulatory* rule of promising; it is not essential to promising.

Predicting the future is something we ordinarily associate with mystics or charlatans, but promising, contracting, and many other institutions help us *construct* and so *predict* the future. If we could not reliably plan future activities with others, cooperative behavior would be confined to what two or more people could accomplish in the immediate present. As North argued, secure property rights and a reliable court system were important ingredients in the development of England because these institutions created a relatively secure future. Let us look more closely at how we use promising and contracts to construct and predict the future.

If someone promises to meet you for lunch, that promise is made in accord with a complex set of social rules that specify compliance except in unusual and drastic circumstances. When you accept the promise, you do several things you would not do otherwise; for example, you rearrange another meeting, do not eat lunch at home, travel to a particular restaurant, etc. If the person does not show up, that does not mean the person broke the promise. If the person had to give CPR to a heart attack victim, we would say that the person had not fulfilled the promise, but had not broken it either, since standard social rules allow us to miss a luncheon engagement to save a life. In fact, anyone who let someone die to keep a luncheon engagement would be, at the very least, ethically suspect. If, however, we do not fulfill promises because we are tired, or we want to watch a soap opera, that would normally constitute promise breaking.

Contracts are government-backed promises. The government steps in to reduce uncertainty when promises put valuable property and opportunity at risk. A contract, just like a promise, should be fulfilled except under unusual and somewhat drastic circumstances (see Chapter 5).

The above discussion illustrates three important things. First, it shows how we use institutions to construct the future and so reduce uncertainty. Second, it shows how institutions integrate different ethical values, as promising integrates and ranks the values of life over luncheon agreements. Third, it shows that institutions are *partly constituted by*, or made up of, ethical features: the essence of an institution is that it tells us what we *should* do. This "should" is part of the institution, not something external to it.[7]

To say that ethical features are built into institutions does not mean that the *resolutions* to all the problems that can arise within and between institutions are also built in. In the S and R case, Jameson and Mamet do not see how they can continue to follow institutional expectations regarding their families, shareholders, labor, suppliers, and the community. The institutions regarding care and concern for their families appear to conflict with economic institutions regarding the property rights of shareholders. Labor also has rights under current legal institutions. Frieberg has legal and political institutions that give it a range of choices that can help or harm S and R. As we have described the case, Jameson and Mamet have internalized many of the values of these institutions. Their internal emotional conflicts mirror the external institutional conflicts.

EVALUATING CONSTITUTIVE AND REGULATIVE RULES

We use constitutive rules to evaluate regulative rules. Suppose, in an economic system based on private property, someone proposed a regulative law taxing inheritance at 100% in order to redistribute wealth. Apart from the political impossibility of passing such a law in most representative democracies, we could argue that this tax would violate the very concept of private property. Part of what it means to have property is to have control over bequeathing one's property: a 100% tax interferes with this condition. Further, to make such a law work, other laws would be needed to prevent people from transferring their wealth before they die. These secondary laws would also interfere with property rights. In this case, we use a constitutive rule to evaluate a regulative rule.

If constitutive rules are the standards we use to evaluate regulative rules, where can we find standards to evaluate the constitutive rules themselves? This is not merely a problem for understanding and evaluating economic institutions and the systems they constitute; it arises in all institutions and systems that have constitutive rules.

To see how we might evaluate constitutive rules and principles, we will examine a very different kind of system, axiomatic geometry, which in the past 150 years has had serious challenges to its constitutive foundations. The problems of axiomatic geometry are similar to and different from the problems we have evaluating economic systems. Examining these similarities and differences will help us understand how to evaluate constitutive economic rules and principles.

EVALUATING FORMAL SYSTEMS: THE EVOLUTION OF AXIOMATIC GEOMETRY

The proposition, "Given a straight line and a point outside that line, one and only one line can be drawn through that point that is parallel to the given line," is an axiom of Euclidean geometry.[8] This is a constitutive rule of geometry just as the right to control one's property is constitutive of the institution of private property. This axiom will shape the kinds of proofs (transactions) that can take place within this system. However, suppose someone were to ask whether the parallel axiom is a *good* axiom? What does it mean to ask this question? Axioms are not good or bad, we might respond, they simply are given or assumed. Axioms are the fundamental standards by which we accept or reject hypotheses. In fact, there is no way even to pose the question of the adequacy of the axioms within an axiomatic geometric system.[9]

That we cannot evaluate axioms within the system they constitute does not mean that there are no standards for evaluating them; it means only that we must seek these standards outside the system. This is just what happened to geometry in the nineteenth and twentieth centuries, when the parallel axiom, above, was challenged. The history of this debate can help us search for standards to evaluate the constitutive aspects (axioms) of economic systems.

In the nineteenth century, two mathematicians, Lobachevski and Reimann, developed consistent non-Euclidean geometries, each offering a different version of the parallel axiom. Lobachevski developed a geometric system that changed the parallel axiom to the following: given a straight line and a point outside that line, more than one parallel line could be drawn through the point. Reimann developed a consistent system that stated that no parallel lines could be drawn through the afore-mentioned point. These systems caused a great deal of discussion in and outside the mathematical community because Euclidean geometry, which had stood for over 2000 years, seemed to be in doubt. This doubt was magnified in the twentieth century when Einstein developed his theory of relativity. In dealing with interstellar distances, in which spatial distortions made by the gravitational forces of stars and galaxies became noticeable, Reimannian geometry was easier to use than Euclidean geometry.

Before the development of relativity theory, the question of which geometric system was best had no clear answer. As mathematical systems, they were all equally good. However, as a way to deal with the everyday world, Euclidean geometry seemed to have the edge. Euclidean geometry was a practical tool we used to help build houses and to give accurate predictions about the position of the planets in our solar system. However, with the advent of relativity theory, Reimannian geometry seemed superior, at least for interstellar calculations. Einstein himself preferred Reimannian geometry because it was more useful for explaining and predicting phenomena on the basis of relativity theory. One way, then, to evaluate systems and the axioms that ground them is to see how well these systems serve human needs and purposes.

EVALUATING ECONOMIC INSTITUTIONS AND SYSTEMS

There is an important difference between geometric systems and economic systems. Whereas human needs and purposes are *external* to geometric systems, they are *internal* to economic systems.

That economic institutions have internal values makes the task of *finding* standards easier than in the case of geometry. Standards are easy to identify because they come with the institution to be evaluated (see Pluralism in Chapter 2, and Bowie "The Moral Obligations of Multinational Corporations" in Chapter 9). Further, given the important role of the constitutive values, they have an initial plausibility.

That economic institutions have internal values makes the task of *justifying* these standards more difficult than in the case of geometry. To point out that a system adheres to a set of values expressed by its constitutive rules shows that an institution is internally consistent, but it does not justify those rules. This is the nub of the problem. As was mentioned before, constitutive rules are the fundamental way in which we evaluate what occurs in an economic system. Where can we find standards to evaluate these standards?

One way to evaluate the internal standards of economic institutions is to interpret, compare, and contrast rules and principles of different institutions. For example, the U.S. Supreme Court evaluated the relationships between the institution of private property and the institution of free competition when it refused to reverse a lower court ruling that broke up AT&T in 1984. The Court decided that competition, with its constituent values, *was more important than* the values of private property that enabled AT&T to become a monopoly. The Court's decision forced AT&T to spin-off its local phone services and to lease its long distance lines to other providers.

Evaluating and modifying an economic system by its constituent values are part of the on-going project of adjusting institutions to changing social and technological settings. These adjustments are not the result of a mechanical process. They involve moral reasoning as discussed in Chapter 2, an assessment of ethical values as discussed in

Chapter 3, an assessment of the economic relationships we will discuss in this chapter, and an assessment of the legal institutions we will discuss in Chapter 5.

INSTITUTIONS AND MARKET CONDITIONS: PROPERTY, RISK–REWARD RELATIONSHIPS, INFORMATION, AND COMPETITION

As we defined them in Chapter 1,

> Institutions are . . . complexes of norms and behaviors that persist over time by serving collectively valued purposes.

Institutions shape markets by influencing choice sets that give us opportunities and limits (North, Part I). Institutions can be *practices* such as promising, *documents* such as the working constitution of a country, *roles* such as church leader, and *organizations* such as the Supreme Court. Institutions from the infrastructural background that makes economic activity possible.

In what follows we will examine institutional aspects of

1. Property rights
2. Links between risks and rewards
3. Information distribution and quality
4. Competitive relationships

Every social system, from the smallest hunter–gatherer tribe to the largest industrial state and trading block, has institutions that specify these four economic conditions. Property rights, which can be private, public, or mixed, specify what is exchanged and who the parties to the exchange are. Risk–reward links specify what is at stake in production and exchange. Information is necessary to produce and distribute goods.

Competition is easily misunderstood, and deserves special comment. Competition occurs whenever we have scarce resources: the question is not whether a social system will have competition, but how it organizes it. Although competition is a necessary feature of all economic systems, it is not a necessary feature of *every aspect* of an economic system. For example, competition may be useful for getting producers of grain to behave efficiently, and less useful within organizations that produce grain. In a different kind of case, Paul Krugman has argued that competition is a bad criterion for evaluating economic relationships between nations.[10]

In this section we will examine how the four economic conditions rely on ethical values, how these economic conditions can fail, and how individuals, organizations, and society use ethical values to assess these failures.

Property

CONSTITUTIVE PRACTICES AND RULES

Property rights define a sphere of control and security over scarce resources. Ideally, they promote individual and social good. *Individually,* we use property rights to help create a life for ourselves, family, and friends. Property rules not only define what belongs to whom, but specify how we exchange these rights. To see the importance of property rights, imagine what life would be like without them. Hobbes argued that without property, life would be "poor, nasty, brutish, and short," as each person would be at war with all others in a fight for survival.[11]

Socially, secure property rights are necessary for the conservation of resources and for production. Without property rights, whatever improvements or savings we make will be quickly appropriated by others. Consider the growth of private property in English villages in the middle ages. When cattle and sheep were few, common grazing lands served everyone's needs. However, as the number of cattle and sheep increased, the grazing land became overused. This overuse was not the result of greedy livestock owners. These owners simply realized that whatever grass they saved by reducing their grazing could easily be used by others. Since all understood this, they grazed as much as possible to get what they could before the grass was gone. If they did not, their livestock would starve, albeit sooner rather than later. The solution to this problem can still be seen today. The British Isles are covered with stone fences and hedgerows that mark off plots for individual grazers. As long as a family had the rights to one or more clearly identifiable plots, it had an incentive to conserve resources for the future.[12]

Property rights can also promote innovation and efficiency as individuals use their property as factors of production. Every society has a large number of property rules and laws that help promote production and order. Together, these rules and laws form the institution of property. This institution, in turn, partially constitutes the economic systems in which individuals and organizations make decisions. Societies make different decisions about how to treat property. Cuba and North Korea give productive property rights to the state. China and Vietnam once gave productive property rights to the state, but appear to be moving away from that system. Most other countries have various combinations of individual, corporate, and state property rights.

Property systems and technology tend to mature together. Copyrights were not an issue until the printing press; the need to protect trademarks grew with large markets; the need to assign property rights underground grew as the need for oil and minerals developed.

Another type of technology, social technology,[13] also spurs the creation of new property rights. Social technology refers to the way societies structure economic, legal, and ethical institutions and relationships to solve problems. Social technology can be as simple as a coin flip or as complex as a national government. One of the most important pieces of social technology is the corporation, a relatively new form of property.

The Development of the Corporation: Splitting the Atom of Property

The corporation, as a type of organization, is a social institution. This was not always so. In the the United States, in the late eighteenth and early nineteenth centuries, there were very few corporations, and those that existed were governed by strict rules.[14] Corporations were founded by charters that had to be approved by the *legislature* of the state of incorporation.[15] These early corporations were formed to provide infrastructural goods, such as canals, that required large amounts of capital. These charters varied from state to state, but were often highly specific: they identified what kind of business would be engaged in, the number of shares to be issued, who the officers would be, how profits were to be distributed, and how corporate property would be distributed in case of bankruptcy.[16] Substantial changes in the charter required the *unanimous* vote of shareholders.[17] For example, if a corporation that ran ferries wanted to run carriages to transport people to and from the ferry sites, a single shareholder could block this plan.

Today, corporations can start or buy other businesses whether or not those businesses are in a similar industry. Internally, corporations can refocus their efforts on new products that are very different from their old products. Corporations can completely re-organize their capital structure. These decisions are made by managers who have little or no long-term property interests in the corporations they manage. Of course, some of the actions mentioned above require board or stockholder approval, but it is rare for boards or stockholders to prevent managers from doing what they want. In practice, the kinds of actions mentioned above are in the control of management.

Berle and Means argue that the rigid control of early corporations was designed to protect the "general public, the corporate creditors, and (to a lesser extent), the corpo-rate shareholders."[18] State governments imposed these rules because they believed that these new business entities posed risks to the general public and to creditors that were different from, and greater than, the risks posed by noncorporate businesses. This in-creased risk is a result of the way that corporate property restructures risks and rewards.

The corporation creates two new kinds of property owners: the corporation itself and the shareholder. It is not clear that the old property rules will work when a legal en-tity and not a human being(s) owns property. Because the corporation owns property, it also bears the losses and the benefits of corporate activity. This allows managers and owners to extract the benefits from the corporate entity while leaving the corporation with the losses.

Berle and Means argued that this new arrangement of risks and rewards "splits the atom of property," destroying the "very foundation on which the economic order of the past three centuries has rested."[19] The atom of property, which Adam Smith presupposed in his thesis that self-interest promotes the common good, is the seemingly natural tie between *owning* property, *managing* property, and the *consequences* of managing it well or badly. The atom of property was the "foundation of economic order" because the owner/manager of productive property had powerful incentives to manage their prop-erty in a way that increased, or at least preserved, its value. An owner/manager must pay creditors and avoid harming the general public to continue production and avoid being sued for hearth and home. Because it is in the owner's interest to maintain a stable busi-ness, this incentive has a salutary effect on society by providing steady employment, a flow of goods, and a reliable tax base.

The corporate financial structure splits the atom of property because it separates owners from managers, and separates each of them from risk by making the corporation the main bearer of liability. Although risk is reduced, owners and managers remain closely connected to the rewards of business activity: owners get dividends and capital growth and mangers get compensation packages. Because the corporation separates risks and rewards, the self-interest of the owners and managers can easily diverge from the interest of the corporation in ways we do not find in a noncorporate environment. Hence, we cannot expect that corporate property will be guided by the incentives that made the traditional institution of private property so useful.

Berle and Means do not argue that shareholders bear no risk, only that their risk is limited to the price they paid for their shares and their corresponding opportunity costs. However, the benefits they can receive have no fixed limit, as the early buyers of Kodak and Microsoft can testify. Further, managers who destroy their businesses lose their jobs, which is an incentive to keep a company going. Berle and Means argue only that the risks of owners and managers are lower in a corporate environment, and that these lower risks are not bought at the expense of lower returns because the risks are transferred to parties external to the corporation.

To understand why corporate property poses greater risks than noncorporate enti-ties to external parties, such as the general public and creditors, we do not need to im-port any new ethical criteria or radical social views. We need rely only on the age-old assumption that in economic matters we can expect people to act from their perceived economic interest. Since it is possible for managers of corporations to maximize their wealth at the expense of the corporation, the general public, creditors, shareholders, or all four, we should expect managers to exploit these opportunities. For example, managers who want to keep their job have an incentive to turn down a buyout offer even though selling would be good for the owners and employees. In a different case, managers may alter the capital structure of a company through a leveraged buyout, transferring a great deal of the corporation assets to themselves. To expect managers to act otherwise would require us to believe they are altruistic.

It was for these reasons that states required such strict rules for the first U.S. corporations. However, this control was short-lived. New York passed a law in 1811 allowing some kinds of business to incorporate without legislative approval.[20] Many other states soon followed and extended New York's lead, giving this opportunity to all kinds of businesses. These laws were administered by a state official, usually the secretary of state; the transformation was fairly well completed by the end of the nineteenth century.[21] By allowing corporations to be formed more easily, and by allowing them to guide their own behavior much more freely, the state began to treat corporations more like noncorporate businesses. Common, statute, and regulatory law still had to pay attention to the special problems and relationships that arose in corporate ownership and management, but the law did this *ex post,* not *ex ante.*

The number and size of corporations in the United States grew rapidly as it became easier to incorporate. Corporations, once formed to supply fundamental infrastructural goods, were in every sector of the economy by the early twentieth century. The reduction of risk and the possibilities of amassing great wealth attracted the talent and capital that played a major role in the development of the United States. The corporation was in many ways the perfect engine to drive the development of a new country that seemed to have limitless resources. It was not until the work of Berle and Means, published 3 years after the worldwide depression hit the United States, that individuals started to reflect on how the corporate financial structure had changed the institution of property.

As societies depend more and more on corporations to create wealth in the form of goods, jobs, and tax revenues, and the social stability that these factors promote, it is not surprising that the corporation has become the center of battles concerning the regulation of business. These conflicts are a part of the process of evaluation, discussed above, by which societies determine how their wealth will be produced and distributed. As we discussed earlier in this chapter, the corporation is the place where the ethical values of markets, societies, families, and individuals intersect. When these values conflict, we need a way to resolve them. An important step in understanding and resolving these conflicts is to remember that the corporation is created by society to serve certain purposes; it did not arise out of nature. Since it is an entity created by social decision making, it is appropriate to ask *why* it was created and *how* it was and can be justified.

The development of corporations in the United States illustrates the foundational role of property in establishing a socioeconomic system. It is hard to imagine what life in the United States or in other industrialized countries would be like without corporations. It is not farfetched to say that there would be no industrialized countries without corporations, at least none with the scope and power that characterize countries such as the United States, Germany, and Japan.

The creation and growth of the corporation illustrate how the rules of property and liability have ethical features and ramifications. In Chapter 6, Milton Friedman, Philip L. Cochran, and R. Edward Freeman propose different views about the ethical, economic, and legal aspects of the corporation. For now, we can say that when property ownership, management, and liability rest with one person or group, self-interest can provide incentives that promote both individual and social welfare. Unfortunately, this property structure is not very good at utilizing resources of large markets, and so actually impedes the well-being of large groups. The corporation is able to bring together large amounts of capital and talent to meet the needs of large markets. However, it also gives individuals more opportunity to exploit the system in a way that harms society.

We can understand corporate regulation, then, as an attempt to restore the incentives that were present when the atom of property was whole, while not losing the individual and social benefits of corporations. This is a very delicate task. Too much regulation or regulation of the wrong kind can severely reduce the benefits of corporations. Too little regulation, on the other hand, can result in substantial risks for the public, creditors, and shareholders, and ultimately for managers themselves.

In the face of such a delicate balancing act, we might wish to retreat to a position in which government simply lets business alone. This is not possible. If we took this position seriously, there would be no corporations, since they cannot exist without the constitutive legal rules that make them possible. Further, the fundamental role of government in the creation of corporations implies that government bears some responsibility for the economic environment that results from them. If the corporate setting generates harms that could not occur without government-enforced constitutive rules, then government has a *prima facie* responsibility to address those harms. In Chapter 5 we will see how the public and special interest groups use this kind of reasoning to pressure government to maintain or alter public policy.

The Unitary and Bundle Views of Property:
A Constitutive Analysis of Government Regulation

Our attitude toward government regulation is influenced by our view of property. We can view property as a *unitary* or a *complex* relationship. Locke and Blackstone viewed property as a unitary or simple relationship between a person and an object of value. Take the relationship between you and this book (assuming that you bought, not borrowed, this book). On the unitary view, you have a direct relationship to this book that gives you a variety of rights: to use it when you want, to write in it, to sell it, and the list goes on. In Chapter 2 we saw how Locke, and Nozick after him, used this view of property to justify the existence and limits of government.

Justice Cardozo argued that property is a complex relationship, which he characterized as a "bundle of sticks." Property is a *collection* of rights to use something of value.[22] Your property relationship to this book is not something that gives you rights, but merely *is* the collection of those rights. Societies construct these bundles to serve certain purposes. As needs change, societies rearrange the bundles.[23]

Berle and Means' analysis of corporations seems to fit better with the bundle of sticks view. When most production in the United States was agricultural, the owner/manager/consequence-bearer was the same person or family. This bundle of property rights continued to work even in the early stages of the industrial revolution. However, as new technology, expanding markets, and the correlative needs for capital, talent, and coordinated information grew, the old bundle of rights became difficult to use. The response was a new bundle of property rights: the corporation.

The proper role of government will be understood differently on the unitary and complex views of property. On the unitary view, government regulation of corporations is a violation of the rights of those who own the corporation. This violation can be justified if it protects other, more important rights. For example, pollution control (see Chapter 6) is justified if it clearly prevents the death of innocent people, as in the case of regulating mercury disposal. However, pollution control is much harder to justify if the goal is to make people happier or better off. In traditional rights theory (see Chapter 3, Locke and Nozick), it is wrong to take one person's property to make others happy. On the bundle of sticks view, however, we can justify both types of regulation by arguing that society is adjusting what it created in the first place. If the corporation is a bundle of rights designed to serve a social function, society can alter that bundle to serve that function better.

REGULATIVE PRACTICES AND RULES: WHEN PROPERTY FAILS

We have discussed how ethical values underlie property rights. We will now focus on problems that arise when these property rights fail. We will examine a form of property failure commonly referred to as *externalities,* which can be negative or positive.

Negative Externalities

Negative externalities occur when a transaction harms those who are not *voluntary* parties to the transaction. When negative externalities arise, those internal to the transaction impose costs on those outside the transaction. It does not matter whether this harm is intentional or not. It does not even matter if those within the transaction attempt to avoid harming those external to the transaction. The essence of a negative externality is not the intentions of those inflicting the harm, but *the lack of consent* of those who are harmed. Again, we see the importance of voluntariness and autonomy to a fundamental economic notion.

Pollution cases present some of the clearest examples of negative externalities. A large steel plant, for example, can cause air and water pollution that harm the health and property of many people. In an unregulated environment, pollution costs are borne by those outside the transactions that occur in the production and sale of the steel. This violates the property rights of those harmed by the pollution unless they agree to be so harmed. The negative impact of these externalities is not reduced if those suffering from the pollution get benefits from the steel business in the form of jobs and tax revenues, since those benefits have nothing to do with the fact that their property rights are being violated against their will. These problems are exacerbated when property rights are unclear or not enforced.

Consider a similar case in which the receipt of benefits does not in itself compensate harm. Suppose that an eccentric neighbor decides to give you an expensive gift every month for no reason. Every month, there is a gift on you front porch. However, several months later, he pours a mild acid on your car that dulls and pits the finish, he uses a yard blower to blow dirt and soot into your windows, and he dumps his garbage on your lawn. The gifts have no mitigating effects on the property damage he has done. If you try to recover your losses in court, the court will not count the gifts the neighbor has given you against your costs. What legitimizes the loss of property rights is not the benefits one might receive or have received from the person who caused the harm, but the consent of the owner to give up those property rights.

An important difference between the steel mill case and the eccentric neighbor case is that it is usually much harder to show the steel mill caused the damage than the neighbor. There are a great number of polluters, and it is often impossible to tie pollution damage to just one of them. Further, even if the source of pollution can be established, it is often difficult to prove that the damage was done by *that* pollution.

Civil and criminal law provide incentives for individuals not to harm the property of others.[24] However, since it is difficult to determine the origin of pollutants and to show a casual link between pollutants and harm, polluting firms can escape detection. When we combine this with the fact that managers are often not personally liable for the damage that results from pollution, there can be economic incentives to pollute. Hence, laws that apply only after harm is done are often ineffective. To limit pollution, environmental regulation tries to prevent harm before it occurs.

International environmental problems are often more difficult than domestic ones. These difficulties are addressed in Chapter 6 by David P. Hanson in "The Ethics of Development and the Dilemmas of Global Environmentalism" and by Colum Lynch in the case "U.S. and Mexico Confront a Toxic Legacy." Without institutions to protect property rights, competitive pressures can create environmental nightmares.

Environmental regulations can be justified from all four ethical orientations: the self-interest of the harmed parties, care, the welfare of the group, and the rights of those harmed. However, we could use the same ethical concerns to argue that government should *not* impose pollution regulation because it interferes with the self-interest of managers and shareholders, the ability of families to support themselves, the wealth of the community, and the rights of shareholders.

This is the kind of maddening situation that gives ethics a bad name, but the situation is not as irresolvable as it seems. First, that we have two arguments that show that these ethical criteria *can* justify opposite conclusions (regulate and do not regulate) does not show that these criteria *do* justify opposite conclusions. We can make these two contrary arguments because there are many constituencies involved in resolving a problem such as pollution, all of whom have legitimate needs and interests. If we focus on people and groups external to the corporation, we can easily favor them; if we focus on people and groups internal to the corporation, we can easily favor them. The difficulty arises when we try to include all relevant constituencies. If we include both constituencies, our decision is more complex and harder to reach, but we will have more relevant information.

Because cases differ, we cannot judge before a conflict arises whether or not regulation of business is justified. The legitimacy of regulation depends on the regulation and/or regulatory agency; the types of behavior to be regulated; the ethical, economic, and legal institutional settings; the state of technology, and more. However, we can examine general features of cases and how they arise out of ethical, economic, and legal institutions and values. Once we become comfortable with these institutions and values, we can use them to evaluate cases.

Positive Externalities

Positive externalities occur when a transaction *benefits* those who are not voluntary parties to the transaction. Perhaps the clearest cases of positive externalities are pure public goods, such as national defense, the monetary system, and the court system. Assuming that these are benefits, we benefit from them whether or not we pay for them. We will discuss public goods in the next section.

Education has substantial positive externalities. Although education clearly benefits the educated person through better jobs and pay, there are also several other constituencies who benefit. Society as a whole benefits since educated people not only tend to improve social conditions, but tend to commit fewer crimes. The ability of educated people to read, write, and solve problems promotes the good of everything from family life to the workplace to society.

Ordinary business transactions can also have positive externalities. When Disney built Disneyland in Anaheim, California, the property values surrounding the park increased substantially. Disney learned from this experience. When they built Disney

World in Orlando, Florida, they bought up a great deal of the surrounding property. This allowed Disney to internalize much of the property value increases, but not all. The fact the Disney was bidding on land raised the prices Disney paid, giving those landowners positive externalities. Further, since Disney could not buy all the land that increased in value, those landowners benifitted.

Externalities and Prices

Externalities skew prices, and so alter supply and demand. Negative externalities are desirable from the point of view of the business generating them, since others pay for parts of the production process. In an unregulated environment the price for a good whose production has significant negative externalities does not reflect the true costs of production. Since the price is artificially low, more of the good is produced than would be produced at a price that reflected the actual costs of production. This added production results in more negative externalities and opportunity costs of other needed goods and services.

Goods that have significant positive externalities will be underproduced. Because not all the benefits from an education redound to the person paying for the education, the supply of education will be too low. Students are willing to pay a cost that is commensurate with the benefits they believe they will receive, but they are not willing to pay the cost for the benefits others will receive. This is the standard explanation of why societies need to subsidize education. The government supplies the funds to make up the difference between what the student is willing to pay and what the education costs. Without this subsidy, education would be underproduced, to the detriment of all.

Underlying both kinds of externalities is the function and value of property. Negative externalities are violations of property rights and the autonomy of rights holders, both of which are essential to efficient markets. Positive externalities are based on the inability to control all the benefits of one's property, resulting in demand being underserved.

When we use law to define and enforce property rights, it serves a *constitutive* function. In its constitutive role, law is a set of rules that helps create, shape, and maintain a social and business environment. In this capacity, law creates opportunities; it is not an instrument that keeps reasonable people from doing what they want.

Chapter 6 contains articles and cases relevant to property. Milton Friedman discusses the ethical presuppositions and ramifications of the shareholder/property rights view. Philip L. Cochran agrees that property relationships include rights and responsibilities, but argues that the firm can be financially structured to give employees, labor, and even the community property rights. R. Edward Freeman argues that all stakeholders have basic rights that management should respect, regardless of their property interests.

William F. Baxter argues that business can have an obligation to protect the environment, but that these obligations are dependent on the human values expressed through market demand. Norman E. Bowie argues that business has no special obligation to the environment, but that it does have a special obligation not to interfere with the political process that generates environmental regulations. The Diablo Canyon Case shows what happens when stakeholders have conflicts that existing institutional frameworks cannot handle.

Richard De George argues that international business has special problems because there are no effective background institutions for the protection of the environment. Patricia H. Werhane focuses on MNC behavior in host countries, and offers six guidelines for respecting the institutional values of a host country without violating basic rights.

Manuel G. Velasquez argues that analyses like De George's and Werhane's are good, but that they do not include issues of fairness and justice. Without these central values, many issues in international business cannot be understood or resolved. David P. Hanson argues that global environmental damage is one of our most pressing issues. His solution, in terms of the institutional framework we are discussing, is that international organizations and trade regimes should help establish and protect property rights.

Risk–Reward Links

CONSTITUTIVE PRACTICES AND RULES

In this section we will look at ethical values underlying risk–reward relationships. We will assume that economic systems need to provide a close and perceivable link between risk and reward.

The link between risk and reward seems to occur naturally in simple economic systems, so it seems odd to say that the rules governing risk–reward links are constitutive. However, by rules we mean both formal and informal rules. We can speak of constitutive rules of unplanned social institutions when we refer to the informal cultural norms that govern those relationships. As a system develops complex entities such as corporations, labor unions, and a variety of governmental organizations, formal rules are needed to define, enforce, and manage the risk–reward link. Minimum wage laws, the National Labor Relations Act, and bankruptcy laws all establish risk–reward links.

The development of the corporation is a concrete example of how society uses constitutive rules to establish risk–reward relationships. As we saw above, the corporation is a form of property that reassociates risk and reward by "splitting the atom of property." This reduces the risks, but not the potential rewards, of capital investment. This attractive arrangement brings together tremendous amounts of capital and talent, enabling corporations to create great benefits for, and impose great risks on, a variety of stakeholders.

While the property rules that form the foundation of an economic system make some risk–reward relationships possible, they prohibit others. Consider the productive practices of Cuba and the United States. One of the main differences between these two economic systems is the role of productive property. Since about 1962, productive property in Cuba has been owned and managed by the state. In 1989, Cuba changed its property laws to allow foreign corporations to own parts of Cuban enterprises. These changes in property ownership were made possible by a change in property laws.[25]

Risk–reward relationships can be justified by the four kinds of ethical values we have discussed. Self-interest can justify close and predictable risk–reward links. Without this information, we could have no way to calculate the effects on our interests. For example, if we are offered a promotion that requires us to relocate to an unstable foreign country, we cannot make an accurate self-interested decision without some idea of our physical and property risks of living in this country and the risk to our career should we refuse. The care perspective, interestingly enough, is much like the egoistic perspective, except that the good that is being promoted is not the good of oneself, but the good of one's relationships. Having clear rules governing the risk–reward relationship will help individuals evaluate how the risks they take will affect their relationships. For example, consider the relocation problem just described, but add in the issues of family and children.

From a utilitarian perspective, a society will be better off having a close link between risk and reward for at least two reasons. First, as Hume emphasized, these rules help maintain order and promote industry. Second, as Mill emphasized, having clear rules will help us evaluate the rules and modify them to promote social well-being. From the perspective of intrinsic value, the closeness of the link allows individuals to evaluate their behavior in terms of duty, fairness, and rights. Second, having clear rules helps us to evaluate and modify these links if they do not respect the intrinsic value of human beings.

From a pluralistic perspective, close risk–reward relationships are necessary for structuring our lives to develop our talents and foster healthy personal, work, and civic relationships, as described by the four kinds of ethical values.

Not only do different ethical views justify risk–reward relationships in different ways, they highlight and ignore different information about the risk–reward relationship. For example, a person with a self-interested point of view would not consider factors that dealt primarily with fairness unless they were instrumental to promoting the interests of the self. Similarly, a utilitarian such as Hume would not consider facts about distributive justice unless they threatened social order. A pluralist would argue that each of the four kinds of ethical values is important because each helps us gather relevant information.

REGULATIVE PRACTICES AND RULES: WHEN RISK–REWARD RELATIONSHIPS FAIL

Traditional economic analyses of the risk–reward link concentrate on capital markets. However, the risk–reward link is also an important aspect of factor, labor, and consumer markets. For example, when individuals take jobs, they suffer opportunity costs that need to be balanced against the rewards they will receive. Further, if there are patterns of employment that discriminate against groups in the workforce, there are opportunity costs to the society in terms of lost talent, increased welfare payments, and the social unrest that occurs when people cannot compete fairly for the rewards of their economic system. However, as was discussed above, there are also costs of regulating risk–reward relationships that have economic, legal, and ethical dimensions. In Chapter 5 we will discuss how stakeholders with opposing interests can use the institutions of representative democracy to pursue their goals.

The Case of Public Goods: The Failure of Risk–Reward Links and Constitutive Market Responses

Public goods are goods such that if they can be used by one person they can be used by all persons. Examples are the legal system, the monetary system, and national defense. Because there is no direct link between the risk of producing these goods and the reward for that production, public goods will not be produced in the quantity demanded, and perhaps will not be produced at all. Some public goods, such as the legal system and the monetary system, are necessary conditions for the existence of markets. Hence, the constitutive rules of these two systems constitute market behavior. This shows that not all responses to market failure are regulative; some responses are constitutive.

Public goods are necessary, but why should individuals pay their fair share? If the public good is not there, an individual's small contribution will not deliver it. If the public good is already there, one gets the public good whether or not one pays for it; this is the basis of the free-rider effect. Table 4.1 illustrates the relative desirability of choices from the point of view of a self-interested consumer who wants to maximize wealth.

In Table 4.1, the first choice is for others to pay so that the good is provided, but to

TABLE 4.1
Relative Desirability of Choices

	I Pay	I Don't Pay
Others pay, public good provided	2	1
Others do not pay, public good not provided	4	3

avoid payment yourself. The second choice is for everyone to pay. The third choice is for no one to pay. The fourth and worst choice is when others do not pay and you do, since you are paying for a good you will not get. Table 4.1 shows that whether we get a public good depends completely on what others do, *as a group;* it has nothing to do with an individual's behavior. Under the assumption of rational self-interest, very few, if any, consumers will pay for a public good. Since public goods are necessary for markets, rational consumers will agree to a tax system that distributes burdens (fairly?) among all users. This is the only way to ensure that "others pay."

There is another way we can explain the free-rider effect. Consumers know how they can benefit using the money they would otherwise spend on a public good. However, it is difficult to calculate the benefits, personal or social, that will result from paying their individual fair share. As we just discussed, one's individual payments have *no effect* on the delivery of the public good. Free-riding can be explained by the desire of consumers to be relatively sure that they will receive something for their payment. The less sure they are of the link between their payment and what they get, the less likely they are to pay. Hence, we do not have to assume wealth-maximizing behavior to explain the free-rider effect. We can also explain it in terms of the desire not to harm oneself or to waste one's resources.

We can strengthen the non-self-interested interpretation of free-riding by noting that rational altruists will also be free-riders. Rational altruists, faced with a decision to pay or not pay for a public good, will see that their payment has nothing to do with the delivery of the public good, so that their payments will yield little or no benefit. Hence, altruists should not pay for a public good, but should spend their money in ways that are more likely to help others.

The need to fund public goods with taxes, then, is not necessarily the result of a selfish public; it can also be explained by the lack of compelling risk–reward link. However, taxes also interfere with the risk–reward link, since they take some of the reward that people risk their resources to get. Burdensome or misplaced taxes can inhibit the risk–reward links they are intend to promote.

In the right conditions, private organizations may provide public goods. Coase has argued that shipping companies may find it cost effective to build a lighthouse to keep their ships from going aground, even though they cannot capture the benefits other companies and individuals get.[26] In our discussion of oligopolies, below, we will see that the same incentives drive corporations to invest in R&D even though they cannot capture all the benefits from it.

The ethical aspects of public goods are fairly easy to see. Public goods serve vital social needs that make economic activity possible. Without public goods, there would be no markets. This is true even in hunter–gatherer societies, in which tradition and custom are the public goods that stabilize society. As we have discussed, all five ethical orientations can be used to justify markets, although each orientation will point to different aspects of markets.

Besides the traditional examples of public goods just discussed, social practices such as truthtelling and promise keeping are also public goods. They are available to all, but not everyone must contribute to them. If enough of us defect, however, they will disappear, and so will the economic institutions that they support.

Chapter 7 focuses on risk–reward relationships in employment, production for international markets, and making payments to foreign officials to create business opportunities. The first topic is discussed in terms of employment at will and whether government should regulate this traditional employment relationship. The second topic concerns the production of medicine for those too poor to pay for it. The third topic discusses the costs and benefits of regulations imposed by the Foreign Corrupt Practices Act and its 1988 Amendments. All three topics raise the question of market failure and success by examining the values that underlie and are promoted by markets.

Information

CONSTITUTIVE PRACTICES AND RULES

A certain amount of reliable information is *constitutive* of market activity. If we cannot trust any information about a transaction, we will not participate in it. In large, impersonal markets, institutions arise to guarantee or validate information, especially with products that are hard to evaluate or with exchanges that occur only once. A wide variety of public and private institutions and organizations perform this service: social practices such as truthtelling and promise keeping, government organizations such as the courts and federal and state legislatures, private industrial and professional associations, and magazines such as *Consumer Reports* and *PC World*.

We cannot say in advance how much or what kind of information a market needs for exchanges to occur. The quality and quantity of information will vary for capital, factor, labor, and consumer markets; for local, national, and global markets; and for the various kinds of competitive markets that exist, from pure competition to monopolies. We do know that there will be a demand for good information, and that the demand will be shaped and served by social institutions.

REGULATIVE PRACTICES AND RULES: WHEN INFORMATION FAILS

Fraud and less serious cases of misinformation are some of the most obvious cases of information failure. In fraud, a product is so misrepresented that buyers get little or nothing of what they expect. If consumers are not buying what they think they are buying, they harm themselves and send the wrong signals to producers. Consumers may tell the producer about the failure of the product. However, this secondary transaction concerning the failure of the product is inefficient.

We can understand a firm's incentive to defraud customers or misrepresent a product as a way to internalize benefits and externalize costs. In fraud, money is received by the firm but benefits are not given. In subtler cases of misrepresentation, this is not so blatant. Rather, consumers get some of what they expect, but not all. Consumers have to decide whether the discrepancy is due to a misrepresented or faulty product, or whether they misinterpreted reasonable information.

Information can fail in unintentional ways, too. Contracts are information about what will occur in the future. However, circumstances can change that make it difficult for one or both parties to fulfill their obligations. The institutions governing contracts will usually require that these contracts be met. If the losses are very great, however, these same institutions can provide relief.

All the ethical orientations can justify laws against fraud, although as we have seen, each orientation would point to different aspects of fraud to explain why it should be prohibited. Pluralism would integrate these four ethical considerations in ways we have already discussed.

Regulative law is not the primary way a voluntary market encourages reliable information. There is no way a government or private organization could monitor the trillions of exchanges that occur yearly in advanced economies. The social training that we receive as we grow up plays a significant role in promoting good information. Competition, the last market condition we will discuss, can also promote good information.

Although it is easy to speak in these generalities, the readings and cases in Chapter 8 show that the complexity of the real world does not always admit of easy solutions. Chapter 8 contains cases and readings on advertising, whistleblowing, and the kinds of information needed in international business. The first topic concerns how far advertisers should go in their attempt to represent their products as better than the competition and whether consumers can rationally evaluate information from advertising. The second topic addresses the issue of whether employee loyalty is or should be a determining factor in revealing information about improper corporate behavior. The third topic concerns the type of information businesses should give to host countries and their employees when exporting or producing dangerous products.

Competition

The two most common explanations of what drives an economic system—self-interest and competition—are related. Most economic theories rely on self-interest as the basic human motivation. As important as self-interest is, focusing on it can obscure the fact that competition results from a scarcity of desired goods, not self-interest.

To see the important role of scarcity, consider three examples. First, if there were no scarcity of desired goods, self-interested beings would not compete, since it would not be in their self-interest to do so: why would they compete for a good they can get without competition? Second, imagine a state of scarcity in which everyone is altruistically motivated to promote the good of their kinship group. In this case, people would compete to get as much as possible for their own groups. (See Hume, Chapter 2, for similar examples.)

The third example concerns computerized markets for controlling large systems, which, because of their mechanical nature, have no place for motivation of any kind, not even self-interest. The Xerox Corporation developed a computerized market system for distributing heat to large buildings that is 10% more efficient than conventional distribution methods. Each heating area is given a certain amount of "capital" and thermostats "bid" for hot or cool air, along with all other heating areas. The computer delivers more of the scarce resource to higher bidders. There are 1500 auctions a day. To make this work, certain standards and market rules are programmed into the system. There is an ideal temperature against which bids are measured. Also, bidding units cannot build up excessive capital because they happen to be in areas that need less heating or cooling.[27]

This market system for heating and cooling eliminates the need for a hierarchy program that tries to anticipate heating needs. In large systems, of which this is just one example, there is too much information, even for a computer, for central planning to work. This computerized market system has distribution and reallocation rules that intersect with bids to redistribute heating and cooling about once a minute—the *motive* behind the bidding is irrelevant to the outcome.

Competition is a dynamic of a distribution system, whereas self-interest is a dynamic of individual choice. In principle they are separable. Realistically, however, these two dynamics fit together.

CONSTITUTIVE PRACTICES AND RULES

Competition promotes allocative efficiency as long as there are clear and enforceable property rights, clear and close links between production and reward, and reliable information. Allocative efficiency within an otherwise equitable economic infrastructure would be a highly desirable state of affairs (see Appendix). Equitable market conditions legitimize demand–supply relationships, which allocative efficiency indicates are satisfied. Adam Smith made this argument more than two hundred years ago (see Chapter 3).

From the point of view of self-interest, equitable markets maximize one's opportunities. From the point of view of care, one is free to form and participate in voluntary relationships of one's choice, and one has the opportunity to design one's nonvoluntary relationships in a variety of ways. From the point of view of utility, the system is justified in at least two ways. First, people get their needs met, and so the good of all is promoted. Second, resources are not wasted, avoiding opportunity costs. From the point of view of intrinsic value, this system treats consumers fairly, since they are likely to get what they pay for. In general, competition can promote a robust economic setting in which all have the opportunity to flourish.

As good as competition is under ideal conditions, ideal conditions rarely obtain. Without clearly defined and enforced property rights, competition can lead to negative externalities, such as the destruction of natural resources (Chapter 6), and it can provide incentives to externalize risks (Chapter 7) and give inaccurate information (Chapter 8). Competition will not satisfy the demand for public goods. As economic systems become more complex, individuals and organizations can find more ways to promote their interests at the expense of others and the group as a whole.[28]

Four Competitive Market Structures

Not all goods are produced and distributed in the same competitive environment. Some are best produced in systems of perfect competition, others in monopolistic competition, others in oligopolistic competition, and some in natural monopolies. These four competitive environments are described below.

Perfect competition exists when there are so many sellers of an undifferentiated product, such as grain, that no seller can affect the price. Of course, this does not mean that nothing can affect the price. Government import and export policies, agricultural subsidies, currency inflation, and natural disasters all affect price. Perfect competition can be affected only by forces large enough to affect the overall market, and individual producers, as a rule, are too small to do this. From the point of view of social welfare, this is a good feature of perfect competition. Individual producers cannot manipulate the system to their benefit, imposing costs on others.

Monopolistic competition occurs when there are many firms selling similar products that are differentiated only by things such as brand name, delivery, or service. Dry cleaners and branded sporting goods shops are in monopolistic competition. These businesses are monopolies because no firm offers exactly what the others do, but they compete with each other because the differences between their products are small enough so that consumers can find substitutes. Typically, barriers to entry are low, so there are many businesses.

Oligopolistic competition arises when high entry costs and economies of scale make it difficult for more than a small number of suppliers to succeed. Oligopolistic competition occurs in industries such as automobile manufacturing and commercial airlines. The production and pricing policies of one firm in an oligopoly can easily affect the pricing and production policies of other firms. Since each firm supplies a large percentage of the demand, there are huge gains to be made from manipulating the market.

Natural monopolies occur when entry costs are so high that only one producer is possible in a distribution area, as was thought to be the case with utilities. These monopolies are called natural because the monopolies result from market forces, not the influence of suppliers.

Since the court-imposed breakup of AT&T in 1984, natural monopolies no longer seem so natural. The fate of AT&T has shown that the delivery system of utilities can be altered to open the door to competition. In April 1996, the Federal Energy Regulatory Commission required electric utilities to open up their transmission lines to other producers. This applies only to the wholesale level, but it is estimated that this will save consumers billions of dollars.[29] Government implements these changes by altering the property rights utilities have to their physical infrastructure. In the past, utilities used their property rights to exclude other producers from using their transmission lines. To promote competition, government has modified that right.

REGULATIVE PRACTICES AND RULES: WHEN COMPETITION FAILS

Given these four kinds of competitive environments, what counts as competitive failure? Using perfect competition as our standard, the last three market structures are *all* forms of market failure. In each case, sellers can get prices that are higher than they would be in a perfectly competitive environment. We can also view these latter three market structures as different *successful* markets, each of which can fail in its own way. Adopting this latter point of view can help us understand why government does not regulate competitive relationships in two of four market structures, and of those markets it does regulate, why it regulates them differently.

In perfect competition and monopolistic competition, the number of firms and low entry costs keep production high and prices low. Government regulation to maintain competitive markets is directed largely at firms in oligopolies and monopolies. It is only in these kinds of markets that firms can affect the overall market.

One way the United States regulates oligopolistic markets is with antitrust law. The Sherman Act (1890), for example, was enacted to prevent monopolistic business activities. The Act was a political response to the public belief that monopolies were unfair and economically inefficient. The Sherman Act prevented business from engaging in some types of wealth-generating behavior, but like all policies, it had some unexpected consequences. Businesses with labor problems used the Sherman Act to end strikes, arguing that union activity was a form of monopoly. The Clayton Act (1914) prevented using the Sherman Act this way. The move to protect labor was further amplified by the Wagner Act (1935), passed during the Depression when public trust of business was low. The Wagner Act, businesses argued, gave unions monopolistic power that could harm workers and business: it allowed unions to force all workers to join the union, and it gave unions the right to strike in sectors that were crucial to national interests. In an attempt to address this, Congress passed the Taft–Hartley Act (1947), which, among other things, allowed nonunion workers to work in a union shop and gave the U.S. Attorney General the power to order an 80-day cooling off period for strikes that affected the national interest.

The 57 year progression from the Sherman Act to the Taft–Hartley Act represents the way a representative democracy shapes economic relationships. How a society can and should integrate the interests of relevant stakeholders is a function of institutional and more transient social, political, legal, economic, and technological factors. These factors are impossible to predict because they are complex and constantly changing. Hence, situations such as the one above, in which one law corrects for the unexpected consequences of another, do not necessarily show that regulation is hopelessly confused; this kind of adjustment is what we should expect in a rapidly changing representative democracy.

In oligopolies, government uses rules and fines to prevent anticompetitive behavior. In natural monopolies, government participates directly in regulating prices and supply, usually through state public utility commissions. In neither case does the government try to transform the *structure* of these oligopolistic or monopolistic markets into perfectly competitive structures. Oligopolies and monopolies produce goods that have supply and demand characteristics that make pure competition impossible. Because of this, imperfect markets are the most efficient way to supply these goods. Government regulation and court action try to provide incentives within these imperfect markets to encourage firms to produce and price their goods as they would in a perfectly competitive market.

The view that cars and electricity cannot be produced in a perfectly competitive environment is almost too trivial to mention, expect that it gives us a different way to think about market success and failure. If cars and electricity can be produced *only* in oligopolies or monopolies, it is odd to say that these markets are failures, and that a perfect market that could not produce these goods is our standard for success.

This odd statement makes sense, however, if we distinguish between market outcomes and market structures. We can use perfect competition to evaluate production and pricing *outcomes* in these imperfect markets. We should not use perfect competition to evaluate the *structure* of these imperfect markets. Referring to oligopolistic and monopolistic market structures as failures can blur the distinction between two kinds of market failures that we need to keep distinct. Let us call these *contingent* and *structural* market failure.

Contingent market failure results from market behavior that is not intrinsic to the structure of the market. For example, there is nothing in the structure of the consumer lending market that implies that lenders will deceive borrowers or that borrowers will deceive lenders. The problem of deceptive practices in consumer lending is contingent on how the motives of decision makers intersect with market institutions and incentives. Since market structures and processes need good information, we can use perfect information to evaluate the outcomes *and* structure of markets. For example, truthtelling is important when lenders advertise their services, when borrowers give information about the purpose of the loan, and in determining the final price of the loan.

Structural market failure results from behavior that is intrinsic to the structure of particular markets. Generating electricity and automobile manufacturing have intrinsic features that make perfectly competitive markets impossible. For structural market failure, perfect competition can serve as a standard to evaluate production and pricing outcomes, but not to evaluate the market structures and processes that generate those outcomes.

Oligopolies and monopolies produce technological innovation with significant positive externalities. Joseph Schumpeter and John Kenneth Galbraith argue that firms in an oligopoly are more likely to engage in research and development for two related reasons: they have the resources to do so, and they are in a position to recover more benefits from their innovations than they would be if there were many producers.[30] This innovation is valuable to society as whole, generating returns that have been estimated to be three times the value captured by the producer.[31] In general, the more benefits a firm can appropriate from R&D, the more likely they are to do it. As Samuelson and Nordhaus point out, not all innovation comes from large corporations,[32] but even if only half of all innovation comes from large firms, that is a benefit we must consider when evaluating the impacts of an oligopolistic market structure.

There is also reason to believe that oligopolistic and monopolistic behavior is not as inefficient as we might think. One study puts the overall market loss from monopolies at less than 0.1% of GNP, and another puts the loss between 0.5 and 2% of GNP, with data pointing to the lower number.[33] These costs are very low. When we add the benefit of innovation, it is hard to justify using government resources to further reduce these costs.

There are two ways we can account for the surprisingly low costs of monopolies. The first is that these studies were done in the United States, which has had broad and wide ranging antitrust legislation since 1890. Allowing for the fact that Republican and Democratic administrations have enforced these laws differently, they still provide an incentive for large firms to act in ways that do not invite government action. Second, the low costs are consistent with the general view that markets will tend to find the most efficient ways to produce goods. As messy as business–government relationships are in the United States, these studies suggest that the outcomes of these relationships, at least regarding competition, are fairly good.

In Chapter 9, James H. Michelman argues that the duties and values of competition are incompatible with the ethical values of care and compassion. Tom L. Beauchamp's case seems to support Michelman's view. However, as we discussed, there are several kinds of competition. We have also seen that competition is only one feature of economic markets: property rights must be secured, risk relationships must be defined, and information must be reliable. The pieces by Michelman and Beauchamp need to be analyzed using these standards, too. Norman E. Bowie's article takes a broader understanding of markets. He argues that competition in the international arena has special problems because property, risk–reward relationships, and information are treated differently in different countries. This allows competitive practices to erode these market conditions, as in the case "Tee-Shirts and Tears." Competition also gives large corporations, such as Boeing and Microsoft, incentives to modify market conditions to promote their own perceived good. Bowie goes on to argue that international trade regimes and organizations are beginning to secure these market conditions and their underlying ethical values.

INDIVIDUALS IN ORGANIZATIONS: GOALS OR CONTRACTS?

This section examines how the ethical values imbedded in the four market conditions are inherited by organizations. The ethical values and goals of organizations, in turn, are inherited by the individuals within it. The arrow of inheritance also moves directly from markets to individuals. These relationships are portrayed in Figure 4.1.

The arrow of inheritance also points in the other direction. In Chapters 1 and 2 we saw that individuals bring values and patterns of behavior into organizations (see the Feuerstein example in the section on Intrinsic Value, Chapter 3). Organizations influence markets in several ways: advertising, R&D, promoting production and distribution efficiencies, pricing-policies, and shaping government policy. In some instances, individuals can affect markets. These relationships are portrayed in Figure 4.2.

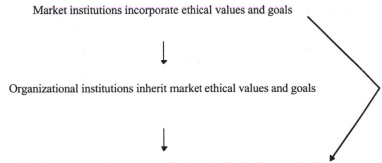

Market institutions incorporate ethical values and goals

Organizational institutions inherit market ethical values and goals

Individuals inherit market and organizational ethical values and goals

Figure 4.1

Many social and political issues, such as those concerned with race, gender, and family structure, arise in organizational contexts. There are at least four reasons for this. First, as Figures 4.1 and 4.2 illustrate, organizations are the place where individual, family, civic, and market values intersect. Second, organizations distribute scarce resources for which there is enormous competition. Third, because organizations must constantly decide how to act, they need to resolve basic value conflicts that inhibit action. Fourth, unlike the larger society, organizations are small enough to enact and monitor programs to deal with problems.[34] This makes organizations especially useful for those who want to pursue larger social goals. On the institutional view, organizational conflicts are not isolated instances; they reflect conflicting values in the institutional environment.

Consider the S and R case. Jameson and Mamet are dealing with conflicting institutional values. *No matter what decision they make, they take an ethical position.* Relocation, to promote shareholder value, suggests that shareholders are most important, as illustrated in Figure 4.3. Staying in Frieberg, to promote the well-being of their families and of the community, suggests family and community values are most important, as illustrated in Figure 4.4. On the institutional view, Jameson and Mamet's decision will be *case specific.* It will reflect their view of how the institutions and facts intersect at the time they are making the decision. In a different situation, they could rank the values differently.

Jameson and Mamet are facing a conflict between ethical principles, not a conflict

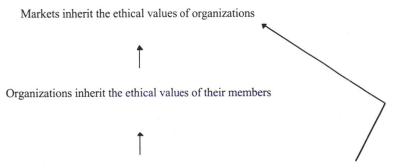

Markets inherit the ethical values of organizations

Organizations inherit the ethical values of their members

Individuals are guided by the ethical values of self-interest, family-friends, group welfare, and/or intrinsic value (Each person has a unique interpretation and mix of these four principles.)

Figure 4.2

Market institutions incorporate the value of promoting shareholder interest

As officers, Jameson and Mamet rely on the value of promoting the interests of
shareholders

Jameson and Mamet value family and community

Figure 4.3

between ethics and economics. In the language of Chapter 2, the two officers are experiencing cognitive disequilibrium because the decision-making strategies that have worked in the past fail in this case. Cognitive–developmental theory suggests they will seek a new strategy to reduce their disequilibrium. To do this they need to reevaluate the facts of the case, the organizational setting, and/or the institutional setting. Cognitive–developmental theory also suggests Jameson and Mamet will not reject troublesome principles that have worked in the past. Instead, they will look for a way to incorporate their previous decision-making principles—self, care, group welfare, and intrinsic value—in a new way. This new reasoning strategy does not have to satisfy all four sets of principles in every case. The new strategy only has to give Jameson and Mamet a way to handle their present dilemma in a way that preserves the integrity of these four principles (see introduction to pluralism in Chapter 3).

The multidirectional value influence that occurs between individuals, organizations, and markets is especially prominent in international business. An organization that develops within one institutional setting will often have to make adjustments when moving to a country with different institutional values and expectations (see the articles by De George and Werhane in Chapter 6). Doing business in a foreign country can change the business, individuals, and organizations in the foreign country, and even the foreign country itself.

A word of caution: individuals, organizations, and markets are constantly affecting and being affected by each other in a number of ways. The static relationships portrayed in Figures 4.1–4.4 are snapshots of processes that are always in motion. Taking a snap-

Markets incorporate ethical values and goals, one of which is to promote the interests of
shareholders

As officers, Jameson and Mamet rely on the value of promoting family and community

Jameson and Mamet value family and community

Figure 4.4

shot can help us understand how a process works as long as we remember that the goal is to understand the process, not the snapshot.

Two Views of Organizations: Contracts and Goals

There are two different views of economic organizations: the goal-seeking view and the contract view. Both views are founded on well-known institutional values. According to the *goal view,* organizations are hierarchical decision-making entities with functional areas designed to reach a goal. Organizational members should be motivated by the institutional values of loyalty and teamwork, not by self-interest.[35] We evaluate an organization by how efficiently it reaches its goals.

The *contract view* asserts that corporations are created and maintained by individuals who contract with each other to pursue their own individual interests.[36] The contract view also holds that organizations are hierarchical decision-making entities with functional areas designed to reach a goal, but that the goal is valuable only because it helps individuals to pursue their individual interests. There is no loyalty to the corporation itself, which is nothing more than a nexus of contracts. (See Duska, "Whistleblowing and Employee Loyalty," in Chapter 8 for some implications of this view.) We evaluate an organization by how well it satisfies the interests of its members.

The goal and contract views appeal to different institutions and values. The goal-directed view emphasizes group value, teamwork, and respect for authority. Depending on how the contract view is constructed, it can emphasize self-interest, individual rights, and/or personal integrity.

THE GOAL-BASED VIEW OF ORGANIZATIONS

The goal-directed view of organizations is the oldest and most influential view of corporations. Max Weber argued that we need to distinguish business organizations from societies because the former are goal directed whereas the latter are not.[37] Herbert Simon has argued that it is a corporation's goal that differentiates it from other corporations. The goal is the corporation's "ethical premise," which is given to, but not evaluated by, its members.[38] We use this ethical premise to evaluate the corporation's functional structure and the behavior of its officers and employees. Of the four ethical orientations—self-interest, care, formal groups and their interests, and intrinsic human value—the goal view takes the third value as dominant, but limits it to the level of organizations.

The structure of the corporation depends on the nature of its product, the state of technology, and the market and institutional structures in which it operates. An efficient corporation in an oligopolistic market will be different from an efficient corporation in a perfect market. For example, automobile manufacturers have functional areas devoted to political relationships because public policy affects their product and market. Small farms, on the other hand, will not have this functional area, although they may belong to a trade association that does.

Market structure alone does not determine organizational structure. For example, in early 1996, Microsoft had twice the market value of GM, and had a near monopoly in personal computer operating systems. Despite its large size and virtual monopoly, Microsoft spent very little on lobbying, placing its first lobbyist in Washington, D.C. in 1995.[39] It did not need lobbyists because there was little public pressure to regulate Microsoft. Microsoft's strong market position did not clearly threaten important social institutions: it was not a necessary good, as was electricity; it posed no risk to public or personal safety, as did automobiles; its price was usually imbedded in the computer, so consumers were not aware of it; and its price seemed reasonable when bought separately. Microsoft does, however, face many legal issues about protecting its products from illegal copying, its large market share, and its marketing practices. It retains batteries of law firms to handle these issues. (See "Two Roads to China: Nice, and Not So Nice" in Chapter 9, for Microsoft's strategy dealing with China.)

Just as market structure influences corporate behavior, corporate structure influences individual behavior. Corporate members are supposed to promote the goal of the corporation. However, only a few upper-level corporate officers deal with this goal directly. Most officers and employees work to promote the goals of their functional areas. If the organization's structure fits its product, technology, and market, promoting the goals of one's functional area promotes the corporate goal.

Corporate structure can break down at three different levels. At the *market–organization* level, a corporation may fail to adapt to changing demand, technology, or institutional market and political structures. At the *organizational–functional unit* level, different functional areas may compete with each other in ways that work against corporate goals. At the *functional unit–individual person* level, individuals may work to promote their individual interests at the expense of their functional unit. This last concern, known as an agency problem, deserves extra attention.

Agency problems arise when the interests of a manager, who is an agent for the owners, conflict with corporate goals. For example, suppose that a company wants to buy S and R. According to goal theory, Jameson and Mamet should do what is best for S and R's owners. However, if selling S and R would have bad consequences for Jameson and Mamet, they have strong incentives to act as agents for themselves, not the owners.

Agency problems also interfere with a firm's ability to gather and distribute information. For example, if Jameson and Mamet reject an offer to buy the company that would be good for shareholders, they will have to misrepresent the information they give to shareholders. Since information comes in networks, and not in discrete packets, they will have to withhold or misrepresent many facts to the Board of Directors and the owners, who will have bad information for making other decisions (see Paine, Part I). Further, Jameson and Mamet will have to make side-deals with other officers who must collude with them to misrepresent the facts. These officers are likely to demand compensation for their risks, further draining corporate resources. Finally, all the officers involved must interfere with the internal monitoring systems to prevent their collusion from being revealed. Although this example uses upper-level officers, agency problems can arise at all levels of management.

Another kind of conflict with corporate goals occurs because professionals in functional areas such as law, accounting, and engineering have responsibilities that extend beyond the corporation. As an officer of the court, for example, a general counsel has a responsibility to report wrongdoing that other officers do not. When faced with corporate wrongdoing, a general counsel may have to violate his duty to the company or his duty to the court. Whether or not the general counsel's action is self-interested is irrelevant from the point of view of corporate goals. What matters is that the behavior interferes with corporate goals.

When individual values conflict with organizational values, what should the organization do? Utilitarianism provides one answer to this question. It defines the good in terms of a goal. If we apply this to corporations, then corporate members should promote corporate goals. This does not mean that we have to rely on people's ethical commitment to the firm's well-being. We can find other ways to encourage people to promote corporate goals. For example, if we think people are self-interested, we should reward them, perhaps in terms of compensation, for promoting corporate goals. If we think people are committed to their families, we might offer better benefits packages and leave allowances. The best situation is when people are loyal to a firm, since fewer resources are needed to encourage them to be team players. If we believe that people are primarily interested in being treated fairly, we will make it clear how our hiring, promotion, and compensation strategies are based on fairness. In Cuba, for example, a manager of a Spanish-owned luxury hotel has monthly meetings with all employees, including maids and gardeners, in which he opens the books and explains the hotel's finances. These meetings are not required by the Cuban government, but he believes it shows the staff that they are being treated fairly.[40]

Although utilitarianism can help us understand the dynamics of goal-seeking corporations, it is less helpful for understanding how corporate goals themselves are formed and evaluated. Simon said that a corporate goal is *given* to the members of the corporation, but someone or some group must decide what that goal is. In the early days of corporate activity it was easy to identify corporate goals. Corporations were formed to provide specific goods such as canals and ferries. These corporate charters were accepted by state legislatures on utilitarian grounds: the goals they pursued promoted group welfare. Today, however, corporate charters do not specify corporate goals in this way. How are corporate goals chosen?

John Ladd, relying on Simon's view of the corporation, argues that corporate goals are determined mechanistically within a corporation.[41] Because of this, these goals have no moral status or content. Kenneth Goodpaster, responding to Ladd, argues that corporate goals are not mechanistically generated. Goodpaster argues that corporate goals are influenced by the values of the decision makers.[42] These decision makers can, if they desire, establish ethical corporate goals, such as not exploiting the poor. For example, Levi-Strauss has a commitment not to exploit third world workers: it has refused some low-cost opportunities as a result.[43] In another case, B. Dalton, Booksellers contributed money and management expertise to literacy campaigns.[44]

Milton Friedman also believes that corporations have a moral impact on society, but that if corporate leaders try to promote ethical values directly, they will do more harm than good (Chapter 6). Friedman argues that the best thing business people can do in a free market is to provide a good product at a good price. This strategy will satisfy demand with minimal use of resources, and so will yield the most profits. Helping the poor, giving aid to education, or supporting the ballet are worthy causes, but businesses should not do these things for three major reasons. First, the money belongs to the owners, so managers have no right to give it away (intrinsic value theory). Second, business leaders have no expertise in these matters, so they are likely to waste resources that could be used for the common good (utilitarianism). Finally, corporate leaders are not elected officials, and so they have no right to transform society. If citizens want a social transformation, they can vote for it (intrinsic value theory tied to a view of representative democracy).

Friedman uses utilitarian and rights reasoning to support his view: first, we will all be better off if business sticks to business, and second, doing otherwise violates the rights of shareholders and citizens. Let us focus on the utilitarian reasoning. Friedman argues that corporate goals fit into the larger social goal of producing goods and services. It is this larger social goal that legitimizes corporate goals. His argument is similar to Hume's and Mill's (Chapter 2), who argued that the best way to promote the good of all, at least in most cases, is to follow accepted rules and practices. These rules and practices survive *because* they are useful. Mill believed that we should change rules when doing so would clearly benefit all, but we should change the rules in accordance with clear legal and legislative constraints that keep such changes orderly. Only in the most exceptional and drastic circumstances should we actively break rules. Friedman's view, applied to the S and R case, would imply that Jameson and Mamet should make the best business decision for S and R, and let society take care of the rest.

Utilitarianism also directs us to look at the society in which the corporation is embedded. If corporate goals conflict with more important social goals, the corporation can lose. Let us consider an easy case first: child pornography. Child pornography violates and abuses children, and panders to some of our worst qualities. Despite the amount of money that can be made from this material, most societies believe that the product is so harmful that they should not allow it to be produced or sold. There is no public debate about this issue because we agree that stopping child pornography is sensible and necessary.

A case that is not quite so clear concerns the "cop killer" bullet. Cop killer bullets are designed to penetrate body armor, like bulletproof vests, that police use in raids. Few criminals wear body armor. There is a federal law that prohibits the public sale of these bullets. In 1994, a company designed a body armor piercing bullet that does not fall under the federal law because it is made of plastic, not metal as specified by the legislation. The manufacturer argued it was legal, so it could sell it.[45]

Government officials and the press viewed this as a conflict between the company's sales goals and the need for public safety. Most uses of utilitarian reasoning would argue against producing, or at least selling this bullet. The manufacturer temporarily stopped all sales of the bullet until Congress could look at the issue again. The goal of the manufacturer to create and dominate a new market niche for these bullets was overridden by the social goal to protect police officers in dangerous situations. When the manufacturer saw this, it revised its corporate goals to become a "good corporate citizen."[46] In this case, corporate goals were chosen that would fit better with dominant social institutions and values.

The goal view of corporations helps us understand and evaluate corporate behavior at the market–organizational level and at the organization–functional unit level. There are, however, empirical and conceptual problems with the goal view of corporations that limit its usefulness. The central empirical problem is locating the goal. Keeley gives several reasons why it is difficult to show that organizational members share a common corporate goal.[47] He argues that what we take to be corporate goals are the goals that a few executives have *for* the corporation. These are not goals *of* the corporation. We need to understand more than these goals to understand corporate behavior. We also need to understand the interests and goals of groups and individuals that influence corporate activity, such as labor, suppliers, consumers, and owners.

Critics of the goal approach argue that corporations are better understood as instruments that people use to fulfill a variety of individual goals.[48] On this view, corporations are systems created by contracts for the pursuit of personal interests. These corporate systems provide an institutional context in which members determine corporate goals, strategy, labor relationships, and all the other corporate activities and relationships.

THE CONTRACT-BASED VIEW OF ORGANIZATIONS

If we could contract for everything we need, we would not need corporations. For example, if we were producing a product by ourselves and wanted to expand production, or needed accounting help, we would contract with others to provide these services. These people, in turn, could contract with others to supply their needs. Everything could be produced by these loose aggregates of individual contracts.

Unfortunately, loose aggregates of contracts have three connected problems: (1) collecting and distributing information, (2) agency problems, and (3) liability problems. Formal organizations help reduce these problems.

Information Problems

Let us go back to the beginning of corporate life in the United States. Imagine that you are entrepreneur in the late 1700s and that you have contracted with a city to build a canal. To build the canal using individual contracts, you must contract with several individuals to provide different services: acquiring capital, research into other canal projects, locating equipment, labor needs, surveyors, and the list goes on. If a new need arises, you will have to revise existing contracts or form new ones. Information will travel along contractual connections. If you want to get a message to someone who is five contractual connections away, then that information will be transmitted four times before it gets to the person who needs it. If inconsistent information comes to that person from a different source, you and the person who sent the inconsistent information will have to use existing or new contractual relationships to resolve the issue.

You cannot solve this information problem by hiring someone to skip the intermediate steps to give information to your distant contractual cousin, since there is no contract between you and your distant contractual cousin. If you form such a contract, you will have to make sure it does not violate or interfere with intermediary contractual connections. There will also have to be some method for monitoring the accuracy and use of the information. This will result in high *transaction costs*. A transaction cost is what it costs to transfer a good or a service from one process or entity to another.[49]

Corporations reduce transaction costs by substituting a hierarchy for the loose aggregate of contracts. This hierarchy is responsible for transmitting, coordinating, and monitoring the use of information. One officer is in charge of the organization, who is answerable to a board of directors. A number of secondary officers run various functional areas: finance, accounting, production, labor, etc. Each of these officers has subordinates to perform specific tasks. These functional areas collect, interpret, and transmit information. Whenever a corporation can produce a product less expensively than an aggregate of individual contracts, corporations will drive out the loose aggregates, as long as there is a social and legal infrastructure that makes corporations possible.

In general, the larger the corporation, the more difficult informational problems will be. In 1995 Monsanto lost a big sale to a competitor because of internal information problems. A salesperson was worried that the sale might fall apart, but he could not get this information to the right people in time to save the sale. In response to these kinds of problems, Monsanto and other large corporations have created a new functional area: information distribution, the head of which is called the Chief Information Officer. The CIO does not deal with the technology of information distribution, but with the informational needs and relationships between different functional areas.[50]

Agency Problems

Oliver E. Williamson argues that corporations are necessary to monitor and control the self-interested motivations of individuals.[51] In an open contracting environment, there are many opportunities for people to break agreements without detection. In the Canal case, suppose you have contracted with a person to travel to different cities to investigate canal building technology. The person asks for payment that will cover travel and opportunity costs. You give some of this money at the time the contract is signed. According to agency theory, this person now has an incentive to visit fewer cities and to collect less information on the visits the person does make. When the person returns with a report and demands final payment, you cannot easily tell if the report is accurate and well researched unless you spend time and money doing so. If you spend money and time to evaluate the information seriously, the value to you of the previous transaction is reduced. If you contract with someone else to evaluate the information, this again adds to the cost, and you face agency problems with this new person.

There is another problem. If you find out that the person did not fulfill all aspects of the contract, your options for recovery are limited and costly. If you find out this information before making final payment, and you do not pay, the person may sue you in civil court to enforce the contract. If you have already paid, you can sue in civil court to recover your payment. You may lose, however; and even if you win you still need to get payment from the person. This may require you to go back to court. If you try to avoid these postcontract problems *ex ante* by building monitoring and evaluation into the contract, you pay the transaction costs sooner rather than later.

The corporation reduces these problems by using hierarchies to monitor and enforce agreements. Although corporations can be more efficient than loose aggregates of individual contracts, they are not without their own costs. Adding a layer of management to coordinate production and information requires more payroll and a way to organize and integrate the management layer itself. The more complex the governance system, the more it costs to maintain and coordinate it. Despite this, corporations can still be less costly than loose aggregates of contracts. When these cost savings are present, individuals have incentives to form them.

Liability Problems

In a loose aggregate of contracts, mistakes can result in great personal losses for the contractors. If, in the course of building the canal, you damage property or harm someone, you can be sued in civil court. Corporations transfer this risk from the owners and officers to the corporation (see the discussion of how corporate structure limits liability in the discussion of property, above).

A Deeper Look at the Contract View: The Negotiated
Interactive System View of Corporations

According to the negotiated interactive system (NIS) view of corporations, a corporation is a micromarket created by contracts. This micromarket is an interactive system of relationships in which people negotiate for rights and benefits by taking on responsibilities and burdens. This interactive system *is* the corporation; there is nothing over and above it that has goals. Organizational goals exist, but they are expressions of what the controlling parties want for the organization. Unity of action results from agreement about which activities to undertake. As those agreements change, so do the organizational goals.[52] Of the four kinds of ethical values we examined—promoting self-interest, care, promoting group interest, and respecting intrinsic human value—the NIS view takes the first and fourth values as organizationally dominant.

Michael Keeley argues that the NIS view accounts better for the diversity of goals we find in organizations.[53] Organizations can provide their members with pay, security, prestige, career enhancement, and medical and retirement benefits. Employees trade their time and talent for different subsets of these goods. On this view, it is the rich diversity of what people can get from a corporation that makes it viable.

Manuel Velasquez argues that the NIS view is superior in another way, too. The contract model explains better how people use alliances and information to increase their bargaining power in organizations.[54] If goals define the corporations, these alliances would be abhorred. Agency problems are viewed differently in the NIS than in the goal view. For the NIS, we expect agency problems, and internal contracts will try to correct for them. For the goal view, agency problems are external to true corporate activity. They can be dealt with by training or other methods to get employees to identify more closely with the firm.

As micromarkets, corporations control scarce internal resources by setting up an institutional infrastructure that defines and enforces property rights, controls risk–reward relationships, distributes and monitors information, and defines the competitive climates between and within the various functional areas. Unfortunately, we cannot evaluate micromarkets as we do macromarkets. In macromarkets efficiency can be achieved only if contracting parties have roughly equal power. Otherwise, powerful contractors can force deals that are good for them, but undesirable for others and for the group as a whole, which leads to allocative inefficiency.

In a corporate micromarket we know in advance that internal contracts will be made between people with different organizational powers. It is these power differentials that make the corporation more efficient than unorganized contracting in an open market, as we discussed above. These power relationships can change through renegotiation, but there must be some power relationships, or we do not have an organization at all.

The NIS view of the corporation seems to present us with a paradox. The corporation is organized along market principles, but the inherent inequality of power prevents us from evaluating it as a market. If we cannot use market principles to evaluate corporate micromarkets, how can we evaluate them? Zammuto suggests four ways to do this.

Four Ways to Evaluate NISs.   Zammuto argues that we can interpret NISs as relative systems, developmental systems, power-driven systems, or microsocial systems.[55] Each interpretation carries with it different evaluate standards.

A Relativistic Approach to NIS.   Connally, Conlon, and Deutsch argue that there is no reason to favor any one of the many constituencies that make up a corporation.[56] To rank them by using one value or another would arbitrarily make one group more important than the other. All we can do is describe what goes on.

Keeley argues that the relativistic approach makes an ethical claim in spite of itself, viz., everyone is equal, and so no one has the right to give one group more power than others.[57] However, as we have noted, the corporation is an entity in which some people control the property, influence the risks, regulate the information, and control the competitive environment of others. It may be that in an abstract sense we are all equal, but we are not all equal when we show up for work. We have an organizational place defined by powers and limitations.

Wielding power is not limited to executives. In a tight labor market, workers can easily drive up wages and switch companies often. This may be good for their careers, but not always for the companies they leave behind. Suppliers and buyers can also have conflicts. Suppose S and R tells one of its suppliers it is moving to Taiwan in 6 months, and the supplier raises prices in violation of their contract. By the time S and R can get court action to order delivery at the contract price, they will not need the supplier anymore. To continue with production, they pay the higher price.

Is paying off the supplier the best way to handle the problem? The relativistic approach has no answer, since to give an answer would arbitrarily favor one group. Would it have been wrong for S and R to retaliate with a hostile takeover? Again, the relativistic approach can have no answer. Going back to the case as described in S and R (A), saying that all parties are equal does not help Jameson and Mamet solve their problem.

On the contrary, their problem rests, in part, on their belief that the competing interests, if not equal, all deserve consideration.

The inability of the relativistic view to guide decision making is a central weakness from a management point of view. Managers do not have the luxury of contemplating abstract equality. They need a way to evaluate information so they can choose a course of action.

A Developmental Approach to NIS.   The developmental approach, which Zammuto prefers, is the view that corporations should try to meet as many of its constituents' expectations as possible. Like the relativistic approach, no constituency is valued more than others, but it does give management some direction in making decisions. The right corporate decision is the one that satisfies the most constituencies. Too often, managers see conflict as a win–lose situation. The developmental approach urges managers to expand or alter corporate relationships so that conflicts are reduced or disappear[58] (see the discussion of moral imagination in Chapter 1).

Keeley argues that the developmental view gives us no way to evaluate the preferences of various constituencies. Suppose S and R stays in Frieberg and at the next negotiation labor wants more money, more benefits, and a shorter work week, and there is nothing in the labor market that would warrant this preference. Or what about an ineffective executive who will leave only with an exorbitant severance package? These are preferences of constituencies, but should management satisfy them?

The developmental approach also does not help managers when they are faced with true win–lose situations. Jameson and Mamet see no options other than staying or relocating, and each option has bad consequences for different groups. It is because they are implicitly using a developmental approach that Jameson and Mamet are having such problems.

A Power-Oriented Approach to NIS.   Power in an organization can stem from several sources. In this discussion we will focus on the power people have because they control resources critical to the firm. These people have a bargaining position superior to those who do not control such resources. On this view, powerful people get more, but they *deserve* more, because without them the company would fail.[59]

In a perfect market in which capital, labor, and information flow freely, this would be a plausible model. People who were uniquely talented would know their value and so would others. Giving more to them would seem justified. However, we are not in a perfect market, and people can acquire power by controlling scarce resources for all sorts of reasons. Consider the case of "greenmail." In the 1980s, corporate raiders would sometimes raid a company they did not intend to acquire. They would buy enough stock to make their takeover bid credible, and use their voting power to cause trouble for management. Their real goal was to get management to buy back their stock at a premium, or get some other lucrative deal.[60]

These raiders held critical voting resources. Their power stemmed not from what they added, however, but from what they could take away. They could interfere with corporate operations in a way that would eventually lower the value of the company. To avoid harm to the company and themselves, rational managers bought out the greenmailers as soon as they could. On the power analysis, greenmailers deserve their money just as much as marketing executives who triple sales.

At first glance, Jameson and Mamet have the power to make the relocation decision. However, other stakeholders also have the power to affect the decision. Unions, and perhaps the community, can use legal institutions to interfere with the move. Suppliers could make life very difficult for S and R in the time between the decision to move and the move itself. Workers could slow down in a variety of undetectable ways. Sabotage is also possible. CMP tools have very low tolerances. If the parts are just outside specifications, they may work for the first 5000 to 6000 operations, but then will begin to deteriorate. Because the manufacturing process is so complex, this deterioration will be difficult to detect until the part fails completely.[61] Shipping defective units could ruin the reputation of S and R.

The power approach will not help Jameson and Mamet make their relocation decision, but using it as a tool of analysis can help them gather relevant information. Part of what they need to do is resolve the conflicts between groups that have power to affect the decision.

A Microsocial Approach to NIS.   This approach, which Keeley favors, uses traditional standards of justice to evaluate corporate relationships.[62] Keeley argues that how we are treated in the workplace is crucial to individual well-being. We spend a great deal of time at work, and our job affects how others view us. Pay scales determine where our children go to school and where we live, both of which can affect our rights and well-being. Labor does not move as fast as capital, and this power imbalance is a part of the market. Corporations inherit these imbalances. According to the microsocial approach, we need some standards that guide internal corporate relationships to make sure that no party can arbitrarily use power to satisfy ends that harm all or impinge on the rights of others. It does not matter whether the person arbitrarily using power is a labor leader or business executive, janitor or board member.

Keeley's point is as much a descriptive point as a prescriptive one. The agreements that we make in a corporation will affect the rights and duties, benefits and burdens of ourselves and others. We choose one distribution over another because we prefer it. Keeley asks us to examine what determines our preferences for one distribution over another. He answers using familiar terms: our preferences are determined by self-interest, care, group welfare, and considerations of human intrinsic value. Although these values are violated at times, few of us are willing to give them up.

One problem with the microsocial view is that it is unlikely that these standards can be applied within corporations as they are applied outside corporations. As we have seen, the purpose of the corporation is to create power relationships that do not occur in an open contracting environment. It is this power to decide and monitor that reduces transaction costs. It is not at all clear how to apply standards such as justice in artificial social environments such as corporations. If we take the evolutionary view of ethics suggested by Mary Midgley (Chapter 2, Care), we can put the point this way. Justice and fairness developed within social institutions in which people were assumed to be equal in some fundamental sense. There is no reason to think that these concepts apply in the same ways to social systems that are unequal by design and that people join voluntarily. (See Werhane on employment at will in Chapter 7.)

The contractual view of the corporation has become more popular, but has not supplanted the older and more traditional goal view. In what follows, we will see if there is a way to integrate these two views.

GOALS AND CONTRACTS: AN INTEGRATED PERSPECTIVE

Herbert Simon and Douglass North can help us integrate some of the insights of the goal view and the contract view of organizations. We will begin with Simon.

Simon argues that the contract view, as espoused by Williamson, cannot explain how authority, reward, identification, and coordination work in organizations.[63]

Authority Relationships

According to Williamson, employees are hired using "incomplete contracts" because employee tasks cannot be fully specified in advance. Hierarchical authority is necessary to make sure that people do their jobs in the most efficient way possible. In the absence of authority, employees will shirk, increasing transaction costs.

Simon argues that authority–employee relationships do not work in this way. Typically, authorities ask employees to reach some goal: fix this hinge, reach a sales quota, design a circuit. The employee must decide the best way to achieve that goal. *How* the employee achieves the goal is crucial. The employee can reach the goal quickly and efficiently or slowly and inefficiently. If this process is to be monitored closely enough to avoid shirking, managers will spend all of their time monitoring employees. But they do not spend all of their time this way.

According to Simon, the main purpose of authority is to transmit information about "decision premises," not to prevent self-interested shirking.[64] Decision premises give employees a set of standards for making decisions that will promote organizational goals. These standards are part of the organizational institutions that define and regulate organizational behavior.

Rewards

Simon denies the contract view that economic rewards are the primary source of motivation. Given the complexity and interdependence of employees, it is very hard to measure the amount each employee adds to organizational success or failure. Edwin Hartman makes this point when he argues that the corporation is a commons.[65] Of course, we can usually tell if someone is not working at all, and it is often clear when an individual is a legitimate star. But most employees do reasonably well. In this large group, we cannot identify those who contribute the most and so we cannot reward them for their contribution.

Loyalty: Identification with Organizational Goals

Simon argues that the empirical evidence that employees are loyal to organizations is overwhelming.[66] He does not argue for the obviously false thesis that people will give complete loyalty to the organization, but only that without some loyalty, organizations cannot exist. The need for loyalty rests on the difficulty of measuring how much individual employees contribute to organizational goals. These measurement problems mean that monitoring alone cannot force workers to act in ways that promote organizational goals. Measurement problems also make it difficult for rewards to adequately reflect and reinforce actions that promote organizational goals. Like Hartman, Simon characterizes the corporation as a commons, and as such, it is subject to overuse.[67] Successful organizations, Simon argues, are those in which employees go beyond the requirements of the job to protect and improve the commons. Loyalty can explain this; contracts and monitoring cannot.

Coordination

Simon argues that coordination of information and behavior, not monitoring, is the main advantage organizations have over markets.[68] It is this coordination that makes rational action possible. In an organization, individuals and functional units need to be aware of what other individuals and functional units are doing. For example, when planning S and R's expenses, accounting and finance need to be aware of the many different aspects of the relocation decision. Human relations also must be involved. These and other functional areas supply information and decision-making criteria that Jameson and Mamet need. No one in this web of relationships can act rationally without knowing, at least to some degree, what the others are planning and doing.

Simon compares these interactions to driving an automobile: it is rational to drive on the right only if everyone else does. In England and Japan, where they drive on the left, it would be irrational to drive on the right. Simon's point is that the rationality of actions is not a function of the act itself, but of how it *coordinates* with the action of others in institutional settings. Unless you know what others will or are likely to do, there is no rational action, except perhaps, exit. B. J. Diggs cites a case in which the English and the French claimed the same Pacific Island after World War II.[69] Before they settled their dispute, the rule was to drive on the left *and* to drive on the right—perhaps the rational driver stayed off the road.

Organizations, like roads, need rules and institutions that establish basic patterns of interaction. Within these, individuals can determine the best route for achieving the goal. Establishing and maintaining these institutions is the primary and most important job of management. Of course, management must also monitor, punish, and reward, but these are regulatory actions that take place within a set of constitutive rules and practices.

Douglass North argues for a contract view of organizations that can account for many of the empirical phenomena that Simon thinks the contract view cannot explain. Like Simon, North explains the advantage of the corporation over the market in terms of coordination of information and behavior. North also can explain organizational behavior in terms of loyalty to, and identification with, the organization because contracts are made within social institutions. If loyalty is an institutional value in the society, the organization and its contracts can inherit this value.

MAKING DECISIONS WITHIN ECONOMIC INSTITUTIONS

Economic institutions at the social and organizational levels serve all four of the purposes we have been discussing.

1. Institutions create opportunities for pursuing self-interest.
2. Institutions create opportunities for developing family relationships and friendships.
3. Institutions create opportunities for developing formal groups and promoting their interests.
4. Institutions create opportunities for pursuing fairness, justice, and human rights.

How we should use these institutional opportunities depends on our ethical point of view. Egoists argue that we should focus on 1, care theorists argue for 2, utilitarians for 3, and intrinsic value theorists for 4. Pluralists argue that all four types of opportunities are equally important, but that in particular situations, we should favor one or the other.

In the S and R case, Jameson and Mamet feel external and internal pressure to promote all four institutional purposes. Unfortunately, they see no way to do this regarding relocation. Further complicating the issue, as we saw in Chapter 2, is that each of these four values can be interpreted in different ways. In the next chapter we will see how law selects and reinforces particular interpretations of these values.

SUMMARY AND TRANSITION TO CHAPTER 5

In this chapter we examined how individual decision making relies on ethical values embedded in economic institutions and organizations. Some central points are as follows:

- Markets influence organizations, which influence individuals.
  - *Markets are ethical engines.* They direct behavior according to a set of institutional values that constitutes and regulates self-interest, personal relationships, group well-being, and intrinsic value.
  - Descriptive and normative economics cannot be separated. At the level of theory, descriptive economics relies on normative values, such as autonomy. At the level of practice, managers use descriptive economics to pursue normative goals.
  - The ethical foundation of an economic system is determined by how the four market conditions—property, risk–reward relationships, information, and competition—are defined and enforced.
  - *Organizations* are microethical engines. To succeed, they must act in accord with the basic institutional values expressed in the four market conditions.
  - In the United States, institutional values support both the contract and goal views of organizations.
  - *Individuals,* to be successful, must act in accord with basic values in markets and organizations. How these basic market and organizational values are interpreted will depend, in part, on whether individuals adopt a contract or a goal view of organizations.
- Individuals influence organizations, which influence markets.
  - *Individuals* have values that can be different from market and organizational values. This can result in organizational and even institutional change.
  - *Organizations* can have values that are different from their market settings. This can result in *market* change.
- Organizations are at the center of social conflict.
  - They determine the way wealth and power are distributed in societies.
  - They are the place where impersonal market values intersect with the personal values of organizational members.
- International business also involves value transmissions between markets, organizations, and individuals, but without the institutional stability often found in nation-states.

The values that guide market, organizational, and individual decision making are in constant flux. For individuals to make informed decisions about future activities, however, they need to be relatively sure of the institutions and values that will govern behavior in the future. Law is an instrument that reinforces particular interpretations of the values underlying institutions. When successful, law creates a secure environment that allows the long-term planning necessary to achieve the four institutional purposes. How law does this is the subject of the next chapter.

APPENDIX: PARETO EFFICIENCY

Normative Elements within Descriptive Economics

Consider a standard definition of Pareto or allocative efficiency:

> Allocative efficiency occurs when there is no possible [voluntary] reorganization of pro-
> duction that would make everyone better off—the poor, the rich, the wheat and shoe
> producer, etc. Under conditions of efficiency, therefore, one person's utility can be in-
> creased only by lowering someone else's utility.[70]

If we assume that we are not willing to make trades that make us worse off, a state
of Pareto efficiency is obtained when no more voluntary trades are possible. Pareto efficiency relies on the ethical principle of autonomy and it assumes the legitimacy of the
four market conditions.

Pareto Efficiency as an Evaluative Tool

Relying on the role of autonomy in Pareto efficiency, we can formulate the following argument.

Pareto efficiency is a state in which all the demand that can be satisfied is satisfied.
Satisfying demand, that is, providing goods and services to individuals to satisfy their
needs and wants, is one of the primary ways in which an economic system respects the
individuals within it. Since a Pareto-efficient state maximizes output while exhibiting a
respect for individuals, it is the only standard we need to evaluate an economic system.

This is a compelling argument. It fails, however, because Pareto efficiency is indifferent to the way in which basic property rights are *defined* and *distributed.* Consider the
following scenarios.

Suppose that at a particular point in time before the Civil War the United States was
allocatively efficient. That is, all voluntary trades had been made. Of course, some of the
trades that created this state of affairs were the morally abhorrent trades of human beings, who were not part of the trading community, but part of the traded community. The
trade in human beings was made possible by the property laws defined and enforced by
government.

The slavery example shows that allocative efficiency says nothing about how property laws stipulate *what* is being traded or *who* is allowed to trade; Pareto efficiency concerns only the utility of those doing the trading. Hence, there is an important difference
between allocative efficiency, which measures the utility of traders, and *social economic
well-being,* which measures the utility of all those affected by an economic system. We
do not need an extreme example such as slavery to differentiate between allocative efficiency and social economic well-being. Infants and the very ill are not traders either, so
their welfare and needs cannot be captured in the notion of allocative efficiency, except
derivatively by those who make trades for them.

Pareto efficiency also has problems with the distribution of wealth. An extreme but
theoretically plausible example of this is an allocatively efficient economic system in
which 1% of the population is very rich and 99% is very poor. For this system to be allocatively efficient we need only imagine that the rich and the poor can find no trading

partners to increase their individual welfare, and so no voluntary trades are possible. Since the total output would be quite low compared to what it could be in a more equal distribution of wealth and education, we see again that allocative efficiency is an incomplete measure of economic welfare.

Notes

1. Paul A. Samuelson and William D. Nordhaus. *Economics,* 3rd ed. New York: McGraw-Hill, 1985, p. 4.
2. Frank Knight. "Freedom as Fact and Criterion." *The International Journal of Ethics* XXXIX:2 (Jan. 1929), pp. 129–147.
3. *Ibid.,* p. 142.
4. Also see Douglass North. *Institutions, Institutional Change and Economic Performance.* Cambridge: Cambridge University Press, 1990, pp. 113–116.
5. There are many more factors involved in the development of England and Spain. This does not, however, diminish the importance of cultural practices and relationships.
6. These are the functions that cognitive–developmental theorists claim for moral reasoning. The overlap here is not coincidental. Moral reasoning has as its content the rules and laws that govern social activity. Hence, it is not surprising we use moral reasoning to understand and evaluate constitutive and regulative institutional rules.
7. See Nozick's point in Chapter 2 that Locke's Proviso is part of the nature of property, not an external constraint on the use of property.
8. Actually, Euclid's formulation is different, and more complicated. This formulation is, however, logically equivalent to Euclid's formulation.
9. One might argue that the consistency of the axioms is a question that can arise within an axiomatic system. However, if an inconsistency is discovered, the axiomatic system does not have the resources to specify how to resolve that inconsistency. Further, even if an axiomatic system is consistent, there are likely to be ways to change the axioms that still result in a consistent system. Once again, the system itself has nothing to say about which axiom set one should choose.
10. Benjamin M. Friedman. "Must We Compete?" Review of *Peddling Prosperity: Economic Sense and Nonsense in the Ages of Diminished Expectations,* by Paul Krugman. *The New York Review of Books* October 20, 1994.
11. Thomas Hobbes. *Leviathan.* Indianapolis: Bobbs-Merrill, 1958, p. 107.
12. James D. Gwartney and Richard Stroup. *Economics: Private and Public Choice,* 3rd ed. New York: Academic Press, 1982, p. 614.
13. David Messick. "Equality, Fairness, and Social Conflict." *Social Justice Research* 8:2 (1995), pp. 165–171.
14. Adolf Berle and Gardiner Means. *The Modern Corporation and Private Property,* revised edition. New York: Harcourt Brace and World, 1968, pp. 119–140.
15. *Ibid.,* pp. 121–122.
16. *Ibid.,* p. 122.
17. *Ibid.,* pp. 123–124.
18. *Ibid.,* p. 122.
19. *Ibid.,* p. 8.
20. *Ibid.,* p. 121.
21. *Ibid.,* pp. 119, 127.
22. Benjamin N. Cardozo. *The Paradoxes of Legal Science.* New York: Columbia University Press, 1928, p. 129.
23. The bundle of sticks view fits well with Hume's view of property. Hume argues that property is a piece of social technology that exists to manage scarcity. Because societies have different scarcities, technologies, political structures, social structures, and physical environments, they develop different systems of property.
24. These incentives, though important and indispensable, are not the foundation for the stability of property, and hence for the economic activity that a system of property provides. The most powerful and pervasive reason why property is secure is the general disposition to respect it that is inculcated in moral training. If that disposition did not exist, there would be no enforcement system that would work. There are two reasons why punitive incentives will not work without a general disposition to respect property. First, we would need to have everyone under constant surveillance,

which is impossible. Second, we would need to be able to trust those in the surveillance system, which is also impossible. Punitive incentives are needed only for that small portion of the population that has a tendency to violate property rights. If this group gets too large, society will crumble.

25. Author's field research.
26. Coase has argued that there are exceptions to this, such as when a shipping company needs a lighthouse, and can recoup enough benefits from building it. Coase's insight is that there are two aspects to a public good: the use that a producer gets from it and the use that free-riders get from it. If the first factor is significant enough, the public good will be produced. Even in these cases, however, we would expect the public goods to be underproduced. See "The Lighthouse and Economics" in Ronald Coase. *The Firm, the Market and the Law.* Chicago: University of Chicago Press, 1988.
27. J. Markoff. "Can Xerox Auction off Hot Air?" *New York Times,* National edition, June 24, 1996, C7.
28. For more on this, see Douglass North, *op. cit.,* especially Chapter 7.
29. A. Salpukis. "Electric Utilities to Provide Access for Competitors." *New York Times,* National edition, April 25, 1996, A1.
30. Paul A. Samuelson and William D. Nordhaus, *op. cit.,* pp. 540–541.
31. *Ibid.,* p. 540.
32. *Ibid.,* p. 541.
33. *Ibid.,* pp. 519–520.
34. John Dienhart. "Rationality, Ethical Codes and an Egalitarian Justification of Ethical Expertise: Implications for Professions and Organizations." *Business Ethics Quarterly* 5:3 (1995), pp. 419–450.
35. Michael Keeley. *A Social Contract Theory of Organizations.* Notre Dame: Notre Dame Press, 1988, p. 83.
36. Ronald Coase. "The Nature of the Firm." and Oliver Williamson. "The Logic of Economic Organization." Both articles appear in *The Nature of the Firm.* Eds. Oliver Williamson and G. Winter. New York: Oxford University Press, 1993.
37. Keeley, *op. cit.,* p. 79.
38. H. Simon. *Administrative Behavior,* 3rd ed. New York: The Free Press, 1976, p. 50.
39. See *New York Times,* Oct. 7, 1996, Section 4, p. 13 and Catherine Yang. "The Other Bill Goes to Washington." *Business Week* n3475 (May 13, 1996), p. 57.
40. Author's field research.
41. John Ladd. "Morality and the Ideal of Rationality in Formal Organizations." *The Monist* 54 (1970), pp. 488–516.
42. Kenneth Goodpaster. "Morality and Organization." In *Ethical Issues in Business: A Philosophical Approach.* Eds. Thomas Donaldson and Patricia Werhane. Englewood Cliffs, NJ: Prentice Hall, 1979.
43. See Lynne Paine and J. Katz. "Levi Strauss & Co.: Global Outsourcing." Harvard Case Study #395127, 1994.
44. See John Dienhart. "Charitable Investments: A Strategy for Improving the Environment of Business." *The Journal of Business Ethics* 7 (1988), pp. 63–71.
45. "Designer of New Ammunition Is On Defensive After Criticism." *New York Times,* January 1, 1995, Section 1, p. 7.
46. *Ibid.,* p. 7.
47. Keeley, *op. cit.,* p. 82. Herbert Simon mentions this himself, but does not think it is a problem. See Simon, *op. cit.,* p. 262 n.
48. Keeley, *op. cit.,* pp. 34–35, 98–99.
49. Oliver Williamson. *The Economic Institutions of Capitalism.* New York: The Free Press, 1985, p. 1.
50. Lea Beth Ward. "In the Executive Alphabet, You Call Them CLO's." *New York Times,* National edition, February 4 1996, Section 3, p. 12.
51. Oliver Williamson. "The Logic of Economic Organization," in Oliver Williamson and G. Winter, *op. cit.,* pp. 92–93.
52. Keeley, *op. cit.,* pp. 47–49.
53. *Ibid.,* pp. 190–191.
54. M. Velasquez. *Business Ethics: Concepts and Cases.* Englewood Cliffs, NJ: Prentice Hall, 1992, pp. 392–394, 414–420.
55. R. Zammuto. *Assessing Organizational Effectiveness.* Albany: SUNY Press, 1982. Cited in Keeley, *op. cit.,* p. 192. Zammuto, and Keeley after him, call this fourth interpretation the "Social Justice Approach." I think the less ethically loaded term "microsocial system" is better.

56. T. Connally, E. Conlon, and S. Deutsch. "Organizational Effectiveness: A Multiple Constituency Approach." *Academy of Management Review* 5: 1980. Cited in Keeley, *op. cit.,* p. 192.
57. Keeley, *op. cit.,* pp. 193–195.
58. Zammuto, *op. cit.,* pp. 195–199.
59. J. Pfeffer and G. Salancik. *The External Control of Organizations.* New York: Harper & Row, 1978. Cited by Keeley, *op. cit.,* pp. 199–203.
60. For an example, see T. Shale. "Boone of Contention. (T. Boone Pickens' Acquisition of Koito Manufacturing Stock)." *Euromoney* (April 1990), p. 19.
61. This is a hypothetical example.
62. Keeley, *op. cit.,* pp. 203–208.
63. H. Simon. "Organizations and Markets." *Journal of Public Administration Research and Theory* 5:3 (1995), pp. 273–293.
64. *Ibid.,* p. 281.
65. Edwin Hartman. *Organizational Ethics and the Good Life.* New York: Oxford University Press, 1996. See Chapter 3.
66. Simon. "Organizations and Markets," *op. cit.,* pp. 283–285.
67. *Ibid.,* p. 283.
68. *Ibid.,* pp. 288–293.
69. Author's class notes, University of Illinois, 1976.
70. Samuelson and Nordhaus, *op. cit.,* p. 483.

Law and Ethical Decision Making

INTEGRATING ETHICAL, ECONOMIC, AND LEGAL PRINCIPLES

Jameson and Mamet, like all business people, make decisions within legal systems that define and regulate property rights, risk–reward relationships, information, and competition. In the last chapter, we saw that these conditions are shaped by institutions and their underlying economic and ethical values. In this chapter we will examine how law clarifies and reinforces these ethical and economic values. We will then examine some of the legal and economic institutional settings in which Jameson and Mamet will make their decision.

There can be no better example of the importance of legal institutions than the fall of communism in Eastern Europe and the former USSR. State ownership of productive property, the arbitrary links between production and reward, the restriction and distortion of information, and the elimination of competition at the factor and production levels made it impossible for the system to produce enough food, clothing, medical care, and housing, and so increased competition at the consumer level.

The current struggle of these new countries reflects how difficult it is to create a completely new economic infrastructure through law. Economic activity relies on institutional practices and relationships, reinforced by law, to ensure market stability. In the absence of secure institutions,[1] economic relationships can change overnight. Because the future is uncertain, these economic systems still produce at levels well below their potential. The Republics of the former USSR are in a position that is a little like rebuilding the hull of a ship while at sea. Ideally, you want to do it bit by bit, but they do not have that luxury.

Preview of Chapter

"The Reinforcement View of Law: Institutions and Social Stability" and "The Content of Law: Reinforcing Ethical Values and Economic Relationships" examine how law clarifies and reinforces the ethical and economic values and relationships we discussed in Chapters 2–4. According to the reinforcement view, law is a proper subset of the values, rules, and practices that make up institutions. "The Challenge of Public Choice Theory" discusses the claim that narrow self-interest directs public policy in representative democracies.

"A Closer Look at Government Regulation: Three Views" examines government regulation from the traditional supply and demand perspective, the public choice perspective, and the reinforcement perspective. "Environmental Regulatory Law: Command and Control, Market Based, and Reflexive" introduces the concept of reflexive regulations. Reflexive regulations encourage firm and industry self-regulation in ways that try to avoid the prisoners' dilemma and free riding problems.

"S and R Electronics (B): Integrating Individuals, Organizations, and Markets" shows how business decision making relies on legal and economic systems to weave together individual, organizational, and market values and demands. Jameson and Mamet use international and national rules and laws, along with features of the semiconductor manufacturing market, to generate alternatives that can resolve some of the competing interests in the relocation decision.

THE REINFORCEMENT VIEW OF LAW: INSTITUTIONS AND SOCIAL STABILITY

Social institutions tell us what we should do in a variety of situations. If we make a promise, we should keep it; if a family member is ill, we should come to their aid; if we have children, we should care for them. Because institutions tell us what we should do, they create expectations in others about our future behavior. It is this ability of institutions to "create the future" that makes them so powerful. Without them, social relationships—and the business that occurs within them—would be impossible.

While institutions are necessary for social life, it is also true that some are more important than others. The reinforcement view of law, developed below, states that societies use law to reinforce ethical and economic values that underlie social institutions. Since law is costly, it is mainly used to reinforce values and relationships that are necessary for social stability and well-being. For example, fulfilling a contract to supply steel for an office building is more important for social stability and well-being than keeping a promise to meet someone for lunch. As a result, we have a great deal of law concerning contracts, and none concerning ordinary luncheon promises. To take a different case, making sure that a divorced parent makes child support payments is more important than ensuring that the divorced parent attends the child's sporting events. Hence, we have laws concerning the former, but not the latter.[2]

If the reinforcement view is correct, there is no sharp division between ethics and law; law is based on ethical values that partially constitute social institutions. Many laws, of course, are not mere reinforcements of ethical norms. Traffic laws, such as the law that automobiles should stay on the right, have no ethical analogue. Yet, even in these cases, the rationale of the law is to avoid death, injury, and property damage, while still allowing for efficient travel, all of which are supported by standard ethical values.

In the United States, law is determined by courts, legislatures, regulatory agencies, and executive orders. Each one of these institutions is itself governed by procedural rules that determine how law can be made.

Law: Procedural Elements

Governmental powers are established by three kinds of rules:

* Rules of recognition
* Rules of change
* Rules of adjudication[3]

These rules are usually found in a nation's constitution. *Rules of recognition* define the powers of governmental offices and determine the standards for valid laws. In the United States, for example, the House and Senate must cast a majority vote for a bill to become law. *Rules of change* define how we can change our laws. For example, to amend the constitution, two-thirds of the Senate and the House must approve the amendment, or the amendment must be proposed by a constitutional convention called for by at least two-thirds of the states. The amendment must then be ratified by three-fourths of the states. *Rules of adjudication* determine procedures to settle conflicts. The United States has a variety of federal, administrative, and state courts, and a growing arbitration system to handle conflicts of various kinds.

For a proposal to become law, it must satisfy the procedural requirements specified by the rules of recognition. As important as these procedural requirements are, they do not tell us what the *content* of law is or should be. To understand and evaluate the content of law, we need to examine how law functions to define and regulate economic and ethical institutions.

Law: Constitutive and Regulative Elements

CONSTITUTIVE LAW

In a representative democracy, voters choose government officials to use the rules of recognition, change, and adjudication to create *constitutive law.* Constitutive law establishes the four conditions of an economic infrastructure.

* **Condition 1:** Property rights
* **Condition 2:** Risk–reward relationships
* **Condition 3:** Information distribution and quality
* **Condition 4:** Competitive market structures

This constitutive legal system is based on broad goals and values regarding self-interest, personal relationships, group well-being, and intrinsic value (see Chapter 4).

REGULATIVE LAW

Within this constitutive legal environment, government uses *regulatory law* to modify outcomes of the constitutive system. The standards that guide regulatory law are based on the market conditions themselves (see Chapter 4 for more on how economics relies on internal standards). As we have discussed, when the courts broke up AT&T, they altered AT&T's corporate property rights (Condition 1) to promote a more competitive environment (Condition 4).

TWO KINDS OF CONSTITUTIVE LAW

We have distinguished constitutive and regulative law. We now distinguish two kinds of constitutive law: logically constitutive law and contingently constitutive law. *Logically constitutive* (LC) law clarifies and/or creates the rules and practices that define business entities, activities, or relationships. For example, a country's constitution and laws authorizing incorporation are logically constitutive because they create the possibility of specific kinds of entities and behavior. *Contingently constitutive* (CC) law preserves the rules and practices that define business entities, activities, or relationships in the face of contingent threats such as rule breaking or lack of coordination. Laws that protect property from theft and laws that set standards for bankruptcy procedures are contingently constitutive.

Regulative (R) law shapes market behavior in ways that are not necessary for preserving the rules and practices that define business entities, activities, or relationships. Regulations from the Occupational Health and Safety Administration (OSHA) requiring businesses to tag failed hydraulic jacks and the Food and Drug Administration's (FDA) food labeling laws are regulative. LC, CC, and R law are not discrete categories of law; they form a continuum, as portrayed in Figure 5.1.

As we move right on this continuum, laws will be less crucial to maintaining an existing economic system; as we move left, laws become more crucial.

The distinction between constitutive and regulative law shows that law is not primarily an instrument that restricts business behavior, but an instrument that creates the very possibility of business behavior. The basic legal infrastructure determines the general ways that we can and cannot promote self-interest, develop personal relationships, promote group welfare, and respect intrinsic value.

According to the reinforcement view, law reinforces the ethical and economic values and practices that make up social institutions. Since our focus is business, we are interested primarily in how law reinforces the institutions that define and regulate the four conditions of the market.

Logically constitutive (LC) law helps establish the four market conditions that make business transactions possible. Although LC law establishes the foundation of business activity, it is shaped by the needs of business and society. An example of this is the growth of the corporation—changing social needs led to the development of this new kind of business entity (Chapter 4). In another case, the growth of mining required LC laws that stipulated and clarified belowground property rights. More recently, the Internet is creating new issues regarding copyrights. Unless secure and reasonable property rights are determined, the information output in this medium will not reach its potential.[4] A similar problem is occurring with computer software development. Patent law in the United States is still unclear how to treat software instruction programs. Again, until secure and reasonable property rights are determined, software development will not reach its potential.[5]

Logically Constitutive	Contingently Constitutive	Regulatory
LC	CC	R

Figure 5.1

The reinforcement view of law predicts that changes in LC law will be based on the four sets of values—self-interest, care, group well being, and intrinsic value—that underlie institutions. In our discussion of public choice theory, below, we will see how these values are interpreted and implemented to provide a stable business environment.

Changing LC law is the most drastic way to deal with social and technological changes. CC law and R law attempt to manage the application or interpretation of LC law without changing LC law in itself.

Contingently constitutive (CC) law tries to prevent contingent failures that attack the very basis of one or more of the four market conditions. CC law can prevent these failures in at least two ways: by equilibrating conflicts in LC law and by discouraging violations of LC law.

Equilibrating Conflicts in LC Law

Market conditions can conflict in two ways. First, two or more market conditions can conflict with each other. For example, businesses in oligopolies can use their legally defined property rights (Condition 1) to limit supply and increase their rewards (altering Condition 2). Successfully limiting supply usually requires manipulating information (altering Condition 3). These actions reduce competition (altering Condition 4). To promote competition, antitrust laws restrain how businesses in oligopolies use their property. If successful, these laws reinforce the values of freedom, autonomy, and efficiency that underlie competition. Antitrust laws are *constitutive* because they address a serious challenge to the four market conditions; they are *contingent* because it is not necessary that the market should fail in this way.

Second, market conditions can sometimes conflict with themselves. Consider gun use in Zimmerman, Minnesota, a town about 50 miles outside of St. Paul-Minneapolis. Zimmerman was a rural area that is now being developed for residential use. Residents had been able to walk out their front doors and hunt on their own farms. However, as houses were built closer together, the property rights of landowning hunters began to conflict with the property rights of homeowners on standard lots. The tradition in the United States is to restrict the right to hunt on one's own property in these conditions. This solution reinforces the widely held belief that the ethical values of life and economic development override more discretionary activities such as hunting.[6]

Discouraging Violations of LC Law

CC law also discourages law breaking that attacks basic market conditions. The laws against fraud and breaking contracts are prime examples. On the reinforcement view, these laws reinforce the institutions of truthtelling and promise keeping. The law does not reinforce these rules when we lie about how someone looks or if we break a promise to meet someone for lunch. However, when secure expectations are necessary for business transactions, law reinforces the conditions necessary for these transactions to take place.

It is not always clear whether a law is LC or CC. The reconstruction amendments to the U.S. constitution (thirteenth, fourteenth, and fifteenth amendments), the 1964 and 1991 Civil Rights Acts, and the 1954 and 1971 Supreme Court decisions requiring integrated schools and legalizing abortion seem to be CC laws. They secure property, employment, housing, education, and privacy rights that were already present in LC law. At least this was the reason given by the legislators and judges who voted in favor of these amendments, laws, and decisions. These rules are constitutive because they were deemed necessary to preserve the basic values embedded in the LC infrastructure. They are contingent because they arose from the widespread violation of these values.

Opponents argue that these amendments, laws, and decisions *change* the fundamental values present in LC law, and so are really examples of LC law. The Reconstruction Amendments violate state autonomy, the Civil Rights Acts violate personal and
corporate property rights, and the abortion decision violates the right to life.

According to the reinforcement view, both sides of the debate have legitimate points
because the values on which they rely *are* embedded in LC law. Because of this, the reinforcement view would reject the claim that either side is simply creating values to justify their own unique points of view. According to the reinforcement view, laws do not
copy or create ethical values; they *interpret* these values. Ethical values that underlie social institutions do not come in neat packages, ready for codification (the same is true of
economic values, see Chapter 4).

When institutional values conflict, society uses its legal institutions to choose which
institutional values to support and which to subordinate. The Civil Rights Act of 1964
interpreted equal opportunity in a way that allowed for quotas. The Civil Rights Act of
1991 reinterpreted the notion of equal opportunity to exclude quotas.[7] This revision reflected the values of the country, which had begun to see quotas as conflicting directly
with individual freedom.

Given a particular legal infrastructure made up of LC and CC laws, regulative law
fine-tunes individual and organizational behavior according to the values underlying
those laws. In the United States, OSHA regulates business activity that affects worker
safety and health. OSHA argues that these regulations are necessary to protect our workforce, and so promote individual and group welfare. R laws also fine-tune LC and CC
laws in centrally planned economies. In 1995 the Cuban government passed regulative
laws to tax gas and electricity. The government argued that these funds were necessary
to ensure service, and so promote group welfare. The government also argued that these
taxes did not violate the socialist values that such basic goods should be free. The goods
are free, the government argued; the people are only paying for their distribution.[8]

The reinforcement view does not by itself predict how a society will interpret and
enforce institutional values. These choices are the result of shifting, complex coalitions.
Insofar as they can be predicted, this is the province of social science.

In the next section we will examine how societies use specific ethical and economic
values to create and modify law.

THE CONTENT OF LAW: REINFORCING ETHICAL
VALUES AND ECONOMIC RELATIONSHIPS

According to the reinforcement view, law is a product of how societies interpret economic and ethical institutional relationships and values. We can represent this in Table
5.1.

Table 5.1 will be different for different countries, and different for the same country at different times. Further, reasonable people can disagree about how to fill it in to
represent a particular state of affairs. Still, we can use it as a tool to understand the ethical and economic values that ground a country's legal system. Table 5.2 illustrates how
we could use this table in the United States. To keep things simple, we will use standard
interpretations of economic and ethical categories. We will also give only one example
per cell to illustrate how law can *support* or *conflict* with institutional values, practices,
and relationships.

Most laws can be supported and criticized by several ethical orientations. For example, the child labor restrictions cited in the Personal Relationships column can be sup-

TABLE 5.1
Legal Intersection of Ethics and Economics

	Self-interest	Personal relationships	Group interest	Intrinsic value	
				Property rights	Fairness
Property	Laws	Laws	Laws	Laws	Laws
Risk–Reward relationships	Laws	Laws	Laws	Laws	Laws
Information	Laws	Laws	Laws	Laws	Laws
Competition	Laws	Laws	Laws	Laws	Laws

ported by the other three ethical orientations, but for different reasons. Egoists could argue that children are not able to make rational decisions about their interests. Utilitarians could argue that groups need to educate children to create sound labor markets, and rights theorists could argue that children are too young to make an informed, rational choice about going to work and forsaking an education, and so the practice violates childrens' autonomy.

Table 5.2 shows how law integrates ethical values and beliefs about economic mechanisms and causation. Individuals and groups can disagree with the status quo be-

TABLE 5.2
Legal Intersection of Ethics and Economics for the United States

	Self-interest	Personal relationships	Group interest	Intrinsic value	
				Property rights	Fairness
Property	Private property laws and corporate charter laws reflect value of self-interest	Inheritance laws promote family continuity	Legislation to provide public goods promotes group well-being	Private property laws and corporate charter laws reflect value of property rights	Due process laws help ensure fair procedures
Risk–Reward relationships	Taxes interfere with the pursuit of wealth and security for oneself	Family Leave Bill promotes caring family relationships	Environmental laws protect public resources	Taxes interfere with property rights	Reduction in voting age from 21 to 18 allowed those drafted to vote on national policy
Information	Privacy laws prevent disclosure of trade secrets	Food labeling, private medical information promote family well-being	Freedom of information necessary for economic growth	Privacy laws protect property rights	Information about important harms and opportunities helps people direct their own lives
Competition	Open markets allow individuals to pursue their self-interest	Child labor restrictions promote family stability, protect children	Allowing some monopolies optimizes output	Market regulations interfere with property rights	Regulating natural monopolies ensures fair(er) prices

cause they reject the economic assumptions, the ethical assumptions, or both. When those who disagree try to change the laws, they appeal to the legislative and/or the judicial system. We can think of these governmental systems as markets, each with its own structure and incentive systems.

There is not much disagreement that the rows in Table 5.2 represent the four basic conditions of the market. There is considerable disagreement, however, about how these conditions should be interpreted and enforced. Table 5.2 shows that these disagreements have an ethical component. If we could resolve ethical disagreements so that we would have one column instead of five, this would make it much easier to interpret and enforce the economic conditions. Can we do this?

In Chapter 2, we saw that ethical theorists tend to argue for a single ethical principle, such as self-interest, care, group interest, or fairness, and to reject or subordinate the other ethical principles. If this single-principle strategy were successful, it would simplify Table 5.2 considerably: we would have four cells instead of 20. Unfortunately, this strategy has not succeeded. The result is a public debate that includes the 20 cells, and usually more.[9] As this public debate goes on, we have a *de facto* integration of ethical values and economic conditions that guide our everyday activities.

How we should fill in this table will be a function of our ethical view. According to ethical pluralism, each of the four ethical orientations serves important individual and social functions. Pluralism does not assert that one orientation always trumps the others, instead it tries to integrate them. Table 5.3 is an example of how pluralism would alter Table 5.2. The real challenge, though, is to find a way to intergrate these values.

Pluralism can use the psychological, ethical, and economic beliefs and theories covered in the first three chapters to ground an integrative strategy. Most of the psychological and ethical theories we examined view human beings as rational problem solvers,[10] but argue that our rationality is limited, or "bounded" by time constraints, incomplete information, and limited calculating power.[11] Another common theme is that we are social, relationship creatures.[12]

Our limited rationality and our need for human relationships make institutions such as government, family, and promising very important. If we had to use our rational powers to continually evaluate and monitor our personal and professional relationships, we would have time for little else. Institutions set up a social infrastructure so that we can be reasonably certain of how people will behave in a variety of conditions.[13] Once we understand the social infrastructure, we can devote our limited rational powers to understanding and constructing our individual lives in concert with family, friends, business, and government. Kohlberg and Gilligan explain moral development in just this way: first we come to understand our basic social infrastructure, then we use that knowledge to direct our lives (hopefully) to suit our particular needs and talents and to develop fulfilling relationships.[14]

Let us apply this pluralistic view to the issue of child labor using two of the four basic ethical values: self-interest and group interest. For most of human history, child labor has not been an issue. In tribes and villages, children worked to help supply the needs of their family and group. This work prepared them for their adult roles and contributed to the welfare of the group: self-development and communal welfare were promoted by the same activities. Contemporary economic systems often separate self-development from communal welfare. Children working in factories may contribute to the group good, but are not prepared for their roles as adults. They are denied an education and an environment suitable for social and physical development. Further, child labor eventually harms the group because it lowers the quality of the labor market, makes family life more difficult, and increases health care costs if the children do not

TABLE 5.3
Legal Intersection of Ethics and Economics: A Pluralistic Approach

| | **Ethical pluralism helps us integrate different ethical values** | | | | |
| | | | | **Intrinsic value** | |
	Self-interest	**Personal relationships**	**Group interest**	**Property rights**	**Fairness**
Property	Private property laws and corporate charter laws reflect value of self-interest	Inheritance laws promote family continuity	Legislation to provide public goods promotes group well-being	Private property laws and corporate charter laws reflect value of property rights	Due process laws help ensure fair procedures
Risk–Reward relationships	Taxes interfere with the pursuit of wealth and security for oneself	Family Leave Bill promotes caring family relationships	Environmental laws protect public resources	Taxes interfere with property rights	Reduction in voting age from 21 to 18 allowed those drafted to vote on national policy
Information	Privacy laws prevent disclosure of trade secrets	Food labeling, private medical information promote family well-being	Freedom of information necessary for economic growth	Privacy laws protect property rights	Information about important harms and opportunities helps people direct their own lives
Competition	Open markets allow individuals to pursue their self-interest	Child labor restrictions promote family stability, protect children	Allowing some monopolies optimizes output	Market regulations interfere with property rights	Regulating natural monopolies ensures fair(er) prices

develop well physically. In an industrial society, laws restricting child labor promote individual development and group welfare.

Pluralism by itself does not specify how societies should use law to integrate the four ethical values to promote individual and community good. As the above example shows, how these values should be integrated depends on economic, technological, and social conditions, and the values we use to understand these conditions.

THE CHALLENGE OF PUBLIC CHOICE THEORY

Public choice theory appears to challenge the reinforcement view of law. According to public choice theory, law is driven by power and self-interest, not by ethical values. However, there are good reasons to believe that public choice theory is compatible with the reinforcement view.

The Basic Principles of Public Choice Theory

The foundation of public choice theory is simple and compelling:

People reason and behave similarly in private and public sectors.

If we assume that people in business promote their own interest, it is reasonable to assume that people in the public sector do the same. This assumption implies that candidates run for office because they believe it will promote their interests, and citizens vote for the candidate they believe will promote their interests.

However, as we saw in the discussion of moral psychology in Chapter 2 and the discussion of egoism in Chapter 3, the definition of self-interest is a function of one's view about oneself, one's family, one's society, and the perceived relationships between these elements. Since there are a number of viable ways to interpret and integrate these elements, we cannot assume that self-interest will be understood in the same way by all candidates and voters. Yet, the variety of ways in which politicians and voters view their self-interest is not necessarily a problem. Public choice theory does not attempt to say how people conceive of their self-interest, only that they are motivated by self-interest, however they understand it.

One of the most fundamental principles of public choice theory is embodied in *the rational ignorance effect.* Given the infinitesimal probability that one vote will change the result of an election, people do not seek information about candidates, since they can do other things that will be more productive, more enjoyable, or both. For example, if a worker must choose between putting in overtime at $20 an hour or going to the library to examine congressional voting records, the theory predicts the worker will put in the overtime. Or, if the choice is between enjoying a movie or going to the library to examine congressional voting records, the theory predicts that the person will go to the movie. For the most part, people will spend time and resources on the activity that they believe will net them the greatest return. Since most activities for most people are more productive or enjoyable than political research, it is not rational for them to seek information about political candidates. They are ignorant of political matters, but rationally so.

Self-interested candidates are "political entrepreneurs." Political entrepreneurs seek votes just as private sector entrepreneurs seek dollars. Because it is not rational for voters to seek political information, candidates must supply information to the voters through television, radio, and newspapers—media that voters attend to for other reasons. Also, the information must be presented in a way that is persuasive and memorable. Hence, entertaining "sound-bites," designed to simultaneously identify issues and suggest solutions, are especially important. Reagan's "Are you better off than you were four years ago?" and Clinton's "Its the economy, stupid" were especially effective.

Political advertising has another goal besides getting votes for a candidate, and that is to get voters to the polls. People will not vote for the same reason they will not seek political information: other activities are more productive, enjoyable, or both. Political advertising addresses this problem in two ways. First, it often includes statements about how every vote is important, simply denying the unimportance of one vote. Second, political advertising tries to encourage a sense of loyalty toward the candidate and the issues the candidate supports. In this way, political advertising uses some of the techniques of sports advertising. Since it is unrealistic to suppose that one's attendance at a sporting event will change the outcome, sports advertising often focuses on team and regional loyalty. Political advertising tries to tap into similar sentiments.

Politicians need funds to supply political information to voters. If government does not fully fund campaign expenses, candidates must seek money from outside sources. Private campaign funding creates the special interest effect. Special interest groups are the primary source of funds. Groups such as labor and agriculture can deliver funds and votes. Industry and consumer special interest groups generally have only funds. Special interest groups also give candidates free information about issues and about the needs and interests of those whom the interest groups and the candidates represent.

The special interest effect is compounded by the concealed cost effect. The concealed cost effect refers to the ease of hiding the costs of public policy. For example, U.S. protection of the sugar industry, which includes subsidies of 1.4 billion dollars, is supposed to support the U.S. sugar industry and preserve U.S. jobs. It undoubtedly does this. The price of sugar, however, is increased, costing consumers several billion dollars a year. Further, it is estimated that 40% of these subsidies go to the "largest 1% of sugar farms."[15] The U.S. Commerce Department, citing the presence of sugar in many foods, characterizes this as a regressive tax.[16]

The several billion dollars in increased consumer spending is concealed because it results largely from small increases in prices that are spread over millions of consumers who may or may not notice the higher prices. Even if consumers do notice the higher prices, they may or may not know that the higher prices result from subsidies. Finally, even if consumers know that the price rise is a result of subsidies, the amount of the price increase is usually so small that it is not rational for consumers to spend their time and resources trying to eliminate it.

Voters are also subject to the shortsightedness effect, which is the tendency to over-value present benefits and to discount future costs too much. This provides an incentive for politicians to support public policy that delivers present benefits in a way that trans-fers costs and risks to future generations.

Finally, there is the low marginal cost of law. Although maintaining a governmen-tal system to establish and enforce law is very costly, the cost of adding one new law is usually very small.

Understandably, public choice theorists are wary of government intervention in the market. When we combine the rational ignorance effect with the special interest effect, the concealed cost effect, the shortsightedness effect, and low marginal cost of law, we can see how easy it is for policymakers to shift benefits from the taxpaying public to spe-cial interests and to shift burdens in the opposite direction. The result is an economic system that performs below capacity and violates the basic values of a free market econ-omy. Nozick, for example, would not say these transfers were merely inefficient, he would say they are theft (Chapter 3).

It is important to note that public choice theory does not need to assume that peo-ple are selfish, only that they are reasonably self-interested. We can interpret reasonable self-interest as the desire to live at least moderately well and to avoid harming oneself. Further, we do not have to assume that all voters, candidates, and lawmakers act in ways that public choice theory suggests, only that enough people act this way to influence public policy.[17]

Public Choice and the Reinforcement View of Law

Public choice theory asserts that government is driven by self-interest whereas the rein-forcement view asserts that laws reflect the institutional ethical values of society. We can reconcile this apparent inconsistency in two ways. First, self-interest is an important in-stitutional value, at least in western countries. Second, and more decisively, the *goal* of public choice theory is to reinforce the ethical norms associated with self-interest, sta-ble personal relationships, group interest, and intrinsic value.

Public choice theorists argue that policies that are supposed to promote ethical out-comes, such as welfare programs to help single parents, will instead hide transfers of wealth to a few special interests. The best way to prevent this, and therefore to promote individual well-being, family well-being, group welfare, and fairness, is to reduce or eliminate government action in economic markets. Table 5.4 represents a public choice analysis of welfare for single parents.

TABLE 5.4
A Public Choice Critique of Aid to Single Parents

	Self-interest	Personal relationships	Group interest	Intrinsic value	
				Property rights	Fairness
Property	Taxes are raised, giving working people less money to promote their interest	Funds benefit housing and food industries more than poor families	Housing and food markets are artificially bid up, causing inflation and opportunity costs	Taxes collected to support welfare violate property rights	Transfers of funds from taxpayers to business without the consent of taxpayers
Risk–Reward relationships	Reduces incentive to work for taxpayers and recipients	Drives fathers out of homes	Creates incentives for groups to use public policy to enrich themselves	Taxes to support welfare interfere with risk-reward relationship	Taxes to support welfare deprive people of a fair return on their investments
Information	Information about welfare programs are withheld or distorted, limiting taxpayers ability to pursue their own interests	Information is withheld and distorted, preventing families from improving their lot	Information is withheld and distorted, preventing efficient public policy	Information is withheld and distorted to justify taxes, preventing informed, free use of property	Information is withheld and distorted, preventing rational, free consent
Competition	Increased taxes interfere with competition for scarce resources, and so harms self-interest	Poor families are encouraged to spend time getting welfare funds, not education, making it harder for them to compete for scarce resources	Labor markets are smaller than they would be, bidding up labor costs, and losing talented workers to welfare	Increased taxes lowers capital investments	Segmentation of society prevents people from participating in the political process

As Table 5.4 shows, public choice theory would reject this welfare program because it conflicts with the ethical values in the column headings. The best way to support these values is to let the market work on its own. Public choice theorists are not against ethical government. They are against sham ethical public policy.

Of course, public choice theory does not rule out all government action in markets. If people are as self-interested as public choice theory assumes, government must at least establish and enforce the four market conditions.

A CLOSER LOOK AT GOVERNMENT REGULATION: THREE VIEWS

Government Regulation: The Traditional View

In representative democracies, government regulation is usually a response to economic and social problems. Regulation is sometimes divided into two categories: economic and social. *Economic regulation* is supposed to keep markets running smoothly and efficiently. It is a response to the failure of one or more of the four market conditions and their constituent values. For example, the Federal Aviation Administration (FAA) and the Securities and Exchange Commission (SEC) are supposed to make air travel and securities transactions safer and more predictable. This allows individuals and organizations to pursue their interests in a climate of fairness, which in turn increases travel miles and securities transactions, which, all other things being equal, tends to promote group economic well-being. *Social regulation,* of the kind issued by OSHA and the Equal Employment Opportunity Commission (EEOC), is supposed to improve the quality of life, not to improve market efficiency. On the traditional view, economic regulation can be justified if it promotes one or more of the four market conditions. Social regulation imposes costs and reduces efficiency, and is much harder to justify.

Regulatory standards can emanate from statutes, from regulatory agencies that are established by statute, or both (Table 5.5).

THE PUBLIC DEMAND FOR ECONOMIC AND SOCIAL REGULATION

Most U.S. economic regulations were laid down between 1890 and 1950. In Chapter 4, we saw how the Sherman Act (1890) was spurred by public pressure to end the monopolistic activity of trusts. In the 1930s, the New Deal was a response to public pressure to end the Great Depression. Franklin Delano Roosevelt was elected president to change the economic infrastructure of the land. Relying on Keynes' view that government action could reduce the severity of business cycles, the New Deal set forth a number of permanent regulatory agencies to oversee foundational sectors of the economy. For example, the Securities and Exchange Commission was established to oversee the stock market and the Federal Deposit Insurance Corporation was established to restore trust in banks. Keynes' views also began to be used by the Federal Reserve System, which was established in 1913, to control growth and recession. These actions, and many others like them, were supposed to increase the stability of the basic economic infrastructure.

Most social legislation arose between 1960 and 1975. Lyndon Johnson's Great Society was instituted to promote racial equality and opportunity for the impoverished. The Civil Rights Act of 1964 was a major part of that program. The Environmental Protection Agency (EPA), EEOC, OSHA, and the Consumer Product Safety Commission (CPSC) also came out of this era. These agencies and the regulations they promulgated are primarily intended to promote human well-being, not to promote efficient markets.

If government imposes regulations in response to public pressure, business has an incentive to regulate itself, and so prevent the problems to which the public reacts. Unfortunately, businesses face a difficult problem in coordinating their behavior. This difficulty is similar to the one described in the prisoners' dilemma.

TABLE 5.5
Regulatory Standards

	Regulatory agencies	Regulatory statutes
Economic	FAA, SEC	Sherman Act, Wagner Act
Social	OSHA, EEOC	Civil Rights Acts

TABLE 5.6
The Prisoner's Dilemma

	A does not confess	A confesses
B does not confess	A: 1 year B: 1 year	A: 3 months B: 10 years
B confesses	A: 10 years B: 3 months	A: 5 years B: 5 years

PRISONERS' DILEMMA

There are some situations in which cooperative behavior would result in minimal harm to all participants, yet, since participants cannot be assured that others will cooperate, they must act in a way that is harmful to themselves in order to avoid an even greater harm that will befall them if they cooperate and others do not. The interesting feature of the prisoners' dilemma is that all participants know that they are acting in suboptimal ways, but see no way to avoid it.

The traditional prisoners' dilemma goes like this. Two suspects of an armed robbery are apprehended and put in different rooms. They are both told, truthfully, that even if they do not confess, the state has enough evidence to send them to jail for 1 year. However, they are also told that if one confesses and the other does not, the one who confesses will serve only 3 months, whereas the one who keeps quiet will serve 10 years. If both confess, each will serve 5 years in prison (Table 5.6). What should each of them do?

If neither of them confesses, each will serve 1 year in jail. However, by not confessing, they run the risk of serving 10 years in jail. Since neither can control what the other will do, they will both confess, and each will serve 5 years in jail. If they could have cooperated and not confessed, they could have reduced their stay in jail by a substantial amount. Yet, it is not rational to cooperate, given the great risk involved.

To see how the prisoners' dilemma case applies to the regulation of business, consider the following example. Suppose we have three chemical companies, each polluting the environment equally, and each with roughly equal costs, revenues, profit margins, and market shares. Each business knows that if they agree to reduce pollution as a group, they can avoid government regulation. They will all have to raise prices, and that will reduce revenues, but none of them lose market share to the others. Yet, no corporation has the power to monitor the others or to ensure their cooperation. Since each corporation has an incentive to internalize benefits and externalize costs, each will have an incentive to *appear* to reduce pollution without doing so, or at least to appear to reduce it more than they do.

If a chemical company installs pollution reduction devices, it will have to raise prices. The company that does not install these devices or installs devices of lower quality can keep prices lower than the others, but still higher than before. Hence, the defecting firm can increase market share, revenues, and profit margins. Since companies can predict this will happen, they do not cooperate to reduce pollution, and become subject to government regulation. All participants know that they could reduce their harm significantly by cooperating, but are unable to do so.

There is another problem in voluntary pollution reduction plans that is connected with the problem of noncooperation. Suppose a privately owned firm believed that it could survive with a lower market share if other firms did not cooperate, and so unilaterally imposes costs on itself to reduce pollution. As altruistic as this unilateral action may be, there is good reason to believe that it would have little effect on pollution. Pollution is a system-wide problem, and actions by particular firms, good or bad, may have very little effect on the overall outcome. In this case, the company could harm itself and its stakeholders with no benefit to others.

BUSINESS DEMAND FOR ECONOMIC AND SOCIAL REGULATION

The prisoner's dilemma shows that self-regulation in the absence of external monitoring and enforcement is not likely to work. However, business can regulate itself indirectly by appealing to government. This approach allows business some control of the regulatory process as it taps into the government's ability to monitor and control firms. The Civil Aeronautics Board (CAB) was created in part as a result of airline pressure. For 50 years, the CAB preserved near monopolistic markets for air carriers, regulating prices, schedules, and entry and exit.

In the late 1970s, as deregulation became a public value, The CAB came under attack. The airlines that had monopolistic power over their regions supported the CAB, and they fought to keep it. Not all businesses supported the CAB, however. Groups who wanted to start new airlines opposed the CAB. Businesses whose members travel a great deal were in favor of deregulation. The public also seemed to want deregulation. The budget of the CAB was cut in 1979, and the agency was gone by the end of 1985.[18]

Regulation can coordinate information and create a uniform playing field in other ways. International companies, who once scoffed at international ethical codes for employment and the environment, now advocate these codes. These companies face considerable pressure at home and in the countries where they do business. International codes are a way to avoid a different set of standards in each country.[19]

Government Regulation: The Public Choice View

Public choice theory also argues that government regulation is a response to political demand, but characterizes the demand differently than the traditional view. Public choice theory argues that government regulation responds to the self-interest of those who exert the demand.

Public choice challenges the distinction between economic and social regulation. For example, aid to the sugar industry has the avowed purpose of promoting a strong business climate. Public choice would argue that it really helps the owners and upper management of the sugar businesses. Public choice would make the same argument for social regulation, like the public housing and food stamp programs of the 1960s. Public choice views these programs as a way to promote the good of the housing and the food industries, not the poor. For public choice theory, economic and social regulation are different means to the same end: self-interest.

Government Regulation: The Reinforcement View

The reinforcement view combines the traditional and public choice views of government regulation. According to the reinforcement view, law rests on established social institutions. Hence, when special interests, like the sugar industry, want to maintain or increase subsidies, they appeal to current social institutions. They argue that subsidies preserve U.S. industry, increase U.S. jobs, and promote a stable supply of high-quality sugar to consumers. Public choice argues that these goals are window dressing, and that self-interest, channeled through business organizations, is the foundation of the sugar industry's demand for government aid.

According to the reinforcement view, the pursuit of self-interest is itself a social institution. Corporate subsidies, then, are well within the U.S. institutional framework. There are, however, other institutional forces that are inconsistent with corporate subsidies. Populist political movements, which have an egalitarian core, oppose corporate subsidies. Populists argue that the proper role of the government is to guarantee fair markets in which all can participate. Populism was part of the driving force behind the Sherman Antitrust Act, the pure food and drug laws at the turn of the century, the New Deal, and the reaction against layoffs and high corporate salaries that became an issue in the 1996 U.S. Presidential primary elections.

ENVIRONMENTAL REGULATORY LAW: COMMAND AND CONTROL, MARKET BASED, AND REFLEXIVE

According to the reinforcement view of law, the wide array of environmental laws and agencies reflects the public value of maintaining a clean environment. However, as we have seen, government regulation of business to protect the environment can violate other institutional values, such a personal freedom, the right to use one's property as one wishes, and promoting national wealth. Eric W. Orts lists three types of environmental regulatory law: command and control, market based, and reflexive.[20] Each of these types of regulation aims to protect the environment, but each does so by reinforcing and subordinating different ethical and economic values and relationships.

Command and control law sets standards for pollution and imposes fines and penalties for companies that exceed those standards. From a regulator's point of view, this type of regulation can be seen as following the ethical mandate to strictly enforce the public's desire for a clean environment. However from the point of a business person, this type of regulation can be oppressive and unrealistic, and violates the freedom of business managers and owners. Orts states four objections to the command and control approach to environmental law.

1. "Command-and-control depends too much on administrative agencies which are vulnerable to [political influence]."[21] For example, environmental protection can be severely weakened if the President appoints directors who do not care about the environment.

2. "Command and control is too static."[22] Technology changes, and regulatory agencies cannot keep pace. Another problem is how to set the proper standards for pollution. How do we know what the right amount of pollution is?

3. "Command and control becomes too complex and unwieldy.'[23]' Regulatory agencies churn out more and more rules, until it becomes virtually impossible to keep track of them.

4. "Command and control is too harsh and punitive."[24] Instead of rewarding and encouraging good environmental behavior, it punishes bad environmental behavior.

Orts notes that there are some instances in which command and control regulations are in order. They work, for example, if we are dealing with a highly toxic material, such as mercury, that can kill human beings in very small doses. The value of protecting human life clearly outweighs our freedom to dispose of mercury in landfills or waterways.

In other areas, such as controlling emissions of coal-fired utility plants, Orts notes that the command-and-control approach has given way to a market-based approach.

This approach reinforces the values of autonomy and freedom, but it has limitations as well. Orts raises concerns about four issues.

1. "Pollution charges and taxes."[25] Companies must pay for the privilege of polluting the environment. This can make markets more efficient (see the discussion of negative externalities in Chapter 4). One problem with this approach is knowing how to define the proper charges and tax levels.

2. "Expanding property rights to include the natural environment."[26] If we can define property rights for endangered environments, we can use existing controls, such as the courts, to protect the environment. Unfortunately, some environmental problems, such as air pollution, are not easily recast in terms of property rights.

3. "Tradable Pollution Rights."[27] Companies can trade the pollution rights they buy on the open market, allowing pollution to be controlled in the most efficient way. This can work for oligopolies, where the traders are few. It would be unwieldy for dry cleaners, though.

4. "Environmental marketing regulation."[28] Government or nongovernmental organizations certify products as environmentally friendly. This allows consumers to buy those products that harm the environment less than other products. There are at least two problems with this. First, how do we set standards for "environmentally friendly"? Second, this will work only if consumers are willing to select products on the basis of the environment.

Despite their problems, market-based approaches try to work within common business incentives. By allowing businesses to buy and trade pollution rights, the environment is treated more like other factors of production. It also allows managers more freedom to tailor their environmental plans to their particular production and location characteristics, and it does so without the extreme restrictions on managerial freedom of the command-and-control approach.

Reflexive environmental law tries to work within the institutional environment not only of business, but also of the society in which business operates. Reflexive law tries to set up an institutional environment that reinforces autonomy *and* a clean environment. Orts states:

> By reflexive environmental law, I mean . . . [an] approach to regulation that seeks to encourage self-reflective and self-critical processes within social institutions concerning the effects they have on the natural environment . . . reflexive environmental law aims to establish internal evaluative procedures and patterns of decision making within institutions to lessen environmental harm and to increase environmental benefit. The idea is to employ law not directly in terms of giving specific orders or commands, but indirectly to establish incentives and procedures that encourage institutions to think critically, creatively, and continually about how their activities affect the environment and how they may improve their environmental performance.

> Reflexive law recognizes the complexity of social life and the diversity of the many institutions created to achieve various ends. It aims to guide rather than to suppress the social complexity of institutions. Reflexive law . . . attempts to off-load some of the burdens of direct regulation to encourage self-regulation of social institutions.[29]

Orts cites five examples of how the reflexive model is beginning to be used by government agencies. We will look at three of them.

1. "Environmental Auditing and Enforcement Policies." The EPA, which began as a command and control agency, has issued a *Voluntary Environmental Self-Policing and Self-Disclosure Interim Policy.* This policy allows companies who police themselves and who disclose their own infractions to reduce their penalties for infractions of command-and-control environmental regulations.[30]

2. "Environmental Sentencing Guidelines for Organizations." These proposed guidelines rely on the same principle as the EPA policy just discussed. If the company makes good faith efforts to adhere to environmental laws, court-imposed sentences can be reduced.[31]

3. "Environmental Management and Audit Systems." The European Union has established a voluntary program for firms that want to be environmentally sound. It requires members to release their own audits of how they affect the environment, and it requires these audits to be verified by third parties. This program works like the U.S. securities regulations that require public companies to have their financial audits confirmed by third parties, usually accounting firms.[32]

As these examples show, reflexive law works within institutional and organizational structures to encourage decision making that protects the environment. It allows managers to use moral imagination (Chapter 2) to come up with creative ways to protect the environment.

We should not be fooled into thinking that reflexive law is never punitive. On the contrary, companies can be penalized if they set up internal policing controls that they know to be ineffective or if they release environmental audits they know to be false. What differentiates reflexive law from the other two kinds of law is that it gives corporate decision makers more flexibility to use the special characteristics of their business in its institutional settings. Insofar as it does this, reflexive law promotes managerial freedom and a clean environment.

S AND R ELECTRONICS (B): INTEGRATING INDIVIDUALS, ORGANIZATIONS, AND MARKETS

In this section we will use the reinforcement view of law to examine how national and international rules, rule setting practices, and organizations can affect Jameson's and Mamet's decision to relocate S and R.

Jameson and Mamet hired a consulting firm, the International Consultant Ensemble (ICE), to help with the relocation decision. ICE was started by former executives of international companies in the electronics industries. They have considerable experience in setting up production facilities along the Pacific Rim. The ICE consultants are helping Jameson and Mamet with many of the issues pertaining to relocation. We will cover four of these issues. In each case we will describe the institutional background of the issue, and then describe the ICE recommendations.

We begin with the General Agreement on Tariffs and Trade (GATT), the largest and most pervasive international trade regime. We then examine the Foreign Corrupt Practices Act (FCPA), which prohibits U.S. business representatives from bribing foreign officials. Next, we look at the Federal Sentencing Guidelines for Corporations, which is designed to make executives more accountable for company decisions and actions. We end our discussion with a look at some structural aspects of the semiconductor manufacturing market to get a better idea of S and R's options.

S and R Electronics (B)

THE GENERAL AGREEMENT ON TARIFFS AND TRADE

Jameson and Mamet are making their relocation decision against a background of international trade relationships that did not exist 50 years ago. For their move to succeed, they need to be relatively certain that the future of international trade will be guided by secure institutions. The General Agreement on Tariffs and Trade (GATT) is an agreement that helps create and ensure such institutions. Here is some background.

History

GATT was founded after World War II to promote world stability through international trade. It was widely believed that the trade restrictions of the 1920s and 1930s exacerbated the depth and length of the worldwide depression. This depression, in turn, was an important cause of World War II. In the waning years of the War, the United States and other Allied countries met to rough out the general principles that became GATT. The goal was to create a strong global economy that would make trade flourish and war less likely. Although GATT has had and continues to have problems, it is generally acknowledged to have been a central component of global economic growth.

GATT is a voluntary organization whose rules apply to signatory countries, although some countries participate informally. Following Steven Krasner, Stephanie Lenway argues that GATT is a *regime* made up of principles, norms, and rules. Krasner defines a regime as follows:

> Regimes can be defined as sets of implicit or explicit principles, norms, rules, and decision-making procedures around which actors' expectations converge in a given area of international relations.

- *Principles* are beliefs of fact, causation, and rectitude.
- *Norms* are standards of behavior, defined in terms of rights and obligations.
- *Rules* are specific prescriptions or proscriptions for actions.
- *Decision-making procedures* are prevailing practices for making and implementing collective choice.[33] (reformatted here for emphasis)

Principles

GATT's principles of *fact* and *causation* rest on the theory of comparative advantage, first described by Adam Smith.[34] According to the theory of comparative advantage, countries should specialize in what they can produce most efficiently, trading for other needed goods. Comparative advantage can lie in labor (skilled or unskilled), natural resources, capital, and other areas. GATT's principles of *rectitude* can be explained in terms of the four kinds of ethical values discussed so far. GATT relies on utilitarian concerns (we are all better off as we increase economic welfare in the absence of war) and fairness (free trade gives people an equal opportunity to compete). Fair international markets should also create opportunities to promote individual and family well-being. Ethical and economic goals and values, then, form the heart of GATT.

Norms and Rules

Lenway argues that GATT rests on four *norms:* nondiscrimination, multilateralism, reciprocity, and a commitment to the progressive liberalization of trade.[35] The first three norms are based on fairness and equality. Nondiscrimination and multilateralism norms encourage signatories to apply the same tariffs to all member countries. Reciprocity can be positive or negative. Positive reciprocity occurs when a nation reduces its tariffs in response to reductions in other countries. Negative reciprocity occurs when a country retaliates against unfair trade practices of a member nation.

GATT expresses its norms in *rules*.[36] The two most significant sets of rules are those concerning dispute resolution and the rules enabling periodic multilateral trade negotiations, or "Rounds," in which member countries meet to discuss and reduce trade barriers. The rules regarding disputes allow GATT to set up panels made up of member countries who are not part of the dispute. These panels hear evidence and recommend resolutions. These resolutions, in turn, must be passed unanimously by GATT's members. This method for resolving conflicts seldom succeeded, since the countries in dispute were among those voting on whether to accept the findings of the panel. The losing country was not likely to vote for resolutions that harmed it.

Rounds have been more effective. The Kennedy Round (1964–1967) achieved radical reductions in tariffs. The Tokyo Round (1973–1979) reduced tariffs further, and also dealt with nontariff barriers to trade, such as subsidies, trade licenses, and technical barriers. The progress on these nontariff barriers is less than had been achieved with tariffs. The Uruguay Round (1986–1993) addressed all the issues of the Tokyo Round, along with some special issues, such as financial services and intellectual property rights. It is estimated that the Uruguay Round will reduce tariffs by over 700 billion dollars and increase world income by over 500 billion dollars per year. These are impressive numbers.[37] In the long run, however, the most significant outcome of the Uruguay Round may be the creation of two new organizations: the World Trade Organization and the World Trade Organization Appellate Body.

The Uruguay Round established the World Trade Organization (WTO) to increase the effectiveness of GATT. It's main duties are to make policy recommendations and to gather and distribute information to member countries. The WTO Appellate Body is a court that was created to resolve conflicts between nations over trade issues. The Appellate Body works quite differently from the old method of conflict resolution described above. In the old system, a dispute resolution could be rejected if one country voted against it. The resolutions of the WTO Appellate Body, however, are in force unless there is a unanimous vote to *reject* them. Since the winning nation gets to vote on this issue, it is unlikely that very many recommendations will be rescinded.[38]

The long-range effects of the WTO and the WTO Appellate Body are unclear, but there is some indication of the principles they will use to make decisions. The WTO is likely to continue to use the basic ethical, political, and economic principles that have guided GATT since its inception. The WTO Appellate Court, however, may focus more on economic concerns and the standard utilitarian values about aggregate wealth creation (see Chapters 3 and 4 about how utilitarian values underlie economic reasoning; compare this with intrinsic value ethical views that are more concerned with distributive issues in wealth creation).[39]

Presently, only sovereign states can bring disputes before the WTO Appellate Body. If businesses or individuals want to bring issues before the Body, they must get a nation to do this for them. This practice might change in the future. The European Union (EU), for example, now has mechanisms for individuals and businesses to bring trade disputes directly to EU organizations.[40] The WTO now has informal meetings with labor, environmental organizations, and other stakeholder groups to help it gather information and analyze trade policy.[41]

GATT and the WTO influence Jameson and Mamet both directly and indirectly. Indirectly, GATT helped create the international trade environment that makes the relocation desirable in the first place. If trade relationships were as unstable as they were in the 1920s and 1930s, it would be too risky to make large capital investments overseas for mid-size companies such as S and R. Larger companies such as GM and Phizer can take some of these risks because their markets are already overseas, they have a larger capital base, and they have their own political avenues they can use to protect themselves.[42] However, even the larger companies would have less of an international presence without GATT.

GATT also has a direct influence on Jameson and Mamet's decision to relocate. ICE predicts that continuing world trade spurred by GATT will raise the incomes and needs of people throughout Asia. Chips will be needed not only for computers, but for literally thousands of consumer goods—watches, radios, televisions—that people in these developing countries will buy long before they purchase a computer. If S and R is in Taiwan, it can position itself to supply these factor markets.

GATT also helps reduce market failure, which is to S and R's advantage. It has been estimated that computer software piracy results in annual losses of $12 billion.[43] The Uruguay Round gives more protection to intellectual property. Senior executives at Novell and Lotus argue that these new protections will lower prices and increase software development.[44] Advanced software, in turn, will spur demands for more powerful computers and for the technology to build them. Being in Taiwan will position S and R to be a major player in the computer manufacturing factor market.

THE FOREIGN CORRUPT PRACTICES ACT OF 1977 AND 1988

Jameson and Mamet know that business practices in Taiwan are different from those in the United States. Specifically, they are worried about having to make questionable payments to secure licenses and permits to do business. They both remember the Lockheed scandal in the 1970s when the CEO of Lockheed paid large bribes to Japanese government officials to secure airplane deals. When the bribes became public, both the CEO of Lockheed and the Prime Minister of Japan had to resign.

Jameson became alarmed when she read about a company owned by Boeing that bribed Canadian officials to secure an airplane deal.[45] She asked ICE to advise her on this issue. ICE responded that they were already preparing a report on it. Here is some background.

Congress passed the Foreign Corrupt Practices Act (FCPA) in 1977. The FCPA was prompted, in part, by the Lockheed bribery scandal. The Lockheed affair caused problems in the United States and Japan, and with other U.S. trading partners. In Japan, the image of U.S. businesses manipulating high-level government officials was an attack on national pride. The United States and Japan have important political, military, and economic relationships that both countries want to preserve. A strong United States–Japan relationship is considered essential for the political stability of the region. The U.S. Congress wanted to send a message to Japan and the rest of the world that the United States is opposed to antimarket tactics such as bribery, that it does not want U.S. companies meddling in the political affairs of host countries, and that it is firmly committed to the principles of free trade, including fair competition. As, always, international trade and international politics are intertwined.

Another political motivation for the FCPA was the lack of public trust in big business prevalent in the 1970s. By passing the FCPA, members of Congress wanted to show their constituents and the global trading community that they were taking a stand against corrupt business practices. If Congressional incumbents did not make this clear, their political challengers would. However, the FCPA was not just a knee-jerk reaction to public pressure. It reflects widely held economic and ethical beliefs and values that underlie market, organizational, and individual behavior.

Markets

The ethical values of fairness and group well-being that underlie the FCPA are similar to those that underlie GATT. The United States has backed GATT since its inception. The guiding principle of GATT is that open markets help all countries, at least in the long term. In each Round of GATT since its inception, tariff and nontariff barriers have been reduced.

Using the Lockheed case as an example, we begin with how the FCPA supports the free market values that also underlie GATT.

- **Competition.** In the case of commercial aircraft sales, the people making the buying decision are not the primary users of the product. This fact alone can cause the sale to be based on issues other than price and quality. Bribery further distorts competition because products are not judged primarily by their price and quality, but by the amount of the bribe.

- **Risk–Reward Relationship.** Bribery distorts this condition by reducing risks to producers and increasing risks to consumers. Lockheed was able to reduce its risk by using bribes to secure sales. The risk to consumers increased because the purchase was based on nonproduct concerns.

- **Information.** Bribery gives false price information to the market, since the bribe is not usually recorded as an expense. These purchases send signals to the market that the product is a good value, when it is the bribe that is successful, not the product. The FCPA helps ensure that accurate information goes to the market.

- **Property.** The effect of the FCPA on property is determined by the three other conditions. For example, the distorted information misdirects stockholders of Lockheed about the quality of Lockheed's products. Passengers on Lockheed planes give up their money under false pretenses.

Organizations

To maintain free market standards, the FCPA alters the incentives of organizations. Corporations can be fined up to 2 million dollars. With multiple counts and multipliers, the fines can reach 25 million dollars or more. However, organizations may assume these risks if the benefits are great enough. To reduce this problem, the FCPA reaches inside organizations.

Individuals

Organizations are chartered by laws that shield officers from many kinds of liability. The FCPA pierces this liability shield by assessing criminal penalties, in the form of fines and *prison sentences,* for U.S. citizens who bribe foreign officials in the course of doing business for a U.S. company. Individuals can be fined up to $100,000 and given up to 5 years in prison. Civil penalties can be as high as $10,000. Fines for individuals *cannot* be paid by the businesses they represent.[46]

The FCPA also makes U.S. business people responsible for the actions of their host country consultants. When companies enter foreign markets, they often hire local consultants to help them negotiate the social, legal, and political environment. This is legitimate, and almost always necessary. Local consultants are given budgets to conduct their business. Before the FCPA, consultants did not always have to account for their expenditures. This allowed consultants to bribe officials without the explicit knowledge of their U.S. principals. To combat this problem, the FCPA requires companies to "make and keep books, records, and accounts, which, in reasonable detail, accurately and fairly reflect the transactions and dispositions of the assets of the issue."[47] It also requires that all transactions be authorized using normal procedures.

In 1988 the FCPA was amended to take care of problems that arose in applying the 1977 Act. We will mention two of the most important problems. First, it was soon discovered that doing business in some countries required payments that would be illegal in the United States. It is not uncommon to pay a special fee or to give a gift to government officials in other countries to get telephone service, routine licenses to construct buildings, or to get customs approval to bring goods across the border even though all of the paperwork is in order. These payments, sometimes called "facilitating payments" or "grease payments," are necessary to do business. They are not paid to get special favors, but to secure routine services. These grease payments have been compared with "tipping" in restaurants.

The 1988 amendment allowed facilitating payments. Although allowing these payments made the FCPA more workable, it also made it difficult for business people to know whether a payment was allowable or not. This led to the second change of the 1988 amendment that allows companies to get a judgment from the Department of Justice about the legality of payments *before* making them.[48] Prior judgment regarding criminal matters is very unusual.

Table 5.7 illustrates the goals of the FCPA and the incentives to follow them. The three right-most columns focus on markets and the two left-most columns focus on individuals.

We should note three things about Table 5.7. First, the law works at the individual and organizational and market levels. This is a common feature of regulatory law. To regulate markets and organizations, law must reach down to the individuals who make organizational decisions. Second, the explanations in both Intrinsic Value columns are the same because these two categories focus on the value of human beings. Third, the motivations for obeying the law in the Self-Interest and Personal Relationships column are the same. Our interests and the interests of friends and family are intertwined, and what harms us as individuals often harms our relationships.

ICE informed Jameson and Mamet of the main features of the FCPA. They have assured them that Taiwan—a center for international business and a world leader in the manufacturing of semiconductor chips—does not put up too many roadblocks for U.S. businesses opening manufacturing plants. ICE has helped several companies set up manufacturing in Taiwan. They have a number of reputable local consultants who also know about the FCPA. They have advised Jameson and Mamet that S and R will probably have to hire two or three local advisors, since manufacturing, and its attendant import and export activities, require authorization from government agencies in different parts of the country.

U.S. FEDERAL SENTENCING GUIDELINES FOR ORGANIZATIONS

Several of the professional newsletters and magazines that Jameson and Mamet receive have had articles on the U.S. Sentencing Guidelines for Corporations. They do not plan on doing anything illegal, but they are confused about what the law requires. They have asked ICE to advise them on this issue. Here is some background.

In 1909, the United States Supreme Court decided that organizations could be held liable for breaches of federal criminal law.[49] However, there are two problems in applying criminal law to corporations.[50] In standard criminal law, individuals are guilty of a serious crime only if they *intend* to do something wrong. Since corporations are merely

TABLE 5.7
The Foreign Corrupt Practices Act

| Economic conditions at stake | Ethical values at stake | | | | |
| | | | | Intrinsic value | |
	Self-interest	Personal relationships	Group interest	Property rights	Fairness
Competition	Jail sentences and fines to individuals help preserve this condition	Risk of disrupting personal relationships helps preserve this condition	Preserving a competitive environment promotes low prices and high quality	Everyone is measured by the same standards—the product quality/price ratio—providing a fair playing field	Everyone is measured by the same standards—the product quality/price ratio—providing a fair playing field
Information	Jail sentences and fines to individuals help preserve this condition	Risk of disrupting personal relationships helps preserve this condition	Accurate information about products promotes efficiency	Accurate information about products allows investors to make informed investment decisions	Accurate information about products allows investors to make informed investment decisions
Risk–Reward	Jail sentences and fines to individuals help preserve this condition	Risk of disrupting personal relationships helps preserve this condition	Tying market success to product quality increases product quality	Everyone is measured by the same standards—the product quality/price ratio—enabling reasonable assessments of risk and reward	Everyone is measured by the same standards—the product quality/price ratio—enabling reasonable assessments of risk and reward
Property	Jail sentences and fines to individuals help preserve this condition	Risk of disrupting personal relationships helps preserve this condition	The support of the other market conditions promotes efficient capital distribution	People invest property in a fair system	People invest property in a fair system

legal persons, corporations cannot intend anything, only officers can. Second, imprisonment, the main punishment for criminal law, is not available for corporations. The only remedy available is a fine. Statute and case law on fines are not always effective when applied to corporations. A fine that would be very large for an individual would mean nothing to many corporations.

In November 1991, the U.S. Federal Sentencing Guidelines for Organizations came into effect to address these two problems.[51] These guidelines use a mitigated strict-liability approach. The sentencing guidelines impose strict liability because, in general, they hold corporations responsible for criminal violations of their officers even if the officer acts alone. This seems unfair, since it holds corporations liable for actions they cannot prevent.[52] To mitigate this problem, the Guidelines use two tactics. First, they make exceptions for a true rogue employee as long as there was no reason to suspect the person would break the law. Second, corporations can reduce their fines by up to 95% if they have exerted due diligence in preventing criminal behavior. Due diligence is determined by seven criteria.

1. The organization must have established compliance standards and procedures to be followed by its employees and other agents that are reasonably capable of reducing the prospect of criminal conduct.

2. Specific individual(s) within high-level personnel of the organization must have been assigned overall responsibility to oversee compliance with such standards and procedures.

3. The organization must have used due care not to delegate substantial discretionary authority to individuals whom the organization knew, or should have known through the exercise of due diligence, had a propensity to engage in illegal activities.

4. The organization must have taken steps to communicate effectively its standards and procedures to all employees and other agents, e.g., by requiring participation in training programs or by disseminating publications that explain in a practical manner what is required.

5. The organization must have taken reasonable steps to achieve compliance with its standards, e.g., by utilizing monitoring and auditing systems reasonably designed to detect criminal conduct by its employees and other agents and by having in place and publicizing a reporting system whereby employees and other agents could report criminal conduct by others within the organization without fear of retribution.

6. The standards must have been consistently enforced through appropriate disciplinary mechanisms, including, as appropriate, discipline of individuals responsible for the failure to detect an offense. Adequate discipline of individuals responsible for an offense is a necessary component of enforcement.

7. After an offense has been detected, the organization must have taken all reasonable steps to respond appropriately to the offense and to prevent further similar offenses—including any necessary modifications to its program to prevent and detect violations of law.[53]

These criteria can be used by small companies and large companies alike. A small company can take a few small measures that will meet these standards, whereas a large company will probably have to develop a complex program[54] (see Paine, Part I). Given S and R's size, a senior officer with an extra assistant could coordinate policies to meet these criteria.

ICE summed up these facts for Jameson and Mamet. They told Jameson and Mamet that ICE's report on the Sentencing Guidelines, once accepted by S and R, will serve as the first official document that supports S and R's commitment to meet the seven criteria. ICE is ready to help S and R develop a program that meets the guidelines. Once the program is in place, the FCPA forbids ICE from administering it. Still, ICE can act as consultants, reducing the time S and R spends on the program.

THE SEMICONDUCTOR MANUFACTURING MARKET

Jameson and Mamet are very familiar with the semiconductor manufacturing market. They worked with ICE to find the best way to position S and R in this market. What they discovered convinced them that moving was moderately risky, but that the returns could

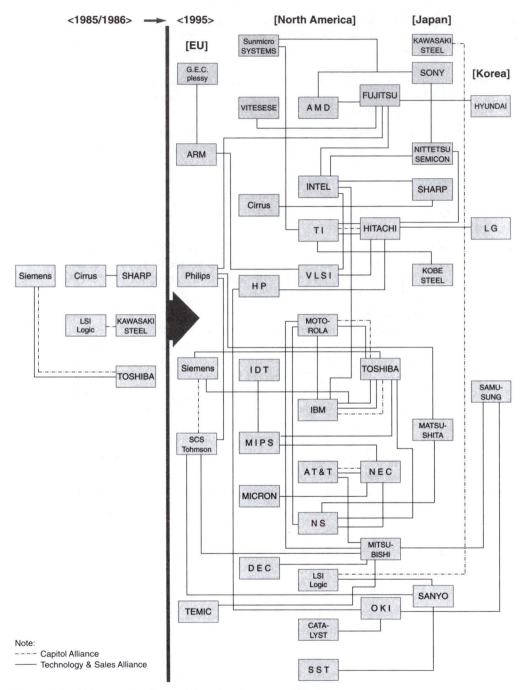

Figure 5.2   Alliances of major world semiconductor manufacturers.
(Used with the kind permission of the Electronic Industries Association of Japan.)

be great. If they did not move overseas, their only U.S. competitor, Integrated Process Equipment, would. Jameson and Mamet wanted to get overseas first.

The interconnected semiconductor manufacturing market gives Jameson and Mamet several options that make it possible to serve more of the competing stakeholders than they had originally thought (Figure 5.2[55]).

When Jameson and Mamet discussed it together and with ICE, the conclusion seemed clear: they should try to form an alliance with one or more semiconductor companies, or with the suppliers to these companies, that already have experience in the Asian market.

Jameson and Mamet began with a list of 10 companies that had Asian experience and who also had executives that either Jameson or Mamet knew and trusted. After making cautious, exploratory phone calls, this list was whittled down to two companies: PRI Automation, where Mamet had a contact, and Applied Materials, where Jameson had a contact.

PRI, located in Billerica, Massachusetts, specializes in making "clean rooms" and robotics for moving silicon chips in the production process. It is expanding rapidly. In July 1996 they came out with an entire automation system for moving silicon chips through the production process. This allows a manufacturer to come to one vendor, PRI, for all its automation needs. They have a strong presence in Japan, but not in Taiwan. Mamet contacted the CFO at PRI, who told them that PRI is interested in the Taiwan market, and that an exploratory meeting could be scheduled to talk about combining their efforts.

Applied Materials, located in Santa Clara, California, supplies equipment that performs six of the eight basic steps in chip manufacturing. It is one of the largest companies in the industry. They, too, have experience in Japan, but not in Taiwan. Jameson, who knows the CFO at Applied, got a cordial reception when she suggested exploring a joint project.

Jameson and Mamet would like to tie the overseas joint venture with a U.S. joint venture. Both PRI and Applied Materials have heavy service and distribution demands in the United States that S and R can help satisfy. This would give S and R's development team new projects, and give new jobs to the highly skilled labor now used to produce CMP tools. The joint venture could also relieve some of Jameson's and Mamet's family pressures, since it would reduce the time they need to spend overseas.

Jameson and Mamet are not at all sure they will have a fairy tale ending, but they are satisfied at this point that they are doing what good managers should do. If some stakeholders lose, it will at least be from a process that considered their interests.

SUMMARY OF CHAPTER 5 AND TRANSITION TO PART III

Chapter 5 discussed how law provides a predictable business environment by reinforcing the economic and ethical values that underlie institutions. Some key points are as follows:

- Law reinforces central ethical values and economic relationships.
  - Constitutive law sets up the basic system that makes business transactions possible.
  - Regulative law tries to ensure that business behavior is consistent with ethical and economic institutional values

- Public choice theory rests on the ethical values of self-interest, care, group well-being, and intrinsic value.
- Managers need to integrate a wide variety of ethical, economic, and legal concerns.
  — Laws can serve as important information-gathering and integration tools.
- International business is more difficult because of the diversity of institutional values.
- International organizations and trade regimes are developing to create stable institutions to govern international trade. These organizations and regimes attempt to reinforce a set of ethical and economic values and conditions.

This concludes our investigation into the ethical, economic, and legal aspects of social institutions. We turn now to Part III, which contains cases and articles that discuss and illustrate many of the concepts, principles, and relationships we have examined. Cases describe situations in which managers must decide how to resolve conflicts between ethical, economic, and legal institutional values, whereas articles argue for a specific way to interpret and integrate ethical, economic, and legal institutional values.

Notes

1. Institutions are not secure by definition. In a changing cultural environment, institutions can become insecure before they completely lose their institutional character.
2. In particular cases, attendance at social functions may be a part of a child custody arrangement.
3. H. L. A. Hart. *The Concept of Law.* Oxford: Clarendon Press, 1961, pp. 92–96.
4. Seth Schiesel. "Global Agreement Reached to Widen Law on Copyright." *The New York Times,* National edition, December 21 1996, p. 1; for a list of resources pertaining to this topic see Jeff Frentzen. "How Copyright Laws Will Affect On-line Data." *PC Week* 11:148 (5 December 1994), p. 17.
5. Frentzen, *op. cit.,* p. 15.
6. I would like to thank Wendy Boucher for this example.
7. This was the official interpretation of the 1991 Act. Whether it really does exclude quotas is still debated.
8. Author's field notes. I leave it to the reader to evaluate this argument.
9. In fact, the number of cells in the real debate is much larger, since the ethical orientation in each column has a number of interpretations. This can easily expand the number of columns to 15 or 20, generating 60 to 80 cells.
10. See Chapter 3: Kohlberg, Epicurus, Rand, Mill, Kant, Rawls, and Aristotle.
11. See Chapter 3: Hume, Mill, Aristotle, and most current economic theories. This is widely accepted by the psychological, economic, and management literature.
12. See Chapter 2: Gilligan; and Chapter 3: Hume and Aristotle.
13. See discussion of scripts and schemas in Chapter 2. Scripts and schemas mirror institutional expectations.
14. If we are rational relationship-building creatures whose limitations require a social infrastructure, our good would be promoted by institutional values that encourage our rational and social development. The ethical theorists we examined generally agreed that the four ethical orientations, if interpreted correctly, promote our rational and social development. They disagreed about the importance of these four elements.
15. Stephen Moore and Dean Stansel. "Ending Corporate Welfare as We Know It." *Policy Analysis* 225 (May 12, 1995), Cato Institute: Internet pages 2 and 6.
16. *Ibid.,* p. 6.
17. James D. Gwartney and Richard Stroup. *Economics: Private and Public Choice,* 3rd ed. New York: Academic Press, 1982, p. 647.
18. Donna Wood. "Deregulating the Airlines." In *Business and Society,* 2nd ed. New York: Harper Collins, 1994, pp. 423–428.
19. *Economist* 340:7975 (July 26, 1996), pp. 15, 51, 52.

20. E. Orts. "A Reflexive Model of Environmental Regulation." *Business Ethics Quarterly* 5:4 (1995), pp. 779–794.
21. *Ibid.*, p. 781.
22. *Ibid.*, p. 782.
23. *Ibid.*, p. 782.
24. *Ibid.*, p. 782.
25. *Ibid.*, p. 783.
26. *Ibid.*, p. 783.
27. *Ibid.*, p. 784.
28. *Ibid.*, p. 784.
29. *Ibid.*, p. 780.
30. *Ibid.*, p. 785.
31. *Ibid.*, p. 785.
32. *Ibid.*, p. 786.
33. Stephanie Lenway. *The Politics of U.S. International Trade: Protection, Expansion, and Escape.* Boston: Pitman, 985, p. 5.
34. *Ibid.*, p. 5.
35. *Ibid.*, p. 6.
36. *Ibid.*, p. 7.
37. G. Shell. "Trade Legalism and International Relations Theory: An Analysis of the World Trade Organization." *Duke Law Journal* 44:5 (March 1995), pp. 829–927.
38. *Ibid.*, p. 832.
39. *Ibid.*, pp. 890, 892.
40. *Ibid.*, pp. 917–919.
41. *Ibid.*, p. 923.
42. See Chapter 9: "Two Roads to China: Nice, and Not So Nice."
43. *Congressional Quarterly Weekly Report* 52:29 (23 July 1995), p. 2006.
44. *PC Week, op. cit.*
45. J. Sterngold. "Canadian Bribe Inquiry Said to Focus on Boeing; a 1990 Jet Deal with Bahamasair Brings Scrutiny and a Lawsuit." *New York Times* National edition, February 13, 1996, C1.
46. Amarjeet S. Bhachu. "Foreign Corrupt Practices Act. (Tenth Survey of White Collar Crime)." *American Criminal Law Review* 32:2 (Winter 1995), pp. 445–455, Section IV, part C (retrieved from an electronic database).
47. *Ibid.*, Section II, part A.
48. *Ibid.*, Section IV, part B.
49. The main points in these introductory remarks are taken from Otto G. Obermaier. "A Practical Partnership." *The National Law Journal* 14:10 (November 11, 1991), p. 13, col. 1.
50. The U.S. Federal Sentencing Guidelines for Organizations apply to organizations of all types. We will focus on corporations.
51. These guidelines were the result of four years of work by the Federal Sentencing Commission, which was originally charged with making federal sentences for individuals more uniform.
52. For other reasons why these guidelines may seem unfair, see Marianne Lavelle. "Sentencing Guidelines Called Unfair." *National Law Journal* 15:52 (August 30, 1993), p. S7, Col. 2.
53. *United States Sentencing Commission Manual.* Sj8A1.3 (1 November 1991), p. 352.
54. See Robert J. Rafalko. "Remaking the Corporation: The 1991 U.S. Sentencing Guidelines." *Journal of Business Ethics* 13 (1994), pp. 626–636.
55. Electronic Industries Association of Japan <http://www.eiaj.org/charts/alliance.html>, July 1997.

PART

III

Applying the Framework: Cases and Articles

INTRODUCTION

The cases and articles in Part III are organized by the four economic conditions discussed in Chapter 3: property, risk–reward relationships, information, and competition. For example, pollution problems are discussed in terms of externalities, and so are put in the chapter on property. Employee rights are discussed in the chapter on risk and reward; whistleblowing and marketing are in the chapter on information; competitive practices, such as moving to lesser developed countries to save on labor costs, are in the chapter on competition.

While categorizing cases and articles by the four market conditions can be helpful, we need to remember that most of the issues we will discuss involve all four conditions. For example, discussions of competition always assume the use of property in a structure of risk and rewards about which participants have incomplete information. Despite this interconnectedness, issues often have central features that command our attention.[1]

Cases are presented to illustrate different decision-making contexts. *Articles* serve four connected roles. First, many of the articles provide backgrounds and surveys of issues. Second, they help identify and integrate central concepts and principles raised by a case. Third, they interpret information. Finally, they supplement and sometimes challenge the views in Parts I and II. The articles are not intended, however, to give "answers" to cases.

Read these chapters as an ongoing conversation that gets broader and deeper. The opening case and articles in Chapter 6 on The Control and Use of Corporate Property offer four different views of how ethical, economic, and legal concerns can and should be integrated at the market, organizational, and individual decision-making levels. These four articles provide focal points around which the reader can interpret and evaluate subsequent readings. The reverse is also true: subsequent readings provide information and arguments that may prompt a reevaluation of the opening articles.

The chapters in Part III get progressively shorter. Property is taken as the central market condition, and so the most space is devoted to it. Issues regarding risk and reward connect to property issues; issues regarding information connect to risk–reward relationships and property; issues concerning competition connect to the previous three topics. The four topics are best seen as interlaced, like a tapestry, with property rights serving as the foundational threads.

A final note. There is no attempt to cover all the issues that fall under the topics of the following four chapters. There is a brief discussion at the beginning of each chapter of other issues that fall under that topic to place the chapter's readings in context.

USING THE FRAMEWORK DEVELOPED IN PART II TO UNDERSTAND AND EVALUATE CASES AND ARTICLES

Applying the Framework to Cases

Cases *describe* conflicts in institutional settings.[2] To understand and resolve these conflicts, we need to understand and be willing to modify the ethical, economic, and legal relationships that make up these settings. The decision-making strategy introduced in Chapter 2 can help us do this.

A DECISION-MAKING STRATEGY FOR CASES

1. Identify stakeholders (people, groups, organizations who have a stake in the problem and its resolution) who are central to the conflict.

2. Describe the institutions and relationships that tie the stakeholders together. Specify the ethical, economic, and legal–political values that form the basis of these institutions and relationships.

3. Show how the conflict arose as the stakeholders acted on the values you have identified. (At this point, you may want to modify your responses to 1 and 2.)

   Be wary of vagueness and ambiguity. For example, do the stakeholders have clear and shared understandings of the ethical, economic, and legal values they use to direct their behavior?

4. Evaluate the institutional settings and relationships using ethical, economic, and legal values.

5. Identify a set of alternatives that can be implemented in the institutional setting out of which the conflict arose. Make sure these alternatives pay attention to the ethical, economic, and legal–political values you discussed in 4.

   Take the point of view of different stakeholders to see what alternatives they would suggest. When possible, get the information directly from stakeholders, rather than imagining what they would say or want.

6. Choose the alternative that best resolves the current conflict, that will prevent similar conflicts in the future, and that will not cause other significant conflicts. Defend your choice in terms of the ethical, economic, and legal values you discussed in 4.

7. Develop and implement a plan to monitor results. Clearly specify the values you will use to evaluate the results.

How we use this strategy will depend on our ethical, economic, and legal points of view. How can we proceed if we cannot show that one ethical, economic, and legal view is superior to others? We can avoid this problem by using ethical pluralism in Steps 1–5 *without* committing ourselves to pluralistic ethics.

In S and R (A) Jameson and Mamet used a kind of uncommitted pluralism as they considered the relocation decision. They identified a group of stakeholders and some of the ethical, economic, and legal relationships between them (Steps 1 and 2). In doing this, they took the claims of all stakeholders to be compelling, but none dominant, as pluralism would prescribe. In S and R (B), they acquired information that helped them formulate alternatives (Step 5). These alternatives took the form of making alliances with other companies in ways that could satisfy the interests of legitimate stakeholders. They did not think very much about how they got into this problem (Step 4), so at this point they cannot tell how to prevent such problems in the future. They also did not explicitly evaluate their institutional setting or relationships (Step 5). They are not ready to choose a course of action or a monitoring plan (Steps 6 and 7).

Once Jameson and Mamet get enough information and alternatives to make a decision, they *will* need to adopt some ethical, economic, and legal point of view. As far as ethics goes, they can use any one of the five ethical views discussed in Chapters 1 and 2, combining it with an economic and legal view. Though they are forced to take an ethical view to make this decision, *they are not forced to hold that view in the future.* Looking back to Kohlberg and Gilligan, we can view ethical decisions as provisional ways to understand and act within ambiguous situations. As we live with the consequences of our decisions, we get information we can use to evaluate our decision.

Applying the Framework to Articles

Articles describe and *evaluate* conflicts between individuals, markets, and organizations in their institutional settings. Often, articles go on to *prescribe* a solution to the conflict. The solution will be put in terms of modifying the ethical, economic, and legal relationships in the institutional settings of the problem. We can modify the decision-making strategy for cases to help us evaluate articles.

A STRATEGY FOR ANALYZING ARTICLES

1. Whom do the authors identify as stakeholders? Have they left anyone out, or included anyone who should not be included?

2. How do the authors describe the institutions and relationships that tie the stakeholders together? How do they specify the ethical, economic, and legal–political values that form the basis of these institutions and relationships? Is the description complete and accurate?

3. How do the authors think the conflict(s) arose as the stakeholders acted in accord with the institutions, relationships, and values identified in the previous step?

4. How do the authors use ethical, economic, and legal criteria to evaluate the institutions and relationships? Do they value some criteria more than others? Do you agree with the authors?

5. What alternatives do the authors suggest? Can they be implemented in the institutional setting out of which the conflict arose? Have alternatives been left out?

6. What resolution do the authors suggest? Can this resolution resolve the current problem and prevent such problems in the future; will it cause other problems? Is their choice consistent with the values identified in 4? Do you agree with the authors?

7. Do the authors have a plan to monitor results if their resolution is adopted? If so, evaluate the plan. If not, can you devise such a plan?

As mentioned above, articles are not intended to give final answers to dilemmas and problems. Rather, they are intended to provide interpretations we can use to develop and defend our own point of view.

Ethical Displacement

Ethical displacement is a decision-making tool that complements the above strategies for analyzing cases and articles. Richard De George defines ethical displacement as follows:

> Ethical displacement consists of resolving a dilemma—or sometimes an ethical problem—by seeking a solution on a level other than the one on which the dilemma or problem appears.[3]

For example, S and R's problem first arose as a conflict between promoting the interests of different stakeholders: owners, managers, labor, suppliers, and the local community. In S and R (B), Jameson and Mamet appealed to different macrolevels: Federal statutes governing overseas business, international trade agreements that affect the risks and rewards of the move, and the structure of the semiconductor industry. Factoring in information from these levels gave them a better understanding of the problem and a broader set of alternatives.

Jameson and Mamet also considered some microissues, such as the ability to hire representatives in Taiwan in a way consistent with the Foreign Corrupt Practices Act. They will also have to look at other microissues before they can make a final decision. For example, to deal successfully with labor they will have to understand the officers and the structure of the labor union.

Ethical displacement is available to all decision makers, from temporary workers who clean floors to CEOs of large corporations. It enables decision makers to get a sense of the institutional settings out of which conflicts arise and helps to examine the values that underlie those institutional settings.

The cases and articles in Part III are followed by discussion questions. These questions can be used independently or to complement the above strategies for analyzing cases and articles.

Notes

1. As we noted in the introduction to the text, disagreement about the placement of an issue is not a problem in itself, since such disagreements enter into the kind of dialogue this book is designed to promote.
2. Cases assume an interpretation of the institutional setting, and so they are not purely descriptive. Because of this, the difference in the evaluative content in cases and articles is a matter of degree. Still, matters of degree can matter.
3. Richard De George. *Competing with Integrity in International Business*. New York: Oxford University Press, 1993.

CHAPTER 6

Property

INTRODUCTION

The cases and articles in this chapter examine the control and use of corporate property in domestic and international arenas, with special attention to the environment. Environmental problems are treated as property failures.

There are many other issues that could be included under the topic of property. Some of these are the role and proper composition of boards of directors, rules regarding stockholder initiatives, standards for and the enforcement of patents at the domestic and international levels, and differences between personal and corporate property rights. There are many introductory business ethics and business and society texts that provide a good starting place to investigate these topics.

As we saw in Chapters 4 and 5, there is general agreement that property rights are at the heart of the institutional settings in which business operates. There is also general agreement that property rights have ineliminable ethical aspects: they specify what we may and should not do with our property, and they impose duties on others not to interfere with the legitimate use of our property.

These points of agreement set the stage for disagreements about the specific nature of property rights. These disagreements are especially volatile regarding corporate property. There are at least three reasons for this. First, as Berle and Means pointed out, the corporation is a relatively new invention (Chapter 4), so it and the institutions governing it are still evolving. Second, many corporations are international, where the institutional settings are relatively weak. Third, there is intense competition for the economic and political power of corporations.

The rest of this introduction consists of brief descriptions of the cases and articles in this chapter.

THE CONTROL AND USE OF CORPORATE PROPERTY

This section begins with H. Jeff Smith's case, "Agrico, Inc.—A Software Dilemma." A newly hired MIS officer of Agrico, Inc., must decide whether to copy the source code of a software program his company is buying. This software will handle all of the basic transactions of the firm. His company has agreed to purchase the software, but the vendor will not sell the source code. The source code is necessary to fix problems with the software. Because the relationship with the vendor has not gone well, the MIS officer believes that having access to the source code is vital to the continued success of his firm. Company counsel tells him that if he copies the source code and the vendor sues, a jury could side with Agrico. What should he do?

The four articles that follow this case discuss basic ethical, economic, and legal principles managers can use to make decisions. In "The Social Responsibility of Business Is to Increase Its Profits," Milton Friedman argues for a shareholder view of corporate property: managers should act as agents to maximize the financial returns of the owners. Using corporate property to pursue social goals violates the rights of the owners. It is also likely to have bad consequences, since managers have no expertise regarding social and political issues. To support his view, Friedman appeals directly to rights and utility as discussed in Chapter 3.

In "Deriving Ethical Principles from Theories of the Firm," Philip L. Cochran agrees with Friedman that managers should promote the interests of the owners, but he points out that owners come from many different stakeholder groups. Some corporations are owned by employees, some are owned by customers (cooperatives), while others are owned by consumers. Cochran argues that these different patterns of ownership result in different views about the legitimate uses of corporate property. At the end of the article, Cochran suggests that the growth of mutual funds and pension funds in corporate equity markets results in firm ownership, directly or indirectly, by employees, customers, shareholders, and others in the community in which the firm does business. Because all of these groups have property interests in corporations, managers should act as agents to promote the interests of all these stakeholders.

In "A Stakeholder Theory of the Modern Corporation," R. Edward Freeman argues for a stakeholder view of corporate property, but he bases it on the Kantian and Rawlsian principles discussed in Chapter 3, not on property interests. Management should coordinate the interests of stakeholders. Stakeholders are important because they are people, and have dignity and rights that must be respected. Freeman argues that economic and legal rules and institutions are changing to reflect this broad view of corporate property.

In "Getting Real: Stakeholder Theory, Managerial Practice, and the General Irrelevance of Fiduciary Duties Owed to Shareholders," Richard C. Marens and Andrew D. Wicks argue that the fiduciary duty of managers is not to maximize shareholder financial interests, but only not to act in ways that would clearly and measurably harm shareholder financial interests. Under this view, which they support with an examination of relevant law, managers are free to promote the interests of nonowning stakeholders by giving to charity, paying more than standard labor rates, and a variety of other things.

PROPERTY AND THE ENVIRONMENT

Protecting the natural environment is one of the standard reasons for limiting the use of corporate property. A. R. Gini's "Diablo Canyon: Nuclear Energy and the Public Welfare" describes some of the problems Pacific Gas and Electric had in bringing a nuclear plant on line. Environmental groups challenged the plant from the beginning. As their protests continued, information was discovered that made the plant more suspect than opponents had originally thought. This case raises all of the stakeholder issues discussed above as well as specific environmental concerns.

In "People or Penguins: The Case for Optimal Pollution" William F. Baxter asks what is bad about environmental pollution. Relying on Kantian standards discussed in Chapter 3, Baxter argues that pollution is bad only if it harms human beings; pollution is not bad because it harms penguins, tidal pools, or redwoods unless human beings value these things enough to pay to protect them. Baxter argues that corporations should be able to use the environment to benefit its stakeholders until what it destroys is more valuable than what is produced. He argues that this is not the mean cost–benefit view it seems to be, since the cost of controlling pollution has to be measured in terms of goods we are *not* buying, such as education and health care.

In "Morality, Money, and Motor Cars," Norman Bowie argues that corporations have no special duty to protect the environment beyond the requirements of law. However, Bowie does argue that business is wrong to influence government policy regarding pollution. He notes that the demand for a clean environment cannot express itself well in economic markets because the environment is a public good (Chapter 4). The only way that this demand can be expressed is through government, but if business intervenes in this expression, it distorts the demand.

INTERNATIONAL: THE CONTROL AND USE OF CORPORATE PROPERTY

In the case, "Plasma, International," T. W. Zimmerer and P. L. Preston describe a company that is chastised by the press for making large profits from the sale of blood. Plasma International, which is located in Tampa, Florida, gets its blood from third world countries because the blood is good quality and the costs are low. The company made huge profits when a natural disaster in Nicaragua increased the demand for blood. The local press and Tampa residents complained that the company was "selling life and death." Plasma's management could not understand what all the fuss was about—they run a business just like any other business.

In "Ethical Dilemmas for the Multinational Enterprise: A Philosophical Overview," Richard De George argues that multinational corporations (MNCs) face conflicting demands because of the lack of background institutions, such as an established system of courts, government agencies, financial institutions, and professional organizations that guides business behavior. International organizations such as the United Nations and the World Trade Organization are trying to fill this vacuum, but the rules of these and similar organizations are weak. Background institutions establish public expectations about MNC behavior. Without these institutions, critics tend to use highly idealized views to critique MNC behavior. The lack of global background institutions also gives MNCs the ability to pursue their interests in ways that harm third parties by emitting excessive pollution, paying low wages, manipulating information, and engaging in monopolistic behavior. De George suggests seven guidelines MNCs can use to guide their behavior and so mitigate these problems. These guidelines represent a pluralistic approach to ethics (Chapter 3).

In "The Moral Responsibility of Multinational Corporations to Be Socially Responsible," Patricia H. Werhane argues against a Friedmanesque view that MNCs should simply obey local customs and law. The fact that a country allows slavery, child labor, and racial discrimination does not mean that it is all right for MNCs to participate in these practices or pretend they do not exist. On the other hand, MNCs are guests in the host countries, and as guests, their right to promote social change is more limited than local organizations. Political activity in host countries can be paternalistic and violate the country's sovereignty. Werhane lists six questions that can help MNCs decide how to operate in host countries.

In "International Business Ethics: The Aluminum Companies in Jamaica," Manuel Velasquez examines three different approaches to evaluating MNC behavior in host countries: Tom Donaldson's rights approach, Gerald Efstrom's utilitarian approach, and De George's pluralistic approach. Using Jamaica's relationships with aluminum producers, Velasquez argues that although all three approaches help us evaluate important elements of the case, they all fail to grapple with the full range of justice issues. He argues for a pluralistic approach of the kind he develops in his book, *Business Ethics: Concepts and Cases.*[1]

International: Property and the Environment

In his article, "U.S. and Mexico Confront a Toxic Legacy," Colum Lynch talks about the environmental problems surrounding the Mequiladora program, which allows non-Mexican companies to operate assembly plants in a narrow strip of land along the Mexican–U.S. border. These companies pay lower tariffs, but still have access to inexpensive Mexican labor. Unfortunately the Mexican laws against pollution are rarely enforced, and toxic wastes are dumped near housing and water supplies.

In "The Ethics of Development and the Dilemmas of Global Environmentalism," David P. Hanson argues that the problems facing the global environment are overwhelming. Population growth and economic development have created great demands for our limited resources. Hanson argues that it may be necessary to limit MNC behavior and intervene in the actions of sovereign nations. He believes that such actions can be initiated through what he calls "supranational organizations" such as the International Monetary Fund and the General Agreement on Tariffs and Trade (now administered by the World Trade Organization). If we compare Hanson's argument with the work of North in Part I, and De George in this chapter, we can understand these supranational bodies as an attempt to provide institutional frameworks for business behavior.

Note

1. M. Velasquez. *Business Ethics: Concepts and Cases.* Englewood Cliffs, NJ: Prentice Hall, 1992.

CASE: **Agrico, Inc.—A Software Dilemma**
         H. Jeff Smith

George P. Burdelle, vice president of information systems at Agrico, Inc., walked into
the computer room with his systems and programming manager, Louise Alvaredo, at
6:30 P.M. on Wednesday, May 27, 1987. Alvaredo typed a few keystrokes on a systems
computer console and turned to Burdelle. "So, as you can see, Jane Seymour [the software engineer for Agrico's new AMR system] left the source code on our computer
when she left for dinner." She paused, and then asked, "Should I copy it to tape and ship
it to our off-site storage facility?"

Agrico's $500 million portfolio of farm-management properties was set for con-
version to the new computer system over the upcoming weekend. AMR, a vendor of
farm-management software, had been selected to provide the software for the new system. The previous summer AMR had agreed to supply the object code for the system but
had been quite reluctant to release the source code to Agrico.[1] The software purchase
agreement between Agrico and AMR provided that the source code be placed in escrow
to provide protection in case of a natural disaster or in the event of AMR's bankruptcy
or inability to provide adequate support for the software. But, despite repeated attempts,
Burdelle had been unable to reach an acceptable arrangement with the software company regarding the escrow of the source code.

Burdelle and Alvaredo knew that Agrico would have certain access to the most recent version of the source code should they choose to copy it now and secure it. Given
his experience with AMR over the past year, Burdelle was not confident that AMR's proposed arrangements to escrow the source code were adequate. And if Agrico's $500 mil-
lion portfolio were converted to the new computer system and something happened to
the existing object code, the possibility existed that the object code could not be reproduced.

Furthermore, Burdelle had an operational concern. He wanted to be sure that any
future modifications to the software were made using the most recent version of the
source code, which included all previous modifications. Otherwise, there was a risk that
the portfolio data could be altered—or, corrupted—without anyone's knowledge.

He recalled the words of Agrico's attorney from a discussion held earlier that week:

> What if you *could* get a copy of their source code through some means? The contract
> states we cannot have a copy of the software without AMR's written permission. On the
> other hand, the agreement clearly calls for an escrow agreement that is acceptable both
> to AMR and to Agrico. If it ever got to court that we took their source code, the judge
> or jury could well side with us, especially when we explained the trouble we have had
> with AMR and their unsatisfactory response to our concerns. Still, a lawsuit would be
> bad publicity and would consume a lot of everyone's time, even if we won. If we lost,
> it is not clear what the impact might be.

Now, because of an AMR employee's oversight, Burdelle had access to the source
code.

"When do you need a decision?" Burdelle asked his systems manager. "Jane said she'd be back from dinner by eight o'clock," Alvaredo replied, "so I need to know in an hour or so."

"I'll give you an answer at 7:30," responded Burdelle, as he walked to his office.

AGRICO—COMPANY BACKGROUND

Agrico, Inc., started by two farmers in Des Moines, Iowa, in 1949, provided farm and ranch management services for 691,000 acres of land in several midwestern states. With market value of its portfolio at $500 million by 1987, Agrico ranked as one of the nation's larger agricultural management firms. Maintaining four regional offices housing an average of five farm managers each, Agrico was able to provide cost-effective management services for more than 350 farms and ranches. The company, acting as an agent, bought equity interests in farms and ranches for their clients (usually pension funds) and managed them to provide operating cash flow and capital appreciation.

Agrico had three different arrangements for the properties. Under crop-share lease arrangements, which represented 47% of their portfolio, tenant farmers would agree to farm land managed by Agrico in return for a portion of each year's crops, which Agrico would ultimately sell in commodity markets. Under cash-rent leases (51% of the portfolio), farmers made cash payments for use of the land. Agrico also directly managed a few properties (about 2% of its total).

AGRICO'S NEW COMPUTER SYSTEM

During their 1985 business planning process, Agrico's executives decided that their existing arrangement for computer services—an agreement with a nearby commercial real estate concern that provided all services for a yearly fee—was not adequate for their present or future needs. The same year they also identified a need for office automation to improve productivity. Their local contract for computer services expired on September 30, 1987, and as summers were traditionally slow (buying, selling, and leasing of farms took place in the winter and spring and supervising of crop harvests in the fall), June 1, 1987 was set as the target conversion date.

Since Agrico had no internal computer systems staff, they contracted with a large computer consulting firm for recommendations on their computing needs and responsibility for them. The consulting firm assigned several of its employees to the project, including a project manager—George P. Burdelle, a mid-1970s graduate of Georgia Tech who had received his MBA from the Harvard Business School shortly thereafter. The results of the systems planning project indicated that Agrico should do in-house data processing. But as they had little expertise, and to minimize cost and installation lead time, it was recommended that they use a software package rather than attempt to develop a custom-coded system. Thus, a software selection and systems design project was begun in March 1986.

Functional requirements for the system were very complex, since it was expected that a single software package would be used for all three property arrangements under Agrico management. The cash-rent leases offered few problems—that accounting was fairly straightforward. The directly managed properties, though few in number, required a different focus—"all the logistics of running a farm or ranch," according to Burdelle. As for the crop-share leases, since Agrico not only shared all expenses and revenues from these farms, but also often received part of the crops for payment, it was heavily involved in farm commodity markets. So, in addition to the program requirements needed to manage the receiving, selling, and delivering of its portion of the crops, the software had to accommodate the commodity market information.

Agrico insisted that these software requirements be met by a single vendor offering an integrated package. From an initial list of more than 40 potential vendors, only two were identified; each was asked to submit a bid in a "request for proposal" (RFP) process. Agrico selected AMR for their software. As Burdelle later explained:

> When you came down to it, it was a relatively straightforward decision for Agrico. AMR had 12 clients up and running, and they had excellent references. We visited two clients and saw demonstrations of features we knew we needed. The software ran on a mini-computer that also provided excellent office automation capabilities. The only major risk we saw was the fact that AMR was a small company.
>
> Our second choice vendor—a mid-sized software house with about 120 employees—sold software that met most of our functional requirements, but they had only sold three copies, none of which were in production yet. Their software ran on a mainframe, with heavy systems support and operations expertise requirements. In addition, the main-frame had very limited ability to support office automation.

A number of modification and enhancement requirements were identified for the AMR software during the selection process, and the cost and completion schedule were included in the RFP response from the vendor. Work on the system installation project began in July 1986.

Throughout this period Agrico was impressed with Burdelle's grasp of its complex system needs; they offered him the position of vice president of information systems, and Burdelle accepted on July 11, 1986. He said:

> Agrico had a need for someone to build a systems department, and I enjoyed working with the company personnel. The June 1, 1987, conversion target date allowed us ade-quate time for the installation, and we had the ability to run parallel with the old system before cutting over.

THE AMR RELATIONSHIP

AMR, a small software outfit headquartered in Omaha, Nebraska, had been founded in 1977 by A.M. Rogers. It sold only one software package—a system for managing farm and ranch portfolios. With 12 clients in nine states, AMR appeared to hold the solution for Agrico. Burdelle described them:

> They were a small company with 10 employees, including Rogers himself. We called every one of their customers and got the same story: positive experiences. Rogers was the core of AMR and had his hand in everything, from marketing to software design and programming. The other employees were systems people, but they were more "carpen-ters" than "architects."

Also in July, Agrico and AMR signed an agreement stating that AMR would pro-vide software consistent with Agrico's needs; AMR would be required to make modifications to its software package. The total purchase price for the software, including modifications, was approximately $200,000. Agrico would also pay one percent of this amount monthly as a maintenance fee. The modified object code was to be delivered to Agrico no later than October 1, 1986; the agreement stated that Agrico's access to the source code was limited to "viewing listings reasonably necessary the system." Only AMR was allowed to make modifications to the code. Commented Burdelle:

> We realized that a good percentage of Rogers's revenue came from modifying the software to meet unique client requirements, so we offered to pay more to buy the source code. We acknowledged that if we modified his source he would not be responsible for retrofitting our changes to his new software releases. However, he apparently was afraid that someone would steal a copy of his software. We offered to sign nondisclosure agreements, whatever, but Rogers was really irrational about keeping the source code.

The software purchase agreement required AMR to maintain the software in escrow with a third party to insure adequate backups.

THE SOFTWARE EXPERIENCE

AMR delivered the object code, as promised, by October. It was installed on Agrico's new computer, which had been delivered in late September. During this same time, Burdelle completed the hiring of his systems staff, which included a systems and programming manager, two programmers, and two operators.

The software acceptance test followed. Both the new Agrico staff and the consultants were involved in the testing. Burdelle related the experience:

> We quickly discovered that all was not right. There was no standard software, as AMR had installed 12 versions—one for each of its clients—around the country. No two were the same—the AMR programmers added or deleted code based upon the needs of each client. We wanted to use practically all of their options, and apparently none of their clients had used them all together. While the individual options worked, they did not always work correctly when combined. We also found out that a number of functions had never been thoroughly tested anywhere.
>
> As it turned out, AMR usually installed and converted the software and then fixed bugs when they were discovered by the client. We were not willing to live with that approach.
>
> Given this situation, we rearranged our schedule to provide more time for software acceptance testing. Our purchase contract required us to pay 20% of the software price upon contract signing, 60% of it 30 days after completion of software acceptance testing, and the remaining balance 90 days after system conversion. We had AMR's attention, because they did not get most of their money until the software passed our acceptance test. I was not going to jeopardize our clients' assets with bug-filled software. Furthermore, I began to see that the escrow of our software was very important, since a standard version literally did not exist.

From October through January, the Agrico team worked at the AMR offices in Omaha. Significant flaws were identified in the software, but AMR had successfully corrected them by March, and Jane Seymour from AMR had begun working on Agrico's computer in Des Moines. But this testing and repair process had exacted its toll on the relationship between Rogers and Burdelle. A contentious tone had crept into their correspondence, which was frequent. On one occasion Rogers complained about the Agrico project team's "tiger testing" of the software, and Burdelle noted, "I instructed the team to be ruthless in identifying bugs. I refused to sign off on the acceptance test until the software was perfect. It was not a pleasant experience."

OFF-SITE ESCROW

During this same period, Burdelle began lengthy discussions with Rogers to define the specific arrangements for the escrow of the object and source code. Burdelle explained:

> When we realized that every one of AMR's installations was unique, we understood just how important it was to have copies of the unique source code for our system stored for backup purposes. Without source code, there was potential for our being forever locked into the existing system with no chance for enhancements or modifications. It was possible we would have to go through the detailed software acceptance testing process again if any changes were made. Given our experience with AMR to date, I was not willing to take it on faith that our source code was adequately protected.
>
> Rogers claimed that we should be satisfied with his backup plan, in which he occasionally took tapes to his bank's vault in Omaha. However, we had no independent way to verify that the source code AMR stated as our escrow copy was in fact the source code that generated our object code. There are companies that store computer tapes in special facilities, like the one we employed in Des Moines for our data tapes, and we wanted that kind of security. Plus, we wanted an independent third party to insure that the latest version was available. The easiest way: escrow the source in the off-site facility we already used.
>
> But Rogers was afraid that we'd modify or sell his source code if it was in the same off-site facility we use, and he was paranoid about keeping control. We talked and talked with him, but our discussions came up empty. He said he thought our concerns about backup procedures were overblown.

Concerned that the June 1 conversion date was fast approaching with backup procedures for code storage still unclear, Burdelle discussed the situation with Agrico's attorney on Tuesday, May 26:

> The attorney said that we had a classic problem of ambiguity. The contract did require AMR to provide us with access to the source code so that we could understand it, but only AMR had the right to copy and store it. Yet, AMR was supposed to store it in a "satisfactory" manner; apparently, we each defined "satisfactory" differently. The attorney felt that if we could get access to the source code we might have a good court argument for storing it ourselves. But technically getting and storing the code did violate the contract.

Burdelle had also considered other solutions, such as discontinuing the relationship with AMR and looking for other vendors. He said:

> Many times along the way, I thought about telling AMR "thanks but no thanks." I realized that the expenses we had incurred were really sunk costs: things like our consult-

ants' bills for debugging the software, which by then had accumulated to $75,000. The biggest problem was that there were few other options: we already knew there was only one other vendor that had even a remotely similar software package, and it used different hardware.

Time was of the essence; any delays in converting to the new system would cost Agrico dearly. We did not want to start over and develop a custom system; that would have been a monumental project. I was confident that the software now worked as it should, but I was concerned about future modifications.

We had also created much ill will with Rogers, and he was becoming even more irrational as the days went by.

In contrast to the deteriorating relationship with Rogers, Agrico had developed great rapport with Jane Seymour. On Wednesday, May 27, Alvaredo said, in fact, that she believed Seymour may have "looked the other way" in leaving the source code on the computer when she went to dinner. "I think Jane knows the bind we are in with Rogers," she told Burdelle.

BURDELLE'S DECISION

Burdelle, alone in his office, pulled the AMR contract from his file cabinet and read again the words concerning access to source code. He thought once more about the attorney's advice, and he quickly reviewed the ramifications of the potential need for modifications to the software. "While we've had more than our share of disagreements, I have always been honest with Rogers, and I've tried to prove that he had no reason to distrust us," Burdelle mused. "I want to abide by the terms of the contract, but I don't want to jeopardize Agrico's clients' assets."

At 7:30 P.M., Burdelle walked to the computer room to give Alvaredo his decision.

Note

1. *Source code* contained a computer program's statements written by programmers in high-level programming languages like BASIC, COBOL, FORTRAN, PL/I, C, etc. It could be printed out on paper or shown on a display terminal and read much like text. A compiler (a special computer program) translated the source code into *object code,* which was in a binary format executed by the computer. Usually, object code could not be read by programmers or easily modified. To make changes to an existing program, programmers usually changed the source code and then recompiled the program, thus creating a new version of the object code. (Most computer software packages purchased by consumers, e.g., LOTUS 1-2-3, contained only the object code. The source code was seldom distributed in such packages.)

Study Questions

1. Describe the ethical, economic, and/or legal principles that suggest Burdelle should copy the source code. How do they fit together?

2. Describe the ethical, economic, and/or legal principles that suggest Burdelle should not copy the source code. How do they fit together?

3. What institutional mechanisms exist to resolve Burdelle's conflicts? To what extent can Burdelle predict the outcomes of these mechanisms?

4. To what extent can post-conventional reasoning (in the broad sense discussed at the end of Chapter 1) help Burdelle resolve this problem?

5. What decision-making pitfalls should Burdelle try to avoid? (See Paine, Messick and Bazerman, Trevino, Gioia.)

6. What ethical, economic, and/or legal stand will Burdelle take if he copies the software? If he does not copy the software?

Milton Friedman

The Social Responsibility of Business Is to Increase Its Profits

When I hear businessmen speak eloquently about the "social responsibilities of business in a free-enterprise system," I am reminded of the wonderful line about the Frenchman who discovered at the age of 70 that he had been speaking prose all his life. The businessmen believe that they are defending free enterprise when they declaim that business is not concerned "merely" with profit but also with promoting desirable "social" ends; that business has a "social conscience" and takes seriously its responsibilities for providing employment, eliminating discrimination, avoiding pollution and whatever else may be the catchwords of the contemporary crop of reformers. In fact they are—or would be if they or anyone else took them seriously—preaching pure and unadulterated socialism. Businessmen who talk this way are unwitting puppets of the intellectual forces that have been undermining the basis of a free society these past decades.

The discussions of the "social responsibilities of business" are notable for their analytical looseness and lack of rigor. What does it mean to say that "business" has responsibilities? Only people can have responsibilities. A corporation is an artificial person and in this sense may have artificial responsibilities, but "business" as a whole cannot be said to have

responsibilities, even in this vague sense. The first step toward clarity to examining the doctrine of the social responsibility of business is to ask precisely what it implies for whom.

Presumably, the individuals who are to be responsible are businessmen, which means individual proprietors or corporate executives. Most of the discussion of social responsibility is directed at corporations, so in what follows I shall mostly neglect the individual proprietors and speak of corporate executives.

In a free-enterprise, private-property system, a corporate executive is an employee of the owners of the business. He has direct responsibility to his employers. That responsibility is to conduct the business in accordance with their desires, which generally will be to make as much money as possible while conforming to the basic rules of the society, both those embodied in law and those embodied in ethical custom. Of course, in some cases his employers may have a different objective. A group of persons might establish a corporation for an eleemosynary purpose—for example, a hospital or a school. The manager of such a corporation will not have money profit as his objectives but the rendering of certain services.

In either case, the key point is that, in his

capacity as a corporate executive, the manager is the agent of the individuals who own the corporation or establish the eleemosynary institution, and his primary responsibility is to them.

Needless to say, this does not mean that it is easy to judge how well he is performing his task. But at least the criterion of performance is straightforward, and the persons among whom a voluntary contractual arrangement exists are clearly defined.

Of course, the corporate executive is also a person in his own right. As a person, he may have many other responsibilities that he recognizes or assumes voluntarily—to his family, his conscience, his feelings of charity, his church, his clubs, his city, his country. He may feel impelled by these responsibilities to devote part of his income to causes he regards as worthy, to refuse to work for particular corporations, even to leave his job, for example, to join his country's armed forces. If we wish, we may refer to some of these responsibilities as "social responsibilities." But in these respects he is acting as a principal, not an agent; he is spending his own money or time or energy, not the money of his employers or the time or energy he has contracted to devote to their purposes. If these are "social responsibilities," they are the social responsibilities of individuals, not of business.

What does it mean to say that the corporate executive has a "social responsibility" in his capacity as businessman? If this statement is not pure rhetoric, it must mean that he is to act in some way that is not in the interest of his employers. For example, that he is to refrain from increasing the price of the product in order to contribute to the social objective of preventing inflation, even though a price increase would be in the best interests of the corporation. Or that he is to make expenditures on reducing pollution beyond the amount that is in the best interests of the corporation or that is required by law in order to contribute to the social objective of improving the environment. Or that, at the expense of corporate profits, he is to hire "hardcore" unemployed instead of better qualified available workmen to contribute to the social objective of reducing poverty.

In each of these cases, the corporate executive would be spending someone else's money for a general social interest. Insofar as his actions in accord with his "social responsibility" reduce returns to stockholders, he is spending their money. Insofar as his actions raise the price to customers, he is spending customers' money. Insofar as his actions lower the wages of some employees, he is spending their money.

The stockholders or the customers or the employees could separately spend their own money on the particular action if they wished to do so. The executive is exercising a distinct "social responsibility," rather than serving as an agent of the stockholders or the customers or the employees, only if he spends the money in a different way than they would have spent it.

But if he does this, he is in effect imposing taxes, on the one hand, and deciding how the tax proceeds shall be spent, on the other.

This process raises political questions on two levels: principle and consequences. On the level of political principle, the imposition of taxes and the expenditure of tax proceeds are governmental functions. We have established elaborate constitutional, parliamentary and judicial provisions to control these functions, to assure that taxes are imposed so far as possible in accordance with the preferences and desires of the public—after all, "taxation without representation" was one of the battle cries of the American Revolution. We have a system of checks and balances to separate the legislative function of imposing taxes and enacting expenditures from the executive function of collecting taxes and administering expenditure programs and from the judicial function of mediating disputes and interpreting the law.

Here the businessman—self-selected or appointed directly or indirectly by stockholders—is to be simultaneously legislator, executive and jurist. He is to decide whom to tax by how much and for what purpose, and he is to spend the proceeds—all this guided only

by general exhortations from on high to restrain inflation, improve the environment,
fight poverty and so on and on.

The whole justification for permitting
the corporate executive to be selected by the
stockholders is that the executive is an agent
serving the interests of his principal. This justification disappears when the corporate executive imposes taxes and spends the proceeds for "social" purposes. He becomes in
effect a public employee, a civil servant, even
though he remains in name an employee of a
private enterprise. On grounds of political
principle, it is intolerable that such civil servants—insofar as their actions in the name of
social responsibility are real and not just window dressing—should be selected as they are
now. If they are to be civil servants, then they
must be elected through a political process. If
they are to impose taxes and make expenditures to foster "social" objectives, then political machinery must be set up to make the assessment of taxes and to determine through a
political process the objectives to be served.

This is the basic reason why the doctrine
of "social responsibility" involves the acceptance of the socialist view that political mechanisms, not market mechanisms, are the appropriate way to determine the allocation of
scarce resources to alternative uses.

On the grounds of consequences, can the
corporate executive in fact discharge his alleged "social responsibilities"? On the one
hand, suppose he could get away with spending the stockholders' or customers' or employees' money. How is he to know how to
spend it? He is told that he must contribute to
fighting inflation. How is he to know what action of his will contribute to that end? He is
presumably an expert in running his company—in producing a product or selling it or
financing it. But nothing about his selection
makes him an expert on inflation. Will his
holding down the price of his product reduce
inflationary pressure? Or, by leaving more
spending power in the hands of his customers, simply divert it elsewhere? Or, by
forcing him to produce less because of the
lower price, will it simply contribute to short-

ages? Even if he could answer these questions, how much cost is he justified in imposing on his stockholders, customers, and employees for this social purpose? What is his
appropriate share and what is the appropriate
share of others?

And, whether he wants to or not, can he
get away with spending his stockholders',
customers' or employees' money? Will not
the stockholders fire him? (Either the present
ones or those who take over when his actions
in the name of social responsibility have reduced the corporation's profits and the price
of its stock.) His customers and his employees can desert him for other producers and
employers less scrupulous in exercising their
social responsibilities.

This facet of "social responsibility" doctrine is brought into sharp relief when the
doctrine is used to justify wage restraint by
trade unions. The conflict of interest is naked
and clear when union officials are asked to
subordinate the interest of their members to
some more general purpose. If union officials
try to enforce wage restraint, the consequence is likely to be wildcat strikes, rank-
and-file revolts and the emergence of strong
competitors for their jobs. We thus have the
ironic phenomenon that union leaders—at
least in the U.S.—have objected to Government interference with the market far more
consistently and courageously than have
business leaders.

The difficulty of exercising "social responsibility" illustrates, of course, the great
virtue of private competitive enterprise—it
forces people to be responsible for their own
actions and makes it difficult for them to "exploit" other people for either selfish or un-
selfish purposes. They can do good—but
only at their own expense.

Many a reader who has followed the argument this far may be tempted to remon-
strate that it is all well and good to speak of
Government's having the responsibility to
impose taxes and determine expenditures for
such "social" purposes as controlling pollution or training the hard-core unemployed,
but that the problems are too urgent to wait on

the slow course of political processes, that the exercise of social responsibility by business-men is a quicker and surer way to solve press-ing current problems.

Aside from the question of fact—I share Adam Smith's skepticism about the benefits that can be expected from "those who affect to trade for the public good"—this argument must be rejected on the grounds of principle. What it amounts to is an assertion that those who favor the taxes and expenditures in ques-tion have failed to persuade a majority of their fellow citizens to be of like mind and that they are seeking to attain by undemocra-tic procedures what they cannot attain by democratic procedures. In a free society it is hard for "evil" people to do "evil," especially since one man's good is another's evil.

I have, for simplicity, concentrated on the special case of the corporate executive, except only for the brief digression on trade unions. But precisely the same argument applies to the newer phenomenon of calling upon stock-holders to require corporations to exercise so-cial responsibility (the recent G.M. crusade for example). In most of these cases, what is in effect involved is some stockholders trying to get other stockholders (or customers or em-ployees) to contribute against their will to "so-cial" causes favored by the activists. Insofar as they succeed, they are again imposing taxes and spending the proceeds.

The situation of the individual proprietor is somewhat different. If he acts to reduce the returns of his enterprise in order to exercise his "social responsibility," he is spending his own money, not someone else's. If he wishes to spend his money on such purposes, that is his right, and I cannot see that there is any ob-jection to his doing so. In the process, he, too, may impose costs on employees and cus-tomers. However, because he is far less likely than a large corporation or union to have mo-nopolistic power, any such side effects will tend to be minor.

Of course, in practice the doctrine of so-cial responsibility is frequently a cloak for ac-tions that are justified on other grounds rather than a reason for those actions.

To illustrate, it may well be in the long-run interest of a corporation that is a major employer in a small community to devote re-sources to providing amenities to that com-munity or to improving its government. That may make it easier to attract desirable em-ployees, it may reduce the wage bill or lessen losses from pilferage and sabotage or have other worthwhile effects. Or it may be that, given the laws about the deductibility of cor-porate charitable contributions, the stock-holders can contribute more to charities they favor by having the corporation make the gift than by doing it themselves, since they can in that way contribute an amount that would otherwise have been paid as corporate taxes.

In each of these—and many similar—cases, there is a strong temptation to rational-ize these actions as an exercise of "social responsibility." In the present climate of opin-ion, with its widespread aversion to "capital-ism," "profits," and the "soulless corporation" and so on, this is one way for a corporation to generate goodwill as a by-product of expendi-tures that are entirely justified in its own self-interest.

It would be inconsistent of me to call on corporate executives to refrain from this hyp-ocritical window-dressing because it harms the foundations of a free society. That would be to call on them to exercise a "social re-sponsibility"! If our institutions, and the atti-tudes of the public make it in their self-interest to cloak their actions in this way, I cannot summon much indignation to re-nounce them. At the same time, I can express admiration for those individual proprietors or owners of closely held corporations or stock-holders of more broadly held corporations who disdain such tactics as approaching fraud.

Whether blameworthy or not, the use of the cloak of social responsibility, and the non-sense spoken in its name by influential and prestigious businessmen, does clearly harm the foundations of a free society. I have been impressed time and again by the schizo-phrenic character of many businessmen. They are capable of being extremely far-sighted and clearheaded in matters that are in-ternal to their businesses. They are incredibly short-sighted and muddle-headed in matters that are outside their businesses but affect the possible survival of business in general. This short-sightedness is strikingly exemplified in the calls from many businessmen for wage and price guidelines or controls or income policies. There is nothing that could do more in a brief period to destroy a market system and replace it by a centrally controlled system than effective governmental control of prices and wages.

The short-sightedness is also exemplified in speeches by businessmen on social responsibility. This may gain them kudos in the short run. But it helps to strengthen the already too prevalent view that the pursuit of profits is wicked and immoral and must be curbed and controlled by external forces. Once this view is adopted, the external forces that curb the market will not be the social consciences, however highly developed, of the pontificating executives; it will be the iron fist of Government bureaucrats. Here, as with price and wage controls, businessmen seem to me to reveal a suicidal impulse.

The political principle that underlies the market mechanism is unanimity. In an ideal free market resting on private property, no individual can coerce any other, all cooperation is voluntary, all parties to such cooperation benefit or they need not participate. There are no values, no "social" responsibilities in any sense other than the shared values and responsibilities of individuals. Society is a collection of individuals and of the various groups they voluntarily form.

The political principle that underlies the political mechanism is conformity. The individual must serve a more general social interest—whether that be determined by a church or a dictator or a majority. The individual may have a vote and say in what is to be done, but if he is overruled, he must conform. It is appropriate for some to require others to contribute to a general social purpose whether they wish to or not.

Unfortunately, unanimity is not always feasible. There are some respects in which conformity appears unavoidable, so I do not see how one can avoid the use of the political mechanism altogether.

But the doctrine of "social responsibility" taken seriously would extend the scope of the political mechanism to every human activity. It does not differ in philosophy from the most explicitly collectivist doctrine. It differs only by professing to believe that collectivist ends can be attained without collectivist means. That is why, in my book *Capitalism and Freedom,* I have called it a "fundamentally subversive doctrine" in a free society, and I have said that in such a society, "there is one and only one social responsibility of business—to use its resources and engage in activities designed to increase its profits so long as it stays within the rules of the game, which is to say, engages in open and free competition without deception or fraud."

Study Questions

1. What ethical, economic, and legal principles and rules does Friedman use to support his stockholder view of managerial responsibility and decision making?

2. If you used these principles to identify important information in the Agrico case, what information are you likely to collect and what information are you likely to miss?

3. Does Friedman assume, tacitly or explicitly, that the institutional setting of managerial decision making is Pareto efficient? (See Appendix to Chapter 4.) Does your answer to this question affect your view of his argument?

4. How could you use Friedman's view to advise Burdelle in the Agrico Case?

Philip L. Cochran

Deriving Ethical Principles from Theories of the Firm

Theories of the firm describe the relationship between the firm and its various constituencies. At their core theories of the firm describe and define the rationale for the very existence of the firm. A rich variety of theories of the firm exist. These include but are not limited to neoclassical (investor owner), worker owner, consumer owner (also known as the consumer cooperative), societal owned (public) firms. These theories of the firm all focus on a single, homogeneous groups of principals and posit that the firm is or should be managed in the sole interests of those principals.

Aoki (1984: 7) underlines this point when he states that orthodox theories of the firm have in common the assumption that the firm is being managed ". . . in the sole interests of a particular group of its participants, identified as either shareholders, managers, or workers. They try to capture the essence of the firm by focusing their analytical attentions on the utility maximization of a dominant class of participants. . . ."

If one carefully examines a particular theory of the firm it should be possible to derive certain ethical principles from it. Theories of the firm, by their very nature, suggest different obligations to various constituency groups of the firm. Some of these obligations can, in turn, have ethical overtones.

Theories of the firm can usefully be divided into two broad categories: naive and sophisticated. The naive theories look at only a single connection between the firm and its owners. In the interest of parsimony the primary interest of the major group of principals is the only interest recognized by the theory. The sophisticated theories recognize that a firm's principals may be impacted by a firm's activities along a number of dimensions.

NAIVE THEORIES OF THE FIRM

Naive Neoclassical Theory

The naive neoclassical theory of the firm implicitly assumes that the firm is owned by a group of investors whose only links with the firm are financial. These investors join together voluntarily and pool their resources in order to achieve certain ends, i.e. increasing their wealth. The one and only goal of the firm is to engage in those activities which most increases the value of the owners' shares (Brealey and Myers, 1981, p. 21.)

Given this premise, one is led logically to the conclusion that firms have no ethical obligations beyond those to their shareholders. It is for this reason that Milton Friedman argued that "there is one and only one social responsibility of business—to use its resources and engage in activities designed to increase its profits so long as it stays within the rules of the game" (Friedman, 1962, p. 133). Neoconservatives, such as Friedman, contend that it is the role of government to write the "rules of the game" and that business should adhere narrowly to its prescribed role, namely maximizing corporate profits.

However, even neoconservatives such as Friedman recognize that management should engage in certain activities (such as selling a safer product or providing a less hazardous workplace) to the extent that such activities increase profits by reducing legal expenses, increasing goodwill, increasing sales, and so on. Note, however, that the only justification for engaging in any activities that others might call "socially responsible" is return to shareholders. If these activities do not translate directly to the "bottom line" then they should not be conducted.

Thus, if increased investment in worker safety programs increases shareholder wealth by reducing the chances of expensive future lawsuits or by increasing worker loyalty then this activity should be supported. If, however, such activities can be clearly shown to decrease shareholder wealth then they should not be undertaken.

Likewise, if it can be shown that customers will pay a premium for safer products then safer products should be produced. For example, a number of firms such as Johnson and Johnson have learned that a reputation for safe products can be a positive marketing tool. Some analysts attribute Tylenol's rapid return to its pre-poisoning market share to Johnson and Johnson's positive public image. People didn't blame the company for the poisonings nor did they see the poisonings as evidence of poor quality control. Johnson and Johnson's quick and very public reaction to the poisonings was to immediately recall all the Tylenol on store shelves and to offer to buy back any Tylenol that consumers had already purchased. This reaction was applauded in many circles as being "socially responsible." However, a neoconservative could easily argue that this quick reaction strategy led to a much better effect on the "bottom line" than would a policy of legalistic responses and slow reaction.

What are the ethical responsibilities of such a firm? Clearly, under this scenario the principal, perhaps only, direct responsibility of such a firm is to its investors or stockholders. What responsibilities does such a firm have for worker or customer safety? Generally the only direct ethical responsibilities of such firms will be to invest resources into worker or customer safety to the extent to which such investments increase the firm's profits (thus increasing the return to shareholders.) That is, continue investing until the marginal cost of investments in safety equals the marginal cost of bad publicity, lawsuits, etc.

Naive Worker Owner Theory of the Firm

A worker owned firm is a firm in which the workers and only the workers hold residual property rights to the firm. That is, all the profits go to the workers. There are a few such firms in the U.S. and in other countries.

However, this was the national model in the ex-Yugoslavia. In 1958 Benjamin Ward published a now classic paper in the *American Economic Review* entitled "The Firm in Illyria: Market Syndicalism" in which he demonstrated that the objective function of a worker owned firm would not be the same as that of an investor owned firm. Whereas in an investor owned firm the objective function would be profit maximization, in a worker owned firm the objective function would be profit maximization per worker. This would occur because every time a new worker was hired he or she would have a claim on the total residual profits of the firm. An implication of this finding is that worker owned firms would be more capital intensive than investor owned firms.

Under this model a worker owned firm would have motivations similar to that of an investor owned firm with respect to product safety. That is, it would continue to invest in product safety until the marginal cost of the additional investment equals the marginal returns of the additional investment.

With respect to worker related issues such as worker safety the naive model would yield a result similar to that of the investor owned firm. Though this is clearly flawed it is nonetheless a logical extension of the theory.

Naive Customer Owner Theory of the Firm

A customer owned firm is a firm in which the customers and only the customers receive the residual profits. Consumer cooperatives are one category of employee owned firms. Consumer cooperatives are organizations established to purchase and distribute goods and services to their members. The distinguishing characteristic of the consumer cooperative is that the customers are in most cases members of the organization. Though not widespread in the United States some consumer cooperatives have become reasonably large. For example, Recreational Equipment Incorporated, the largest consumer cooperative in the U.S., had 1993 gross sales of over $100 million.

Though there are a number of ways that consumer cooperatives are organized, the most common plan is known as the Rochdale Plan. The Rochdale Plan calls for open membership with each member receiving one vote. Sales are made only to members. Membership requires a nominal capital investment. Goods are priced at market levels and dividends (patronage refunds) are paid in proportion to members' purchases.

The naive objective function of a consumer owned firm is minimization of the cost to the consumer. Thus with respect to any ethical obligations to workers the consumer owned firm would look similar to an investor owned firm.

Even with respect to consumer issues if the only link between the consumer and the firm is a financial link then issues such as truth in advertising, product safety, and so on should be no more relevant for a consumer owned firm than for an investor owned firm.

See Table 1 for an explication of the naive theories of the firm. The obvious weaknesses that are imposed by the core assumption of these theories (that the only relationship between the firm and its principal constituency group is financial) leads to what I have termed the sophisticated theories of the firm.

SOPHISTICATED THEORIES OF THE FIRM

Sophisticated Neoclassical Theory

Even before we relax the simplifying assumption that the only link between the firm and its shareholders is financial it is important to recognize that not all shareholders necessarily have the same financial goals. Depending on an individual's risk preferences he or she might prefer higher or lower risk investments. Depending on an individual's tax bracket she or he might prefer a different mix of dividends and appreciation. Depending on an individual's age he or she may be more or less inclined toward stability of future earnings. Thus even under a naive neoclassical model management must still attempt to balance the interests of various constituents within the shareholder group.

Similar arguments could also apply to worker and consumer owned firms. For example, in a worker owned firm there might be some workers (say younger workers) who would prefer that the firm invest more heavily into research and development that might show significant returns in a decade or two. On the other hand, an older worker might be more interested in earnings stability and thus

TABLE 1
Naive Theories of the Firm

	Obligations to investors	Obligations to workers	Obligations to customers	Obligations to society
Investor owner	Maximize profits	None	None	None
Worker owner	Not applicable	Max. profits per worker	None	None
Customer owner	Not applicable	None	Minimum prices	None
Society owner	Not applicable	Possible	Possible	Maximize social return

might opt for an investment strategy that emphasized mature markets.

When one drops the simplifying assumption made in the naive neoclassical model that the only link between the investors and the firms is a financial link then one can build a more sophisticated and realistic—but still neoclassical—model. For example, imagine that the owners of a factory have homes built on the same river as the factory but downstream from the factory. Assume that the owners and their families use this river for recreation including swimming. Assume that they draw their drinking water from the river.

It would seem intuitively obvious that these owners would be interested in more than just the profits flowing from the firm. They would also be concerned about the pollutants potentially flowing into the river. Thus there are a set of links between the firm and the investor owners. Clearly one of the links is financial. But just as clearly, another is through the effects that the firm has on the environment. If some of the owners also work at the firm then there is yet another link.

Sophisticated Worker Owner Theory of the Firm

If we extend Ward's logic one step further— management of an employee owned firm has a stronger obligation to provide a safe workplace for its workers than does management of a similar, but investor owned, firm. If management of a worker owned firm had the choice of adopting a set of work rules that increased the probability of worker injuries but also increased profits (and thus financial return to the workers) it would have a difficult tradeoff. The workers might be willing to accept greater risk for higher returns. Certainly management would have an obligation to fully inform workers regarding the nature of any such tradeoff.

On the other hand, in an investor owned firm (operated according to neoclassical economic principles) the primary responsibility of management is to its investors. Under these circumstances management might engage in some sort of cost/benefit calculus weighing the additional revenues from such new work rules against the increased probability of lawsuits, bad publicity, decreased worker morale, and so on resulting from the higher probability of worker injuries. It would be less inclined to fully disclose the potential dangers to its workers. In sum, though the decisions reached by such firms may be similar and in some cases identical, the decision making calculus is different because the constraints are different.

In numerous, but less dramatic situations, such as worker training and job enrichment programs the management of an employee owned firm would in all likelihood choose solutions different than would the management of a pure investor owned firm. For example, job enrichment can be justified in an investor owned firm if and only if it has a positive impact on the bottom line. However, in a worker owned firm job enrichment might be seen as an end itself. Increasing worker utility is a firm objective.

Sophisticated Consumer Owner Theory of the Firm

Some of the early literature on consumer cooperatives contended that they were superior to investor owned firms in a number of dimensions including "the elimination of many competitive practices, such as misleading advertising or 'high pressure' selling. . . . the elimination of many of the motives for fraud . . . the elimination of accounting inaccuracies" and so on (Warne, 1923, pp. 4–5).

In a more recent context, the emphasis is more likely to be on product quality and safety. For example, REI maintains a staff of quality control engineers in order to adequately evaluate merchandise prior to offering it for sale to its members. This staff is maintained as a *duty* to REI's customer/members. Its existence is not predicated upon any assumptions regarding the profitability of this unit. In a similar, but investor owned, firm such a staff would have to be justified on the basis of return to stockholders.

The pure customer owned firm's primary obligation is to its customers. If such a firm had a choice between making a substantial profit (after legal expenses, bad public relations costs, and so on) by selling a product that would injure some of its customers or making only a marginal profit by selling a safer product it would clearly be obligated to do the former. In this case (provided that the firm is within the law) there is no separate class of investors who have claims that conflict with those of the customers, no case can be made for the latter alternative. That is, the firm would have no *direct* obligations. See Table 2 for a summary of the sophisticated theories of the firm.

COMBINED THEORIES OF THE FIRM

What happens when you begin to combine these uni-owner theories of the firm? Aoki proposed a so called "J Model" firm. He argued that such a firm closely mirrors the model of the Japanese firm. In such a firm the objective function is a joint function of investor and worker interests.

Aoki states that "in the neoclassical theory, only the shareholders (entrepreneurs) are explicitly recognized as rational maximizers." He goes on to point out that missing is an explicit treatment of interactions among shareholders, managers and employees and it is difficult to maintain that firm-specific resources are endowed in a single, monolithic agent such as the entrepreneur (as a proxy for the body of shareholders). The firm must be viewed as a sort of coalition of financial as well as human resource-holders.

In a recent work that has received wide publicity, Kotter and Heskett (1992) argue that "firms with cultures that emphasized all key managerial constituencies (customers, stockholders, and employees) . . . outperformed firms that did not have these cultural traits by a huge margin" (p. 11). Though their study investigated the effects of corporate culture and though they used the term "constituencies" and not "stakeholders" their results are consistent with the growing literature on stakeholders. One could view Kotter and Heskett's work as a model for a firm that tried to maximize the returns to three constituencies: customers, stockholders, and employees. Aoki suggested that his "J-model," which sought to balance owner and employee interests, "is perhaps fated to be subsumed under the yet to be developed general theory of the firm. . . ." See Table 3 for a summary of the combined models.

ACTUAL OWNERSHIP PATTERNS

In 1976 Peter Drucker published a controversial new book, *The Unseen Revolution: How Pension Fund Socialism Came to America*. In this work he presented the then startling argument that American workers were rapidly becoming the real owners of corporate America. He based his thesis on the fact that in 1975 pension funds owned 25% of the equity capi-

TABLE 2
Sophisticated Theories of the Firm

	Obligations to investors	Obligations to workers	Obligations to customers	Obligations to society
Investor owner	Maximum owner utility	None	None	None
Worker owner	Not applicable	Maximum worker utility	None	None
Customer owner	Not applicable	None	Maximum customer utility	None
Society owner	Not applicable			Maximum societal utility

TABLE 3A
The Coalition (J Model) Theory of the Firm

	Obligations to investors	Obligations to workers	Obligations to customers	Obligations to society
Investor owner	Maximize returns to shareholders and to workers		None	No direct

TABLE 3B
The TriPartite (Kotter and Heskitt) Theory of the Firm

	Obligations to investors	Obligations to workers	Obligations to customers	Obligations to society
Investor owner	Maximize returns to shareholders, workers, and customers			No direct

tal of American business. In 1976 Drucker predicted that the percentage of stock owned by pension funds would soar to 50% by 1985 and to more than 66% by 1995 (1976, p. 1).

By 1985 fully 49% of the stock of the *Fortune* 500 firms for which data were available was owned by institutional investors. Since the beneficial owners of such pension funds are American workers and their families they are, in fact, the real owners of American industry. Drucker's prediction has proven to be uncannily accurate.

TOWARD A STAKEHOLDER THEORY OF THE FIRM

Most theories of the firm have a basic shortcoming—a failure to fully incorporate the diverse interests and values of all their principal stakeholders. Fama (1980) puts it this way,

> . . . ownership of capital should not be confused with ownership of the firm. Each factor in a firm is owned by somebody. The firm is just the set of contracts covering the way inputs are joined to create outputs and the way receipts from outputs are shared among inputs. In this 'nexus of contracts' perspective, ownership of the firm is an irrelevant concept.

If ownership is irrelevant and the "nexus

of contracts" is a better model then we seem to inevitably be led to a stakeholder model in which the firm is part of a web of obligations among a wide range of constituencies. The first authors to explicitly discuss a stakeholder theory of the firm were Evan and Freeman (1988) in their article "A Stakeholder Theory of the Modern Corporation: Kantian Capitalism." In this work Evan and Freeman propose "the bare bones of an alternative theory, a stakeholder theory of the modern corporation" (Evan and Freeman, 1988: 97). In this theory the authors suggest that the neoclassical concept that the sole responsibility of managers should be to the firm's stockholders should be replaced by a broader theory that managers should be responsible to a wide range of stakeholders.

Evan and Freeman argue that firms are already, in effect, managed in the interests of a wide range of constituents beyond just the firm's stockholders. They note that laws have seriously constrained the ability of managers to manage the affairs of the firm solely in the interests of the stockholders. They contend that externalities, moral hazards, and monopoly power has led to still further constraints on the freedom of managers.

They then go on to propose two stakeholder management principles:

> P1: The corporation should be managed for the benefit of its stakeholders: its

customer, suppliers, owners, employees, and local communities. The rights of these groups must be ensured, and, further, the groups must participate, in some sense, in decisions that substantially affect their welfare.

P2: Management bears a fiduciary relationship to stakeholders and to the corporation as an abstract entity. It must act in the interest of the stakeholders as their agent, and it must act in the interests of the corporation to ensure the survival of the firm, safeguarding the long-term stakes of each group. (Evan and Freeman, 1988: 103)

In his 1991 article Goodpaster attacked the idea that managers have a fiduciary responsibility to non-stockholder stakeholders (though he did not refer to the Evan and Freeman article). Goodpaster contends that any theory that management has any fiduciary responsibilities to non-stockholder stakeholders (in his terminology "multi-fiduciary stakeholder" approach) is fundamentally flawed. He asserted that:

The relationship between management and stockholders is ethically different in kind from the relationship between management and other parties (like employees, suppliers, customers, etc.), a fact that seems to go unnoticed by the multi-fiduciary approach. If it were not, the corporation would cease to be a private sector institution—and what is now called business ethics would become a more radical critique of our economic system than is typically thought. On this point, Milton Friedman must be given a fair and serious hearing. (Goodpaster, 1991: 69)

This is an important, but fundamentally unsatisfying, thesis. It is often difficult, if not impossible, to separate fiduciary from non-fiduciary responsibilities. In today's world most stakeholders are also stockholders—if not directly then certainly indirectly. The average American has a pension fund or funds which hold portfolios of common stock that tend to mirror the stockmarket. As a result virtually all workers of any given major firm are either primary or secondary stockholders in that firm. That is they either own actual shares or the rights to shares of their firm (often acquired through employee stock ownership plans) or they hold the stock indirectly through the company's pension fund or through private IRAs or other mutual fund investments. The same argument holds for consumers—the majority of consumers of the products of the major firms also own stock (directly or indirectly) in the firms that make the products which they buy—as well as virtually any other stakeholder group.

It is unrealistic to assume that firms can produce different products for stockholder-consumers than for nonstockholder-consumers. Likewise it is impractical for firms to create different working conditions for stockholder-employees than for non-stockholder-employees. The same argument could obviously be made with respect to any other stakeholder groups. Thus this implicit assumption of the neoclassical theory (that only financial links exist between the shareholders and the firm) is incorrect. Thus, on occasion, those legal and moral obligations of the firm to one or more stakeholders might supersede the financial claims of stockholders.

This led in 1992 to Brenner and Cochran's paper in which they called for a more complete stakeholder theory of the firm. In 1995 the *Academy of Management Review* published an important set of articles in this area including articles by Clarkson, Donaldson and Preston, as well as by Quinn and Jones. See Table 4 for a preliminary summary of how a stakeholder theory of the firm might inform the field of business ethics.

The stakeholder theory of the firm as discussed in this paper is an attempt to better explain firms in the modern world. These firms are discovering that they are subject to the demands of various stakeholders playing out their values in a myriad of interactions. Where the limits of this stakeholder concept end is difficult to determine.

One well known example of a firm which placed obligations to stakeholders above

TABLE 4
A Generalized Stakeholder Theory of the Firm

	Obligations to investors	Obligations to workers	Obligations to customers	Obligations to society
Dispersed ownership	Satisfactory profit	Safety, job satisfaction	Safety, value, honesty	Environmental obligations

those to shareholders is the Merck Co. At a cost of over $10 million Merck developed a drug to combat a vicious tropical disease, River Blindness. River Blindness afflicts millions of people every year. If not treated it eventually leads to total blindness.

However, a simple and effective drug developed by Merck cures the disease and prevents its recurrence. After Merck developed the drug it tried to find some agency to purchase and distribute the drug. Unable to find any agency to do so Merck vowed to do so itself. At a cost in excess of $10 million per year it distributes the drug itself.

Merck has no expectation whatsoever of recouping either their original investment or their ongoing distribution costs. This is clearly a case of a firm recognizing obligations to tertiary stakeholders that exceed those to their stockholders.

References

ABBOTT, WALTER F. AND MONSEN, R. JOSEPH. "On the Measurement of Corporate Social Responsibility: Self Report Disclosure as a Method of Measuring Social Involvement." *Academy of Management Journal,* 22(3), 1979, 501–515.

AOKI, M. *The Co-operative Game Theory of the Firm.* New York: Oxford University Press, 1984.

AOKI, M. "The Japanese Firm in Transition." In K. Yamamura and Y. Yasuba, editors. *The Political Economy of Japan (Volume 1).* Stanford: Stanford University Press, 1987.

AOKI, M. "Toward an Economic Model of the Japanese Firm." *Journal of Economic Literature,* XXVII, 1990, 1–27.

BARNEA, AMIR, HAUGEN, ROBERT, AND SENBET, LEMMA. "Market Imperfections, Agency Problems, and Capital Structure: A Review." *Financial Management,* Summer 1981, 7–22.

BREALEY, RICHARD AND SENBET MYERS. *Principals of Corporate Finance.* New York: McGraw-Hill Book Company, 1981.

BRENNER, STEVEN AND COCHRAN, PHILIP L. "The Stakeholder Theory of the Firm: Implications for Business and Society Theory and Research." In *Contemporary Issues in Business and Society,* Dean Ludwig and Karen Paul, editors. Mellon Publishing, June 1992.

CLARKSON, MAX B.E. "A Stakeholder Framework for Analyzing and Evaluating Corporate Social Performance." *Academy of Management Review,* January 1995, 92–117.

COCHRAN, PHILIP L. AND WOOD, ROBERT A. "Corporate Social Responsibility and Financial Performance." *Academy of Management Journal,* March 1984, 42–56.

DEGEORGE, RICHARD D. *Business Ethics,* New York: Macmillan Publishing Co., 1982.

DONALDSON, THOMAS. *Corporations and Morality.* Englewood Cliffs, NJ: Prentice Hall, 1982.

DONALDSON, THOMAS AND PRESTON, LEE. "The Stakeholder Model of the Corporation: Concepts, Evidence, and Implications." *Academy of Management Review,* January 1995, 65–91.

DRUCKER, PETER. *The Unseen Revolution: How Pension Fund Socialism Came to America.* New York: Harper and Row, 1976.

EVAN, W. M., AND FREEMAN, R. E. "A Stakeholder Theory of the Modern Corporation: Kantian Capitalism." In *Ethical Theory and Business.* T. L. Beaucamp and N. E. Bowie, editors. Englewood Cliffs, NJ: Prentice Hall, 1988.

FREEMAN, R. EDWARD, *Strategic Management: A Stakeholder Approach.* Marshfield, MA: Pitman Publishing Inc., 1984.

FRIEDMAN, MILTON. *Capitalism and Freedom.* Chicago: University of Chicago Press, 1962.

GATEWOOD, ELIZABETH AND CARROLL, ARCHIE B. "The Anatomy of Corporate Social Response: The Rely, Firestone 500, and Pinto

Cases," *Business Horizons,* 24 (September/October, 1981), 9–16.

GOODPASTER, K. E. "Business Ethics and Stakeholder Analysis." *Business Ethics Quarterly,* 1, 1991, 53–73.

HILL, CHARLES W. L. AND JONES, THOMAS M. "Stakeholder-Agency Theory." *Journal of Management Studies,* 29(2), 1992, 131–154.

PALMER, JAMES L. "Can Consumer Cooperation Correct Important Defects in Marketing?" *The Journal of Marketing,* April 1937, 390.

QUINN, DENNIS P. AND JONES, THOMAS M. "An Agent Morality View of Business Policy." *Academy of Management Review,* January 1995, 22–42.

STRAND, R. "A Systems Paradigm of Organizational Adaptations to the Social Environment." *Academy of Management Review,* 1, 1983, 90–96.

WARD, BENJAMIN. "The Firm in Illyria: Market Syndicalism." *American Economic Review,* 66(4), 1958, 373–386.

WARNE, COLSTON E. *Consumer's Cooperative Movement in Illinois.* Chicago: University of Chicago Press, 1923.

Study Questions

1. How does Cochran use ethical, economic, and legal principles and rules to explain his view of managerial responsibility and decision making?

2. If you used these principles and rules to identify important information in the Agrico case, what information are you likely to collect and what important information are you likely to miss?

3. What assumptions do you think Cochran makes about the institutional environment of business. Compare and contrast these with Friedman's assumptions. In your view, which set of assumptions is more realistic? Why?

4. How could you use Cochran's view to advise Burdelle in the Agrico Case?

R. Edward Freeman

A Stakeholder Theory of the Modern Corporation

INTRODUCTION

Corporations have ceased to be merely legal devices through which the private business transactions of individuals may be carried on. Though still much used for this purpose, the corporate form has acquired a larger significance. The corporation has, in fact, become both a method of property tenure and a means of organizing economic life. Grown to tremendous proportions, there may be said to have evolved a "corporate system"—which has attracted to itself a combination of attributes and powers, and has attained a degree of prominence entitling it to be dealt with as a major social institution.[1]

Despite these prophetic words of Berle and Means (1932), scholars and managers alike continue to hold sacred the view that managers bear a special relationship to the stockholders in the firm. Since stockholders own shares in the firm, they have certain rights and privileges, which must be granted to them by management, as well as by others. Sanctions, in the form of "the law of corporations," and other protective mechanisms in the form of social custom, accepted management practice, myth, and ritual, are thought to reinforce the assumption of the primacy of the stockholder.

The purpose of this paper is to pose several challenges to this assumption, from within the framework of managerial capitalism, and to suggest the bare bones of an alternative theory, *a stakeholder theory of the modern corporation*. I do not seek the demise of the modern corporation, either intellectually or in fact. Rather, I seek its transformation. In the words of Neurath, we shall attempt to "rebuild the ship, plank by plank, while it remains afloat."[2]

My thesis is that I can revitalize the concept of managerial capitalism by replacing the notion that managers have a duty to stockholders with the concept that managers bear a fiduciary relationship to stakeholders. Stakeholders are those groups who have a stake in or claim on the firm. Specifically I include suppliers, customers, employees, stockholders, and the local community, as well as management in its role as agent for these groups. I argue that the legal, economic, political, and moral challenges to the currently received theory of the firm, as a nexus of contracts among the owners of the factors of production and customers, require us to revise this concept. That is, each of these stakeholder groups has a right not to be treated as a means to some end, and therefore must participate in determining the future direction of the firm in which they have a stake.

The crux of my argument is that we must reconceptualize the firm around the following question: For whose benefit and at whose expense should the firm be managed? I shall set forth such a reconceptualization in the form of a *stakeholder theory of the firm*. I shall then critically examine the stakeholder view and its implications for the future of the capitalist system.

THE ATTACK ON MANAGERIAL CAPITALISM

The Legal Argument

The basic idea of managerial capitalism is that in return for controlling the firm, management vigorously pursues the interests of stockholders. Central to the managerial view of the firm is the idea that management can pursue market transactions with suppliers and customers in an unconstrained manner.

The law of corporations gives a less clearcut answer to the question: In whose interest and for whose benefit should the modern corporation be governed? While it says that the corporations should be run primarily in the interests of the stockholders in the firm, it says further that the corporation exists "in contemplation of the law" and has personality as a "legal person," limited liability for its actions, and immortality, since its existence transcends that of its members. Therefore, directors and other officers of the firm have a fiduciary obligation to stockholders in the sense that the "affairs of the corporation" must be conducted in the interest of the stockholders. And stockholders can theoretically bring suit against those directors and managers for doing otherwise. But since the corporation is a legal person, existing in contemplation of the law, managers of the corporation are constrained by law.

Until recently, this was no constraint at all. In this century, however, the law has evolved to effectively constrain the pursuit of stockholder interests at the expense of other claimants on the firm. It has, in effect, required that the claims of customers, suppliers, local communities, and employees be taken into consideration, though in general they are subordinated to the claims of stockholders.

For instance, the doctrine of "privity of contract," as articulated in *Winterbottom v.*

Wright in 1842, has been eroded by recent developments in products liability law. Indeed, *Greenman v. Yuba Power* gives the manufacturer strict liability for damage caused by its products, even though the seller has exercised all possible care in the preparation and sale of the product and the consumer has not bought the product from nor entered into any contractual arrangement with the manufacturer. Caveat emptor has been replaced, in large part, with caveat venditor.[3] The Consumer Product Safety Commission has the power to enact product recalls, and in 1980 one U.S. automobile company recalled more cars than it built. Some industries are required to provide information to customers about a product's ingredients, whether or not the customers want and are willing to pay for this information.[4]

The same argument is applicable to management's dealings with employees. The National Labor Relations Act gave employees the right to unionize and to bargain in good faith. It set up the National Labor Relations Board to enforce these rights with management. The Equal Pay Act of 1963 and Title VII of the Civil Rights Act of 1964 constrain management from discrimination in hiring practices; these have been followed with the Age Discrimination in Employment Act of 1967.[5] The emergence of a body of administrative case law arising from labor-management disputes and the historic settling of discrimination claims with large employers such as AT&T have caused the emergence of a body of practice in the corporation that is consistent with the legal guarantee of the rights of the employees. The law has protected the due process rights of those employees who enter into collective bargaining agreements with management. As of the present, however, only 30 percent of the labor force are participating in such agreements; this has prompted one labor law scholar to propose a statutory law prohibiting dismissals of the 70 percent of the work force not protected.[6]

The law has also protected the interests of local communities. The Clean Air Act and Clean Water Act have constrained management from "spoiling the commons." In an historic case, *Marsh v. Alabama,* the Supreme Court ruled that a company-owned town was subject to the provisions of the U.S. Constitution, thereby guaranteeing the rights of local citizens and negating the "property rights" of the firm. Some states and municipalities have gone further and passed laws preventing firms from moving plants or limiting when and how plants can be closed. In sum, there is much current legal activity in this area to constrain management's pursuit of stockholders' interests at the expense of the local communities in which the firm operates.

I have argued that the result of such changes in the legal system can be viewed as giving some rights to those groups that have a claim on the firm, for example, customers, suppliers, employees, local communities, stockholders, and management. It raises the question, at the core of a theory of the firm: In whose interest and for whose benefit should the firm be managed? The answer proposed by managerial capitalism is clearly "the stockholders," but I have argued that the law has been progressively circumscribing this answer.

The Economic Argument

In its pure ideological form managerial capitalism seeks to maximize the interests of stockholders. In its perennial criticism of government regulation, management espouses the "invisible hand" doctrine. It contends that it creates the greatest good for the greatest number, and therefore government need not intervene. However, we know that externalities, moral hazards, and monopoly power exist in fact, whether or not they exist in theory. Further, some of the legal apparatus mentioned above has evolved to deal with just these issues.

The problem of the "tragedy of the commons" or the free-rider problem pervades the concept of public goods such as water and air. No one has an incentive to incur the cost of clean-up or the cost of nonpollution, since the marginal gain of one firm's action is small. Every firm reasons this way, and the result is pollution of water and air. Since the industrial revolution, firms have sought to internalize the benefits and externalize the costs of their actions. The cost must be borne by all, through taxation and regulation; hence we have the emergence of the environmental regulations of the 1970s.

Similarly, moral hazards arise when the purchaser of a good or service can pass along the cost of that good. There is no incentive to economize, on the part of either the producer or the consumer, and there is excessive use of the resources involved. The institutionalized practice of third-party payment in health care is a prime example.

Finally, we see the avoidance of competitive behavior on the part of firms, each seeking to monopolize a small portion of the market and not compete with one another. In a number of industries, oligopolies have emerged, and while there is questionable evidence that oligopolies are not the most efficient corporate form in some industries, suffice it to say that the potential for abuse of market power has again led to regulation of managerial activity. In the classic case, AT&T, arguably one of the great technological and managerial achievements of the century, was broken up into eight separate companies to prevent its abuse of monopoly power.

Externalities, moral hazards, and monopoly power have led to more external control on managerial capitalism. There are de facto constraints, due to these economic facts of life, on the ability of management to act in the interests of stockholders.

A STAKEHOLDER THEORY OF THE FIRM

The Stakeholder Concept

Corporations have stakeholders, that is, groups and individuals who benefit from or are harmed by, and whose rights are violated or respected by, corporate actions. The concept of stakeholders is a generalization of the notion of stockholders, who themselves have some special claim on the firm. Just as stockholders have a right to demand certain actions by management, so do other stakeholders have a right to make claims. The exact nature of these claims is a difficult question that I shall address, but the logic is identical to that of the stockholder theory. Stakes require action of a certain sort, and conflicting stakes require methods of resolution.

Freeman and Reed (1983)[7] distinguish two senses of *stakeholder.* The "narrow definition" includes those groups who are vital to the survival and success of the corporation. The "wide-definition" includes any group or individual who can affect or is affected by the corporation. I shall begin with a modest aim: to articulate a stakeholder theory using the narrow definition.

Stakeholders in the Modern Corporation

Figure 1 depicts the stakeholders in a typical large corporation. The stakes of each are reciprocal, since each can affect the other in terms of harms and benefits as well as rights and duties. The stakes of each are not univocal and would vary by particular corporation. I merely set forth some general notions that seem to be common to many large firms.

Owners have a financial stake in the corporation in the form of stocks, bonds, and so on, and they expect some kind of financial return from them. Either they have given money directly to the firm, or they have some historical claim made through a series of morally justified exchanges. The firm affects their livelihood or, if a substantial portion of their retirement income is in stocks or bonds, their ability to care for themselves when they can no longer work. Of course, the stakes of owners will differ by type of owner, preferences for money, moral preferences, and so on, as well as by type of firm. The

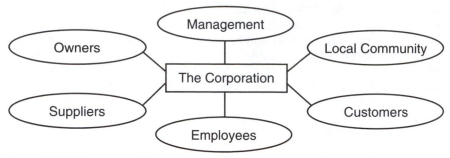

Figure 1   A Stakeholder model of the corporation.

owners of AT&T are quite different from the owners of Ford Motor Company, with stock of the former company being widely dispersed among 3 million stockholders and that of the latter being held by a small family group as well as by a large group of public stockholders.

Employees have their jobs and usually their livelihood at stake; they often have specialized skills for which there is usually no perfectly elastic market. In return for their labor, they expect security, wages, benefits, and meaningful work. In return for their loyalty, the corporation is expected to provide for them and carry them through difficult times. Employees are expected to follow the instructions of management most of the time, to speak favorably about the company, and to be responsible citizens in the local communities in which the company operates. Where they are used as means to an end, they must participate in decisions affecting such use. The evidence that such policies and values as described here lead to productive company-employee relationships is compelling. It is equally compelling to realize that the opportunities for "bad faith" on the part of both management and employees are enormous. "Mock participation" in quality circles, singing the company song, and wearing the company uniform solely to please management all lead to distrust and unproductive work.

Suppliers, interpreted in a stakeholder sense, are vital to the success of the firm, for raw materials will determine the final product's quality and price. In turn the firm is a customer of the supplier and is therefore vital to the success and survival of the supplier. When the firm treats the supplier as a valued member of the stakeholder network, rather than simply as a source of materials, the supplier will respond when the firm is in need. Chrysler traditionally had very close ties to its suppliers, even to the extent that led some to suspect the transfer of illegal payments. And when Chrysler was on the brink of disaster, the suppliers responded with price cuts, accepting late payments, financing, and so on. Supplier and company can rise and fall together. Of course, again, the particular supplier relationships will depend on a number of variables such as the number of suppliers and whether the supplies are finished goods or raw materials.

Customers exchange resources for the products of the firm and in return receive the benefits of the products. Customers provide the lifeblood of the firm in the form of revenue. Given the level of reinvestment of earnings in large corporations, customers indirectly pay for the development of new products and services. Peters and Waterman (1982)[8] have argued that being close to the customer leads to success with other stakeholders and that a distinguishing characteristic of some companies that have performed well is their emphasis on the customer. By paying attention to customers' needs, management automatically addresses the needs of suppliers and owners. Moreover, it seems that the ethic of customer service carries over to the community. Almost without fail the "excellent companies" in Peters and Waterman's study have good reputations in the community. I would argue that Peters and Waterman have found multiple applications of Kant's dictum, "Treat persons as ends unto themselves," and it should come as no surprise that persons respond to such respectful treatment, be they customers, suppliers, owners, employees, or members of the local community. The real surprise is the novelty of the application of Kant's rule in a theory of good management practice.

The local community grants the firm the right to build facilities and, in turn, it benefits from the tax base and economic and social contributions of the firm. In return for the provision of local services, the firm is expected to be a good citizen, as is any person, either "natural or artificial." The firm cannot expose the community to unreasonable hazards in the form of pollution, toxic waste, and so on. If for some reason the firm must leave a community, it is expected to work with local leaders to make the transition as smoothly as possible. Of course, the firm does not have perfect knowledge, but when it discovers some danger or runs afoul of new competition, it is expected to inform the local community and to work with the community to overcome any problem. When the firm mismanages its relationship with the local community, it is in the same position as a citizen who commits a crime. It has violated the implicit social contract with the community and should expect to be distrusted and ostracized. It should not be surprised when punitive measures are invoked.

I have not included "competitors" as stakeholders in the narrow sense, since strictly speaking they are not necessary for the survival and success of the firm; the stakeholder theory works equally well in monopoly contexts. However, competitors and government would be the first to be included in an extension of the this basic theory. It is simply not true that the interests of competitors in an industry are always in conflict. There is no reason why trade associations and other multi-organizational groups cannot band together to solve common problems that have little to do with how to restrain trade. Implementation of stakeholder management principles, in the long run, mitigates the need for in-

dustrial policy and an increasing role for government intervention and regulation.

The Role of Management

Management plays a special role, for it too has a stake in the modern corporation. On the one hand, management's stake is like that of employees, with some kind of explicit or implicit employment contract. But, on the other hand, management has a duty of safe-guarding the welfare of the abstract entity that is the corporation. In short, management, especially top management, must look after the health of the corporation, and this involves balancing the multiple claims of conflicting stakeholders. Owners want higher financial returns, while customers want more money spent on research and development. Employees want higher wages and better benefits, while the local community wants better parks and day-care facilities.

The task of management in today's corporation is akin to that of King Solomon. The stakeholder theory does not give primacy to one stakeholder group over another, though there will surely be times when one group will benefit at the expense of others. In general, however, management must keep the relationships among stakeholders in balance. When these relationships become imbalanced, the survival of the firm is in jeopardy.

When wages are too high and product quality is too low, customers leave, suppliers suffer, and owners sell their stocks and bonds, depressing the stock price and making it difficult to raise new capital at favorable rates. Note, however, that the reason for paying returns to owners is not that they "own" the firm, but that their support is necessary for the survival of the firm, and that they have a legitimate claim on the firm. Similar reasoning applies in turn to each stakeholder group.

A stakeholder theory of the firm must redefine the purpose of the firm. The stockholder theory claims that the purpose of the firm is to maximize the welfare of the stockholders, perhaps subject to some moral or social constraints, either because such maxi-mization leads to the greatest good or because of property rights. The purpose of the firm is quite different in my view.

"The stakeholder theory" can be un-packed into a number of stakeholder theories, each of which has a "normative core," inex-tricably linked to the way that corporations should be governed and the way that man-agers should act. So, attempts to more fully define, or more carefully define, a stake-holder theory are misguided. Following Don-aldson and Preston, I want to insist that the normative, descriptive, instrumental, and metaphorical (my addition to their frame-work) uses of 'stakeholder' are tied together in particular political constructions to yield a number of possible "stakeholder theories." "Stakeholder theory" is thus a genre of stories about how we could live. Let me be more specific.

A "normative core" of a theory is a set of sentences that includes among others, sen-tences like:

1. Corporations ought to be governed . . .

2. Managers ought to act to . . .

where we need arguments or further narra-tives which include business and moral terms to fill in the blanks. This normative core is not always reducible to a fundamental ground like the theory of property, but certain norma-tive cores are consistent with modern under-standings of property. Certain elaborations of the theory of private property plus the other institutions of political liberalism give rise to particular normative cores. But there are other institutions, other political conceptions of how society ought to be structured, so that there are different possible normative cores.

So, one normative core of a stakeholder theory might be a feminist standpoint one, re-thinking how we would restructure "value-creating activity" along principles of caring and connection.[9] Another would be an eco-logical (or several ecological) normative cores. Mark Starik has argued that the very idea of a stakeholder theory of the firm ig-nores certain ecological necessities.[10] Table 1 is suggestive of how these theories could be developed.

In the next section I shall sketch the nor-mative core based on pragmatic liberalism. But, any normative core must address the questions in columns A or B, or explain why these questions may be irrelevant, as in the ecological view. In addition, each "theory," and I use the word hesitantly, must place the normative core within a more full-fledged ac-count of how we could understand value-creating activity differently (column C). The only way to get on with this task is to see the stakeholder idea as a metaphor. The attempt to prescribe one and only one "normative core" and construct "a stakeholder theory" is at best

TABLE 1
A Reasonable Pluralism

	A. Corporations ought to be governed . . .	B. Managers ought to act . . .	C. The background disciplines of "value creation" are . . .
Doctrine of fair contracts	. . . in accordance with the six principles.	. . . in the interests of stakeholders.	—business theories —theories that explain stake holder behavior
Feminist standpoint theory	. . . in accordance with the principles of caring/connection and relationships.	. . . to maintain and care for relationships and networks of stakeholders.	—business theories —feminist theory —social science understand-ing of networks
Ecological principles	. . . in accordance with the principle of caring for the earth.	. . . to care for the earth.	—business theories —ecology —other

a disguised attempt to smuggle a normative core past the unsophisticated noses of other unsuspecting academics who are just happy to see the end of the stockholder orthodoxy.

If we begin with the view that we can understand value-creation activity as a contractual process among those parties affected, and if for simplicity's sake we initially designate those parties as financiers, customers, suppliers, employees, and communities, then we can construct a normative core that reflects the liberal notions of autonomy, solidarity, and fairness as articulated by John Rawls, Richard Rorty, and others.[11] Notice that building these moral notions into the foundations of how we understand value creation and contracting requires that we eschew separating the "business" part of the process from the "ethical" part, and that we start with the presumption of equality among the contractors, rather than the presumption in favor of financier rights.

The normative core for this redesigned contractual theory will capture the liberal idea of fairness if it ensures a basic equality among stakeholders in terms of their moral rights as these are realized in the firm, and if it recognizes that inequalities among stakeholders are justified if they raise the level of the least well-off stakeholder. The liberal ideal of autonomy is captured by the realization that each stakeholder must be free to enter agreements that create value for themselves, and solidarity is realized by the recognition of the mutuality of stakeholder interests.

One way to understand fairness in this context is to claim à la Rawls that a contract is fair if parties to the contract would agree to it in ignorance of their actual stakes. Thus, a contract is like a fair bet, if each party is willing to turn the tables and accept the other side. What would a fair contract among corporate stakeholders look like? If we can articulate this ideal, a sort of corporate constitution, we could then ask whether actual corporations measure up to this standard, and we also begin to design corporate structures which are consistent with this Doctrine of Fair Contracts.

Imagine if you will, representative stakeholders trying to decide on "the rules of the game." Each is rational in a straightforward sense, looking out for its own self-interest. At least *ex ante*, stakeholders are the relevant parties since they will be materially affected. Stakeholders know how economic activity is organized and could be organized. They know general facts about the way the corporate world works. They know that in the real world there are or could be transaction costs, externalities, and positive costs of contracting. Suppose they are uncertain about what other social institutions exist, but they know the range of those institutions. They do not know if government exists to pick up the tab for any externalities, or if they will exist in the night-watchman state of libertarian theory. They know success and failure stories of businesses around the world. In short, they are behind a Rawls-like veil of ignorance, and they do not know what stake each will have when the veil is lifted. What groundrules would they choose to guide them?

The first groundrule is "The Principle of Entry and Exit." Any contract that is the corporation must have clearly defined entry, exit, and renegotiation conditions, or at least it must have methods or processes for so defining these conditions. The logic is straightforward: each stakeholder must be able to determine when an agreement exists and has a chance of fulfillment. This is not to imply that contracts cannot contain contingent claims or other methods for resolving uncertainty, but rather that it must contain methods for determining whether or not it is valid.

The second groundrule I shall call "The Principle of Governance," and it says that the procedure for changing the rules of the game must be agreed upon by unanimous consent. Think about the consequences of a majority of stakeholders systematically "selling out" a minority. Each stakeholder, in ignorance of its actual role, would seek to avoid such a situation. In reality this principle translates into each stakeholder never giving up its right to participate in the governance of the corporation, or perhaps into the existence of stakeholder governing boards.

The third groundrule I shall call. "The Principle of Externalities," and it says that if a contract between A and B imposes a cost on C, then C has the option to become a party to the contract, and the terms are renegotiated. Once again the rationality of this condition is clear. Each stakeholder will want insurance that it does not become C.

The fourth groundrule is "The Principle of Contracting Costs," and it says that all parties to the contract must share in the cost of contracting. Once again the logic is straightforward. Any one stakeholder can get stuck.

A fifth groundrule is "The Agency Principle" that says that any agent must serve the interests of all stakeholders. It must adjudicate conflicts within the bounds of the other principals. Once again the logic is clear. Agents for any one group would have a privileged place.

A sixth and final groundrule we might call, "The Principle of Limited Immortality." The corporation shall be managed as if it can continue to serve the interests of stakeholders through time. Stakeholders are uncertain about the future but, subject to exit conditions, they realize that the continued existence of the corporation is in their interest. Therefore, it would be rational to hire managers who are fiduciaries to their interest and the interest of the collective. If it turns out the "collective interest" is the empty set, then this principle simply collapses into the Agency Principle.

Thus, the Doctrine of Fair Contracts consists of these six groundrules or principles:

1. The Principle of Entry and Exit
2. The Principle of Governance
3. The Principle of Externalities
4. The Principle of Contracting Costs
5. The Agency Principle
6. The Principle of Limited Immortality

Think of these groundrules as a doctrine which would guide actual stakeholders in devising a corporate constitution or charter. Think of management as having the duty to act in accordance with some specific constitution or charter.

Obviously, if the Doctrine of Fair Contracts and its accompanying background narratives are to effect real change, there must be requisite changes in the enabling laws of the land. I propose the following three principles to serve as constitutive elements of attempts to reform the law of corporations.

The Stakeholder Enabling Principle

Corporations shall be managed in the interests of its stakeholders, defined as employees, financiers, customers, employees, and communities.

The Principle of Director Responsibility

Directors of the corporation shall have a duty of care to use reasonable judgment to define and direct the affairs of the corporation in accordance with the Stakeholder Enabling Principle.

The Principle of Stakeholder Recourse

Stakeholders may bring an action against the directors for failure to perform the required duty of care.

Obviously, there is more work to be done to spell out these principles in terms of model legislation. As they stand, they try to capture the intuitions that drive the liberal ideals. It is equally plain that corporate constitutions which meet a test like the doctrine of fair contracts are meant to enable directors and executives to manage the corporation in conjunction with these same liberal ideals.[12]

Notes

1. Cf. A. Berle and G. Means, *The Modern Corporation and Private Property* (New York: Com-

merce Clearing House, 1932), 1. For a reassess-
ment of Berle and Means' argument after 50
years, see *Journal of Law and Economics* 26
(June 1983), especially G. Stigler and C. Friedland, "The Literature of Economics: The Case of
Berle and Means," 237–68; D. North, "Comment on Stigler and Friedland," 269–72; and G.
Means, "Corporate Power in the Marketplace,"
467–85.

2. The metaphor of rebuilding the ship while afloat
is attributed to Neurath by W. Quine, *Word and
Object* (Cambridge: Harvard University Press,
1960), and W. Quine and J. Ullian, *The Web of
Belief* (New York: Random House, 1978). The
point is that to keep the ship afloat during repairs
we must replace a plank with one that will do a
better job. Our argument is that stakeholder capitalism can so replace the current version of managerial capitalism.

3. See R. Charan and E. Freeman, "Planning for the
Business Environment of the 1980s," *The Journal of Business Strategy* 1 (1980): 9–19, especially p. 15 for a brief account of the major developments in products liability law.

4. See S. Breyer, *Regulation and Its Reform* (Cambridge: Harvard University Press, 1983), 133,
for an analysis of food additives.

5. See I. Millstein and S. Katsh, *The Limits of Corporate Power* (New York: Macmillan, 1981),
Chapter 4.

6. Cf. C. Summers, "Protecting All Employees
Against Unjust Dismissal," *Harvard Business
Review* 58 (1980): 136, for a careful statement of
the argument.

7. See E. Freeman and D. Reed, "Stockholders and
Stakeholders: A New Perspective on Corporate
Governance," in C. Huizinga, ed., *Corporate
Governance: A Definitive Exploration of the Is-
sues* (Los Angeles: UCLA Extension Press,
1983).

8. See T. Peters and R. Waterman, *In Search of Excellence* (New York: Harper and Row, 1982).

9. See, for instance, A. Wicks, D. Gilbert, and E.
Freeman, "A Feminist Reinterpretation of the
Stakeholder Concept," *Business Ethics Quar-*

terly, Vol. 4, No. 4, October 1994; and E. Freeman and J. Liedtka, "Corporate Social Responsibility: A Critical Approach," Business Horizons,
Vol. 34, No. 4, July–August 1991, pp. 92–98.

10. At the Toronto workshop Mark Starik sketched
how a theory would look if we took the environment to be a stakeholder. This fruitful line of
work is one example of my main point about
pluralism.

11. J. Rawls, *Political Liberalism,* New York: Columbia University Press, 1993; and R. Rorty,
"The Priority of Democracy to Philosophy" in
*Reading Rorty: Critical Responses to Philoso-
phy and the Mirror of Nature (and Beyond),* ed.
Alan R. Malachowski, Cambridge, MA: Blackwell, 1990.

Study Questions

1. What ethical, economic, and legal principles and rules does Freeman use to
support his stakeholder view of managerial responsibility and decision making?

2. If you used these principles and rules to
identify important information in the
Agrico case, what information are you
likely to collect and what important information are you likely to miss?

3. What assumptions do you think Freeman makes about the institutional environment of business. Compare and
contrast these with Friedman's and
Cochran's assumptions. In your view,
which set of assumptions is more realistic? Why?

4. How could you use Freeman's view to
advise Burdelle in the Agrico Case?

Richard C. Marens and Andrew D. Wicks

Getting Real: Stakeholder Theory, Managerial Practice, and the General Irrelevance of Fiduciary Duties Owed to Shareholders

INTRODUCTION

Over the last several years, business ethicists (Goodpaster, 1991; Boatwright, 1994; Freeman, 1994; Goodpaster and Holloran, 1994; Donaldson and Preston, 1995) have disputed the implications for stakeholder theory of the fiduciary obligations owed by corporate management to shareholders. They have argued extensively as to whether this duty privileges shareholders and whether public policy could or should recalibrate the balance vis-à-vis other groups. The actual impact of these fiduciary responsibilities upon real-world business practice has received comparatively little attention. This paper attempts to address this neglect through a thorough examination of the relevant case law. In doing so, the authors have arrived at two conclusions. The first is that the existence of a fiduciary duty owed to stockholders presents few practical problems for a management team that wishes to implement a stakeholder-oriented approach to business. Second, the specific responsibilities generated by this fiduciary duty are in no way "over and above" the kind of treatment shareholders could reasonably expect to receive under a stakeholder regime.

Although stakeholder groups other than shareholders may not be able to enforce a fiduciary duty against corporate management, this legal reality does not preclude managers from behaving *as if* they were actually under such obligations. Legal relationships, and particularly legal relationships that emerge under a common law system, are not based on complete, elegant, and consistent sets of principles. They are instead the result of incremental modification of often vague and overlapping doctrines that must be selectively applied toward solving practical business problems or settling a variety of disputes. As a result, the precise legal doctrines that define the relationships between top corporate management and the various groups holding a stake in the firm's performance will differ from stakeholder group to stakeholder group *precisely* because each group holds a different economic and social relationship to the firm.

This axiom of legal realism generates two important results for stakeholder theory. First, as Goodpaster argued (1991), legal obligations subsumed under the rubric of *fiduciary* will not readily lend themselves to all stakeholder relationships. Second, there is no reason to assume, and empirical reasons to doubt, that owing a duty to one class of stakeholders creates serious practical constraints upon how the law allows managers to treat other groups.

This paper develops this argument through five sections. We begin by summarizing the discussion of the "stakeholder paradox" that allegedly arises from the fiduciary duties of corporate managers. This is followed by an explanation of the precise nature of these duties owed to stockholders. Next, the paper will argue that a century of legal precedent generally permits management the freedom to adopt and implement a stakeholder approach with regard to various constituencies. We then show that while fiduciary obligations do little to limit managerial autonomy to do so, no current statute or common law principles compel a full-scale stakeholder approach. The paper then proposes a new extension of legal doctrine to encourage such an approach and finally concludes by discussing implications for theory and teaching.

THE "STAKEHOLDER PARADOX"

Since Freeman's (1984) seminal article on stakeholder theory appeared in print, scholars of business ethics have increasingly used stakeholder theory as a conceptual framework to discuss the ethical dimensions and implications of corporate activity. Freeman began the discussion by arguing that successful managers must systematically attend to the interests of various stakeholder groups. Later pieces, including contributions by Freeman himself (Evan and Freeman, 1988; Freeman and Gilbert, 1988; Donaldson and Preston, 1995), moved beyond this "enlightened self-interest" position by taking the more radical position that the interests of stakeholders have intrinsic worth irrespective of whether these advance the interests of shareholders. Under this view, the success of a firm is not merely an end in itself but should also be seen as providing a vehicle for advancing the interests of stakeholders other than shareholders.

Since each class of stakeholder has a different legal, economic, and social relationship to a particular business, a general stakeholder approach does not explain how managers should balance different *kinds* of dependencies. Particularly troublesome is the legal reality that managers owe shareholders a "fiduciary" duty not generally granted to any other group. While Donaldson and Preston (1995) are correct in pointing to contractual obligations and regulatory responsibilities designed to protect other groups from specific malefeasances such as discrimination or pollution, we argue below that Goodpaster (1991) and Goodpaster and Holloran (1994) were also accurate in characterizing the duty to stockholders as more general and proactive than what other constituencies can claim.

Goodpaster, however, goes further then this by insisting on a potential conflict arising out of this legal asymmetry, arguing for the existence of a "stakeholder paradox" where corporate management would find themselves (under all but the most ideal circumstances) having to choose between fulfilling this fiduciary duty and serving the interests of other stakeholders. Boatright (1994) argued that this paradox could be overcome by extending this fiduciary duty to cover other stakeholders, a suggestion criticized by Goodpaster and Holloran (1994) as both impractical and potentially unwise.

Freeman (1994), however took a different track, claiming that the existence of any fiduciary duty owed stockholder is theoretically irrelevant to the normative justification for stakeholder theory since such duties do not give license to corporate managers to violate normative ethics in interactions with non-stockholders (see also Jones, 1995). Donaldson and Preston (1995) go even further by suggesting that the legislation of protections to other groups implies that the broader norms of ethical behavior are consistent with stakeholder philosophy.

Not all behavior, however, that might be defensible as consistent with normative ethics will always prevail in a court of law, the arena in which legal rights are established and applied. Consequently, directors and managers might rightly concern themselves with their legal as well as their ethical position in relating to various stakeholder groups. As this paper will make clear, however, they have little to fear. An examination of the origin and meaning of fiduciary responsibility shows that this duty does little to threaten managers who set out to implement stakeholder-oriented policies.

THE ASYMMETRY OF LEGAL RELATIONSHIPS WITHIN THE CORPORATE "WEB"

Courts did not historically encumber corporate management with a fiduciary duty toward company stockholders in order to privilege shareholders vis-à-vis other stakeholder groups. Rather, it was designed to prevent self-dealing on the part of directors and top management that fell short of criminal behavior such as embezzlement (Brudney, 1985; Clark, 1985). Traditionally, this meant preventing business decisions, typically involving expenditures, that were made *primarily* because they personally benefited top managers or their friends (Berle and Means, 1933), while more recent charges of malfeasance tend to focus on managerial entrenchment as much as enrichment.

When conflict of interest is not at issue, no case law or corporate statute argues that management's fiduciary duty should be equated with a right of stockholders to oversee managerial decision-making (Brudney, 1985; Mitchell, 1992). If business ethicists seem to implicitly assume otherwise, the source of this misconception is not hard to deduce. Stakeholder theory is, at least in part, a response to neo-classical theories of the firm which impose an empirically false symmetry of legal relationships among corporate constituencies. By assuming that there might be some truth to such legal chimeras as "nexus of contracts" and "agency theory," stakeholder theorists would reasonably counter that these legal relationships are inadequate to support a stakeholder approach to business management. If stakeholder theorists erred, it was in assuming that these hypothesized relationships had some basis in law.

Corporations are not, in any meaningful legal sense, nexi of contracts, nor are directors agents of stockholders. To take the second point first, "agency" (Clark, 1985) is a highly specific two-way relationship in which the principal can direct or override the agent and the agent can, under highly restricted circumstances, legally bind or create liabilities for the principal. Neither directional arrow holds, in any meaningful way, between stockholder and director. Not only do individual stockholders lack legal standing to specify details of how a business should be managed, directors and top managers can neither bind individual shareholders to contracts with third parties or generate personal liabilities

for them through debt or tort.[1] On the other hand, directors (and *their* agents, high-level managers) *can* legally bind the corporate entity as a whole to either contractual obligations or financial liability.

This distinction is not merely semantic. The duties required of a fiduciary are not to obey a person, as an agent might, but to make every effort to protect their property, in this case the funds or other assets the stockholder has exchanged for corporate shares. As a fiduciary, a corporate director's relationship is not with the shareholder personally but with her *investment*.

Not only is this relationship not that of agency, it is also not contractual in any legally meaningful way. The general fiduciary obligation is one of fulfilling a normatively-defined level of *responsibility* toward beneficiaries with little connection to contract law and its underlying presumption of voluntary bargaining between informed parties (Mitchell, 1992). By contrast, the fiduciary principle evolved from the far older law of property, which directs *trustees* to manage property in the interest of those judged incompetent to do so themselves, historically because of age, gender, or infirmity (Mennell, 1994; Mitchell, 1992). Fiduciary duties were imposed on these trustees in order to protect legal owners who were not in a position to manage their own affairs from the unscrupulous self-dealing of those administrators the incompetent were *forced* to rely upon (Johnston, 1988; Mennell, 1994). This is a set of circumstances that would describe any outside corporate investor, whose involvement in the business is based upon the expectation of a financial return through either dividends or sale of the security, and who is almost never in a position to oversee that this investment is neither negligently handled nor exploited for personal gain by the handler.

The beneficiary/fiduciary relationship is considerably more straightforward than those derived from contract in which parties negotiate some terms and explicitly or implicitly adopt others from extant regulations or currently accepted practices (Mitchell, 1992).

The typical penalty for breach of contract involve monetary damages, making all but the most egregious breaches a kind of business decision as to whether cost of the penalty (and, possibly, damage to reputation) exceeds the gain from repudiation. By contrast, the fiduciary duties required of trustees: honesty, adequate care for the entrusted property, providing the owner with any relevant information, avoiding any unauthorized personal gain even when such gain does not hurt the beneficiary (Block et al, 1989), are not typically subject to negotiation, and a judge would carefully scrutinize the circumstances of any claim that a beneficiary freed the fiduciary from any of these duties (Mitchell, 1992).

As result, contractual duties and fiduciary duties are measured differently. Contractees are expected to complete certain acts while fiduciaries are required to act under certain *motives*. In the corporate setting, fiduciary duties do not impose a requirement that a business be run in a certain manner. No court equates this duty with "maximizing shareholder value"[2] even assuming such an indeterminate concept could be estimated. What the duty does require is honesty and candor in the relationship with the stockholder and a general avoidance of using one's office for illegitimate personal gain. Traditionally such illegitimate self-dealing might have meant dealing with another company *because* a director has some financial interest in the other concern. A more modern application might mean keeping stockholders from voting on a tender offer because the inside directors fear for their jobs. There is nothing in the relationship that absolutely bars acts of generosity on the part of fiduciaries who are not themselves the beneficiary of the act, unless such generosity can be shown to harm the beneficiary.

Given the modest nature of this duty list, there are at least three reasons to doubt that they provide any serious obstacle to the implementation of stakeholder principles. First, it is not obvious that the right of shareholders to expect honesty, candor, and care on the part of management gives them a higher level of protection than the legal rights available to other stakeholders. Creditor interests, for example, are protected by bankruptcy law. Suppliers and customers can seek redress under the Uniform Commercial Code or more recent statutes such as "lemon laws" that cover used car sales. Tort victims are the beneficiaries of insurance requirements for various kinds of businesses. And employees can enlist government assistance in collecting unpaid wages or compensation for income-diminishing injuries and can demand fiduciary protection for pension assets and other benefits (Donaldson and Preston, 1995).

Second, courts are starting to impose on corporate management fiduciary duties with regard to other groups under certain circumstances. Last year, the Supreme Court ruled in *Varity v. Howe* (1996) that a corporation that reorganized all of its money-losing ventures into a single subsidiary that eventually went bankrupt (leaving a healthy surviving parent) had breached its fiduciary duty to the employees of the subsidiary. The company had not only urged employees to transfer to the subsidiary (without disclosing its precarious condition), it even transferred the benefit administration of several retirees to the subsidiary without their knowledge. As a result the parent corporation and several of its executives were found to have violated duties created under the Employee Retirement Income Security Act (ERISA) and assumed by corporations that administer their own benefit plans. The Court just recently extended this reasoning to the protection of non-retirement benefits when it found for employees dismissed after refusing to accept employment with another company, but a company with whom their original employer had arranged for them to do exactly the same work but with reduced benefits (*Intermodal v. Sante Fe Railroad,* 1997).

And finally, as we will demonstrate in detail below, when stockholders have attempted to challenge managerial behavior as being overly generous toward another constituency, they have almost always lost.

BUT WHAT ABOUT
DODGE BROS. V. FORD?

Stakeholder theorists who argue that share-holder interests are (fortunately or unfortunately) paramount typically cite the famous dictum from the Michigan case *Dodge Bros. v. Ford* that "the corporation exists for the benefit of the shareholders" (Goodpaster, 1991; Boatright, 1994) as evidence of a restraint on the discretion of management. Leaving aside the question as to whether dicta from a state court decision remains influential after seventy-five years, an examination of the context of the statement and the circumstances of the law suit makes it clear that this perspective was not meant to empower the shareholder at the expense of managerial discretion.

The law suit was aimed at Henry Ford's tightfisted dividend policy. Ford Motors had become one of the world's most profitable companies and was literally piling up unspent cash that it could not invest fast enough, yet was recently refusing to pay out much more than 1% of its net income in dividends. Because it was the company's principal share-holder, Henry Ford, who managed the company, this was a classic case of upholding the rights of minority shareholders against the tyranny of a majority investor. Ford Motors was, at the time, a privately-held corporation and courts have been particularly sensitive to protect minority interests in such firms (Mitchell et al, 1996), such as the Dodge brother plaintiffs. Unlike holders of publicly traded shares, minority shareholders in a private corporation are not usually in a position to readily sell-out and thereby exit from an unsatisfactory relationship[3] and by definition minority holders possess little or no power to replace an unsatisfactory board of directors with one more amenable to their perspective. One might, in fact, argue that the stockholders of privately held companies deserve more consideration as stakeholders than their public counterparts. Because minority shareholders in a privately-held company are far less free to exit the relationship if management makes a decision they find objectionable,

they are more dependent upon a right to have their interests considered by management.

The court rejected Henry Ford's defense that "my ambition is to employ still more men, to spread the benefits of this industrial system to the greatest possible number, to help them build up their lives and their homes" (*Dodge Bros. v. Ford,* 1919: p. 505). While his assertion is usually taken at face value to violate accepted norms of proper business purpose, the court may well have been aware that he was speaking with dubious sincerity (Nevins, 1954). Testimony indicates that Ford Motors had issued higher dividends in the past, suggesting perhaps that Ford's primary motive in refusing to pay-out was to prevent the Dodge Brothers from funding a competitive company, which, in fact, they eventually did. But whatever Ford's true motives were, it would be difficult to imagine that any normative stakeholder theory would deny shareholders the right to share in some of the prosperity generated by a successful business.

It should also be noted that the court did not hold that investors could interfere with managerial business planning or insist that their immediate financial gain become the only consideration of the board of directors. The judge actually dismissed most of the complaints filed by the Dodge Brothers, holding for example, that Ford and his fellow directors had the right to plan the business as they judged best, free from second guessing on such business decisions as expanding production and smelting his own iron, and certainly under no obligation to forego these in favor of distributing further dividends.

Moreover, there is no evidence that the decision in any way affected Henry Ford's peculiar brand of paternalism in relations toward his employees. The court did not prevent Ford from continuing to pay higher-than-market wages or prevent him from subjecting them to speed-ups, invasions of privacy, and expectations of social conformity that went far beyond what was attempted by other employers. Working for Ford remained a tradeoff of high wages and tight behavioral restriction (Meyer, 1981).

Reading the case, one might reasonably conclude that it strongly confirmed the principle that shareholders cannot interfere with managerial decisions that can be plausibly justified as enhancing business performance. The court acknowledged that Ford could build new plants, vertically integrate, or otherwise run the business as he saw fit. What they forbid was the company's decision to sit on a mountain of cash for allegedly philanthropic, not business, purposes, particularly when the court had reasons to doubt Ford's candor regarding his actual motive.

In fact, since *Dodge Bros. v. Ford* courts have proven very reluctant to force a corporation to pay-out additional dividends or otherwise examine the economic wisdom of business decisions (Brudney, 1980).[4] In *Grobow v. GM* (1988), the board of directors was permitted to exercise its collective Judgement that paying H. Ross Perot seven hundred million dollars in order to remove him from the board of directors was in the best interest of the corporation. In finding a legitimate business purpose in spending these funds to eliminate Perot's unflagging dissension (as opposed to larger dividends or new investments), the highly influential Delaware Supreme Court implied that there would be few decisions not involving outright self-dealing that stockholders could enjoin boards from making.

DOING WELL BY DOING GOOD

An examination of a century of case law under circumstances less dramatic than what faced the Michigan Court in 1919 demonstrates that corporate managers have successfully defended generosity and consideration toward non-shareholding constituents. In the process, courts have often accepted arguments that anticipated instrumental stakeholder theory (see Jones, 1995). Whatever skepticism the court expressed in Dodge Bros. v. Ford toward charitable giving has largely disappeared in American jurisprudence since A.P. Smith v. Barlow recognized in 1953 an enlightened self-interest rationale

for spending profits in this manner (Von Stange, 1994). Similarly, courts established long ago that corporations can voluntarily agree to pay a tax bill that is higher than the law might strictly require as part of a political compromise with local communities (*Kelly v. Bell,* 1969). General Motors recently applied this principle, when, having won the right in court to disregard its own promises made in return for a property tax reduction, it agreed to a new investment program with the offended community (Hattori, 1994).

Historically, generosity toward employees has almost always won when, unlike in *Dodge Bros.* the generous treatment is justified as a means of improving efficiency or productivity. A century ago, in *Steinway v. Steinway & Sons* (1909), a family shareholder lost his court challenge to the building of a company town for manufacturing employees on the grounds that such an act of communitarianism would improve labor relations, and, as the court noted, help keep out unions. Later, corporations routinely defeated challenges by stockholders to various bonus and profit-sharing plans when justified by creating incentives for better corporate performance (*Diamond v. Davis,* 1935; *Gallin v. National City Bank,* 1945) until they too became legally unassailable.

ESOPS, or Employee Stock Ownership Plans, might appear to be theoretically more vulnerable to challenge since they often require the assumption of debt or the dilution of current stock holdings to implement them. Yet, except in very rare cases in which the ESOP was thrown together at the last minute to prevent a takeover (more on this below), ESOPS have been consistently upheld by courts as consistent with management's right to set personnel policy and select means of raising productivity (see *Herald v. Seawall,* 1972). One court (*In re* Dunkin Donuts, 1990) even accepted management's argument that an ESOP plan would help heal the effects of a corporate downsizing on surviving employees.

One might argue that the need to justify acts of generosity through a finding of a rational business purpose such as higher productivity, long-term earning horizons or beneficial public relations limits a stakeholder approach to a very timid instrumental use of the concept. However, it is also important for stakeholder theorists to understand that court rooms are not forums for the expression of deeply held moral philosophy. Lawyers are trained to make the most conservative, precedent-supported argument that can plausibly defend a particular act or policy.

No competent attorney would allow her client to argue in court that their corporation made a decision because it "was the right thing to do" in the face of evidence that management knew of legal alternatives whose impact on the bottom line, short term and long term, was indisputably superior. It may smack of moral cowardice, but given the uncertainty of what sustains and makes a business profitable over a period of years, virtually any act that does not financially threaten the survival of the business could be construed as in the long-term best interest of shareholders.

TAKEOVERS AND THE PURSUIT OF A RATIONAL BUSINESS PLAN

If board fiduciary duties toward stockholders prove significant in any issue of corporate policy it is in their treatment of takeover bids. Top managers might reasonably see such takeovers or mergers as a threat to their continued tenure in well-paid and fulfilling jobs. Consequently, the appearance of a tender offer might tempt them into a breech of their fiduciary duty by looking for ways to cling to their high-paying jobs rather than making decisions based on a judgment as to what furthers the financial interests of stockholders.

The structure of a large portion of takeover efforts made it relatively simple for management to defend their resistance in terms other than self-entrenchment.[5] To begin with, not all tender offers will necessarily make most stockholders better off. A corporate board could reasonably find some tender offers *coercive* of shareholders, as, for example, a two-tiered offer which promises a premium to the first stockholders to sell, whose purpose is to create to a stampede of acceptance on the part of those who fear being the ones to miss out (e.g.: *Baron v. Strawbridge,* 1986). In addition, any offer that is so poorly financed that the long-term survival of the firm is put in doubt arguably triggers a fiduciary duty to reject it in order to protect the interests of any shareholder who does not wish to sell (e.g., *Amanda v. Universal Foods,* 1989). Such judgments gain credibility when they are made by directors of demonstrable stature and independence without employment or other significant financial ties to the company. These "outside" directors are presumably more disinterested than "inside" directors who risk losing a managerial position in a takeover battle.

But on numerous occasions courts have also found for boards of directors that have rejected tender offers that are neither patently manipulative or clearly fiscally unsound. The language of the judicial opinions in several of these cases sounds remarkably similar to that of a normative stakeholder approach. The Supreme Court of Delaware, by far the most influential state court with respect to corporation and securities law, has consistently rejected the notion that directors have a duty to sell the company whenever a takeover proposal offers a premium over current market value of company stock (*Paramount v. Time,* 1989: p. 1144), and the court has even established a positive duty to "adopt defensive measures to defeat a takeover attempt contrary to the best interests of the corporation *and* its shareholders" (*Revlon v. MacAndrews,* 1986, p. 184). The court had implicitly defined these corporate, but non-shareholder interests, very broadly when it had ruled the previous year in *Unocal v. Mesa Petroleum* (1985) that boards might consider impact on "customers, creditors, employees, and perhaps *even* the community generally" (p. 955, italics mine).

Numerous courts decisions in other jurisdictions have concurred by supporting the right of boards to choose the continuation of corporate policies over obtaining premium stock price for shareholders. Companies could refuse highly leveraged offers likely to put an end to philanthropic and research policies (*Amanda v. Universal,* 1989) or fight to keep a company independent when it rationally saw such independence as vital for customer, community and employee relations (*Baron v. Strawbridge Clothier,* 1986). One court, for example, upheld a bank's decision to choose one takeover "suitor" over another, explicitly accepting as legitimate the bank's justification that the winning bidder was better on "social issues," including the prospect of creating more opportunity for the company's employees (*Kayser v. National Finance,* 1987, p. 265).

On one of the few occasions that the Supreme Court has spoken to the three-way relationship between directors, shareholders and other stakeholders (*CTS v. Dynamics Corp.,* 1987), it upheld a state anti-takeover statute that allowed a corporate board to fight off such an attempt.[6] Its justification rejected the need for state legislatures to follow "any one particular economic theory of the firm" (p. 92) such as shareholder supremacy, while acknowledging a state interest in "maintaining stable relationships between *parties involved in corporations*" (Id., p. 90). Another court went further by actually finding a proactive duty to protect employee benefits such as pensions and severance pay by eschewing mergers or takeovers that might threaten these (*GAF v. Union Carbide,* 1985). This case first established the duty that the Supreme Court more recently extended in *Varity* and *Intermodal* to transactions that did not involve takeovers.

One the other hand, the potential for self-dealing implicit in takeover defenses has provided virtually the only circumstance where stockholders can challenge the legitimacy of establishing an ESOP. ESOPS sometimes serve as a form of takeover defense, either because the debt, cash, or dilution required to create an ESOP might scare away suitors, or because the management-appointed trustees of the plan (and eventually, the vested employees) could probably be expected to vote with management.

ESOPS upheld by courts despite their concurrence with a hostile takeover are typically rationalized in stakeholder terms. Xerox, for example, could triple the size of its existing ESOP in response to a takeover bid, because the ESOP could be characterized with some credibility as part of a long-running program of building a "partnership" relationship with employees in order to improve productivity (Monks and Minow, 1991). Moreover, *current* Xerox shareholders would not have been hurt by the plan since employees would pay for most of it with pay cuts, a move employees might prefer to losing their jobs in a hostile takeover. ESOPS that materialize at the "last minute," however, have, on occasion, been ruled a breach of fiduciary duty (see e.g., Yoshihashi, 1992; *Franz Mtg. v. EAC Industries,* 1985).

A similar split has occurred regarding the enforcement of "tin" parachutes, generous severance packages for non-executive employees triggered only by hostile takeovers. They were upheld, for example, in *GAF v. Union Carbide.* Other courts, however, have thrown them out when such generosity was never extended to employees laid-off (Block et. al., 1989, 1991).

While the precise details are complex and frequently mind-numbing, a legal conclusion can be drawn from these various results. Management, almost by definition, has a personal stake in opposing unsolicited takeover offers. Nonetheless, if benefits to a defense can reasonably be construed as beneficial to other stakeholder groups, and the defensive strategy is not clearly detrimental to stockholders, managers do not entirely surrender the legal autonomy allowed them in making virtually any other class of common corporate decisions.

COMPELLING A STAKEHOLDER APPROACH

If American corporate law does little to inhibit a stakeholder orientation on the part of corporate managers, it also does little to compel one. Management teams exercise a wide range of discretion as to whether to embrace a

stakeholder view of constituencies when instituting major corporate changes. While National Steel worked with employees and the
Weirton community to sell them its steel plant
when it became unprofitable for the company
to operate (Lieber, 1995), U.S. Steel chose
only a few years earlier to shutdown its
Youngstown, Ohio facility rather than risk
creating competition by selling it to its employees (*USW v. U.S. Steel Corp.*, 1980), a decision recently emulated by British Petroleum
regarding one of *its* refineries (Cooper, 1997).

This autonomy vis-à-vis stakeholders has
not been altered by the rash of corporate constituency statutes passed by the majority of
state legislatures in recent years (Fort, 1995).[7]
This result is not surprising considering that
all but one of these laws (the exception being
Connecticut's) only permit directors to take
the interests of customers, creditors, employees, or the community into consideration; they
do not compel such concern, and even Connecticut law does not create a specific cause-
of-action on which stakeholders can sue. Nor
has any court extrapolated such a right
(Singer, 1993). While Maine's corporate constituency law has been one of only three that
has ever been cited by a court in finding in
favor of a *managerial* decision (*Georgia Pacific v. Great Northern*, 1989), seven years
later the same court could still assert that no
Maine statutory or case law allowed an *employee or creditor* to sue for breach of fiduciary duty (*Tiernan v. Barresi*, 1996, p. 37).

The 100,000 complaints of age discrimination that have been filed with the Equal
Employment Opportunity Commission during this decade also supports this conclusion.
Although a sizable fraction resulted from either downsizing or reorganization following
a merger or acquisition (Grimsley, 1997), not
a single aggrieved workers has sued on the
basis of a corporate constituency statute.
Given the numbers involved, it seems highly
implausible that no attorney would have attempted to sue on these statutes if there was a
realistic hope that these statutes might be
used to challenge, as well as defend, the policies pursued by corporate management.

It is perhaps not surprising, then, that the
three instances where such statutes have been
used in appellate decisions all involved directors resisting takeover bids. Even here, these
statutes provided only secondary support for
a more central justification. This supporting
role is demonstrated by the way each court introduced its use of the relevant stakeholder
statute, using the words "[f]urthermore"
(*Kayser v. Commonwealth National Financial Corp.*, 1987, p. 265), "[i]n addition"
(*Abrahamson v. Wadell*, 1992, p. 272) and
"[t]his is particularly so [in light of the stakeholder statute]" (*Georgia Pacific Corp. v.
Great Northern Nakoosa Corp*, 1992, p. 33).
If constituency statutes have had any impact
it has probably been the informal one of giving directors, who might be confused regarding their legal obligations and possibly worried about personal liability, a degree of legal
cover for taking the interests of other stakeholders into consideration (Lorsch, 1989).

The record of legislation aimed to protect *specific* classes of stakeholders has had a
mixed record. In general, the more specific
and less intrusive into managerial decision-
making the legislation, the greater its even-
tual impact, in part because the more ambitious legislation has been overturned. While
the Supreme Court upheld a Maine law in
Halifax Packing-Co.-v.-Coyne (1987) that required severance payments to victims of a
plant closing calculated by a fixed formula
based on years of service, other courts have
thrown-out more complex and ambitious
statutes: a Massachusetts law that required
severance for layoffs after *any* change in control (*Simas-v.-Quaker-Fabric-Corp.*, 1993),
and a Hawaiian law that compelled severance
for virtually any layoff that could be connected to some structural change in the business (*Akau v. Tel-A-Com*, 1990).

In a parallel fashion, Federal WARN legislation requiring notification of employees
of impending layoffs has become accepted as
part of the business landscape, in part because
of its many exceptions and loopholes in case
of a business emergency. On the other hand,
courts have generally refused to find age discrimination when older unionized employees
are discarded in favor of operating newer

plants staffed by younger non-union employees (*Allen v. Dierbold,* 1994). The court reasoned that if a company wishes to replace more expensive unionized employees with cheaper non-unionized ones by switching production to another plant, it is not discriminating merely because the average age is significantly higher in the first group.

A similar spectrum is evident in cases centered on community responsibility of corporations that accept government aid. The more specific the requirement, the easier it is to enforce. In a case involving development bonds, issued by the State of Minnesota with the explicitly stated intention to help investors buy troubled firms in order to preserve jobs, a court found for the state and against an investor who used the subsidizes of these bonds to buy and dismantle a factory in order to ship its assets to North Carolina (*In re Duluth,* 1989). On the other hand, although the City of Yonkers condemned some land to enable Otis Elevator to expand and stay in the city, this deal did not require Otis to continue investing and manufacturing in Yonkers when Otis Elevator could show a few years later that this particular plant was becoming increasingly unprofitable to operate (*Yonkers v. Otis Elevator,* 1988). Similarly, the Michigan Supreme Court would not hold General Motors to its promise to perpetually manufacture a particular automobile model in Ypsilanti Township in return for tax benefits (Hattari, 1994).

Unions are certainly one stakeholder group recognized by law as entitled to exercise power in limiting employer discretion regarding compensation, working conditions, and work rules. However, a Supreme Court decision twelve years ago, *First Maintenance v. NLRB* (1981), denies unions any legal right to participate in other kinds of corporate decision-making, including some categories that directly affect employees. As a result, unions have little pressure to exert regarding mergers, downsizing, layoffs or contracting-out work previously performed by union members unless they can show that such acts were committed out of an anti-union animus. It is long established law that unions can not

prevent a company from abandoning a plant in the middle of a contract period in favor of another more profitable site, and even concessions granted in the middle of a contract period do not obligate the employer to continue to recognize the union at the end of the period (*Marine Transport Lines v. International Organization of Masters,* 1986).

Unions are, of course, entitled to bargain for severance pay and other layoff benefits should reorganization cost jobs, but one survey found that only 40% of union contracts actually include a severance package (Summers, 1995). Moreover, unions who have managed to bargain for job-security provisions in their contracts have often found it difficult to enforce these in court (Stone, 1991). And should even such mild limitations on managerial autonomy be found intolerable, a generation of declining rates of private-sector unionization suggests that management is often in a position to "rid themselves of these meddlesome stewards."

MOVING THE COMMON LAW IN A STAKEHOLDER DIRECTION

The common law system, with its selective use of precedent in both deciding cases and interpreting legislation, is a mix of tradition and improvisation capable of generating a great deal of innovation, albeit at an uncertain rate and with somewhat unpredictable results. As the law evolves, there are arguments attorneys can make that, by building on analogy, might move the law incrementally toward compelling recalcitrant managers toward more consideration of stakeholder interests without radically interfering with the general independence of management to run a business as it feels best.

One is the general extension of fiduciary duty to other financial participants (Boatwright, 1994). This has begun to happen in conjunction with the previous mentioned fiduciary duties created by ERISA. As the law now stands, corporations can not make business decisions to avoid their responsibilities to their present and future pension beneficiaries and now with *Inter-modal,* this has been extended to forbid business decisions that disregard duties to recipients of other kinds of benefits such as medical insurance, sick leave and overtime pay that is more generous than the legal minimum.

Theoretically, fiduciary duties might be imposed on corporations that benefit from the various investment decisions stakeholders must routinely make when relying on the representations of a particular business. Businesses routinely benefit from the investments made by others: suppliers who install new machinery to meet the company's requirements; retailers who invest in advertising, training, and store modifications to accommodate their products; communities who build roads, establish educational programs and make various sorts of civic improvements; and customers who pay with their cold hard cash. Law professor Katherine Stone (1991) has proposed that internal labor market theory, which asserts that employers pay below marginal value for neophytes with an implicit promise to overpay after years of commitment to a particular firm, presents courts with a fiduciary rationale for protecting employee "investments" of years or decades of service in hopes of such a payoff.

These arguments for extending a fiduciary duty, however, are likely to require more of a stretch than most courts are comfortable making, particularly when extant law in contracts, torts, and employment already covers some of the same territory. Stone's proposal in particular requires the acceptance of an economic theory that has hardly achieved universal legitimacy.

A less conceptually radical way of covering much of the same territory has been suggested by O'Neil (1993) in connection with the employment relationship. Rather than trying to analogize too broadly and perhaps inappropriately from the narrow property orientation of fiduciary duties, he suggests modifying a legal obligation already embedded in the employment law. Currently, employers can demand a duty of loyalty from their employees derived from the original law of "master and servants." Employees can be

sued for acts of disloyalty that are not actually criminal, such as revealing secrets or "stealing" business opportunities, learned about through one's job, away from the employer. O'Neill proposes making this duty reciprocal so that employers can not take advantage of their workers through deliberately misleading them or unnecessarily disregarding their interests in making decisions.

Such a reciprocal duty of loyalty might enjoin a profitable employer from laying-off employees if it can offer no rational business purpose beyond that of trying to convince investors to bid-up the price of the stock. Similarly, corporations would be held accountable for lying to employees regarding their future relationship, or replacing permanent employees with temporaries or part-timers in order to avoid paying benefits. Loyalty defined as honest communication and the avoidance of corporate enrichment at employee expense would go a long way toward creating fiduciary-like protections for employees. At the same time, managers would not be constrained from any ethically justifiable business decisions, including such unpleasant ones as downsizing in order to stay competitive. Moreover, if compelled by threat of law suit to behave ethically toward employees and other stakeholder groups, many firms might actually discover that two-way loyalty creates no impediments to long-term profitability (Jones, 1995).

A similar duty might be extended to the communities. Communities could rely and, if necessary, sue upon promises made by businesses in return for tax favors or infrastructural investment. Companies would be forced to temper their requests with realism and honesty. Some might argue that these new legal duties place corporate boards and top executives under "too many masters." But as Macy and Miller point out (1993), corporate leaders already serve many masters, and it is difficult to see that requiring that they treat those from whom they expect cooperation with honesty and care would be unduly burdensome. Moreover, even if such behavior does, in some instances, raise the cost of doing business, it is difficult to understand why society as a whole would not be better served with slightly higher prices here and there, if they were the by-product of more dependable and trustworthy interactions.

CONCLUSION: IMPLICATIONS FOR STAKEHOLDER THEORY AND PRACTICE

If a corporate board's fiduciary duty to stockholders amounts to little more than protecting their investments from self-dealing, . . . then what are the implications of this reality for stakeholder theory?

To begin with, our analysis suggests that . . . meeting fiduciary duties to shareholders does not entail that managers must side with shareholders and against stakeholders. Firms have the legal autonomy to act proactively and advance the interests of a number of stakeholders simultaneously . . .

Though there are clearly some cases where the firms have to make hard choices among the interests of various stakeholders, this reading suggests that such cases are the exception rather than the rule. Thus researchers would do well to drop the idea of a stakeholder paradox, spend less time worrying about fiduciary duties as a significant problem for the theory, and re-focus inquiry in ways that avoid these conceptual roadblocks. . . .

A final and equally important challenge lies in education. If our analysis is correct, and the presumed legal obstacles to stakeholder theory are largely absent, this suggests that while conflict between the interests of shareholders and other stakeholders will not disappear, they need not be structurally inevitable or as unreconciliable as many would assume. Arguably, managers and much of the public have accepted a relatively unquestioned and problematic ideology that defines the shareholder/manager relationship as that of principle/agent, assuming, perhaps naively, that it was based on deep social consensus and legal precedent. In that case, a major challenge for ethicists and business schools lies in exposing this myth to students and the public at large

and clarifying that whatever differences exist between stakeholder and shareholder theorists, these are ideologically based and thus contestable. Students and managers also need to know that they do not risk violating the law or well-founded social norms should they choose to manage their firms in a manner that weighs the interests of other groups with the same gravity that they bring to questions of shareholder value. Specifically, education should include the following:

1. The stakeholder paradox is largely a false, ideologically created and avoidable problem since managers are not compelled to choose between the law and stakeholder ethics.

2. Managers have considerable freedom regarding firm operations and investments and are not legally-bound to reach decisions *purely* on the basis of their impact on shareholders.

3. Stakeholder theory need not be the antithesis or response to Friedman's shareholder theory, but can serve as a more compelling, inclusive, and realistic account of how business organizations can and should operate. . . .

Notes

1. In the rare case that a court will "pierce the corporate veil" and find a stockholder personally liable for a tort committed by a corporation, the stockholder is almost invariably involved in the tortuous behavior and/or has clearly aimed to use incorporation as a personal shield to avoid personal liability for highly negligent or reckless behavior.
2. See *Paramount v. Time* (1989) for a refutation of the idea that the primary legal duty of corporate boards is to achieve the highest possible stock price.
3. Stakeholder theorists have been less than careful about making this distinction between private and publicly-traded corporations. The text of most stakeholder proposals seem to assume a publicly-traded status for the object of the theories, but, arguably, there is no reason that stakeholder principles might not be applied to the privately-held company.
4. While courts have occasionally ruled on divi-

dend policy over the last eighty years, the most important decisions have focused on payouts so *generous* that plaintiff stockholders have claimed that they threatened the survival of the business. Even then, judges have generally avoided interference, and in the leading case (*Sinclair Oil,* 1971) the court decided that firm-bankrupting dividends were permissible as long as minority shareholders were not discriminated against in the looting of the till.

5. Brudney (1985), suggests that courts have in recent years erected procedural barriers limiting plaintiffs' ability to challenge self-dealing by shifting the burden of showing improper motive onto the plaintiff. See *Buffalo Forge v. Ogden,* 1983.

6. These statutes, typically passed during the early 1980s, legalized various measures corporate boards could take to "defend" the firm from hostile takeover attempts. These statutes tended to be narrower and more technical than the corporate constituency statutes that began to appear a few years later.

7. States that have passed corporate constituency statutes include: Connecticut, Florida, Georgia, Hawaii, Idaho, Illinois, Indiana, Iowa, Kentucky, Louisiana, Maine, Massachusetts, Minnesota, Mississippi, Missouri, Nebraska, New Jersey, New Mexico, New York, Ohio, Oregon, Pennsylvania, Rhode Island, South Dakota, Tennessee, Wisconsin, Wyoming.

References

BERLE, ADOLF A. & GARDINER C. MEANS. 1933. *The Modern Corporation and Private Property.* New York: Commerce Clearing House.

BLOCK, DENNIS J., NANCY E. BARTON AND STEPHEN A RADIN. 1989 (suppl. 1991). *The Business Judgment Rule: Fiduciary Duties of Corporate Directors.* Englewood Cliffs, NJ: Prentice Hall Law & Business.

BLOCK, DENNIS J., NANCY E. BARTON AND STEPHEN A RADIN. 1989 (suppl. 1991). *The Business Judgment Rule: Fiduciary Duties of Corporate Directors.* Englewood Cliffs, NJ: Prentice Hall Law & Business.

BOATRIGHT, JOHN. 1994. "What's So Special about Shareholders?" *Business Ethics Quarterly* 4: 393–408.

BRUDNEY, VICTOR. 1985. "Corporate Governance, Agency costs, and the Rhetoric of Contract." *Columbia Law Review* 85: 1403–1444.

BRUDNEY, VICTOR. 1980. "Dividends, Discretion, and Disclosure." *Virginia Law Review* 66: 85–129.

CLARK, ROBERT C. 1985. "Agency Costs versus Fiduciary Duties." In *Principals and Agents,* John Pratt and Richard Zeckhauser (eds.). Boston: Harvard University Press.

COLEMAN, DENNIS R. 1996. Fort Halifax progeny—benefits sans plans. *Benefits Law Journal* 9: 71–79.

COOPER, MARC. 1997. "A Town Betrayed." *The Nation* (July 14) 11.

DONALDSON THOMAS, AND L.E. PRESTON. 1995. "The Stakeholder Theory of the Corporation: Concepts, Evidence, and Implications." *American Management Review* 20: 65–91.

EVAN, WILLIAM AND R. EDWARD FREEMAN. 1993. "A Stakeholder Theory of the Modern Corporation: Kantian Capitalism." In Tom L. Beauchamp and Norman Bowie (eds), *Ethical Theory and Business:* 75–84. Englewood Cliffs, NJ: Prentice Hall.

FORT, TIMOTHY L. 1995. "Corporate Constituency Statutes: A Dialectical Interpretation." *Journal of Law and Commerce* 15: 257–294.

FREEMAN, EDWARD R. 1994. "The Politics of Stakeholder Theory: Some Future Directions." *Business Ethics Quarterly* 4: 409–422.

GOODPASTER, KENNETH. 1991. "Business Ethics and Stakeholder Analysis." *Business Ethics Quarterly* 1: 69–77.

GOODPASTER, KENNETH AND THOMAS E. Holloran. 1994. "In Defense of a Paradox." *Business Ethics Quarterly* 4: 423–430.

GRIMSLEY, KIRSTIN DOWNEY. 1997. "Next for Boomers? Battles against Age Bias." *Washington Post* (Feb. 2) H1.

HATTORI, APRIL. 1994. "General Motors Agrees to Seek New Use for Shuttered Plant." *The Bond Buyer* (April 15) 6.

JARDIM, ANNE. 1970. *The First Henry Ford: A Study in Personality and Business Leadership.* Cambridge, MA: MIT Press.

JOHNSTON, DAVID. 1988. *Roman Law of Trusts.* Oxford: Claredon Press.

JONES, TOM. 1995. "Instrumental Stakeholder Theory: A Synthesis of Ethics and Economics." *American Management Review* 20: 404–437.

LIEBER, JAMES. 1995. *Friendly Takeover: How an Employee Buyout Saved a Steel Town.* New York: Viking Press.

LORSCH, JAY W. WITH ELIZABETH. 1989. *Pawns or Potentates: The Reality of America's Corporate Boards.* Boston, MA: Harvard Business School Press.

MACY, JONATHAN, AND JEFFREY MILLER. 1993. "Corporate Stakeholders a Contractual Perspective." *University of Toronto Law Journal* 63: 401–424.

MENNELL, ROBERT L. 1994. *Wills and Trusts in a Nutshell*. St. Paul: West Pub. Co..

MEYER, STEPHEN. 1981. *The Five Dollar Day: Labor Management and Social Control in the Ford Motor Company*. Albany: S.U.N.Y. Press.

MITCHELL, LAWRENCE E. 1992. "The Economic Structure of Corporate Law." *Texas Law Review* 71: 217–242.

MITCHELL, LAWRENCE E., LAWRENCE A. CUNNINGHAM, AND LEWIS SOLOMON. 1996. *Corporate Finance and Governance: Cases, Materials, and Problems*. Durham, NC: Carolina Academic Press.

MONKS, R. AND NELL MINOW. 1991. *Power and Accountability*. New York: HarperBusiness.

NEVINS, ALLAN. 1954. *Ford*. New York: Scribner.

O'NEILL, TERRY A. 1993. "Employees' Duty of Loyalty and the Corporate Constituency Debate." *Connecticut Law Review* 25: 681–716.

SINGER, JOSEPH WILLIAM. 1988. "The Reliance Interest in Property." *Stanford Law Review* 40: 611–751.

———. 1993. "Jobs and Justice: Rethinking the Stakeholder Debate." *University of Toronto Law Journal* 63(3): 475–510.

SHEIN JAMES B. 1996. "A Limit on Downsizing: Varity Corp. v. Howe." *Pepperdine Law Review* 24: 1–35.

STONE, KATHERINE VAN WEZEL. 1991. "Employees as Stakeholders under State Nonshareholder Constituency Statutes." *Stetson Law Review* 21(1): 45–72.

SUMMERS, CLYDE. 1995. Worker Dislocation: "Who Bears the Burden: A Comparative Study of Social Values in Five Countries." *Notre Dame Law Review* 70: 1033–1078.

SWOBODA, FRANK. 1995. "How to Protect your 401(k) Piggy Bank." *Washington Post* (Dec. 3) H4.

VON STANGE, GARY. 1994. "Corporate Social Responsibility through Constituency Statutes: Legend or Lie?" *Hofstra Labor Law Journal* 11: 461–497.

YOSHIHASHI, PAULINE. 1992. "Lockheed Ordered to Pay $30 Million to NL Industries." *Wall Street Journal* (Dec. 8) A10.

Cases

Abrahamson v. Wadell, 624 NE2d 1118 (Ohio 1992)

Akau v. Tel-A-Com, 5 BNA IER CAS 488 (D.Ha. 1990)

Allen v. Dierbold, 33 F.3d 674 (6th Cir. 1994)

Amanda Corp v. Universal Foods, 708 F.Supp. 984 (E.D.Wisc. 1989)

A.P. Smith Manufacturing v. Barlow, 98 A.2d 581 (N.J. 1953)

Baron v. Strawbridge, 646 F.Supp. 690 (Penn. 1986)

Buffalo Forge v. Ogden Corp., 717 F.2d 757 (2nd Cir. 1983)

CTS v. Dynamics Corp., 481 US 69 (1987)

Diamond v. Davis, 62 N.Y.S.2d 181 (1945)

Dodge Bros. v. Ford Motor Co., 170 N.W. 668 (Michigan, 1919)

First National Maintenance Corp. v. NLRB, 452 U.S. 666 (1981)

Franz Mtg. v. EAC Industries, 501 A2d 401 (Del 1985)

GAF v. Union Carbide, 624 F.Supp. 1016 (S.D.N.Y. 1985)

Gallin v. National City Bank, 273 NYS 87 (1935)

Gelco v. Coniston Partners, 652 F.Supp. 829 (D.Minn. 1986)

Georgia Pacific Corp. v. Great Northern Nakoosa Corp., 727 F.Supp. 31 (D.Me. 1989)

Grobow v. General Motors Corp., 539 A2d 180 (Del. 1988)

Halifax Packing Co. v. Coyne, 482 U.S. 1 (1987)

Herald Co. v. Seawell, 472 F.2d 1081 (10th Cir. 1972)

In re City of Duluth (Triangle Corp.), 437 N.W.2d 430 (Minn.App. 1989)

In re Dunkin Donuts, Fed. Sec. L. Rep. (CCH) P95,725 (Del.Ch. 1990)

In the matter of Federated Dept. Stores, 135 Bankr. 950 (S.D.Oh. 1992)

Intermodal Rail Employees Association v. Atchison, Topeka & Santa Fe Railway Co., 117 S.Ct. 1513 (1997).

Kayser v. Commonwealth National Financial Corp., 675 F.Supp 238 (D.C.Penn. 1987)

Kelly v. Bell, 254 A.2d 62 (Del.Ch. 1969)

Marine Transport Lines v. International Organization of Masters, 636 F.Supp. 384 (S.D.N.Y. 1986)

Minstar Acquiring Corp. v. AMF, 628 F.Supp. 1252 (S.D.N.Y. 1985)

Paramount Communication v. Time Inc., 571 A.2d 1140 (Del. 1989)

RCM Securities v. Stanton, 928 F.2d 1318 (2d Cir. 1991)

Revlon v. McAndrews & Forbes Holding Co., 506 A.2d 173 (Del. 1986)

Simas v. Quaker Fabric Corp., 6 F.3d 849 (1st Cir. 1993)

Sinclair Oil Corp. v. Levien, 280 A.2d 717 (Del. 1971)

Steinway v. Steinway & Sons, 40 N.Y.S. 649
   (1909)

Tiernan v. Barresi, 944 F.Supp. 35 (D.Me. 1996)

Unocal v. Mesa Petroleum, 493 A2d 946 (Del.
   1985)

United Steelworkers v. United Steel Corp., 631
   F.2d 1264 (6th Cir. 1980).

Varity Corp. v. Howe, 1016 Sup.Ct. 1065 (1996)

Yonkers v. Otis Elevator Corp., 844 F.2d 42 (2nd
   Cir. 1988)

Study Questions

1. How do Marens and Wicks use ethical,
   economic, and legal principles and rules
   to explain their view of managerial responsibility and decision making?

2. If you used these principles and rules to
   identify important information in the
   Agrico case, what information are you
   likely to collect and what important information are you likely to miss?

3. What assumptions do you think Marens
   and Wicks make about the institutional
   environment of business. Compare and
   contrast these with Friedman's, Cochran's, and Freeman's assumptions. In
   your view, which set of assumptions is
   more realistic? Why?

4. How could you use Marens and Wicks
   view to advise Burdelle in the Agrico
   Case?

CASE: Diablo Canyon: Nuclear Energy and the Public Welfare
A. R. Gini

The Diablo Canyon Nuclear Reactor is located on a rocky cove just outside of San Luis Obispo, California and midway between Los Angeles and San Francisco. In September of 1981 Diablo Canyon was the scene of the final showdown between the Abalone Alliance (a coalition of anti-nuclear groups), the powerful Nuclear Regulatory Commission (NRC) and California's single largest producer of energy, the Pacific Gas and Electric Company (PG&E). The confrontation that ensued during the next three months was in fact the culmination of twelve years of protest and legal maneuverings which had kept the plant idle since its completion in 1979.

The Diablo reactor is the largest and most sophisticated of three nuclear plants to be designed and built by PG&E. The 735 acre shoreline site seemed to be an ideal location in 1968 when construction began. It was far from the big cities, had unlimited supplies of cooling water and the cost was put at a modest $350 to $450 million. To the nearby town of San Luis Obispo, population 40,000, it meant new jobs.

The plant itself is made up of two separate nuclear reactors and electric generating systems with the combined output of 2,200,000 kilowatts of electricity. The two units were designed to produce 33% of the projected energy resources of PG&E in the 1980s. It is estimated that once in operation the plant would save the equivalent of 20 million barrels of fossil fuels per year and over $2 billion in customer services charges in the first five years of operation.

PG&E has steadfastly claimed that the Diablo reactor was the cheapest, most efficient and ecologically safest means to meet the increasing volume of energy demanded by its customers. They maintain that the reactor is the finest example of the "state of the art" in the nuclear energy industry. PG&E claims that the plant contains every possible safety device, and that the construction of the plant was designed to take into account the geological abnormalities of the California coastline. Specifically, they claim to have intentionally designed and "over constructed" the plant in order to withstand a 6.75 earthquake as measured on the Richter scale. This was done in order to compensate for any possible "ripple effects" from seismic reactions emanating from three major fault zones located between 15 and 60 miles due east of the plant (Sur-Nacimiento Fault Zone, Rinconada Fault and San Andreas Fault).

At the time construction began there was no organized anti-nuclear power movement and environmental groups voiced little or no opposition. Utility officials predicted that the plant could start producing electricity within two to four years. These projections, however, proved to be at least five years off the mark as one series of design and construction problems after another added both to the postponement of the completion date and to increased building costs. PG&E's difficulties were multiplied when in 1973 geologists discovered an active fault (Hosgri Fault) in the Pacific seabed just 2.5 miles west of Diablo Canyon. Both federal and state authorities ordered that the plant be structurally reinforced to withstand an earthquake of 7.5 magnitude. These modifications took nearly three years at a cost of well over $200 million. Further costs and delays were incurred in various lawsuits and injuctions as well as over 190 days of public hearings defending the safety of the plant. In March of 1979 yet a new setback occurred when the nuclear plant at Three Mile Island near Harrisburg, Pennsylvania was shut down by the

NRC because of serious design errors, inadequate emergency procedures and deficiencies in operating techniques. The NRC immediately suspended the licensing of all new plants and ordered sweeping changes in equipment and operating procedures, changes that added $100 million to the cost of Diablo Canyon.

As a result of all of this, the initial projected costs of the plant zoomed from $350 million to well over $2.5 billion—an almost 800 percent cost overrun. In May of 1981 Barton W. Schakelford, president and chief operating officer of PG&E, estimated that his company was spending over $500,000 a day in interest charges alone on money borrowed to continuously up-grade a plant which has yet to produce one kilowatt hour of electricity.

By mid-1981 PG&E had completed "retrofitting" the Diablo reactor to meet the specifications of the NRC both in regard to the Hosgri Fault as well as the new requirements imposed on all plants because of the near tragedy of Three Mile Island. On July 17, 1981, PG&E announced that the "Atomic Safety and Licensing Appeal Board" of the NRC had found that "the (Diablo Canyon) plant (is) adequately designed to withstand any earthquake that can be reasonably expected." The NRC stated that its staff and their technical consultants had conducted the most "extensive and exhaustive" seismic review ever undertaken, and that they had complete confidence in the Board's decision.[1]

Even before this report had been issued Dr. John A. Blume, internationally recognized seismologist and primary consultant for PG&E, flatly stated that the containment structures at Diablo Canyon were the "strongest man-made structures in the world." Dr. Blume was convinced that no other building in the world was better designed or had more strength. He was confident that the plant would survive unimpaired a quake of an 8.25 magnitude.[2] Given all of this data a senior spokesman for PG&E stated that as far as the company was concerned all the evidence to date indicated that "Diablo Canyon is without question the most thoroughly studied power plant in the nation's history. The plant is safe from any earthquake that can occur in the area."[3]

Working from this body of evidence PG&E in August 1981 initiated procedures for petitioning the NRC for a "limited license" to begin the loading of atomic fuel into one of the plant's reactors and to commence with low level (5% capacity) power testing operations. After the successful completion of these preliminary tests PG&E would be eligible to apply for a full commercial operator's license. If all went well the plant manager, Robert Thornberg, felt that the facility could be generating electricity by January of 1982.

However, the opposition was simply not convinced of the overall safety of the plant, and the anti-nuclear forces under the direction of the Abalone Alliance began to activate plans for a final assault on Diablo. The Abalone Alliance was formed in 1977 and although its roots are in California it grew to become the parent body for a nationwide coalition of 58 anti-nuclear organizations. It takes its name from the thousands of abalone mollusks that were killed during the testing of the plant's cooling system. While the alliance was organized to protest the completion of the Diablo Canyon reactor the overall goals of the group are much larger. As Claude Steiner, a spokesman for the alliance, put it, "Our purpose goes beyond blockading Diablo; we want to halt all U.S. nuclear power development."[4] Specifically, the alliance believes that all nuclear energy is inherently unsafe because of the complexity of their overall systems, the problems involved with the disposal of radio-active wastes and because of the possibility, no matter how slim, of a "melt down" or uncontrolled nuclear accident. The alliance also believes that nuclear reactors are inextricably linked to the nuclear armaments race, at least insofar as the fissionable material needed to make an atomic bomb comes from reprocessing the uranium in spent fuel rods into plutonium. And finally, the alliance believes that the Diablo Canyon site is a certain disaster simply waiting for an opportunity to occur!

The alliance contends that PG&E's initial decision in 1968 to build the plant within 60 miles of three separate fault zones may ultimately be proven to be a well-warranted risk, for which PG&E took all necessary precautions. However, they feel that the utility's decision in 1973 to carry on with construction after the discovery of the Hosgri Fault just 2.5 miles to the west is both morally indefensible and technically impossible to justify. The site, they argue, is simply too dangerous. They appealed to the federal government to deny any form of license to PG&E because of the serious seismic, emergency preparedness and related safety issues that still remained to be explored and resolved. The alliance felt that if one must be built, there are much better places to build nuclear plants. Dr. John Gofman, a nuclear industry expert from the University of California Medical Center in San Francisco, claims that the plant is unsafe because quakes are too unpredictable in regard to their duration and intensity. He argues that if the NRC allows the Diablo plant to operate, then in effect it is saying that "people in this area are expendable and that they are willing to write us off." Professor Gofman went on to suggest that the best-laid plans of mice and men have gone wrong so often that if they had any common sense, they wouldn't build a plant there![5]

In September 1981 after one year of intensive preparation, numerous successful rallies publicizing the events, and countless grass-roots organizational meetings, the various forces, factions and friends of the alliance began to arrive at a thirty acre tent village set up on private property northeast of the plant. Their strategy was to blockade the plant compound by land and sea. The blockade was to include groups of people scaling the entrance gate, groups of individuals lying down in the middle of the access roads to the plant and a mini-fleet of rubber rafts and scuba divers who would try to penetrate the plant's perimeter along the coastline. It was their hope to make the plant's start-up as difficult as possible and to stop the loading of the atomic fuel which is the first necessary step for the proposed low level power testing. The alliance, however, was determined to keep violence from marring the demonstrations. They adopted a code which prohibited property damage, verbal or physical violence and the carrying of weapons while taking part in any form of protest. Their goal was to focus world attention on what was happening at Diablo Canyon. However, the leaders of the alliance realized from the beginning that their blockade was nothing more than a "symbolic effort." The blockade was "symbolic" in two senses:

1. The atomic fuel necessary for testing had already been stored in the plant for a period of five years, and, therefore, the chances of stopping the actual loading operations were very small.

2. The plant area was being patrolled and protected by an estimated 1,000 local police, state sheriffs and the National Guard. The leaders of the protest realized that at best their efforts could forestall but not entirely prohibit the operational status of the plant.

By September 14, the tent city had only grown to 3,000 people. This figure was far below the 30,000 that the alliance had initially estimated. Officials of PG&E were overjoyed by the sparse turnout of protestors. They felt that such a small turnout helped to substantiate their belief that the Abalone Alliance only represented a minority opinion in regard to nuclear energy and that most people had confidence in PG&E claims for the safety of the twin reactor complex. Fearful of losing their momentum the leaders of the alliance announced that the blockade of Diablo would begin on the morning of September 15. On the first day of the blockade the press clearly outnumbered the protestors and only 300 people were arrested for blocking or scaling the facility's entrance. It was also estimated that twenty-five more people were arrested for trespassing after reaching the beach front side of the plant in rafts. In no way did the protestors deter the busing of 700 PG&E workers into the plant. As far as the plant manager was concerned, "It was business as usual around here!"[6] The police also grew in confidence after the first encounter. They felt that the protestors were unorganized and undermanned and that they, the police, would be able to handle all eventualities. Nevertheless, they warned that they would remain on the scene. "If it lasts a month," said Glen Craig, commissioner of the California Highway Patrol, "we are prepared to deal with it for a month."[7]

By September 18, the ranks of the alliance had already dwindled to approximately 1,500 people and yet each day the number of people arrested grew. Although few new people were joining the protestors, the same group of people kept getting re-arrested. By the end of the month while less than 300 protestors remained at the campsite, over 1,893 arrests had been made. Yet even with these disappointing figures, the Abalone Alliance vowed to continue its vigil. PG&E at this point felt that it had survived the gauntlet of trial by public opinion and had won. Now all that was needed was approval by the NRC to begin testing.

Approval by the NRC came on September 21 when the full board unanimously voted to grant PG&E a license to test the first of its two reactors. Work began immediately at the plant on a final checklist in preparation for the loading of atomic fuel and preliminary testing. Suddenly, PG&E was beset with a series of unexpected reversals. On September 28, PG&E announced that fuel loading would be delayed because "a discrepancy" had been found in a checklist stress analysis of part of the plant's containment structures. By the very next day PG&E was forced to admit that the start up of the Unit One reactor would be "indefinitely suspended" after finding that the structural supporter of Unit One did not conform to the design plans as approved by the NRC. To simplify, when PG&E upgraded the seismic-support systems around the reactors after the discovery of the Hosgri Fault, the reconstruction plans intended for Unit One were in fact used on Unit Two and vice versa. The critical point is that the possible seismic stress that each reactor could absorb would be different because they are approximately 200 feet apart. This seemingly minor separation would mean that each reactor would be exposed to a different degree of "vertical earthquake motion." Therefore, it is possible that the containment structures could be damaged, thereby violating the integrity of the reactor's cores. The containment structures in question are also part of the reactor's heat removal system. This system, in addition to its normal role in dispersing residual heat when a reactor is shut down for refueling, functions as a back-up cooling device in the event of a nuclear accident.

This first unexpected setback was by no means the end of PG&E's problems. By October 1, the utility discovered serious design problems in four other systems within the reactor containment structure that are vital parts of a network of devices necessary to shut down or cool off the reactor in case of emergency. October 2 brought yet new disclosures by PG&E of structural errors in the support systems that hold the electronic cables attached to the reactors. Officials indicated that the improper construction of the cable supports could result during an earthquake in the loss of the electrical power needed to control the reactors and their emergency monitoring devices. The coup de grace came on October 24 when James Hanchett, a spokesman for the San Francisco office of NRC, announced that PG&E was unable to demonstrate that the weights it calculated for the equipment located in the reactor areas were correct. If these calculations were incorrect it would mean that the floors of the reactor areas were not sufficiently reinforced to sustain the trauma of a seismic shock. If the accusation was accurate the NRC felt that this error was potentially more significant and more dangerous than any of the mistakes that had been earlier identified at the Diablo Canyon plant.[8]

Throughout all of this PG&E had voluntarily postponed all testing procedures as a precautionary measure, but steadfastly maintained that even if these errors had gone undetected the plant would not have been endangered because of the extremely conservative design criteria used.[9] Officials of PG&E including its president claimed before the press and the NRC that the problems were ultimately minor ones isolated to one area of the plant, and that repairs could be completed within a matter of months so that testing could resume.

The response of the Abalone Alliance to these claims was expected. One member of the alliance stated that the discovery of these errors "affirms what we have been saying all along-that the plant is structurally not safe."[10] The alliance felt that PG&E's overall response to the situation typified the disregard that the utility has for public safety and welfare. What PG&E really is interested in is recouping and making a profit on the more than $2.5 billion they have invested into the Diablo project. As far as the alliance is concerned, PG&E has been both cavalier and criminal in its construction of so delicate a plant so close to a fault.

From the first report by PG&E of the discovery of a "slight discrepancy" in September, the NRC began to analyze and re-analyze all the relevant data. NRC officials were dispatched from their offices in Washington and San Francisco to Diablo Canyon for an endless series of on-site inspections. At the same time PG&E officials were being summoned to Washington to explain and justify the various discoveries as they occurred. By November the newly installed chairman of the NRC, Nunzio J. Palladino, called for a closed-door session of the commission to study "the many structural deficiencies that have come to light." Following three days of debate, on November 19, Mr. Palladino announced that "the commission doesn't like what it's seen" and because it does not feel that PG&E can live up to "efficiency standards" and "quality control" requirements the NRC has voted to suspend the license of the Diablo Canyon reactor.[11] One board member of the NRC, Peter A. Bradford, asserted that the reported "discrepancies" at the Diablo reactor had been a "first rate screw-up" since day one. He found it unbelievable that so many errors could occur in the most controversial area of the most controversial plant in the country.[12] The action to suspend the license of PG&E represents the first time a license to load fuel has been revoked, and it makes Diablo Canyon the most conspicuous and embarrassing reversal that the nuclear energy industry has suffered to date.

Clearly, throughout this prolonged multilateral confrontation the NRC tried to walk a fine line between public safety on the one hand and the danger of a huge financial loss by PG&E on the other. The NRC's other major concern was the ripple effect that the Diablo decision would have on the entire industry. Ironically, in early October of 1981 President Reagan ordered the NRC and its chairman to speed up procedures for the licensing of nuclear plants so that the time from first blueprint to the start of electricity production, now as long as 14 years, could be cut to six to eight years. Also, Reagan ordered the NRC to work with industry on developing safe methods for the permanent disposal of nuclear wastes.[13] The motivation behind the President's pro-nuclear policy statement was to make America more energy independent, to create a more amiable climate for the construction of atomic plants and to take some pressure off the financially strapped industry.

Since the March 1979 accident at Three Mile Island the growth of nuclear power has been slowing steadily and in some places in the country completely stopped. In the months preceding the final NRC ruling on Diablo Canyon at least ten atomic plants closed or had their completion plans terminated because of design problems, escalating costs and public concern about location and safety. With the setback at Diablo Canyon most experts now feel that it is highly questionable whether the President's program will bring relief to the atomic industrial community.

On December 1, 1981, at the annual conference of the Atomic Industrial Forum, Mr. Palladino told executives of the nation's utilities and builders of nuclear power plants that while excessive governmental regulations are partially responsible for the present position of atomic energy, they too were responsible because of their poor workmanship and the "inexcusable" standards of quality assurance programs. "During my first five months as NRC chairman," said Palladino, "a number of deficiencies in some plants have come to my attention which show a surprising lack of professionalism in the construction and preparation for operation of nuclear facilities. The responsibility for such deficiencies rests squarely on the shoulders of management." Palladino went on to say that "there have been lapses of many kinds—in design analyses resulting in built-in design errors, in poor construction practices, in falsified documents, in harassment of quality control personnel and in inadequate training of reactor operators. Quality cannot be inspected into a plant," Mr. Palladino said. "Quality must be built into the plant. All of you, I am sure, would say that you know this, but the practices at some plants do not confirm that the importance of this principle is always understood."

Mr. Palladino went on to suggest that because of Three Mile Island and Diablo Canyon "the industry and the NRC have suffered a loss of credibility that can only be regained over time. The responsibility for regaining public confidence rests with the utilities who finance and operate the plants and the construction companies that build them, as well as with government regulators." He called on the utility companies to examine their policies on quality control. He stressed that just as all utilities have certified independent financial audits of their fiscal activities, there should also be similar audits of their quality control measures. "I believe," said Mr. Palladino, "that credibility will be regained if the future brings safe and economic nuclear power along with (the) elimination of shoddy workmanship and poor practices. Well managed utilities cannot afford to let the poor performers jeopardize public safety and undermine public confidence in the industry."[14]

Whatever the ultimate outcome of Mr. Palladino's chastisement, the future of the Diablo Canyon nuclear power plant remains in doubt. If nothing else, the confrontation at Diablo Canyon has served to make the American public aware of the benefits, issues and dangers at stake in the use of atomic energy. For some, Diablo Canyon has been a valuable lesson from which the entire industry can profit and grow. For others, Diablo Canyon symbolizes the end of an overly ambitious and expensive experiment. As one cynical observer put it, "At the present time, nuclear power is dead in the United States. The economics and politics of it rule out the construction of more plants."[15]

Notes

1. *Diablo Canyon Info,* PG&E Public Information Department, July 17, 1981.
2. "PG&E Interviews Dr. John A. Blume," PG&E Public Information Dept., 1981.
3. *New York Times,* August 24, 1981, sec. 2, p. 10.
4. *Maclean's: Canada's Weekly News Magazine,* September 28, 1981, p. 40.
5. *Newsweek,* August 10, 1981, p. 51.
6. *New York Times,* September 15, 1981, sec. 4, p. 28.
7. *Newsweek,* September 28, 1981, p. 38.

8. *New York Times,* October 25, 1981, sec. 1, p. 24.
9. *New York Times,* November 4, 1981, sec. 1, p. 18.
10. *New York Times,* September 30, 1981, sec. 1, p. 20.
11. *New York Times,* November 20, 1981, sec. 1, p. 1.
12. *New York Times,* October 1, 1981, sec. 1, p. 1.
13. *Time,* October 26, 1981, p. 18.
14. *New York Times,* December 12, 1981, sec. 1, pp. 1 and 19.
15. *U.S. News & World Report,* April 6, 1981, p. 59.

Study Questions

1. Describe how this problem arose at the individual, organizational, industrial, and market levels.

2. Describe the way the stakeholders used institutional mechanisms and opportunities to pursue their interests. Do you think that these mechanisms and opportunities played any part in shaping the interests of the stakeholders?

3. Compare and contrast how the three views of managerial responsibility discussed above can help you understand this case. Which view is the most useful? Why?

4. Are there any institutions that are supposed to help coordinate the interests of these various stakeholders? If so, did they work in this case?

William F. Baxter

People or Penguins: The Case for Optimal Pollution

I start with the modest proposition that, in dealing with pollution, or indeed with any problem, it is helpful to know what one is attempting to accomplish. Agreement on how and whether to pursue a particular objective, such as pollution control, is not possible unless some more general objective has been identified and stated with reasonable precision. We talk loosely of having clean air and clean water, of preserving our wilderness areas, and so forth. But none of these is a sufficiently general objective: each is more accurately viewed as a means rather than as an end.

With regard to clean air, for example, one may ask, "how clean?" and "what does clean mean?" It is even reasonable to ask, "why have clean air?" Each of these questions is an implicit demand that a more general community goal be stated—a goal sufficiently general in its scope and enjoying sufficiently general assent among the community of actors that such "why" questions no longer seem admissible with respect to that goal.

If, for example, one states as a goal the proposition that "every person should be free to do whatever he wishes in contexts where his actions do not interfere with the interests of other human beings," the speaker is unlikely to be met with a response of "why." The goal may be criticized as uncertain in its implications or difficult to implement, but it is so basic a tenet of our civilization—it reflects a cultural value so broadly shared, at least in the abstract—that the question "why" is seen as impertinent or imponderable or both.

I do not mean to suggest that everyone would agree with the "spheres of freedom" objective just stated. Still less do I mean to suggest that a society could subscribe to four or five such general objectives that would be adequate in their coverage to serve as testing criteria by which all other disagreements might be measured. One difficulty in the attempt to construct such a list is that each new goal added will conflict, in certain applications, with each prior goal listed; and thus each goal serves as a limited qualification on prior goals.

Without any expectation of obtaining unanimous consent to them, let me set forth four goals that I generally use as ultimate testing criteria in attempting to frame solutions to problems of human organization. My position regarding pollution stems from these four criteria. If the criteria appeal to you and any part of what appears hereafter does not, our disagreement will have a helpful focus: which of us is correct, analytically, in supposing that his position on pollution would better serve these general goals. If the criteria do not seem acceptable to you, then it is to be expected that our more particular judgments will differ, and the task will then be yours to identify the basic set of criteria upon which your particular judgments rest.

My criteria are as follows:

1. The spheres of freedom criterion stated above.
2. Waste is a bad thing. The dominant feature of human existence is scarcity—our available resources, our aggregate labors, and our skill in employing both have always been, and will continue for some time to be, inadequate to yield to every man all the tangible and intangible satisfactions he would like to have. Hence, none of those resources, or labors, or skills, should be wasted—that is, employed so as to yield less than they might yield in human satisfactions.
3. Every human being should be regarded as an end rather than as a means to be used for the betterment of another. Each should be afforded dignity and regarded as having an absolute claim to an even-handed application of such rules as the community may adopt for its governance.
4. Both the incentive and the opportunity to improve his share of satisfactions should be preserved to every individual. Preservation of incentive is dictated by the "no-waste" criterion and enjoins against the continuous, totally egalitarian redistribution of satisfactions, or wealth; but subject to that constraint, everyone should receive, by continuous redistribution if necessary, some minimal share of aggregate wealth so as to avoid a level of privation from which the opportunity to improve his situation becomes illusory.

The relationship of these highly general goals to the more specific environmental issues at hand may not be readily apparent, and I am not yet ready to demonstrate their pervasive implications. But let me give one indication of their implications. Recently scientists have informed us that use of DDT in food production is causing damage to the penguin population. For the present purposes let us accept that assertion as an indisputable scientific fact. The scientific fact is often asserted as if the correct implication—that we must stop agricultural use of DDT—followed from the mere statement of the fact of penguin damage. But plainly it does not follow if my criteria are employed.

My criteria are oriented to people, not penguins. Damage to penguins, or sugar pines, or geological marvels is, without more, simply irrelevant. One must go further, by my criteria, and say: Penguins are important because people enjoy seeing them walk about rocks; and furthermore, the well-being of people would be less impaired by halting use of DDT than by giving up penguins. In short, my observations about environmental problems will be people-oriented, as are my criteria. I have no interest in preserving penguins for their own sake.

It may be said by way of objection to this position, that it is very selfish of people to act as if each person represented one unit or importance and nothing else was of any importance. It is undeniably selfish. Nevertheless I think it is the only tenable starting place for analysis for several reasons. First, no other position corresponds to the way most people really think and act—i.e., corresponds to reality.

Second, this attitude does not portend any massive destruction of nonhuman flora and fauna, for people depend on them in many obvious ways, and they will be preserved because and to the degree that humans do depend on them.

Third, what is good for humans is, in many respects, good for penguins and pine trees—clean air for example. So that humans are, in these respects, surrogates for plant and animal life.

Fourth, I do not know how we could administer any other system. Our decisions are either private or collective. Insofar as Mr. Jones is free to act privately, he may give such preferences as he wishes to other forms of life: he may feed birds in winter and do with less himself, and he may even decline to resist an advancing polar bear on the ground that the bear's appetite is more important than those portions of himself that the bear may choose to eat. In short my basic premise does not rule out private altruism to competing life-forms. It does rule out, however, Mr. Jones' inclination to feed Mr. Smith to the bear, however hungry the bear, however despicable Mr. Smith.

Insofar as we act collectively on the other hand, only humans can be afforded an opportunity to participate in the collective decisions. Penguins cannot vote now and are unlikely subjects for the franchise—pine trees more unlikely still. Again each individual is free to cast his vote so as to benefit sugar pines if that is his inclination. But many of the more extreme assertions that one hears from some conservationists amount to tacit assertions that they are specially appointed representatives of sugar pines, and hence that their preferences should be weighted more heavily than the preferences of other humans who do not enjoy equal rapport with "nature." The simplistic assertion that agricultural use of DDT must stop at once because it is harmful to penguins is of that type.

Fifth, if polar bears or pine trees or penguins, like men, are to be regarded as ends rather than means, if they are to count in our calculus of social organization, someone must tell me how much each one counts, and someone must tell me how these life-forms are to be permitted to express their preferences, for I do not know either answer. If the answer is that certain people are to hold their proxies, then I want to know how those proxy-holders are to be selected: self-appointment does not seem workable to me.

Sixth, and by way of summary of all the foregoing, let me point out that the set of environmental issues under discussion—although they raise very complex technical questions of how to achieve any objective—ultimately raise a normative question: what *ought* we to do. Questions of *ought* are unique to the human mind and world—they are meaningless as applied to a nonhuman situation.

I reject the proposition that we *ought* to respect the "balance of nature" or to "preserve the environment" unless the reason for doing so, express or implied, is the benefit of man.

I reject the idea that there is a "right" or "morally correct" state of nature to which we should return. The word "nature" has no normative connotation. Was it "right" or "wrong" for the earth's crust to heave in contortion and create mountains and seas? Was it "right" for the first amphibian to crawl up out of the primordial ooze? Was it "wrong" for plants to reproduce themselves and alter the atmospheric composition in favor of oxygen? For animals to alter the atmosphere in favor of carbon dioxide both by breathing oxygen and eating plants? No answers can be given to these questions because they are meaningless questions.

All this may seem obvious to the point of being tedious, but much of the present controversy over environment and pollution rests on tacit normative assumptions about just such nonnormative phenomena: that it is "wrong" to impair penguins with DDT, but not to slaughter cattle for prime rib roasts. That it is wrong to kill stands of sugar pines with industrial fumes, but not to cut sugar pines and build housing for the poor. Every man is entitled to his own preferred definition of Walden Pond, but there is no definition that has any moral superiority over another, except by reference to the selfish needs of the human race.

From the fact that there is no normative definition of the natural state, it follows that there is no normative definition of clean air or pure water—hence no definition of polluted air—or of pollution—except by reference to the needs of man. The "right" composition of the atmosphere is one which has some dust in it and some lead in it and some hydrogen sulfide in it—just those amounts that attend a sensibly organized society thoughtfully and knowledgeably pursuing the greatest possible satisfaction for its human members.

The first and most fundamental step toward solution of our environmental problems is a clear recognition that our objective is not pure air or water but rather some optimal state of pollution. That step immediately suggests the question: How do we define and attain the level of pollution that will yield the maximum possible amount of human satisfaction?

Low levels of pollution contribute to human satisfaction but so do food and shelter and education and music. To attain ever lower levels of pollution, we must pay the cost of having less of these other things. I contrast that view of the cost of pollution control with the more popular statement that pollution control will "cost" very large numbers of dollars. The popular statement is true in some senses, false in others; sorting out the true and false senses is of some importance. The first

step in that sorting process is to achieve a clear understanding of the difference between dollars and resources. Resources are the wealth of our nation; dollars are merely claim checks upon those resources. Resources are of vital importance; dollars are comparatively trivial.

Four categories of resources are sufficient for our purposes: At any given time a nation, or a planet if you prefer, has a stock of labor, of technological skill, of capital goods, and of natural resources (such as mineral deposits, timber, water, land, etc.). These resources can be used in various combinations to yield goods and services of all kinds—in some limited quantity. The quantity will be larger if they are combined efficiently, smaller if combined inefficiently. But in either event the resource stock is limited, the goods and services that they can be made to yield are limited; even the most efficient use of them will yield less than our population, in the aggregate, would like to have.

If one considers building a new dam, it is appropriate to say that it will be costly in the sense that it will require x hours of labor, y tons of steel and concrete, and z amount of capital goods. If these resources are devoted to the dam, then they cannot be used to build hospitals, fishing rods, schools, or electric can openers. That is the meaningful sense in which the dam is costly.

Quite apart from the very important question of how wisely we can combine our resources to produce goods and services, is the very different question of how they get distributed—who gets how many goods? Dollars constitute the claim checks which are distributed among people and which control their share of national output. Dollars are nearly valueless pieces of paper except to the extent that they do represent claim checks to some fraction of the output of goods and services. Viewed as claim checks, all the dollars outstanding during any period of time are worth, in the aggregate, the goods and services that are available to be claimed with them during that period—neither more nor less.

It is far easier to increase the supply of

dollars than to increase the production of goods and services—printing dollars is easy. But printing more dollars doesn't help because each dollar then simply becomes a claim to fewer goods, i.e., becomes worth less.

The point is this: many people fall into error upon hearing the statement that the decision to build a dam, or to clean up a river, will cost $X million. It is regrettably easy to say: "It's only money. This is a wealthy country, and we have lots of money." But you cannot build a dam or clean a river with $X million—unless you also have a match, you can't even make a fire. One builds a dam or cleans a river by diverting labor and steel and trucks and factories from making one kind of goods to making another. The cost in dollars is merely a shorthand way of describing the extent of the diversion necessary. If we build a dam for $X million, then we must recognize that we will have $X million less housing and food and medical care and electric can openers as a result.

Similarly, the costs of controlling pollution are best expressed in terms of the other goods we will have to give up to do the job. This is not to say the job should not be done. Badly as we need more housing, more medical care, and more can openers, and more symphony orchestras, we could do with somewhat less of them, in my judgment at least, in exchange for somewhat cleaner air and rivers. But that is the nature of the trade-off, and analysis of the problem is advanced if that unpleasant reality is kept in mind. Once the trade-off relationship is clearly perceived, it is possible to state in a very general way what the optimal level of pollution is. I would state it as follows:

People enjoy watching penguins. They enjoy relatively clean air and smog-free vistas. Their health is improved by relatively clean water and air. Each of these benefits is a type of good or service. As a society we would be well advised to give up one washing machine if the resources that would have gone into that washing machine can yield greater human satisfaction when diverted into pollution control. We should give up one hospital if the resources thereby freed would yield more human satisfaction when devoted to elimination of noise in our cities. And so on, trade-off by trade-off, we should divert our productive capacities from the production of existing goods and services to the production of a cleaner, quieter, more pastoral nation up to—and no further than—the point at which we value more highly the next washing machine or hospital that we would have to do without than we value the next unit of environmental improvement that the diverted resources would create.

Now this proposition seems to me unassailable but so general and abstract as to be unhelpful—at least unadministerable in the form stated. It assumes we can measure in some way the incremental units of human satisfaction yielded by very different types of goods. The proposition must remain a pious abstraction until I can explain how this measurement process can occur. In subsequent chapters I will attempt to show that we can do this—in some contexts with great precision and in other contexts only by rough approximation. But I insist that the proposition stated describes the result for which we should be striving—and again, that it is always useful to know what your target is even if your weapons are too crude to score a bull's eye.

Study Questions

1. How does Baxter use Kant to support his views? Could you support his views using one or more of the other ethical views discussed in Chapter 2?

2. Whose view fits best with Baxter's arguments: That of Friedman, Cochran, or Freeman?

3. Use Baxter to analyze the Diablo Canyon case.

Norman Bowie

Morality, Money, and Motor Cars

Environmentalists frequently argue that business has special obligations to protect the environment. Although I agree with the environmentalists on this point, I do not agree with them as to where the obligations lie. Business does not have an obligation to protect the environment over and above what is required by law; however, it does have a moral obligation to avoid intervening in the political arena in order to defeat or weaken environmental legislation. In developing this thesis, several points are in order. First, many businesses have violated important moral obligations, and the violation has had a severe negative impact on the environment. For example, toxic waste haulers have illegally dumped hazardous material, and the environment has been harmed as a result. One might argue that those toxic waste haulers who have illegally dumped have violated a special obligation to the environment. Isn't it more accurate to say that these toxic waste haulers have violated their obligation to obey the law and that in this case the law that has been broken is one pertaining to the environment? Businesses have an obligation to obey the law—environmental laws and all others. Since there are many well-publicized cases of business having broken environmental laws, it is easy to think that business has violated some special obligations to the environment. In fact, what business has done is to disobey the law. Environmentalists do not need a special obligation to the environment to protect the environment against illegal business activity; they need only insist that business obey the laws.

Business has broken other obligations beside the obligation to obey the law and has harmed the environment as a result. Consider the grounding of the Exxon oil tanker *Valdez* in Alaska. That grounding was allegedly caused by the fact that an inadequately trained crewman was piloting the tanker while the captain was below deck and had been drinking. What needs to be determined is whether Exxon's policies and procedures were sufficiently lax so that it could be said Exxon was morally at fault. It might be that Exxon is legally responsible for the accident under the doctrine of respondent superior, but Exxon is not thereby morally responsible. Suppose, however, that Exxon's policies were so lax that the company could be characterized as morally negligent. In such a case, the company would violate its moral obligation to use due care and avoid negligence. Although its negligence was disastrous to the environment, Exxon would have violated no special obligation to the environment. It would have been morally negligent.

Environmentalists, like government officials, employees, and stockholders, expect that business firms and officials have moral obligations to obey the law, avoid negligent behavior, and tell the truth. In sum, although many business decisions have harmed the environment, these decisions violated no environmental moral obligations. If a corporation is negligent in providing for worker safety, we do not say the corporation violated a special obligation to employees; we say that it violated its obligation to avoid negligent behavior.

The crucial issues concerning business obligations to the environment focus on the

From *Business, Ethics, and the Environment: The Public Policy Debate,* eds. W. Michael Hoffman, Robert Frederick, and Edward Petry, Jr. (New York, Quorum Books 1990) 89–97 © The Center for Business Ethics at Bentley College. Reprinted by permission of the Center for Business Ethics at Bentley College and Greenwood Publishing Group, Inc. Westport, CT.

excess use of natural resources (the dwindling supply of oil and gas, for instance) and the externalities of production (pollution, for instance). The critics of business want to claim that business has some special obligation to mitigate or solve these problems. I believe this claim is largely mistaken. If business does have a special obligation to help solve the environmental crisis, that obligation results from the special knowledge that business firms have. If they have greater expertise than other constituent groups in society, then it can be argued that, other things being equal, business's responsibilities to mitigate the environmental crisis are somewhat greater. Absent this condition, business's responsibility is no greater than and may be less than that of other social groups. What leads me to think that the critics of business are mistaken?

William Frankena distinguished obligations in an ascending order of the difficulty in carrying them out: avoiding harm, preventing harm, and doing good. The most stringent requirement, to avoid harm, insists no one has a right to render harm on another unless there is a compelling, overriding moral reason to do so. Some writers have referred to this obligation as the moral minimum. A corporation's behavior is consistent with the moral minimum if it causes no avoidable harm to others.

Preventing harm is a less stringent obligation, but sometimes the obligation to prevent harm may be nearly as strict as the obligation to avoid harm. Suppose you are the only person passing a 2-foot-deep [wading] pool where a young child is drowning. There is no one else in the vicinity. Don't you have a strong moral obligation to prevent the child's death? Our obligation to prevent harm is not unlimited, however. Under what conditions must we be good samaritans? Some have argued that four conditions must exist before one is obligated to prevent harm: capability, need, proximity, and last resort. These conditions are all met with the case of the drowning child. There is obviously a need that you can meet since you are both in the vicinity and have the resources to prevent the drowning with little effort; you are also the last resort.

The least strict moral obligation is to do good—to make contributions to society or to help solve problems (inadequate primary schooling in the inner cities, for example). Although corporations may have some minimum obligation in this regard based on an argument from corporate citizenship, the obligations of the corporation to do good cannot be expanded without limit. An injunction to assist in solving societal problems makes impossible demands on a corporation because at the practical level, it ignores the impact that such activities have on profit.

It might seem that even if this descending order of strictness of obligations were accepted, obligations toward the environment would fall into the moral minimum category. After all, the depletion of natural resources and pollution surely harm the environment. If so, wouldn't the obligations business has to the environment be among the strictest obligations a business can have?

Suppose, however, that a businessperson argues that the phrase "avoid harm" usually applies to human beings. Polluting a lake is not like injuring a human with a faulty product. Those who coined the phrase *moral minimum* for use in the business context defined harm as "particularly including activities which violate or frustrate the enforcement of rules of domestic or institutional law intended to protect individuals against prevention of health, safety or basic freedom." Even if we do not insist that the violations be violations of a rule of law, polluting a lake would not count as a harm under this definition. The environmentalists would respond that it would. Polluting the lake may be injuring people who might swim in or eat fish from it. Certainly it would be depriving people of the freedom to enjoy the lake. Although the environmentalist is correct, especially if we grant the legitimacy of a human right to a clean environment, the success of this reply is not enough to establish the general argument.

Consider the harm that results from the production of automobiles. We know statistically that about 50,000 persons per year will die and that nearly 250,000 others will be seriously injured in automobile accidents in the

United States alone. Such death and injury, which is harmful, is avoidable. If that is the case, doesn't the avoid-harm criterion require that the production of automobiles for profit cease? Not really. What such arguments point out is that some refinement of the moral minimum standard needs to take place. Take the automobile example. The automobile is itself a good-producing instrument. Because of the advantages of automobiles, society accepts the possible risks that go in using them. Society also accepts many other types of avoidable harm. We take certain risks—ride in planes, build bridges, and mine coal—to pursue advantageous goals. It seems that the high benefits of some activities justify the resulting harms. As long as the risks are known, it is not wrong that some avoidable harm be permitted so that other social and individual goals can be achieved. The avoidable-harm criterion needs some sharpening.

Using the automobile as a paradigm, let us consider the necessary refinements for the avoid-harm criterion. It is a fundamental principle of ethics that "ought" implies "can." That expression means that you can be held morally responsible only for events within your power. In the ought-implies-can principle, the overwhelming majority of highway deaths and injuries is not the responsibility of the automaker. Only those deaths and injuries attributable to unsafe automobile design can be attributed to the automaker. The ought-implies-can principle can also be used to absolve the auto companies of responsibility for death and injury from safety defects that the automakers could not reasonably know existed. The company could not be expected to do anything about them.

Does this mean that a company has an obligation to build a car as safe as it knows how? No. The standards for safety must leave the product's cost within the price range of the consumer ("ought implies can" again). Comments about engineering and equipment capability are obvious enough. But for a business, capability is also a function of profitability. A company that builds a maximally safe car at a cost that puts it at a competitive disadvantage and hence threatens its survival is building a safe car that lies beyond the capability of the company.

Critics of the automobile industry will express horror at these remarks, for by making capability a function of profitability, society will continue to have avoidable deaths and injuries; however, the situation is not as dire as the critics imagine. Certainly capability should not be sacrificed completely so that profits can be maximized. The decision to build products that are cheaper in cost but are not maximally safe is a social decision that has widespread support. The arguments occur over the line between safety and cost. What we have is a classical trade-off situation. What is desired is some appropriate mix between engineering safety and consumer demand. To say there must be some mix between engineering safety and consumer demand is not to justify all the decisions made by the automobile companies. Ford Motor Company made a morally incorrect choice in placing Pinto gas tanks where it did. Consumers were uninformed, the record of the Pinto in rear-end collisions was worse than that of competitors, and Ford fought government regulations.

Let us apply the analysis of the automobile industry to the issue before us. That analysis shows that an automobile company does not violate its obligation to avoid harm and hence is not in violation of the moral minimum if the trade-off between potential harm and the utility of the products rests on social consensus and competitive realities.

As long as business obeys the environmental laws and honors other standard moral obligations, most harm done to the environment by business has been accepted by society. Through their decisions in the marketplace, we can see that most consumers are unwilling to pay extra for products that are more environmentally friendly than less friendly competitive products. Nor is there much evidence that consumers are willing to conserve resources, recycle, or tax themselves for environmental causes.

Consider the following instances reported in the *Wall Street Journal*. The restaurant chain Wendy's tried to replace foam plates and cups with paper, but customers in the test markets balked. Procter and Gamble offered Downey fabric softener in concentrated form that requires less packaging than ready-to-use products; however the concentrate version is less convenient because it has to be mixed with water. Sales have been poor. Procter and Gamble manufactures Vizir and Lenor brands of detergents in concentrate form, which the customer mixes at home in reusable bottles. Europeans will take the trouble; Americans will not. Kodak tried to eliminate its yellow film boxes but met customer resistance. . . .

Data and arguments of the sort described should give environmental critics of business pause. Nonetheless, these critics are not without counterresponses. For example, they might respond that public attitudes are changing. Indeed, they point out, during the Reagan deregulation era, the one area where the public supported government regulations was in the area of environmental law. In addition, Fortune predicts environmental integrity as the primary demand of society on business in the 1990s.

More important, they might argue that environmentally friendly products are at a disadvantage in the marketplace because they have public good characteristics. After all, the best situation for the individual is one where most other people use environmentally friendly products but he or she does not, hence reaping the benefit of lower cost and convenience. Since everyone reasons this way, the real demand for environmentally friendly products cannot be registered in the market. Everyone is understating the value of his or her preference for environmentally friendly products. Hence, companies cannot conclude from market behavior that the environmentally unfriendly products are preferred.

Suppose the environmental critics are right that the public goods characteristic of environmentally friendly products creates a market failure. . . .

Traditionally it is the function of the government to correct for market failure. If the market cannot register the true desires of con-sumers, let them register their preferences in the political arena. Even fairly conservative economic thinkers allow government a legitimate role in correcting market failure. Perhaps the responsibility for energy conservation and pollution control belongs with the government.

Although I think consumers bear a far greater responsibility for preserving and protecting the environment than they have actually exercised, let us assume that the basic responsibility rests with the government. Does that let business off the hook? No. Most of business's unethical conduct regarding the environment occurs in the political arena.

Far too many corporations try to have their cake and eat it too. They argue that it is the job of government to correct for market failure and then use their influence and money to defeat or water down regulations designed to conserve and protect the environment. They argue that consumers should decide how much conservation and protection the environment should have, and then they try to interfere with the exercise of that choice in the political arena. Such behavior is inconsistent and ethically inappropriate. Business has an obligation to avoid intervention in the political process for the purpose of defeating and weakening environmental regulations. Moreover, this is a special obligation to the environment since business does not have a general obligation to avoid pursuing its own parochial interests in the political arena. Business need do nothing wrong when it seeks to influence tariffs, labor policy, or monetary policy. Business does do something wrong when it interferes with the passage of environmental legislation. Why?

First, such a noninterventionist policy is dictated by the logic of the business's argument to avoid a special obligation to protect the environment. Put more formally:

1. Business argues that it escapes special obligations to the environment because it is willing to respond to consumer preferences in this matter.

2. Because of externalities and public

goods considerations, consumers cannot express their preferences in the market.

3. The only other viable forum for consumers to express their preferences is in the political arena.

4. Business intervention interferes with the expression of these preferences.

5. Since point 4 is inconsistent with point 1, business should not intervene in the political process.

The importance of this obligation in business is even more important when we see that environmental legislation has special disadvantages in the political arena. Public choice reminds us that the primary interest of politicians is being reelected. Government policy will be skewed in favor of policies that provide benefits to an influential minority as long as the greater costs are widely dispersed. Politicians will also favor projects where benefits are immediate and where costs can be postponed to the future. Such strategies increase the likelihood that a politician will be reelected.

What is frightening about the environmental crisis is that both the conservation of scarce resources and pollution abatement require policies that go contrary to a politician's self-interest. The costs of cleaning up the environment are immediate and huge, yet the benefits are relatively long range (many of them exceedingly long range). Moreover, a situation where the benefits are widely dispersed and the costs are large presents a twofold problem. The costs are large enough so that all voters will likely notice them and in certain cases are catastrophic for individuals (e.g., for those who lose their jobs in a plant shutdown).

Given these facts and the political realities they entail, business opposition to environmental legislation makes a very bad situation much worse. Even if consumers could be persuaded to take environmental issues more seriously, the externalities, opportunities to free ride, and public goods characteristics of the environment make it difficult for even enlightened consumers to express their true preference for the environment in the market. The fact that most environmental legislation trades immediate costs for future benefits makes it difficult for politicians concerned about reelection to support it. Hence it is also difficult for enlightened consumers to have their preferences for a better environment honored in the political arena. Since lack of business intervention seems necessary, and might even be sufficient, for adequate environmental legislation, it seems business has an obligation not to intervene. Nonintervention would prevent the harm of not having the true preferences of consumers for a clean environment revealed. Given business's commitment to satisfying preferences, opposition to having these preferences expressed seems inconsistent as well.

The extent of this obligation to avoid intervening in the political process needs considerable discussion by ethicists and other interested parties. Businesspeople will surely object that if they are not permitted to play a role, Congress and state legislators will make decisions that will put them at a severe competitive disadvantage. For example, if the United States develops stricter environmental controls than other countries do, foreign imports will have a competitive advantage over domestic products. Shouldn't business be permitted to point that out? Moreover, any legislation that places costs on one industry rather than another confers advantages on other industries. The cost to the electric utilities from regulations designed to reduce the pollution that causes acid rain will give advantages to natural gas and perhaps even solar energy. Shouldn't the electric utility industry be permitted to point that out?

These questions pose difficult questions, and my answer to them should be considered highly tentative. I believe the answer to the first question is "yes" and the answer to the second is "no." Business does have a right to insist that the regulations apply to all those in the industry. Anything else would seem to violate norms of fairness. Such issues of fairness do not arise in the second case. Since natural gas and solar do not contribute to acid rain and since the costs of acid rain cannot be fully captured in the market, government intervention through regulation is simply correcting a market failure. With respect to acid rain, the electric utilities do have an advantage they do not deserve. Hence they have no right to try to protect it.

Legislative bodies and regulatory agencies need to expand their staffs to include technical experts, economists, and engineers so that the political process can be both neutral and highly informed about environmental matters. To gain the respect of business and the public, its performance needs to improve. Much more needs to be said to make any contention that business ought to stay out of the political debate theoretically and practically possible. Perhaps these suggestions point the way for future discussion.

Ironically business might best improve its situation in the political arena by taking on an additional obligation to the environment. Businesspersons often have more knowledge about environmental harms and the costs of cleaning them up. They may often have special knowledge about how to prevent environmental harm in the first place. Perhaps business has a special duty to educate the public and to promote environmentally responsible behavior.

Study Questions

1. What presuppositions do you think Bowie makes about the purpose of business organizations and institutions? Do you agree with him?

2. What presuppositions do you think Bowie makes about the purpose of government organizations and institutions? Do you agree with him?

3. Whose view fits best with Bowie's arguments: That of Friedman, Cochran, or Freeman?

4. Use Bowie to analyze the Diablo Canyon case.

CASE: Plasma International
T. W. Zimmerer and P. L. Preston

The Sunday headline in the Tampa, Florida, newspaper read:

Blood Sales Result in Exorbitant Profits for Local Firm

The story went on to relate how the Plasma International Company, headquartered in Tampa, Florida, purchased blood in underdeveloped countries for as little a 90 cents a pint and resold the blood to hospitals in the United States and South America. A recent disaster in Nicaragua produced scores of injured persons and the need for fresh blood. Plasma International had 10,000 pints of blood flown to Nicaragua from West Africa and charged hospitals $150 per pint, netting the firm nearly 1.5 million dollars.

As a result of the newspaper story, a group of irate citizens, led by prominent civic leaders, demanded that the City of Tampa, and the State of Florida, revoke Plasma International's licenses to practice business. Others protested to their congressmen to seek enactment of legislation designed to halt the sale of blood for profit. The spokesperson was reported as saying, "What kind of people are these—selling life and death? These men prey on the needs of dying people, buying blood from poor, ignorant Africans for 90 cents worth of beads and junk, and selling it to injured people for $150 a pint. Well, this company will soon find out that the people of our community won't stand for their kind around here."

"I just don't understand it. We run a business just like any other business; we pay taxes and we try to make an honest profit," said Soi Levin as he responded to reporters at the Tampa International Airport. He had just returned home from testifying before the House Subcommittee on Medical Standards. The recent publicity surrounding his firm's activities during the recent earthquakes had once again fanned the flames of public opinion. An election year was an unfortunate time for the publicity to occur. The politicians and the media were having a field day.

Levin was a successful stockbroker when he founded Plasma International Company three years ago. Recognizing the world's need for safe, uncontaminated, and reasonably priced whole blood and blood plasma, Levin and several of his colleagues pooled their resources and went into business. Initially, most of the blood and plasma they sold was purchased through store-front operations in the southeast United States. Most of the donors were, unfortunately, men and women who used the money obtained from the sale of their blood to purchase wine. While sales increased dramatically on the basis of an innovative marketing approach, several cases of hepatitis were reported in recipients. The company wisely began a search for new sources.

Recognizing their own limitations in the medical-biological side of the business they recruited a highly qualified team of medical consultants. The consulting team, after extensive testing, and a worldwide search, recommended that the blood profiles and donor characteristics of several rural West African tribes made them ideal prospective donors. After extensive negotiations with the State Department and the government of the nation of Burami, the company was able to sign an agreement with several of the tribal chieftains.

As Levin reviewed these facts, and the many costs involved in the sale of a commodity as fragile as blood, he concluded that the publicity was grossly unfair. His thoughts were interrupted by the reporter's question: "Mr. Levin, is it necessary to sell a vitally needed medical supply, like blood, at such high prices especially to poor people in such a critical situation?" "Our prices are determined on the basis of a lot of costs that we incur that the public isn't even aware of," Levin responded. However, when reporters pressed him for details of these "relevant" costs. Levin refused any further comment. He noted that such information was proprietary in nature and not for public consumption.

Study Questions

1. What values of what institutions are coming into conflict?

2. Do the management and town have different views about the nature and purpose of the institution of business? If so, how could you use these different perceptions to help the two sides understand each other better? (Assume you are a well-known and respected public figure.)

3. Are there any national or international institutions that guide Plasma International's acquisition and pricing behavior outside the United States? (These institutions can be formal or informal.) If so, are they legitimate? If not, should any institutions be implemented?

Richard T. De George

Ethical Dilemmas for Multinational Enterprise: A Philosophical Overview

First World multinational corporations (MNCs) are both the hope of the Third World and the scourge of the Third World. The working out of this paradox poses moral dilemmas for many MNCs. I shall focus on some of the moral dilemmas that many American MNCs face.

Third World countries frequently seek to attract American multinationals for the jobs they provide and for the technological transfers they promise. Yet when American MNCs locate in Third World countries, many Americans condemn them for exploiting the resources and workers of the Third World. While MNCs are a means for improving the standard of living of the underdeveloped countries, MNCs are blamed for the poverty and starvation such countries suffer. Although MNCs provide jobs in the Third World, many criticize them for transferring these jobs from the United States. American MNCs usually pay at least as high wages as local industries, yet critics blame them for paying the workers in underdeveloped countries less than they pay American workers for comparable work. When American MNCs pay higher than local wages, local companies criticize them for skimming off all the best workers and for creating an internal brain-drain. Multinationals are presently the most effective vehicle available for the development of the Third World. At the same time, critics complain that the MNCs are destroying the local cultures and substituting for them the tinsel of American life and the worst aspects of its culture. American MNCs seek to protect the interests of their shareholders by locating in an environment in which their enterprise will be safe from destruction by revolutions and confiscation by socialist regimes. When they do so, critics complain that the MNCs thrive in countries with strong, often right-wing, governments.[1]

The dilemmas the American MNCs face arise from conflicting demands made from opposing, often ideologically based, points of view. Not all of the demands that lead to these dilemmas are equally justifiable, nor are they all morally mandatory. We can separate the MNCs that behave immorally and reprehensibly from those that do not by clarifying the true moral responsibility of MNCs in the Third World. To help do so, I shall state and briefly defend five theses.

Thesis I: Many of the moral dilemmas MNCs face are false dilemmas which arise from equating United States standards with morally necessary standards.

Many American critics argue that American multinationals should live up to and implement the same standards abroad that they do in the United States and that United States mandated norms should be followed.[2] This broad claim confuses morally necessary ways of conducting a firm with United States government regulations. The FDA sets high standards that may be admirable. But they are not necessarily morally required. OSHA specifies a large number of rules which in general have as their aim the protection of the worker. However, these should not be equated with morally mandatory rules. United States wages are the highest in the world. These also should not be thought to be the morally necessary norms for the whole world or for

United States firms abroad. Morally mandatory standards that no corporation—United States or other—should violate, and moral minima below which no firm can morally go, should not be confused either with standards appropriate to the United States or with standards set by the United States government. Some of the dilemmas of United States multinationals come from critics making such false equations.

This is true with respect to drugs and FDA standards, with respect to hazardous occupations and OSHA standards, with respect to pay, with respect to internalizing the costs of externalities, and with respect to foreign corrupt practices. By using United States standards as moral standards, critics pose false dilemmas for American MNCs. These false dilemmas in turn obfuscate the real moral responsibilities of MNCs.

Thesis II: Despite differences among nations in culture and values, which should be respected, there are moral norms that can be applied to multinationals.

I shall suggest seven moral guidelines that apply in general to any multinational operating in Third World countries and that can be used in morally evaluating the actions of MNCs. MNCs that respect these moral norms would escape the legitimate criticisms contained in the dilemmas they are said to face.

1. *MNCs should do no intentional direct harm.* This injunction is clearly not peculiar to multinational corporations. Yet it is a basic norm that can be usefully applied in evaluating the conduct of MNCs. Any company that does produce intentional direct harm clearly violates a basic moral norm.

2. *MNCs should produce more good than bad for the host country.* This is an implementation of a general utilitarian principle. But this norm restricts the extent of that principle by the corollary that, in general, more good will be done by helping those in most need, rather than by helping those in less need at the expense of those in greater need. Thus the utilitar-

ian analysis in this case does not consider that more harm than good might justifiably be done to the host country if the harm is offset by greater benefits to others in developed countries. MNCs will do more good only if they help the host country more than they harm it.

3. *MNCs should contribute by their activities to the host country's development.* If the presence of an MNC does not help the host country's development, the MNC can be correctly charged with exploitation, or using the host country for its own purposes at the expense of the host country.

4. *MNCs should respect the human rights of its employees.* MNCs should do so whether or not local companies respect those rights. This injunction will preclude gross exploitation of workers, set minimum standards for pay, and prescribe minimum standards for health and safety measures.

5. *MNCs should pay their fair share of taxes.* Transfer pricing has as its aim taking advantage of different tax laws in different countries. To the extent that it involves deception, it is itself immoral. To the extent that it is engaged in to avoid legitimate taxes, it exploits the host country, and the MNC does not bear its fair share of the burden of operating in that country.

6. *To the extent that local culture does not violate moral norms, MNCs should respect the local culture and work with it, not against it.* MNCs cannot help but produce some changes in the cultures in which they operate. Yet, rather than simply transferring American ways into other lands, they can consider changes in operating procedures, plant planning, and the like, which take into account local needs and customs.

7. *MNCs should cooperate with the local government in the development and enforcement of just background institutions.* Instead of fighting a tax system that

aims at appropriate redistribution of incomes, instead of preventing the organization of labor, and instead of resisting attempts at improving the health and safety standards of the host country, MNCs should be supportive of such measures.

Thesis III: Wholesale attacks on multinationals are most often overgeneralizations. Valid moral evaluations can be best made by using the above moral criteria for context-and-corporation-specific studies and analysis.

Broadside claims, such that all multinationals exploit underdeveloped countries or destroy their culture, are too vague to determine their accuracy. United States multinationals have in the past engaged—and some continue to engage—in immoral practices. A case by case study is the fairest way to make moral assessments. Yet we can distinguish five types of business operations that raise very different sorts of moral issues: (1) banks and financial institutions; (2) agricultural enterprises; (3) drug companies and hazardous industries; (4) extractive industries; and (5) other manufacturing and service industries.

If we were to apply our seven general criteria in each type of case, we would see some of the differences among them. Financial institutions do not generally employ many people. Their function is to provide loans for various types of development. In the case of South Africa they do not do much—if anything—to undermine apartheid, and by lending to the government they usually strengthen the government's policy of apartheid. In this case, an argument can be made that they do more harm than good—an argument that several banks have seen to be valid, causing them to discontinue their South African operations even before it became financially dangerous to continue lending money to that government. Financial institutions can help and have helped development tremendously. Yet the servicing of debts that many Third World countries face condemns them to impoverishment for the foreseeable future. The role of financial institutions in this situation is crucial and raises special and difficult moral problems, if not dilemmas.

Agricultural enterprises face other demands. If agricultural multinationals buy the best lands and use them for export crops while insufficient arable land is left for the local population to grow enough to feed itself, then MNCs do more harm than good to the host country—a violation of one of the norms I suggested above.

Drug companies and dangerous industries pose different and special problems. I have suggested that FDA standards are not morally mandatory standards. This should not be taken to mean that drug companies are bound only by local laws, for the local laws may require less than morality requires in the way of supplying adequate information and of not producing intentional, direct harm.[3] The same type of observation applies to hazardous industries. While an asbestos company will probably not be morally required to take all the measures mandated by OSHA regulations, it cannot morally leave its workers completely unprotected.[4]

Extractive industries, such as mining, which remove minerals from a country, are correctly open to the charge of exploitation unless they can show that they do more good than harm to the host country and that they do not benefit only either themselves or a repressive elite in the host country.

Other manufacturing industries vary greatly, but as a group they have come in for sustained charges of exploitation of workers and the undermining of the host country's culture. The above guidelines can serve as a means of sifting the valid from the invalid charges.

Thesis IV: On the international level and on the national level in many Third World countries the lack of adequate just background institutions makes the use of clear moral norms all the more necessary.

American multinational corporations operating in Germany and Japan, and German and Japanese multinational corporations operating in the United States, pose no special moral problems. Nor do the operations of

Brazilian multinational corporations in the United States or Germany. Yet First World multinationals operating in Third World countries have come in for serious and sustained moral criticism. Why?

A major reason is that in the Third World the First World's MNCs operate without the types of constraints and in societies that do not have the same kinds of redistributive mechanisms as in the developed countries. There is no special difficulty in United States multinationals operating in other First World countries because in general these countries do have appropriate background institutions.[5]

More and more Third World countries are developing controls on multinationals that insure the companies do more good for the country than harm.[6] Authoritarian regimes that care more for their own wealth than for the good of their people pose difficult moral conditions under which to operate. In such instances, the guidelines above may prove helpful.

Just as in the nations of the developed, industrial world the labor movement serves as a counter to the dominance of big business, consumerism serves as a watchdog on practices harmful to the consumer, and big government serves as a restraint on each of the vested interest groups, so international structures are necessary to provide the proper background constraints on international corporations.

The existence of MNCs is a step forward in the unification of mankind and in the formation of a global community. They provide the economic base and substructure on which true international cooperation can be built. Because of their special position and the special opportunities they enjoy, they have a special responsibility to promote the cooperation that only they are able to accomplish in the present world.

Just background institutions would preclude any company's gaining a competitive advantage by engaging in immoral practices. This suggests that MNCs have more to gain than to lose by helping formulate voluntary, UN (such as the code governing infant formulae),[7] and similar codes governing the conduct of all multinationals. A case can also be made that they have the moral obligation to do so.

Thesis V: The moral burden of MNCs do not exonerate local governments from responsibility for what happens in and to their country. Since responsibility is linked to ownership, governments that insist on part or majority ownership incur part or majority responsibility.

The attempts by many underdeveloped countries to limit multinationals have shown that at least some governments have come to see that they can use multinationals to their own advantage. This may be done by restricting entry to those companies that produce only for local consumption, or that bring desired technology transfers with them. Some countries demand majority control and restrict the export of money from the country. Nonetheless, many MNCs have found it profitable to engage in production under the terms specified by the host country.

What host countries cannot expect is that they can demand control without accepting correlative responsibility. In general, majority control implies majority responsibility. An American MNC, such as Union Carbide, which had majority ownership of its Indian Bhopal plant, should have had primary control of the plant. Union Carbide, Inc. can be held liable for the damage the Bhopal plant caused because Union Carbide, Inc. did have majority ownership.[8] If Union Carbide did not have effective control, it is not relieved of its responsibility. If it could not exercise the control that its responsibility demanded, it should have withdrawn or sold off part of its holdings in that plant. If India had had majority ownership, then it would have had primary responsibility for the safe operation of the plant.

This is compatible with maintaining that if a company builds a hazardous plant, it has an obligation to make sure that the plant is safe and that those who run it are properly trained to run it safely. MNCs cannot simply transfer dangerous technologies without consideration of the people who will run them,

the local culture, and similar factors. Unless MNCs can be reasonably sure that the plants they build will be run safely, they cannot morally build them. To do so would be to will intentional, direct harm.

The theses and guidelines that I have proposed are not a panacea. But they suggest how moral norms can be brought to bear on the dilemmas American multinationals face and they suggest ways out of apparent or false dilemmas. If MNCs observed those norms, they could properly avoid the moral sting of their critics' charges, even if their critics continued to level charges against them.

Notes

1. The literature attacking American MNCs is extensive. Many of the charges mentioned in this paper are found in Richard J. Barnet and Ronald E. Muller, *Global Reach: The Power of the Multinational Corporations,* New York: Simon & Schuster, 1974, and in Pierre Jalee, *The Pillage of the Third World,* translated from the French by Mary Klopper, New York and London: Modern Reader Paperbacks, 1968.
2. The position I advocate does not entail moral relativism, as my third thesis shows. The point is that although moral norms apply uniformly across cultures, U.S. standards are not the same as moral standards, should themselves be morally evaluated, and are relative to American conditions, standard of living, interests, and history.
3. For a fuller discussion of multinational drug companies see Richard T. De George, *Business Ethics,* 2nd ed., New York: Macmillan, 1986, pp. 363–367.
4. For a more detailed analysis of the morality of exporting hazardous industries, see my *Business Ethics,* 367–372.
5. This position is consistent with that developed by John Rawls in his *A Theory of Justice,* Cambridge, Mass.: Harvard University Press, 1971, even though Rawls does not extend his analysis to the international realm. The thesis does not deny that United States, German, or Japanese policies on trade restrictions, tariff levels, and the like can be morally evaluated.
6. See, for example, Theodore H. Moran, "Multinational Corporations: A Survey of Ten Years' Evidence," Georgetown School of Foreign Service, 1984.
7. For a general discussion of UN codes, see Wol-

fang Fikentscher, "United Nations Codes of Conduct: New Paths in International Law," *The American Journal of Comparative Law,* 30 (1980), pp. 577–604.

8. The official Indian Government report on the Bhopal tragedy has not yet appeared. The Union Carbide report was partially reprinted in the *New York Times,* March 21, 1985, p. 48. The major *New York Times* reports appeared on December 9, 1984, January 28, 30, and 31, and February 3, 1985.

Study Questions

1. Can you use one or more of the seven guidelines to analyze the Plasma case?

What benefit and what problems come from using the guidelines in this case?

2. How could the management of Plasma International use these guidelines to improve their relationship with the town (assuming they should care about this relationship).

3. What if Plasma is selling life and death? Why is this wrong? Isn't this what hospitals do when they charge money for life saving procedures, like heart transplants? How is the Plasma case different?

Patricia H. Werhane

The Moral Responsibility of Multinational Corporations to Be Socially Responsible

There is a truism that multinational corporations should act like good corporate citizens in the host countries and cities in which they operate. The grounds for this truism and the extent of these obligations have been variously spelled out by a number of thinkers. These arguments include the idea that multinational corporations have a moral imperative to be socially responsible, which has sometimes been traced to a notion of a social contract.[1] The claim is that multinationals have at least implicit contracts to act in a morally decent manner in the countries and cities that allow them to do business. In return for the opportunity to exist and do business, corporations, like ordinary citizens, have obligations to contribute to the well-being of the community.

Alternately, one can develop an argument that as guests in a host country, corporations have special duties to their host—not merely to behave appropriately within the customs or mores of the host country, but, as guests, to contribute positively to the social well-being of that society.

One could also appeal to a rights theory or a sense of justice. As members of the universal community of human beings, and organizations created by human beings, multinationals have responsibilities to respect basic rights wherever they operate, including obligations not to cause harm, obligations to respect freedoms, and obligations to act in a fair manner in business dealings with all stakeholders. Such a position appears in at least two guises: (1) that a multinational has positive obligations to the community, or (2) that a multinational has merely negative obligations not to violate more rights nor to create more harm than the status quo.

Finally, one could take up a Friedmanesque argument that the social responsibility of managers of multinationals is to increase the return on investment for their shareholders within the restraints of law and custom. So, while a multinational's responsibility is to operate within the law and customs of the host country, it has no further commitments to social responsibility. Indeed, it would be a violation of fiduciary duties to extend such responsibilities.

All of these elaborations of the moral responsibility of multinationals to be socially responsible, are interesting and important, and they have been developed by a number of theoreticians. This chapter, however, deals with a more specific problem. If we assume that multinationals have some responsibilities to the communities in which they do business, what is the extent and limits of those responsibilities?

To begin, let's briefly discuss and eliminate from consideration the Friedmanesque position. This view has been labeled "Friedmanesque" because it is a caricature of Milton Friedman's much more carefully argued theses; but it is one that is often attributed to him. This position, in the exaggerated manner in which I have stated it, is problematic. If the primary responsibility of business is defined in terms of its fiduciary corporate-shareholder relationship, this conclusion allows corporations to do business under morally reprehensible conditions if those conditions do not violate law or custom of the host country. So one would have been allowed to practice apartheid in South Africa, to discriminate against women in the workplace in Saudi Arabia, not to hire Palestinian PLO members in Israel, use dangerous pesticides, or market untested drugs in some Third World countries where such products are not illegal. Moreover, such a thesis does not take into account the consideration of customers, employees, or citizens of the host community as stakeholders, except when the well-being of those

stakeholders directly affects the interests of the shareholders. So a multinational could pollute, export a country's natural resources, discriminate against some of its citizens, hire away its skilled laborers and professionals to work in the corporate home country, or produce or sell dangerous products, without impunity. This is not to argue that multinationals do this or that these activities are all always morally wrong. But each of these examples raises ethical issues which, if one takes a Friedmanesque position seriously, are not to be counted as important considerations in corporate decision making except as they affect fiduciary interests or violate law or custom.

A less offensive but restrained approach to the question of multinational social responsibilities emanates from a negative rights theory. In brief, if each of us has the right to be left alone and the right not to be interfered with, so too, nations have such rights. No institution, then, has a right to disturb that communal equilibrium or create harm to the citizens of that community. Therefore, as long as a company does not contribute to the further harm of a community (e.g., by adding to pollution, by creating more joblessness, interfering with local politics, not honoring contracts, or disobeying the law), and as long as that company does not contribute to further violations of human rights, a multinational would be fulfilling its social obligation to that host community.

Now there is nothing wrong with this point of view. But we tend to ask more of multinationals than that they merely mind their own business and do not create further harms. The question then becomes, what is the "more" we demand?

Let us look at the question of social responsibility from a more positive perspective. Let us consider the argument that corporations, like good citizens, have positive social responsibilities to the long-term viability and well-being of the community in which they operate, as well as ordinary moral obligations to other stakeholders (e.g., employees, customers, suppliers, and shareholders). It will turn out that while one is often worried that a Friedmanesque or a negative rights approach does not demand enough of multinational business, one must be equally cautious in spelling out the nature and extent of positive social responsibilities. For if one demands too much of business, and if a corporation accedes to our demands, a corporation could become overly paternalistic or politically embroiled in community affairs, an involvement that is neither desirable for the corporation nor the host community. In the case of multinationals, it shall be argued, its responsibility as a "guest" in another community is more restricted than that of a corporate citizen in its home country.

To attempt to answer the question, "What is the extent of moral responsibility of a multinational corporation to be socially responsible?," let us look at a concrete example—the famous Sullivan Principles and their adoption by American multinationals operating in South Africa. The original principles made six demands: (1) integrate workplace, washrooms, and eating facilities; (2) provide equal and fair employment practices for all employees; (3) provide equal pay for equal or comparable work; (4) expand training programs for non-whites; (5) increase non-whites in supervisory and managerial positions; and (6) improve housing and education opportunities for employees outside the workplace. These principles should like motherhood and apple pie. But the sixth principle demands that companies be proactive in improving the quality of life outside the workplace. Generalized, this is the requirement that corporations contribute to the viability and long-term well-being of the community in which they operate. . . .

Obviously, most corporations are not experts at political interference. This is neither their aim nor expertise and not their responsibility. Such demands not only ask too much of business—if corporations begin to engage in local politics of a host community they are overstepping their bounds as multinational visitors. If successful, a multinational company might succeed in interfering with the political balance of that community. One need only to be reminded of ITT's interac-

tions with the Chilean government in the 1970s to worry about this possibility.

But, one might protest, if there are obvious social ills or political evils in a country in which one is doing business, if these violate rights of citizens of that country, and if a multinational has the power and resources to make improvements in these malaises, is it not its responsibility to do so? I would argue that even if totalitarianism, apartheid, human rights violations, lack of democratic procedures, etc. are evils, one surely questions the interference of one nation with another except on very stringent moral grounds. There is a presumption for national political sovereignty unless circumstances are most abhorrent. Nations are independent states. Because states are made up of individuals who have autonomous moral standing, they too have such standing. They are collectives made up of individuals whose autonomy is defined both by international law and by moral principle. Except in the most inhumane circumstances, a nation's right to self-determination ordinarily overrides most arguments for intervention.[2] If a nation seldom has justifiable moral grounds for intervening with the autonomy of another nation, a multinational corporation's positive moral responsibilities to become engaged in politics is an even more questionable conclusion. The fact that some multinationals have enormous capital resources, sometimes greater than the community in which they are conducting business, should give further strength to the arguments defending the presumption of sovereignty. The revised Sullivan Principles, then, ask too much of business, and its demands are antithetical both to the role of business and to political sovereignty.

While one can make a viable argument that corporations have social responsibilities to their home communities, one must take care in transferring those same sorts of obligations to multinational settings. One is tempted to use a model such as the Lilly Corporation which has been very proactive in improving job opportunities and education in the Indiana community in which it is headquartered. Its aim has been to create a stable community, which is to its and the community's benefit.[3] But Lilly is a citizen of that community. There is a fine line, not merely between honoring one's obligations to a community and paternalism, but also between operating and interfering in a community where one is a guest rather than a citizen. To illustrate, the Minneapolis-based H. B. Fuller company opened a glue manufacturing plant in Honduras, offering industrialization and a number of new jobs to that poor country. Unfortunately, the glue they manufactured became the "drug of choice" for street children who sniffed it and became addicted.[4] What is Fuller's social responsibility in this case? If Fuller stops manufacturing glue in Honduras, there is a loss of over a thousand jobs in a country with little industry and high unemployment. But if it engages in drug education and social reform in that country, it may overstep the bounds of being a "good guest," because these activities can entail interferences with the autonomy and politics of Honduras.

What, then, is the extent of the moral responsibility of multinationals to be socially responsible in a host community? How can we hold multinationals responsible for what they do without extending that requirement to duties that involve them in political and social activities in which they have no skills and which extend their power beyond that of corporate guest status in a host country? First, and most obviously, as a guest, a multinational has a social responsibility to obey the laws and respect the customs of the host country, except where exceptions are allowed and encouraged. The American corporations who practiced the Sullivan Principles within their company in South Africa are evidence of such an exception, because the South African government condoned the practice. Even so, a number of American companies did not have South African offices rather than either obey or disobey South African apartheid laws. Second, it is not the duty nor the privilege of multinationals to engage in political activities in another country or community where they are not citizens. The revised Sullivan Principles asked too much of corporations.

Third, if a corporation cannot uphold its own policies and code of ethics while operating in a foreign context, it should not engage in activities there. For example, if a corporation has an explicit affirmative action policy, it should think carefully before operating in Saudi Arabia.

Fourth, if what a company is engaged in, produces, or affects causes more harms to the citizens of a host country than the present status quo in that country, the multinational has a responsibility either to stop that activity or redress these harms. So H. B. Fuller, for example, must engage in some set of proactive activities that either prevents further uses of its glue as a drug or withdraw from Honduras. However, when those proactive activities involve interference with social or political life of a host country, one should only engage in such activities with utmost restraint.

How can one test whether a particular set of activities is required, desirable, or questionable as part of multinational social responsibility? One might ask the following types of questions:

1. Is this set of activities necessary? "Necessity" is often defined as: what is needed in order to do business in that community. But, in order to justify engaging in allegedly socially responsible activities in a host country a multinational must consider two other provisos: is the activity necessary to redress harms created by the company and/or necessary because of the laws and expectations of that community.[5] With these provisos one should ask:

2. Can this activity be carried out without interfering with the political sovereignty or social fabric of the host country?

3. If this activity requires social change, can it be carried out without violence to the acceptable practices of that society? Or, more simply put, would such a set of activities be acceptable to dispassionate rational persons in that society, even when performed by "foreigners"?

4. Does this set of activities pass a "public-

ity" test? That is, can these activities be made public in the community in which they are to occur? Can they be made public internationally?

5. Does this set of activities coincide with, or not contradict, common sense moral principles by which the corporation operates in its home country?

6. Can such activities be conducted in cooperation with the host country or are there conflicts?

The sixth question is very important, because often one can engage in socially responsible activities (or avoid morally questionable ones) by making agreements with the host country. In the case of H. B. Fuller, Fuller now works with the Honduras government in drug education; it assists but does not take the lead in such activities. It also packages the glue in larger, more expensive, containers not readily affordable by children.

In conclusion, one must be unduly cautious in ascribing social responsibilities to multinationals, particularly when they are guests in another community. Proactivism should be restrained. When there appear to be social ills that need redress, social ills caused by, or within the purview of, the multinational in question, social activism should be tempered by quiet cooperation with host country agencies. Problems of paternalism, political and social interference, threats to national sovereignty, and lack of expertise are such that the moral responsibility of a multinational corporation may be simply not to interfere or even not to do business in a particular milieu. This conclusion may seem too harsh both to those corporations wishing to expand economically and to those companies that take proactive social responsibility as part of doing business, but it is required of morally responsible corporations in transnational business environments.

Notes

1. See, for example, Thomas Donaldson, *Corporations and Morality* (Englewood Cliffs, N.J.: Prentice-Hall, 1982). Donaldson uses the social contract argument to support the claim that corporations have moral responsibilities. He does not focus so much on the social obligations of such institutions.
2. See Michael Walzer, *Just and Unjust Wars* (New York: Basic Books, 1977), especially Chapters 4 and 6 for an expansion of this argument.
3. See "Eli Lilly Corporation," in Robert D. Hay, Edmund R. Gray, and Paul H. Smith, eds., *Business and Society* (Cincinnati: South-Western Publishing, 1976) 17–24.
4. See Norman Bowie and Stephanie Lenway, "H.B. Fuller in Honduras," in Thomas Donaldson and Patricia Werhane, eds., *Ethical Issues in Business,* 4th Ed. (Englewood Cliffs, N.J.: Simon and Schuster, 1993) forthcoming.
5. See Thomas Donaldson, *The Ethics of International Business* (New York: Oxford Univ. Press, 1989), especially Chapter Six.

Study Questions

1. How does Werhane build a framework for understanding international business based on the strengths of different views? How does she use this framework to understand issues in international business?

2. Can we use Werhane's six questions to understand better the institutional environments of business?

3. How do Werhane's six questions compare and contrast with De George's seven guidelines?

Manuel Velasquez

International Business Ethics: The Aluminum Companies in Jamaica

Abstract: I evaluate the adequacy of the three models of international business ethics that have been recently proposed by Thomas Donaldson, Gerard Elfstrom and Richard De George. Using the example of the conduct of the aluminum companies in Jamaica, I argue that these three models fail to address the most important of the ethical issues encountered by multinationals because they focus too narrowly on human rights issues and on utilitarian considerations. In addition I argue that these models also evidence an inadequate understanding of microeconomic theory. I end by proposing that these defects can be remedied by a model of ethics that incorporates a theory of moral rights, a utilitarian-based theory of the market, and a theory of justice.

I want to evaluate the principles that philosophers Thomas Donaldson, Gerard Elfstrom, and Richard De George claim should be used to evaluate the ethics of international business activities.[1] My approach here will be to ask whether the principles suggested by our three philosophers are adequate for dealing with the moral issues raised by a particular historical episode: the operations of the aluminum companies in Jamaica before and during the so-called Manley period, i.e., during the 1960s and 1970s. I will argue that the ethical issues raised by this episode are the more important of the many moral issues international businesses face. Yet, I will argue, the principles suggested by the three philosophers fail to address these central issues, or do so inadequately. I will end with some suggestions of what a more adequate approach to international business ethics would have to look like.

I focus on the aluminum companies in Jamaica for two reasons. First, the case is one about which a great deal of public information now exists. Michael Manley, prime minister of Jamaica during the 1970s, in particular has written extensively about these events.[2] But there also exist a number of studies of the aluminum industry that shed additional light on these events.[3] Secondly, as I will argue, the case raises exactly the kinds of ethical issues that most frequently and most seriously afflict companies operating in less developed nations.

Philosophers, of course, are not the first to have addressed international business ethics. During the 1970s a number of works on multinationals appeared, most critical of them,[4] but some favorable.[5] More recent assessments of multinationals have tended to favor them[6] although critical voices are still heard.[7] A new approach to international business ethics that is extremely promising is one which takes as its starting point the codes of ethics that have been proposed by international bodies such as the United Nations and the OECD.[8] Although the codes are both valuable and useful, still, because of their political origins, complete reliance on these codes, I believe, carries with it a number of risks; however, I will say little about these codes except in passing.[9]

I. THE ALUMINUM COMPANIES IN JAMAICA: 1960–1980

Jamaica is a small island in the Caribbean with a population of about 2 million people, 90 percent of whom are black descendants of the African slaves that once labored on the country's sugar plantations. Colonized by the Spanish in the sixteenth century, it was captured by the British in the seventeenth, and remained a British possession until 1962 when it became an independent nation. Through the first half of the twentieth century, conditions on the island were abysmal: unemployment was high, poverty, malnutrition, disease, and illiteracy were rampant. Workers on the sugar plantations earned a few pennies a day, and peasants made barely a subsistence living farming the island's rocky hillsides. Then the aluminum companies arrived.

Aluminum ore was discovered in Jamaica in 1942 when a wealthy landowner, Alfred D'Costa wondered why his imported grass would not grow in the deep red soil on his land. When D'Costa had his soil analyzed, he discovered he was sitting on one of the few known major deposits of bauxite, the ore from which aluminum is produced. By the early 1950s three of the world's six major aluminum companies had bought up the land in which Jamaica's bauxite was buried: Reynolds and Kaiser (both U.S. companies), and ALCAN (a Canadian company).[10] The American companies set up mining operations, and shipped the bauxite ore to the United States where it was converted into finished aluminum. ALCAN, however, with more sensitivity to local needs, did not merely mine the bauxite, but also processed the bauxite into alumina within Jamaica.

To understand the moral and strategic significance of these decisions, it is important to understand the industrial processes that underlie the aluminum industry. Aluminum is produced through a four-stage process.[11] The first stage is the mining of bauxite ore, a technologically simple process. At the second stage the bauxite is chemically treated and baked to produce alumina, a white powder. This stage requires more labor and a larger capital investment than the first stage. The third stage is the conversion of alumina powder into aluminum metal through an electrolyte smelting process that requires tremendous amounts of energy to run the smelters.

The fourth stage is the metalworking processes—rolling, casting, extruding, and so on—that work the aluminum into the finished form in which it is marketed to manufacturers—car, truck, and aircraft companies, construction companies, and container manufacturers. The six aluminum companies, of course, had each integrated backward and forward and so controlled all four stages, including the final marketing of aluminum metal, through the global cartel they had formed.

Each of the later stages in this four-stage process requires a more sophisticated technology than earlier stages, and each later stage adds more value to the product, and so is more profitable, than earlier stages. Thus by restricting their operations in Jamaica to the first or mining stage, the American companies were electing not to share with Jamaica the more advanced industrial technologies of the later stages; they were electing to give Jamaica only the earliest and so least profitable stages of aluminum production; and they were electing to minimize the amount of capital they invested in Jamaica. The Canadian company, by contrast, had elected to transfer to Jamaica the technology involved in the first two stages of production, and so allow it to share in more value-added processing than mere mining; and it had elected to invest more capital in Jamaica. Nevertheless all three companies kept the most profitable and technologically advanced parts of the process at home. When a fourth major aluminum company, ALCOA, arrived in Jamaica, in 1962, it continued this pattern, confining its Jamaican operations to mining bauxite until 1972 when, like ALCAN, it opened an alumina processing plant and began shipping alumina. It may be argued that the companies did not open aluminum smelting plants in Jamaica because it had no ready source for the enormous quantities of energy consumed by aluminum smelting, but in the 1950s and 1960s energy was still readily and cheaply available on world markets and the aluminum companies were building coal-based smelters in the U.S., and coal-based, oil-based and nuclear-power based smelters in Europe.[12]

The aluminum companies, then, gave impoverished and underdeveloped Jamaica the bottom-most dregs of the processing stages of this highly profitable industry. What else did Jamaica get? In 1950 and 1957 the companies negotiated agreements to pay Jamaica a royalty on each ton of bauxite and alumina shipped and to pay a corporate tax on each ton of bauxite based on the "profit" the government and the companies jointly agreed to attribute to each ton. And, finally the companies agreed to pay an income tax on the net profits earned by their local subsidiaries. Significantly, during this period none of the American companies declared a net taxable profit from their Jamaican subsidiaries and so they paid no income taxes.[13] Shipments, of course, could be easily monitored at Jamaican ports, so royalties and taxes on shipments could be accurately levied. However, since the prices of goods and services transferred internally between the subsidiaries and affiliates of a multinational are set by the multinational itself, the aluminum companies were able to set whatever accounting prices they chose on the alumina and bauxite they transferred from their Jamaican subsidiaries to their American subsidiaries; moreover, they could also set whatever arbitrary prices they chose on services, overhead, licenses, and other costs that were charged back to their Jamaican subsidiaries. The accuracy of these transfer prices, of course, could not be monitored by the Jamaican government, particularly because the companies refused to provide the government with complete financial statements on their global operations. Through transfer price manipulation, then, the companies were able to claim low revenues and high costs at their Jamaican subsidiaries and thereby declare a lack of profits and escape taxes.[14] Only ALCAN, the Canadian company, paid its fair share of income taxes.

To get an idea of the benefits the aluminum companies derived from the bauxite they took out of Jamaica (at least until 1974) relative to the payments they made to Jamaica for this fundamental source of their aluminum, consider that the total annual royalties and taxes paid by all the aluminum companies put together peaked at only $36 million in 1970 and thereafter began to decline.[15] On the other hand, ALCOA's annual revenues during this period were about $2.9 billion; ALCAN's were $2.6 billion; Reynolds were $2.1 billion; and Kaiser's were $1.8 billion.[16] The four companies, then, that were relying primarily on Jamaica's bauxite for their products, were making a total of close to $10 billion, an amount that dwarfs the $36 million they paid Jamaica for the bauxite.

There were, of course, a few other benefits Jamaica derived from the aluminum companies. In 1972, for example, the companies paid a total of about $54 million in wages and salaries to Jamaican workers, and purchased an additional $46 million in local goods and services. In each of these transactions, however, the companies received labor, goods, or services that were worth what the companies paid. In fact, the wages and salaries the aluminum companies paid workers in Jamaica were barely about subsistence level. In the 1950s the Jamaican National Worker's Union had calculated that the minimum wage needed to support a Jamaican family was 56 cents an hour. The companies, however, set wages at 26 cents an hour, a level slightly above prevailing wage scales.[17] Comparable subsistence wages characterized the companies throughout this period.

Thus, although Jamaica by 1970 was producing about 20 percent of the ore that was the source of one of the world's most indispensable and strategically important metals, although the aluminum companies continued to make sizable profits even during recessionary periods, and although Jamaica had a relatively small population, the country remained mired in abject poverty. Unemployment remained at about 24 percent. Infant mortality and malnutrition soared. Illiteracy, poor housing, and inadequate medical care were endemic.

In 1972 Jamaica elected a new government under the leadership of Michael Manley whose avowed aim was to address unemployment, poverty, and inequality.[18] Manley implemented numerous social programs to achieve these ends. Schools were expanded and made available to all, nurses and doctors were brought to the countryside, and government employment programs were set up. Where was the money for all this to come from? Manley turned to the taxes being paid by the aluminum companies. In 1974 Manley, through government fiat raised the levies on Bauxite and entered negotiations to purchase the local operations of the aluminum companies. The companies refused at first, but then, beginning with Reynolds, they one by one accepted the new levies. Moreover, although the companies refused to part with their alumina refining plants, they agreed to sell all or part of their mining operations to the Jamaican government over a period of ten years. Government revenues on bauxite and alumina rose from $28 million in 1972 to $187 million in 1974.[19] The Jamaican government became owner of all the land and 51 percent of the mining operations that had formerly belonged to the aluminum companies.[20]

The aluminum companies did not take this lying down and soon retaliated. Multinationals are not only able to transfer goods and services among their various subsidiaries in different countries, their global presence also allows them to shift operations from one country to another. And this they did. To retaliate against the Manley government, the companies gradually shifted their bauxite operations out of Jamaica and into Guinea in Africa as well as into Australia. The Jamaican government's bauxite revenues dropped rapidly over the next several years as the companies contracted their operations in Jamaica even as they expanded them elsewhere. Moreover, although Jamaica now owned its bauxite mining operations, the aluminum companies retained the core technologies involved in turning bauxite into finished aluminum, and retained full control of world markets for bauxite so the Jamaicans were unable to sell the bauxite they were mining. To make matters worse for Jamaica, prices for imported goods now began to inflate as the result of the 1973 oil price increases, while the partially administered world price

of bauxite fell as the world entered a recessionary phase.

The rest of this story is quickly told. Conditions in Jamaica gradually worsened even farther and in 1977 Manley was forced to turn to the International Monetary Fund to borrow funds to buy the goods the country was no longer able to buy on its own. The Fund imposed gradually harsher conditions on the country as it slowly slid into debt. Under the austerity regime mandated by the Fund the government was forced to curtail its social services, limit wage increases to 7 percent in the face of inflation rates of 30 percent, and raise taxes sharply. Enforced devaluation cut the value of its bauxite exports even farther. On October 31, 1980, the Manley government was swept out of power in a violent election. Unemployment was now at 30 percent, living standards were lower in 1980 than they had been in 1960, inflation had reached levels as high as 47 percent, inequality had worsened, violence and acute shortages of food and other basics were common, and the country had an enormous debt.[21] Conditions there today are not much better, but that is another story.

It should be emphasized that the aluminum companies were not solely to blame for the terrible state that the country found itself in at the end of the 1970s. Much of the blame for Jamaica's problems can be attributed to mistaken government policies. However, we are not discussing the ethics of government, but of business, so we will focus here on the ethical issues raised by the operations of the aluminum companies.

Several ethical issues stand out in this episode and it will help to identify them explicitly. First is the issue of technology transfer. Was it right for the aluminum companies to consistently refuse to share with Jamaica any but the most primitive and least value-added aluminum processing technologies, while they took from her the raw materials on which their business depended in an essential way? Second is the issue of the manipulation of transfer prices. Was it ethical for the aluminum companies to manipulate the accounting prices set on the goods transferred between their affiliates and subsidiaries so as to avoid paying their taxes to Jamaica? Third is the issue of the transfer of their operations. Was it right that at the very moment that Jamaica was struggling to create a more equitable society, the aluminum companies retaliated against the new taxes the government imposed by moving their operations out of Jamaica, thereby helping to plunge the country even more deeply into an economic quagmire from which it has not yet emerged? Fourth is the issue of balance between the benefits Jamaica provided for the aluminum companies, and the benefits the companies provided for the people of Jamaica. Was it fair or just that Jamaica made relatively little from the aluminum ores it supplied the companies, while the companies reaped enormous profits from those ores? Fourth is the issue of monopoly power. Is the kind of economic power that the aluminum industry possess—it is a monopolistic industry organized as an international cartel that can set prices for its goods and for those who supply it with its raw materials—moral? Sixth is the issue of financial disclosure. Were the companies justified in failing to provide full disclosure of their global operations? Seventh is the issue of employee wages and working conditions. Was it ethical for the companies to pay less than workers needed to provide themselves with a decent standard of living?

But this is enough on Jamaica and the ethical issues raised by the operations of the aluminum companies. Let me turn now to look at several philosophers' suggestions about the appropriate criteria for answering questions about the morality of international business practices such as these.

II. DONALDSON AND HUMAN RIGHTS

Thomas Donaldson is currently perhaps the most well-known American theorist on international business ethics. Donaldson argues, on the basis of a social contract model of ethics, that international ethical issues should be solved by appealing to a "minimalist"

ethics consisting of ten "fundamental international rights" that are supposed to be obligatory across all nations provided the rights are "affordable in relation to resources, other obligations, and fairness in the distribution of burdens."[22] Donaldson's preferred list of fundamental international rights include the rights to: (1) freedom of physical movement, (2) ownership of property, (3) freedom from torture, (4) a fair trail, (5) nondiscriminatory treatment, (6) physical security, (7) freedom of speech and association, (8) minimal education, (9) physical security, (7) freedom of speech and association, (8) minimal education, (9) political participation, and (10) subsistence. Donaldson does not think that businesses have a positive duty to secure these rights for people. He writes that it would be "unfair, not to mention unreasonable" to expect "the profit-making corporation, in contrast (to government)" to secure these rights. So the corporation has only the negative duty to avoid doing things that would deprive others of these rights.

Donaldson suggests an "algorithm" that is supposed to guide the application of these rights to particular situations. When a multinational corporation is evaluating the morality of a questionable practice that is prevalent in a host country—such as bribery or wages that are less than subsistence level—Donaldson suggests that the multinational must first ask whether it is possible to conduct business in the host country without engaging in the practice. If it is not possible to do business without the practice, then the multinational must ask a second question: does the practice violate any of the fundamental international rights? If the practice violates one or more of these rights, the multinational must ask, thirdly, whether the rationale for the local practice is related to the host country's relative level of economic development. If so, then "the practice is permissible if and only if the members of the home country would, under conditions of economic development relevantly similar to those of the host country, regard the practice as permissible." In short, one should avoid practices that violate human rights, except when such practices are essential to a country's economic development.

Donaldson's approach is both valuable and useful. It is provides a narrow and easily mastered set of ethical criteria that do not place unreasonable burdens on corporations. Moreover, his "algorithm" integrates the troubling issue of uneven economic development into his moral calculus. Nevertheless, his approach can and has been subjected to a number of damaging criticisms.[23]

But the question I want to ask here is whether his approach helps us deal with the ethical issues raised by the operations of the aluminum companies in Jamaica? The answer is that, by and large, Donaldson's approach does not address the central issues raised by such cases. The trouble is that Donaldson's theory is restricted to human rights issues. While human rights are certainly an important part of ethics, and perhaps the most prominent part of international ethics, it is a mistake to think that they are its only part, even its only "minimalist" part or its most basic part.[24] In fact, the prevalent issues in international business ethics in general, and in the Jamaican case in particular, are issues that have little to do with human rights and that are therefore unresolvable from Donaldson's perspective. Among these are the issues of monopoly profits and monopolization of markets, transfer price manipulation and tax avoidance, corporation limitations placed on the transfer of technology, and failure to disclose financial information to host governments. Practices like these violate economic efficiency, and they present major obstacles to a nation's programs of social development. For these utilitarian reasons such practices are generally condemned as unethical even though they do not typically involve the violation of any fundamental human rights. Because Donaldson's approach is so narrowly restricted to human rights, however, it has little to say about these and the many other similar sorts of financial, accounting, reporting, and market issues that more commonly face businesses especially in their relationship to less developed host economies.

Donaldson's approach does have some-thing to say about one of the issues raised by the Jamaica case, and that is the issue of wages and employee rights. In Jamaica the aluminum companies persistently paid less than subsistence wages and did little to improve employee working conditions. Donaldson tells us that to evaluate the issue of wages and other employee rights issues we should go through his four-step "algorithm." Questionable employee practices, he tells us, are "permissible if and only if the [corporate] members of the home country would, under conditions of economic development relevantly similar to those of the host country, regard the practice as permissible." In short, would the managers of the aluminum companies have regarded the subsistence wages as necessary for Jamaica's economic development. The problem with this approach is, of course, its obvious ethnocentrism. Donaldson asks us to judge the ethics of such practices from the standpoint of American corporate management, not from the standpoint of Jamaican locals.

The upshot, then, is that Donaldson's human rights approach is ethnocentric, but, more importantly, it is too narrow to provide much help in answering most of the kinds of economic, developmental, and financial ethical issues raised by the activities of the aluminum companies in Jamaica during the period we have examined. It may be suggested at this point that perhaps the issues raised by the Jamaican case are unusual, and that the ethical issues that international companies more often face are human rights issues and not the sorts of ethical economic issues that are raised in the Jamaican case. But this suggestion is mistaken.

First, although human rights violations are the more sexy issues that are more often reported in the popular press, such issues arise in only a few parts of the world and they are raised for only a few businesses in those regions. On the other hand, every single company that operates subsidiaries in two or more countries has to face the issue of transfer price manipulation. Every single company operating in a consolidated or oligopoly global industry has to deal with the issue of monopolistic pricing. Every single large company that bases its success on proprietary technologies has to decide how much of this technology it will share with its host countries. Every single company operating in a foreign country has to decide how much information about its global operations it will disclose to its host governments. And every single company operating abroad has to decide what employee policies it will follow in the various parts of the world in which it operates. In short the issues that are raised in the Jamaican case are issues that are integral to the core operations of a business in an international environment. But the human rights issues which Donaldson's theory is designed to address are issues that are peripherally and tangentially related to the core business functions.

Secondly, if one examines the codes of ethics that international bodies have developed for multinational business enterprises, it is clear that the issues on which Donaldson focuses are not in their judgment the central issues. The *OECD Guidelines for Multinational Enterprises,* for example, which was adopted in 1976 by the nations of the Organization for Economic Co-Operation and Development,[25] makes no mention of human rights and in fact refers to rights only five times, none of which occurrences refer to the rights that appear on Donaldson's list. The issues that the *OECD Guidelines* to address—and address at considerable length—are precisely those issues that appeared in the Jamaican case: the obligation of multinationals to give due consideration to host countries' developmental and social needs; the obligation to provide adequate disclosure of information; the obligation to avoid monopolistic practices and participation in cartels; the obligation to pay one's fair share of taxes; the obligation to provide fair working conditions, and the obligation to transfer technology on reasonable terms and conditions.[26] Thus, it is the considered judgment of the OECD and its member countries that the crucial issues in international business ethics are exactly those issues which were raised by the operations of the aluminum companies in Jamaica. . . .

III. ELFSTROM AND UTILITARIANISM

Gerard Elfstrom, another ethicist who has recently turned his attention to international business ethics, takes an approach that is quite different from Donaldson's.[27] Elfstrom rejects appeals to rights because they are either too "abstract" or, when rendered sufficiently specific, they become too riddled with "conflicts." Only the ethical theory of utilitarianism he says, can provide us with a "well-defined normative foundation." Utilitarianism is the theory that our only moral obligation is to promote the greatest good for the greatest number. Elfstrom suggests (claiming R. M Hare as an authority) that what is good should be defined in terms of the preferences people hold.[28] Since "the great majority of people . . . have very strong interests in life and the means required to sustain it," he concludes that the duty "to provide the greatest good for the greatest number of people, therefore, amounts to a fundamental obligation to preserve human life and its means." Among the means that Elfstrom thinks we are obligated to provide for society, he includes "a diet sufficient for normal activity, as well as shelter, clothing and basic medical care." Less important and therefore less obligatory than the satisfaction of such "basic wants," is the satisfaction of "secretary" wants such as for "flavor and variety in food, . . . [and] clothes and shelter which are stylish or luxurious." Our basic ethical obligation, then, apparently is to preserve human life and provide everyone with a minimum level of food, shelter, clothing, and basic medical care.

One would expect that Elfstrom's approach would lead to maximal obligations on corporations. That is, since Elfstrom claims to be a utilitarian, one would expect him to make the standard utilitarian claim that businesses and agents in general have the duty to provide for people's basic wants right up to the point where the costs begin to outweigh the benefits. But this, of course, would impose extremely heavy and implausible burdens on businesses. For example, so long as corporate assets could provide greater utility by being used to provide food for the needy than to provide advertising, pure utilitarians would say that it would be wrong to use them for such corporate purposes. The unrealistic nature of the obligations that pure utilitarianism implies forces Elfstrom to abandon the logic of utilitarianism by arguing (in a manner that is reminiscent of Donaldson) that private corporations are "not accountable to the larger public in the way a governmental agency might be," and so "governments and not corporations should take the initiative in addressing social ills and improving human life." Like Donaldson, elfstrom concludes that corporations have no positive duty to provide the means to human life, but only the negative duty to "avoid actions and policies which are likely to deprive people of their lives or means to life."[29] Thus for Elfstrom, companies do not have a positive obligation to give people the means to life, nor, in fact, any obligations to provide people with any goods at all. Instead, companies merely have a negative obligation to refrain from activities that are likely to kill people, and to avoid taking away from people the means to life. In short, companies have no obligations to provide anything, just obligations not to take things away.

Elfstrom's version of utilitarianism, then, leaves him with a normative theory that is even narrower than Donald's since the only ethical duty of corporations that Elfstrom officially recognizes is the duty to "avoid activities that endanger human life and well-being." Does this theory help us deal with the international ethical issues raised by the operations of the aluminum companies in Jamaica? I suggest that it doest not. We may be sure that with rare exceptions, the aluminum companies operating in Jamaica did not directly take people's lives nor did they directly endanger human lives nor did they directly take any goods away from people. Refraining from disclosing financial information, engaging in transfer price manipulation, participating in monopolistic practices and cartels, refraining from paying one's fair share of taxes, failing to provide fair working conditions, and failing to transfer technology to a devel-

oping country—all these are negative actions or omissions, and so all of them are consistent with Elfstrom's negative utilitarianism which imposes no positive duties on corporations. None of these practices directly endangers human life and none of them directly takes away the means to human life, and so none of them would be touched by Elfstrom's negative utilitarianism. . . .

Elfstrom's approach then, like that of Donaldson, is too narrow. Where Donaldson's approach is too narrowly focused on rights, Elfstrom's is too narrowly focused on negative utility and, consequently, there are significant multinational ethical issues that Elfstrom's approach cannot adequately address. In particular, it has little to say about the ethical issues that were raised by the aluminum companies in Jamaica. Moreover, even if Elfstrom were to rely on a more traditional form of utilitarianism, his approach would still need to incorporate an analysis of markets and market behaviors, something that is entirely missing from his discussion.

IV. DE GEORGE AND GUIDELINES FOR MULTINATIONALS

A third and refreshingly different approach is provided by Richard De George who addresses many of the core ethical issues Donaldson and Elfstrom ignore.[30] De George develops seven basic "guidelines" for American multinationals operating in less developed countries: (1) Multinationals should do no intentional direct harm; (2) Multinationals should produce more good than harm for the host country; (3) Multinationals should contribute by their activity to the host country's development; (4) Multinationals should respect the human rights of their employees; (5) To the extent that local culture does not violate ethical norms, multinationals should respect the local culture and work with and not against it; (6) Multinationals should pay their fair share of taxes; (7) Multinationals should cooperate with the local government in developing and enforcing just background institutions. De George goes on to give four more guidelines that "extend" the original seven, plus ten additional "strategies" for dealing with corruption.

Unlike Donaldson and Elfstrom, De George's discussions of these guidelines address many of the issues that are apparent in the Jamaica case. His discussions, although often briefer than their subject matter merits, include discussions of transfer price manipulation, financial disclosure, technology transfer, the development objectives of less developed nations, and employee wages and working conditions. Missing from his discussion, however, is an issue that was at the core of the Jamaica case, and that is present, at least as an underlying theme, in all discussions of multinational ethics: monopolistic power and behavior. I will return to this issue later. For now, we should also note that, unlike Elfstrom, De George recognizes the significance of human rights particularly in relation to employee issues (guideline 4). Yet, unlike Donaldson, his analysis is not restricted to human rights, but also incorporates several norms that are frankly utilitarian (guidelines 1 and 2). Moreover, also unlike Donaldson, De George's approach is sensitive to the issue of ethnocentrism with its insistence that multinationals should "respect local culture" (guideline 5).

At first sight, then, De George's guidelines are generally prudent, sensible, and cover many of the important issues raised by multinational business operations. Closer inspection, however, reveals a number of problems. Because of space constraints, I confine myself to discussing only De George's first three guidelines. This discussion will, I think, bring out the basic problems with De George's approach.

De George's first guideline states that companies should do no intentional direct harm. This seems true enough except that the exact meaning of this guideline becomes crucially unclear when it is applied to market behaviors: exactly what is the difference between direct and indirect (or non-direct?) harm when companies are operating in free markets? For example, when a multinational drives out native competitors by offering bet-

ter service, lower prices, and higher quality goods, with the intention of monopolizing the local market, are the competitors being directly harmed or only indirectly? If competition that drives out weaker competitors is an instance of direct harm, then De George's guideline unrealistically makes immoralists out of virtually all superior businesses; but if this is not an instance of direct harm, then by what criteria are we to decide which harms are direct and which are not direct? Although unfair competition against indigenous businesses was not a central issue throughout much of the Jamaica case, the issue points to a failing that afflicts much of De George's approach: he fails to take into account the importance of markets in evaluating the behaviors of companies. The nature and significance of this will, I think, become clearer soon.

Let us turn to De George's second guideline: multinationals should produce more good than harm in less developed countries. This may appear to be good advice. But a closer look again reveals problems. First: exactly what does it mean? For example, how much "more good" is a multinational supposed to produce before its inevitable "harm" (e.g., consumption of local resources) is justified? But there is a deeper problem here. Economics tells us that in any voluntary market exchanges, such as were involved in the dealings of the aluminum companies with Jamaica, both parties benefit and so utility is necessarily increased. But if so, then, all multinationals, provided no coercion is involved, virtually always produce more economic benefits than harm for their host countries: customer utility is improved since otherwise customers would not have purchased the product; worker utility is increased since otherwise workers would not have taken the jobs; the host country gains since otherwise it would not give the multinational a license to operate in return for the benefits the multinational provides; and the multinational gains since otherwise it would not remain in business there. All of these factors were at work in Jamaica since, everyone will agree, Jamaica was better off with the aluminum companies there than it would have been without their presence at all. But then, it is not at all clear whether De George's second guideline would ever apply in the voluntary market exchanges that are characteristic of virtually all multinational operations.

Readers familiar with elementary economics will suggest that perhaps De George's second guideline is supposed to rule out exchanges in imperfect markets or market failures. Although De George never says as much, and is perhaps not aware of it, the examples he cites of cases where his guideline applies are all either cases of market failures ("pollution, rapid depletion of its resources, deforestation that leads to natural disasters"[31]) or of market imperfections ("deceptive subterfuge," "failing to disclose the real effects of a drug,"[32]). But if this guideline is supposed to rule out such cases, then what is called for is not this broad and unclear guideline: what we need is a narrower, and clearer, criterion that tells us that certain specific market failures and imperfections render exchanges unethical; in particular that harmful externalities, information asymmetries, and anticompetitive market conduct is wrong. If De George's approach incorporated an adequate treatment of markets, then it would provide a clearer and more adequate analysis of exactly those issues that were paramount in the Jamaica case, where the aluminum companies provided deceptive or incomplete information on the real value of their operations in Jamaica, where they engaged in monopolistic control of markets, and where their activities had some harmful external effects. The problems that De George is correctly trying to address with his second guideline, then, are primarily the kinds of conduct that appear when markets fail or when they are imperfect. Unfortunately, De George fails to frame the issues as the market issues that they in fact are, and instead offers us this guideline which is unclear, misleading, and incomplete.

There's yet another deep problem with this second guideline, a problem that can teach us something important about another significant defect in De George. The problem will become apparent if we look at the argument that De George gives in support of his second guideline:

> This second norm presents a special instance of the application of a utilitarian analysis: it does not allow the multinational to justify harm to the host country by appeal to the greater good produced for it or for the United States. To do so would increase the disparity between the status of the host country and that of the United States; it would benefit the well off at the expense of the poorly off; it would increase the dependence of the LDCs on the more developed countries; and it would eventually contribute to heightened world-wide tensions. This is enough to preclude the action on a straight utilitarian calculation, since overall the action would produce more harm than good. This norm is derived from that calculation.[33]

This is a very strange passage since on its face it is clearly mistaken. On a "straight utilitarian calculation," the "greater good" an action produces justifies any harm, so long as its net utility outweighs the net utility any other action could provide. Utilitarianism does not give any preference to the utility of less developed countries over that of the more developed ones.

But De George wants to claim in this passage that when the benefits of a multinational's operations accrue to the more developed country and the harms to the less developed one, the result is always "more harm than good." This, I believe, can be shown to be false. De George claims that when developed countries benefit at the expense of undeveloped countries, this always leads to "heightened world-wide tensions." But there are many examples of the exploitation of small nations where such world-wide tensions did not result. Moreover, even when such harmful tensions do result, they do not necessarily outweigh the benefits that derived from the activities that produced those tensions. Consider, for example, how the American aluminum companies for decades got more out of Jamaica than Jamaica got from them. Moreover, the transportation industry of the industrialized nations especially, but also its construction and container industries, all benefited enormously from the aluminum provided by Jamaica's ores, while Jamaica's economy was gradually devastated, and its people remained mired in poverty, unable to lift themselves up on the relatively limited funds it derived from its participation in the aluminum industry. Yet it is at least arguable that the enormous industrial benefits that the huge populations of the more developed world derived from the exploitation of Jamaica's bauxite far outbalanced the harm that the relatively small population of Jamaica suffered. Moreover, although the gap between Jamaica and the United States widened, "world-wide tensions" were hardly affected because Jamaica was and has remained a fairly tiny political and economic power, and its tensions hardly affect that world. Thus, in this obvious instance right at our doorstep, it is hardly true that when a more developed country benefits at the expense of a less developed one, the result always will be "more harm than good."

Now there is a real moral problem here, of course, in the relations between a country like Jamaica and a country like the United States, and, more generally, in the relations between the poorer and the richer nations of the world, and De George is right to be concerned about it. But it is a problem that utilitarian theory cannot handle, although De George mistakenly tries to use utilitarianism to deal with it. The problem that worries De George are the injustices that are created by the unequal sharing of benefits and burdens between the rich and poor nations of the world. He sees correctly that there is something wrong with a situation in which a rich nation like the United States benefits at the expense of a poor one like Jamaica. He correctly sees that when the rich nations benefit at the expense of the poor, the gap between them widens. And this too seems wrong. But he misdiagnoses the problem by falsely claiming that such situations always produce "more harm than good." Obviously, inequalities can and often do produce more benefits

than harm. The inequalities, however, are still wrong. But they are wrong, not because they violate utilitarianism, but because they violate justice. And that is the problem with De George's approach. While he explicitly acknowledges the importance of human rights and of utilitarianism, his approach fails to take seriously the importance of justice in evaluating the activities of multinationals, particularly as this relates to their activities in less developed nations.

Finally, consider De George's third principle on development: "Multinationals should contribute by their activity to the host country's development." This guideline may ask too much of the corporation. While it was the duty of the Jamaican government to actively promote development of its own country, it is not at all apparent that the aluminum companies had any positive duties to provide assistance in this regard. Both Donaldson and Elfstrom, recall, explicitly argue that corporations have no positive duties to provide such assistance, both holding that corporations have only negative duties where development is concerned. Donaldson points out that the corporation is organized as a profit-making institution and is therefore ill-equipped to take development as one of its aims; Elfstrom argues that development should be the prerogative of elected or representative agents such as government and not of private parties such as a corporation. Both of these considerations are persuasive. De George, however, seems oblivious to the need to provide arguments for his view, and oblivious to the controversial nature of his claims about development.

If we look at the situation in Jamaica, of course, what we see is a situation in which the aluminum companies did in fact make positive contributions to the economic development of Jamaica through the royalties they paid and capital investments they brought. Apparently, then, they behaved ethically according to De George's guidelines. But the ethical demands of the situation were much more complex. First, what less developed countries need desperately if they are to industrialize is access to industrial technology and to markets. Jamaica, in particular, needed the refining technologies involved in the later stages of aluminum production and capital investment in these technologies, as well as access to world markets for whatever bauxite, alumina, or aluminum ingot they might have been able to produce. But, as we have seen, the aluminum companies decided to withhold these from Jamaica and because the industry was monopolized, there was little Jamaica could do. Secondly, the important ethical issue, as we have seen, is not whether the aluminum companies made any contributions to Jamaica's development. The real ethical issue is the meager contribution they made relative to the enormous revenues they collected.

De George's approach, then, also fails to adequately deal with the ethical issues raised by Jamaica and the operations of the aluminum companies. De George's approach must be augmented with a set of principles of justice. Moreover, his approach must incorporate a more adequate treatment of markets and the ethics of various forms of market behaviors.

V. CONCLUSION

What can be concluded from this overview of recent philosophical approaches to international business ethics? Our discussion suggests, first, that an adequate approach to ethics in international contexts requires broader criteria than the narrow focus on human rights that Donaldson provides; broader than the mere reliance on negative utilitarianism that Elfstrom provides, and broader even than the focus on utilitarianism and rights that De George suggests. Our discussion, particularly of De George suggests, secondly, that addressing the issues raised by the operations of international corporations also requires a set of more or less clearly articulated principles of justice, in addition to utilitarian and moral rights principles. And, finally, our discussions of both Elfstrom and De George suggests that utilitarian principles by themselves are incapable of providing clear and non-ambiguous criteria for evaluating the operations of multinationals. Utilitarian theory has to be joined to

microeconomic theory if it is to shed light on the ethical nature of market behaviors, precisely the kinds of behaviors that are characteristic of corporations.

What approach, then, should be taken when confronting the moral issues raised by the activities of multinationals? The kind of approach that I believe is needed has been elaborated elsewhere, and space prevents me from presenting it here.[34] Suffice it to say that an adequate theory of international business ethics must incorporate a theory of moral rights that includes the right of national self-determination and employee rights such as those relating to child labor, the right to a living wage, and the right to unionize; it must incorporate a theory of justice that is powerful enough to deal with the complex problems of development and of the inequalities between rich and poor nations; and it must include a utilitarian-based theory of the market that will enable us to deal with issues related to the efficiency of markets such as market externalities, information asymmetries, anticompetitive market conduct, and anticompetitive market structure. Anything less, if we heed the example of the aluminum companies in Jamaica, will be inadequate.

Notes

1. T. Donaldson, *The Ethics of International Business* (New York: Oxford University Press, 1989); G. Elfstrom, *Moral Issues and Multinational Corporations* (New York: St. Martin's Press, 1991); R. T. De George, *Competing with Integrity in International Business* (New York: Oxford University Press, 1993).

2. Michael Manley, *Jamaica: Struggle in the Periphery* (London, 1982); Michael Manley, *Up the Down Escalator: Development and the International Economy* (Washington, D.C.: Howard University Press, 1987); Michael Manley, *The Poverty of Nations: Reflections on Underdevelopment and the World Economy* (Concord, MA: Pluto Press, 1991).

3. See, Ronald Graham, *The Aluminum Industry and the Third World* (London: Zed Press, 1982); Merton J. Peck, ed., *The World Aluminum Industry in a Changing Energy Era* (Washington, D.C.: Resources for the Future, 1988); H. D. Huggins, *Aluminum in Changing Communities* (London: Andre Deutsche Limited, 1965).

4. Richard Barnet and Ronald Muller, *Global Reach: The Power of the Multinational Corporations* (New York: Simon & Schuster, 1974).

5. Ray Vernon, *Storm Over the Multinationals: The Real Issues* (London: Macmillan Press, 1977); H. May, *Multinational Corporations in Latin America* (New York: Council of the Americas, 1975).

6. Alex Rubner, *The Might of the Multinationals: The Rise and Fall of the Corporate Legend* (New York: Praeger Publishers, 1990).

7. Rachael Kamel, *The Global Factory* (Philadelphia: American Friends Service Committee, 1990); Janet Lowe, *The Secret Empire, How 25 Multinationals Rule the World* (Homewood, IL: Business One Irwin, 1992).

8. See, for example, William C. Frederick, "The Moral Authority of Transnational Corporate Codes," *Journal of Business Ethics,* 10:165–177; Kathleen A. Getz, "International Codes of Conduct: An Analysis of Ethical Reasoning," *Journal of Business Ethics,* 9:567–577; Claes Hagg, "The OECD Guidelines for Multinational Enterprises, A Critical Analysis," *Journal of Business Ethics,* 3:71–76. A number of international bodies have in fact developed codes of ethics for multinationals including: the United Nations (The Proposed Text of the Draft UN Code of Conduct on Transnational Corporations, not yet formally adopted), the International Chamber of Commerce (The ICC Guidelines for International Investment, 1972), the Organization for Economic Cooperation and Development (the OECD Guidelines for Multinational Enterprises, 1976), and the International Labor Organization of the UN (the UN International Labor Office Tripartite Declaration of Principles Concerning Multinational Enterprises and Social Policy, 1977).

9. For an analysis of these codes see John M. Kline, *International Codes and Multinational Business* (Westport, CO: Quorum Books, 1985).

10. The big six are Alcan (Canada), Alcoa (U.S.), Kaiser (U.S.), Pechiney (France), Reynolds (U.S.), and Alusuisse (Switzerland).

11. Peck, *ibid.,* pp. 4–8.

12. Peck, *ibid.,* p. 33, 78.

13. Manley, 1987, p. 54: ". . . none of the American-based companies ever declared a net, taxable profit on their Jamaica operations. Even when the bauxite production was running at record levels in 1973, no company, save ALCAN, confessed a profit."

14. Manley, 1987, p. 54: ". . . to say nothing of the notional and highly fictional prices which were set by the companies for moving bauxite and alumina between their various affiliated bodies."

15. Manley, 1987, p. 38.

16. Manley, 1987, p. 197.

17. Manley, 1987, pp. 33–34; Manley notes, that such low wages were prevalent in Jamaica at the time. Although the companies could easily have afforded much more, they decided to pay only the local prevailing wage. Huggins, 1965, p. 121 writes: "the workers through their unions pressed for rates of pay on a par with those paid to bauxite and alumina employees in Canada and the United States. The companies resisted this claim, but the compromise reached has given the bauxite workers a lead over other industrial workers in the island."

18. Anthony Payne, "Jamaica: The 'Democratic Socialist' Experiment of Michael Manley," in Anthony Payne and Paul Sutton, *Dependency Under Challenge: The Political Economy of the Contemporary Commonwealth Caribbean* (Manchester, U.K.: Manchester University Press, 1984), pp. 18–42.

19. Manley, 1987, pp. 38, 61.

20. Payne, *ibid.,* p. 28.

21. Derick A. C. Boyd, *Economic Management, Income Distribution, and Poverty in Jamaica* (New York: Praeger Publishers, 1988).

22. Donaldson's theory is elaborated in his 1989 book, *The Ethics of International Business,* cited above; many of the main ideas in this book were first outlined in his "Multinational Decision-Making: Reconciling International Norms," *Journal of Business Ethics,* 4 (1985), 357–366; a short popularized version of his main claims can be found in his "Can Multinationals Stage a Universal Morality Play," *Business and Society Review* (1992), 51–55. Donaldson claims in his book that a social contract theory of ethics will imply "that a productive organization should refrain from violating minimum standards of justice and of human rights in any society in which it operates" (p. 54). The ten "fundamental rights" are supposed to specify what these rights must be, although, surprisingly, Donaldson never gives an argument to show that these particular ten rights would be chosen from a social contract perspective.

23. See Norman Bowie, "Moral Decision Making and Multinationals," *Business Ethics Quarterly,* v. 1, no. 1, 1991, pp. 223–32.

24. For evidence of the importance of rights in international contexts one need look no farther than the United Nations Declaration of Human Rights. Nevertheless, other international codes, particularly those which deal with multinationals, are not focused on human rights issues. In fact, the fundamental value that has pride of place in almost every international code of ethics is economic or social development, which is a utilitarian value, not one of human rights.

25. These nations include: Austria, Belgium, Canada, Denmark, France, Germany, Greece, Iceland, Ireland, Italy, Luxembourg, the Netherlands, Norway, Portugal, Spain, Sweden,

Switzerland, Turkey, the United Kingdom, the United States, Japan, Finland, Australia, New Zealand, and Yugoslavia.

26. Organization for Economic Co-operation and Development, *the OECD Guidelines for Multinational Enterprises* (Paris: OECD, 1986).

27. Elfstrom's theory is elaborated in his 1991 book, *Moral Issues and Multinational Corporations,* cited above.

28. There is a question here as to whether Elfstrom is reading Hare correctly; Hare's view—like that of Bentham—is that satisfaction of the actual preferences of every individual must be maximized, while Elfstrom's view—much closer to Mill's—is that those goods in which the majority of people have strong interests must be maximized.

29. This is, of course, a strange conclusion for a utilitarian, since exactly the same argument could be made about any private individual, thereby absolving every individual of any positive utilitarian duties.

30. De George's theory is elaborated in his 1993 book, *Competing with Integrity in International Business,* cited above; De George's approach was first described in "Ethical Dilemmas for Multinational Enterprises: A Philosophical Overview," in *Ethics and the Multinational Enterprise,* ed. by W. Michael Hoffman, Anne E. Lange, and David A. Fedo (Washington, D.C.: University Press of America, 1986), 39–46.

31. *Ibid.,* p. 48.

32. *Ibid.,* p. 61, 62.

33. *Ibid.,* p. 48.

34. See Manuel Velasquez, *Business Ethics: Concepts and Cases* (Englewood Cliffs, NJ: Prentice-Hall, 1992).

Study Questions

1. Why does Velasquez believe that the rights approach, the utilitarian approach, and De George's pluralistic approach are not sufficient for understanding and resolving problems in international business? Do you agree with him? Why?

2. How does Velasquez want to remedy the problems of these three approaches? To what extent is his answer based on institutional concerns and changes?

3. Use Velasquez's approach to analyze the Plasma case. Is his approach clearly better than the other three he discusses?

CASE: **U.S. and Mexico Confront a Toxic Legacy**
Colum Lynch

Here at the Otay Mesa industrial park on the outskirts of Tijuana, subsidiaries of dozens of US corporations sit like a great industrial fortress overlooking Ejido Chilpancingo, a small working-class barrio situated in a valley near the Tijuana River.

Since the industrial park opened over a decade ago, residents of Ejido Chilpancingo say, they have been living in the shadow of a chemical nightmare. Their livestock feed on toxic waste, their air is often blackened by pollutants and their water supply has been fouled by a network of open drainage pipes that poke out over the town from a bluff beneath the industrial park. Its tenants include subsidiaries to such corporate giants as Mobil Oil and Pepsi and to American Optical Corp., a Southbridge, Mass. -based firm that manufactures lenses.

When rain falls upon Ejido Chilpancingo, plant workers release into drainage pipes stockpiled industrial detergents, solvents, heavy metals and petroleum products. The outflow empties into dozens of meandering creeks, rivulets and gulleys before emptying into a river where the town residents bathe.

Ultimately the contaminated waters reach the Rio Tijuana and then flow north back into the United States.

In February, when President George Bush visited Los Angeles and San Antonio to mobilize support for a North American Free Trade Agreement among the United States, Mexico and Canada, he argued that the agreement was the antidote to the environmental problems that afflict communities like Ejido Chilpancingo. By providing benefits to US corporations, he reasoned, the agreement would raise living standards for Mexicans and Americans alike, and "higher standards of living . . . will help people keep the air and water cleaner on both sides of the border."

The agreement has to be ratified by the US Congress, which is unlikely to deal with it until after the November elections.

To deal with the immediate problems, which will cost billions to clean up, Bush has proposed what he called an Integrated Border Plan and asked the US Congress to appropriate $250 million to fund a series of clean-up operations along the US side of the border. (The proposal is now before the House Appropriations Committee.) At the same time, President Carlos Salinas de Gortari promised to commit $460 million over the next three years for environmental clean-up and to improve Mexico's capacity to monitor rampant illegal chemical dumping by foreign corporations along his side of the border.

At Ejido Chilpancingo, where an experiment in free trade has already been going on for over a decade, residents say they can't wait for any benefits from a free trade agreement to trickle down into their community.

US, Japanese and Mexican corporations have already transformed their town into an environmental junk yard. From the Otay Mesa industrial park, poisonous plumes of black smoke rise from the industrial waste being illegally burned, emitting an acrid odor of rubber and sulphur. The open-air grounds of a nearby factory are covered with a snowy layer of lead sulphate dust, a compound found in corroded batteries that attacks the central nervous system. Puddles of yellow water collect on the dirt roads of the town square.

Down the road from the square, Jose Juan de Vora, 11, sits wearily on the edge of the single bed in his small one-bedroom home. The boy fell sick months ago. Clumps of his hair have fallen out, a skin infection covered much of his body, and he no longer plays. A rash extends from the top of his ear to his cheekbone.

The boy's mother, Dona Rosa de Vora, 42, says her three granddaughters and many other children of Ejido Chilpancingo have been racked by similar ailments. She says a doctor believes the town's communal water, which often stings the skin upon touch, is responsible for the problems.

The foreign companies that have set up shop at Ejido Chilpancingo over the last 10 years are part of Mexico's *maquiladora* program. The program allows foreign companies to set up *maquiladoras,* or assembly plants, along a 65-mile corridor on the US-Mexico border, and to reap the benefits of low tariffs and cheap Mexican labor. It has drawn hundreds of US firms that manufacture everything from Barbie Dolls to parts for Patriot Missiles. It has also lured hundreds of thousands of Mexican laborers from the interior to take advantage of nearly 100 percent employment, and wages that exceed Mexico's $3 a day minimum.

Under Bush's Free Trade Agreement, towns like Ejido Chilpancingo would sprout up throughout Mexico.

No one is certain what impact the dumping and the fouled waters of Ejido Chilpancingo will ultimately have on the health of residents, but reports of a rare and fatal brain disease among newborns in Brownsville, Tex., which specialists suspect may be linked to pollution, has sent a chill the length of the 2,000-mile US-Mexico border.

A recent study of water samples taken by the Autonomous University of Baja California from one creek in Ejido Chilpancingo found dangerous levels of lead (more than 100 times acceptable levels), zinc, cadmium and chromium (commonly linked to some skin problems) in one stream that runs into the village.

A 1990 government study by Mexico's State Workers Institute of Social Security found that 16.4 percent of the community suffer from skin diseases, and 8.5 percent from respiratory ailments.

"They wouldn't do this in San Diego," thunders Maurilio Pachuca, a crafts merchant who has been organizing residents to stop the toxic dumping in his town. "Well, we're human beings, too!"

But the environmental damage created by industry in Otay Mesa doesn't stop at Ejido Chilpancingo.

On the US side of the border, Jesse Gomez, manager of the Effie May Organic Farm, grows cabbage, beets, carrots, lettuce and broccoli for American consumers on a 130-acre farm along the Rio Tijuana. When heavy rains flood the river, the contaminated water spreads over the land. Business is booming, though he worries that one day his crops will not meet environmental standards if the contamination isn't brought under control.

Gomez says his hopes lie in the construction of a monumental $200 million sewage treatment plant that will process 12 million gallons of raw sewage and toxic soup that run into the United States through the Rio Tijuana. The plant, which would be completed in 1995, is one of the cornerstones of the Bush administration's proposed solution to border pollution.

Some environmentalists say the sewage treatment plant won't solve Gomez's problems. "It's amazing how people in the US could ever feel safe when massive environmental contamination is happening on the other side of an imaginary political line," says Marco Kaltofen, an author of a study for the Boston-based National Toxic Campaign Fund on the impact of the *maquiladora* industry on water pollution along the border.

Kaltofen says sewage treatment plants cannot control the flow of industrial residues like petroleum, heavy metals and pesticides that pollute the Rio Tijuana. "The issue of toxic waste management has to be dealt with in the plants where the chemical waste originates," he says. Otherwise, "It's out the drain one day, on your dinner table in New York a week later," citing the movement of toxic chemicals from the factories into the food chain through farms along the Rio Tijuana.

The Integrated Environmental Plan, as the scheme is officially called, is designed to erect a line of defense against a number of polluted water-ways like the Rio Tijuana that flow into the United States. The plan also includes $75 million to improve drinking water and sewage systems in the hundreds of shanty towns that have sprung up along the US side in the last decade. Another $50 million would finance limited air-pollution management, training for Mexican inspectors, and a system for tracking the movement of raw chemicals imported into Mexico for manufacturing purposes.

Under Mexican law, US manufacturers in Mexico are required to return imported raw chemical waste and solvents used in the manufacturing process in the nation of origin. Only a tiny percentage of the chemical waste, however, finds its way back to the United States. As in the Otay Mesa industrial park, much of it is simply poured down drains, dropped in clandestine garbage dumps or buried in canyons. The estimated cost of cleaning up the border area run as high as $9 billion.

J. Michael McCloskey, chairman of the Sierra Club, calls the plan "short-sighted," because it confronts only the existing problem and fails to provide a long-term strategy for increasing funding as free trade extends throughout Mexico.

He also said the plan lacks an "action-forcing mechanism" to require industry to comply with Mexican or US environmental laws. Mexico has a notoriously poor track record on environmental enforcement. And so far, the US Environmental Protection Agency has only asked manufacturers to take voluntary steps to contain illegal dumping and to reduce the use of toxic materials.

According to Kaltofen, who led the water pollution study, the EPA has refused to sanction US corporate dumpers or even to acknowledge the extent of the US corporations' role in creating a toxic waste disaster zone along the border. The EPA, he says, treats pollution as a "made in Mexico" problem.

EPA spokesman Luke Hester acknowledges that border pollution is a "horrendous problem," and he says Mexico is improving its standards daily. Mexico, he says, has doubled the number of border environmental inspectors to 200, and earlier this month the government shut down eight facilities for environmental violations. "We're not going to turn Mexico around overnight," he says, "but there is movement. There's progress."

Environmentalists, meanwhile remain skeptical. Once a free trade agreement is signed, they fear President Bush will lose sight of his vision of a sound environment.

"What assurances," McCloskey asks, "do we have that all of these promises won't be quickly forgotten?"

Study Questions

1. What institutional practices and values helped create this problem?

2. Can those same institutional practices and values help resolve this problem, or will we need to use other values to instill new practices? Explain your answer.

3. Compare and contrast how De George, Werhane, and Velasquez would analyze this case. Which provides the best analysis? Why? Can you combine these approaches to develop a fuller view?

David P. Hanson

The Ethics of Development and the Dilemmas of Global Environmentalism

Environmentalism is a pledge to preserve the possibilities of our world for future generations. It is based on an acceptance of interdependence and the need for self-restraint in the interests of those yet to come. The environmental ethic forces us to confront the economists' truth: resources are limited, and not all interests can be satisfied. Whose interests shall we defend? What resources are we willing to sacrifice?

Environmental problems are increasingly matters of international concern. They are the result in large part of well-established patterns of economic development. In considering what to do, we should evaluate environmental issues in the broadest possible context by looking at the impact of historical patterns of global economic and social change to determine if the present rate of economic development can be sustained.

A strong argument can be made that the poorer countries have a moral right to economic development. The technological and economic developments of the last century have led to a moral revolution in Western societies. From the perspective of those who are accustomed to developed standards of living, the lives of most people in traditional societies are nasty, brutish, and short. Economic and technological development has produced enormous advances in basic human values: nutrition, sanitation, health, longevity, education, and overall security.

Economic development has also brought a moral resolution in social relations. In traditional agricultural societies, the control of land has been a major basis for social power. The pace of technological change has generally been very slow. In the short term, potential production has been constant. As a result, peasant and master have generally fought over a fixed quantity, where the gains of one come at the expense of the other. In this struggle, landlords had the superior position as long as there were too many peasants and a scarcity of arable land. As a result, class relations in traditional societies have often been characterized by violence and exploitation by the few, who are very rich, against the many, who are very poor.

Resources in the developed societies are produced by larger groups of people acting in cooperation. Competition in the market economies occurs as much among these competing corporate bureaucracies as between individual producers. The competitive position of companies in the market economies is increasingly determined by the judgment and skill employees bring to the production process. Even in the traditional manufacturing industries, quality and design have become as important as the more traditional criteria of cost and volume.

The increasing dependence of managerial elites on the commitment and skill of subordinates has led to increased demands for highly qualified personnel. Over the last fifty years, these processes have led to the development of a large middle class made up of managers, professionals, technicians, and skilled workers. With this has also come the development of a social ethic based on the acceptance of interdependency, consensus, professionalism, and the need for self-restraint.[1]

The reality of rapid and sustained economic growth in the Western societies has also transformed social conflicts. With economic growth, all can benefit in the long run. Social conflict becomes a barrier to the welfare of all rather than a tool for the prosperity of a few. The results of this transformation can be seen in the institutionalization of the welfare state and a general acceptance of environmental ideals.

The existing patterns of economic and technological development are historically unique. With few exceptions, the conditions of life for most people, in, for example, Mesopotamia in 2000 B.C. were not significantly different from the living standards of the average French citizen in the year 1500 A.D.

The pace of economic and technological development has accelerated dramatically in the last fifty years. Per capita energy consumption, a reasonable measure of technological and economic development, has risen thirty-fold in North America between 1870 and the present.[2]

If population growth can be curtailed, the availability of raw materials need not pose an obstacle to continued economic development. If we take care of the land, fertility can be sustained indefinitely. Few materials are ever lost from human use, they are only transformed and transported into different forms. The transformation of ore into iron, for example, does not make the metal any less available.

The major barriers to continued development are environmental. The traces of carbon dioxide (CO_2) and related gases in the atmosphere block the radiation of energy from the earth into space. Any significant increases in the atmospheric concentration of these gases will result in rising temperatures on earth.[3]

Unfortunately, the major energy source for economic development has been based on the conversion of mineral carbon into gaseous CO_2. Every year, we are dumping between 6 billion and 10 billion cons of CO_2

into the air. The amount of CO_2 in the atmosphere is increasing by almost 1 percent per year. If this rare of CO_2 dumping continues, we can expect an increase of 6 to 9 degrees Fahrenheit in the mean temperature of the earth over the next fifty years.[4]

The consequences for the human community are generally unfavorable. Climate zones should shift toward the poles. Both precipitation and the length of the growing season at high latitudes should increase. The increases should be most pronounced at higher latitudes. Arabic lands located around 30 degrees north-south latitude are likely to become increasingly arid. A most serious consequence is likely to be the melting of the polar icecaps and the rising level of the ocean. A 3-foot rise in the water level would make many cities uninhabitable and, in many parts of the world, could significantly reduce the amount of arabic land.[5]

The processes of climactic change will lead to environmental stress quite apart from the increase in final equilibrium temperatures. There will inevitably be a lag between the death of existing plant, animal, and human communities and the reestablishment of new species and technologies for life.

Unless we are willing to discount the welfare of future generations against our own, there is a compelling case for reducing the emission of carbon-based gases down to the level at which these gases are being removed from the atmosphere. Dumping at any higher level than zero net emission will slow the pace of change but may not change the result.[6]

Energy utilization in the developed economics can be reduced by at least half through conservation without significantly altering standards of living. Roughly equal amounts of energy are used for manufacturing, transportation, and heating and cooling. Major cuts in the amount of energy required for transportation and heating and cooling can be achieved through increased utilization of existing technology and through changes in the criteria and processes of public planing.[7]

There are limits to what can be achieved

toward energy conservation in manufacturing. The amount of energy required to produce the steel, aluminum, and cement for building new houses, roads, and cars is fixed by the laws of chemistry and physics. There do not seem to be any viable low-energy substitutes for these materials in the construction of the public and private goods we associate with economic development.

To an extent, we can shift over to less polluting energy sources. Solar power might be able to supply up to one-quarter of all electric energy needs.[8] Biomass could also provide a closed-cycle, carbon-based fuel source. Geothermal, wind, and ocean thermal energy conversion processes may replace carbon fuels.

A changeover from carbon-based fuels is not likely to be easy or cheap. Many of these technologies are best suited for the production of electricity, which has the problem of high capital costs and low conversion efficiencies. The initially promising option of nuclear power has already been derailed by a record of high costs, high risks, and high opposition. Solar power will not be feasible in many parts of the world or for many industrial applications. Raising crops, such as sugar cane, for conversion to fuels will take abundant supplies of land, capital, and labor.

A failure to restrict carbon utilization while promoting worldwide economic development will severely complicate the problems of the greenhouse effect. Raising worldwide per capita consumption of carbon-based energy to just one-fourth of current U.S. levels would increase aggregate CO_2 production by almost 90 percent. Even if the developed countries then reduced their per capita carbon consumption to the "one-quarter U.S." level, the aggregate result would still be a 26 percent increase in global CO_2 emissions.[9]

Maintaining a balance between economic development and energy conservation will be far more difficult for the poorer countries. Among the developed countries of the Organization for Economic Cooperation and Development, there is no relation between per capita income and per capita energy consumption. The correlation between per capita income and energy consumption for all nations though is 0.88.[10]

In effect, the demand for material- and energy-intensive goods in the developed countries is becoming satiated. Much of the growth in the developed economics is in the design, manufacture, and distribution of intellect-intensive goods, such as computers and aircraft.[11] The relation between energy consumption and economic development is much stronger for poorer nations. The demand for energy-intensive basic construction materials and manufactured goods, such as houses, roads, telephone systems, airports, and cars, has not yet been met.

In the developed world, a transition to a low-pollution economy for a given level of economic development could be implemented relatively easily. The resources of capital and technology are readily available. Rising costs of energy production could be offset through the adoption of conservation technologies in housing and transportation. The problems posed by changing energy sources will be far more severe in the developing countries. The poorer countries have tended to specialize in the production of basic minerals and agricultural goods, surprisingly energy-intensive processes. World markets in most of these goods are highly price competitive. Poorer countries that unilaterally restrict their rate of carbon utilization are likely to face increasingly severe competitive disadvantages.

Population size is another long-term limit to environmental protection and economic development. For a given level of technology and per capita income, the level of CO_2 production will be directly related to population size. Thus, we may be able to maintain a smaller population at a higher standard of living, subject to the constraints of carbon utilization.

Population growth tends to be quite high in the poorer countries and almost zero in the developed countries. In the poorest countries, the rate of increase may be as high as 3.5 to 4 percent per year, and the population will double every seventeen to twenty-two years. Thus, the social dislocations caused by population growth are far greater in the poorer countries, which have the fewest resources, and far less in countries with abundant resources. The imposition of pollution restraints on developing countries, leading to an increased demand for scarce intellectual and capital resources, is likely to accentuate these difficulties.

Rapid population growth in the poorer countries compounds the social problems of economic development. The work force is usually divided between a large traditional agricultural sector and a small, relatively modernized urban sector. Population growth in the traditional sector generally outpaces economic growth in the modern sector. At the same time, the modernization of agriculture often leads to the displacement of inefficient, labor-intensive share-cropping systems for more productive plantations using seasonal wage labor. The results of these two trends are seen in rising unemployment levels, the explosive growth of the urban population, and widening gaps between rich and poor.[12]

Population growth in poorer countries often leads to greater pressures on land utilization. In parts of Africa and Latin America, overpopulation and population growth have led to overcultivation, erosion, and an actual drop in per capita agricultural production. In Latin America, Africa, and Southeast Asia, this has led to a search for new agricultural land through the widespread destruction of the rain forests. Between 15 and 30 percent of total CO_2 production is caused by this deforestation.[13]

The moral importance of encouraging development in the Third World must therefore be balanced against the practical imperative of limiting atmospheric pollution. Progress on either goal will require effective action on population growth. Can any of these goals be achieved?[14]

An honest answer is not a comforting one. The problems of population control, economic growth, and atmospheric pollution require effective responses that must be based on what will be possible, which is not necessarily what will be fair or equitable.

The priorities for action can be evaluated according to the consequences of failure. A failure to stabilize atmospheric CO_2 levels will lead to a progressive deterioration in the conditions of life for all—rich and poor alike.

Partial solutions that only slow the rate of CO_2 buildup will merely postpone the greenhouse effects; they will not avoid them.

This is not true for the problem of population growth. To an extent, the problems of rapid population growth can potentially be offset by rapid economic and technological development. While a failure to control population growth is likely to result in a progressive immiseration of life, the effects will generally be confined to the poorer countries, where the population growth is outstripping resource development.

From a global perspective, the problems of economic development are less pressing. Like the issue of population growth, the consequences of a failure to develop are largely local. If we can solve the population problem, then a failure to promote economic development results in the persistence of the status quo rather than in a progressive reduction of human welfare. Furthermore, economic development is not an all-or-nothing proposition any increase in income will potentially increase social welfare.

There are also differences in the capacities of government for effective action on these three issues. Our capacity for effective action on the tasks of economic development, population control, and pollution abatement is significantly limited by our reliance on the independent nation-state as the fundamental political unit. The division of the world into many small administrative units has created an incentive for governments to emphasize local over global issues. In both the developed and underdeveloped world, governments generally respond to local interests over international concerns. We cannot expect governments to act where the local costs significantly outweigh local benefits.

The division of the world into rich and poor states also poses problems. The invention of guns, large sailing ships, the factory system, and the corporation gave the European powers a vast military and economic advantage over the traditional societies. The result was the global expansion of Europe through colonialism and empire. The benefits to the home countries came in the forms of cheap resources and guaranteed markets.

Colonialism broke down because the costs of occupation outstripped the benefits of market domination. It became easier to turn local administration over to local elites while maintaining ties of trade and investment.

The moral results of decolonization have been mixed. Independence is consistent with the strong ethical claim of all people for autonomy and self-determination. Forceful intervention by a stronger country into the affairs of a weaker one, even if the motives were to be good and results beneficial, is morally unacceptable. However, the colonial powers often turned authority over to local elites, who were likely to safeguard the interests of the colonial government in trade and investment ties. The end of colonialism has too often resulted in the emergence of ineffective or corrupt institutions of governance. Political control over trade ties with the outside world has often become a new source of power rivaling the traditional control over land. The results have often added a barrier to development: a tendency for Third World governments to emphasize short-term political and class interests over long-term popular development interests.

The end of colonialism has also put a new perspective on the roles of the Western powers. It is now the responsibility of the newly independent governments, not the colonial powers, to promote the interests of the developing societies. It is true, though, that lip service has been paid to international development efforts. Poor people can neither produce nor buy very much. Poor countries tend to be unstable and politically troubled. However, the desire of foreign governments to maintain existing military alliances, trade ties, and investment security guarantees encourages an accommodation with elites who may have little concrete interest in development.

The social and political interests of the upper classes in many developing countries also constitute major barriers to economic growth. Raising the income of the poor usually implies a radical shift in the positions and interests of the rich. If so, then development assistance programs will not be effective unless they are accompanied by substantial political changes in both the developing and the developed countries.[15]

What is to be done? How do we achieve the antithetical goals of restraining atmospheric pollution and promoting economic development? How can we encourage progress on population control, which may be a precondition for progress on either goal?

It is unrealistic to expect strong action by the poorer countries on problems of global pollution. On one hand, their contribution to both the magnitude of the problem and the effectiveness of the response are likely to be low. On the other hand, the costs to the poorer countries of limiting carbon-gas emissions, relative to available resources, are likely to be high. Countries that do not impose these costs on their local economies potentially enjoy cost advantages in international markets.

It is unlikely that the developed countries will be able to promote economic development effectively in the Third World. To the extent that the social structure and government policies of the developing countries constitute major impediments to development, the role of the developed countries is limited to encouragement and support. To the extent that these changes would upset existing political and economic ties, the developed countries are unlikely to support development efforts.

It is even more difficult for foreign governments to promote population control in the developing world. Economic development has a major effect on reducing family size. Where they are effective, family planning programs also reduce population growth. The effectiveness of these programs, however, depends heavily on an involved commitment by government and other social institutions. Neither economic development nor the necessary commitment to population control can be mandated from the outside.

It will be up to the developed countries to take effective leadership on the issue of carbon buildup in the atmosphere while essentially leaving the problems of population control and economic development to the poorer states.

The effectiveness of the response from the developed countries on the issue of pollution control will depend on their capacity for concerted action. Only by applying uniform rules for all developed countries can we avoid the conflict between economic advantage and environmental progress. Therefore, the desirability of program alternatives must be matched against the reasonable availability of international institutions through which they will be administered.

Fortunately, a major consolidation of political units at the supranational level has taken place among the developed nations over the last fifty years. World governance in the post-World War II period has been characterized by the development of specialized institutions such as the General Agreement on Tariffs and Trade, and International Monetary Fund (IMF), and the International Maritime Organization (IMO), which have been surprisingly effective. It is possible that institutions will develop to regulate global environmental conditions similar to the effective role played by the IMO in regulating oceanic pollution.

This does not answer the question of how the developed countries can encourage the less developed nations to follow suit. One possible tool is through influence over international energy markets and prices. Historically the consumption rate of carbon-based fuel in the developing world has declined when energy prices on international markets increased. The generally cooperative relation between the developed countries and the Organization of Petroleum Exporting Countries provides an example of how these market prices could be managed.

Unfortunately our ability to block the utilization of domestic coal or oil resources in countries such as China or to prevent deforestation in countries such as Brazil is limited given our lack of political control and their need for additional land and cheap energy. Other tools may be needed to encourage developing countries to pursue a domestic policy of environmental restraint.

The incentive might be based on a conditional acceptance of programs for capital subsidy and commodity price stabilization that many developing countries have been advocating in the United Nations and elsewhere. The penalty for noncompliance could come through conditional restrictions imposed by the developed countries on international credits and market access. The model for these programs could be taken from the role played by the IMF in encouraging domestic fiscal restraint.

Another key might be through technology transfer. Western countries could encourage the utilization of energy-efficient production techniques by reducing restrictions on the diffusion of the relevant technologies and by subsidizing the capital costs of energy-efficient equipment. A similar program of technology transfer has already been incorporated into the Law of the Sea treaty.

Another strategy might be to encourage developing countries to break away from the production of basic agricultural and industrial materials. Countries such as Mexico and Hong Kong have based development programs in large part on low-energy, labor-intensive manufacturing and assembly operations. Tourism and banking services are becoming increasingly important in many developing countries. Industries such as programming and software development are both highly labor intensive and potentially portable across national boundaries.

These programs are likely to be, at best, only partially effective. The experience of the IMF has shown that short-term considerations of domestic politics often override long-term incentives for reform from international agencies. Countries such as the People's Republic of China and the Soviet Union that have traditionally pursued policies of autarky are less likely to be swayed by incentives and penalties imposed by international institutions.

Even if the developing countries concentrated on low-pollution industries and adopted the best available technologies, development is likely to increase pollution levels. Development implies the acquisition of manufactured goods and a dramatic expansion of civil construction. The production of these goods is still energy intensive. In short, there are no easy solutions.

Notes

1. Rheinhard Bendix, *Work and Authority in Industry* (New York: Wiley, 1956); Amatai Etzioni, *The Comparative Analysis of Complex Organizations* (New York: Free Press, 1961).
2. Chauncey Starr, "Energy and Power," *Scientific American* (September 1971): 37–50.
3. C. Genthon et al., "Vostok Ice Core: Climate Response to CO_2 and Orbital Forcing Changes Over the Last Climactic Cycle," *Nature,* October 1, 1987, pp. 414–418. Other gases besides CO_2, such as methane and Freon, contribute significantly to the greenhouse effect. The concentrations of these gases have also been rising steadily in recent years, largely as a result of human activity. The distinctions among the sources and effects of these gases are not particularly relevant for this argument and will be ignored in the balance of this chapter. V. Ramanathan et al., "Trace Gas Trends and Their Potential Role in Climate Change," *Journal of Geophysical Research,* June 20, 1985, pp. 5547–5556.
4. Stephen H. Schneider, "The Changing Climate," *Scientific American* (September 1989): 70–79.
5. Michael Malik, "Fear of Flooding: Global Warming Could Threaten Low Lying Asia-Pacific Countries," *Far Eastern Economic Review,* December 22, 1988, pp. 20–21.
6. It is not clear how much CO_2, if any, we can safely release into the atmosphere. There are 740 million tons of CO_2 in the atmosphere. Each year natural processes release and absorb roughly 400 million tons of CO_2. The contribution from human activity is therefore a very small percentage of the total interchange. Schneider, "Changing Climate," p. 73.

    Other factors complicate predictions about climate changes. The earth has been unusually warm for the last few thousand years. It is possible that any temperature rise induced by human activities will be offset by a naturally occurring shift toward a colder climate. Finally, mathematical models are still too imprecise to allow for confident predictions about the long-term results of atmospheric changes. Particularly troublesome are the effects of cloud cover and estimates on the rate at which CO_2 will be taken up by the oceans. The analysis in this chapter reflects the predominant view. See James E. Hansen, director, Goddard Institute for Space Studies, "The Greenhouse Effect: Impacts on Global Temperatures and Regional Heat Waves," testimony before U.S. Senate, Committee on Energy and Natural Resources, June 23, 1988.

7. Earl Cook, "The Flow of Energy in an Industrial Society," *Scientific American* (September 1971): 135–144; Arthur Rosenfeld and David Hafemeister, "Energy Efficient Buildings," *Scientific American* (April 1988): 78–85.
8. Yoshihiro Hamakawa, "Photovoltaic Power," *Scientific American* (April 1987): 92.
9. Calculations based on data in John H. Gibbons, Peter D. Blair, and Holly L. Gwin, "Strategies for Energy Use," *Scientific American* (September 1989): 136–143.
10. Between 1980 and 1986, the U.S. gross national product grew by 16 percent. During this period, steel consumption dropped by 7 percent, and energy consumption declined by 3 percent. Data from *Statistical Abstract of the United States, 1988* (Washington, D.C.: U.S. Government Printing Office, 1989), pp. 422, 681, 741.
11. Calculations based on data from *ibid.,*pp. 805, 816.
12. James Clad and Margot Cohen, "Genesis of Dispair," *Far Eastern Economic Review,* October 20, 1988, pp. 24–30; "Development and Income Inequality Revisited," *Applied Economics* (April 1988): 509–531.
13. Schneider, "Changing Climate," p. 73; Lester A. Brown, Christopher Flavin, and Sandra Postel, "A World at Risk," in Lester A. Brown et al., *State of the World: 1989* (New York: Norton, 1989), pp. 1–20.
14. Several representatives from developing countries argued vigorously at a 1971 international conference in Founex, Switzerland, that the pollution and exhaustion of resources caused by economic activity in the developed countries are major barriers to the growth of the undeveloped economies. See "The Founex Report on Development and the Environment," *International Conciliation,* no. 586 (January 1972): 7–36; Miguel A. Ozorio de Almeida "The Confrontation between Problems of Development and the Environment," *International Conciliation,* no. 586 (January 1972): 37–56.
15. For a discussion of this point from the Alliance for Progress, see Walter LaFeber, "The Alliance in Retrospect," in Andrew MacGuire and Janet Welsh, eds., Bordering on Trouble: Resources and Politics in Latin America (Bethesda: Adler and Adler, 1986), pp. 337–388.

Study Questions

1. How does Hanson describe the present institutional environment of international business?

2. What new institutions does Hanson say we need to cope with the problem of global pollution? Are the values underlying these new institutions also new?

3. Who and what will promote the creation of Hanson's preferred institutions? Who and what will try to stop the creation of Hanson's preferred institutions? Explain your answer using an institutional framework. (See Frederick's article in the next chapter.)

4. Why can't the problem be solved by nations cleaning up their own backyards? If every nation did this, wouldn't the problem be eliminated?

CHAPTER 7

Risk–Reward
Relationships

INTRODUCTION

The articles and cases in this chapter examine the risk–reward relationship in two areas: employment and international investment in product development and production. These issues build on our discussion in Chapter 6 about the control and use of corporate property.

There are many other topics that could be included in this chapter: corporate mergers and acquisitions, insider trading, individual investment in financial instruments, socially responsible investing, and product liability, to name a few. There are many introductory business ethics and business and society texts that provide a good starting place to investigate these topics.

EMPLOYMENT

In the case of "Kate Simpson," by Cara F. Jonassen, a new employee is asked to reveal information that she believes is confidential. She likes her job and her boss, but she is angry at being put in this situation. There is no mention of any internal institutions she could use to get advice about what to do. One of the reasons her job is at risk is the Employment at Will doctrine.

In "Employment at Will and Due Process," Patricia H. Werhane and Tara J. Radin examine several reasons to support the doctrine of employment at will (EAW). EAW allows employers to fire employees without justification and it allows employees to quit without notification. EAW applies only to employer–employee relationships that are not protected by employment contracts, statute, or public policy. Werhane and Radin focus on the right of employers to sever the employment relationships without cause. They examine several reasons why employers may have such a right. They are based on property (Chapters 4 and 5), reciprocity, autonomy (Chapter 3), efficiency (Chapter 4), and utility (Chapter 3). They examine each of these reasons and find them only partially correct. They propose an analysis that gives employees more rights while still respecting basic values that underlie managerial discretion.

Anne T. Lawrence's case, "Johnson Controls and Protective Exclusion from the Workplace," concerns excluding women from certain production areas because of potential harm to their fetuses should they become pregnant. Some women underwent voluntary sterilization. Other women sued, arguing that the company policy violated their civil rights.

In "The Right to Risk Information and the Right to Refuse Workplace Hazards," Ruth R. Faden and Tom L. Beauchamp argue that business, government, and employees agree about the *general* right of employees to know about workplace hazards. The problem concerns the standards for disclosing this kind of information. One issue concerns proprietary information. Must a company disclose information that can put it at a competitive disadvantage? This can be especially difficult if the danger to employees is small and uncertain. Another issue concerns overlapping rules. The right to leave a dangerous job setting without being fired is defined in at least three different ways by different government statutes and regulatory agencies. Faden and Beauchamp point out that the search for standards often begins with the literature in medicine on informed consent. They note that the institutional settings of medicine are quite different from the institutional settings of business, and so the way the medical establishment has handled this issue may not be directly applicable to business and its institutional settings.

INTERNATIONAL

The case "Merck & Co., Int." by the Business Enterprise Trust, describes how Merck, one of the largest pharmaceutical companies in the world, had to decide whether to fund research for a drug that could cure "river blindness." River blindness afflicts a large population, but a population that is too poor to pay for the drug. Should Merck use its resources to do research on this drug? If successful, should they bear the cost of making and distributing it?

In "The Moral Authority of Transnational Corporate Codes," William C. Frederick argues that ethical principles are embedded in several key "multilateral compacts" (see the discussion of GATT in Chapter 5 for a similar approach). He compares and contrasts six multilateral agreements, showing that they have guidelines that are designed to protect employees, consumers, and the environment; to form strong market structures; and to reduce bribery. He argues that these guidelines are based on human rights and fundamental freedoms.

From the institutional perspective, Frederick is talking about the growth of international institutions to direct world trade. These institutions grow because governments, businesses, concerned citizens, and nongovernmental organizations (NGOs) *demand* them. Since none of these constituencies has the power to impose an institutional environment, they must negotiate the terms of that environment together. These multilateral compacts may represent early steps in the progression to worldwide institutions guiding business practice.

In "Wait International and Questionable Payments," Charles R. Kennedy, Jr., describes how the external legal and political environment and the interpretation of this environment by members of a firm can affect decision making in an MNC. The case describes how the 1988 Amendments to the FCPA influence changes in Wait International's Code of Conduct.

In "The Foreign Corrupt Practices Act Amendments of 1988: 'Death' of a Law,"

Bartley A. Brennan states that the 1988 amendments to the 1977 FCPA were justified on the grounds that the 1977 Act was inefficient, imposed U.S. values on other cultures, and was too vague to follow. Brennan argues that a closer examination of the relevant ethical, economic, and legal institutions and values shows that these reasons do not hold up. His discussion includes many topics we have discussed. Some of these are utility, rights, and fairness (Chapter 3), efficiency (Chapter 4), the reinforcement view of law, public choice theory, the FCPA (Chapter 5), the articles by De George and Werhane (Chapter 6), and in this chapter, the article by Frederick.

CASE: Kate Simpson
Cara F. Jonassen

Kate had joined the investment banking firm of Lawton Medical Financing, Inc., just four days earlier and was in the process of adjusting to her new working pace. Although the subsidiary of a larger firm, Lawton was still quite small, numbering only 60 people nationwide. The Atlanta branch, where Kate was working, consisted of three professionals and two secretaries. It was a young and rapidly growing enterprise that had an "all hands on deck" sort of atmosphere that Kate found both exhilarating and exhausting.

The senior vice president, David Moore, was intelligent, affable, and possessed of an almost obnoxious amount of energy. He seemed to have entered the field in part because of rather altruistic feelings; the idea of financing not-for-profit hospitals appealed to him. On the other hand, he was clearly a very savvy businessman whose relationships with his lenders were the envy of all his competitors. Having spoken with him several times before she even applied for a job, Kate had the impression that David had a very strong moral sense, yet he also had the pragmatic streak necessary for success. She wondered whether there were times when that pragmatism crossed the line to expediency.

Bill Hillman, the company's vice president, was only a few years younger than David, although his boyish appearance and rather brash manner made him seem quite a bit younger. He had joined the firm some 18 months earlier and had been transferred from New York to Atlanta about four months ago. He made it clear that he had no intention of moving back to New York and seemed to spend a lot of time on contingency plans to be implemented should the firm try to transfer him from Atlanta.

While David could analyze the numbers involved in a deal very quickly, he really enjoyed coming out with new approaches to financing and actually getting people to sit down and agree to his plans. Bill did not have the same diplomatic abilities, but he liked to make the numbers work and was actively involved in the solicitation of new business.

Kate, as the new associate, had ostensibly been assigned to do a massive spreadsheet on the details of all the deals done in hospital financing over the past two years. It was already becoming apparent, however, that she was really supposed to be available to help out in whatever capacity was needed. At one moment she might be researching some legislation for David, at the next she could be running an amortization schedule for Bill. Both of the men were anxious to teach her, and she was looking forward to learning as much as possible before returning to graduate business school in six months.

This morning had provided a new source of excitement. She would be making her first business trip the next day. As David had explained it, they were to help a hospital client in Nashville choose a consultant to do the feasibility study for the planned takeover of another facility. There were to be four consultants presenting proposals; she and David were to hear the presentations and summarize the differences among the proposals to the hospital's board of directors.

She had spent all morning poring over the three proposals they had received thus far. Of those three, the one by Roberts and Company had emerged as the best study for the least amount of money. She supposed that part of their job would be to help the administrator of the hospital keep the board of directors from automatically choosing the least expensive study; each of the three fees quoted probably far exceeded the annual salary of any of the board members. It was obvious that a study would never have been approved had it not been required for the official Certificate of Need, which itself was required for the acquisition.

Kate was annoyed when she glanced up and realized that it was already 3 P.M. Rice, Mitchell & Co., the fourth consulting firm, had promised her a copy of its proposal by 2:30 that afternoon. David would be back in the office at 4:30, expecting her to have finished her part of the assessment. When she called her secretary to see whether the proposal had arrived, she discovered that Bill, who she thought was not involved in this project, was on the phone with Bob Smythe, his counterpart at Rice, Mitchell, at that very moment. As she wandered over to Bill's office to find out what was going on, she felt a little annoyed since Smythe knew perfectly well from their conversation that morning that the preliminary work on this project was her responsibility.

Bill was about to hang up the phone as she entered. "Fine, Bob. You owe me one, but don't worry about it. Good luck getting the thing cranked out by morning."

She watched Bill slide the Roberts and Company proposal into a crisp envelope with Lawton Medical Financing emblazoned across the flap. "Those guys at Rice really like to run it down to the wire," he said. "Bob's just starting on the Nashville proposal. I told him we'd let him glance at Roberts's version of the thing. Why don't you run it upstairs for him? You can wait and make sure we get it back."

As she headed for the elevator, Kate was furious with Bill for having placed her in this situation. She had only a few moments to decide what she should do.

Study Questions

1. What additional information does Simpson need to make an informed decision?

2. What assumptions about the bidding process is she making?

3. What assumptions about the labor market did you make when you read this case for the first time?

4. Are there any internal institutions or practices she can use to guide her decision? If not, should there be?

5. What constitutes a wrong decision in this case? A right decision?

Patricia H. Werhane and Tara J. Radin

Employment at Will and Due Process

In 1980, Howard Smith III was hired by the American Greetings Corporation as a materials handler at the plant in Osceola, Arkansas. He was promoted to fork-lift driver and held that job until 1989, when he became involved in a dispute with his shift leader. According to Smith, he had a dispute with his shift leader at work. After work he tried to discuss the matter, but according to Smith, the shift leader hit him. The next day Smith was fired.

Smith was an "at will" employee. He did not belong to, nor was he protected by any union or union agreement. He did not have any special legal protection, for there was no apparent question of age, gender, race, or handicap discrimination. And he was not alleging any type of problem with worker safety on the job. The American Greetings Employee Handbook stated that "We believe in working and thinking and planning to provide a stable and growing business, to give such service to our customers that we may provide maximum job security for our employees." It did not state that employees could not be fired without due process or reasonable cause. According to the common law principle of Employment at Will (EAW), Smith's job at American Greetings could, therefore, legitimately be terminated at any time without cause, by either Smith or his employer, as long as that termination did not violate any law, agreement, or public policy.

Smith challenged his firing in the Arkansas court system as a "tort of outrage." A "tort of outrage" occurs when employer engages in "extreme or outrageous conduct" or intentionally inflicts terrible emotional stress. If such a tort is found to have occurred, the action, in this case, the dismissal, can be overturned.

Smith's case went to the Supreme Court of Arkansas in 1991. In court the management of American Greetings argued that Smith was fired for provoking management into a fight. The Court held that the firing was not in violation of law or a public policy, that the employee handbook did not specify restrictions on at will terminations, and that the alleged altercation between Smith and his shift leader "did not come close to meeting" criteria for a tort of outrage. Howard Smith lost his case and his job.[1]

The principle of EAW is a common-law doctrine that states that, in the absence of law or contract, employers have the right to hire, promote, demote, and fire whomever and whenever they please. In 1887, the principle was stated explicitly in a document by H. G. Wood entitled *Master and Servant.* According to Wood, "A general or indefinite hiring is prima facie a hiring at will."[2] Although the term "master-servant," a medieval expression, was once used to characterize employment relationships, it has been dropped from most of the recent literature on employment.[3]

In the United States, EAW has been interpreted as the rule that, when employees are not specifically covered by union agreement, legal statute, public policy, or contract, employers "may dismiss their employees at will . . . for good cause, for no cause, *or even for causes morally wrong,* without being thereby guilty of legal wrong."[4] At the same time, "at will" employees enjoy rights parallel to employer prerogatives, because employees may quit their jobs for any reason whatsoever (or no reason) without having to give any notice to their employers. "At will" employees range from part-time contract workers to CEOs, including all those workers and managers in the private sector of the economy not covered by agreements, statutes, or contracts. Today at least 60% of all employees in the private sector in the United States are "at will" employees. These employees have no rights to due process or to appeal employment decisions, and the employer does not have any obligation to give reasons for demotions, transfers, or dismissals. Interestingly, while employees in the *private* sector of the economy tend to be regarded as "at will" employees, *public*-sector employees have guaranteed rights, including due process, and are protected from demotion, transfer, or firing without cause.

Due process is a means by which a person can appeal a decision in order to get an explanation of that action and an opportunity to argue against it. Procedural due process is the right to a hearing, trial, grievance procedure, or appeal when a decision is made concerning oneself. Due process is also substantive. It is the demand for rationality and fairness: for good reasons for decisions. EAW has been widely interpreted as allowing employees to be demoted, transferred or dismissed without due process, that is, without having a hearing and without requirement of good reasons or "cause" for the employment decision. This is not to say that employers do not have reasons, usually good reasons, for their decisions. But there is no moral or legal obligation to state or defend them. EAW thus sidesteps the requirement of procedural and substantive due process in the workplace, but it does not preclude the institution of such procedures or the existence of good reasons for employment decisions.

EAW is still upheld in the state and federal courts of this country, as the Howard Smith case illustrates, although exceptions are made when violations of public policy and law are at issue. According to the *Wall Street Journal,* the court has decided in favor of the employees in 67% of the wrongful discharge suits that have taken place during the past three years. These suits were won not on the basis of a rejection of the principle of EAW but, rather, on the basis of breach of contract, lack of just cause for dismissal when a company policy was in place, or violations of public policy. The court has carved out the "public policy" exception so as not to encourage fraudulent or wrongful behavior on the part of employers, such as in cases where employees are asked to break a law or to violate state public policies, and in cases where employees are not allowed to exercise fundamental rights, such as the rights to vote, to serve on a jury, and to collect worker compensation. For example, in one case, the court reinstated an employee who was fired for reporting theft at his plant on the grounds that criminal conduct requires such reporting.[5] In another case, the court reinstated a physician who was fired from the Ortho Pharmaceutical Corporation for refusing to seek approval to test a certain drug on human subjects. The court held that safety clearly lies in the interest of public welfare, and employees are not to be fired for refusing to jeopardize public safety.[6]

During the last ten years, a number of positive trends have become apparent in employment practices and in state and federal court adjudications of employment disputes. Shortages of skilled managers, fear of legal repercussions, and a more genuine interest in employee rights claims and reciprocal obligations have resulted in a more careful spelling out of employment contracts, the development of elaborate grievance procedures, and in general less arbitrariness in employee treatment.[7] While there has not been a universal revolution in thinking about employee rights, an increasing number of companies have qualified their EAW prerogatives with restrictions in firing without cause. Many companies have developed grievance procedures and other means for employee complaint and redress.

Interestingly, substantive due process, the notion that employers should give good reasons for their employment actions, previously dismissed as legal and philosophical nonsense, has also recently developed positive advocates. Some courts have found that it is a breach of contract to fire a long-term employee when there is not sufficient cause— under normal economic conditions even when the implied contract is only a verbal one. In California, for example, 50% of the implied contract cases (and there have been over 200) during the last five years have been decided in favor of the employee, again, without challenging EAW.[8] In light of this recognition of implicit contractual obligations between employees and employers, in some unprecedented court cases *employees* have been held liable for good faith breaches of contract, particularly in cases of quitting without notice in the middle of a project and/or taking technology or other ideas to another job.[9]

These are all positive developments. At the same time, there has been neither an across-the-board institution of due process procedures in all corporations nor any direct challenges to the *principle* (although there have been challenges to the practice) of EAW as a justifiable and legitimate approach to employment practices. Moreover, as a result of mergers, downsizing, and restructuring, hundreds of thousands of employees have been laid off summarily without being able to appeal those decisions.

"At will" employees, then, have no rights to demand an appeal to such employment decisions except through the court system. In addition, no form of due process is a requirement preceding any of these actions. Moreover, unless public policy is violated, the law has traditionally protected employers from employee retaliation in such actions. It is true that the scope of what is defined as "public policy" has been enlarged so that "at will" dismissals without good reason are greatly reduced. It is also true that many companies have grievance procedures in place for "at will" employees. But such procedures are voluntary, procedural due process is not *required*, and companies need not give any reasons for their employment decisions.

In what follows we shall present a series of arguments defending the claim that the right to procedural and substantive due process should be extended to all employees in the private sector of the economy. We will defend the claim partly on the basis of human rights. We shall also argue that the public/private distinction that precludes the application of constitutional guarantees in the private sector has sufficiently broken down so that the absence of a due process requirement in the workplace is an anomaly.

EMPLOYMENT AT WILL

EAW is often justified for one or more of the following reasons:

1. The proprietary rights of employers guarantee that they may employ or dismiss whomever and whenever they wish.
2. EAW defends employee and employer rights equally, in particular the right to freedom of contract, because an employee voluntarily contracts to be hired and can quit at any time.
3. In choosing to take a job, an employee voluntarily commits herself to certain responsibilities and company loyalty, in-

cluding the knowledge that she is an "at will" employee.

4. Extending due process rights in the workplace often interferes with the efficiency and productivity of the business organization.
5. Legislation and/or regulation of employment relationships further undermine an already overregulated economy.

Let us examine each of these arguments in more detail. The principle of EAW is sometimes maintained purely on the basis of proprietary rights of employers and corporations. In dismissing or demoting employees, the employer is not denying rights to *persons*. Rather, the employer is simply excluding that person's *labor* from the organization.

This is not a bad argument. Nevertheless, accepting it necessitates consideration of the proprietary rights of employees as well. To understand what is meant by "proprietary rights of employees" it is useful to consider first what is meant by the term "labor." "Labor" is sometimes used collectively to refer to the workforce as a whole. It also refers to the activity of working. Other times it refers to the productivity or "fruits" of that activity. Productivity, labor in the third sense, might be thought of as a form of property or at least as something convertible into property, because the productivity of working is what is traded for remuneration in employee-employer work agreements. For example, suppose an advertising agency hires an expert known for her creativity in developing new commercials. This person trades her ideas, the product of her work (thinking), for pay. The ideas are not literally property, but they are tradable items because, when presented on paper or on television, they are sellable by their creator and generate income. But the activity of working (thinking in this case) cannot be sold or transferred.

Caution is necessary, though, in relating productivity to tangible property, because there is an obvious difference between productivity and material property. Productivity requires the past or present activity of working, and thus the presence of the person performing this activity. Person, property, labor, and productivity are all different in this important sense. A person can be distinguished from his possessions, a distinction that allows for the creation of legally fictional persons such as corporations or trusts that can "own" property. Persons cannot, however, be distinguished from their working, and this activity is necessary for creating productivity, a tradable product of one's working.

In dismissing an employee, a well-intentioned employer aims to rid the corporation of the costs of generating that employee's work products. In ordinary employment situations, however, terminating that cost entails terminating that employee. In those cases the justification for the "at will" firing is presumably proprietary. But treating an employee "at will" is analogous to considering her a piece of property at the disposal of the employer or corporation. Arbitrary firings treat people as things. When I "fire" a robot, I do not have to give reasons, because a robot is not a rational being. It has no use for reasons. On the other hand, if I fire a person arbitrarily, I am making the assumption that she does not need reasons either. If I have hired people, then, in firing them, I should treat them as such, with respect, throughout the termination process. This does not preclude firing. It merely asks employers to give reasons for their actions, because reasons are appropriate when people are dealing with other people.

This reasoning leads to a second defense and critique of EAW. It is contended that EAW defends employee and employer rights equally. An employer's right to hire and fire "at will" is balanced by a worker's right to accept or reject employment. The institution of any employee right that restricts "at will" hiring and firing would be unfair unless this restriction were balanced by a similar restriction controlling employee job choice in the workplace. Either program would do irreparable damage by preventing both employees and employers from continuing in voluntary employment arrangements. These arrangements are guaranteed by "freedom of contract," the right of persons or organiza-

tions to enter into any voluntary agreement with which all parties of the agreement are in accord.[10] Limiting EAW practices or requiring due process would negatively affect freedom of contract. Both are thus clearly coercive, because in either case persons and organizations are forced to accept behavioral restraints that place unnecessary constraints on voluntary employment agreements.[11]

This second line of reasoning defending EAW, like the first, presents some solid arguments. A basic presupposition upon which EAW is grounded is that of protecting equal freedoms of both employees and employers. The purpose of EAW is to provide a guaranteed balance of these freedoms. But arbitrary treatment of employees extends prerogatives to managers that are not equally available to employees, and such treatment may unduly interfere with a fired employee's prospects for future employment if that employee has no avenue for defense or appeal. This is also sometimes true when an employee quits without notice or good reason. Arbitrary treatment of employees *or* employers therefore violates the spirit of EAW—that of protecting the freedoms of both employees and employers.

The third justification of EAW defends the voluntariness of employment contracts. If these are agreements between moral agents, however, such agreements imply reciprocal obligations between the parties in question for which both are accountable. It is obvious that, in an employment contract, people are rewarded for their performance. What is seldom noticed is that, if part of the employment contract is an expectation of loyalty, trust, and respect on the part of an employee, the employer must, in return, treat the employee with respect as well. The obligations required by employment agreements, if these are free and noncoercive agreements, must be equally obligatory and mutually restrictive on both parties. Otherwise one party cannot expect— morally expect—loyalty, trust, or respect from the other.

EAW is most often defended on practical grounds. From a utilitarian perspective, hiring and firing "at will" is deemed necessary in productive organizations to ensure maximum efficiency and productivity, the goals of such organizations. In the absence of EAW unproductive employees, workers who are no longer needed, and even troublemakers, would be able to keep their jobs. Even if a business *could* rid itself of undesirable employees, the lengthy procedure of due process required by an extension of employee rights would be costly and time-consuming, and would likely prove distracting to other employees. This would likely slow production and, more likely than not, prove harmful to the morale of other employees.

This argument is defended by Ian Maitland, who contends,

> [I]f employers were generally to heed business ethicists and institute workplace due process in cases of dismissals and take the increased costs or reduced efficiency out of workers' paychecks— then they would expose themselves to the pirating of their workers by other employers who would give workers what they wanted instead of respecting their rights in the workplace. . . . In short, there is good reason for concluding that the prevalence of EAW does accurately reflect workers' preferences for wages over contractually guaranteed protections against unfair dismissal.[12]

Such an argument assumes (a) that due process increases costs and reduces efficiency, a contention that is not documented by the many corporations that have grievance procedures, and (b) that workers will generally give up some basic rights for other benefits, such as money. The latter is certainly sometimes true, but not always so, particularly when there are questions of unfair dismissals or job security. Maitland also assumes that an employee is on the same level and possesses the same power as her manager, so that an employee can choose her benefit package in which grievance procedures, whistleblowing protections, or other rights are included. Maitland implies that employers might include in that package of benefits their rights to practice the policy of unfair dis-

missals in return for increased pay. He also at least implicitly suggests that due process precludes dismissals and layoffs. But this is not true. Procedural due process demands a means of appeal, and substantive due process demands good reasons, both of which are requirements for other managerial decisions and judgments. Neither demands benevolence, lifetime employment, or prevents dismissals. In fact, having good reasons gives an employer a justification for getting rid of poor employees.

In summary, arbitrariness, although not prohibited by EAW, violates the managerial ideal of rationality and consistency. These are independent grounds for not abusing EAW. Even if EAW itself is justifiable, the practice of EAW, when interpreted as condoning arbitrary employment decisions, is not justifiable. Both procedural and substantive due process are consistent with, and a moral requirement of, EAW. The former is part of recognizing obligations implied by freedom of contract, and the latter, substantive due process, conforms with the ideal of managerial rationality that is implied by a consistent application of this common law principle.

EMPLOYMENT AT WILL, DUE PROCESS, AND THE PUBLIC/PRIVATE DISTINCTION

The strongest reasons for allowing abuses of EAW and for not instituting a full set of employee rights in the workplace, at least in the private sector of the economy, have to do with the nature of business in a free society. Businesses are privately owned voluntary organizations of all sizes from small entrepreneurships to large corporations. As such, they are not subject to the restrictions governing public and political institutions. Political procedures such as due process, needed to safeguard the public against the arbitrary exercise of power by the state, do not apply to private organizations. Guaranteeing such rights in the workplace would require restrictive legislation and regulation. Voluntary market arrangements, so vital to free enterprise and guaranteed by freedom of contract, would be sacrificed for the alleged public interest of employee claims.

In the law, courts traditionally have recognized the right of corporations to due process, although they have not required due process for employees in the private sector of the economy. The justification put forward for this is that since corporations are public entities acting in the public interest, they, like people, should be afforded the right to due process.

Due process is also guaranteed for permanent full-time workers in the public sector of the economy, that is, for workers in local, state and national government positions. The Fifth and Fourteenth Amendments protect liberty and property rights such that any alleged violations or deprivation of those rights may be challenged by some form of due process. According to recent Supreme Court decisions, when a state worker is a permanent employee, he has a property interest in his employment. Because a person's productivity contributes to the place of employment, a public worker is entitled to his job unless there is good reason to question it, such as poor work habits, habitual absences, and the like. Moreover, if a discharge would prevent him from obtaining other employment, which often is the case with state employees who, if fired, cannot find further government employment, that employee has a right to due process before being terminated.[13]

This justification for extending due process protections to public employees is grounded in the public employee's proprietary interest in his job. If that argument makes sense, it is curious that private employees do not have similar rights. The basis for this distinction stems from a tradition in Western thinking that distinguishes between the public and private spheres of life. The public sphere contains that part of a person's life that lies within the bounds of government regulation, whereas the private sphere contains that part of a person's life that lies outside those bounds. The argument is that the portion of a person's life that influences only that person should remain private and outside the purview of law and regulation, while the portion that influences the public welfare should be subject to the authority of the law.

Although interpersonal relationships on any level—personal, family, social, or employee-employer—are protected by statutes and common law, they are not constitutionally protected unless there is a violation of some citizen claim against the state. Because entrepreneurships and corporations are privately owned, and since employees are free to make or break employment contracts of their choice, employee-employer relationships, like family relationships, are treated as "private." In a family, even if there are no due process procedures, the state does not interfere, except when there is obvious harm or abuse. Similarly, employment relationships are considered private relationships contracted between free adults, and so long as no gross violations occur, positive constitutional guarantees such as due process are not enforceable.

The public/private distinction was originally developed to distinguish individuals from the state and to protect individuals and private property from public—i.e., governmental—intrusion. The distinction, however, has been extended to distinguish not merely between the individual or the family and the state, but also between universal rights claims and national sovereignty, public and private ownership, free enterprise and public policy, publicly and privately held corporations, and even between public and private employees. Indeed, this distinction plays a role in national and international affairs. Boutros Boutros-Ghali, the head of the United Nations, recently confronted a dilemma in deciding whether to go into Somalia without an invitation. His initial reaction was to stay out and to respect Somalia's right to "private" national sovereignty. It was only when he decided that Somalia had fallen apart as an independent state that he approved U.N. intervention. His dilemma parallels that of a state, which must decide whether to intervene in a family quarrel, the alleged abuse of a spouse or child, the inoculation of a Christian Scientist, or the blood transfusion for a Seventh-Day Adventist.

There are some questions, however, with

the justification of the absence of due process with regard to the public/private distinction. Our economic system is allegedly based on private property, but it is unclear where "private" property and ownership end and "public" property and ownership begin. In the workplace, ownership and control is often divided. Corporate assets are held by an ever-changing group of individual and institutional shareholders. It is no longer true that owners exercise any real sense of control over their property and its management. Some do, but many do not. Moreover, such complex property relationships are spelled out and guaranteed by the state. This has prompted at least one thinker to argue that "private property" should be defined as "certain patterns of human interaction underwritten by public power."[14]

This fuzziness about the "privacy" of property becomes exacerbated by the way we use the term "public" in analyzing the status of businesses and in particular corporations. For example, we distinguish between privately owned business corporations and government-owned or -controlled public institutions. Among those companies that are not government owned, we distinguish between regulated "public" utilities whose stock is owned by private individuals and institutions; "publicly held" corporations whose stock is traded publicly, who are governed by special SEC regulations, and whose financial statements are public knowledge; and privately held corporations and entrepreneurships, companies and smaller businesses that are owned by an individual or group of individuals and not available for public stock purchase.

There are similarities between government-owned, public institutions and privately owned organizations. When the air controllers went on strike in the 1980s, Ronald Reagan fired them, and declared that, as public employees, they could not strike because it jeopardized the public safety. Nevertheless, both private and public institutions run transportation, control banks, and own property. While the goals of private and public institutions differ in that public institutions are allegedly supposed to place the public good

ahead of profitability, the simultaneous call for businesses to become socially responsible and the demand for governmental organizations to become efficient and accountable further question the dichotomy between "public" and "private".

Many business situations reinforce the view that the traditional public/private dichotomy has been eroded, if not entirely, at least in large part. For example, in 1981, General Motors (GM) wanted to expand by building a plant in what is called the "Poletown" area of Detroit Poletown is an old Detroit Polish neighborhood. The site was favorable because it was near transportation facilities and there was a good supply of labor. To build the plant, however, GM had to displace residents in a nine-block area. The Poletown Neighborhood Council objected, but the Supreme Court of Michigan decided in favor of GM and held that the state could condemn property for private use, with proper compensation to owners, when it was in the public good. What is particularly interesting about this case is that GM is not a government-owned corporation; its primary goal is *profitability,* not the common good. The Supreme Court nevertheless decided that it was in the *public* interest for Detroit to use its authority to allow a company to take over property despite the protesting of the property owners. In this case the public/private distinction was thoroughly scrambled.

The overlap between private enterprise and public interests is such that at least one legal scholar argues that "developments in the twentieth century have significantly undermined the 'privateness' of modern business corporations, with the result that the traditional bases for distinguishing them from public corporations have largely disappeared."[15] Nevertheless, despite the blurring of the public and private in terms of property rights and the status and functions of corporations, the subject of employee rights appears to remain immune from conflation.

The expansion of employee protections to what we would consider just claims to due process gives to the state and the courts more opportunity to interfere with the private economy and might thus further skew what is seen by some as a precarious but delicate balance between the private economic sector and public policy. We agree. But if the distinction between public and private institutions is no longer clear-cut, and the traditional separation of the public and private spheres is no longer in place, might it not then be better to recognize and extend constitutional guarantees so as to protect all citizens equally? If due process is crucial to political relationships between the individual and the state, why is it not central in relationships between employees and corporations since at least some of the companies in question are as large and powerful as small nations? Is it not in fact inconsistent with our democratic tradition not to mandate such rights?

The philosopher T. M. Scanlon summarizes our intuitions about due process. Scanlon says,

> The requirement of due process is one of the conditions of the moral acceptability of those institutions that give some people power to control or intervene in the lives of others.[16]

The institution of due process in the workplace is a moral requirement consistent with rationality and consistency expected in management decision-making. It is not precluded by EAW, and it is compatible with the overlap between the public and private sectors of the economy. Convincing business of the moral necessity of due process, however, is a task yet to be completed.

Notes

1. *Howard Smith III v. American Greetings Corporation,* 304 Ark. 596: 804 S.W. 2d 683.
2. H. G. Wood. *A Treatise on the Law of Master and Servant* (Albany, N.Y.: John D. Parsons, Jr., 1877), p. 134.
3. Until the end of 1980 the *Index of Legal Periodicals* indexed employee-employer relationships under this rubric.
4. Lawrence E. Blades. "Employment at Will versus Individual Freedom: On Limiting the Abusive Exercise of Employer Power," *Columbia Law Review,* 67 (1967), p. 1405, quoted from *Payne v. Western,* 81 Tenn. 507 (1884), and *Hutton v. Watters,* 132 Tenn. 527, S.W. 134 (1915).
5. *Palmateer v. International Harvester Corporation,* 85 Ill. App. 2d 124 (1981).
6. *Pierce v. Ortho Pharmaceutical Corporation* 845 NJ 58 (NJ 1980), 417 A.2d 505. See also Brian Heshizer, "The New Common Law of Employment: Changes in the Concept of Employment at Will," *Labor Law Journal,* 36 (1985), pp. 95–107.
7. See David Ewing, *Justice on the Job: Resolving Grievances in the Nonunion Workplace* (Boston: Harvard Business School Press, 1989).
8. See R. M. Bastress, "A Synthesis and a Proposal for Reform of the Employment at Will Doctrine," *West Virginia Law Review,* 90 (1988), pp. 319–51.
9. See "Employees' Good Faith Duties," *Hastings Law Journal,* 39 (198). See also *Hudson v. Moore Business Forms,* 609 Supp. 467 (N.D. Cal. 1985).
10. See *Lockner v. New York,* 198 U.S. (1905), and Adina Schwartz, "Autonomy in the Workplace," in Tom Regan, ed., *Just Business* (New York: Random House, 1984), pp. 129–40.
11. Eric Mack, "Natural and Contractual Rights," *Ethics,* 87 (1977), pp. 153–59.
12. Ian Maitland, "Rights in the Workplace: A Nozickian Argument," in Lisa Newton and Maureen Ford, eds., *Taking Sides* (Guilford, CT: Dushkin Publishing Group), 1990, pp. 34–35.
13. Richard Wallace, "Union Waiver of Public Employees' Due Process Rights," *Industrial Relations Law Journal,* 8 (1986), pp. 583–87.
14. Morris Cohen, "Dialogue on Private Property," *Rutgers Law Review* 9 (1954), p. 357. See also *Law and the Social Order* (1933) and Robert Hale, "Coercion and Distribution in a Supposedly Non-Coercive State," *Political Science Quarterly,* 38 (1923), p. 470; John Brest, "State Action and Liberal Theory," *University of Pennsylvania Law Review* (1982), pp. 1296–1329.
15. Gerald Frug, "The City As a Legal Concept," *Harvard Law Review,* 93 (1980), p. 1129.
16. T. M. Scanlon, "Due Process," in J. Roland Pennock and John W. Chapman, eds., *Nomos XVIII: Due Process* (New York: New York University Press, 1977), p. 94.

Study Questions

1. How do Werhane and Radin use ethical, economic, and legal concepts to critique the traditional employment at will doctrine?

2. How do they use these same concepts to

suggest changes to the employment at will doctrine?

3. Are Werhane and Radin suggesting regulative or constitutive changes to the institutional environment of business (see Chapters 3 and 4)? Explain.

4. Use Werhane and Radin's analysis to evaluate the Kate Simpson case.

CASE: **Johnson Controls and Protective Exclusion from the Workplace**

Anne T. Lawrence

In 1990, Cheryl Cook was employed in a nontraditional job: She ran the ball mill, a two-story-tall machine that made lead oxide at the Johnson Controls automotive battery plant in Bennington, Vermont. To get the job, the 34-year-old mother of two had had to undergo surgical sterilization. Under a "fetal protection" policy, adopted in 1982, Johnson Controls had decided to hire only infertile women for production jobs, because of the possible effects of maternal exposure to lead on unborn children. The United Auto Workers, the union representing most of the company's production workers, believed that the company's policy was illegal. In 1984, the union filed suit on behalf of all adversely affected employees, charging sex discrimination under Title VII of the Civil Rights Act. Like many women who worked for Johnson Controls, Cheryl Cook expressed resentment at the company's assumption that she was unable to make responsible reproductive decisions on her own. "[Y]ou should choose for yourself," she told a reporter. "Myself, I wouldn't go in there if I could get pregnant. But they [company managers] don't trust you."[1]

Johnson Controls, for its part, vigorously defended its policy of protective exclusion, despite the apparently discriminatory impact of the policy and the tough decisions it forced many female job applicants and employees to make. Medical evidence clearly showed, the company believed, that maternal exposure to lead could interfere with fetal development, causing neurological damage and other birth defects. "To knowingly poison unborn children," the company reasoned, was "morally reprehensible."

Moreover, the company argued that it had a legitimate right to protect itself from the expensive liability lawsuits that could result if a child were born with impairments traceable to its mother's occupational exposure. The company, which was in compliance with Occupational Safety and Health Administration (OSHA) lead standards for adult exposure, maintained that there was no technologically or economically feasible way to reduce lead levels in the battery-making process sufficiently to eliminate risk to the fetus.

After a long journey through the judicial system, the dispute between Johnson Controls and employees who believed themselves victimized by its policy came before the U.S. Supreme Court. In March 1991, after a series of contradictory decisions by lower courts, the high court would decide the legality of the Johnson Controls policy of protective exclusion in a land-mark case that appeals court Judge Frank Easterbrook called "likely the most important sex discrimination case in any court since 1964, when Congress enacted Title VII [of the Civil Rights Act]." In the balance hung not only the fate of female employees and job applicants at Johnson Controls, but also that of perhaps as many as 20 million other women whose jobs exposed them to substances potentially hazardous to the fetus.

Originally presented at a meeting of the North American Case Research Association, November 1991. Research was supported in part by the San Jose State University College of Business. This case was written from public sources, without the cooperation of management, solely for the purpose of stimulating student discussion. All events and individuals are real. Copyright © 1993 by the *Case Research Journal* and Anne T. Lawrence.

JOHNSON CONTROLS, INC.

At the time of the Supreme Court decision, Johnson Controls, Inc., was one of the nation's leading manufacturers of automotive lead batteries, particularly for the replacement parts market. Between its founding at the turn of the century and the late 1970s, Johnson Controls was engaged chiefly in the production of environmental controls, automotive seating, and miscellaneous plastic products. In 1978, the company purchased Globe Union, Inc., an independent battery manufacturer that had been in business for over 50 years. In 1990, the Globe Battery Division of Johnson Controls operated fourteen plants, extending from Bennington, Vermont, to Fullerton, California, and accounted for 16 percent of Johnson's sales and 20 percent of its income. That year, the company as a whole posted sales of $4.5 billion and employed 43,500 workers—approximately 5400 of them in the battery division.

Prior to the 1960s, few if any women worked in production jobs at Globe Union, reflecting long-standing historical patterns of gender segregation in which men worked in production jobs and women in office and support roles. In the 1970s, at Globe Union—as in many other businesses in those years—women began moving in increasing numbers into traditionally male occupations. Even by the mid-1980s, however, only a small percentage of women had production jobs. In the Bennington, Vermont, plant, for example, only 5 percent of the production work force was female. Women never penetrated the top echelons of the company: In 1990, the company's fifteen top executives and twelve directors were all men.

The production process used in Johnson's Globe Battery Division plants necessarily entailed exposure to lead, which is the element that enables an automotive battery to store and deliver electricity. As Denise Zutz, director of corporate communications at Johnson, bluntly put it, "[Without lead] no one would be driving a car."[2] To make a battery, Johnson Controls workers mixed lead oxide to form a paste, which was then compressed to form lead plates in the core of the battery. Lead dust and vapors were produced at multiple points in the production process. Johnson Controls, like other battery manufacturers, had made numerous efforts to develop a nonlead-based battery. Although several alternatives were currently in the experimental stage—including a zinc-bromide battery that Johnson had been researching for several years—none had yet been successfully developed for commercial use.

LEAD TOXICITY

Lead, a heavy metal, is one of the oldest known toxins. When lead particles are inhaled or ingested, they damage the central nervous, immune, reproductive, cardiovascular, and excretory systems of the body. At low levels, lead causes fatigue and irritability; at high levels, loss of consciousness, seizures, and eventually death. Lead-exposed individuals run a heightened risk of heart attack and stroke. According to the Centers for Disease Control (CDC), lead becomes dangerous to adults at blood levels of 50 micrograms per deciliter (μg/dl). Children suffer toxic effects from lead at even lower levels. Lead poisoning in children is caused mainly by inhaling leaded gasoline fumes and by swallowing peeling, leaded paint in older, poorly maintained buildings. At blood levels of around 25 μg/dl, children begin to show characteristic signs of lead poisoning: irritability, hyperactivity, lowered attention span, and learning difficulties. Higher doses, as in adults, can have even more serious consequences.

Lead also adversely affects the unborn. Lead in a pregnant woman's bloodstream crosses the placenta and enters the fetus's blood, at concentration levels similar to the mother's. Because its central nervous system develops rapidly, the fetus is particularly sensitive to lead. Exposure in the womb may lead to irreversible brain damage, resulting in intellectual and motor retardation, behavioral abnormalities, and learning deficiencies. It can also cause spontaneous abortion, low birth weight, premature delivery, and stillbirth. Adverse effects to the fetus have been detected at blood levels as low as 10 μg/dl, well below the CDC standard for adults.

One of the special difficulties with protecting the fetus is that lead is an accumulative toxicant, building up over time in the blood, soft tissues, and bones. Lead's half-life in the body is 5 to 7 years, and it often remains long after an individual has been removed from a high-lead environment. By a cruel twist of medical fate, pregnancy may actually increase levels of lead in the blood, since bones often decalcify during pregnancy to provide calcium to the developing fetus, mobilizing lead stored in the bones. Studies have shown that maternal lead blood levels may as much as double during pregnancy, even without additional exposure. Thus removing a woman from a high-lead workplace when a pregnancy is discovered—or even when one is planned—does not eliminate the risk of lead-caused damage to the fetus.

The effects of lead on male reproductive health are less well understood and more controversial. Lead affects male reproductive capacity: Lead-exposed men may experience reduced sexual drive and, at high levels, impotence. Lead may also cause genetic damage to sperm, leading to birth defects. Most of the evidence for male-mediated effects comes from animal studies. A 1990 University of Maryland study, for example, found that lead-exposed male rats mated with unexposed females produced offspring whose brains developed abnormally. The researchers were unable to explain the biological mechanisms by which such male-mediated effects occurred, however, and the results of this study were not confirmed for humans.

GOVERNMENT REGULATION OF LEAD EXPOSURE

In view of the medical evidence on the hazards of lead, the Occupational Safety and Health Administration (OSHA) in 1978 adopted a standard requiring that employees be removed from worksites when their blood levels reached 50 μg/dl, based on an average of three consecutive blood tests. These employees were permitted to return when their blood levels fell to 40 μg/dl or below.

In setting its lead standard, OSHA also considered the impact of lead exposure on the fetus and the possible need to exclude pregnant or fertile women from high-lead workplaces. The agency concluded:

> [T]here is no basis whatsoever for the claim that women of child-bearing age should be excluded from the workplace in order to protect the fetus or the course of pregnancy.[3]

OSHA did not set a separate standard for fetal exposure. However, the agency did recommend that individuals of both sexes who planned to conceive a child maintain blood levels below 30 μg/dl "because of the demonstrated adverse effects of lead on reproductive function in both males and females as well as the risk of genetic damage of lead on both the ovum and sperm."[4]

THE JOHNSON CONTROLS LEAD HYGIENE PROGRAM

Well before the OSHA lead standard was established, Globe Union and its successor, Johnson Controls, moved to protect their employees from the adverse effects of lead. In 1969 Dr. Charles Fishburn, then working for Globe Union and later the chief architect of Johnson's fetal protection policy, introduced a comprehensive lead hygiene program at the company. Globe (and later Johnson) instituted "housekeeping" measures and engineering controls to reduce lead dust and vapors in the air. For example, the company installed pumps to supply clean air to workstations and central vacuum systems and powered floor scrubbers and sweepers to keep its plants as free as possible of lead dust.

To prevent workers from carrying home lead particles, work clothing and footwear were provided by the company, and employees were given paid time at the day's end to shower and change into their personal attire. The company provided respirators and taught employees how to use them. Johnson maintained an active program of blood testing, and employees with blood levels above 50 µg/dl were transferred without loss of pay or benefits to jobs where the average level of workers was below 30. After purchasing Globe in 1978, Johnson invested $15 million in additional environmental engineering controls at its battery division plants.

Many observers, including those from the union, agreed that Globe Union, and later Johnson Controls, made significant progress in their industrial hygiene programs during the 1970s and 1980s. During this period, the company remained in substantial compliance with OSHA lead standards.[5]

INSTITUTING A VOLUNTARY POLICY

In 1977, partly in response to the growing number of women in production jobs in its plants, Globe Union established its first policy on women in lead-exposed jobs. In promulgating this policy, the company noted:

> [Protection] of the unborn child is the immediate and direct responsibility of the parents. While the medical profession and the company can support them in the exercise of this responsibility, it cannot assume it for them without simultaneously infringing their rights as persons. . . .
>
> Since not all women who can become pregnant wish to become mothers, . . . it would appear to be illegal discrimination to treat all who are capable of pregnancy as though they will become pregnant.[6]

Observing that scientific evidence at that time had not conclusively established the risk of lead exposure to the fetus, the company did not officially exclude women capable of bearing children from jobs that exposed them to lead. However, the company issued the following warning:

> [We] do feel strongly that those women who are working in lead exposure . . . and those women who wish to be considered for employment be advised that there is risk, [and] . . . we recommend not working in lead if they are considering a family.[7]

The company also required each woman to sign a statement saying that she understood the company's recommendation.

Globe Union did not guarantee transfers for women requesting removal from high-lead-exposure jobs, nor did it guarantee equal wage rates for those who did transfer.

THE 1982 FETAL PROTECTION POLICY

In 1982, the company—now under the management of Johnson Controls—instituted a new "fetal protection" program in all its battery plants. Citing its ethical obligation not to engage in any activity threatening the well-being of any person, Johnson reversed its voluntary policy and announced its intention to exclude all fertile women from high-lead-exposure jobs in its battery manufacturing plants. It stated its policy as follows:

> [I]t is the [Globe Battery] Division's policy that women who are pregnant or who are capable of bearing children will not be placed into jobs involving lead exposure or which could expose them to lead through the exercise of job bidding, bumping, transfer or promotion rights. This policy is intended to reduce or eliminate the possible unhealthy effects of lead on the unborn children of pregnant employees or applicants.[8]

Johnson defined as "capable of bearing children" any woman under the age of 70 who could not provide medical documentation of sterility, regardless of her age, marital status, sexual orientation, fertility of her partner, use of contraception, or intention to bear children. The company explicitly stated that it was not its intention to encourage surgical sterilization:

> [The policy] is in no way intended to support or encourage women of child-bearing capability to seek to change this status. Employees are strongly advised against such action.[9]

For women already employed in lead-exposed positions, Johnson Controls applied a "grandfather" clause: They could continue to work at their present positions as long as they were able to maintain blood levels below 30 µg/dl in regular tests. If blood levels rose, they were permitted to transfer to other jobs without loss of pay, seniority, or benefits.

The fetal protection policy applied to all jobs in which any employee had recorded a blood level over 30 µg/dl, or where any air sample had exceeded 30 µg per cubic meter, during the previous year. Such high-lead-exposure jobs typically made up less than half of all production jobs. In practice, however, Johnson Control's new policy excluded fertile women from virtually all production jobs, since most positions—even if not lead-exposed—were connected by chains of job bidding, transfer, or promotion to jobs that were exposed.

JUSTIFYING THE NEW POLICY

In justifying its move from a voluntary policy to one of protective exclusion, the main argument of Johnson Controls was that the old policy had not worked. Between 1977 and 1982, at least six women in high-lead positions had become pregnant while maintaining blood levels above 30 µg/dl. One of the children born to these mothers, according to the company's occupational physician, showed some signs of hyperactivity, although this condition was never definitively traced to the mother's occupational

exposure to lead. In addition, the company claimed that increased scientific understanding of the risk of lead exposure to the fetus since 1977 had heightened its concern for
fetal health.

The company informed its employees that it had considered and rejected several
less discriminatory policies, including voluntary exclusion, limiting exclusion to women
actually pregnant or planning to become so, and transferring women whose blood lead
levels rose above certain levels. Many pregnancies are unplanned, the company argued.
Moreover, women often are unaware of pregnancy during the initial weeks, and—in any
case—removal from the job after pregnancy has begun may be insufficient to eliminate
fetal risk. To protect the unborn, therefore, Johnson officials argued they had no choice
but to bar fertile women from high-lead jobs altogether.

Although the main stated reason of Johnson Controls for adopting an exclusionary
policy was its concern for the unborn, the company was also influenced by fears of liability lawsuits from children adversely affected by their mother's occupational exposure
to lead. The company believed it had a legal obligation to avoid injuries to "third parties," such as fetuses, resulting from the hazards of its manufacturing operations. In a
brief filed later before the Supreme Court, the company's attorneys maintained:

> In this day and age, it cannot seriously be disputed that a company's desire to avoid di-
> rect harm to its employees and their families, its customers, and its neighbors from its
> own toxic hazards goes to the heart of its "normal operation."

The brief went on to quote with approval an opinion in an earlier court decision:

> [The] normal operation of a business encompasses ethical, legal and business concerns
> about the effect of an employer's activities on third parties. An employer might be
> validly concerned on a variety of grounds both practical and ethical with the hazards of
> his workplace on the children of his employees.[10]

Although it delicately avoided addressing the issue directly, the company's point
was clear: It was concerned about potential liability risk.

In assessing the extent of the company's exposure to possible liability lawsuits,
Johnson Controls managers faced considerable uncertainty. Although employee suits
against employers for injury at work are preempted by workers' compensation laws,
most states permit the live-born child of an employee to sue its mother's employer for
injuries caused in utero by the employer's negligence. Such suits, however, have historically been difficult to win. The causes of most birth defects are elusive. Moreover, in a
situation in which an employer had followed all OSHA regulations and warned the
mother of known hazards, a child would be hard-pressed to prove employer negligence.
Prior to the time the Supreme Court considered the Johnson Controls case, in only one
instance had a child sued an employer for its mother's occupational exposure to lead;
this case had resulted in a jury verdict in favor of the employer, even though the employer had violated OSHA's maximum exposure rules.[11]

WOMEN'S WORKPLACE RIGHTS

Johnson Controls' new policy of protective exclusion—at the time probably the most
comprehensive of any in place in U.S. industry—represented a bold challenge to the
Civil Rights Act of 1964 and its subsequent amendments. The company's position raised

serious questions about the nature of women's rights in the workplace, and how these were to be balanced against possible rights of the fetus and the employer.

Title VII of the Civil Rights Act of 1964 prohibits discrimination in employment on the basis of sex, as well as on the basis of race, color, religion, and national origin. In 1978, Congress passed the Pregnancy Discrimination Act (PDA), which amended Title VII by providing that the term "on the basis of sex" include "because of or on the basis of pregnancy, childbirth, or related medical conditions." That is, pregnant workers (and others distinguished by "related" conditions, such as potential for pregnancy) must, for all employment purposes, be afforded the same treatment as other workers with similar abilities.

In interpreting Title VII, as amended, the courts subsequently developed two frameworks for analyzing discrimination claims. If an employment policy is discriminatory on its face—for example, if it overtly excludes women from a particular job—it is permitted only if the employer can demonstrate that gender is a bona fide occupational qualification (BFOQ). In practice, the courts have interpreted BFOQs narrowly. For example, a department store may legitimately hire only men to model male fashions, but a fire department may not hire only men as fire fighters simply because the position is physically demanding.

On the other hand, if an employment policy is neutral on its face but in fact has an adverse impact on members of a protected class, the courts apply a weaker standard. In such so-called "disparate impact" cases, the employer need only demonstrate that its policy is dictated by a "business necessity." According to the United States Court of Appeals for the Fourth Circuit, "[The] test is whether there exists an overriding legitimate business purpose such that the practice is necessary to the safe and efficient operation of the business."[12]

In practice, the courts have held that employment practices that have a disparate impact are defensible only if they are clearly job-related. For example, a police department may be permitted to use written employment tests, even if minorities perform less well on them than do whites, if it can demonstrate that the tests accurately predict successful job performance.

The entry of increasing numbers of women into hazardous jobs in the 1970s and 1980s—and the subsequent efforts of employers to exclude them in the name of fetal protection—called the legal question: Were gender-based policies of exclusion to protect the unborn legal or illegal? And should specific policies be judged under the more restrictive BFOQ or the less restrictive "business necessity" standard? In 1982, when Johnson Controls managers adopted their fetal protection policy, these difficult matters of law remained unresolved.

THE UNITED AUTO WORKERS LAWSUIT

The union representing Johnson Controls employees, the United Auto Workers (UAW), believed that protective exclusion was unfair—and illegal. In 1984 the union filed suit, charging that Johnson's fetal protection policy constituted illegal sex discrimination under Title VII and the Pregnancy Discrimination Act. Individual plaintiffs in the case included Mary Craig, a young woman who underwent sterilization in 1983 to keep her job; Elsie Nason, a 50-year-old divorcee whose pay was cut when she was forced to transfer out of a high-lead-exposure job; and Donald Penney, who was denied a transfer out of a high-lead area that he requested because he intended to start a family.

The union's key argument was that the policy of Johnson Controls violated Title VII of the Civil Rights Act because sterility was not a bona fide occupational qualification. The UAW brief argued that the company's policy was discriminatory on its face:

> Because Johnson Controls policy excludes women—and only women—from certain jobs precisely because of their capacity to bear children—that policy is facially discriminatory under the statute [Title VII] as amended by the PDA [the Pregnancy Discrimination Act].[13]

Therefore, Johnson Controls would have to demonstrate a BFOQ. But sterility, the union insisted, had nothing to do with battery-making: "Fertile women . . . produce batteries as efficiently and proficiently as anyone else."[14]

Since fertile women were just as capable of effectively performing the work as were men and infertile women, the employer had not demonstrated a BFOQ. In response to the contention of Johnson Controls that reproductive risks were mediated exclusively through the mother, the union presented medical evidence showing that lead posed a reproductive hazard for men as well as for women. Thus, the appropriate response was not to exclude women, but to reduce workplace exposures to lead for all workers, male and female. The union did not dismiss the employer's concern for fetal health as trivial or insincere. Indeed, the UAW acknowledged in its brief that "certain ethical and moral goals, including promoting child and fetal health, are widely accepted in this society."[15] However, it maintained that the determinants of fetal health were complex and influenced by many factors in addition to workplace hazards. In fact, the union argued, exclusionary policies themselves may be hazardous to fetal health, by pushing women out of jobs with good pay and medical benefits:

> [T]he relationship between fetal health and female employment is a complex one. There are . . . fetal risks both in the processes and materials used in many workplace situations and in depriving fertile and pregnant women of income through denial of employment opportunities.[16]

The plaintiffs also attacked the policy for assuming that women were unable to make independent, intelligent decisions about the conditions under which to bear children. The plaintiffs' attorney, Marsha Berzon, stated in her oral argument before the Supreme Court:

> The policy . . . is based on a negative behavioral stereotype about how women who are faced with possible fetal harm will behave. . . . In today's day and age, women in general can control whether or not they are going to have children.[17]

The mother, not the employer, she maintained, was best situated to assess possible risks and what was best for the child.

The union also argued that the fetal protection policy violated women's privacy. The UAW brief stated:

> Requiring proof of sterility as a precondition to obtaining or retaining a job is, in itself, a serious intrusion into very sensitive matters, even for those whose personal reproductive situation conforms to the employer's requirement.

The policy had the effect, furthermore, of pressuring some women to undergo sterilization, although the company explicitly denied that this was their intent.

Some women workers, the union noted, "are as a practical matter forced to choose between their job opportunities and their childbearing capacity. Since many women are economically dependent on their jobs, putting women to that choice conditions employment for women, but not for men, upon the ability to exercise 'the right to have offspring . . . one of the basic civil rights of man.' "[18]

Finally, the union argued that the policy of Johnson Controls, if upheld, would open the door to the exclusion of women from a very wide range of jobs entailing possible hazards to the fetus, thus effectively resegregating the work force. According to studies by the Bureau of National Affairs cited by the union, as many as 20 million jobs held by women involved exposure to possible fetotoxins; many millions more involved exposure to other risks, such as infectious agents, stress, noise, radiation, or even ordinary physical accidents such as falls or automobile accidents.

The union also noted that in practice fetal protection policies had generally been limited to male-dominated occupations. For example, policies like Johnson's were most common in production facilities in the chemical, automotive, and paint industries—all areas in which women constituted a minority. By contrast, women had rarely, if ever, been excluded on the basis of fetal protection from surgical nursing, childcare, or secretarial jobs, where they dominate the work force—even though anesthetic gases, rubella viruses, and radiation emitted by video display terminals were all documented fetal hazards. The union maintained that employers had not excluded women from these work settings, despite the possibility of fetal risk, for the simple reason that women were indispensable.[19]

If upheld by the courts, the union argued, fetal protection policies would therefore have the practical effect of reversing many of the gains women had made in the 1970s and 1980s in moving into formerly male-dominated occupations and industries. Union attorney Berzon told the court:

> The net effect of upholding a policy of this type . . . would be the resegregation of the work force, particularly because the economics of the situation are that employers are going to install fetal protection policies in instances in which they are not dependent on women workers for the work force and not instigate them where they are highly dependent on women workers, because they would have nobody to do the job.[20]

By upholding the position of Johnson Controls, the union concluded, the court would "cut the heart out of Title VII and out of the Pregnancy Discrimination Act."

Notes

1. Peter T. Kilborn. "Who Decides Who Works at Jobs Imperiling Fetuses." *The New York Times,* 2 September 1990: Al, A12.
2. Cathy Trost. "Business and Women Anxiously Watch Suit on 'Fetal Protection.'" *The Wall Street Journal,* 8 October 1990:A3.
3. Brief for the Petitioners at 2–3. International Union, United Automobile, Aerospace, and Agricultural Implements Workers of America. *UAW v. Johnson Controls, Inc.,* 111 S. Ct. 1196 (1991) (No. 89–1215).
4. *International Union UAW v. Johnson Controls,* 886 F. 2d 871, 918 (7th Cir. 1989), rev'd., 111 S. Ct. 1196 (1991).
5. Kilborn, A1.
6. Brief for the Petitioners, at 2.
7. *International Union UAW v. Johnson Controls,* 886 F. 2d, at 876.
8. *International Union UAW v. Johnson Controls,* 886 F. 2d, at 877.

9. *International Union UAW v. Johnson Controls,* 886 F. 2d, at 878.
10. Brief for the Petitioners, at 18–19.
11. The case was *Security National Bank v. Chloride, Inc.,* 1985; it is discussed in the circuit court opinion in *International Union UAW v. Johnson Controls,* 886 F. 2d, at 886.
12. Margaret Post Duncan. "Fetal Protection Policies: Furthering Sex Discrimination in the Marketplace." *Journal of Family Law,* 28 (1989–1990): 733.
13. Brief for the Petitioners, at 20.
14. Brief for the Petitioners, at 31.
15. Brief for the Petitioners, at 37.
16. Brief for the Petitioners, at 39.
17. Official Transcript of Proceedings before the U.S. Supreme Court, at 8. *International Union UAW v. Johnson Controls,* No. 89–1215, October 10, 1990.
18. Brief for the Petitioners, at 16.
19. For further discussion of this point, see Mary E. Becker, "From *Muller v. Oregon* to Fetal Vulnerability Policies," *University of Chicago Law Review,* 53 (1986); M. Paul, C. Daniels, and R. Rosofsky, "Corporate Responses to Reproductive Hazards in the Workplace: Results of the Family, Work, and Health Survey," *American Journal of Industrial Medicine,* 16 (1989); and Deborah A. Stone, "Fetal Risks, Women's Rights: Showdown at Johnson Controls," *American Prospect,* Fall 1990.
20. Official Transcript of Proceedings before the U.S. Supreme Court, at 11–12. *International Union UAW v. Johnson Controls,* No. 89–1215, October 10, 1990.

Study Questions

1. What ethical and economic relationships did the company try to reinforce by excluding women from areas of production that could harm ova?

2. What ethical and economic relationships and outcomes did the women's law suit attempt to reinforce?

3. Does this conflict between women employees and the management of Johnson Controls mirror larger institutional conflicts in society? Explain your answer using the reinforcement view of law.

Ruth R. Faden and Tom L. Beauchamp

The Right to Risk Information and the Right to Refuse Workplace Hazards

In recent years, the right of employees to be informed about health hazards in the workplace has become a major issue in occupational health policy. We focus on several philosophical and policy-oriented problems concerning the right to know and correlative obligations to disclose relevant information. Related rights are also addressed, including the right to refuse hazardous work and the right of workers to contribute to workplace safety standards. . . .

I

A diverse set of recent U.S. laws and federal regulations reflect the belief that citizens in general, and workers in particular, have a right to learn about significant risks. These include The Freedom of Information Act, The Federal Insecticide, Fungicide, and Rodenticide Amendments and Regulations, The Motor Vehicle and School Bus Safety Amendments, The Truth-in-Lending Act, The Pension Reform Act, The Real Estate Settlement Procedures Act, The Federal Food, Drug, and Cosmetic Act, The Consumer Product Safety Act, and The Toxic Substances Control Act. Taken together, this legislation communicates the message that manufacturers and other businesses have a moral (and often a legal) obligation to disclose information needed by individuals to decide about their participation, employment, or enrollment.

Recent developments in the right to know in the workplace have consistently held to this general trend towards disclosure and have included an expanded notion of corporate responsibility to provide adequate information to workers. These developments could revolutionize corporate workplace practices. Until the 1983 OSHA Hazard Communication Standard (HCS) went into effect in 1986 for the manufacturing sector and in 1988 for the non-manufacturing sector,[1] workers did not routinely receive extensive information from many employers.

Today, by contrast, some corporations have established model programs. For example, the Monsanto Company has a right-to-know program in which it distributes information on hazardous chemicals to its employees, and both notifies and monitors past and current employees exposed to carcinogenic and toxic chemicals. Hercules Inc. has videotape training sessions that incorporate frank discussions of workers' anxieties. The tapes depict workplace dangers and on-the-job accidents. Those employees who have seen the Hercules film are then taught how to read safety data and how to protect themselves.[2]

Job-training programs, safety data sheets, proper labels, and a written program are all now HCS-mandated. According to the present standards, all employers must "establish hazard-communication programs to transmit information on the hazards of chemicals to their employees." The training of new employees must occur before they are exposed to hazardous substances, and each time a new hazard is introduced. Each employee must sign a written acknowledgment of training, and OSHA inspectors may interview employees to check on the effectiveness of the training sessions.[3]

The sobering statistics on worker exposure and injury and on dangerous chemicals in the workplace make such corporate programs essential. The annual Registry of Toxic Effects of Chemical Substances lists over 25,000 hazardous chemicals, at least 8,000 of which are present in the workplace. As OSHA mentioned in the preamble to its Hazard Communication Standard, an estimated 25 million largely uninformed workers in North America (1 in 4 workers) are exposed to toxic substances regulated by the federal government. Approximately 6,000 U.S. workers die from workplace injuries each year, and perhaps as many as 100,000 deaths annually are caused to some degree by workplace exposure and consequent disease. One percent of the labor force is exposed to known carcinogens, and over 44,000 U.S. workers are exposed full time to OSHA-regulated carcinogens.[4]

Despite OSHA's HCS regulations, compliance problems persist. By March, 1989, OSHA had recorded over 49,000 HCS violations in the workplace. The agency described the non-compliance rate as "incredible."[5] Part of the problem stems from ignorance both about the dangers and current OSHA requirements.

II

The most developed models of general disclosure obligations and the right to know are presently found in the extensive literature on informed consent, which also deals with in-

formed refusal. Physicians have broadly recognized moral and legal obligations to disclose known risks (and benefits) that are associated with a proposed treatment or form
of research. No parallel obligation has traditionally been recognized in relationships between management and workers. Workmen's
compensation laws originally designed for
problems of accident in instances of immediately assessable damage handled risks in
this environment. Obligations to warn or to
disclose were irrelevant under the "no-fault"
conception in workmen's compensation.

However, needs for information in the
workplace have gradually become associated
with occupational disease. In particular,
knowledge is needed about the serious long-
term risks of injury, disease, and death from
exposure to toxic substances. These risks to
health carry increased need for information
on the basis of which a person may wish to
take various actions, including choosing to
forgo employment completely, to refuse certain work environments within a place of
employment, to request improved protective
devices, and to request lowered levels of exposure. Notification of workers should provide benefits of early disease diagnosis and
prevention and promote needed lifestyle as
well as occupational changes. Information
should also improve workers' opportunities
for appropriate compensation.[6]

Employee-employer relationships—
unlike physician-patient relationships—are
often confrontational and present to workers
a constant danger of undisclosed or under-
disclosed risk. This danger and the relative
powerlessness of employees may not be sufficient to justify employer disclosure obligations in all circumstances, but placing relevant information in the workers' hands seems
morally required in all hazardous conditions.
By what criteria, then, shall such disclosure
obligations be determined?

One plausible argument is the following:
Because large employers, unions, and government agencies must deal with multiple
employees and complicated causal conditions, no standard should be more demanding
than the so-called reasonable person stan-

dard. This standard is what a fair and informed member of the relevant community
believes is needed. Under this standard, no
employer, union, or other party should be
held responsible for disclosing information
beyond that needed to make an informed
choice about the adequacy of safety precautions, industrial hygiene, long-term hazards,
and the like, as determined by what the reasonable person in the community would
judge to be the worker's need for information
material to a decision about employment or
working conditions.

However, this reasonable person standard of disclosure is not adequate for all
disclosures. In the case of serious hazards—
such as those involved in short-term, concentrated doses of radiation—a standard tied to
individual persons may be more appropriate.
When disclosures to individual workers may
be expected to have a subjective impact that
varies with each individual, the reasonable
person standard should be supplemented by a
standard that addresses each worker's personal informational needs.

Perhaps the best solution to the problem
of a general standard is a compromise between a reasonable-person and a subjective
standard: Whatever a reasonable person
would judge material to the decision-making
process should be disclosed, and in addition
any remaining information that is material to
an individual worker should be provided
through a process of asking whether he or she
has any additional or special concerns. This
standard should avoid a narrow focus on the
employer's obligation to disclose information and should seek to ensure the quality of
a worker's understanding and consent. These
problems center on communication rather
than on legal standards of disclosure. The key
to effective communication is to invite participation by workers in a dialogue. Asking
questions, eliciting concerns, and establishing a climate that encourages questions may
be more meaningful than the full corpus of
disclosed information. Different levels of education, linguistic ability, and sophistication
about the issues need to be accommodated.
We need also to consider which groups of

workers will be included. The majority of the nation's workplaces are presently exempted from OSHA regulations, leaving these workers largely uninformed. Even in workplaces that are covered, former workers often have as much of a need for the information as do presently employed workers. The federal government has the names of approximately 250,000 former workers whose risk of cancer, heart disease, and lung disease has been increased by exposure to asbestos, polyvinyl chloride, benzene, arsenic, beta-naphthalamine, and dozens of other chemicals. Employers have the names of several million such workers.

The U.S. Congress has passed a bill to notify those workers at greatest risk, so that checkups and diagnosis of disease can be made before a disease's advanced stage.[7] But at this writing, neither industry nor the government has developed a systematic program. They claim that the expense of notifications would be prohibitive, that many workers would be unduly alarmed, and that existing screening and surveillance programs should prove adequate in monitoring and treating disease. Critics rightly charge, however, that existing programs are inadequate and that workers have a right to know in order to investigate potential problems at their initiative.[8]

III

Despite the apparent consensus on the desirability of having some form of right to know in the workplace, hurdles exist that will make it difficult to implement this right. Complicated questions arise about the kinds of information to be disclosed, by whom, to whom, under what conditions, and with what warrant in ambiguous or uncertain circumstances. Trade secrets have also been a long-standing thorn in the side of progress,[9] because companies resist disclosing information about an ingredient or process claimed as a trade secret. They insist that they should never be required to reveal their substances or processes if their competitors could then obtain the information. For this reason, OSHA has been required

to balance the protection of workers through disclosure against the protection of corporate interests in nondisclosure. Also, economic and related social constraints sometimes inhibit workers from exercising their full range of workplace options. For example, in industries in which ten people apply for every available position, bargaining for increased protection is an unlikely event.

However, we must set these problems aside in order to consider perhaps the most perplexing difficulty about the right to know in the workplace: the right to refuse hazardous work assignments and to have effective mechanisms for workers to reduce the risks they face. Shortly after the Hazard Communication Standard went into effect, labor saw that the right to know was often of little practical use unless some parallel method were in place to modify hazardous working conditions. U.S. law has generally made unsafe working conditions a publishable offense, and the United States Occupational Safety and Health Act of 1970 (OSH Act)[10] limited rights to refuse to work when there is good evidence of life-threatening conditions. Specifically, the OSH Act grants workers the right to request an OSHA inspection if they believe an OSHA standard has been violated or an imminent hazard exists. Under the Act, employees also have the right to "walk-around," i.e. to participate in OSHA inspections of the worksite and to consult freely with the inspection officer. Most importantly, the OSH Act expressly protects employees who request an inspection or otherwise exercise their rights under the OSH Act from discharge or any discriminatory treatment in retaliation for legitimate safety and health complaints.[11]

While these worker rights under the OSH Act are essential, they are not sufficiently strong to assure that all workers have effective mechanisms for initiating inspections of suspected health hazards. The OSH Act does not cover small businesses (those employing fewer than ten workers) or federal, state, and municipal employees. Questions also remain about OSHA's ability to enforce these provisions of the OSH Act. But if workers are to effectively use disclosed information on health hazards, they must have access to a workable and efficient regulatory system. The OSH Act is also written to protect the rights of individuals, not groups. It has no provisions for collective action by workers and does not mandate workplace health and safety committees, as does legislation in some countries.

Workers still need an adequately protected right to refuse unsafe work and a right to refuse an employer's request that they sign OSHA-mandated forms acknowledging that they have been trained about hazardous chemicals. One cannot easily determine the current extent to which these rights are protected.[12] Although the OSH Act does not grant a general right to refuse unsafe work, provisions to this effect exist in some state occupational safety laws. In addition, former Secretary of Labor Ray Marshall issued a regulation that interprets the OSH Act as including a limited right to refuse unsafe work, a right upheld by the U.S. Supreme Court in 1980.[13] The Labor-Management Relations Act (LMRA) also provides a limited right of refusal, which is also included implicitly in the National Labor Relations Act (NLRA).[14]

These statutory protections have not established uniform conditions granting to workers a right to refuse. For example, OSHA regulations allow workers to walk off the job if there is a "real danger of death or serious injury," while the LMRA permits refusals only under "abnormally dangerous conditions."[15] Under the LMRA, the nature of the occupation determines the extent of danger justifying refusal, while under OSHA the character of the threat, or so-called "imminent danger," determines worker action. By contrast, under the NLRA a walk-out by two or more workers may be justified for even minimal safety problems, so long as the action can be construed as a "concerted activity" for mutual aid and protection and a no-strike clause does not exist in any collective bargaining agreements. While the NLRA appears to provide the broadest protection to workers, employees refusing to work under the NLRA can lose the right to be reinstated in their positions if permanent replacements can be hired.

The relative merits of the different statutes are further confused by questions of overlapping authority, called "preemption." It is not always clear (1) whether a worker is eligible to claim protection under a given law, (2) which law affords a worker maximum protections or remedies in a particular circumstance, and (3) whether or under what conditions a worker can seek relief under another law or through the courts, once a claim under a given law has been rejected or invalidated.

The current legal situation concerning the right to refuse hazardous work also fails to resolve other questions. Consider, for example, whether a meaningful right to refuse hazardous work entails an obligation to continue to pay nonworking employees, or to award the employees back-pay if the issue is resolved in their favor. On the one hand, workers without union strike benefits or other income protections would be unable to exercise their right to refuse unsafe work due to economic pressures. On the other hand, to permit such workers to draw a paycheck is to legitimize strike with pay, a practice traditionally considered unacceptable by management and by Congress.

The situation does not resolve whether the right to refuse unsafe work should be restricted to cases of obvious, imminent, and serious risks to health or life (the current OSHA and LMRA position) or should be expanded to include lesser risks and uncertain risks—for example, exposure to suspected toxic or carcinogenic substances that although not immediate threats, may prove more dangerous over time. In order for "the right to know" to lead to meaningful worker action, workers must be able to remove themselves from exposure to suspected hazards, as well as obvious or known hazards.

The question of the proper standard for determining whether a safety walkout is justified is connected to this issue. At least three different standards have been applied in the past: a good-faith subjective standard, which requires only that the worker honestly believe that a health hazard exists; a reasonable person standard, which requires that the belief be reasonable under the circumstances as well as sincerely held; and an objective standard, which requires evidence—commonly established by expert witnesses—that the threat exists. Although the possibility of worker abuse of the right to refuse has been a major factor in a current trend to reject the good faith standard, recent commentary has argued that this trend raises serious equity issues in the proper balancing of this concern with the needs of workers confronted with basic self-preservation issues.[16]

No less important is whether the right to refuse hazardous work should be protected only until a formal review of the situation is initiated (at which time the worker must return to the job) or whether the walk-out should be permitted until the alleged hazard is at least temporarily removed. Requirements that workers continue to be exposed while OSHA or the NLRB conduct investigations is certain to prove unacceptable to workers when the magnitude of potential harm is significant. However, compelling employers to remove suspected hazards during the evaluation period may also result in intolerable economic burdens. This situation is worsened by the fact that workers are often not in a position to act on information about health hazards by seeking alternative employment elsewhere.

We need, then, to delineate the conditions under which workers may be compelled to return to work during an alleged hazard investigation and the conditions that can compel employers to remove alleged hazards.

IV

Legal rights will prove useless if workers remain ignorant of their options. Despite recent requirements that employers initiate training programs, it remains doubtful that many workers, particularly nonunion workers and those in small businesses, are aware that they have a legally protected right to refuse hazardous work, let alone that at least three statutory provisions protect that right. Even if workers were to learn of such a right, they could probably not weave their way through the maze of legal options unaided. OSHA officials have acknowledged that both employ-

ers and workers are puzzled about proper strategies of education and compliance.[17] But if the workplace is to have a meaningful right to know, workers must have an adequate program to educate them not only about hazards but about their rights and how to exercise them. In general, they attempt to regulate the workplace rather than to empower workers in the workplace—two very different strategies.

Although the interests in health and safety of business are sometimes in sharp conflict with the interests of workers and society, employers and managers have an obligation to explain the right to notification and the right (at least temporarily) to refuse work under unduly hazardous conditions. Such programs of information and training in hazards are as important for employers and managers as for workers. In several recent court cases corporate executives have been tried—and in some cases convicted—for murder and manslaughter, because they negligently caused worker deaths by failing to notify of hazards. In Los Angeles and Chicago occupational deaths are investigated as possible homicides.[18] An improved system of corporate disclosures of risk and the rights of workers will therefore benefit everyone.

Notes

1. 29 CFR 1910.1200; 48 FR 53, 280 (1983); and see Linda D. McGill, "OSHA's Hazard Communication Standards: Guidelines for Compliance," *Employment Relations Today* 16 (Autumn 1989): 181–87.
2. Laurie Hays, "New Rules on Workplace Hazards Prompt Intensified On the Job Training Programs," *The Wall Street Journal,* July 8, 1986, p. 31; Cathy Trost, "Plans to Alert Workers," *The Wall Street Journal,* March 28, 1986, p. 15.
3. "Hazard Communication," *Federal Register,* August 24, 1987; and see William J. Rothwell. "Complying with OSHA," *Training & Development Journal* 43 (May 1989): 53–54; McGill, "OSHA's Hazard Communication Standards: Guidelines for Compliance," p. 184.
4. See 48 CFR 53, 282 (1983); Office of Technology Assessment, *Preventing Illness and Injury in the Workplace* (Washington: U.S. Government Printing Office, 1985). See also Sheldon W. Samuels, "The Ethics of Choice in the Struggle against Industrial Disease," *American Journal of Industrial*

Medicine 23 (1993): 43–52, and David Rosner and Gerald E. Markowitz, eds. *Dying for Work: Workers' Safety and Health in Twentieth-Century America.* Bloomington: University of Indiana Press, 1987.

5. Current Reports, *O.S.H. Reporter* (March 15, 1989), p. 1747, as quoted in McGill, "OSHA's Hazard Communication Standard," p. 181.

6. See the articles by Gregory Bond, Leon Gordis, John Higgenson and Flora Chu, Albert Jonsen, and Paul A. Schulte in *Industrial Epidemiology Forum's Conference on Ethics in Epidemiology,* ed. William E. Fayerweather, John Higgenson, and Tom L. Beauchamp. New York: Pergamon Press, 1991.

7. High Risk Occupational Disease Notification and Prevention Act, HR 1309.

8. See Cathy Trost, "Plans to Alert Workers to Health Risks Stir Fears of Lawsuits and High Costs," *The Wall Street Journal* March 28, 1986, p. 15; Peter Perl, "Workers Unwarned," *The Washington Post,* January 14, 1985, pp. A1, A6.

9. Under current standards, an employer is not required to disclose the name or any information about a hazardous chemical that would require disclosure of a bona fide trade secret; but in a medical emergency the company must disclose this information to physicians or nurses as long as confidentiality is assured.

10. 29 U.S.C. §651–658 (1970).

11. OSH Act 29 U.S.C. 661(c). If the health or safety complaint is not determined to be legitimate, there are no worker protections.

12. The right to refuse an employer's request to sign a training acknowledgment form is upheld in *Beam Distilling Co. v. Distillery and Allied Workers' International,* 90 Lab. Arb. 740 (1988). See also Ronald Bayer, ed. *The Health and Safety of Workers.* New York: Oxford University Press, 1988; James C. Robinson, *Toil and Toxics: Workplace Struggles and Political Strategies for Occupational Health.* Berkeley: University of California Press, 1991.

13. *Whirlpool v. Marshall* 445 US 1 (1980).

14. See the exposition in Susan Preston, "A Right Under OSHA to Refuse Unsafe Work or A Hobson's Choice of Safety or Job?," *University of Baltimore Law Review* 8 (Spring 1979), pp. 519–550.

15. 29 U.S.C. §143 (1976), and 29 CFR §1977.12 (1979).

16. James C. Robinson, "Labor Union Involvement in Occupational Safety and Health, 1957–1987," *Journal of Health Politics, Policy, and Law* 13 (Fall 1988), p. 463; Nancy K. Frank, "A Question of Equity: Workers' Right to Refuse Under OSHA Compared to the Criminal Necessity Defense," *Labor Law Journal* 31 (October 1980), pp. 617–626.

17. McGill, "OSHA's Hazard Communication Standard," p. 181.

18. See *Illinois v. Chicago Magnet Wire Corporation,* No. 86–114, *Amicus Curiae* for The American Federation of Labor and Congress of Industrial Organizations; R. Henry Moore, "OSHA: What's Ahead for the 1990s," *Personnel* 67 (June 1990), p. 69.

Study Questions

1. How do Faden and Beauchamp argue for limits to employment at will? What ethical, economic, and/or legal principles do they use to make their case?

2. Do the authors argue that employees have a right to all information about dangers in the workplace? If not, how should management limit that information?

3. Does the right to refuse workplace hazards imply anything about the right to *accept* workplace hazards, as in the Johnson Controls case?

4. How well do Faden and Beauchamp's arguments fit with Werhane and Radin's views?

CASE: **Merck & Co., Inc.**
The Business Enterprise Trust

In 1978, Dr. P. Roy Vagelos, then head of the Merck research labs, received a provocative memorandum from a senior researcher in parasitology, Dr. William C. Campbell. Dr. Campbell had made an intriguing observation while working with ivermectin, a new antiparasitic compound under investigation for use in animals.

Campbell thought that ivermectin might be the answer to a disease called river blindness that plagued millions in the Third World. But to find out if Campbell's hypothesis had merit, Merck would have to spend millions of dollars to develop the right formulation for human use and to conduct the field trials in the most remote parts of the world. Even if these efforts produced an effective and safe drug, virtually all of those afflicted with river blindness could not afford to buy it. Vagelos, originally a university researcher but by then a Merck executive, had to decide whether to invest in research for a drug that, even if successful, might never pay for itself.

RIVER BLINDNESS

River blindness, formally known as *onchocerciasis,* was a disease labeled by the World Health Organization (WHO) as a public health and socioeconomic problem of considerable magnitude in over 35 developing countries throughout the Third World. Some 85 million people in thousands of tiny settlements throughout Africa and parts of the Middle East and Latin America were thought to be at risk. The cause: a parasitic worm carried by a tiny black fly which bred along fast-moving rivers. When the flies bit humans—a single person could be bitten thousands of times a day—the larvae of a parasitic worm, *Onchocerca volvulus,* entered the body.

These worms grew to more than two feet in length, causing grotesque but relatively innocuous nodules in the skin. The real harm began when the adult worms reproduced, releasing millions of microscopic offspring, known as microfilariae, which swarmed through body tissue. A terrible itching resulted, so bad that some victims committed suicide. After several years, the microfilariae caused lesions and depigmentation of the skin. Eventually they invaded the eyes, often causing blindness.

The World Health Organization estimated in 1978 that some 340,000 people were blind because of onchocerciasis, and that a million more suffered from varying degrees of visual impairment. At that time, 18 million or more people were infected with the parasite, though half did not yet have serious symptoms. In some villages close to fly-breeding sites, nearly all residents were infected and a majority of those over age 45 were blind. In such places, it was said, children believed that severe itching, skin infections and blindness were simply part of growing up.

In desperate efforts to escape the flies, entire villages abandoned fertile areas near rivers, and moved to poorer land. As a result, food shortages were frequent. Community life disintegrated as new burdens arose for already impoverished families.

The disease was first identified in 1893 by scientists and in 1926 was found to be related to the black flies. But by the 1970s, there was still no cure that could safely be used for community-wide treatment. Two drugs, diethylcarbamazine (DEC) and Suramin, were useful in killing the parasite, but both had severe side effects in infected individuals, needed close monitoring, and had even caused deaths. In 1974, the Onchocerciasis Control Program was created to be administered by the World Health Organization, in the hope that the flies could be killed through spraying of larvacides at breeding sites, but success was slow and uncertain. The flies in many areas developed resistance to the treatment, and were also known to disappear and then reinfest areas.

MERCK & CO., INC.

Merck & Co., Inc. was, in 1978, one of the largest producers of prescription drugs in the world. Headquartered in Rahway, New Jersey, Merck traced its origins to Germany in 1668 when Friedrich Jacob Merck purchased an apothecary in the city of Darmstadt. Over three hundred years later, Merck, having become an American firm, employed over 28,000 people and had operations all over the world.

In the late 1970s, Merck was coming off a 10-year drought in terms of new products. For nearly a decade, the company had relied on two prescription drugs for a significant percentage of its approximately $2 billion in annual sales: Indocin, a treatment for rheumatoid arthritis, and Aldomet, a treatment for high blood pressure. Henry W. Gadsden, Merck's chief executive from 1965 to 1976, along with his successor, John J. Horan, were concerned that the 17-year patent protection on Merck's two big moneymakers would soon expire, and began investing an enormous amount in research.

Merck management spent a great deal of money on research because it knew that its success ten and twenty years in the future critically depended upon present investments. The company deliberately fashioned a corporate culture to nurture the most creative, fruitful research. Merck scientists were among the best-paid in the industry, and were given great latitude to pursue intriguing leads. Moreover, they were inspired to think of their work as a quest to alleviate human disease and suffering world-wide. Within certain proprietary constraints, researchers were encouraged to publish in academic journals and to share ideas with their scientific peers. Nearly a billion dollars was spent between 1975 and 1978, and the investment paid off. In that period, under the direction of head of research, Dr. P. Roy Vagelos, Merck introduced Clinoril, a painkiller for arthritis; a general antibiotic called Mefoxin; a drug for glaucoma named Timoptic; and Ivomec (ivermectin, MSD), an antiparasitic for cattle.

In 1978, Merck had sales of $1.98 billion and net income of $307 million. Sales had risen steadily between 1969 and 1978 from $691 million to almost $2 billion. Income during the same period rose from $106 million to over $300 million. (See Table 1 for a 10-year summary of performance.)

At that time, Merck employed 28,700 people, up from 22,200 ten years earlier. Human and animal health products constituted 84% of the company's sales, with environmental health products and services representing an additional 14% of sales. Merck's foreign sales had grown more rapidly during the 1970s than had domestic sales, and in 1978 represented 47% of total sales. Much of the company's research operations were organized separately as the Merck Sharp & Dohme Research Laboratories, headed by Vagelos. Other Merck operations included the Merck Sharp & Dohme Division, the Merck Sharp & Dohme International Division, Kelco Division, Merck Chemical Manufacturing Division, Merck Animal Health Division, Calgon Corporation, Baltimore Aircoil Company, and Hubbard Farms.

The company had 24 plants in the United States, including one in Puerto Rico, and

TABLE 1
10-Year Summary of Financial Performance*

Merck & Co., Inc. and subsidiaries (dollar amounts in thousands except per-share figures)

	1978	1977	1976	1975	1974	1973	1972	1971	1970	1969
Results of Year										
Sales	$1,981,440	$1,724,410	$1,561,117	$1,401,979	$1,260,416	$1,104,035	$942,631	$832,416	$761,109	$691,453
Materials and production costs	744,249	662,703	586,963	525,853	458,837	383,879	314,804	286,646	258,340	232,878
Marketing/administrative expenses	542,186	437,579	396,975	354,525	330,292	304,807	268,856	219,005	201,543	178,593
Research/development expenses	161,350	144,898	133,826	121,933	100,952	89,155	79,692	71,619	69,707	61,100
Interest expense	25,743	25,743	26,914	21,319	8,445	6,703	4,533	3,085	2,964	1,598
Income before taxes	507,912	453,487	416,439	378,349	361,890	319,491	274,746	252,061	228,555	217,284
Taxes on income	198,100	173,300	159,100	147,700	149,300	134,048	121,044	118,703	108,827	109,269
Net income**	307,534	277,525	255,482	228,778	210,492	182,681	151,180	131,381	117,878	106,645
Per common share**	$4.07	$3.67	$3.38	$3.03	$2.79	$2.43	$2.01	$1.75	$1.57	$1.43
Dividends declared on										
common stock	132,257	117,101	107,584	105,564	106,341	93,852	84,103	82,206	76,458	75,528
Per common share	$1.75	$1.55	$1.42-½	$1.40	$1.40	$1.23-½	$1.12	$1.10	$1.02-½	$1.02-½
Gross plant additions	155,853	177,167	153,894	249,015	159,148	90,194	69,477	67,343	71,540	48,715
Depreciation	75,477	66,785	58,198	52,091	46,057	40,617	36,283	32,104	27,819	23,973
Year-End Position										
Working capital	666,817	629,515	549,840	502,262	359,591	342,434	296,378	260,350	226,084	228,296
Property, plant, and equipment (net)	924,179	846,784	747,107	652,804	459,245	352,145	305,416	274,240	239,638	197,220
Total assets	2,251,358	1,993,389	1,759,371	1,538,999	1,243,287	988,985	834,847	736,503	664,294	601,484
Stockholders' equity	1,455,135	1,277,753	1,102,154	949,991	822,782	709,614	621,792	542,978	493,214	451,030
Year-End Statistics										
Average number of common shares outstanding (in thousands)	75,573	75,546	75,493	75,420	75,300	75,193	75,011	74,850	74,850	74,547
Number of stockholders	62,900	63,900	63,500	63,500	61,400	60,000	58,000	54,300	54,600	53,100
Number of employees	28,700	28,100	26,800	26,300	26,500	25,100	24,100	23,200	23,000	22,200

*The data are as previously reported, restated for poolings-of-interests and stock splits.
**Net income for 1977 and related per-share amounts exclude gain on disposal of businesses of $13.225 and 18c, respectively.

44 in other countries. Six research laboratories were located in the United States and four abroad.

While Merck executives sometimes squirmed when they quoted the "unbusinesslike" language of George W. Merck, son of the company's founder and its former chairman, there could be no doubt that Merck employees found the words inspirational. "We try never to forget that medicine is for the people," Merck said. "It is not for the profits. The profits follow, and if we have remembered that, they have never failed to appear. The better we have remembered it, the larger they have been." These words formed the basis of Merck's overall corporate philosophy.

THE DRUG INVESTMENT DECISION

Merck invested hundreds of millions of dollars each year in research. Allocating those funds amongst various projects, however, was a rather involved and inexact process. At a company as large as Merck, there was never a single method by which projects were approved or money distributed.

Studies showed that, on the average, it took 12 years and $200 million to bring a new drug to market. Thousands of scientists were continually working on new ideas and following new leads. Drug development was always a matter of trial and error; with each new iteration, scientists would close some doors and open others. When a Merck researcher came across an apparent breakthrough—either in an unexpected direction, or as a derivative of the original lead—he or she would conduct preliminary research. If the idea proved promising, it was brought to the attention of the department heads.

Every year, Merck's research division held a large review meeting at which all research programs were examined. Projects were coordinated and consolidated, established programs were reviewed and new possibilities were considered. Final approval on research was not made, however, until the head of research met later with a committee of scientific advisors. Each potential program was extensively reviewed, analyzed on the basis of the likelihood of success, the existing market, competition, potential safety problems, manufacturing feasibility and patent status before the decision was made whether to allocate funds for continued experimentation.

THE PROBLEM OF RARE DISEASES AND POOR CUSTOMERS

Many potential drugs offered little chance of financial return. Some diseases were so rare that treatments developed could never be priced high enough to recoup the investment in research, while other diseases afflicted only the poor in rural and remote areas of the Third World. These victims had limited ability to pay even a small amount for drugs or treatment.

In the United States, Congress sought to encourage drug companies to conduct research on rare diseases. In 1978 legislation had been proposed which would grant drug companies tax benefits and seven-year exclusive marketing rights if they would manufacture drugs for diseases afflicting fewer than 200,000 Americans. It was expected that this "orphan drug" program would eventually be passed into law.

There was, however, no U.S. or international program that would create incentives for companies to develop drugs for diseases like river blindness which afflicted millions of the poor in the Third World. The only hope was that some Third World government, foundation, or international organization might step in and partially fund the distribution of a drug that had already been developed.

THE DISCOVERY OF IVERMECTIN

The process of investigating promising drug compounds was always long, laborious and fraught with failure. For every pharmaceutical compound that became a "product candidate," thousands of others failed to meet the most rudimentary pre-clinical tests for safety and efficacy. With so much room for failure, it became especially important for drug companies to have sophisticated research managers who could identify the most productive research strategies.

Merck had long been a pioneer in developing major new antibiotic compounds, beginning with penicillin and streptomycin in the 1940s. In the 1970s, Merck Sharp & Dohme Research Laboratories were continuing this tradition. To help investigate for new microbial agents of potential therapeutic value, Merck researchers obtained 54 soil samples from the Kitasato Institute of Japan in 1974. These samples seemed novel and the researchers hoped they might disclose some naturally occurring antibiotics.

As Merck researchers methodically put the soil through hundreds of tests, Merck scientists were pleasantly surprised to detect strong antiparasitic activity in Sample No. OS3153, a scoop of soil dug up at a golf course near Ito, Japan. The Merck labs quickly brought together an interdisciplinary team to try to isolate a pure active ingredient from the microbial culture. The compound eventually isolated—avermectin—proved to have an astonishing potency and effectiveness against a wide range of parasites in cattle, swine, horses and other animals. Within a year, the Merck team also began to suspect that a group of related compounds discovered in the same soil sample could be effective against many other intestinal worms, mites, ticks and insects.

After toxicological tests suggested that ivermectin would be safer than related compounds, Merck decided to develop the substance for the animal health market. In 1978 the first ivermectin-based animal drug, Ivomec, was nearing approval by the U.S. Department of Agriculture and foreign regulatory bodies. Many variations would likely follow: drugs for sheep and pigs, horses, dogs, and others. Ivomec had the potential to become a major advance in animal health treatment.

As clinical testing of ivermectin progressed in the late 1970s, Dr. William Campbell's ongoing research brought him face-to-face with an intriguing hypothesis. Ivermectin, when tested in horses, was effective against the microfilariae of an exotic, fairly unimportant gastrointestinal parasite, *Onchocerca cervicalis*. This particular worm, while harmless in horses, had characteristics similar to the insidious human parasite that causes river blindness, *Onchocerca volvulus*.

Dr. Campbell wondered: Could ivermectin be formulated to work against the human parasite? Could a safe, effective drug suitable for community-wide treatment of river blindness be developed? Both Campbell and Vagelos knew that it was very much a gamble that it would succeed. Furthermore, both knew that even if success were attained, the economic viability of such a project would be nil. On the other hand, because such a significant amount of money had already been invested in the development of the animal drug, the cost of developing a human formulation would be much less than that for developing a new compound. It was also widely believed at this point that ivermectin, though still in its final development stages, was likely to be very successful.

A decision to proceed would not be without risks. If a new derivative proved to have any adverse health effects when used on humans, its reputation as a veterinary drug could be tainted and sales negatively affected, no matter how irrelevant the experience with humans. In early tests, ivermectin had had some negative side effects on some specific species of mammals. Dr. Brian Duke of the Armed Forces Institute of Pathology in Washington, D.C., said the cross-species effectiveness of antiparasitic drugs are unpredictable, and there is "always a worry that some race or subsection of the human population" might be adversely affected.

Isolated instances of harm to humans or improper use in Third World settings might also raise some unsettling questions: Could drug residues turn up in meat eaten by humans? Would any human version of ivermectin distributed to the Third World be diverted into the black market, undercutting sales of the veterinary drug? Could the drug harm certain animals in unknown ways?

Despite these risks, Vagelos wondered what the impact might be of turning down Campbell's proposal. Merck had built a research team dedicated to alleviating human suffering. What would a refusal to pursue a possible treatment for river blindness do to morale?

Ultimately, it was Dr. Vagelos who had to make the decision whether or not to fund research toward a treatment for river blindness.

Study Questions

1. What internal decision-making standards caused this problem to arise?

2. How would Friedman, Cochran, Freeman, and Marens and Wicks analyze this case? Which of these three points of view is strongest as a descriptive mechanism? As a prescriptive mechanism?

William C. Frederick

The Moral Authority of Transnational Corporate Codes

Moral guidelines for corporations may be found embedded in several multilateral compacts adopted by governments since the end of the Second World War. Taken as a whole, these normative guides comprise a framework for identifying the essential moral behaviors expected of multinational corporations. Corporate actions that transgress these principles are understood to be *de facto,* and in some cases *de jure,* unethical and immoral. This set of normative prescriptions and proscriptions embodies a moral authority that transcends national boundaries and societal differences, thereby invoking or manifesting a universal or transcultural standard of cor-porate ethical behavior. Although this remarkable development has not run its full course and therefore is not yet all-embracing, it is well enough along for its main outlines to be evident and its central normative significance to be clear.

LANDMARK MULTILATERAL COMPACTS

The four decades between 1948 and 1988 have been remarkable for the proliferation of intergovernmental agreements, compacts, accords, and declarations that have been in-

From *Journal of Business Ethics* 10, 165–177, 1991. Used with kind permission of Kluwer Academic Publishers and the author. Copyright © 1991 Kluwer Academic Publishers; all rights reserved.

tended to put on the public record various sets of principles regulating the activities of governments, groups, and individuals. The core concerns of these compacts have ranged from military security to economic and social development, from the protection of national sovereignty to specifying acceptable actions by multinational enterprises, from condemnations of genocide and slavery to the regulation of capital flows and the transfer of technology, from the political rights of women to the movements of refugees and stateless persons, and many others too numerous to list here. They reflect the many kinds of problems and issues that have confronted governments in the last half of the 20th century (United Nations, 1983).

This paper focuses on six of these intergovernmental compacts, which by their nature, purpose, and comprehensiveness might well be considered to be the most generic or archetypal of such agreements. Collectively they proclaim the basic outlines of a transcultural corporate ethic. This ethic effectively lays down specific guidelines for the formulation of multinational corporate policies and practices. These six compacts and their respective dates of promulgation are:

- The United Nations Universal Declaration of Human Rights (1948) [Abbreviated as UDHR]

- The European Convention on Human Rights (1950) [ECHR]

- The Helsinki Final Act (1975) [Helsinki]

- The OECD Guidelines for Multinational Enterprises (1976) [OECD]

- The International Labor Office Tripartite Declaration of Principles Concerning Multinational Enterprises and Social Policy (1977) [ILO]

- The United Nations Code of Conduct on Transnational Corporations (Not yet completed nor promulgated but originating in 1972.) [TNC Code][1]

The first two compacts are clearly normative in focus and intention, emphasizing

human rights, but they are not addressed specifically to multinational enterprises. The principal emphasis of the Helsinki Final Act is the national and political security of the signatory governments, although this accord and its successor protocols carry strong messages concerning human rights and environmental protections, which do concern business operations. The last three compacts are aimed primarily and explicitly at the practices of multinational enterprises across a wide range of issues and problems. While three of the six accords issue primarily from European-North American governments, the other three represent the views of a much wider, even global, range of governments.

NORMATIVE CORPORATE GUIDELINES

By careful reading of these six intergovernmental compacts, one can derive a set of explicitly normative guides for the policies, decisions, and operations of multinational corporations. These guidelines refer to normal business operations, as well as more fundamental responsibilities regarding basic human rights.

Employment Practices and Policies

- MNCs should not contravene the manpower policies of host nations. [ILO]

- MNCs should respect the right of employees to join trade unions and to bargain collectively. [ILO; OECD; UDHR]

- MNCs should develop nondiscriminatory employment policies and promote equal job opportunities. [ILO; OECD; UDHR]

- MNCs should provide equal pay for equal work. [ILO; UDHR]

- MNCs should give advance notice of changes in operations, especially plant closings, and mitigate the adverse effects of these changes. [ILO; OECD]

- MNCs should provide favorable work conditions, limited working hours, holidays with pay, and protection against unemployment. [UDHR]

- MNCs should promote job stability and job security, avoiding arbitrary dismissals and providing severance pay for those unemployed. [ILO; UDHR]
- MNCs should respect local host-country job standards and upgrade the local labor force through training. [ILO; OECD]
- MNCs should adopt adequate health and safety standards for employees and grant them the right to know about job-related health hazards. [ILO]
- MNCs should, minimally, pay basic living wages to employees. [ILO; UDHR]
- MNCSs' operations should benefit lower-income groups of the host nation. [ILO]
- MNCs should balance job opportunities, work conditions, job training, and living conditions among migrant workers and host-country nationals. [Helsinki]

Consumer Protection

- MNCs should respect host-country laws and policies regarding the protection of consumers. [OECD; TNC Code]
- MNCs should safeguard the health and safety of consumers by various disclosures, safe packaging, proper labelling, and accurate advertising. [TNC Code]

Environmental Protection

- MNCs should respect host-country laws, goals, and priorities concerning protection of the environment. [OECD; TNC Code; Helsinki]
- MNCs should preserve ecological balance, protect the environment, adopt preventive measures to avoid environmental harm, and rehabilitate environments damaged by operations. [OECD; TNC Code; Helsinki]
- MNCs should disclose likely environmental harms and minimize risks of accidents that could cause environmental damage. [OECD; TNC Code]
- MNCs should promote the development of international environmental standards. [TNC Code; Helsinki]
- MNCs should control specific operations that contribute to pollution of air, water, and soils. [Helsinki]
- MNCs should develop and use technology that can monitor; protect, and enhance the environment. [OECD; Helsinki]

Political Payments and Involvement

- MNCs should not pay bribes nor make improper payments to public officials. [OECD; TNC Code]
- MNCs should avoid improper or illegal involvement or interference in the internal politics of host countries. [OECD; TNC Code]
- MNCs should not interfere in intergovernmental relations. [TNC Code]

Basic Human Rights and Fundamental Freedoms

- MNCs should respect the rights of all persons to life, liberty, security of person, and privacy. [UDHR; ECHR; Helsinki; ILO; TNC Code][2]
- MNCs should respect the rights of all persons to equal protection of the law, work, choice of job, just and favorable work conditions, and protection against unemployment and discrimination. [UDHR; Helsinki; ILO; TNC Code]
- MNCs should respect all persons' freedom of thought, conscience, religion, opinion and expression, communication, peaceful assembly and association, and movement and residence within each state. [UDHR; ECHR; Helsinki; ILO; TNC Code]
- MNCs should promote a standard of living to support the health and well-being of

workers and their families. [UDHR; Helsinki; ILO; TNC Code]

- MNCs should promote special care and assistance to motherhood and childhood. [UDHR; Helsinki; ILO; TNC Code]

These guidelines should be viewed as a *collective* phenomenon since all of them do not appear in each of the six compacts. Table 1 reveals that the OECD compact and the proposed TNC CODE provide the most comprehensive coverage of the guideline categories. The relative lack of guidelines in the ECHR compact may be attributable to the considerable membership overlap with the Organization for Economic Cooperation and Development whose members subscribe to the OECD standards for multinationals. Human rights and employment conditions are clearly the leading guideline categories, while consumer protection and corporate political activity appear infrequently. Table 1 suggests that the respective compacts have "specialized" in different types of normative issues involving corporate practices, the most obvious example being the ILO's emphasis on employment issues. The argument of this paper is that the collective weight of the guidelines is more important than the absence of some of them from specific international agreements. Clearly their inclusion across the board would strengthen the case for a global normative system intended to guide corporate practices.

These normative guidelines have direct implications for a wide range of *specific* corporate programs and policies. They include policies regarding child-care, minimum wages, hours of work, employee training and education, adequate housing and health care, pollution control efforts, advertising and marketing activities, severance pay, privacy of employees and consumers, information concerning on-the-job hazards, and, especially for those companies with operations in South Africa, such additional matters as the place of residence and free movement of employees. Quite clearly, the guidelines are not intended to be, nor do they act as, mere rhetoric. Nor do they deal with peripheral matters. They have *direct* applicability to many of the *central* operations and policies of multinational enterprises.

THE NORMATIVE SOURCES OF THE GUIDELINES

These guides for the practices and policies of multinational companies seem to rest upon and be justified by four normative orientations. Given sets of the guidelines can be tied directly to one or more of these moral sources.

National Sovereignty is one such source. All six compacts invoke the inviolability of national sovereignty. In acting on the compacts' principles, each nation is to take care not to infringe on the sovereignty of its neighbors.

TABLE 1
Number of MNC Normative Guidelines by Category for Six Multilateral Compacts

	UDHR	ECHR	Helsinki	OECD	ILO	TNC Code	Total
Employment practices	6	—	—	4	10	—*	20
Consumer protection	—	—	—	1	—	2	3
Environmental protection	—	—	5	4	—	4	13
Political activity	—	—	—	2	—	3	5
Human rights (re: work)	5	2	5	—	5	5	22
Total	11	2	10	11	15	14	63

*It is expected, but is not a foregone certainty, that the Transnational Corporate Code of Conduct will incorporate into its provisions regarding employment practices the bulk and central meaning of those set forth in the ILO Tripartite Declaration. Hence, their omission in this Table should not be construed to mean that they have been ignored or overlooked by the drafters of the TNC Code.

Hence, preservation of a nation's integrity and self-interest appears to be one of the moral foundations on which such multilateral accords rest. Multinational enterprises are urged to respect the aims, goals, and directions of a host-country's economic and social development and its cultural and historical traditions. Companies' plans and goals should not contravene these components of a nation's being and sovereignty. Nor should they interfere in the internal political affairs of host countries through improper political activities, political bribes, or questionable payments of any kind made to political candidates or public officials.

Social Equity is another normative basis underlying some of the specific corporate guidelines. Pay scales are to be established in ways that will insure equity between men and women, racial and ethnic groups, professional and occupational groups, host-country nationals and parent-country expatriates, indigenous employees and migrant workers, and those well-off and those least-advantaged. The same equity principle is advocated for job opportunities, job training, treatment of the unemployed, and the provision of other work-related benefits and services.

Market Integrity is yet another source of moral authority and justification for some of the guidelines identified above, as well as for a large number of other guidelines specified in other agreements that are not treated here which have to do with restrictive business practices, the transnational flow of capital investments, the repatriation of profits, the rights of ownership, and similar matters. Among the normative corporate guidelines listed earlier, those tinged with the notion of market integrity include restrictions on political payments and bribes that might inject non-market considerations into business transactions, a recognition of private collective bargaining (rather than government mandates) as a preferred techniques for establishing pay scales, working conditions, and benefits for employees, and some (but not all)

of the consumer protections sought in the accords.

By far the most fundamental, comprehensive, widely acknowledged, and pervasive source of moral authority for the corporate guidelines is *human rights and fundamental freedoms.* This concept is given eloquent expression in the UN Universal Declaration of Human Rights. It is then picked up and adopted by the framers of four of the other five accords analyzed in this paper. Only the OECD Guidelines for Multinational Enterprises fail to invoke the specific language or the basic meaning of human rights and fundamental freedoms as the normative principle on which these accords are erected, although the OECD Guidelines incorporate some of these rights and freedoms as specific duties and obligations of multinationals. As previously noted, a number of OECD members are signatories to the European Convention on Human Rights, thereby subscribing to the basic principles of the Universal Declaration of Human Rights.

Essentially, the Declaration of Human Rights proclaims the existence of a whole host of human rights and freedoms, saying that they are inherent in the human condition. "All human beings are born free and equal in dignity and rights." "Equal and inalienable rights" are possessed by "all members of the human family" who also manifest an "inherent dignity." Other language speaks of "fundamental human rights," "the dignity and worth of the human person," "the equal rights of men and women," and "fundamental freedoms." These rights and freedoms exist "without distinction of any kind." They are understood as a common possession of humankind, not dependent on membership in any particular group, organization, nation, or society.

This invocation of human rights, as a philosophical principle, owes much to Immanuel Kant. In effect, the Declaration of Human Rights posits the Kantian person as the fundament of moral authority. The human person is said to possess an inherent worth and dignity, as well as inalienable and equal rights and freedoms. This being true of all human beings, correlative duties and obligations are thereby imposed on everyone to respect and not to interfere with the rights of others. No one person is warranted in using another as a means to promote one's own ends and purposes, absent a freely-given informed consent. Hence, a deceptively simple algorithm based on rights and duties sets the stage for the specification of normative rules of conduct for governments, groups, individuals, and—for present purposes—multinational enterprises.[3]

As powerful and compelling as the human rights principle is, it does compete with the other three normative sources—national sovereignty, social equity, and market integrity. This means that human rights are conditioned by political, social, and economic values. Rights do not stand alone or outside the normal range of human institutions, diverse as those institutions are around the globe and from society to society. The nation remains a sacred repository of group allegiance and fierce loyalty, an institution whose leaders at times are fully capable of depriving their own citizens and others of fundamental rights. Witness South Africa's apartheid system, China's brutal suppression of the student-led democracy movement, and the totalitarian excesses of Romania's communist leaders. In all three cases, the state and nation were invoked as ultimate criteria justifying the denial of human rights.

Moreover, societies everywhere erect systems of social status and class, instilling notions of "just claims" and insisting that most people should "know their place." For example, women around the globe find their rights and their life opportunities restricted by male-dominated economic and political systems. The same can be said of the widest variety of ethnic, religious, and racial groups throughout the world, whose fundamental rights and freedoms are often sacrificed on the altar of "social equity" as defined by dominant and competing groups.

Few economic institutions in modern times have appealed more powerfully than markets, whether directed by decentralized economic actors or by centralized states. Those who safeguard the integrity of markets, including officials responsible for high-level governmental or corporate policies, frequently accept the "market necessity" of closing a plant, shifting operations to lower-wage areas, or "busting" a trade union—all in the alleged interest of "allowing the market to work" or "enhancing national and corporate productivity." Doing so may deprive employees of jobs, living wages, retirement security, and other workplace rights.

Hence, in these several ways, rights everywhere are hedged in by such political, social, and economic features of human society. The behavioral guidelines for multinational corporations seem to have been woven, not from a single philosophic principle but by a blending of normative threads. At the pattern's center stand human rights and fundamental freedoms, for in the international compacts reference is found most frequently to this normative marker. But the strands of national sovereignty, social equity, and market integrity are woven into the overall pattern, coloring and giving form to the expression of human rights. Thus are human rights conditioned by societal factors.

One important trait is responsible for the normative dominance of the human rights principle. The human rights spoken of in the Universal Declaration of Human Rights are transcultural. As a principle, human rights span and disregard cultural and national boundaries, class systems, ethnic groupings, economic levels, and other human arrangements which for a variety of reasons differentiate between individuals and groups. Human rights are just that—human. They inhere in *all* humans, regardless of imposed societal classifications and exclusions. They can be defined, disregarded, or violated but they cannot be eradicated.

A transcultural character cannot be claimed for the other three normative sources. National sovereignty is by definition bound to and expressive of the nation. If "nation" is understood to embrace, not only the nation-state but also identification with and allegiance to an ethnic grouping, then it might be more accurate to speak of "socio-ethnicity" as the kind of sovereignty whose protection is sought. In any event, neither "nation-state" nor "socio-ethnic group" is or can be transcultural.

Similarly, social equity meanings rarely if ever span cultural boundaries, in spite of Marxist class theory to the contrary or even the mightiest efforts of Third World nations to see and organize themselves as the world's exploited underclass. That they *are* a global underclass, mistreated, and denied many opportunities by their more prosperous neighbors has not yet bound them together into a solid bloc that could be called transcultural.

Market integrity remains tied firmly to nation-states, even as regional interstate markets such as the European Common Market and the Andean Common Market emerge. Economic systems based on the market principle bear the marks of their national parent's political and ideological institutions. The relatively freer markets that have emerged during the 1980s in the Soviet Union, Eastern Europe, and China are heavily conditioned by the prevailing governmental philosophies of the respective countries, and their operation is not permitted to contravene the perceived needs of the state. The same may be said of markets in the United States, as one observes the ideological swings that accompany successive presidential administrations, legislative elections, and judicial decisions. United States government-imposed commercial sanctions against South Africa, the Soviet Union, Poland, Cuba, Nicaragua, Libya, and other nations reveal the nation-bound character of market operations.

Except for the human rights principle, all other normative sources that undergird the multinational corporate guidelines are thus culture bound, unable to break out of their respective societal contexts. By contrast, human rights are seen to be transcultural. They are the glue or the linchpin that holds the entire normative system together in a coherent international whole. While conditioned by desires for national (or socio-ethnic) sovereignty, social equity, and market integrity—thus finding their operational meaning within a societal context—human rights express attitudes, yearnings, and beliefs common to all humankind. In that sense, they form the core of a global system whose normative aim is to regulate the practices of multinational corporations.

This rights-based normative system finds justification in two ways. One is through deontological obligations implicit in human rights. Here, the philosopher speaks to us. The other justification is more directly operational, taking the form of lessons learned from human experience about the formation and sustenance of human values. These lessons are taught by social scientists. Each of these rationales calls for further elaboration.

RATIONALE I: DEONTOLOGICAL NORMS

The normative corporate guidelines may be seen as extensions and manifestations of broad deontological, i.e., duty-based, principles of human conduct. These principles provide a philosophic basis for defining the duties and obligations of multinational enterprises.

The concurring governments, in the several compacts mentioned here, are saying to multinational enterprises:

• Because your employees have rights to work, to security, to freedom of association, to healthful and safe work conditions, to a pay scale that sustains them and their families at a dignified level of subsistence, to privacy, and to be free from discrimination at work, the managers of multinational corporations incur duties and obligations to respect such rights, to promote them where and when possible, and to avoid taking actions that would deny these rights to the corporation's employees and other stakeholders.

• Because humans and their communities have rights to security, to health, and to the opportunity to develop themselves to their fullest potentials, corporations have an obligation to avoid harming the ecological balance on which human community life and health depend and a positive duty to promote environmental conditions conducive to the pursuit and protection of human rights.

• Because consumers have rights to safe and effective products and to know the quality and traits of the products and services they need to sustain life, companies are obligated, i.e., they have a duty, to offer such products for sale under conditions that permit a free, uncoerced choice for the consumer.

• Because human beings can lay claim to a set of human rights and fundamental freedoms enumerated in the Universal Declaration of Human Rights, multinational corporations are duty-bound to promote, protect, and preserve those rights and freedoms and to avoid trampling on them through corporate operations. The corporations' Kantian duty is implied in the Kantian rights held by all.

A moral imperative is thus imposed on corporations. The source of this deontological imperative is the rights and freedoms that inhere in all human persons. The corporation is bound, by this moral logic, to respect all persons within the purview of its decisions, policies, and actions. In some such fashion as this, the Universal Declaration of Human Rights serves as the deontological fount, the moral fundament, that defines a corporation's basic duties and obligations toward others. The Declaration's moral principles have been extended to many if not most of the multilateral compacts of the past 40 years, many of whose specific provisions take the form of normative guides for corporate actions across a large range of issues. So goes the moral logic of the accords and compacts.

This philosophic position is compelling and convincing. However, the case for a transcultural corporate ethic need not rest on philosophical arguments alone, or, more positively, the deontological position can be considerably enriched and strengthened by considering the role of human experience as a creator of human values.

RATIONALE II: EXPERIENCE-BASED VALUES

Respect for persons, respect for community integrity, respect for ecological balance, and respect for tested human experience in many spheres of life can be understood both deontologically and as adaptive human value orientations. As value phenomena, they are compatible with the needs and experiences of the world's peoples in a technological era. The need to proclaim many of the rights that appear in the Universal Declaration of Human Rights grew directly out of the gross violations of human rights during the pre-war and war periods of the 1930s and 1940s. Those experiences inspired most of the world's governments to take collective action, in the form of a proclamation, to define an acceptable number of such rights and to urge all to nourish and safeguard them.

Since that time, societies around the globe have felt the bite and seen the promise of technology spawned and applied by multinational corporations and governments. They have experienced the benefits, and have often borne the costs, of business operations undertaken without much regard for environmental, human, and community interests. These experiences have been as compelling, if not as traumatic, as those of the pre-war and war years when human rights were trampled. They have generated widespread agreement and belief in a network of experienced-based values that sustain the lives of individuals, their communities, and their societies. It is these values that have found their way into the several multilateral compacts and accords discussed here. Corporations are urged, not just to tend to their deontological duties but also to support, and not to override, the values that have been found through experience to undergird human flourishing.

Speaking of the role played by experience in formulating value standards, sociologist Robin Williams (1979: 22, 45) reminds us that

. . . values are learned. This means that they are developed through some kind of experience. . . . Similar repeated and pervasive experiences are often characteristic of large numbers of persons similarly situated in society; such experiences are described, discussed, and appraised by the persons involved. The communication of common appraisals eventually builds value standards, which often become widely accepted across many social and cultural boundaries. . . .

. . . value orientations, repeatedly experienced and reformulated by large numbers of persons over extended periods, will eventually become intellectualized as components of a comprehensive world view.

The gathering together of such experience-derived values concerning the human condition has produced "a comprehensive world view" of what is thought to be morally acceptable behavior by multinational enterprises. The specific "components" of that world view are the normative corporate guidelines described earlier. Humankind is speaking here, making known the basic, minimum, socially acceptable conditions for the conduct of economic enterprise. It is a voice that speaks the language of philosophically inspired rights and duties, as well as the language of a social-scientific conception of experienced-based, adaptive human values. The outcome in both cases is movement toward a transcultural corporate ethic, which is manifested in the six multilateral compacts or codes of conduct discussed here.

Another observer (Dilloway, 1986a: 427) reveals the transcultural moral potential of such international accords:

The final justification, therefore, for a code of rights is, first, that it defines the conditions in which human potential can develop peacefully in an interdependent milieu; and, second, that such a code, whether for the individual or for interstate relations, offers the only frame of common ideas that can span the diversity of cultures, religions, living standards, and political and economic sys-

tems to create a common nexus of humane practice for an emergent world community.

This view is echoed by Richard Falk (1980:67, 108):

To think of human rights in the world as a whole . . . is itself a reflection of the emergence, however weakly, of a planetary perspective based on the notion that persons . . . warrant our normative attention.

Nor is there is any reason to restrict this "frame of common ideas"—this morality of the commons—to multinational enterprises alone. It would apply with equal force to domestic and multinational companies. Where nations have been able to identify and agree upon common ethical principles and common values that reflect the experience of even the most diverse cultures, a moral minimum has been established. It remains within the power of some governments and their citizens and businesses to exceed this minimum, while other governments' powers may be insufficiently dedicated to meet even the minimum moral standards. But this minimum—the international common morality, the "common nexus of humane practice," the planetary perspective—stands as a benchmark to be striven for. While it exists, no corporation, domestic or multinational, can legitimately claim the right to operate without referring its policies and practices to this basic moral standard, this morality of the commons that has been writ large upon the global . . .

LESSONS FOR POLICY MAKERS

Those who set policies, whether for public or private institutions, can find some important lessons in these multinational codes of conduct.

The most compelling lesson is that highly diverse governments and societies have been able to reach a workable consensus about some core normative directives for multinational enterprises. That should send a strong message to corporate leaders everywhere that the world's peoples, speaking through their governments, are capable of setting standards intended to guide corporate practices and policies into morally desirable channels. As noted, there continues to be much disagreement among governments about many of these issues, but failure to agree on everything should not be allowed to cloak an achieved consensus on many other issues.

Wise corporate leaders will be able to interpret this consensus as a framework of public expectations on which the policies of their own companies can be based. Global stakeholders have set out their positions on a large range of problems and issues that matter to them. In effect, corporations are being offered an opportunity to match their own operations to these public expectations. The best ones will do so. The others may wish they had if, in failing to heed the normative messages, they encounter rising hostility and increased governmental intervention in their affairs.

For public policy makers, these agreements betoken a growing consensus among the world's peoples about what is thought to be morally desirable action by governments. It would be as perilous for political leaders to ignore this rising tide of global agreement as for corporate policy makers to turn their backs upon it. The authority and legitimacy of these central economic and political institutions are frequently at risk, as illustrated so dramatically in Eastern Europe in 1989 and 1990. Therefore, it will be vitally important for those charged with making institutional policies to guide their respective societies in ways acceptable to their citizens.

Acting to promote this normative consensus can be encouraged if policy makers understand both the philosophic roots and the experience-based values from which these international agreements draw their meaning and strength. The philosophic concept of the human person that one finds in these multilateral compacts, and the human and humane values that grow out of shared global experiences, are no mere passing fancy of a planetary people. Building policy on these twin foundations will bring government and business into alignment with the deep structure of human aspirations.

BEYOND MULTINATIONALS: THE CULTURE OF ETHICS

The transcultural corporate ethic described here is only one part of a much more comprehensive, universal moral order whose shadowy outlines are only partially apparent. This broader "culture of ethics" includes all of those fundamental values and moral orientations that have been proven through long experience to contribute to the sustenance and flourishing of human persons within their communities (Frederick, 1986). It will be important, and increasingly apparent, that all economic enterprises, public and private, domestic and multinational, are bound to acknowledge the moral force of this culture of ethics and to shape their policies and practices accordingly. This "moral dimension" of economic analysis and corporate decision making can no longer be set aside or treated as a peripheral matter (Etzioni, 1988). As human societies are drawn ever closer together by electronic and other technologies, and as they face the multiple threats posed by the unwise and heedless use of these devices, it will become ever more necessary to reach agreement on the core values and ethical principles that permit a humane life to be lived by all. Such planetary agreement is now visible, though yet feeble in its rudiments. This broadscale culture of ethics draws upon many societal, religious, and philosophical sources. It is a great chorus of human voices, human aspirations, and human experiences, arising out of societal and cultural and individual diversity, that expresses the collective normative needs of a global people.

Notes

1. The successor protocols subsequently attached to some of these compacts are not treated here,

although doing so would strengthen the paper's argument. Of particular importance are the International Covenant on Economic, Social, and Cultural Rights; the International Covenant on Civil and Political Rights; and the Optional Protocol to the International Covenant on Civil and Political Rights. These three instruments, which were adopted by the United Nations General Assembly in 1966, transformed the general principles of the Universal Declaration of Human Rights into legal obligations of the ratifying states. By 1985, about half of the governments had ratified these covenants (Dilloway 1986 b: 458–459). Three additional documents, two of them intergovernmental and one privately proclaimed, all with obviously normative messages for multinational corporations, have not been included. They are the World Health Organization's International Code on the Marketing of Breast-milk Substitutes (1981), the European Economic Community's Code of Conduct for Companies with Interests in South Africa (1977), and The Sullivan Principles concerning U.S. corporate operations in South Africa (1977). The normative principles on which these three documents are based are entirely consistent with those found in the six compacts that are the focus of this paper. Hence, the case being made here for the emergence of a normative system of global dimensions is predictably stronger than the evidence adduced.

2. The Helsinki Final Act, the ILO Tripartite Declaration, and the UN Code for Transnational Corporations incorporate a general statement accepting the UN Universal Declaration of Human Rights; hence, each of these accords is shown as expressing those guidelines that are derived from the UN Declaration.

Of the numerous human rights and freedoms identified in the UN Declaration, only those are included here whose observance or violation would be most closely tied to corporate operations. Many rights and freedoms with a "political" content are thereby not treated here, although it could be further argued that corporate influence on the public policies and political processes of host nations exerts both direct and indirect effect on such rights and freedoms.

It also should be noted that the UN Universal Declaration of Human Rights takes the form of a resolution of the General Assembly and is not a convention, treaty, or accord to which government representatives affix their signatures. Therefore, it is not technically correct to refer to the "signatories" of the Universal Declaration. Where that usage is employed here, it should be understood as meaning only that the then-voting members of the General Assembly agreed to the Declaration's central message.

3. The algorithm is "deceptively simple" by seeming to overlook the enormous volume of argumentation, qualifications, and exceptions to Kant's views that has been produced by succeeding generations of philosophers. Extended discussion of theories of human rights may be found in Shue (1980) and Nickel (1987). Thomas Donaldson (1989) has developed a far more sophisticated view of ethical algorithms than the one offered here, and I am indebted to him for both the concept and the phrase itself.

References

DILLOWAY, A. J.: 1986a, 'Human Rights and Peace', in Ervin Laszlo and Jong Youl Yoo (eds.), *World Encyclopedia of Peace*. vol. 1 (Pergamon Press, Oxford), p. 427.

DILLOWAY, A. J.: 1986b, 'International Bill of Rights,' in Ervin Laszlo and Jong Youl Yoo (eds.), *World Encyclopedia of Peace*, vol. 1 (Pergamon Press, Oxford), pp. 458–9.

DONALDSON, THOMAS: 1989, *The Ethics of International Business* (Oxford University Press, New York).

DWORKIN, RONALD: 1977, *Taking Rights Seriously* (Harvard University Press, Cambridge).

ETZIONI, AMITAI: 1988, *The Moral Dimension: Toward a New Economics* (Free Press, New York).

FALK, RICHARD: 1980, 'Theoretical Foundations of Human Rights', in Paula Newberg (ed.): *The Politics of Human Rights* (New York University Press, New York).

FELD, WERNER J.: 1980, *Multinational Corporations and U.N. Politics: The Quest for Codes of Conduct* (Pergamon Press, New York).

FREDERICK, WILLIAM C.: 1986, 'Toward CSR3: Why Ethical Analysis is Indispensable and Unavoidable in Corporate Affairs', *California Management Review* 28(3), 126–41.

KOHLBERG, LAWRENCE: 1981, *The Philosophy o f Moral Development* (Harper & Row, San Francisco).

NICKEL, JAMES W.: 1987, *Making Sense of Human Rights: Philosophical Reflections on the Universal Declaration of Human Rights* (University of California Press, Berkeley).

ROBERTSON, A. H.: 1977, *Human Rights in Europe*. 2nd edition (Manchester University Press, Manchester).

ROKEACH, MILTON: 1973, *The Nature of Human Values* (Free Press, New York).

ROKEACH, MILTON: 1979, *Understanding Human Values: Individual and Societal* (Free Press, New York).

ROWAN, RICHARD L. AND DUNCAN C. CAMPBELL: 1983, 'The Attempt to Regulate Industrial Relations through International Codes of Conduct', *Columbia Journal of World Business* 18(2), 64–72.

SHUE, HENRY, 1980, *Basic Rights: Subsistence, Affluence, and U.S. Foreign Policy* (Princeton University Press, Princeton, N.J.).

UNITED NATIONS: 1983, *Human Rights: A Compilation of International Instruments* (United Nations, New York).

UNITED NATIONS: 1988, *Transnational Corporations in World Development: Trends and Prospects* (United Nations, New York).

WALDMAN, RAYMOND J.: 1980. *Regulating International Business through Codes of Conduct* (American Enterprise Institute, Washington, D.C.).

WALLACE, CYNTHIA DAY: 1982, *Legal Control of the Multinational Enterprise: National Regulatory Techniques and the Prospects for International Controls* (Martinus Nijhoff, The Hague).

WINDSOR, DUANE AND LEE E. PRESTON: 1988. 'Corporate Governance, Social Policy and Social Performance in the Multinational Corporation', in Lee E. Preston (ed.), *Research in Corporate Social Performance and Policy,* vol. 10 (JAI Press, Greenwich, Conn.).

WILLIAMS, ROBIN: 1979, 'Change and Stability in Values and Value Systems', in Milton Rokeach, *Understanding Human Values* (Free Press, New York).

Study Questions

1. How does Frederick relate ethical principles to rules? Use the reinforcement view of law to explain your answer.

2. Is Frederick arguing for the creation of an international institutional environment as De George does in Chapter 6? Is this realistic? What benefits and problems would arise in such an environment? For example, what happens to national sovereignty?

3. Use Frederick's analysis to evaluate the Merck case.

CASE: Wait International and Questionable Payments
Charles R. Kennedy, Jr.

In January 1990, Bill Glade, Director of Internal Audit for Wait International, Inc., had been asked to review the company's code of conduct and to make recommendations concerning questionable payments to government officials, suppliers, and contractors. Because Bill had been recently promoted to this new position, this was his first major assignment. The previous director of internal audit had been promoted to corporate controller.

The company's Board of Directors thought this review was necessary for two reasons: The U.S. Foreign Corrupt Practices Act (FCPA) had been significantly amended last year, and some of the countries where international expansion was planned had a history of demanding payments from foreign companies. In particular, a senior member of Indonesia's Capital Investment Coordinating Board (BKPM) had recently suggested that Wait International could receive "special consideration" under the Foreign Capital Investment Law (FCIL) if certain payments were made. Under FCIL, the following concessions were available to qualified applicants in "priority industries": exemption from import duties on capital equipment, construction materials, and raw materials for three years; exemption from corporate income taxes and dividend withholding for five years; and the right to use accelerated depreciation and loss carryforward in determining income tax liabilities.

Besides these "entry" costs, government officials in Indonesia were also known to routinely demand payment from companies with ongoing operations in the country on such matters as work permits for expatriates, import licenses, brand-name approval, and price increases. To help expedite such matters, one American country manager, with several years' experience in Indonesia, told Bill that his U.S. company had routinely held an annual party for key government officials. These lavish parties included "willing" females. Another country manager for a Japanese firm informed Bill that everything in Indonesia had a fee attached to the approval process. For example, the Japanese manager recently paid an Indonesian official within the Patent and Trademark Office $1,000 to get his company's product's brand name approved for local sales. In another case, a manager for a German company suggested that Wait International should hire the brother of the director of the BKPM, who was a local lawyer with a successful track record in getting concessions under the FCIL. Bill understood that Wait International had planned to hire another local law firm, which had two American-trained partners that in-house counsel had gone to school with. Bill wondered if his company should go with the director's brother instead, even though he charged a 200 percent premium over the American-trained lawyers. In addition, Bill was not sure how the company's current code of conduct applied to these different kinds of payment demands, particularly in light of the amended FCPA, and he knew the company's Board of Directors had similar questions. Besides the legality of the company's position and of its employees, Bill felt the ethical dimension had to be clearly and explicitly addressed as well.

This case was prepared by Charles R. Kennedy, Jr., Babcock School of Management, Wake Forest University. Reprinted by permission of the author.

WAIT INTERNATIONAL, INC.

Wait International, Inc., is a billion-dollar-plus company that is a diversified manufacturer of consumer and light-industrial products. The company is incorporated and headquartered in the United States, but half of its sales and profits are from outside the United States. The company's normal international operation is a self-contained manufacturing and sales operation in each nation. Thus, subsidiaries in foreign countries are separate profit centers, headed by a country president who reports to a group officer in charge of a single product in a geographic area (e.g., the vice president of Far East operations for a product). At present, Wait International, Inc., has operations in England, Italy, Spain, France, Germany, Argentina, Brazil, Mexico, Japan, South Korea, Taiwan, South Africa, and the Philippines.

Wait International was a fast-growing, profitable company. Sales had climbed nearly 12 percent between 1988 and 1989, which exceeded a 10 percent average for the entire 1980s. Net income to sales was also over 8 percent in the last two years. Much of this growth and profitability was due to international operations, where sales had grown nearly 20 percent in the last ten years on net profit margins of over 12 percent. Because of this success, Wait International planned to expand into countries where it currently did not have operations. As a general rule, such an expansion would require capital investments of at least $5 million in each country in which it opened a new operation.

QUESTIONABLE PAYMENTS AT WAIT INTERNATIONAL

Unlike some other U.S. multinationals, Wait International had avoided major legal problems with questionable payments abroad. To some degree this was explained by the nature of the businesses that the company was in. For example, bribery and illegal payments to foreign officials have been most common in oligopolistic industries handling large, capital-intensive products; these would include aerospace, construction, and energy companies. In fact, the bulk of more than 400 U.S. corporations who voluntarily admitted over $300 million worth of questionable payments to U.S. government investigators in 1976 came from such industries. Exxon disclosed payments of $59.4 million; Lockheed, $55 million; Boeing, $50.4 million; and Northrop, $34.3 million. Wait International, being primarily a manufacturer of consumer and light-industrial products, was not subject to the same kind of pressures and temptations as were other companies.

Another factor helping to explain Wait International's relatively clean record on questionable payments is that the company before 1977, when the original FCPA was passed, did not operate in countries where demands for questionable payments were typically high. Investments in the developing countries of Argentina, Brazil, Mexico, South Korea, Taiwan, and the Philippines were not made until the late 1970s and early 1980s. By that time, the company had established a code of conduct that was vigorously enforced (see Exhibit 1).

Several country presidents of overseas subsidiaries were often frustrated and confused by the company's code of conduct statement. For one thing, the statement was very general and hard to interpret. In terms of the "payments and gifts" section, what did "significant value" actually mean? When did customary business entertainment become improper? Was impropriety mainly an issue of perception? Country presidents in Latin American and Asia found the issues to be particularly important because of how business in those areas was normally conducted. Facilitating or "grease" payments were expected by many government workers for the most routine decisions, including such a

---

EXHIBIT 1   CODES OF ETHICAL AND LEGAL CONDUCT

Code of Conduct: The highest standard of individual conduct is expected at all times from each employee and any of its subsidiaries, not only in matters of financial integrity, but in every aspect of business relationships.

Compliance with the Law: First and foremost, pertinent laws of every jurisdiction in which the company operates must be followed. Each employee is charged with the responsibility of sufficient knowledge of the law in order to recognize potential dangers and to know when to seek legal advice.

Competition: Competition based on quality, service, and price is the heart of the free enterprise system, and the company enthusiastically accepts this challenge and competes on a positive basis.

Conflicts of Interest: Employees are required periodically to read and verify their compliance with a policy that is intended to avoid actual or apparent impropriety. Favoritism, preferential treatment, and unethical business practices are to be avoided at all costs.

Payments and Gifts: Payment or receipt of kickbacks, bribes, or undisclosed commissions is contrary to company policy. Giving and receiving business gifts of nominal value, while discouraged, is permissible where customary. Giving or receiving gifts of significant value is prohibited. Customary business entertainment is proper; impropriety results when the value or cost is such that it could be interpreted as affecting an otherwise objective business decision.

The company will comply with the U.S. Foreign Corrupt Practices Act. This Act generally prohibits payments or gifts to any official of any government entity, or department, agency, or instrumentality thereof, illegally or corruptly to influence the act or decision of the government or official in order that the company can obtain or retain business or have business directed to it.

Company Assets and Transactions: Compliance with prescribed accounting procedures is required at all times. In all instances, employees having control in any manner over company assets and transactions are expected to handle them with the strictest integrity and to accurately and fairly record them in reasonable detail on the company's books.

---

mundane task as when a telephone would be installed or serviced. Did the code-of-conduct statement forbid these kinds of payments? Certainly, the document was not very specific on such matters. Informally, the company allowed each country president a great deal of leeway in deciding what an acceptable gift or entertainment expense was and how to interpret the FCPA. Nearly all country presidents reacted by being very wary of questionable practices. If there was any doubt at all in their minds about the impropriety of a particular payment or gift, it was not made. Consequently, business was at times adversely affected because either deals were not made or operations were disrupted owing to a slowdown in bureaucratic decision making.

FCPA

Before making a recommendation, Bill needed to understand fully the FCPA, as amended in the Omnibus Trade and Competitiveness Act of 1988. The FCPA attacks the problem of corporate bribery abroad in a twofold approach: first by banning certain types of foreign payments and second by requiring U.S. firms to keep accurate records and to maintain adequate internal accounting controls. The antibribery provisions of the act prohibit firms from paying foreign officials in order to obtain or retain business. The accounting provisions deter bribery by imposing an affirmative requirement on firms and managers to keep books and records that accurately reflect an entity's transactions (including any questionable payments) and to maintain an adequate system of internal controls to assure that the entity's assets are used for proper corporate purposes. Individuals violating the antibribery or the accounting provisions can be fined up to $100,000, imprisoned for up to five years, or both for each offense. Corporations, on the other hand, can be fined up to $2 million for criminal violations of the act.

The antibribery provisions of the Foreign Corrupt Practices Act thus criminalize certain questionable payments. The provisions apply to all corporations with reporting obligations to the SEC or whose securities are registered with the SEC *and* to all "domestic concerns." The FCPA defines "domestic concerns" as all citizens, nationals, or residents of the United States and all business entities organized under the laws of any state, territory, or possession, or having its principal place of business in the United States.

This definition would appear to exclude from the jurisdiction of the FCPA foreign subsidiaries of American corporations that are organized under the laws of a foreign country and that have their principal place of business outside the United States. However, the FCPA as amended in 1988 makes it unlawful to make, offer, or authorize payments to "any person while knowing that all or a portion of such money or thing will be offered or given or promised, directly or indirectly, to any foreign official . . . for purposes of . . . influencing any act or decision of such foreign official." Because *knowing* is defined as specific awareness or "willful blindness," U.S. corporations will typically be held responsible for illegal payments made by their foreign subsidiaries, particularly those that are wholly or majority-owned. For minority-owned subsidiaries, on the other hand, the corporation must act in good faith to use its influence on the subsidiary to comply with the law.

Besides defining the scope of the law in terms of the party making the payment, the FCPA also addresses the issue of who is being paid and why. If payments are made to foreign officials in order to expedite routine government action, such a payment is legal under the FCPA. Routine government action is defined as

> an action which is ordinarily and commonly performed by a foreign official in—
>
> (i) obtaining permits, licenses or other official documents to qualify a person to do business in a foreign country;
>
> (ii) processing government papers such as visas and work orders;
>
> (iii) providing police protection, mail pick-up and delivery or scheduling inspections associated with contract performance or inspections related to transit of goods across country;
>
> (iv) providing phone service, power and water supply, loading and unloading cargo or protecting perishable products or commodities from deterioration; or
>
> (v) actions of similar nature.

Congress's interpretation of the law, as expressed by the Senate-House Conference Report, however, specifically excluded from routine action any decision that had the functional equivalent of "obtaining or retaining business for or with or directing business to any person." For example, payments to a ministry official responsible for authorizing price increases for a product would still be illegal under the FCPA because that would constitute an attempt to influence the discretionary power of a foreign official in order to gain or retain business.

Thus the intent of the law is that payments must be made "corruptly" in order to be considered a violation; an individual or entity making a payment would be held liable under the act only if he or she were found to possess "an evil motive or purpose [or] an intent to wrongfully influence the recipient." For example, the legislative history behind the act indicates that "true extortion situations" would not be illegal since "a payment to keep an oil rig from being dynamited should not be held to be made with the requisite corrupt purpose."

The FCPA identifies three classes of foreign individuals or entities to whom payments are prohibited, unless they are for expediting routine government action; these individuals are:

(1) any foreign official;

(2) any foreign political party or official thereof or any candidate for foreign political office;

(3) any person, when a company knows that person will give, promise or offer all or part of the company's payment to a third party who is a foreign official, political party or candidate for political office. The FCPA defines a "foreign official as any officer or employee of a foreign government or any department, agency, or instrumentality thereof, or any person acting in an official capacity for or on behalf of any such government or department, agency, or instrumentality. Such term does not include any employee of a foreign government or any department, agency, or instrumentality thereof whose duties are essentially ministerial or clerical.

By excluding from its definition of "foreign officials" those persons "whose duties are essentially ministerial or clerical," Congress apparently intended to allow under the FCPA so-called facilitating or grease payments made to minor functionaries to persuade them to carry out their customary tasks—such as allowing shipments through customs, issuing construction permits, or giving police protection.

The FCPA thus would not bar large payments to minor officials—as long as their duties are "ministerial or clerical." In addition, the 1988 amendments provide areas of affirmative defense against charges of FCPA violations. For example, a firm could defend itself on the basis that "the payment of a gift, offer or promise of anything of value that was made was lawful under the written laws and regulations of the foreign official's, political party's, party official's or candidate's country." In addition, the 1988 amendments provide an affirmative defense that

the payment, gift, offer or promise of value that was made was a reasonable bona fide expenditure, such as travel and lodging expenses . . . directly related to—

(A) the promotion, demonstration or explanation of products or services; or

(B) the execution or performance of a contract with a foreign government or agency thereof.

The Conference Report, however, explicitly stated that if a gift or payment is corruptly made to obtain or retain business then such a defense would not be acceptable.

Whereas the antibribery provisions apply to all "domestic concerns," whether or not these are businesses registered with the SEC, the accounting provisions cover only companies subject to securities laws—that is, only public companies. In a sense, however, the accounting provisions have a wider scope than the antibribery statutes. Bribery is a rare event, compared to record-keeping and control, which are day-to-day activities.

The accounting provisions as amended in 1988 have the following features. First, the law limits criminal liability for violating the accounting provisions to those who "knowingly circumvent" the system of internal accounting controls or who "knowingly falsify" accounting records or transactions. This legal standard conforms to the earlier SEC announcement that "if a violation was committed by a low level employee, without the knowledge of top management, with an adequate system of internal controls, and with appropriate corrective action taken by the issuer, we do not believe that any action against the company would be called for." Second, the 1988 amendments explicitly define both the "reasonable detail" in which firms must keep their books and the "reasonable assurance" that management has control over corporate assets. The definition employed is "such a level of detail and degree of assurance as would satisfy prudent officials in the conduct of their own affairs having in mind a comparison between benefits to be obtained and costs to be incurred in obtaining such benefits." Again, this definition mirrors earlier SEC statements or interpretations that guided enforcement under the FCPA.

TOWARD A NEW CODE OF CONDUCT

After reviewing and studying the amended FCPA, Bill Glade decided to seek the advice of a lawyer outside the company on legal responsibilities and actions that Wait International should take. The lawyer was asked to address two key issues: what the firm should do if FCPA violation by employees were discovered and what preventative measures should be taken to reduce the likelihood of violations occurring in the first place. The lawyer's report is contained in Exhibit 2.

EXHIBIT 2

MEMO
TO: Bill Glade, Director of Internal Audit
           Wait International, Inc.
FROM: Chedrick R. Kellington
RE: FCPA Compliance
DATE: 1/7/90

You have asked me to address the fundamental issues regarding FCPA compliance by your firm. I understand that you are familiar with the details of the law as amended in 1988, so my comments will be made under that assumption. In particular, you wanted to know your firm's legal responsibilities if violations of the FCPA occur and how to best reduce the chances of such violations occurring. I will address these two interrelated issues in turn.

What should your firm do if suspected violations of the FCPA have occurred? Probably the least painful course for any company discovering its own violations is the SEC's voluntary disclosure program, which started in 1975. If you find yourself in such a situation, the firm can conduct internal investigations, publicly file the material facts (usually on Form 8–K, filed with the SEC), and adopt preventative measures. The SEC requires that the internal investigation be conducted by independent members of the board of directors, with help from the firm's regular external auditing firm. Preventative measures include strengthened internal controls and a corporate policy statement from the board of directors. The policy statement is intended to prevent illegal foreign and domestic political payments as well as false or incomplete books and records.

I also offer the following advice. If managers or auditors of public companies discover possible violations, they should inform inside counsel and the audit committee (or the board itself, if the company has no audit committee) and seek advice from outside counsel. If the lawyers believe that the violations may be significant, the audit committee or the board should authorize an internal inquiry. Investigators should include outside counsel and outside auditors, and they should report directly to the board or to the audit committee. When the inquiry is complete, the audit committee can determine whether or not a corrective Form 8–K must be filed with the SEC. At this point, the company will be able to negotiate with the SEC. The manner of resolution acceptable to the SEC will depend on the seriousness of the violation and the degree of participation by senior managers. A. Clarence Sampson, the SEC's former Chief Accountant, has stated that the SEC would look more kindly on companies that make timely disclosures and take preventative actions on their own. Privately held companies should follow similar internal procedures, conferring instead with the Justice Department on the best means of resolution.

What sorts of preventative measures are possible? Most lawyers urge that a company's first step should be to set up an audit committee of independent and energetic outside directors. Secondly, managers should review existing controls—to avoid violating either the record-keeping or the controls provision. Such a review could begin with the external auditor's criticisms and suggestions. Thus, senior managers, internal counsel, and internal auditors should carefully examine the auditor's suggestions. If managers choose not to make any of the proposed changes, they should record the reasons for that decision.

Controls of certain sensitive transactions should be carefully reviewed whether or not external auditors are critical of them. Such transactions include the following: political contributions; transfers of funds outside of the country; use of tangible corporate assets, such as aircraft, boats, apartments and estates; and possible insider-dealings, such as sales to firms owned in part by corporate officials. In all these instances it is particularly important that the records show not only the amounts but also the circumstances and true purposes of all transactions.

Allowable facilitating payments must also be carefully documented and controlled, to comply with the accounting provisions as well as to ensure that employees do not escalate purported grease payments into bribes. Castle and Cook, Inc., a Honolulu-based diversified food company, has described its methods of controlling facilitating payments. Robert Moore, vice president and general counsel, has told me that the firm draws up careful budgets for all "specially regulated costs." No grease payments may be made unless they have been budgeted. The total budget for facilitating payments is usually over $200,000 per year; the money is used to get local army and police personnel to guard warehouses, to move shipments through customs, and to get ships out of port. Each division's budget for such payments is screened by internal and external legal counsel in the host countries to determine that the payments are legal under local laws. The division's treasurer must certify that the payments are used for the purposes specified. Then the budgets pass up through the ranks to be approved by group managers, internal auditors, general counsel, and the vice president of finance.

Auditors also recommend that certain types of accounts and assets are particularly vulnerable to misappropriation and therefore require stringent controls. For example, political payments have often been made from accounts without tangible assets—such as accounts for consulting expenses, for sales expenses (advertising, commissions, discounts), or for employee remuneration (bonuses, travel, entertainment). Accounts payable have also been drained. Other endangered assets are those that are unrecorded and readily converted to cash—such as scrap, vending machine revenue, sales samples, marketing plans and data lists (lists of stockholders, employees, or customers). Lastly, all payments to third-party intermediaries (sales agents, outside counsel, consultants) need to be carefully controlled and monitored.

In addition to reviewing existing controls and strengthening them if necessary, your firm will want to consider whether the firm's organization fosters compliance. For example, internal auditors are less likely to be influenced if they report directly to the audit committee or to the board than if they report to senior financial managers. Similarly, internal auditors of divisions and subsidiaries are less susceptible if they report to central auditors rather than to divisional or subsidiary managers—although the latter procedure is more often the case. In general, the more decentralized the company and the greater a unit's distance from headquarters, the greater the chances that the unit will disregard corporate controls if they seem to be a nuisance. Because corporations can be held liable for subsidiaries' actions, some companies are now requiring from their subsidiaries quarterly reports documenting and explaining financial conditions, sensitive payments, and irregularities in internal controls.

Your firm should also consider whether or not the climate in the company subtly persuades employees to override controls and resort to creative accounting or bribes. Sometimes overly optimistic forecasts motivate executives to manipulate accounts and falsify reports. Other pressures might include excess capacity, obsolete product lines, unrealistic demands for more profits, and sales dependent on a few customers or transactions.

Finally, written corporate conduct codes will help employees to understand the law and to resist temptation. Although you cannot completely eliminate the actions of dishonest employees, it is crucial that top management record its disapproval of such activity in writing and communicate that policy periodically to all employees. One should also stress that the resulting code of conduct is not only a document of legal compliance but one that sets the tone of ethical business practices as well. It is within that context that compliance with the law and the company's code of conduct is most assured. Employees should know in no uncertain terms that the document is as much a moral as it is a legal statement and that violations of the code will result in immediate dismissal.

I hope this advice has been helpful. If you ever require any additional assistance, please let me know.

After receiving and reading the lawyer's report, Bill was convinced, more than ever, that an amended code of conduct was required. Bill's proposal is contained in Exhibit 3. In particular, the "Payments and Gifts" section of the earlier statement was completely rewritten. This section in the old code of conduct was too vague in Bill's opinion, and if compliance was left up to the interpretation of each country president, the probability of FCPA violations would increase. Bill was concerned this would happen because the amended law seemed to allow many more payments than in the past, and if their country presidents engaged in more questionable payments as a result, then the chances were high that missteps would be made. To counter potential legal problems, the company must be more specific and stringent in what was allowed in the area of questionable payments. Moreover, for Bill this was the ethical approach to take. To pay government officials or workers anything but insignificant sums of money seemed wrong to him. Such payments only encouraged or reinforced unethical behavior.

Bill circulated his proposed changes prior to the upcoming meeting of the Board of Directors. His cover memo for the proposed changes can be seen in Exhibit 4. One mem-

---

EXHIBIT 3   CODE OF CONDUCT COMPLIANCE PROCEDURES RELATING TO QUESTIONABLE PAYMENTS

1. The following Code of Conduct applies to Wait International, Inc., and its subsidiaries and advises employees in management responsibilities throughout the world of the Company's responsibility to comply with the U.S. Foreign Corrupt Practices Act and foreign law; it generally prohibits bribes, kickbacks, or undisclosed commissions. The Code is redistributed annually and recipients are required to acknowledge their receipt, understanding, and agreement to comply therewith.

2. The Wait International Corporate accounting Manual has replicated the content of the Code of Conduct insofar as this subject is concerned.

3. Management advises operating personnel that, while payments to government officials may be legal under U.S. and foreign law ("Facilitating Payments"), the Company's policy is that such Facilitating Payments should not be made. However, Facilitating Payments will be tolerated if necessary to prevent substantial disruption to the business, and then *only* if (i) such payments receive prior approval by the managing director, (ii) any individual payment does not exceed $100 (or its foreign currency equivalent), and (iii) each such payment is reported to the Internal Audit Department.

4. The entry into new countries, or the commencement of large projects in foreign countries, is preceded by researching the local laws as to any prohibitions or permission for the payment of money or giving of gifts to government officials.

5. Any third-party intermediaries whom an operating unit proposes to retain are chosen from those candidates who are highly recommended by reputable sources in the country and who have demonstrated a history of successful efforts with an unblemished reputation for integrity and compliance with the law.

6. Such third-party intermediaries are required to sign contracts containing acknowledgments of the existence of U.S. and foreign laws relating to illegal payments and of the Company's policies regarding compliance with law and the conduct of business, and the intermediary's agreement to comply therewith.

7. Prior to engagement by an operating unit, the proposed compensation for an intermediary is compared to other reasonable and customary charges of known reputable parties in similar circumstances. Actual charges once third parties are retained are audited by local management on a 100% basis, and on a periodic sampling basis by the Internal Audit Department.

8. An intermediary is required to supply detailed written support for each payment to be made by the intermediary to any third party in the course of the contract.

9. Payments deemed questionable under foreign or U.S. law are referred to the Corporate or Operating Unit Law Department for determination as to legality.

10. Matters referred to the Law Department for determination may be further referred to local counsel, as to foreign law matters, or to the U.S. Justice Department for an advisory opinion, as to questions involving the Foreign Corrupt Practices Act.

---

ber of the board, the executive vice president for international affairs, had a very negative reaction. He was so opposed to Bill's recommendation that a stinging memo was written and distributed to other board members before the meeting (see Exhibit 5). Bill wondered whether he had made a political mistake in making his own recommendation and how he should defend himself in the meeting.

EXHIBIT 4

MEMO
TO: Board of Directors, Wait International, Inc.
FROM: Bill Glade, Director of Internal Audit
RE: Proposed Changes in Company's Code of Conduct
DATE: 1/15/90

I've attached my recommended changes to the code-of-conduct statement given my review of the amended FCPA. I should stress that the proposal is meant to replace the "Payments and Gifts" section of the old statement only. I think the new wording has the advantage of being more specific and detailed. Our country presidents certainly need more guidance, especially given the recent changes in the law. Without clearer and stricter guidelines, the probability grows that mistakes will be made, and the company will then face the legal consequences. If adopted, the revised code-of-conduct statement would not only be in full and complete compliance with the law but would also place the company on a high ethical plane. As a general rule, the company should not make payments to government officials or workers who are violating the public trust. I will be glad to explain these recommendations more fully at the upcoming meeting of the board next week.

EXHIBIT 5

MEMO
TO: Board of Directors, Wait International, Inc.
FROM   Bryan C. Wade, Executive Vice President for International Affairs
RE: Bill Glade's Proposed Changes in the Company's Code-of-Conduct Statement
DATE: 1/18/90

Before our meeting next week, I want to express my strong opposition to Bill Glade's proposed changes in the company's code-of-conduct statement. I have several problems with his proposal. First, why would we want to impose a much stricter set of standards than we had earlier when the government has decided to loosen its restrictions? The amended FCPA was in response to the adverse competitive consequences the original law had on American firms abroad. Our firm certainly suffered some negative consequences, as our country presidents avoided any and all payments that might have been even remotely perceived as improper. Now when the amended law clearly says that "facilitating payments" to any government official or worker are legal, irrespective of amount, Bill Glade recommends that such payments not be made a general rule, and even when such payments are "necessary to prevent substantial disruption to the business," they are limited to $100. Why such an arbitrary limit? If the demand is for $101, do we allow our business to be seriously disrupted? If the managing director is getting involved in any case, why can't he decide if the amount is proper and justified? I could imagine many situations where a facilitating payment of several hundred dollars would not only be good business but also clearly within the law.

On another level, I question Bill Glade's imposition of his ethical standards on others. In fact, I'm personally offended by his implication that individuals who support facilitating payments when they are legal and make good business sense are engaged in questionable or unethical behavior. Moreover, if I were a government official or worker in a foreign country, I would find Bill Glade's self-righteous attitude offensive as well. Who are we to tell them that they are engaged in unethical behavior when they ask for customary facilitating payments? In many countries, such payments are accepted as part of the job and have been going on for decades, if not centuries. As long as payments are not used for corrupting purposes, which are true violations of their public trust, money spent to facilitate their normal duties, such as providing import licenses, telephone service, expatriate permits, etc., are completely ethical. Thus I oppose Bill Glade's recommendations on both moral and practical business grounds.

Study Questions

1. How is Wait's policy decision about foreign payments affected by the legal environment at home and abroad?

2. Should Wait obey the letter of the law or the spirit of the law? Use the reinforcement view of law to explain your answer (note: the reinforcement view is broad enough to support either answer).

3. If Frederick were hired as a consultant, what might he tell Wait?

Bartley A. Brennan

The Foreign Corrupt Practices Act Amendments of 1988: "Death" of a Law

The Members of Congress who authored this elimination of the antibribery law chose the perfect vehicle. They needed a big bill that would be handled by a myriad of committees so they could bury the few fatal lines that killed the Foreign Corrupt Practices Act deep in this forest of hundreds of thousands of words. They needed a controversial bill that would concentrate the debate on a series of economic matters that shook and divided the country and distracted the press from the death knell to antiforeign bribery law. What an opportunity to slip through a bribery repealer. The authors of the provision fully understood the gutting provision could not stand by itself. Even in a moderately complex bill the amendment would be vulnerable. But pushed by one of the many committees developing the details of this king size trade bill that was furiously contested by Congress and the President, the press and public could hardly be expected to notice the death of the Foreign Corrupt Practices Act.[1]

INTRODUCTION

An extraordinary eight year effort by some members of Congress and some business lobbyists to amend the Foreign Corrupt Practices

---

From *North Carolina Journal of International Law and Commercial Regulation vol.* 15 (1990). Reprinted by permission of the *North Carolina Journal of International Law and Commercial Regulation.*

Act of 1977 (FCPA or Act) culminated on August 23, 1988, with the enactment of the Omnibus Trade and Competitiveness Act of 1988 (Trade Act). The 1988 FCPA Amendments are only six pages in this approximately four hundred page piece of legislation whose goals only indirectly, at best, were to amend the FCPA. Those seeking to amend the FCPA had, over an eight-year period, failed to obtain passage of such amendments when they were introduced as separate bills. Furthermore, the Trade Act itself was once vetoed by the President and was passed as a result of a series of compromises worked out in a Trade Bill Conference Committee. It is therefore not surprising that proponents of the FCPA, such as Senator Proxmire, have charged those who have been successful in amending the Act with seeking to "gut" the law.

This Article analyzes the major changes that the 1988 Amendments made to the accounting and antibribery sections of the 1977 FCPA. Throughout the discussion particular attention will be given to the way in which the 1988 Amendments address the problems created by the 1977 Act. These problems are identified in a 1981 report issued by the General Accounting Office, which conducted a survey of U.S. corporations. This Article concludes that the 1988 Amendments severely undercut the original objectives of the 1977 Act.

In reviewing the 1988 Amendments to the FCPA, it should be remembered why the 1977 Act was enacted. In the period from 1974 to 1976, approximately 435 corporations voluntarily disclosed to the Securities and Exchange Commission (SEC) that they had made improper or questionable payments to foreign officials or members of foreign political parties. Such bribery led to the ownfall of governments and officials in Japan, the Netherlands, and Korea. By weakening its statute against bribery, the United States does not present itself as a good political and economic model for other nations to follow. This message is especially inappropriate at a time when the Soviet Union and several Eastern European nations are evolving toward economies based on the U.S. model. . . .

THE ANTIBRIBERY PROVISIONS OF THE FCPA

The 1977 Antibribery Provisions

In addition to the accounting provisions of the 1977 FCPA which mandated disclosure of questionable or illegal payments, Congress also provided antibribery provisions which prohibited the bribery of any foreign official. Under this section, not all payments were prohibited. Instead, only those payments that were driven by corrupt intentions, those made to influence certain persons to commit or fail to perform certain acts, and those made for the purpose of retaining business were prohibited.

Corporate and government officials, as well as academicians and lawyers, criticized the bribery sections of the 1977 FCPA for vaguely defining what constituted compliance. Some commentators suggested that this vagueness forced U.S. corporations to forego business opportunities abroad for fear of violating the FCPA and incurring its stiff criminal sanctions. The GAO Report found that of "the 30% of our respondents who reported that the Act had caused a decrease in their overseas business, approximately 70% rated the clarity of at least one of the antibribery provisions as inadequate or very inadequate." The major ambiguities to the antibribery provisions noted by the respondents FCPA were the following:

(1) the degree of responsibility a company has for the actions of the foreign agents;

(2) the definition of the term "foreign official";

(3) whether a payment is a bribe (illegal under the FCPA) or a "facilitating payment" (legal under the FCPA); and

(4) the dual jurisdiction of the SEC and Department of Justice.

The 1988 Amendments to the Antibribery Provisions

The 1988 Amendments change the antibribery provisions of the 1977 FCPA in seven areas.

CORRUPT PAYMENTS

The 1988 Amendments attempt to clarify the definition of what type of payments are prohibited. The Amendments change this definition in two respects. First, payments under the 1977 FCPA were prohibited if their purpose was to influence *"any act or decision of such foreign official in his official capacity, including a decision to fail to perform his official functions."*[2] The 1988 Amendments alter this provision to forbid payments or offers to pay foreign officials for the purpose of *"influencing any act or decision of such foreign official in his official capacity, or inducing such foreign official to do or omit to do any act in violation of the lawful duty of such official."*[3] Thus, it would seem at first glance that the language was changed in order to bring the FCPA into compliance with U.S. bribery laws. However, as one commentator has noted, the conferees failed because our domestic bribery statute forbids *all* corrupt payments intended to influence official functions, while the FCPA, as amended, increases the number of already existing categories of facilitating or "grease" payments.

Second, under the 1977 FCPA, payments were only illegal if made "in order to assist such issuer in obtaining or retaining business. . . ."[4] Some confusion arose as to whether lobbying fell within the definition of "retaining business." Although the Conference Committee rejected a proposed amendment that would have broadened the definition of "retaining business," the Conference Report does attempt to clarify the provision. It states that the conferees:

wish to make clear that the reference to corrupt payments for "retaining business" in present law is not limited to the renewal of contracts or other business, but also included a prohibition against corrupt payments relating to the execution or performance of contracts or the carrying out of existing business, such as a payment to a foreign official for the purpose of obtaining more favorable tax treatment. . . . The term should not, however, be construed so broadly as to include lobbying or other normal representations to government officials.[5]

The Conference Report as noted here sought on one hand to broaden the scope of prohibited payments beyond the purpose of "retaining business" but also to liberalize its interpretation so as not to include lobbying or normal representations. These conflicting objectives may have unfortunate repercussions in light of the expansion of categories of lawfully permitted facilitating or "grease" payments discussed below.

THE "REASON TO KNOW" STANDARD FOR THIRD PARTY PAYMENTS

In addition to prohibiting payments directly to "foreign officials," the 1977 FCPA also prohibited corporate entities or officers from giving anything of value to "any person, while knowing or having reason to know that all or a portion of such money or thing of value will be offered directly or indirectly" to various persons. These payments are referred to as third party payments.

Almost fifty percent of the respondents surveyed by the GAO found the "reason to know" language either "very inadequate" or "marginally inadequate." Lawyers and legal scholars argued that a "reason to know" standard increased the potential liability of a company and its officers for the acts of foreign agents or more closely affiliated third parties even if the company was unable to monitor or control their conduct. Several recurring questions were asked. What does "reason to know" mean? Is "reason to know" something less than full actual knowledge? If so, how much less, and should it be used in prosecution of criminal conduct? Those favoring the language as it stood under the FCPA pointed out that "reason to know" language existed in twenty-nine provisions of other federal laws. An analysis of these provisions, however, showed that thirteen of the twenty-nine provisions were civil or administrative statutes as contrasted with the FCPA, a criminal statute that provided for up to five years imprisonment. The remaining provisions fell into areas relating to federal safety standards or other types of regulatory procedures. Furthermore, similar "reason to know" language is included in eight provisions of the criminal code which has been replaced by the Federal Criminal Code Revisions.

Perhaps the most significant problem was that no precedents existed interpreting the "reason to know" language of the 1977 FCPA. In addition, because both the Department of Justice and the SEC had joint enforcement authority, a question was raised as to whether the agencies had the same interpretation of the "reason to know" language.

The 1988 Amendments delete the "reason to know" language and apply a "knowing" standard, which is defined as follows:

   (A) A person's state of mind is "knowing" with respect to conduct, a circumstance, or a result if—

      (i) such person is aware that such person is engaging in such conduct, that such circumstance exists, or that such result is substantially certain to occur; or

      (ii) such person has a firm belief that such circumstance exists or that such result is substantially certain to occur.

   (B) When knowledge of the existence of a particular circumstance is required for an offense, such knowledge is established if a person is aware of a high probability of the existence of such circumstance, unless the person actually believes that such circumstance does not exist. . . .[6]

The "reason to know" standard has been replaced by a standard that is more difficult for prosecutors to meet. The Conference Report made it clear that "simple negligence" or "mere foolishness" was insufficient for criminal liability. However, the Committee also stated that management will be held liable for "conscious disregard," "willful blindness," or "deliberate ignorance." In other words a "head in the sand" state of mind approach by management will not be tolerated. Citing several federal cases the Conference Report noted that the knowledge requirement is not equivalent to recklessness. It requires "an awareness of a high probability of the existence of the circumstance." The Conference Report goes on to state that the FCPA covers circumstances where any "reasonable person would have realized the existence of the circumstance or result" and the defendant "consciously chose not to ask about what he had reason to believe he would discover." Courts are instructed to use a mix of subjective and objective standards to determine the level of knowledge based on this test.

It would appear that the only circumstance from which a company must now protect itself is the intentional disregarding of some mix of subjective and objective signals that illegal payments were made by an agent or employee to a third party. It is not clear at this point what the signals are. As one commentator has pointed out, the Conference Report does not cite any cases which "suggest liability where the consequences of the factual knowledge possessed by the defendant result in future conduct prohibited by the statute," yet the language of the statute imposes liability in cases where there is an awareness or belief "such result is substantially certain to occur." It would seem clear that the language substituted for the "reason to know" standard may in fact prevent serious prosecution of violators of the FCPA.

FACILITATING PAYMENTS

The Amendments change the exemption for facilitating or "grease" payments. These payments are not made to obtain or retain business but merely to expedite a business activity in which the ministerial level employee is already employed. An example is the payment of thirty dollars to a customs official to move paperwork along so that a shipment of nondurable goods can be unloaded quickly. Many foreign governments permit such facilitating payments even though they are illegal in the United States and several other countries.

Under the 1977 FCPA, facilitating payments were allowed in several ways. The 1977 FCPA defined "foreign official" as any officer or employee of a foreign government or one of its departments, agencies, or instrumentalities. This definition expressly excluded any employee whose duties were "essentially ministerial or clerical." Corporate officials frequently complained that this language was unclear. Are employees of a publicly held nationalized corporation considered "foreign officials?" Is an official, or member of that official's family residing in a foreign country, who is also involved in the private sector a "foreign official?" How should the law treat individuals who simultaneously hold positions in both government and business? Can an excluded "ministerial or clerical" employee be paid a "facilitating payment" to use his influence to induce a "foreign official" to act, as long as the clerical employee does not pay the official from funds received from a U.S. corporation?

As stated above, the 1977 FCPA also proscribed only "corrupt" payments. The legislative history of the FCPA defined a corrupt payment as one made "to induce the recipient to misuse his official position in order to wrongfully direct business to the payor or his client" and requires an "evil motive or purpose." Because ministerial employees were excluded from the definition of foreign official, it is clear the FCPA was not intended to proscribe grease or facilitating payments.

Moreover, social gifts or routine expenditures for marketing products were lawful. However, consistent complaints about enforcement officials' interpretation led to requests for a congressional clarification of the statute.

Despite the apparently clear legislative intent that facilitating payments to ministerial or clerical employees not be proscribed, thirty-eight percent of those responding to the GAO questionnaire rated the clarity of the provisions inadequate. The dilemma raised was that a large corrupt payment to an official with "ministerial" duties might *not* be prohibited while a small payment to expedite customs papers may be prohibited if made to a senior "official." Furthermore, middle-level employees of U.S. corporations did not fully understand what constituted a facilitating payment. The decision to make such a payment would often have to be made quickly because hesitation might cause a delay in transportation or unloading of goods.

The 1988 Amendments now allow payments to any foreign official if they are facilitating or expediting payments for the purposes of expediting or securing the performance of a routine governmental action. "Routine governmental action" is defined as follows:

> an action which is ordinarily and commonly performed by a foreign official in:
>
> (i) obtaining permit[s], licenses, or other official documents to qualify a person to do business in a foreign country;
>
> (ii) processing governmental papers such as visas and work order[s];
>
> (iii) providing police protection, mail pick up and delivery, or scheduling inspections associated with contract performance or inspections related to transit of goods across country;
>
> (iv) providing phone service, power and water supply, loading and unloading cargo, or protecting perishable products or commodities from deterioration; or
>
> (v) actions of a similar nature.

Payments can now be made to *any* foreign official, not just ministerial or clerical persons, as long as they fall within the five categories. This substantially changes the intent of the 1977 FCPA as well as the breadth of the exception. The 1977 FCPA facilitating payments language was directed at the type of foreign official (ministerial or clerical), while 1988 amendments are directed at the type of duties to be performed. The "actions of a similar nature" language greatly expands the types of activities that may be allowed as "grease" or facilitating payments.

AFFIRMATIVE DEFENSES

In addition to expanding the "grease" payment exceptions for criminal prosecution, the 1988 Amendments also provide for two affirmative defenses for those accused of violating the FCPA. First, it is now an affirmative defense if a payment to a foreign official is lawful "under the written laws" of the foreign country. The Conference Report makes it clear "that the absence of written laws in a foreign official's country would not by itself be sufficient to satisfy this defense." Also, in interpreting what is lawful under written law, the conference committee members state that "normal rules of legal construction should apply."

This defense was added in response to complaints that U.S. companies were losing business because actions forbidden by the 1977 FCPA were permitted in foreign countries and undertaken by foreign competitors. A related problem was the lack of uniformity among nations regarding the propriety of facilitating payments. While a foreign agent might legally receive such a payment under the law of his or her country, the U.S. corporation making the payment might be violating the FCPA.

A study by Dr. John Graham of the University of Southern California, which reviewed all available empirical data, concluded that:

(a) During the 1978–1980 period, the FCPA had no negative effect on export performance of American industry. No differences in U.S. markets shown were discovered in nations where the FCPA was reported to be a trade disincentive both in terms of total trade with each country as well as for sales in individual product categories.

(b) During the 1977 statute, U.S. trade with bribe-prone countries has actually outpaced our trade with non-bribe-prone ones.[7]

Dr. Graham further concluded that the FCPA has not hurt the competitive position of U.S. industry. In fact, Dr. Graham's study provides support for the proposition that improper foreign payments are at least unnecessary. He suggests, therefore, that management should question payments to foreign firms on economic as well as ethical grounds.

Another complaint was that the FCPA sought to export U.S. morality. However, David D. Newsome has argued that the corrupt association of a U.S. company and a foreign official carries political implications for both actors which do not concern other foreign multinational corporations. He notes that "American businessmen often ask, 'Why us?' Why should America's multinationals be singled out for restrictions when all around them their competitors operate without such restrictions?"[8] Mr. Newsome concludes that the answer lies in the unique position which U.S. corporations have in world business ventures, coupled with their role in domestic affairs of foreign nations. He states that "[o]ur companies cannot escape the fact that their activities will never be totally detached from local sensitivities relating to United States intervention of any sort in the internal affairs of another country."[9] Thus, from both an economic and a moral viewpoint, this new affirmative defense seems unnecessary and unwise.

The second affirmative defense established by the Amendments allows payments to be made for "reasonable and bona fide expenditures." Examples include travel and lodging expenses incurred by or on behalf of a foreign official, party, party official, or candidate that are "directly related to (A) the promotion, demonstration or explanation of products or services; or (B) the execution or performance of a contract with a foreign government or agency thereof." In general, this second affirmative defense codifies the procedure followed by the Justice Department under the 1977 FCPA.

REPEAL OF THE "ECKHARDT AMENDMENT"

The "Eckhardt Amendment," which was included in the 1977 Act, prevented the prosecution of employees or agents of an issuer or U.S. corporation unless the concern itself was found to have violated the FCPA. The 1988 Amendments delete the language that prevented such prosecution.

Congressman Eckhardt originally proposed such language to prevent senior management of companies from using agents or employees as "scapegoats." Also, the legislative history indicates that the sponsors of the 1977 Act were concerned that agents or employees might not have the resources to defend themselves against charges of violations of the FCPA. The 1988 Amendments now open the door for the "scapegoat" scenario. Therefore, it is now important that individual employees and agents retain their own counsel when any possibility exists of a violation of the FCPA under the "knowing" standard. The repeal of the "Eckhardt Amendment" may create a difficult working environment for employees or agents and their employers or principals. . . .

CONCLUSION

The 1988 Amendments to the FCPA seek to redefine legally and ethically acceptable conduct for U.S. concerns doing business in foreign nations. Those who espouse an efficiency view that the "right to export" is best for the nation have succeeded in "gutting" the FCPA after an eight-year struggle. In the meantime, those who have been concerned about the legal and ethical conduct of U.S. companies doing business abroad have lost the battle to maintain the standards established by the 1977 FCPA. Scientifically sound studies (as opposed to anecdotal comments) indicated that the 1977 FCPA was at most a minor disincentive to export expansion, with other variables being far more important.[10] Moreover, the 1988 Amendments send the wrong signals to U.S. and foreign business communities at a time when new markets are opening in Eastern Europe. If we as a nation wish to encourage the adoption of an economic model based on competition for those who have experienced the poverty of a command model, bribery, under the guise of "facilitating payments," we will only give ammunition to those in Eastern Europe and elsewhere who are opposed to reform. While the proponents of the 1988 Amendments have won in the short run, a return to pre-FCPA (1977) conduct by domestic concerns doing business abroad will lead to more stringent legislation in the long term.

Notes

1. 134 Cong. Rec. S 8528 (daily ed. June 24, 1988) (statement of Sen. Proxmire).
2. 15 U.S.C. § 78dd-2(a)(1)(A) (1982) (emphasis added).
3. *Id.* § 78dd-1(a)(1)(A)(i) (1988) (emphasis added).
4. *Id.* § 78dd-1(a) (1982).
5. H.R. Conf. Rep. No. 576, 100th Cong., 2d Sess., 134 Cong. Rec. H 1863, H 2116 (daily ed. Apr. 20, 1988), *reprinted in* 1988 U.S. Code Cong. & Admin. News 1949, at 918.
6. 15 U.S.C. § 78dd-1(f)(2)(A), (B) (1988).
7. Graham, *Foreign Corrupt Practices: A Manager's Guide,* 18 COLUM. J. WORLD BUS. 89 (1983).
8. *See* Foreign Corrupt Practices Act—Oversight: Hearings Before the Subcomm. on Telecommunications, Consumer Protection, and Finance of the Comm. on Energy and Commerce, House of Representatives, 97th Cong. 1st & 2d Sess. 176 (1981 & 1982), at 391 (statement of D. Newsome).
9. *See id.* at 391–92.
10. *Id.; see* Sternitzke, *The Great American Competitive Disadvantage: Fact or Fiction,* 10 J. INT'L BUS. STUD 25, 32–35 (1979). Sternitzke concludes that "over the last decade the lagging long run growth of American exports has been

due mainly to the lose of competitiveness of American manufacturing goods in affluent markets, and has been attributable only incidentally to commodity structure or mix of American exports." *See* Graham, *Foreign Corrupt Practices: A Manager's Guide,* 18 COLUM J. WORLD BUS. 89 (1983).

Study Questions

1. How does Brennan use ethical, economic, and legal principles to show that the 1988 amendments cripple the original law, passed 11 years earlier? Do you agree with him?

2. Does the reinforcement view of law support or reject Brennan's main point, or is it neutral?

3. What do you think of a national law that governs behavior outside the nation? For example, should behavior in the United States be subject to Chinese, Ugandan, Bolivian, or German law? What ethical, economic, and legal values are at stake?

4. Use Brennan to evaluate the Waite case. Do you agree with this analysis? Explain.

CHAPTER 8

Information

INTRODUCTION

Good information is central to all areas of business. Without good information, we would not put our property at risk to reap potential rewards. The articles and cases in this section concern the role of information in advertising, whistleblowing, and the production and use of dangerous products.

There are many other topics that could be included in this chapter: truthtelling and bluffing, trade secrets, employee privacy, and gathering intelligence on competitors, to name a few. There are many introductory business ethics and business and society texts that provide a good starting place to investigate these topics.

ADVERTISING AND MARKETING

In "Natural Cereals," a case by Norman E. Bowie and Patrick E. Murphy, a newly hired marketing executive must decide between two approaches to a marketing plan. One approach very carefully avoids misleading consumers; the other approach focuses on obeying the letter of the law and following industry practice, even if customers might be misled. Her problem is exacerbated by the fact that one of her superiors supports the first approach and another supports the second approach.

In "Advertising and Behavior Control," Robert L. Arrington argues that most advertising does not coerce or in any other way force consumers to buy products. Arrington focuses on the industry practice of puffery, which is the attempt to enhance a product by linking it with things like adventure and sex. Through an examination of the concepts of free choice, autonomy, and behavior control, he argues that advertising can influence behavior, but not control it.

In "Persuasive Advertising, Autonomy, and the Creation of Desire," Roger Crisp repudiates Arrington's analysis, arguing that persuasive advertising aims at a level of awareness that consumers cannot directly evaluate. Because they can not directly evaluate it, their autonomy is being violated because they are led to make exchanges they would not make if they fully understood their own motives.

WHISTLEBLOWING

In Sally Seymour's "The Case of the Willful Whistle-Blower," a newly appointed middle manager must mediate between one of his engineers, who finds information that the company covered up costly, but not dangerous, product design flaws, and the CEO, who believes that the issue, now 10 years old, should be laid to rest.

In "Whistleblowing and Employee Loyalty," Ronald Duska argues that whistleblowing is not a violation of employee loyalty because there is no good reason for employees to be loyal to their companies. The employee–employer relationship is contractual, trading work for pay; there is nothing more to it. Duska acknowledges that employers try to instill loyalty in their employees, but this is because loyal employees work better for less pay. He also acknowledges that many employees do feel loyal to their companies, but that they are misguided.

INTERNATIONAL

Richard T. De George, in "The Transfer of Dangerous Industries to Underdeveloped Countries" discusses setting up a plant in an underdeveloped country that would violate safety standards in the company's home country. He argues that this can be legitimate under certain conditions.

In "Chemical Exports and the Age of Consent: The High Cost of International Export Control Proposals," Michael P. Walls argues that getting prior informed consent (PIC) from countries importing dangerous chemicals would have bad ethical, economic, and legal consequences (Chapters 3, 4, and 5). Ethically, PIC violates the right of national sovereignty; economically, it will generate costly paperwork and shipment delays without corresponding benefit; legally, it is incompatible with U.S. law and perhaps elements of GATT. There are better ways, Walls argues, to make sure that importing countries, especially third world countries, are not victimized by more developed exporting countries.

CASE: **Natural Cereals**

Norman E. Bowie and Patrick E. Murphy

Breakfast Foods, Inc. (BFI) is a national manufacturer of food products with three dry cereal divisions—children's, family, and natural. BFI also sells frozen breakfast entrees such as waffles and pancakes.

BFI's marketing department has just hired three assistant branch managers. One of these, Sally Thompson, received her MBA from a major mid-western university. Before joining BFI, Sally spent two years with the marketing group of a large food manufacturer. Although her experience at the former firm was educational, Sally often felt frustrated by the lack of responsibility.

Moving to BFI was good for Sally. BFI is a decentralized, progressive company, and management believes in giving people significant responsibility as soon as possible. Sally learned early that BFI management is quick to reward success but does not tolerate those who do not accept responsibility and its ramifications.

THE ASSIGNMENT

Sally's first major project is to improve market share in the adult cereal market through advertising and labeling strategies. Her charge is to suggest a new or modified marketing campaign for the Natural Cereals Division. Natural Cereals' brands are Fiber Rich, Bran Breakfast Flakes, Natural Bran, and Bran Bits. Sally is excited. This project allows her to work with two of the marketing department's best professionals, Tom Miller and Joe Bradley.

Tom Miller, a group product manager for the Natural Cereals Division, is a 20-year veteran of BFI and has greatly influenced company policy. Tom is well-known throughout BFI as a fair, yet demanding, manager with a high degree of integrity. He transferred from the Family Cereals Division five years ago, having made his reputation as the product manager for Winkies, the number-two brand in the company. Since Tom's time is limited, he assigned Joe Bradley to informally supervise Sally on this project.

Joe, recently promoted to product manager, has been with BFI for four and one-half years, most of which were spent in the Family Cereals Division. His best-known campaign was for Sparkles, a children's cereal. Joe joined forces with a well-known toy manufacturer to give away a miniature character toy with each box of Sparkles. The box also contained an order form so parents could purchase the remaining set of characters directly from the manufacturer. This campaign increased market share of Sparkles by 10 percent. Sally knows she can learn a lot from Joe. She also knows he is Tom's friend and protégé. Sally suspects Joe will one day take Tom's position.

Another reason this is the perfect project for Sally is the fact that she is extremely health conscious. She believes too many cereals contain excessive amounts of sugar, which can encourage unhealthy eating habits in children and adults. An avid reader of health food literature, she has seen a number of scientific studies showing a correlation between high fiber and cancer reduction. For example, people who have a diet rich in fiber tend to have a significantly lower incidence of colon cancer.

This case was developed by Norman E. Bowie and Patrick E. Murphy of the Arthur Andersen & Co. Business Ethics Program. Reprinted by permission of Arthur Anderson & Co. SC.

Sally is well aware of the public's fear of cancer and has faced the trauma of cancer herself. She had a lump removed from a breast only a year ago. Fortunately, it was benign. Her father was not so lucky. Three years ago he succumbed to lung cancer. Sally believes cancer shortens lives and, given the agonizing deaths it causes, leaves severe emotional scars on surviving family members. She has such scars, as well as considerable anxiety about her own fate. She is committed to doing whatever she can in the war against cancer.

COMPETITIVE/MARKET ANALYSIS

After consulting Joe, Sally examines a file of articles compiled by her predecessor about competitors in the cereal industry. The articles point out that intense industry competition is due to strong brands and high levels of advertising. Competitors spend $75,000,000 on advertising, two-thirds of which goes for television commercials. The good news is that adult ready-to-eat bran/fiber cereals grew twice as fast as the market, and sales increased over 20 percent last year.

In 1984, one competitor launched the first health claims advertising campaign for any food product—its high fiber bran cereal. The company included information from the National Cancer Institute (NCI) on its packages and its advertising copy, which it had worked out in advance with NCI. The claims linked a specific product with the prevention of a particular disease—cancer. Although the Food and Drug Administration (FDA), which has jurisdiction over health claims, was not completely happy with this ad campaign, they did not block the ads. The following statement appeared on the back of the company's cereal box:

> The National Cancer Institute believes eating the right foods may reduce your risk of some kinds of cancer. Research evidence indicates high fiber foods are important to good health. High fiber foods, like bran cereal, are considered to be part of a healthy diet. Bran cereals are one of the best sources of fiber.

Also, this competitor's television ads made the following claim:

> Cancer! It doesn't worry me as much since I learned that I can fight back by a healthy diet. The National Cancer Institute believes a high fiber, low-fat diet may reduce your risk of some kinds of cancer. High fiber is important to a healthy diet, just like training is important to an athlete. I run, bike, and swim regularly. But that isn't enough. They say it's a matter of eating right too. My health is really important, so I made some changes, like eating foods high in fiber.

This campaign proved quite effective. Annual sales of the company's cereals grew from $2,100,000 in 1983 to $2,800,000 in 1985. Sally found a study in *Public Health Reports*[1] that examined the effect of this campaign on sales. The article showed that in the 24 weeks following the start of the health claim campaign, there was a sharp increase in sales of this competitor's high fiber cereal. Its share of the total cereal market rose from 0.99 to 1.46 percent, a relative increase of 47 percent.

This competitor followed up its initial campaign with other campaigns that made health claims for its other high fiber cereals. Since 1984, the competitor has increased its advertising by one-third and introduced six new brands aimed at adults. These ads using the cancer preventative message were rather controversial. Certain people objected to the ads because they did not say what kinds of cancer they were referring to and how much of the cereal you had to eat. This statement by Dr. Timothy Johnson (medical director for a major television network) on a "Nightline" program raised several additional questions.

> [W]hen it comes specifically to diet and cancer connection, there is considerable uncertainty. I spent several months this past year looking very carefully at this hypothesis and talking literally to cancer experts all over the world, and found that opinion was divided and that the studies were inconsistent. Now, the language of the . . . ad is really quite accurate. It says, "Some studies suggest that it may. . . ." Problem is, there are other studies that suggest it may not. And the evidence is there for inconsistency. Now, you might say, so what? It's a diet that won't hurt, it may help, why not hedge our bets? And I really don't have any problem with that approach, but I do have two further concerns. One is that we may squander our scientific credibility in suggesting certainty where it does not exist, and then when we come to the public and really need to talk to them, they may not believe us. And I worry about what may happen on the fringes, not so much with the . . . ad but in health food stores or in other ways in which products and pills and books are promoted as a surefire answer to cancer with a particular diet program.[2]

Another competitor has also jumped on the fiber bandwagon by introducing four new high fiber products. It has promoted its brands with a health claim using a variation of the initial NCI message on the back panel of its bran cereal package. Although this strategy did not increase total sales, the company was able to hold its market share position.

In studying company and trade data, Sally finds that Breakfast Foods, Inc., has lost two percentage points since 1985 and that its overall cereal market share is currently 14 percent. This is far behind the 40 percent share of the market leader and somewhat lower than its main competitor, which holds 20 percent. The data confirm the company has been losing market share to competitors that make a connection between high fiber cereals and a possible reduction in the risk of getting certain kinds of cancer.

Prepared with these facts and figures, Sally schedules a meeting with Joe. She knows the approach she wants to take but decides it would be best to get Joe's advice before developing her preliminary ad campaign.

PRELIMINARY AD CAMPAIGN

As Sally enters Joe's office, he holds up her analysis summary. "Good work, Sally! Your analysis makes the picture clear. We've got to move before our market share drops any lower, and a health-oriented campaign is the way to go." Joe leans back in his chair, clasps his hands behind his head, and motions for Sally to have a seat.

Sally, pleased by Joe's support, replies, "I think the best approach is to follow our competitors' general strategy. People simply don't know enough about their health. Cancer isn't something to take lightly. People need to become more aware of. . . ."

"You're right," Joe interrupts. "A hard-hitting health campaign is what we need. We've probably benefited from the bran-cancer connection indirectly. Making it official with a clear, powerful message should benefit us even more. What we don't want to do, though, is waste our efforts. Tom just sent this memo us." Joe slides an open trade report across his desk.

Sally picks up the report and reads the part circled in red:

It costs just as much to run a lousy commercial as a good one. More than most products, cereal is "marketing sensitive"; that is, dollars spent on mediocre marketing simply fall into the void, while the same amount spent on a well-aimed pitch can dramatically increase sales.[3]

"This is what it's all about, Sally. We have to come up with a blockbuster campaign for Natural Cereals. Otherwise, we're going to lose our shirts. Let's meet with Tom to get his input. I know he'll support our approach 100 percent."

THE MEETING

Fortunately, Sally and Joe were able to schedule a meeting with Tom for that afternoon. As they walk into Tom's office, Sally feels a little uneasy. She remembers Tom's comments over lunch last week. He had made it very clear he feels marketing and advertising must be truthful as well as persuasive. Sally wonders whether Tom will be concerned by the objections to the competitor's campaign she had read during her analysis.

"Well, this was quick work!" Tom says. "I'm glad to see you've come up with some ideas already. You got my note, I assume. This is going to be one tough campaign—we have to make it count."

"Yeah," says Joe, "Sally has worked around the clock on this. I think you will be pleased with what we've done." Joe smiles and turns to Sally.

Tentatively, Sally begins. "I've read a lot about bran cereals, and it looks like our major competitor has been quite successful. We can build on the health claims they've started. We really wouldn't be providing a new message, but it seems clear health claims will sell."

Tom leans back in his chair, closes his eyes and pauses. After what seems like an eternity to Sally, he says, "I don't know. That's an interesting approach, but it isn't the only one. I'm pretty hesitant about all this new emphasis on health claims. I'm not sure our competitors are presenting the whole picture."

Joe jumps in. "I agree, Tom. I spent a lot of time pondering this issue. But Sally convinced me. I think a carefully developed health campaign is the way to go."

"Well, Sally," says Tom, "I'm not saying no. You've obviously done your homework. But I want to make sure you consider the implications. You know the FDA has been looking into this matter and has issued a directive." Tom rummages through his file drawer, hands Sally a folder, and continues. "Take it and read it. Then come back next Monday with several campaign options. You've put a lot of effort into this so far. Now let's just take some time to consider the alternatives."

CAMPAIGN OPTIONS

Sally goes to work immediately. From the information Tom gave her, she finds that in November 1987 the FDA proposed regulations allowing manufacturers to print messages on food labels about the health benefits of their products. Specifically, the FDA listed four criteria for evaluating health related claims and information on food labeling:

1. Information on the labeling must be truthful and not misleading to the consumer.
2. Information should be based on and be consistent with valid, reliable scientific evidence that is publicly available.

3. Available information regarding the relationship between nutrition and health shows that good nutrition is a function of total diet over time, not of specific foods.

4. The use of health-related information constitutes a nutritional claim that triggers the requirements of FDA's regulations regarding nutrition labeling.

The next morning, Sally makes a copy of the criteria and heads for Joe's office to get his thoughts.

After reading over them, Joe is silent. He shakes his head slightly and says, "I'm not sure these criteria will have any impact on our plans."

"Well," says Sally, "I think we might want to tone down our approach a little, don't you?"

"Not really." Joe smiles. "I did a little research myself last night and I learned the Federal Trade Commission, which regulates advertising, is pretty sympathetic to our competitors' ads. They believe the claim that some people might actually avoid cancer of the colon or rectum by eating their cereals is generally accurate. I think the FTC would allow advertising claims based on this labeling information."

"I don't know how seriously we should take the FDA's position, Joe. But I do know we should stick with the health orientation. Let me think of some specific options and I'll get back to you."

"Okay, it's your show." "But," says Joe, "keep in mind we can't blow this campaign. It's got to have an impact."

Sally feels uneasy as she leaves Joe's office. She knows Joe is right. Her career is at stake. This is a highly visible campaign. Yet, she knows Tom is right too. She starts to think of ideas for her marketing campaign. The FDA proposal would allow her to coordinate packaging and advertising, and that would give consumers a consistent message.

ADVERTISING AND PACKAGING OPTIONS

To determine the best approach, Sally plans to develop several advertising and packaging alternatives for the natural product line. She will take the alternatives to Joe to see what he thinks. She just received from the research department the cereal's side panel containing nutritional and ingredient information (see Exhibit 1). Now she has to work on the marketing options.

Besides the ad linking high fiber cereals with cancer risk reduction she reviewed earlier, she found a recent ad for another product noting it was high in vitamin B and provided an energy boost. As the first option, she thought of a possible hard-hitting strategy using the statement "Vitamin Enriched" on packaging and in advertising.

The report she recently received from BFI's research department indicated that Natural brands contained 13 essential vitamins and minerals. She would feel comfortable putting this on the package and in advertising. In closely investigating the side panel listing nutritional information, she finds that Natural Bran Cereal, by itself, contains no fat. She knows a large part of the market is conscious of the levels of fat in foods. This could be another good claim to make.

But there are problems. Sally knows that the vitamin content is similar in all bran cereals. She also knows from internal company documents that most Americans are not deficient in B vitamins, nor does the amount of B vitamins contained in the cereal give one instant energy.

The second option she thinks of focuses exclusively on the appeal of bran and fiber as possible preventatives to cancer. She learns from company records that the amount of

EXHIBIT 1   EACH SERVING CONTAINS
10 GRAMS OF DIETARY FIBER.

Nutrition Information Per Serving
Serving Size: 1 oz. (About 2/3 Cup) (28.35 g)
Servings Per Package: 20

	1 oz. (28.15 g) Cereal	With 1/2 Cup (118 ml) Vitamin D Fortified Whole Milk
Calories	90	160*
Protein	3 g	7 g
Carbohydrate	28 g	34 g
Fat	0	4 g
Sodium	230 mg	290 mg

Percentages of U.S. Recommended Daily Allowances (U.S. RDA)

Protein	4%	10%
Vitamin A	25%	30%
Vitamin C	**	**
Thiamine	25%	30%
Riboflavin	25%	35%
Niacin	25%	25%
Calcium	**	15%
Iron	45%	45%
Vitamin D	10%	25%
Vitamin B_6	25%	30%
Folic Acid	25%	25%
Vitamin B_{12}	25%	30%
Phosphorus	15%	25%
Magnesium	15%	20%
Zinc	10%	15%
Copper	10%	10%

**Contains less than 2% of the U.S. RDA of these mutrients

Ingredients: Whole Wheat, Wheat Bran, Sugar, Natural Flavoring, Salt and Com Syrup. Vitamins and Minerals: Iron, Vitamin A, Palmitate, Niacinamide, Zinc Oxide (Source of Zinc), Vitamin B_6, Riboflavin (Vitamin B_2), Thiamine Mononitrate (Vitamin B_1), Vitamin B_{12}, Folic Acid, and Vitamin D.

Carbohydrate information

	1 oz. Cereal	with 1/2 Cup Whole Milk
Starch and Related Carbohydrates	13g	13g
Sucrose and Other Sugars	5g	11g
Dietary Fiber	10g	10g
Total Carbohydrate	28g	34g

bran in Natural Cereals has increased by 40 percent in the last two years. One label alternative is: "With 40 Percent More Bran." Sally also knows this amount is equal to the most bran in any cereal. Therefore, another label or ad option is: "Containing the Highest Level of Fiber—Help prevent cancer by eating high fiber foods." She could place these statements in large boldface print on the package label and use them in advertising. This would reiterate the competition's strategy of linking cancer reduction with bran.

Another label she considers as part of this second option uses "natural" in the title for Bran Breakfast Flakes or Bran Bits. The slogan "Fiber for Health" is also a possible package label and advertising tag line.

Although these two options would probably be most effective, the FDA criteria keep running through her mind. As a result, she develops a third option downplaying health claims.

Option Three would point out that her product is a high-fiber, low-fat natural food. The label and the ads would feature energetic, healthy young people eating her breakfast cereals before an early morning tennis match. However, other traditional selling devices would be used, and the link to cancer reduction would not appear. From a marketing standpoint, she believes coupons on the back of the package might appeal to a broader market. She could also promote BFI's new "Resealable Pack," which allows the inside bag to be resealed for freshness. Other possibilities include discounts on a T-shirt and a cookbook featuring recipes using Natural's cereals. All of this would add up to a broad-based marketing appeal without relying totally on fiber and health claims. She thinks Tom might like this approach.

Sally knows these ideas are somewhat sketchy, but she wants Joe's input. She schedules a meeting for the following morning. She grabs a quick sandwich at the cafeteria and goes back to her desk to review her notes and reasoning for the meeting.

EVALUATING THE OPTIONS

Joe listens quietly to Sally's options. As she describes each, he jots down a few notes.

When she finishes, he simply says, "Combine Options One and Two."

"But I'm not sure that's the best way," Sally begins. "They are persuasive, but I think we should consider the implications."

Joe shakes his head. "The implication is that you need to increase market share and increase it quickly. Option Three won't do it. Options One and Two will. Everything we put on the package and the ads will be the truth. We could simply say 'Vitamin Enriched and Contains Vitamin B.' We don't need to say anything about vitamin B and an energy boost. Plus, we know the FTC won't object to cancer-reduction claims.

"There is nothing wrong with this approach. Besides, as you said yourself, we're doing people a favor. It isn't our responsibility to make people health experts. That's not our job, but selling cereal is."

Sally frowns. "What do you think Tom will say?"

"Look," Joe responds, "I talked with Tom about this over dinner. He said, basically, what I decide goes. Even if he doesn't agree totally, he won't overrule me. Tom is an excellent manager but doesn't have to concern himself with the details. The bottom line is that if we don't go with a hard-hitting campaign, we're going to lose our shirts. I've made my reputation around here, Sally. Now it's your turn. I want you to develop a full campaign combining Options One and Two."

Sally walks out of Joe's office. The project she wanted so badly isn't turning out the way she expected. She knows that, technically, Joe is supposed to just advise her, but could she realistically ignore his request? Besides, maybe he is right. What he said makes sense. Options One and Two are literally true. And is it her responsibility to make people health experts?

She sits down at her desk and begins to clear her mail. An envelope there from Tom contains a note and list of questions:

SALLY/JOE:

Here are a list of questions I use to evaluate the legal and ethical impact of advertising I have done. Please look them over. We do not want any legal or pressure-group problems!

- Are your claims accurate?

- Do you have competent and reliable evidence to support your claims? It should be evidence that the scientific or medical community is willing to support.

- Have you disclosed important limitations or qualifications to the claims you have made about your product?

- Have you misrepresented or cited out of context the contents of a report or scientific study? Have you suggested there is a consensus of medical opinion on an issue when there is not?

- Have you suggested that a report is government sponsored when it is not

- Is your advertising inconsistent with information on the label? Has FDA found the food ingredient in your product to be ineffective for your advertising purpose?[4]

Sally quickly scans the list. Exasperated, she phones Joe and blurts out, "Have you read the note from Tom?"

"Yes, Sally, I did," sighs Joe. "I read it this morning, and my position is the same. We can answer yes to each question." Sally slowly replaces the receiver and thinks aloud, "Now what?"

Notes

1. Alan S. Levy and Raymond C. Stokes, "Effects of Health Promotion Advertising on Sales of Ready-To-Eat Cereals," *Public Health Reports,* July-August 1987, pp. 398–403.
2. Transcript of "Nightline," program 1181. December 2, 1985, ABC News.
3. Quoted in Pamela Sherrid, "Fighting Back at Breakfast," *Forbes,* October 7, 1985, p. 127.
4. Dianne L. Taylor, "Health-Related Food Advertising: 'The Time Is Ripe for Change,'"*Food Engineering,* December 1984, p. 21.

Study Questions

1. What exactly is the problem(s) Sally Thompson faces?

2. What attracted Thompson to BFI? Does the structure of BFI shape the problem(s) she faces?

3. Tom Miller and Joe Bradley seem to have different views about the ethical, economic, and legal infrastructure in which cereal marketing occurs. Explain their views, using the reinforcement view of law.

Robert L. Arrington

Advertising and Behavior Control

Consider the following advertisements:

1. "A Woman in *Distinction Foundations* is so beautiful that all other women want to kill her."

2. Pongo Peach color from Revlon comes "from east of the sun . . . west of the moon, where each tomorrow dawns." It is "succulent on your lips" and "sizzling on your finger tips (And on your toes, goodness knows)." Let it be your "adventure in paradise."

3. "Musk by English Leather—The Civilized Way to Roar."

4. "Increase the value of your holdings. Old Charter Bourbon Whiskey—The Final Step Up."

5. Last Call Smirnoff Style: "They'd never really miss us, and it's kind of late already, and its quite a long way, and I could build a fire, and you're looking very beautiful, and we could have another martini, and it's awfully nice just being home . . . you think?"

6. A Christmas Prayer. "Let us pray that the blessings of peace be ours—the peace to build and grow, to live in harmony and sympathy with others, and to plan for the future with confidence." New York Life Insurance Company.

These are instances of what is called puffery—the practice by a seller of making exaggerated, highly fanciful, or suggestive claims about a product or service. Puffery, within ill-defined limits, is legal. It is considered a legitimate, necessary, and very successful tool of the advertising industry. Puffery is not just bragging; it is bragging carefully designed to achieve a very definite effect. Using the techniques of so-called motivational research, advertising firms first identify our often hidden needs (for security, conformity, oral stimulation) and our desires (for power, sexual dominance and dalliance, adventure) and then they design ads which respond to these needs and desires. By associating a product, for which we may have little or no direct need or desire, with symbols reflecting the fulfillment of these other, often subterranean interests, the advertisement can quickly generate large numbers of consumers eager to purchase the product advertised. What woman in the sexual race of life could resist a foundation which would turn other women envious to the point of homicide? Who can turn down an adventure in paradise, east of the sun where tomorrow dawns? Who doesn't want to be civilized and thoroughly libidinous at the same time? Be at the pinnacle of success—drink Old Charter. Or stay at home and dally a bit—with Smirnoff. And let us pray for a secure and predictable future, provided for by New York Life, God willing. It doesn't take very much motivational research to see the point of these sales pitches. Others are perhaps a little less obvious. The need to feel secure in one's home at night can be used to sell window air conditioners, which drown out small noises and provide a friendly, dependable companion. The fact that baking a cake is symbolic of giving birth to a baby used to prompt advertisements for cake mixes which glamorized the "creative" housewife. And other strategies, for example involving cigar symbolism, are a bit too crude to mention, but are nevertheless very effective.

Don't such uses of puffery amount to

manipulation, exploitation, or downright control? In his very popular book *The Hidden Persuaders,* Vance Packard points out that a number of people in the advertising world have frankly admitted as much:

> As early as 1941 Dr. Dichter (an influential advertising consultant) was exhorting ad agencies to recognize themselves for what they actualy were—"one of the most advanced laboratories in psychology." He said the successful ad agency "manipulates human motivations and desires and develops a need for goods with which the public has at one time been unfamiliar—perhaps even undesirous of purchasing." The following year *Advertising Agency* carried an ad man's statement that psychology not only holds a promise for understanding people but "ultimately for controlling their behavior."[1]

Such statements lead Packard to remark: "With all this interest in manipulating the customer's subconscious, the old slogan 'let the buyer beware' began taking on a new and more profound meaning."[2]

B. F. Skinner, the high priest of behaviorism, has expressed a similar assessment of advertising and related marketing techniques. Why, he asks, do we buy a certain kind of car?

> Perhaps our favorite TV program is sponsored by the manufacturer of that car. Perhaps we have seen pictures of many beautiful or prestigeful persons driving it—in pleasant or glamorous places. Perhaps the car has been designed with respect to our motivational patterns: the device on the hood is a phallic symbol; or the horsepower has been stepped up to please our competitive spirit in enabling us to pass other cars swiftly (or, as the advertisements say, 'safely'). The concept of freedom that has emerged as part of the cultural practice of our group makes little or no provision for recognizing or dealing with these kinds of control.[3]

In purchasing a car we may think we are free, Skinner is claiming, when in fact our act is completely controlled by factors in our environment and in our history of reinforcement. Advertising is one such factor.

A look at some other advertising techniques may reinforce the suspicion that Madison Avenue controls us like so many puppets. T.V. watchers surely have noticed that some of the more repugnant ads are shown over and over again, *ad nauseam.* My favorite, or most hated, is the one about A-1 Steak Sauce which goes something like this: Now, ladies and gentlemen, what is hamburger? It has succeeded in destroying my taste for hamburger, but it has surely drilled the name of A-1 Sauce into my head. And that is the point of it. Its very repetitiousness has generated what ad theorists call *information.* In this case it is indirect information, information derived not from the content of what is said but from the fact that it is said so often and so vividly that it sticks in one's mind—i.e., the information yield had increased. And not only do I always remember A-1 Sauce when I go to the grocers, I tend to assume that any product advertised so often has to be good—and so I usually buy a bottle of the stuff.

Still another technique: On a recent show of the television program "Hard Choices" it was demonstrated how subliminal suggestion can be used to control customers. In a New Orleans department store, messages to the effect that shoplifting is wrong, illegal, and subject to punishment were blended into the Muzak background music and masked so as not to be consciously audible. The store reported a dramatic drop in shoplifting. The program host conjectured whether a logical extension of this technique would be to broadcast subliminal advertising messages to the effect that the store's $15.99 sweater special is the "bargain of a lifetime." Actually, this application of subliminal suggestion to advertising has already taken place. Years ago in New Jersey a cinema was reported to have flashed subthreshold ice cream ads onto the screen during regular showings of the film—and, yes, the concession stand did a landslide business.

Puffery, indirect information transfer, subliminal advertising—are these techniques of manipulation and control whose success shows that many of us have forfeited our autonomy and become a community, or herd, of packaged souls?[4] The business world and the advertising industry certainly reject this interpretation of their efforts. *Business Week,* for example, dismissed the charge that the science of behavior, as utilized by advertising, is engaged in human engineering and manipulation. It editorialized to the effect that "it is hard to find anything very sinister about a science whose principle conclusion is that you get along with people by giving them what they want.[5] The theme is familiar: businesses just give the consumer what he/she wants; if they didn't they wouldn't stay in business very long. Proof that the consumer wants the products advertised is given by the fact that he buys them, and indeed often returns to buy them again and again.

The techniques of advertising we are discussing have had their more intellectual defenders as well. For example, Theodore Levitt, Professor of Business Administration at the Harvard Business School, has defended the practice of puffery and the use of techniques depending on motivational research.[6] What would be the consequences, he asks us, of deleting all exaggerated claims and fanciful associations from advertisements? We would be left with literal descriptions of the empirical characteristics of products and their functions. Cosmetics would be presented as facial and bodily lotions and powders which produce certain odor and color changes; they would no longer offer hope or adventure. In addition to the fact that these products would not then sell as well, they would not, according to Levitt, please us as much either. For it is hope and adventure we want when we buy them. We want automobiles not just for transportation, but for the feelings of power and status they give us. Quoting T. S. Eliot to the effect that "Human kind cannot bear very much reality," Levitt argues that advertising is an effort to "transcend nature in the raw," to "augment what nature has so crudely fashioned." He maintains that "everybody every-

where wants to modify, transform, embellish, enrich and reconstruct the world around him." Commerce takes the same liberty with reality as the artist and the priest—in all three instances the purpose is "to influence the audience by creating illusions, symbols, and implications that promise more than pure functionality." For example, "to amplify the temple in men's eyes, (men of cloth) have, very realistically, systematically sanctioned the embellishment of the houses of the gods with the same kind of luxurious design and expensive decoration that Detroit puts into a Cadillac." A poem, a temple, a Cadillac—they all elevate our spirits, offering imaginative promises and symbolic interpretations of our mundane activities. Seen in this light, Levitt claims, "Embellishment and distortion are among advertising's legitimate and socially desirable purposes." To reject these techniques of advertising would be "to deny man's honest needs and values."

Phillip Nelson, a Professor of Economics at SUNY-Binghamton, has developed an interesting defense of indirect information advertising.[7] He argues that even when the message (the direct information) is not credible, the fact that the brand is advertised, and advertised frequently, is valuable indirect information for the consumer. The reason for this is that the brands advertised most are more likely to be better buys—losers won't be advertised a lot, for it simply wouldn't pay to do so. Thus even if the advertising claims made for a widely advertised product are empty, the consumer reaps the benefit of the indirect information which shows the product to be a good buy. Nelson goes so far as to say that advertising, seen as information and especially as indirect information, does not require an intelligent human response. If the indirect information has been received and has had its impact, the consumer will purchase the better buy even if his explicit reason for doing so is silly, e.g., he naively believes an endorsement of the product by a celebrity. Even though his behavior is overtly irrational, by acting on the indirect information he is nevertheless doing what he ought to do, i.e., getting his money's worth. "'Irrationality' is rational," Nelson writes, "if it is cost-free."

I don't know of any attempt to defend the use of subliminal suggestion in advertising, but I can imagine one form such an attempt might take. Advertising information, even if perceived below the level of conscious awareness, must appeal to some desire on the part of the audience if it is to trigger a purchasing response. Just as the admonition not to shoplift speaks directly to the superego, the sexual virtues of Rx-7's, Pongo Peach, and Betty Crocker cake mix present themselves directly to the id, bypassing the pesky reality principle of the ego. With a little help from our advertising friends, we may remove a few of the discontents of civilization and perhaps even enter into the paradise of polymorphous perversity.

The defense of advertising which suggests that advertising simply is information which allows us to purchase what we want, has in turn been challenged. Does business, largely through its advertising efforts, really make available to the consumer what he/she desires and demands? John Kenneth Galbraith has denied that the matter is as straightforward as this.[8] In his opinion the desires to which business is supposed to respond, far from being original to the consumer, are often themselves created by business. The producers make both the product and the desire for it, and the "central function" of advertising is "to create desires." Galbraith coins the term "The Dependence Effect" to designate the way wants depend on the same process by which they are satisfied.

David Braybrooke has argued in similar and related ways.[9] Even though the consumer is, in a sense, the final authority concerning what he wants, he may come to see, according to Braybrooke, that he was mistaken in wanting what he did. The statement "I want x," he tells us, is not incorrigible but is "ripe for revision." If the consumer had more objective information than he is provided by product puffing, if his values had not been mixed up by motivational research strategies (e.g., the confusion of sexual and automotive values), and if he had an expanded set of

choices instead of the limited set offered by profit-hungry corporations, then he might want something quite different from what he presently wants. This shows, Braybrooke thinks, the extent to which the consumer's wants are a function of advertising and not necessarily representative of his real or true wants.

The central issue which emerges between the above critics and defenders of advertising is this: do the advertising techniques we have discussed involve a violation of human autonomy and a manipulation and control of consumer behavior, or do they simply provide an efficient and cost-effective means of giving the consumer information on the basis of which he or she makes a free choice? Is advertising information, or creation of desire?

To answer this question we need a better conceptual grasp of what is involved in the notion of autonomy. This is a complex, multifaceted concept, and we need to approach it through the more determinate notions of (a) autonomous desire, (b) rational desire and choice, (c) free choice, and (d) control or manipulation. In what follows I shall offer some tentative and very incomplete analyses of these concepts and apply the results to the case of advertising.

(A) AUTONOMOUS DESIRE

Imagine that I am watching T.V. and see an ad for Grecian Formula 16. The thought occurs to me that if I purchase some and apply it to my beard, I will soon look younger—in fact I might even be myself again. Suddenly I want to be myself! I want to be young again! So I rush out and buy a bottle. This is our question: was the desire to be younger manufactured by the commercial, or was it 'original to me' and truly mine? Was it autonomous or not?

F. A. von Hayek has argued plausibly that we should not equate nonautonomous desires, desires which are not original to me or truly mine, with those which are culturally induced.[10] If we did equate the two, he points out, then the desires for music, art, and knowledge could not properly be attributed to a person as original to him, for these are surely induced culturally: The only desires a person would really have as his own in this case would be the purely physical ones for food, shelter, sex, etc. But if we reject the equation of the nonautonomous and the culturally induced, as von Hayek would have us do, then the mere fact that my desire to be young again is caused by the T.V. commercial—surely an instrument of popular culture transmission—does not in and of itself show that this is not my own, autonomous desire. Moreover, even if I never before felt the need to look young, it doesn't follow that this new desire is any less mine. I haven't always liked 1969 Aloxe Corton Burgundy or the music of Satie, but when the desires for these things first hit me, they were truly mine.

This shows that there is something wrong in setting up the issue over advertising and behavior control as a question whether our desires are truly ours or are created in us by advertisements. Induced and autonomous desires do not separate into two mutually exclusive classes. To obtain a better understanding of autonomous and nonautonomous desires, let us consider some cases of a desire which a person does not *acknowledge* to be his own even though he *feels* it. The kleptomaniac has a desire to steal which in many instances he repudiates, seeking by treatment to rid himself of it. And if I were suddenly overtaken by a desire to attend an REO concert, I would immediately disown this desire, claiming possession or momentary madness. These are examples of desires which one might have but with which one would not identify. They are experienced as foreign to one's character or personality. Often a person will have what Harry Frankfurt calls a second-order desire, that is to say, a desire not to have another desire.[11] In such cases, the first-order desire is thought of as being nonautonomous, imposed on one. When on the contrary a person has a second-order desire to maintain and fulfill a first-order desire, then the first-order desire is truly his own, autonomous, original to him. So there is in fact a distinction between desires which are the agent's own and those which are not, but this is not the same as the distinction between desires which are innate to the agent and those which are externally induced.

If we apply the autonomous/nonautonomous distinction derived from Frankfurt to the desires brought about by advertising, does this show that advertising is responsible for creating desires which are not truly the agent's own? Not necessarily, and indeed not often. There may be some desires I feel which I have picked up from advertising and which I disown—for instance, my desire for A-1 Steak Sauce. If I act on these desires it can be said that I have been led by advertising to act in a way foreign to my nature. In these cases my autonomy has been violated. But most of the desires induced by advertising I fully accept, and hence most of these desires are autonomous. The most vivid demonstration of this is that I often return to purchase the same product over and over again, without regret or remorse. And when I don't, it is more likely that the desire has just faded than that I have repudiated it. Hence, while advertising may violate my autonomy by leading me to act on desires which are not truly mine, this seems to be the exceptional case.

Note that this conclusion applies equally well to the case of subliminal advertising. This may generate subconscious desires which lead to purchases, and the act of purchasing these goods may be inconsistent with other conscious desires I have, in which case I might repudiate my behavior and by implication the subconscious cause of it. But my subconscious desires may not be inconsistent in this way with my conscious ones; my id may be cooperative and benign rather than hostile and malign. Here again, then, advertising may or may not produce desires which are 'not truly mine.'

What are we to say in response to Braybrooke's argument that insofar as we might choose differently if advertisers gave us better information and more options, it follows that the desires we have are to be attributed more to advertising than to our own real inclinations? This claim seems empty. It amounts to saying that if the world we lived in, and we ourselves, were different, then we would want different things. This is surely true, but it is equally true of our desire for shelter as of our desire for Grecian Formula 16. If we lived in a tropical paradise, we would not need or desire shelter. If we were immortal, we would not desire youth. What is true of all desires can hardly be used as a basis for criticizing some desires by claiming that they are nonautonomous.

(B) RATIONAL DESIRE AND CHOICE

Braybrooke might be interpreted as claiming that the desires induced by advertising are often irrational ones in the sense that they are not expressed by an agent who is in full possession of the facts about the products advertised or about the alternative products which might be offered him. Following this line of thought, a possible criticism of advertising is that it leads us to act on irrational desires or to make irrational choices. It might be said that our autonomy has been violated by the fact that we are prevented from following our rational wills or that we have been denied the 'positive freedom' to develop our true, rational selves. It might be claimed that the desires induced in us by advertising are false desires in that they do not reflect our essential, i.e., rational essence.

The problem faced by this line of criticism is that of determining what is to count as rational desire or rational choice. If we require that the desire or choice be the product of an awareness of *all* the facts about the product, then surely every one of us is always moved by irrational desires and makes nothing but irrational choices. How could we know all the facts about a product? If it be required only that we possess all of the *available* knowledge about the product advertised, then we still have to face the problem that not all available knowledge is *relevant* to a rational choice. If I am purchasing a car, certain engineering features will be, and others won't be, relevant, *given what I want in a car.* My prior desires

determine the relevance of information. Normally a rational desire or choice is thought to be one based upon relevant information, and information is relevant if it shows how other, prior desires may be satisfied. It can plausibly be claimed that it is such prior desires that advertising agencies acknowledge, and that the agencies often provide the type of information that is relevant in light of these desires. To the extent that this is true, advertising does not inhibit our rational wills or our autonomy as rational creatures. . . .

To the extent that a consumer takes an advertised product to offer a subjective effect and the product does not, it is unlikely that it will be purchased again. If this happens in a number of cases, the product will be taken off the market. So here the market regulates itself, providing the mechanism whereby misleading advertisements are withdrawn and misled customers are no longer misled. At the same time, a successful bit of puffery, being one which leads to large and repeated sales, produces satisfied customers and more advertising of the product. The indirect information provided by such large-scale advertising efforts provides a measure of verification to the consumer who is looking for certain kinds of subjective effect. For example, if I want to feel well dressed and in fashion, and I consider buying an Izod Alligator shirt which is advertised in all of the magazines and newspapers, then the fact that other people buy it and that this leads to repeated advertisements shows me that the desired subjective effect is real enough and that I indeed will be well dressed and in fashion if I purchase the shirt. The indirect information may lead to a rational decision to purchase a product because the information testifies to the subjective effect that the product brings about. . . .

(C) FREE CHOICE

It might be said that some desires are so strong or so covert that a person cannot resist them, and that when he acts on such desires he is not acting freely or voluntarily but is rather the victim of irresistible impulse or an unconscious drive. Perhaps those who condemn advertising feel that it produces this kind of desire in us and consequently reduces our autonomy.

This raises a very difficult issue. How do we distinguish between an impulse we *do* not resist and one we *could* resist, between freely giving in to a desire and succumbing to one? I have argued elsewhere that the way to get at this issue is in terms of the notion of acting for a reason.[12] A person acts or chooses freely if he does so for a reason, that is, if he can adduce considerations which justify in his mind the act in question. Many of our actions are in fact free because this condition frequently holds. Often, however, a person will act from habit, or whim, or impulse, and on these occasions he does not have a reason in mind. Nevertheless he often acts voluntarily in these instances, i.e., he could have acted otherwise. And this is because if there *had been* a reason for acting otherwise of which he was aware, he would in fact have done so. Thus acting from habit or impulse is not necessarily to act in an involuntary manner. If, however, a person is aware of a good reason to do x and still follows his impulse to do y, then he can be said to be impelled by irresistible impulse and hence to act involuntarily. Many kleptomaniacs can be said to act involuntarily, for in spite of their knowledge that they likely will be caught and their awareness that the goods they steal have little utilitarian value to them, they nevertheless steal. Here their "out of character" desires have the upper hand, and we have a case of compulsive behavior.

Applying these notions of voluntary and compulsive behavior to the case of behavior prompted by advertising, can we say that consumers influenced by advertising act compulsively? The unexciting answer is: sometimes they do, sometimes not. I may have an overwhelming, T.V.-induced urge to own a Mazda Rx-7 and all the while realize that I can't afford one without severely reducing my family's caloric intake to a dangerous level. If, aware of this good reason not to purchase the car, I nevertheless do so, this shows that I have been the victim of T.V. compulsion. But if I have the urge, as I assure you I do, and don't act on it, or if in some other possible world I could afford an Rx-7, then I have not been the subject of undue influence by Mazda advertising. Some Mazda Rx-7 purchasers act compulsively; others do not. The Mazda advertising effort *in general* cannot be condemned, then, for impairing its customers' autonomy in the sense of limiting free or voluntary choice. Of course the question remains what should be done about the fact that advertising may and does *occasionally* limit free choice.

In the case of subliminal advertising we may find an individual whose subconscious desires are activated by advertising into doing something his calculating, reasoning ego does not approve. This would be a case of compulsion. But most of us have a benevolent subconsciousness which does not overwhelm our ego and its reasons for action. And therefore most of us can respond to subliminal advertising without thereby risking our autonomy. To be sure, if some advertising firm developed a subliminal technique which drove all of us to purchase Lear jets, thereby reducing our caloric intake to the zero point, then we would have a case of advertising which could properly be censured for infringing our right to autonomy. We should acknowledge that this is possible, but at the same time we should recognize that it is not an inherent result of subliminal advertising.

(D) CONTROL OR MANIPULATION

Briefly let us consider the matter of control and manipulation. Under what conditions do these activities occur? In a recent paper on "Forms and Limits of Control" I suggested the following criteria.[13]

A person C controls the behavior of another person P if

1. C intends P to act in a certain way A;
2. C's intention is causally effective in bringing about A; and
3. C intends to ensure that all of the necessary conditions of A are satisfied.

These criteria may be elaborated as follows. To control another person it is not enough that one's actions produce certain behavior on the part of that person; additionally one must intend that this happen. Hence control is the intentional production of behavior. Moreover, it is not enough just to have the intention; the intention must give rise to the conditions which bring about the intended effect. Finally, the controller must intend to establish by his actions any otherwise unsatisfied necessary conditions for the production of the intended effect. The controller is not just influencing the outcome, not just having input; he is as it were guaranteeing that the sufficient conditions for the intended effect are satisfied.

Let us apply these criteria of control to the case of advertising and see what happens. Conditions (1) and (3) are crucial. Does the Mazda manufacturing company or its advertising agency intend that I buy an Rx-7? Do they intend that a certain number of people buy the car? *Prima facie* it seems more appropriate to say that they *hope* a certain number of people will buy it, and hoping and intending are not the same. But the difficult term here is "intend." Some philosophers have argued that to intend A it is necessary only to desire that A happen and to believe that it will. If this is correct, and if marketing analysis gives the Mazda agency a reasonable belief that a certain segment of the population will buy its product, then, assuming on its part the desire that this happen, we have the conditions necessary for saying that the agency intends that a certain segment purchase the car. If I am a member of this segment of the population, would it then follow that the agency intends that I purchase an Rx-7? Or is control referentially opaque? Obviously we have some questions here which need further exploration.

Let us turn to the third condition of control, the requirement that the controller intend to activate or bring about any otherwise unsatisfied necessary conditions for the production of the intended effect. It is in terms of this condition that we are able to distinguish brainwashing from liberal education. The brainwasher arranges all of the necessary conditions for belief. On the other hand, teachers (at least those of liberal persuasion) seek only to influence their students—to provide them with information and enlightenment which they may absorb *if they wish.* We do not normally think of teachers as controlling their students, for the students' performances depend as well on their own interests and inclinations.

Now the advertiser—does he control, or merely influence, his audience? Does he intend to ensure that all of the necessary conditions for purchasing behavior are met, or does he offer information and symbols which are intended to have an effect only *if* the potential purchaser has certain desires? Undeniably advertising induces some desires, and it does this intentially, but more often than not it intends to induce a desire for a particular object, *given* that the purchaser already has other desires. Given a desire for youth, or power, or adventure, or ravishing beauty, we are led to desire Grecian Formula 16, Mazda Rx-7s, Pongo Peach, and Distinctive Foundations. In this light, the advertiser is influencing us by appealing to independent desires we already have. He is not creating those basic desires. Hence it seems appropriate to deny that he intends to produce all of the necessary conditions for our purchases, and appropriate to deny that he controls us.

Let me summarize my argument. The critics of advertising see it as having a pernicious effect on the autonomy of consumers, as controlling their lives and manufacturing their very souls. The defense claims that advertising only offers information and in effect allows industry to provide consumers with what they want. After developing some of the philosophical dimensions of this dispute, I have come down tentatively in favor of the advertisers. Advertising may, but certainly does not always or even frequently, control behavior, produce compulsive behavior, or create wants which are not rational or are not truly those of the consumer. Admittedly it may in individual cases do all of these things, but it is innocent of the charge of intrinsically or necessarily doing them or even, I think, of often doing so. This limited potentiality, to be sure, leads to the question whether advertising should be abolished or severely curtailed or regulated because of its potential to harm a few pour souls in the above ways. This is a very difficult question, and I do not pretend to have the answer. I only hope that the above discussion, in showing some of the kinds of harm that can be done by advertising and by indicating the likely limits of this harm, will put us in a better position to grapple with the question.

Notes

1. Vance Packard, *The Hidden Persuaders* (Pocket Books, New York, 1958), pp. 20–21.
2. *Ibid.*, p. 21.
3. B. F. Skinner, "Some Issues Concerning the Control of Human Behavior: A Symposium," in Karlins and Andrews (eds.), *Man Controlled* (The Free Press, New York, 1972).
4. I would like to emphasize that in what follows I am discussing these techniques of advertising from the standpoint of the issue of control and not from that of deception.
5. Quoted by Packard, *op. cit.*, p. 200.
6. Theodore Levitt, "The Morality (?) of Advertising," *Harvard Business Review* (1970). 84–92.
7. Phillip Nelson, "Advertising and Ethics," in Richard T. De George and Joseph A. Pichler (eds.), *Ethics, Free Enterprise, and Public Policy* (Oxford University Press, New York, 1978), pp. 187–98.
8. John Kenneth Galbraith, "The Dependence Effect," *The Affluent Society.*
9. David Braybrooke, "Skepticism of Wants, and Certain Subversive Effects of Corporations on American Values," in Sidney Hook (ed.), *Human Values and Economic Policy* (New York University Press, New York, 1967).
10. F. A. von Hayek, "The *Non Sequitur* of the 'Dependence Effect,'" *Southern Economic Journal* (1961).
11. Harry Frankfurt, "Freedom of the Will and the Concept of a Person," *Journal of Philosophy* LXVII (1971), 5–20.
12. Robert L. Arrington, "Practical Reason. Responsibility and the Psychopath." *Journal for the Theory of Social Behavior* 9 (1979), 71–89.
13. Robert L. Arrington, "Forms and Limits of Control," delivered in the annual meeting of the Southern Society for Philosophy and Psychology, Birmingham, Alabama, 1980.

Study Questions

1. Why does Arrington believe that standard advertising techniques are not coercive?

2. How does he use the concepts of free choice, autonomy, and behavior control to support his view?

3. What psychological and ethical assumptions does Arrington make? What would Messick and Bazerman say about these assumptions?

Roger Crisp

Persuasive Advertising, Autonomy, and the Creation of Desire

In this paper, I shall argue that all forms of a certain common type of advertising are morally wrong, on the ground that they override the autonomy of consumers.

One effect of an advertisement might be the creation of a desire for the advertised product. How such desires are caused is highly relevant as to whether we would de-

From *Journal of Business Ethics* 6 413–418, 1987. Used with kind permission of the author and Kluwer Academic Publishers. Copyright © 1987 Kluwer Academic Publishers; all rights reserved.

scribe the case as one in which the autonomy of the subject has been overridden. If I read an advertisement for a sale of clothes, I may rush down to my local clothes store and purchase a jacket I like. Here, my desire for the jacket has arisen partly out of my reading the advertisement. Yet, in an ordinary sense, it is based on or answers to certain properties of the jacket—its colour, style, material. Although I could not explain to you why my tastes are as they are, we still describe such cases as examples of autonomous action, in that all the decisions are being made by me: What kind of jacket do I like? Can I afford one? And so on. In certain other cases, however, the causal history of a desire may be different. Desires can be caused, for instance, by subliminal suggestion. In New Jersey, a cinema flashed sub-threshold advertisements for ice cream onto the screen during movies, and reported a dramatic increase in sales during intermissions. In such cases, choice is being deliberately ruled out by the method of advertising in question. These customers for ice cream were acting "automatonously," rather than autonomously. They did not buy the ice cream because they happened to like it and decided they would buy some, but rather because they had been subjected to subliminal suggestion. Subliminal suggestion is the most extreme form of what I shall call, adhering to a popular dichotomy, persuasive, as opposed to informative, advertising, Other techniques include puffery, which involves the linking of the product, through suggestive language and images, with the unconscious desires of consumers for power, wealth, status, sex, and so on; and repetition, which is self-explanatory, the name of the product being "drummed into" the mind of the consumer.

The obvious objection to persuasive advertising is that it somehow violates the autonomy of consumers. I believe that this objection is correct, and that, if one adopts certain common-sensical standards for autonomy, non-persuasive forms of advertising are not open to such an objection. Very high standards for autonomy are set by Kant, who requires that an agent be entirely external to the causal nexus found the ordinary empirical

world, if his or her actions are to be autonomous. These standards are too high, in that it is doubtful whether they allow any autonomous action. Standards for autonomy more congenial to common sense will allow that my buying the jacket is autonomous, although continuing to deny that the people in New Jersey were acting autonomously. In the former case, we have what has come to be known in recent discussions of freedom of the will as *both* free will *and* free action. I both decide what to do, and am not obstructed in carrying through my decision into action. In the latter case, there is free action, but not free will. No one prevents the customers buying their ice cream, but they have not themselves made any genuine decision whether or not to do so. In a very real sense, decisions are made for consumers by persuasive advertisers, who occupy the motivational territory properly belonging to the agent. If what we mean by autonomy, in the ordinary sense, is to be present, the possibility of decision must exist alongside.

Arrington (1982) discusses, in a challenging paper, the techniques of persuasive advertising I have mentioned, and argues that such advertising does not override the autonomy of consumers. He examines four notions central to autonomous action, and claims that, on each count, persuasive advertising is exonerated on the charge we have made against it. I shall now follow in the footsteps of Arrington, but argue that he sets the standards for autonomy too low for them to be acceptable to common sense, and that the charge therefore still sticks.

(A) AUTONOMOUS DESIRE

Arrington argues that an autonomous desire is a first-order desire (a desire for some object, say, Pongo Peach cosmetics) accepted by the agent because it fulfils a second-order desire (a desire about a desire, say, a desire that my first-order desire for Pongo Peach be fulfilled), and that most of the first-order desires engendered in us by advertising are desires that we do accept. His example is an advertisement for Grecian Formula 16, which engenders in him a desire to be younger. He desires that both his desire to be younger and his desire for Grecian Formula 16 be fulfilled.

Unfortunately, this example is not obviously one of persuasive advertising. It may be the case that he just has this desire to look young again rather as I had certain sartorial tastes before I saw the ad about the clothes sale, and then decides to buy Grecian Formula 16 on the basis of these tastes. Imagine this form of advertisement: a person is depicted using Grecian Formula 16, and is then shown in a position of authority, surrounded by admiring members of the opposite sex. This would be a case of puffery. The advertisement implies that having hair coloured by the product will lead to positions of power, and to one's becoming more attractive to the opposite sex. It links, by suggestion, the product with my unconscious desires for power and sex. I may still claim that I am buying the product because I want to look young again. But the real reasons for my purchase are my unconscious desires for power and sex, and the link made between the product and the fulfilment of those desires by the advertisement. These reasons are not reasons I could avow to myself as good reasons for buying the product, and, again, the possibility of decision is absent.

Arrington's claim is that an autonomous desire is a first-order desire which we accept. Even if we allow that it is possible for the agent to consider whether to accept or to repudiate first-order desires induced by persuasive advertising, it seems that all first-order desires induced purely by persuasive advertising will be non-autonomous in Arrington's sense. Many of us have a strong second-order desire not to be manipulated by others without our knowledge, and for no good reason. Often, we are manipulated by others without our knowledge, but for a good reason, and one that we can accept. Take an accomplished actor: much of the skill of an actor is to be found in unconscious body-language. This manipulation we see as essential to our being entertained, and thus acquiesce in it. What is important about this case is that there seems

to be no diminution of autonomy. We can still judge the quality of the acting, in that the manipulation is part of its quality. In other cases, however, manipulation ought not to be present, and these are cases where the ability to decide is importantly diminished by the manipulation. Decision is central to the theory of the market-process: I should be able to decide whether to buy product A or product B, by judging them on their merits. Any manipulation here I shall repudiate as being for no good reason. This is not to say, incidentally, that once the fact that my desires are being manipulated by others has been made transparent to me, my desire will lapse. The people in New Jersey would have been unlikely to cease their craving for ice cream, if we had told them that their desire had been subliminally induced. But they would no longer have voiced acceptance of this desire, and, one assumes, would have resented the manipulation of their desires by the management of the cinema.

Pace Arrington, it is no evidence for the claim that most of our desires are autonomous in this sense that we often return to purchase the same product over and over again. For this might well show that persuasive advertising has been supremely efficient in inducing non-autonomous desires in us, which we are unable even to attempt not to act on, being unaware of their origin. Nor is it an argument in Arrington's favour that certain members of our society will claim not to have the second-order desire we have postulated. For it may be that this is a desire which we can see is one that human beings *ought* to have, a desire which it would be in their interests to have, and the lack of which is itself evidence of profound manipulation.

(B) RATIONAL DESIRE AND CHOICE

One might argue that the desires induced by advertising are often irrational, in the sense that they are not present in an agent in full possession of the facts about the product. This argument fails, says Arrington, because if we require *all* the facts about a thing before we can desire that thing, then all our desires will be irrational; and if we require only the *relevant* information, then prior desires determine the relevance of information. Advertising may be said to enable us to fulfil these prior desires, through the transfer of information, and the supplying of means to ends is surely a paradigm example of rationality.

But, what about persuasive, as opposed to informative, advertising? Take puffery. Is it not true that a person may buy Pongo Peach cosmetics, hoping for an adventure in paradise, and that the product will not fulfil these hopes? Are they really in possession of even the relevant facts? Yes, says Arrington. We wish to purchase *subjective* effects, and these are genuine enough. When I use Pongo Peach, I will experience a genuine feeling of adventure.

Once again, however, our analysis can help us to see the strength of the objection. For a desire to be rational, in any plausible sense, that desire must at least not be induced by the interference of other persons with my system of tastes, against my will and without my knowledge. Can we imagine a person, asked for a reason justifying their purchase of Pongo Peach, replying: "I have an unconscious desire to experience adventure, and the product has been linked with this desire through advertising"? If a desire is to be rational, it is not necessary that all the facts about the object be known to the agent, but one of the facts about that desire must be that it has not been induced in the agent through techniques which the agent cannot accept. Thus, applying the schema of Arrington's earlier argument, such a desire will be repudiated by the agent as non-autonomous and irrational.

Arrington's claim concerning the subjective effects of the products we purchase fails to deflect the charge of overriding autonomy we have made against persuasive advertising. Of course, very often the subjective effects will be lacking. If I use Grecian Formula 16, I am unlikely to find myself being promoted at work, or surrounded by admiring members of the opposite sex. This is just straight deception. But even when the effects do manifest themselves, such advertisements have still overridden my autonomy. They have activated desires which lie beyond my awareness, and over behaviour flowing from which I therefore have no control. If these claims appear doubtful, consider whether this advertisement is likely to be successful: "Do you have a feeling of adventure? Then use this brand of cosmetics." Such an advertisement will fail, in that it appeals to a *conscious* desire, either which we do not have, or which we realise will not be fulfilled by purchasing a certain brand of cosmetics. If the advertisement were for a course in mountain-climbing, it might meet with more success. Our conscious self is not so easily duped by advertising, and this is why advertisers make such frequent use of the techniques of persuasive advertising.

(C) FREE CHOICE

One might object to persuasive advertising that it creates desires so covert that an agent cannot resist them, and that acting on them is therefore neither free nor voluntary. Arrington claims that a person acts or chooses *freely* if they can adduce considerations which justify their act in their mind; and *voluntarily* if, had they been aware of a reason for acting otherwise, they could have done so. Only occasionally, he says, does advertising prevent us making free and voluntary choices.

Regarding free action, it is sufficient to note that, according to Arrington, if I were to be converted into a human robot, activated by an Evil Genius who has implanted electrodes in my brain, my actions would be free as long as I could cook up some justification for my behaviour. I want to dance this jig because I enjoy dancing. (Compare: I want to buy this ice cream because I like ice cream.) If my argument is right, we are placed in an analogous position by persuasive advertising. If we no longer mean by freedom of action the mere non-obstruction of behaviour, are we still ready to accept that we are engaged in free action? As for whether the actions of consumers subjected to persuasive advertising are voluntary in Arrington's sense, I am less optimistic than he is. It is likely, as we have suggested, that the purchasers of ice cream or Pongo Peach would have gone ahead with their purchase even if they had been made aware that their desires had been induced in them by persuasive advertising. But they would now claim that they themselves had not made the decision, that they were acting on a desire engendered in them which they did not accept, and that there was, therefore, a good reason for them not to make the purchase. The unconscious is not obedient to the commands of the conscious, although it may be forced to listen.

In fact, it is odd to suggest that persuasive advertising does give consumers a choice. A choice is usually taken to require the weighing-up of reasons. What persuasive advertising does is to remove the very conditions of choice.

(D) CONTROL OR MANIPULATION

Arrington offers the following criteria for control:

A person C controls the behaviour of another person P if

1. **C** intends **P** to act in a certain way **A**

2. **C's** intention is causally effective in bringing about **A**, and

3. **C** intends to ensure that all of the necessary conditions of **A** are satisfied.

He argues that advertisements tend to induce a desire for X, given a more basic desire for Y. Given my desire for adventure, I desire Pongo Peach cosmetics. Thus, advertisers do not control consumers, since they do not intend to produce all of the necessary conditions for our purchases.

Arrington's analysis appears to lead to some highly counter-intuitive consequences. Consider, again, my position as human robot. Imagine that the Evil Genius relies on the fact that I have certain basic unconscious desires in order to effect his plan. Thus, when he wants me to dance a jig, it is necessary that I have a more basic desire, say, ironically, for power. What the electrodes do is to jumble up my practical reasoning processes, so that I believe that I am dancing the jig because I like dancing, while, in reality, the desire to dance stems from a link between the dance and the fulfilment of my desire for power, forged by the electrodes. Are we still happy to say that I am not controlled? And does not persuasive advertising bring about a similar jumbling-up of the practical reasoning processes of consumers? When I buy Pongo Peach, I may be unable to offer a reason for my purchase, or I may claim that I want to look good. In reality, I buy it owing to the link made by persuasive advertising between my unconscious desire for adventure and the cosmetic in question.

A more convincing account of behaviour control would be to claim that it occurs when a person causes another person to act for reasons which the other person could not accept as good or justifiable reasons for the action. This is how brain-washing is to be distinguished from liberal education, rather than on Arrington's ground that the brain-washer arranges all the necessary conditions for belief. The student can both accept that she has the beliefs she has because of her education and continue to hold those beliefs as true, whereas the victim of brain-washing could not accept the explanation of the origin of her beliefs, while continuing to hold those beliefs. It is worth recalling the two cases we mentioned at the beginning of this paper. I can accept my tastes in dress, and do not think that the fact that their origin is unknown to me detracts from my autonomy, when I choose to buy the jacket. The desire for ice cream, however, will be repudiated, in that it is the result of manipulation by others, without good reason. . . .

It seems, then, that persuasive advertising does override the autonomy of consumers, and that, if the overriding of autonomy, other things being equal, is immoral, then persuasive advertising is immoral.

An argument has recently surfaced which suggests that, in fact, other things are not equal, and that persuasive advertising, although it overrides autonomy, is morally acceptable. This argument was first developed by Nelson (1978), and claims that persuasive advertising is a form of informative advertising, albeit an indirect form. The argument runs at two levels: first, the consumer can judge from the mere fact that a product is heavily advertised, regardless of the form or content of the advertisements, that that product is likely to be a market-winner. The reason for this is that it would not pay to advertise market-losers. Second, even if the consumer is taken in by the content of the advertisement, and buys the product for that reason, he is not being irrational. For he would have bought the product *anyway,* since the very fact that it is advertised means that it is a good product. As Nelson says:

> It does not pay consumers to make very thoughtful decisions about advertising. They can respond to advertising for the most ridiculous, explicit reasons and still do what they would have done if they had made the most careful judgements about their behaviour. "Irrationality" is rational if it is cost-free.

Our conclusions concerning the mode of operation of persuasive advertising, however, suggest that Nelson's argument cannot succeed. For the first level to work, it would have to be true that a purchaser of a product can evaluate that product on its own merits, and then decide whether to purchase it again. But, as we have seen, consumers induced to purchase products by persuasive advertising are not buying those products on the basis of a decision founded upon any merit the products happen to have. Thus, if the product turns out to be less good than less heavily advertised alternatives, they will not be disappointed, and will continue to purchase, if subjected to the heavy advertising which induced them to buy in the first place. For this reason, heavy persuasive advertising is not a sign of quality, and the fact that a product is advertised does not suggest that it is good. In fact, if the advertising has little or no informative content,

it might suggest just the opposite. If the product has genuine merits, it should be possible to mention them. Persuasive advertising, as the executives on Madison Avenue know, can be used to sell anything, regardless of its nature or quality.

For the second level of Nelson's argument to succeed, and for it to be in the consumer's interest to react even unthinkingly to persuasive advertising, it must be true that the first level is valid. As the first level fails, there is not even a *prima facie* reason for the belief that it is in the interest of the consumer to be subjected to persuasive advertising. In fact, there are two weighty reasons for doubting this belief. The first has already been hinted at: products promoted through persuasive advertising may well not be being sold on their merits, and may, therefore, be bad products, or products that the consumer would not desire on being confronted with unembellished facts about the product. The second is that this form of "rational irrationality" is anything but cost-free. We consider it a great cost to lose our autonomy. If I were to demonstrate to you conclusively that if I were to take over your life, and make your decisions for you, you would have a life containing far more of whatever you think makes life worth living, apart from autonomy, than if you were to retain control, you would not surrender your autonomy to me even for these great gains in other values. As we mentioned above in our discussion of autonomous desire, we have a strong second-order desire not to act on first-order desires induced in us unawares by others, for no good reason, and now we can see that that desire applies even to cases in which we would *appear* to be better off in acting on such first-order desires.

Thus, we may conclude that Nelson's argument in favour of persuasive advertising is not convincing. I should note, perhaps, that my conclusion concerning persuasive advertising echoes that of Santilli (1983). My argument differs from his, however, in centering upon the notions of autonomy and causes of desires acceptable to the agent, rather than upon the distinction between needs and desires. Santilli claims that the arousal of a desire is not a rational process, unless it is preceded by a knowledge of actual needs. This, I believe, is too strong. I may well have no need of a new tennis-racket, but my desire for one, aroused by informative advertisements in the newspaper, seems rational enough. I would prefer to claim that a desire is autonomous and at least *prima facie* rational if it is not induced in the agent without his knowledge and for no good reason, and allows ordinary processes of decision-making to occur.

Finally, I should point out that, in arguing against all persuasive advertising, unlike Santilli, I am not to be interpreted as bestowing moral respectability upon all informative advertising. Advertisers of any variety ought to consider whether the ideological objections often made to their conduct have any weight. Are they, for instance, imposing a distorted system of values upon consumers, in which the goal of our lives is to consume, and in which success is measured by one's level of consumption? Or are they entrenching attitudes which prolong the position of certain groups subject to discrimination, such as women or homosexuals? Advertisers should also carefully consider whether their product will be of genuine value to any consumers, and, if so, attempt to restrict their campaigns to the groups in society which will benefit (see Durham, 1984). I would claim, for instance, that all advertising of tobacco-based products, even of the informative variety, is wrong, and that some advertisements for alcohol are wrong, in that they are directed at the wrong audience. Imagine, for instance, a liquor-store manager erecting an informative bill-board opposite an alcoholics' rehabilita-

tion center. But these are secondary questions for prospective advertisers. The primary questions must be whether they are intending to employ the techniques of persuasive advertising, and, if so, how these techniques can be avoided.

References

ARRINGTON, R.: 1982, "Advertising and Behaviour Control," *Journal of Business Ethics* I, 1.

DURHAM, T.: 1984, "Information, Persuasion, and Control in Moral Appraisal of Advertising Strategy," *Journal of Business Ethics* III, 3.

NELSON, P.: 1978, "Advertising and Ethics," in *Ethics, Free Enterprise, and Public Police.* (eds.) R. De George and J. Pichler, New York: Oxford University Press.

SANTILLI, P.: 1983, "The Informative and Persuasive Functions of Advertising: A Moral Appraisal," *Journal of Business Ethics* II, 1.

Study Questions

1. Why does Crisp believe that standard advertising techniques are coercive?

2. How does Crisp use the concepts of free choice, autonomy, and behavior control to support his view?

3. What psychological and ethical assumptions does Crisp make? What would Messick and Bazerman say about these assumptions?

4. Does Arrington or Crisp present the stronger case?

CASE: The Case of the Willful Whistle-Blower
Sally Seymour

When Ken Deaver, CEO of Fairway Electric, promoted me to vice president of the nu-clear division, I was on top of the world. Now, just a month later, it feels like the world's on top of me. I'm used to having a team to share the problems, but now I'm on my own. At least Ken's door has always been open to me. He's been my mentor since I began at Fairway eight years ago, and he's really responsible for my success here. I owe him a lot. But when I think back over the last few weeks, I have to wonder whether I should have listened to him on this one.

It started the morning I walked into my office to find one of my old teammates wait-ing for me. He apologized for taking my time but said it was really important. I had worked with Jim for more than four years. If he says it's important, it's important.

"What's up?" I asked.

"Bob," he said, "I've run up against something I can't handle alone. I hate to dump this on you when you're just starting your new job, but it's the sort of thing I should take to my boss, and that's you now."

"Sure, Jim. Whatever it is, you've got my help."

He took a couple of deep breaths before he continued. "You know how we're cramped for space downstairs. Well, yesterday I asked my secretary to clear out any files over five years old. Before she left for the day, she stacked the old files on my desk so I could glance through them. And I couldn't believe what I found."

Jim pulled a red notebook from his briefcase.

"I found this report written 15 years ago by two engineers in the nuclear division. It's about a flaw in our design of the Radon II nuclear reactor. Apparently there was a structural problem in the containment unit that would show up as the power plant was being built. It wasn't a safety hazard, but it would hold up construction and cost a lot to fix. The report says that Fairway was going to rework the design. But listen to this memo from the head of the nuclear division." Jim opened the notebook and read from a sheet stapled to the inside cover.

"The potential problems in the design of the Radon II are disturbing. They do not, however, present a safety hazard. It therefore would be counterproductive to discontinue sales of the design. If there are problems with fittings, they will show up as the plant is built, at which point the necessary corrections can be made. The need for retrofitting is not uncommon. Our experience has been that customers rarely complain about such extra costs."

Jim closed the notebook and looked up.

"This memo makes me sick, Bob. I can't believe Fairway would risk its reputation by selling plans they knew were flawed. Those customers bought the designs thinking they were the best on the market. But the Radon II took longer to build and cost a bunch more money than what Fairway told customers. That's misrepresentation. Maybe the reason the utilities never complained is because they could pass the cost on to the rate payers. But that's a real rip-off, and the top guys at Fairway knew about it."

Jim threw the notebook on my desk and looked at me, his face flushed.

"Don't you think engineering ought to know about this?" he said.

I'd never seen Jim so steamed up. Of course, I was pretty upset myself. That report was new to me too. But I had a lot of faith in Fairway, so I wasn't going to leap to conclusions. I told Jim I'd ask some questions and get back to him by the end of the day.

I headed straight for Ken's office, recalling along the way everything I could about the Radon II reactor. I knew that we'd had problems with it, but it never occurred to me that our original designs were flawed. Jim was right that no one ever complained about the delays and costs of refitting. But I remembered one instance where a utility converted a Radon II to a coal-fired plant because of the cost overruns. In that case, the utility paid for the conversion and it didn't go into the rate base.

When I showed the report to Ken, he recognized it right away.

"How did Jim get ahold of this?" he asked.

"He discovered it by accident—cleaning out old files," I said. "He's pretty disturbed about it, and I can't say I blame him." Ken's office was suddenly very still.

"I thought this report was dead and buried," he said. "Have you read it?"

"Enough to get the drift," I said. "Apparently we sold a power plant design when we knew there were flaws in it."

"Yes, but you've got to understand the context. Back then we were in the middle of an energy crisis. Everyone was rushing to build nuclear power plants. We were under tremendous pressure to come up with a winning design, and Radon II was what we decided on. After a few plants went under construction, some problems surfaced, so we put a couple of engineers on it. But by the time they wrote this report, it was too late for us to go back to the drawing board. We wouldn't have had any customers left. We figured we'd solve the problem as soon as we could, but we'd sell the original design in the meantime. It was basically a very good one. And it was safe."

"I can't believe we would risk our reputation like that."

"I know it's not the way we usually operate, but that shows you the pressure we were under," Ken said. "The whole division would have gone down. There was no other way."

I was uncomfortable putting Ken on the defensive. I'd always trusted his judgment. Who was I to grill him about something that happened 15 years ago when I wasn't even around? Still, I needed to press the point.

"So what do I tell Jim?" I asked.

"Nothing. It's ancient history. The engineers who wrote that report are long gone. Look at it this way, the fact that we ordered a study of the problem shows that we care about quality. We eventually got the bugs out. Besides, it was never a question of safety. It was merely a matter of some extra work during construction."

"But what about all the cost overruns? If Fairway didn't swallow them, someone else must have—like the utilities or their customers."

"Look, Bob, what's past is past. What would we gain by bringing this into the open today? But I guarantee we've got a hell of a lot to lose. The regulators and some shareholders would love to blame us for all the exorbitant cost overruns. And the antinuclear groups would have a field day. We've got enough problems getting licenses as it is.

"We'd lose a lot of business, you know. I'm talking about hundreds of jobs here, and the very survival of this company. Maybe we're not perfect, but we're the most conscientious, quality-conscious corporation I know of."

"And what do I do with this report?" I asked.

"Deep-six it. As we should have done long ago. Tell Jim Bower what I told you, and explain why there's no reason to make an issue of it at this late date."

I nodded in agreement and headed back to my office. I found Jim waiting.

He scowled when I reported Ken's reaction.

"So you're telling me to forget I ever saw the report? And I suppose that means you're going to forget I showed it to you."

"Look, Ken's got some good reasons for not wanting to make an issue of it. I may or may not agree with him, but he's running the show."

"Damn it, Bob!" Jim shouted. "If we go along with this, we're just as guilty as the people who sold those bad designs 15 years ago."

"Cool down, cool down. I know what you're saying, but Ken is just being realistic. After all, no one got hurt, the cost was spread over a lot of people, and the problem's been corrected. If this gets exposed, it could really hurt us."

"No, I won't cool down. Maybe it seems like ancient history to Ken, but unless we make a clean slate now, it could happen again. One of the reasons I took this job is because Fairway is a company I can respect. What am I supposed to think now?"

"I see your point," I replied, "but I also see Ken's. And he's the boss. Maybe you should talk to him."

"If I can't get through to you I don't see how I'll get through to him. So I guess that's it."

As it turned out, that wasn't it. When Jim left my office, he didn't go straight back to work. First he went to the newspaper, and the story appeared two days later.

FAIRWAY SOLD DEFECTIVE REACTORS—REPORT WARNED OF HAZARD

Naturally, the reporter got it all wrong and blew the problem out of proportion. He didn't even have a copy of the report. I suppose we hadn't helped matters though. When the reporter called for a comment, Ken asked him to call back in a couple of hours. Then Ken and I met with our public relations officer, Amy Thone, to discuss how to handle the situation. Amy thought we should come clean—admit we made a mistake and stress the fact that our record for the past five years had been excellent. But Ken felt that the less we said, the sooner it would blow over. I went along with him. When the reporter called back, Ken's response was "no comment."

The article did say that the anonymous source still thought Fairway was a reliable builder of nuclear plants and that it was a good company with many skilled and highly principled employees. The source had gone to the newspaper because he felt it was his ethical duty to the consumers who had been forced to pay for Fairway's mistakes. But that part of the story was buried in the next-to-last paragraph.

Needless to say, the public outcry was intense. Antinuke activists went berserk, and politicians made holier-than-thou speeches. After a couple of days hearing phones ring off the hook, we realized that stonewalling was compounding our problems. So we made a clean breast of it. We drafted a statement to the press saying that Fairway engineers had in fact discovered design flaws in 1973 but that the company had corrected the problem within 14 months. Ken made himself available to answer questions, and he and Amy arranged to meet with community leaders. They even invited experts from the university to answer the technical questions. The thrust of these efforts was to assure the public that no flaws had been discovered since 1973 and that all Fairway's designs were safe.

Thanks to Amy and Ken, the controversy finally died down. I was proud of the way they handled things. I was also glad that Ken didn't fire Jim. At the height of the crisis, someone at headquarters had suggested that he "get rid of the troublemaker," but Ken thought that would only make matters worse. I didn't want to fire Jim either. I felt he was still a valuable employee. I knew he was committed to Fairway, and we sure needed his skills.

We weathered those difficult weeks with only a few outstanding lawsuits, but an ugly incident like that never has a simple ending. It keeps unraveling. Now we have another problem. Word got out that Jim was the whistle-blower, and now his life here is miserable. The feeling is that Jim can't be trusted. Last week, Lorraine Wellman, another former teammate, came to talk to me about the problem.

"You know, it's not that anyone hates Jim for what he did," she said. "It's just that no one can understand why he did it. They could understand it if someone had been hurt or killed because of a bad design, but that wasn't the case. In their minds, he risked their jobs for something that happened ages ago.

"Morale is pretty low in the trenches," she added. "One guy told me he used to be proud of where he worked. Now his neighbors razz him about 'Radongate' and 'Three-Mile Radon.' No one wants to work with Jim, and it's affecting our output."

I felt terrible for Jim. Unlike the others, I understood why he did what he did, and I respected his integrity. On the other hand, I wasn't surprised that his coworkers resented him. I just wished everyone would forget the whole thing and get on with their work. But the situation seemed to be getting worse instead of better.

Yesterday Ken came to see me about the mounting problems in Jim's department. He suggested that Jim might want to resign and that we could give him a very generous package if he did. I knew what Ken was driving at. He didn't want to stir up trouble by firing a whistle-blower, but he thought we could get around it by pressuring Jim to leave on his own. That would solve all our problems. Of course Ken just wanted what was best for Fairway, but I resisted the idea. I asserted that the problems were temporary, and threw in a few remarks about Jim's outstanding performance. I figured I should defend him. After all, Jim had done the noble thing, and it didn't seem right that he should get the shaft. But Ken persisted. He was worried about meeting targets and didn't think one person should be allowed to make everyone else look bad. He asked me to talk to Jim.

Jim had been avoiding me since he showed me the report, and maybe I was avoiding him too. The worst thing about this whole situation is that it ruined our friendship. Still, he agreed to see me in my office. I tried to break the ice by extending my hand and saying that I missed seeing him. But he ignored the gesture and mumbled something about being busy. So I decided to jump right in.

"I've heard about the problems you've been having with the team. This thing is taking its toll—on Fairway, your department, and you."

"I can handle it. Or maybe that's not your point. Are you saying that the company doesn't want me around anymore?"

"Look Jim," I said, "I'm real sorry this happened. I hate to see you and your family suffering like this. Maybe a transfer to another office would be the best thing. There are other divisions that could use your talents."

"You just don't get it, do you, Bob? I haven't done anything wrong, and I'm the one who's suffering. People are blaming me for a report I didn't write and bad designs I didn't push on customers. And now I'm the one you want out. I figured the idea of firing me might occur to someone, but I can't believe you agreed to it. That's one I hadn't expected."

"No one has mentioned firing," I said. "I'm talking about a transfer. I see why you're angry about your teammates giving you a hard time, but why come down on me? I'm one of the few who understand your position, and I've tried to support you."

"You've tried to *support* me? Give me a break! I didn't want to get into this, but now that you've brought it up, I'm going to spell it out for you.

"I didn't ask to see that report. It fell into my hands. But once it did, I couldn't just pretend it wasn't there. What the company did was wrong—you know that and I know that. If someone didn't say something, Fairway could get away with it again.

"But I surely didn't figure you'd make me go this alone. I didn't expect you to run to the newspapers, but I did expect you to make a strong case to Ken for the company coming clean on this. And failing that, I expected you—as my supervisor—to take this off my shoulders by assuming the responsibility yourself.

"You've got more power than I have, and you certainly have more influence with Ken. But you acted like this whole thing had nothing to do with you—like you were just a messenger. You dumped Ken's answer in my lap and washed your hands of the whole affair.

"I never thought I'd say this, but it's beginning to look like you care way too much for your fancy new title and your tight relationship with Ken. Well, I won't quit and I won't transfer!"

Before I could respond, Jim was out the door. I don't know how long I sat at my desk in a daze. After a while I tried to get back to work, but I couldn't concentrate. The whole morning I kept going over what Jim had said. How could I defend Jim and the company at the same time? Was Ken wrong? Had Jim really done the noble thing after all?

Study Questions

1. What exactly is (are) the problem(s) Bob faces?

2. What are the ethical, economic, and legal aspects of revealing this information now?

3. How would Friedman, Cochran, and Freeman analyze this case? Which of these three points of view is strongest as a descriptive mechanism? As a prescriptive mechanism?

4. Are employees like Jim Bower assets or burdens to companies? Would your answer to this depend on whether you adopted a goal or a contract view of the organization?

Ronald Duska

Whistlebowing and Employee Loyalty

Three Mile Island. In early 1983, almost four years after the near meltdown at Unit 2, two officials in the Site Operations Office of General Public Utilities reported a reckless company effort to clean up the contaminated reactor. Under threat of physical retaliation from superiors, the GPU insiders released evidence alleging that the company had rushed the TMI cleanup without testing key maintenance systems. Since then, the Three Mile Island mop-up has been stalled pending a review of GPU's management.[1]

The releasing of evidence of the rushed cleanup at Three Mile Island is an example of whistleblowing. Norman Bowie defines whistleblowing as "the act by an employee of informing the public on the immoral or illegal behavior of an employer or supervisor."[2] Ever since Daniel Ellsberg's release of the Pentagon Papers, the question of whether an employee should blow the whistle on his company or organization has become a hotly contested issue. Was Ellsberg right? Is it right to report the shady or suspect practices of the organization one works for? Is one a stool pigeon or a dedicated citizen? Does a person have an obligation to the public which overrides his obligation to his employer or does he simply betray a loyalty and become a traitor if he reports his company?

There are proponents on both sides of the issue—those who praise whistleblowers as civic heroes and those who condemn them as "finks." Glen and Shearer who wrote about the whistleblowers at Three Mile Island say, "Without the *courageous* breed of assorted company insiders known as whistleblowers—workers who often risk their livelihoods to disclose information about construction and design flaws—the Nuclear Regulatory Commission itself would be nearly as idle as Three Mile Island . . . That whistleblowers deserve both gratitude and protection is beyond disagreement."[3]

Still, while Glen and Shearer praise whistleblowers, others vociferously condemn them. For example, in a now-infamous quote, James Roche, the former president of General Motors said:

> Some critics are now busy eroding another support of free enterprise—the loyalty of a management team, with its unifying values and cooperative work. Some of the enemies of business now encourage an employee to be *disloyal* to the enterprise. They want to create suspicion and disharmony, and pry into the proprietary interests of the business. However this is labelled—industrial espionage, whistle blowing, or professional responsibility—it is another tactic for spreading disunity and creating conflict.[4]

From Roche's point of view, whistleblowing is not only not "courageous" and deserving of "gratitude and protection" as Glen and Shearer would have it, it is corrosive and not even permissible.

Discussions of whistleblowing generally revolve around four topics: (1) attempts to define whistleblowing more precisely; (2) debates about whether and when whistleblowing is permissible; (3) debates about whether and when one has an obligation to blow the whistle; and (4) appropriate mechanisms for institutionalizing whistleblowing.

In this paper I want to focus on the second problem, because I find it somewhat disconcerting that there is a problem at all. When I first looked into the ethics of whistleblowing it seemed to me that whistleblowing was a good thing, and yet I found in the literature claim after claim that it was in need of defense, that there was something wrong with it, namely that it was an act of disloyalty. . . .

In his book *Business Ethics,* Norman Bowie, who presents what I think is one of the finest presentations of the ethics of whistleblowing, claims that "whistleblowing . . . violate[s] a *prima facie* duty of loyalty to one's employer." According to Bowie, there is a duty of loyalty which prohibits one from reporting his employer or company. Bowie, of course, recognizes that this is only a *prima facie* duty, i.e., one that can be overridden by a higher duty to the public good. Nevertheless, the axiom that whistleblowing is disloyal is Bowie's starting point.

Bowie is not alone. Sisela Bok, another fine ethicist, sees whistleblowing as an instance of disloyalty.

> The whistleblower hopes to stop the game; but since he is neither referee nor coach, and since he blows the whistle on his own team, his act is seen as a *violation of loyalty* [italics mine]. In holding his position, he has assumed certain obligations to his colleagues and clients. He may even have subscribed to a loyalty oath or a promise of confidentiality . . . Loyalty to colleagues and to clients comes to be pitted against loyalty to the

public interest, to those who may be injured unless the revelation is made.[5]

Bowie and Bok end up defending whistleblowing in certain contexts, so I don't necessarily disagree with their conclusions. However, I fail to see how one has an obligation of loyalty to one's company, so I disagree with their perception of the problem, and their starting point. The difference in perception is important because those who think employees have an obligation of loyalty to a company fail to take into account a relevant moral difference between persons and corporations and between corporations and other kinds of groups where loyalty is appropriate. I want to argue that one does not have an obligation of loyalty to a company, even a *prima facie* one, because companies are not the kind of things which are proper objects of loyalty. I then want to show that to make them objects of loyalty gives them a moral status they do not deserve and in raising their status, one lowers the status of the individuals who work for the companies.

But why aren't corporations the kind of things which can be objects of loyalty? . . .

Loyalty is ordinarily construed as a state of being constant and faithful in a relation implying trust or confidence, as a wife to husband, friend to friend, parent to child, lord to vassal, etc. According to John Ladd "it is not founded on just *any* casual relationship, but on a specific kind of relationship or tie. The ties that bind the persons together provide the basis of loyalty."[6] But all sorts of ties bind people together to make groups. I am a member of a group of fans if I go to a ball game. I am a member of a group if I merely walk down the street. I am in a sense tied to them, but don't owe them loyalty. I don't owe loyalty to just anyone I encounter. Rather I owe loyalty to persons with whom I have special relationships. I owe it to my children, my spouse, my parents, my friends and certain groups, those groups which are formed for the mutual enrichment of the members. It is important to recognize that in any relationship which demands loyalty the relationship works both ways and involves mutual enrichment. Loyalty is incompatible with self-interest, because it is something that necessarily requires we go beyond self-interest. My loyalty to my friend, for example, requires I put aside my interests some of the time. It is because of this reciprocal requirement which demands surrendering self-interest that a corporation is not a proper object of loyalty.

A business or corporation does two things in the free enterprise system. It produces a good or service and makes a profit. The making of a profit, however, is the primary function of a business as a business. For if the production of the good or service was not profitable the business would be out of business. Since non-profitable goods or services are discontinued, the providing of a service or the making of a product is not done for its own sake, but from a business perspective is a means to an end, the making of profit. People bound together in a business are not bound together for mutual fulfillment and support, but to divide labor so the business makes a profit. Since profit is paramount if you do not produce in a company or if there are cheaper laborers around, a company feels justified in firing you for the sake of better production. Throughout history companies in a pinch feel no obligation of loyalty. Compare that to a family. While we can jokingly refer to a family as "somewhere they have to take you in no matter what," you cannot refer to a company in that way. "You can't buy loyalty" is true. Loyalty depends on ties that demand self-sacrifice with no expectation of reward, e.g., the ties of loyalty that bind a family together. Business functions on the basis of enlightened self-interest. I am devoted to a company not because it is like a parent to me. It is not, and attempts of some companies to create "one big happy family" ought to be looked on with suspicion. I am not "devoted" to it at all, or should not be. I work for it because it pays me. I am not in a family to get paid, but I am in a company to get paid.

Since loyalty is a kind of devotion, one can confuse devotion to one's job (or the ends of one's work) with devotion to a company.

I may have a job I find fulfilling, but that is accidental to my relation to the company. For example, I might go to work for a company as a carpenter and love the job and get satisfaction out of doing good work. But if the company can increase profit by cutting back to an adequate but inferior type of material or procedure, it can make it impossible for me to take pride in my work as a carpenter while making it possible for me to make more money. The company does not exist to subsidize my quality work as a carpenter. As a carpenter my goal may be good houses, but as an employee my goal is to contribute to making a profit. "That's just business!" . . .

The cold hard truth is that the goal of profit is what gives birth to a company and forms that particular group. Money is what ties the group together. But in such a commercialized venture, with such a goal there is no loyalty, or at least none need be expected. An employer will release an employee and an employee will walk away from an employer when it is profitable to do so. That's business. It is perfectly permissible. Contrast that with the ties between a lord and his vassal. A lord could not in good conscience wash his hands of his vassal, nor could a vassal in good conscience abandon his lord. What bound them was mutual enrichment, not profit.

Loyalty to a corporation, then, is not required. But even more it is probably misguided. There is nothing as pathetic as the story of the loyal employee who, having given above and beyond the call of duty, is let go in the restructuring of the company. He feels betrayed because he mistakenly viewed the company as an object of his loyalty. To get rid of such foolish romanticism and to come to grips with this hard but accurate assessment should ultimately benefit everyone.

One need hardly be an enemy of business to be suspicious of a demand of loyalty to something whose primary reason for existence is the making of profit. It is simply the case that I have no duty of loyalty to the business or organization. Rather I have a duty to return responsible work for fair wages. The commercialization of work dissolves the type of relationship that requires loyalty. It sets up merely contractual relationships. One sells one's labor but not one's self to a company or an institution. . . .

Of course if everyone would view business as a commercial instrument, things might become more difficult for the smooth functioning of the organization, since businesses could not count on the "loyalty" of their employees. Business itself is well served, at least in the short run, if it can keep the notion of a duty to loyalty alive. It does this by comparing itself to a paradigm case of an organization one shows loyalty to, the team.

Remember that Roche refers to the "management team" and Bok sees the name "whistleblowing" coming from the instance of a referee blowing a whistle in the presence of a foul. What is perceived as bad about whistleblowing in business from this perspective is that one blows the whistle on one's own team, thereby violating team loyalty. If the company can get its employees to view it as a team they belong to, it is easier to demand loyalty. The rules governing teamwork and team loyalty will apply. One reason the appeal to a team and team loyalty works so well in business is that businesses are in competition with one another. If an executive could get his employees to be loyal, a loyalty without thought to himself or his fellow man, but to the will of the company, the manager would have the ideal kind of corporation from an organizational standpoint. As Paul R. Lawrence, the organizational theorist says, "Ideally, we would want one sentiment to be dominant in all employees from top to bottom, namely a complete loyalty to the organizational purpose."[7] Effective motivation turns business practices into a game and instills teamwork.

But businesses differ from teams in very important respects, which makes the analogy between business and a team dangerous. Loyalty to a team is loyalty within the context of sport, a competition. Teamwork and team loyalty require that in the circumscribed activity of the game I cooperate with my fellow players so that pulling all together, we can win. The object of (most) sports is victory. But the winning in sports is a social convention, divorced from the usual goings on of society. Such a winning is most times a harmless, morally neutral diversion.

But the fact that this victory in sports within the rules enforced by a referee (whistleblower), is a socially developed convention taking place within a larger social context makes it quite different from competition in business, which, rather than being defined by a context, permeates the whole of society in its influence. Competition leads not only to winners but to losers. One can lose at sport with precious few serious consequences. The consequences of losing at business are much more serious. Further, the losers in sport are there voluntarily, while the losers in business can be those who are not in the game voluntarily (we are all forced to participate) but are still affected by business decisions. People cannot choose to participate in business, since it permeates everyone's life.

The team model fits very well with the model of the free-market system because there competition is said to be the name of the game. Rival companies compete and their object is to win. To call a foul on one's own teammate is to jeopardize one's chances of winning and is viewed as disloyalty.

But isn't it time to stop viewing the corporate machinations as games? These games are not controlled and not over after a specific time. The activities of business affect the lives of everyone, not just the game players. The analogy of the corporation to a team and the consequent appeal to team loyalty, although understandable, is seriously misleading at least in the moral sphere, where competition is not the prevailing virtue.

If my analysis is correct, the issue of the permissibility of whistleblowing is not a real issue, since there is no obligation of loyalty to a company. Whistleblowing is not only permissible but expected when a company is harming society. The issue is not one of disloyalty to the company, but the question of whether the whistleblower has an obligation to society if blowing the whistle will bring him retaliation. I will not argue that issue, but merely suggest the lines I would pursue.

I tend to be a minimalist in ethics, and depend heavily on a distinction between obligations and acts of supererogation. We have, it seems to me, an obligation to avoid harm-

ing anyone, but not an obligation to do good. Doing good is above the call of duty. In-between we may under certain conditions have an obligation to prevent harm. If whistleblowing can prevent harm, then it is required under certain conditions.

Simon, Powers and Gunnemann set forth four conditions.[8] need, proximity, capability, and last resort. Applying these, we get the following.

1. There must be a clear harm to society that can be avoided by whistleblowing. We don't blow the whistle over everything.

2. It is the "proximity" to the whistleblower that puts him in the position to report his company in the first place.

3. "Capability" means that he needs to have some chance of success. No one has an obligation to jeopardize himself to perform futile gestures. The whistleblower needs to have access to the press, be believable, etc.

4. "Last resort" means just that. If there are others more capable of reporting and more proximate, and if they will report, then one does not have the responsibility.

Before concluding, there is one aspect of the loyalty issue that ought to be disposed of. My position could be challenged in the case of organizations who are employers in non-profit areas, such as the government, educational institutions, etc. In this case my commercialization argument is irrelevant. However, I would maintain that any activity which merits the blowing of the whistle in the case of non-profit and service organizations is probably counter to the purpose of the institution in the first place. Thus, if there were loyalty required, in that case, whoever justifiably blew the whistle would be blowing it on a colleague who perverted the end or purpose of the organization. The loyalty to the group would remain intact. Ellsberg's whistleblowing on the government is a way of keeping the government faithful to its obligations. But that is another issue.

Notes

1. Maxwell Glen and Cody Shearer, "Going after the Whistle-blowers," *The Philadelphia Inquirer,* Tuesday, Aug.·2, 1983, Op-ed Page, p. 11a.
2. Norman Bowie, *Business Ethics* (Englewood Cliffs, N.J.: Prentice-Hall, 1982), 14C. For Bowie, this is just a preliminary definition. His fuller definition reads, "A whistle blower is an employee or officer of any institution, profit or non-profit, private or public, who believes either that he/she has been ordered to perform some act or he/she has obtained knowledge that the institution is engaged in activities which a) are believed to cause unnecessary harm to third parties, b) are in violation of human rights or c) run counter to the defined purpose of the institution and who inform the public of this fact." Bowie then lists six conditions under which the act is justified. 142–143.
3. Glen and Shearer, "Going after the Whistleblowers," 11a.
4. James M. Roche, "The Competitive System, to Work, to Preserve, and to Protect," *Vital Speeches of the Day* (May 1971), 445. This is quoted in Bowie, 141 and also in Kenneth D. Walters, "Your Employee's Right to Blow the Whistle," *Harvard Business Review,* 53, no. 4.
5. Sisela Bok, "Whistleblowing and professional Responsibilities," *New York University Education Quarterly,* vol. II, 4 (1980), 3.
6. John Ladd, "Loyalty," *The Encyclopedia of Philosophy,* vol. 5, 97.
7. Paul R. Lawrence, *The Changing of Organizational Behavior Patterns: A Case Study of Decentralization* (Boston: Division of Research, Harvard Business School, 1958), 208, as quoted in Kenneth D. Walters, op. cit.
8. John G. Simon, Charles W. Powers, and Jon P. Gunnemann, *The Ethical investor: Universities and Corporate Responsibility* (New Haven: Yale University Press, 1972).

Study Questions

1. Why does Duska think that loyalty is an improper way to understand employee–company relationships?

2. What assumptions does Duska make about the nature of the firm? For example, does he rely on a goal or a contract view of the firm?

3. How would friedman, Cochran, and Freeman analyze Duska's arguments?

4. How does Duska's article relate to Werhane's view about employment at will?

CASE: **The Transfer of Dangerous Industries to Underdeveloped Countries**
Richard T. De George

Consider the following case: Asbestos USA (a fictitious name) produces asbestos products for the U.S. market. It competes with asbestos products made in Mexico. It is able to compete, despite the fact that Mexican labor is so much cheaper than labor in the United States, because it operates more efficiently and with more advanced equipment than do the Mexican companies. We now know that asbestos causes cancer. Those exposed to it for long periods had a significantly higher rate of cancer than others. The rate was especially high for people who worked in asbestos plants. The United States therefore passed legislation requiring the introduction of a series of safeguards for people working in asbestos plants. Asbestos USA calculated the cost of implementing the safeguards and decided it could not implement them and still stay in business. Rather than close down completely, however, it moved its plant to Mexico, which has not passed comparable safety legislation. Asbestos USA continues to market its products in the United States, even though it manufactures its products in Mexico. There, it operates its equipment in the same way (i.e., without safeguards) as it did in the United States; however, it has to pay its workers only the going wage for the industry in Mexico.

By moving its plant to Mexico, is Asbestos USA acting immorally?

Exposure to asbestos tends to produce cancer in a significant number of people. This is the overriding consideration to which the American government reacted when it passed legislation requiring safeguards. No company, it has ruled, has the right to expose its workers to cancer if this can be prevented. The ruling is a defensible one. It applies to all industries and to all asbestos manufacturers. But obviously the U.S. rule applies only in the United States; it does not apply to asbestos factories in other countries. If Asbestos USA's imports were subject to an import duty, it would have little incentive to move to Mexico. But because this is not the case, it moved its plant. This move is better for its shareholders than if the company had gone out of business. The asbestos products would be bought from Mexican firms anyway, so why not have an American company selling asbestos products to the United States, as well as Mexican companies? These considerations, however, fail to respond to the major issue: is it moral to expose employees to the danger of cancer when this can be prevented? If the answer is no, then it is not moral to so expose Mexican workers.

Which second-order principle is applicable to this case? Here is one possible principle: It is immoral to hire anyone to do work that is in some way dangerous to his or her life or health. But the principle, as stated, is too strong. Any job might be dangerous in some way; therefore, if it were immoral to hire someone to do work that was in any way dangerous, no one could be hired to do many jobs that seem perfectly acceptable. But we must also acknowledge that some jobs are more dangerous than others. Firefighters are paid to put out fires, but they know they risk their lives in doing so. Police are also paid to risk their lives. Yet most people would be reluctant to say that hiring people to do these jobs is immoral. The immorality, therefore, does not come from hiring people

From *Business Ethics,* 4th ed., by Richard T. De George. Reprinted by permission of Prentice-Hall, Inc., Upper Saddle River, NJ.

to do work that involves risk to life or health. But we can defend the principle that it is immoral to hire someone to do work that is known to the employer to involve significant risk without informing the prospective employee of that risk. This application of the principle of informed consent is defensible, as guaranteeing a fair exchange between consenting adults.

If we adopt this principle, then Asbestos USA could be morally right in hiring workers in Mexico, with working conditions that would not be allowed in the United States, if the potential workers were warned of the dangers. We can assume that once warned of the dangers, the workers would agree to work in the plant only if they received more pay than they would for comparable work in a factory in which they were not exposed to the danger of cancer. If this were not the case, it would be an indication that the people who were hired were in some way being forced into the jobs—were not free agents, contracting freely and knowingly to do dangerous work at pay they considered appropriate to make up for the increased risk. A contract between employer and employee is fair if both parties enter into the contract with adequate appropriate knowledge and if both freely agree to the terms of the contract.

The critics of Asbestos USA contend that the Mexican workers, even if they are informed of the dangers and are paid somewhat higher wages than other workers are paid (Brazil requires triple pay for dangerous work), are forced because of the lack of work in Mexico to accept employment in asbestos plants, at less than adequate pay. Hence, the critics contend, despite protestations regarding informed consent, the workers are forced to take such jobs and are exploited in them.

Informed consent is necessary if the action is to be moral, but it is not *sufficient*. There are some things (e.g., selling oneself into slavery) to which no one can morally consent. There are also some conditions that are immoral for an employer to impose on his or her workers, even if the latter agree to work under those conditions. Consent is not enough because people who desperately need money may agree to work under almost any conditions. Built into capitalism is the tendency of employers to pay workers as little as possible and to spend as little as possible on a safe work environment. In the United States, this tendency has been offset by unionization and government legislation. In countries where it is not offset, employers can take unfair advantage of workers and engage in immoral practices. If Asbestos USA wishes to operate its plant in Mexico, it can morally do so only if it informs the workers of the risk, in terms they can understand; if it pays them more for undertaking the risk; and if it lowers the risk to some acceptable level. It need not be at the same level demanded by the Occupational Safety and Health Act (OSHA) in the United States, but morally, it cannot be at a level so high that risk is maximized rather than minimized. It would also be immoral not to eliminate risks that could be removed without extravagant cost. If, in Mexican plants, asbestos particles float freely through the air, collecting like cobwebs and if workers are not even given paper masks, it is clear that minimum safety standards are not being observed.

The Mexican government sometimes passes laws concerning health and safety, which are different from those passed in the United States. We cannot conclude that the Mexican government cares less for the welfare of its people than does the American government for its citizens. U.S. industry is more technologically developed than Mexican industry. Mexican industry is more labor-intensive, on the whole, than U.S. industry. Mexico seeks to attract foreign industry to help develop its potential, to train its people in work skills, and to bring in tax and other revenue. Imported industry also provides work for Mexicans who would otherwise be unemployed. Suppose that for these and similar reasons the Mexican government decides that it gains more by allowing somewhat unsafe factory conditions than by setting standards that would preclude the development of industry in the country. Suppose that the workers prefer working in Asbestos USA to not working at all. We can complain that it is unfair for people not to have work or that the contract of employment with such people is not free and hence morally marred. But granting all of this, it might still be true that Mexico and the Mexican people benefit more by Asbestos USA locating its plant in Mexico than by its not being there. If this were the case, then the move of Asbestos USA would not be immoral, providing it fulfilled the foregoing conditions.

Does this mean that it is moral to export cancer-producing industries to Mexico and other countries, where the regulations are more lenient than in the United States? The argument so far has considered Asbestos USA an isolated case. What will be the effect on Mexico and its people twenty years hence if such industries move there in significant numbers? Are the country and the people better off without such industries? How will the cancer cases be treated? What will happen to families of workers who get cancer? Are health provisions and pension plans provided for the workers?

Companies that wish to act morally must consider and attempt to answer these questions.

Ideally, there should be international agreements on minimally acceptable standards of safety in industry. In the absence of such standards moral sense and pressure must function until law can equalize the position of the worker vis-à-vis the employer. But moral sense and pressure seem to play little role in the policies of many international corporations. Paradoxically, some underdeveloped countries see the conditions for moral action, which have been discussed here, as impediments to the development of their countries, as requirements that keep them underdeveloped, and as the moralizing of Americans who are basically well off and do not understand other situations, including the aspirations of other people. The difficulty of knowing what will benefit the people in such countries most and of knowing what the people truly want—as opposed to what some governmental leaders say—is enormous. The difficulty forces us to be careful not to confuse what is morally right with what is proper for Americans. But American companies that are operating abroad and wish to be moral should not ignore the moral dimension of their actions; they should not simply follow the letter of the law in the countries in which they operate.

Is Asbestos USA immoral if it does not pay its Mexican employees the same wages that it paid its U.S. employees? The claim that it is immoral if it does not is a difficult one to sustain. Justice requires that people who do the same work should receive the same pay. A Mexican could rightly complain of injustice if he were paid less than an American for doing similar work in the same factory. But the principle applies only within the same factory, plant, or office.

The desirability of international minimal wage standards is obvious. But there is no visible movement in this direction, and multinational corporations on the whole have not attempted to promote such standards.

Finally, is it immoral for Asbestos USA to produce products in Mexico for sale in the United States? Suppose a German company made cars in the United States exclusively for export to Germany. Would we claim that the German company was exploiting the United States? It is difficult to develop a principle under which we would make such a determination. Earlier, we suggested the principle that unless a foreign company benefits the country in which it operates, it exploits that country for its own advantage and so acts immorally. This rules out as immoral exploitation of one country, *A*, by another, *B*, that dominates *A* in such a way that *B* can force *A* to act contrary to *A*'s own best interests. But if we consider the building of plants in sovereign states by firms from other countries, the host countries are able to prevent and prohibit such exploitation. If Asbestos USA were to force the demise of Mexican asbestos companies, it is difficult to see why it should be tolerated. But if it does not, there are many ways Asbestos USA might help the economy other than by producing its products for the Mexican market. It supplies work for its Mexican employees, teaches skills to the people it employs, pays taxes to the government, provides work for those who must build the plant in the first place, and purchases materials it needs locally to the advantage of the local economy. The workers in turn use their wages to buy goods, food, and shelter and so help support others in the economy. The Mexican government might well consider the trade-off to be to its advantage.

This analysis does not exonerate Asbestos USA on all counts. It has argued that Asbestos USA is not automatically guilty of the immoral practices attributed to it by typical critics.

We have not touched on the question of what the moral obligations of a multinational are in a country in which the government is repressive and in which the leaders care more for their own good and benefit than for the good of their people. If a government itself exploits its people and encourages foreign exploitation of its people by foreign firms that pay taxes to the government, or pay government officials directly, the government acts immorally. If a firm knowingly and willingly exploits its workers, even if it is legal to do so, it also acts immorally. But whether a particular firm is exploiting its workers often requires detailed investigation.

The critics of multinationals will have little patience with the analysis we have given of Asbestos USA. Even if multinationals can operate morally, they would assert that multinationals typically do not act morally. By outlining the conditions under which multinationals might act morally, the critics would maintain, we have given the impression that multinationals do act morally and that attacks on them are unwarranted. Such was not the intent. The temptations to act immorally are great in the international arena, and it would be surprising if many companies did not succumb. If moral restraints are ineffective, then the restraints on such activity must be international restraints. The abuses of multinationals underscore the need for effective international controls— controls, however, that the present international climate has not strongly fostered.

Study Questions

1. How does De George use the concepts of autonomy and informed consent to argue for his point of view?

2. How does De George use economic differences between developed and developing countries to support his point of view?

3. Is the position De George presents here consistent with his article in Chapter 6?

4. Use Messick and Bazerman to examine strengths and weaknesses of De George's view.

Michael P. Walls

Chemical Exports and the Age of Consent: The High Cost of International Export Control Proposals

INTRODUCTION

Throughout the 1980s, an international debate over the proper role of government in regulating exports and imports of hazardous substances, primarily pesticides and industrial chemicals, has been raging. The debate has been characterized by emotional appeals from public interest groups and steadfast opposition by the worldwide chemical industry. Existing information exchange programs, by which regulatory information is transmitted to interested governments, have been criticized as ineffective in protecting the citizens of importing countries from harmful substances. Prior informed consent ("PIC") proposals have been promoted as the single most effective remedy for the problems of unregulated chemicals exports.

Generally, PIC would require an exporter to obtain, via his own government, the express consent of importing countries to accept shipments of "banned" or "severely restricted" chemicals. Exports would be delayed until consent had been received. Although chemicals are exported to virtually every country, great emphasis has been placed on the benefits of an international PIC program, particularly for developing countries. PIC advocates contend that only PIC can help developing countries build the regulatory infrastructures necessary to ensure controlled importation and use of hazardous substances.

PIC has far-reaching consequences for international trade and international law. Export shipments could be subject to delays and trade-facilitating mechanisms, such as letters of credit, could lose their effectiveness. PIC also implicates the sovereignty of developing countries by linking regulatory decisions to the actions of exporting (and therefore probably developed) countries. At the same time, the likely result of a PIC program is that human health and the environment, particularly in developing countries, will receive no greater protection than at the present time. Finally, in this purported "age of consent," those remedies designed to alleviate the root problems of chemical misuse and underdeveloped governmental infrastructures will receive inadequate attention. . . .

PRIOR INFORMED CONSENT: ACCEPTED INTERNATIONAL STANDARD?

Background

The international impetus for PIC began with a 1981 United Nations General Assembly resolution calling for the exchange of information on "banned hazardous chemicals and unsafe pharmaceutical products." The action closely followed the Carter Administration's "Federal Policy Regarding the Export of Banned or Significantly Restricted Substances," which had established an export licensing procedure for certain hazardous substances of U.S. origin. Although the Reagan Administration quickly rescinded this policy, a move which appeared to forestall domestic efforts to implement PIC, the international

From Michael P. Walls, *NYU Journal of International Law and Politics* 20 (1988). Reprinted by permission.

push to adopt a control system for hazardous exports had already gained momentum.

In 1984, the United Nations Environment Programme (UNEP) adopted the Provisional Notification Scheme and issued a report summarizing the national experiences with export notification procedures and the existing information exchange programs for "banned" and "severely restricted" chemicals. In February of 1987, the Provisional Notification Scheme was incorporated by a UNEP Working Group into the London Guidelines for the Exchange of Information on Chemicals in International Trade (London Guidelines) and was formally adopted by the UNEP Governing Council in June of 1987. In 1984, the Organization of Economic Cooperation and Development (OECD) agreed to a Council Recommendation on information exchange for chemical exports. The United Nations Food and Agriculture Organization (FAO) followed suit in 1985 by adopting the International Code of Conduct on the Distribution and Use of Pesticides.

Notably, chemical industry efforts at self-regulation were being undertaken concurrently with the notification programs being developed by the international intergovernmental organizations: the international pharmaceutical associations adopted the Code of Pharmaceutical Marketing Practices in 1981; the International Group of National Associations of Agrochemical Producers (GIFAP) issued guidelines for the safe and effective use of pesticides; the OECD's Business and Industry Advisory Committee (BIAC) gained industry consensus on the BIAC Guides for Manufacturers and Traders Exporting Chemicals in 1985. Numerous additional examples of the chemical industry's recognition of its responsibilities concerning international trade exist.

THE HIGH COST OF REGULATION: THE CASE AGAINST PIC

Legal Impact of PIC

Legal objections to PIC arise on several grounds, both international and domestic.

PIC is inconsistent with the principle of sovereignty, under which a state has the inherent power to regulate its own affairs. By forcing an importing government to rely on the regulatory decisions contained in requests for consent, PIC, in effect, gives extraterritorial effect to the regulations of exporting countries.

Perhaps more significantly, PIC would turn the international principle of state responsibility on its head. The concept of state responsibility dictates that governments are generally responsible only for the acts of those they control. Most governments do not "control" the acts of independent business concerns, at least to the extent of control giving rise to liability on the part of the state. Nevertheless, PIC would force exporting governments to exercise a significant degree of control over the exports of those independent businesses, particularly in situations where the importing government refuses to accept the import.

PIC also has a potential effect on the assessment of liability. Shipments made in violation of a PIC regime, without the consent of the importing country, will presumably subject the exporting company to liability. Therefore, PIC effectively establishes a "multinational enterprise" principle of responsibility.

Furthermore, liability for violations of a PIC regime could presumably be assessed against exporting *countries,* for failure to exercise the requisite degree of control over shipments made without the consent of importing governments. Exporting countries might also be held liable for injuries caused by accepted imports of banned or severely restricted chemicals. The participants in the ongoing debate over PIC have given little consideration to the important issue of the responsibilities of exporting governments under such a system.

PIC is also inconsistent with U.S. law. Seven U.S. statutes, including the Toxic Substances Control Act [(hereinafter TSCA)] and the Federal Insecticide, Fungicide, and Rodenticide Act [(hereinafter FIFRA)], require some form of notification to importing countries when hazardous materials are exported. The U.S. notifications typically exceed the information exchange requirements established under the intergovernmental programs now in effect. In fact, no other country conducts as extensive a notification program as does the United States.

The United States has not adopted a definition of the terms "banned" or "severely restricted." As a result, the U.S. notifies other governments of a wide range of regulatory action taken under TSCA or FIFRA. These notices are sent despite the fact the regulatory action may not constitute a "ban" or "severe restriction" and despite the fact the recipient country may have little knowledge of the statutory, regulatory, or scientific basis for the action. For example, Section 4 of TSCA provides for toxicological testing of certain substances, but such action constitutes neither a ban nor a severe restriction on the chemical. Blanket notifications such as these may only serve to increase anxiety about chemicals in general, particularly those of U.S. origin. Rather, notifications of actions not constituting a ban or severe restriction might be better handled under a separate information exchange program to advise other governments of new health and environmental data.

Economic Impacts of PIC

The economic and trade impact of PIC is difficult to assess with certainty. The difficulty arises primarily from the lack of data on exports of banned or severely restricted chemicals, as there is no consensus on what chemicals are in fact under such regulatory restrictions. Without agreement on what body of chemicals constitute those that are banned or severely restricted, it is difficult to measure the economic impact of exports of such chemicals. It is possible, however, to identify some aspects of PIC's probable significant impact on international chemical trade. For example, depending on the particulars of a stop shipment order executed under a PIC system, and an importing government's subsequent response to similar shipments, PIC may well violate the anti-discrimination provisions of the General Agreement on Tariffs

and Trade (GATT). Letters of credit and import licenses are time-limited instruments which typically expire within a given period. U.S. chemical manufacturers estimate that a three to six month delay in exports will result under PIC. These instruments could expire before the required consent to ship is received. In addition, emergency or seasonal shipments of agricultural and industrial chemicals could be compromised. Delays in export shipments will compound the warehousing and logistical problems inherent in international trade. Some facilities do not have the ability to store chemical substances for long periods of time. In turn, the possibility of increased health and environmental danger due to accidents is raised. At a minimum, PIC can be expected to drive up the cost of chemical exports to reflect the delays.

Practical Impact of PIC

The probable impact of PIC buttresses the conclusion that the proposals are ill-advised. PIC is less likely than the existing notification programs to aide the development of adequate infrastructures in developing countries. Indeed, developing countries, given the great demands on their often limited resources, will have an incentive to rely on the notifications sent under PIC to reduce the cost of an effective regulatory regime geared to the country's specific needs. PIC in no way assures that an importing government has the interest or the ability to respond to consent requests within a given time limit.

In addition, PIC may increase the incentives for illicit trade in banned and severely restricted chemicals. For example, a PIC system provides no assurance that, if the regulatory controls on exports from one country become too burdensome, importers will not seek other, less regulated sources for the chemicals. Companies forced to comply with PIC may be competitively disadvantaged if other, unregulated sources can meet the existing demand for hazardous products. Presently, shipments from the major chemical producing countries are generally accompanied by transport and use information, the companies involved have close relationships with their customers, and any information deemed necessary in the regulatory process is readily available. It is the importation of chemicals from unregulated sources, and the unregulated distribution of the chemicals at the local level, which probably account for the vast majority of problems.

Therefore, by restricting imports from more responsible suppliers, PIC may drive chemical purchasers to unrestricted sources, with a consequent increase in adverse health and environmental impacts. Hence, PIC may have the opposite effect than that intended by its proponents.

PIC ALTERNATIVES: TOWARD IMPROVED REGULATORY RESPONSE AND SAFETY IN CHEMICAL USE

PIC does not help importing countries handle banned or severely restricted chemicals better. Such a system does nothing to assist importing countries to weigh the economic, health, and environmental concerns which factor into decisions about chemical use. In view of the legal, economic, and practical impacts, several efforts to develop alternatives to PIC should result in measurable improvements in a country's ability to deal with hazardous chemicals.

A recent study conducted by the Organization for American States (OAS) indicates that PIC is not the attractive policy option its promoters suggest.[1] The OAS has recommended that the developed countries undertake a plan of action centered around improved notification and technical assistance to importing countries.[2] The key aspect of the work plan is regional seminars and workshops to discuss the decision-making process in regulatory agencies, enforcement procedures, scientific assessment of hazardous materials, institutional aspects of implementation, and communication of hazard information to users.

The Agency for International Develop-

ment (AID), under a provision of the Foreign Assistance Authorization Act of 1986,[3] has convened a Committee on Health and the Environment.[4] The Committee is charged with "examining opportunities for assisting countries in the proper use of agricultural and industrial chemicals. . . ." The Committee's report should provide some guidance in the development and implementation of programs concerning hazardous materials and might be used by AID in U.S. foreign assistance programs.

The UNEP's newest *Ad Hoc* Working Group of Experts should also focus on those "modalities" of information exchange short of PIC which will further the goal of safe chemical use. One notable area for expansion of the Group's mandate is in the implementation of the London Guidelines, because not all countries have designated national representatives for the receipt of regulatory control and export notices. Furthermore, countries should be encouraged to share their experience under the London Guidelines with the International Register for Potentially Toxic Chemicals, the United Nations agency responsible for overseeing the Guidelines. In this manner, appropriate modifications to the Guidelines might be made, rather than totally abandoning a system not yet proven incapable of solving the problem it addresses.

A number of recommendations for improved notifications under the U.S. export programs have been made, which the Environmental Protection Agency has undertaken to study in an effort to make the program more effective.

Additionally, the international intergovernmental organizations, notably UNEP, should undertake to assist developing countries by identifying and anticipating their environmental problems, as well as adopting appropriate regulatory mechanisms. This type of program might be based on the developing country strategy adopted by the Environmental Protection Agency.

Private industry should also have a role in the search for viable alternatives to PIC. Exporting companies already cooperate in providing information on chemical shipments through the existing intergovernmental programs. Further development of this cooperative approach should be explored.

Even if these developments and improvements do occur, the key to success of information exchange is the establishment of infrastructures which give importing governments the ability to make their own regulatory decisions. Once such infrastructures are in place, and not before, the international community can better evaluate the need for stringent export control restrictions such as PIC.

Notes

1. Organization of American States, *Background on the Problem of Trade in Toxic Products Banned or Severely Restricted in the Producing Countries* 1, OAS Doc. OEA/Ser. H/XIII, CIES/CECON/580 (1987) at 15–16.
2. Organization of American States, *Technical Meeting on Toxic Products, Final Report,* OAS Doc. OEA/ser.H/XIII, CIES/CECON/582, at 8–10, (Sept. 3, 1987).

3. Foreign Assistance Authorization Act for Fiscal Year 1987 § 539(i), Pub. L. No. 99-591, 1986 U.S. Code Cong. & Admin. News (100 Stat.) 3341–236.
4. The Committee first met on October 19, 1987, and is expected to publish its report during 1988.

Study Questions

1. Walls talks about the legal, economic, and practical impacts of the PIC. What are the ethical features of these impacts? How are the ethical features related to Walls' evaluation of the legal, economic, and practical impacts of the PIC?

2. What is Walls' view about PIC as an international standard? Do his arguments apply to all international standards? Compare and contrast Walls' view with those of De George and Werhane in Chapter 6.

3. What do you think are the ethical assumptions of Walls' preferred solution?

CHAPTER 9

Competition

INTRODUCTION

Competition is a characteristic of market systems; it is based on scarcity (Chapter 4). Concerns such as self-interest; the desire to promote the good of our families, friends, and communities; and a commitment to principles such as nonviolence and fairness are characteristics of individuals (Chapters 2 and 3). The readings in "Ethics and Competition" explore the relationship between competitive markets and individuals.

There are many other issues that fall under the topic of competition. Some examples are antitrust in the United States, government subsidies and other ways to give domestic companies an advantage in global markets, and the role of international trade organizations and agreements in creating a global competitive environment. There are many introductory business ethics and business and society texts that provide a good starting place to investigate these topics.

ETHICS AND COMPETITION

In Tom L. Beauchamp's case, "Seizure of the S. W. Parcel," the Oklasis Oil Company uses a legal technicality to take producing oil wells away from the European Petroleum Company (EPC). The EPC has invested in the research and development of an oil well located in an area of land referred to as the S. W. Parcel. EPC made a mistake in filing a re-leasing agreement by typing N. W. Parcel instead of S. W. Parcel. The Oklasis Oil Company used this mistake to lease the S. W. Parcel for itself.

In "Some Ethical Consequences of Economic Competition," James H. Michelman reflects on his 25 years in business. He argues that there is very little room for ethics in business because of competition. Competitors cannot be compassionate or they will go out of business. One saving grace in this story is our limited, or bounded, rationality (see Chapter 4). We do not have the power to make purely rational decisions to maximize profit, and this allows our humanity to seep in to the cold calculating world of business.

Michelman's arguments seem incompatible with this book's thesis that business institutions are partly constituted by ethical principles. A closer look, however, shows that there is no incompatibility. Michelman talks about the *rights* of shareholders and the *duty* of managers to work for them. He also speaks of employees as members of a team who have a duty of *loyalty* to the company (see Duska's article in Chapter 8 for a different view of employee loyalty).

Rights, duties, and loyalty are all ethical concepts. Michelman does not characterize these as ethical because he locates the ethical solely in personal relationships, what we talked about in Chapters 2 and 3 as the care ethic. On the more inclusive view of ethics suggested in this book, Michelman is describing a conflict between the ethical imperatives of business and the ethical imperatives of personal relationships.

INTERNATIONAL

Laura B. Pincus' case, "Tee-Shirts and Tears: Third World Suppliers to First World Markets," describes some of the difficult working conditions of third world workers who make clothes and other articles for consumers in richer countries. The efforts of workers to improve their working conditions by appeals to the government or by forming unions are rarely successful.

In "Two Roads to China: Nice, and Not so Nice," David E. Sanger describes the conciliatory approach of the Boeing Company and the confrontational approach of the Microsoft Corporation to trade and investment in China. Each company is trying to establish a competitive advantage in a country that is in political and economic transition. Because of this transition, property rights and contracts are uncertain. Boeing's strategy is to mediate political conflicts between China and the United States. Microsoft's strategy is more confrontational. China's transitional economy poses a direct threat to its current sales and revenues. Computer operating systems can be copied cheaply and easily and, at the time of this article, pirated software in China was the norm. As a result of these copyright violations, Microsoft has used U.S. bargaining power to fight for tough property rules and enforcement in China.

Norman Bowie's "The Moral Obligations of Multinational Corporations" ties together many of the themes we have discussed in this book. Bowie first argues that MNCs have the same general obligations as domestic companies. MNCs are different only because the international context makes it more difficult to act from these duties. He next addresses the issue of whether MNCs should act in accord with the moral norms of the host country. He argues that they should only if ethical relativism is true (see the Introduction and the section on Pluralism in Chapter 3 for more on relativism). He gives several reasons for doubting ethical relativism. Bowie ends the article by arguing that market ethical values (Chapter 4) can supply substantive universal values for international business. Specifically, he argues that successful markets require honesty and trust (Kant and Rawls, Chapter 3). Without secure property rights, contracts (risk–reward relationships), and information, competitive markets will degenerate into anarchy.

CASE: Seizure of the S.W. Parcel
Tom L. Beauchamp

The European Petroleum Consortium (EPC) is a major European oil company with several affiliates and subsidiaries in the United States. In November 1983 EPC leased three contiguous parcels of land near Chico, California—exactly 300 acres, subdivided into three distinct units of 100 acres—from a wealthy farmer, Mr. Buck Wheat, who owned the property. The parties signed three oil and gas leases, one for each of the three contiguous parcels, which were labeled N.W., S.W., and N.E. because of their geographical location.

Within a year a significant gas-producing well had been drilled on the S.W. property, and Mr. Wheat was earning royalties from the gas production. In the four years following the sale, Mr. Wheat earned in excess of $500,000 in royalties from this well. He was already a multimillionaire by virtue of other wells that oil and gas companies had long operated on his property.

Under the terms of the lease, EPC had the option to extend the lease under the original terms of royalty payments for as long as oil or gas was being produced on any parcel of the land that had been leased. If production ever ceased for a period of one year, the agreement would be invalid. If there were no producing wells on a parcel and EPC wished not to extend the lease on that parcel, EPC was required to file a quitclaim deed (a deed of conveyance that is a form of release of rights) to this effect.

In November 1988, five years after the initial agreement, the lease was scheduled to expire. EPC notified Mr. Wheat by a phone call 90 days prior to the expiration date of the lease of its intention to extend the lease on one parcel of land, the S.W. parcel, but not on the other two. Mr. Wheat responded that he naturally was pleased that royalty payments would continue. Under the terms of the lease, EPC had 30 days beyond the date of expiration to record the quitclaim deed with the county and to record the continuation of the lease arrangement. Twenty-two days beyond the expiration date, EPC did file both the quitclaim and the extension, and 29 days beyond the expiration date an EPC official had a copy delivered to Mr. Wheat by a messenger service. EPC was not required by the terms of the lease to deliver this copy, because Mr. Wheat had already been notified by phone of its intentions.

Thirty-one days beyond the expiration date, Mr. Wheat signed an oil and gas lease on all 100 acres of the producing S.W. parcel with Oklasas Oil Company, a small independent headquartered in Anadarko, Oklahoma. That is, Mr. Wheat leased to Oklasas the very same S.W. parcel on which EPC believed it had an exclusive lease. Obviously two leases to competitors on the same property cannot be valid.

Mr. Wheat's new lease of the S.W. parcel and his rapid change in relations with EPC were the result of an inadvertent clerical error and the enterprising activities of Mr. B. Sly, president of the Oklasas Oil Company. He devised a method of acquiring land that is highly unconventional but that has thus far paid off handsomely. He hired a low-salaried clerk to go into several California counties known to have a large number of producing gas wells. The clerk checks all the leases that have been filed, looking for technical violations of the law or for lease loopholes. Whenever a technical violation or potential problem is found on the lease of a producing property, Mr. Sly contacts the

---

owner of the property and makes a lease offer that exceeds the terms found in the original lease. Mr. Sly can afford to give the property owner a much larger percentage of the royalties than is conventional, because he has no drilling costs and encounters no real speculative risk in an industry filled with drilling risk.

Only about 15 percent of the landowners are willing to meet and discuss the possibility of a lease with Mr. Sly because most believe they have a prior commitment to the company with which they have signed an agreement. About 10 percent renegotiate with the company with which they originally signed the lease; they often use Mr. Sly's offer as a way of obtaining better terms in the new lease, although they do not negotiate terms as favorable as Mr. Sly's. Instead of providing the landowner with the standard one-sixth royalty share. Mr. Sly offers one third, doubling the owners' royalties overnight.

Mr. Sly has been able to sign agreements with approximately one third of the 15 percent who are willing to meet with him. Thus, he eventually comes to terms with about 5 percent of his contacts. His clerk finds one promising legal problem or technical violation that suggests an invalid lease for every nine days of full-time research. Mr. Sly is already bringing in over $3 million annually for Oklasas from the wells he has acquired on these properties, and his operating costs are extremely low because he only obtains properties with producing wells.

Very fortunately from Mr. Sly's perspective, his clerk was working in the county offices on the day EPC filed its quitclaim deeds and extension. The clerk's trained eye detected a serious error almost immediately: EPC had inadvertently quitclaimed the S.W. parcel and extended the lease on the nonproducing N.W. parcel. This error resulted from a slip of the pen; the clerk at EPC had written "N.W." on the form rather than "S.W." Although EPC had a system that was set up to avoid such "erroneous legal descriptions," the error passed through six checkpoints in six offices at EPC without detection.

Within two hours of the clerk's discovery of the misfiling in the county office, the relevant papers had been copied and sent by overnight mail to Mr. Sly. Two days later he was in California to pay a visit to Mr. Wheat. After a two-hour meeting they were joined by their lawyers for a lunch and afternoonmeeting, and by 5:00 an agreement had been signed. Neither party had contacted EPC to ascertain whether a mistake had been made, but it was only too obvious to them that a mistake had indeed been made.

Mr. Wheat asked not only for a one-third royalty share but also that Mr. Sly lease, for a sum of $7,500 per year, the N.E. property that had been quit-claimed and drill on that property. (EPC had said several times that it was not interested in drilling on this property after it had discovered gas on the S.W. property.) Mr. Wheat also asked for a full indemnification in the event of a law-suit by EPC. That is, he asked to be fully secured against loss or damage in the event of a lawsuit over the leases, including any loss from the shutdown of operations at the well. Mr. Sly agreed that he would pay all legal costs and reimburse for any loss that Mr. Wheat might incur.

This was not a difficult decision for Mr. Sly. In oil and gas leases, the written record is everything, so far as the law is concerned. One simply cannot tell the legal status of the property unless there is a written legal record. Unrecorded statements of intention and verbal promises count for nothing. Mr. Sly's lawyer was certain that no suit by EPC would stand a chance of success.

The next day lawyers notified EPC of the new arrangement and told it to abandon the property immediately. Within 24 hours EPC replied that it considered the negotiations over this property to have been in bad faith. EPC said it considered any entry upon the land and any drilling to constitute a trespass and also to be in bad faith. EPC added, however, that it was willing to negotiate and settle out of court, because it was responsible for the clerical error. Oklasas replied immediately that it was not interested in negotiation.

Study Questions

1. How does competition intersect with the institution of property in this case?

2. Why do you think so few people take up the Oklasis Oil Company's offer? Does this say anything about self-interest and/or institutional influences on behavior?

3. How would Friedman, Cochran, and Freeman analyze this case?

James H. Michelman

Some Ethical Consequences of Economic Competition

I would like to discuss some fundamental questions regarding business ethics that stem (for me) from personal observations I've made over twenty-five years of responsible activity in the world of free enterprise.

I

First, I note that a conflict exists between attitudes and actions demonstrated by myself and my associates when related to business, and attitudes and actions shown in more private affairs. I am aware of acts of charity, kindness, and public service performed by my co-workers in their private lives. In their dealings with me, they are truthful and faithful; we share common goals. Yet, in our dealings with customers and suppliers neither our truthfulness nor our fidelity can be assumed. If we are truthful and faithful it is because of (economically) rational or sentimental reasons, not because we are determined by moral law. We excuse ourselves by assuming a sim-

ilar lack of truthfulness and fidelity in our trading partners. And they too, we believe, assume the same of us. Sometimes we are dealt with openly—all cards on the table. In that case, we assume laziness or sentimentality. These attitudes, actions, and reactions derive from the many years we have spent surviving in competitive markets. They are pragmatic; they are learned from experience. . . .

The Wall Street Journal, April 2, 1982, headlined 'The Workout Crew. Bankers Who Step In If Loans Go Bad Reveal Lenders' Other Face. There Isn't Any Smile on It; Teams Tell Ailing Clients To Make Changes Or Else. "We See a Management Void'". This long lead article begins by stating that ". . . workout specialists, the bankers who take over when a business loan goes bad" are known as "undertakers, morticians, black hats, or goons". They are dreaded. They force firings. Sometimes they are known by euphemisms because "Sometimes ailing companies extricate themselves from workout at one bank by borrowing from another institu-

From *Journal of Business Ethics 2*, 79–87, 1983. Used with kind permission of the author and Kluwer Academic Publishers. Copyright © 1987 Kluwer Academic Publishers; all rights reserved.

tion. If the new banker, unaware of the customer's less-than-perfect status, calls the old one for information and hears 'workout', he will run the other way." "A [client] company's change in status from master to slave often comes abruptly . . . 'It's always interesting to watch them walk down that corridor, look at that sign (Institutional Recovery Management) [a euphemism] and watch their faces change as it dawns on them they might be in trouble', chuckles [a senior banking officer]." "Bankers say they have only one concern . . . : getting their money back. 'We have the right to get paid and they have an obligation to pay us. . . . The bank didn't cause the company to make bad investments or whatever it was that caused them to lose money'". The sense of this article is fear and humiliation on the part of the executives of the company in difficulty, contempt and rationality by the bankers.

Neither of these articles (nor the others) conveys any feeling that the actions and attitudes of the participators are unacceptable or even unexpected. Their activities are interesting and so newsworthy. But they are not subject to moral judgment. Yet the comparative advertisers are engaging in an obviously maleficent enterprise (even if unacknowledged by themselves). The workout crews—as described in the article—are brutal. These attributes—maleficence and brutality—are not, of course, those that we would wish our friends and neighbors to hold and express in their dealings with us. Nor may they be warranted by reasoning from a certain justifying premise of free enterprise—one that holds least-cost efficiency to be a proper end of economic activity. For in the case of the advertisers, maleficent effort has been expended merely to induce purchasers to substitute one consumer product for a similar one.[1] With respect to the workout crews, brutality is irrelevant. Yet, until we have reason to think that maleficent persons are attracted to the advertising industry and brutal ones to banks, we must concede that maleficence and brutality are characteristics of the job rather than the person. . . .

II

Business competition—free enterprise—is a rational undertaking. Profit maximization is the overriding consideration in the competitive universe, and profit maximization is achieved through rationality. These remarks, common-place in microeconomic theory, may be justified as follows.

Unless a firm can bid successfully for factors of production it cannot survive. And only if it earns at least an average rate of return on its invested capital, will it be able to stay in the auction. The market validates this premise every day. A firm earning less than its competitors loses its ability to pay its more talented employees that wage which they could get elsewhere, and they will leave. Its credit rating sinks; its cost of funds rises. It may have difficulty borrowing regardless of cost. Thus its access to raw materials becomes restricted, and it is unable to pay for new plant and equipment. As a result its unit cost of production increases. These short examples are not exhaustive. But they illustrate real forces which logically must, and ultimately do, drive that firm to bankruptcy or voluntary liquidation.

One could postulate a universe of firms all initially earning about the same rate of return on invested capital but not maximizing income. But this universe would be unstable for unless there were legal constraints on return of capital the very engine of free enterprise—the profit motive—would immediately drive at least some firms to maximize profits. Once these became some small significant fraction, that fraction could, and would, outbid the rest for productive resources. hence, relative stability occurs only when *all* are running their hardest; that is when *all* are seeking to maximize income. The laggards have already fallen by the wayside; future laggards will suffer the same fate.

To maximize profit the firm is obliged to make the most efficient use of its productive factors among which—often the most important—are persons; to choose products for sale which optimize its revenue; to purchase resources—again including persons—at the lowest possible cost, in short, to operate rationally. Else, it is failing to maximize return on invested capital and, sooner or later, must lose out to its competitors and cease to be a firm.

These simple considerations lead to profound ethical consequences.

First, consider our normal sense of what kind of persons we feel we ought to be. What are the attitudes and actions that we would like to think are part of our own moral makeup and that we would wish others to exhibit in their relationships with us? A non-exhaustive list surely includes courage and intelligence, kindness, compassion, honesty, loyalty, respect for others, adherence to the social duties of mutual aid and non-malefi-cence, and self-respect. Call this set of characteristics our *desired moral character* or the *human virtues.*

What characteristics would we look for in the managers of a company in which we held an important stake? Whatever this catalog turns out to be, call it the *desired business character.* It also certainly includes intelligence and a certain type of courage. But here we value intelligence and courage only insofar as they aid our managers to maximize the profits of our firm.

Next, if we analyze the role of persons as employees of firms engaged in free enterprise we discover an immediate moral paradox. Note that treating an employee as other than a productive factor stems from a philanthropic judgment rather than a business one. It may be rational for a firm to treat (some of) its employees considerately and reward them well, but only up to that point where finally there is no marginal benefit from doing so. Considerations of kindness and sympathy, for example, are irrelevant. A manager's obligation is to his firm, not its employees; and as we have already seen, he has no real choice in the matter if his firm is to survive. But it is clear that in following this reasoning we are struck at once with a contradiction which can be expressed by asking the question, What is the manager's duty to himself? If the dis-

charge of his corporate responsibilities requires him to run counter to his desired moral character and so to violate his own basic self, must he do so? The necessity of profit maximization provides the answer. If the firm is to survive, the manager's obligation must be to it, not to himself. It follows, then, that free enterprise can require the violation of the individual's most basic duties to himself.

As a firm thrives, so do its responsible employees. But *regardless of their own well-being* their duty is to act so as to further the firm's interests which are to maximize its income, to make more and more money, amass more and more wealth. It is likely that these goals will be severely limited since all the firm's competitors, having the very same goals, prevent any single firm from outdistancing the others. But if the firm's policies—and so those of its responsible employees—are not fixed on the main chance, it is bound to fail. Once the firm enters the competition, it must abide by the rules of that competition. And all these rules are comprehended by the single Rule: Let the maxim of your action be that which advances the profitability of your firm. It seems a fair argument that once a rational being enters into—becomes an employee—of a firm (putting aside of course his motive for doing so) insofar as he acts *as an employee,* the maxim of his action must ignore his own moral interest and regard only his duty to make his firm as profitable as possible.

Nor is this all. Rationality demands that vendors rationalize their customers (sell at the highest possible price) and users rationalize their suppliers (buy at the lowest possible cost). Rationality demands that competitors seek the same orders, the same resources, the same employees—seek that is, their advantage at the expense of others. Given the set of demands engendered by, and inseparable from, the universe of economic competition, it therefore becomes a clear contradiction for an employee of one firm to act upon the laws generated by competition and will also that his suppliers, his customers, his competitors, act upon, and benefit from, those laws as well. For he then would be willing that they do what they can to negate his will. He would be willing war on himself.[2]

In sum, we find that the responsible firm employee must regard co-workers, vendors, and customers only as means to his firm's advantage; and that he himself is mere means to this end. We may conclude that insofar as he is fulfilling the obligation of his job—doing that for which he draws compensation—a corporate executive (for example) is foreclosed from acting toward his associates (superior, peers, subordinates) out of humane considerations, foreclosed from considering the interests of his suppliers and customers, foreclosed from beneficent acts toward his competitors, or indeed toward anyone with whom he has a commercial relationship. He is also thereby foreclosed from acting in accordance with his own moral character. He may, of course, perform *seeming* acts of beneficence or fidelity toward any of these persons or toward himself, but in that case the acts would be the end of rational calculation. If not seeming, they must be neutral acts or done *in spite of* his duty to his firm.

III

In addition to the general moral consequences of economic competition, we can identify specific consequences. Some of the more apparent are cataloged below.

1. When any business prize—a sale, a purchase, an order to deliver, a contract to perform—is sought by two or more firms, the duties both of mutual aid and of non-maleficence become contradictory. The contradiction of the duty of mutual aid follows at once from the fact of the competition. The impossibility of non-maleficence follows almost as immediately. For under competition there is a winner (or winners), and there is a loser (or losers). Let us think, for example, of two salesmen competing for a contract. The successful salesman, if his compensation is by commission, has benefited directly. It is possible that his life's prospects have been enhanced. If he is a good salesman, that is, a fre-

quent winner, they will have been. But by winning he has hurt his competitor. The loser may suffer real psychic pain, and through loss of prospective income and damaged expectations, real physical injury as well. But all this is of no matter to the winner. For merely by entering the competition he has willed that his competitors be injured.

2. The obligation to tell the truth is contradicted by the requirements of commercial negotiation. We see this by noting that if there is to be negotiation, rather than a fixed or coerced price[3] there must be *room* for negotiation—call it a negotiating range. The range is defined by the highest price the buyer will pay and the lowest the seller will accept. Within those limits a deal can be struck. Now one or the other must make a statement, else the negotiation could not begin. The statement, however, must be misleading. If the buyer reveals the highest price he is willing to pay (the top of the range) the deal will be made at that figure. Nor can the seller reveal the lowest price he will take. The *duty* of either is to make his opposite believe that the top (bottom) of the possible range is lower (higher) than it really is. And to mislead someone is, of course, to tell him an untruth or, at the least, let him infer what is not the truth. Truth in commercial negotiation is a casualty of the responsibility of the participants to the business entity for whom they work.

3. The duty of respect for others is irrelevant in determining product choices. At any time, a firm has a limited product transformation function. It cannot make everything. From those things that it can produce it will select the ones that will maximize its profit. Considerations of social benefit or damage have no place. But ideas of social benefit or damage derive ultimately from the idea of respect for others. Hence respect for others has no place in the free market.

Consider the tobacco industry. Surely this is a paradigm example. There exists substantial respected testimony that blames smoking for significant numbers of deaths from cancer, heart, and other diseases. Recent articles in *The New York Times* report that senior U.S. officials, among them the Surgeon General, testified before a House sub-committee that, ". . . Government findings . . . blame smoking for 340,000 deaths a year and . . . call it the chief preventable cause of illness and premature death in the nation". But the Tobacco Institute fought a proposal for more specific labeling about the dangers from smoking on cigarette packages and in advertising. The "chairman of the institute's executive committee said, that the proposal for five labels . . . was a 'thinly veiled effort further to harass and ultimately eliminate an important American Industry'". The *Times* also reported that a Rockefeller Foundation study found "The beneficiaries [of the tobacco support program] may be farmers, but they are also doctors and lawyers, churches and banks, mill workers and truck drivers, and in many cases, widows".[4]

It simply is impossible to conceive of persons engaging in the production or merchandising of products for smoking and at the same time observing the precepts encompassed by the obligation to respect your fellow. A defense based upon a spurious premise of freedom of choice is, of course, negated by the vigorous advertising and merchandising campaigns conducted by the industry.

IV

. . . We need not stick to particular cases. Ultimately, all firms are engaged in a single overarching competition for capital and return on capital. In any block of time there is only a certain amount of money to be invested or lent, a certain number of good employees to be hired, a certain amount of income to be distributed. As a result of this unremitting, relentless competition, both specific and general, responsible firm members do develop, in greater or lesser amounts, a team morality. It is 'us agin them'. Consequently, the defeat of the opposition becomes a goal in itself. Consequently also, the business characteristics become justified and in terms of the competition they come to be constituents of a certain higher morality. Though

by besting a competitor, whether in a single small event such as getting an order, or in actually driving him out of business, the winner causes the loser real harm, that moral fact never enters the consciousness of the actors as such. The loser does not feel himself ill-used, and as a business competitor he has no moral grounds for resentment. Feelings of beneficence, even of compassion, are effectually blocked; they have no place in this world.

V

If the analyses set down above are correct in the main, what conclusions can we draw from them? The most apparent, and in a way the least helpful, is that free enterprise, like other social schemes in this imperfect world, is a flawed undertaking. Perhaps examining its flaws in some detail will be more helpful.

First, only in the immediate sense is free enterprise free. For, as I have tried to show, it imposes rigid constraints—all stemming from the a priori of profit maximization—on those who operate in its universe. Within a given industry, one firm, by way of policy, may commence to commit what other citizens could look upon as a series of enormities. But if that firm, because of its policy, say, of dumping untreated wastes into rivers and acid particulates into the atmosphere, reduces its cost of production, the others must follow. The remedy, of course, is legislation and enforcement. But, absent that remedy, the executives of the competing firm are choiceless: they too must pollute. Now, even if it is likely that the business characteristics are a part of their settled attitudes, it does not follow that a propensity to poison the environment is ingrained in their psychologies. In fact there is no reason to assume that such an idea is not repugnant to them as moral individuals. To the reader it certainly is repugnant. So the polluters, seeking to maximize the profits of their firms, are forced to attack themselves as moral beings. Justification from considerations of reciprocity becomes in this case very difficult. It appears, in fact, that justification from considerations of corporate survival is the sole possibility. Hence, I suggest that in this example, and in analogous cases, the participants inflict real damage upon their own self-respect. They themselves are damaging perhaps the most important constituent of their own lives.

The demand that participants attack their own self-respect is not limited to some set of corporate executives. We can see this by observing that ultimately all production, except for government use and private investment, is for private consumption; and so firms increase sales and presumably profit by taking measures to increase and differentiate consumption (differentiation being that means of getting off a horizontal demand curve where it is impossible to earn an economic profit and onto a downward sloping curve where, at appropriate volumes, profits are made). Thus all individuals in the free enterprise system are subject to constant substantial pressures to buy. All, but for a few who for one reason or another exhibit a peculiar indifference—or moral strength—of character, will respond to a degree. But this response is equivalent to a need for extra income and wealth and these—in the free market scheme—are gained through competition. No one, whether he is an assembly line worker, a chief operating officer, a licensed professional or an 'investor', sees himself as a producer of social wealth. Rather we view ourselves, and we must view ourselves, as *competitors* for those true economic (scarce) goods, income and jobs to get income. As such we are subject to the laws of competition, and as such our actions are defined at least as much by the devilish among us as by the angelic. The employee always competes with his employer for money, and typically competes with his co-workers as well. If one is an entrepreneur, he competes with the world. Virtue, being displaced by rationality, has no place in this competition; and the individual is obliged to make a choice between virtue and money. We might sketch an indifference function showing virtue vs income. [See Figure 1.]

This curve seems reasonable enough. At high levels of virtue, but low income, it assumes the individual will sacrifice a great

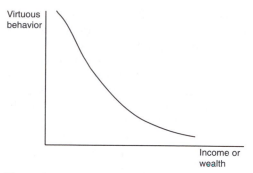

Figure 1

deal of it (and presumably, his self-respect) in order to gain income. If he already has a large income, he probably will not inflict further damage on his self-respect in order to gain more. In fact, he might cede income in order to gain virtue. But if his (perceived) income is low, and by sacrificing (perceived) virtue he can increase it, he probably will do so. At least to a point. For in order to live other than meanly he must have a decent income. In order to have a decent income he is obliged to compete for it. And if the devilish are willing to sacrifice virtue for income, then so must everyone.

Now those who are obliged to sacrifice their humanity, either in the discharge of corporate duties, or in the pursuit of a decent share of material wealth, cannot call themselves free.

Next, I assume—this journal assumes—that most men would wish to lead lives in which they can express in their work the human virtues. Similarly, they would wish to forego behavior which demonstrates hardness, shrewdness, and single-mindedness. And almost everyone would choose to live in that bright world postulated by John Rawls where it is publicly known that the acceptance of the duty of mutual aid brings "a sense of confidence and trust in other men's good intentions and the knowledge that they are there if we need them."[5] The logic of competition shoves all this aside—an intolerable knowledge which men must deny in order to believe themselves truly human.

Thus the compartmentalization of our souls; the acceptance, but non-acknowledge-ment of hypocrisy, and so the impossibility of ever achieving a happy society—which can exist nowhere but in the souls of its members. The reader might here object that no one really is forced into the competition, that one *can* live and not compete, or compete minimally. But this objection would be mistaken. If no one competed, society would no longer be competitive—it would be a different society. And if only the ethically indifferent among us competed, ethical indifference would wholly define our economic universe. But most of us, vigorous competitors or not, are not ethically indifferent. Very few of us make always wholly rational competitive judgements, otherwise we would be monsters, not men. It is *that* dichotomy which finally represents the great flawed detail of free enterprise.

Why stress it so? My answer is that otherwise we must fall into a trap which indeed has snared many. The trap is nothing else but the enchantment of the logical beauty of the free market and the seeming freedom it affords. As we have seen, viewed from the standpoint of individual morality, its freedom is largely illusory. Although, as markets approach the conditions of perfect competition, they approach Paretian efficiency, that fact by itself should not stand as sufficient warrant to build an economy on the foundations of free enterprise. The ethical implications, which I have tried to outline here, ought also to be taken into account.

Now all this does not mean that a society necessarily is to reject free-enterprise in favor of some other economic scheme. For one thing, the system simply works. And regardless of whether society attempts to solve its economic problems by economic competition or in some other fashion, moral dilemmas will inevitably present themselves. For example, if we would avoid the patent evils of a free enterprise system, then we must subject ourselves to the patent evils—loss of liberty—of a command system. Nevertheless, I do not think that the immoralities inherent in economic competition can be overemphasized. For to admit the imperfectability of men and their institutions is not to concede

that they cannot be made better. But first we will have to have a clearer understanding of the nature of our current imperfections. If society is to move forward, it better have some collective awareness of what it is about.

Notes

* I am grateful to John McMurtry for suggesting this paper and for his valued criticisms. I am also indebted to Barbara Kelly for her wise criticism and her constant encouragement.
1. The article lists toilet-bowl cleaners, mouthwashes, soft drinks, pizza, and shampoos among others.
2. It is true that this is a general conclusion which can be drawn from the premises of competition as such, but what we are discussing here is a special kind of competition. It is pervasive, it in large measure defines our lives, and it is impossible to withdraw from it entirely. As we have seen, it forces the competitors to run as fast as they can, without rest. It is well worth focusing on the consequences of *economic* competition, even if some of these may be deduced from the fact of competition itself.
3. A price set by coercion or bribery would itself be the result of an immoral act.
4. Washington, March 11 (UPI). 'U.S. Health Officials Endorse Stronger Cigarette Warnings'.
   Washington, March 12 (AP). 'Tobacco Institute Denounces Cigarette Labeling Proposal'.
   Special to *The New York Times,* Raleigh, N.C., March 8. 'Farmers Back Tobacco Plan They Would Finance'.
5. J. Rawls, *A Theory of Justice* (Harvard University Press, Cambridge, MA, 1971), pp. 338–339.

Study Questions

1. Explain how Michelman relies on the economic institutions that guide business to show that there is no room for ethics.

2. To what extent do these economic institutions themselves rely on ethical values?

3. Analyze Michelman's arguments from the goal view and the contract view of organizations. What are the similarities and differences?

CASE: **Tee-Shirts and Tears: Third World Suppliers to First World Markets**
Laura B. Pincus

> "The hottest places in hell are reserved for those who,
> in a period of moral crisis, maintain their neutrality."
>
> —DANTE

Recent media attention has heightened our awareness of labor conditions in third world countries. While Americans otherwise may have been able to write off substandard labor conditions as another case of cultural variations, these recent cases garnered domestic interest as a result of the parties involved. Their names are about as American as Apple Pie. The Gap. Kathie Lee Gifford. Even Michael Jordan. These are the contractors, the investors, the spokespeople who represent "sweatshops" where, allegedly, young girls are allowed only two restroom visits per day and, allegedly, the days sometimes consist of twenty-one straight hours of work.

LABOR CONDITIONS IN THE UNITED STATES

America's garment industry today grosses $45 billion per year and employs more than one million workers.[1] Uproar began in the Fall of 1995 when Secretary of Labor Robert Reich announced the names of several large retailers who may have been involved in an El Monte, California sweatshop operation. Notwithstanding the fact that the retailers are not liable for the conditions if they have no knowledge of them, the companies involved in this situation agreed to adopt a statement of principles which would require their suppliers to adhere to U.S. federal labor laws.[2]

Reich followed this announcement with an appearance on the *Phil Donahue Show* where he discussed a situation at another plant that employed Thai workers at less than $1.00 per hour and kept its workers behind a barbed wire fence. Retailers respond that it is difficult, if not impossible to police their suppliers and subcontractors, who may total more than 20,000 in some cases. And the pressures of the situation are only becoming worse. The apparel industry, which has borne the brunt of Reich's focus, is highly competitive, and extremely labor-intensive. Competition from companies in other countries that do not impose similar labor condition requirements is fierce. Consequently, one is not surprised to learn that a 1994 Labor Department spot check of garment operations in California found that 93% had health and safety violations.[3]

Manufacturers may have a bit more to be concerned about than retailers. Reich has recently invoked a little-used provision in the Fair Labor Standards Act that hold manufacturers liable for the wrongful acts of their suppliers and that allows for the confiscation of goods produced by sweatshop operations.

Reich has now appealed to the retailers and manufacturers alike to conduct their own random spot checks. "We need to enlist retailers as adjunct policemen. At a time when business says to government, 'Get off our back. We can do it ourselves,' them the opportunity," Reich notes.[4] In June 1995, Reich established to police working conditions made up of manufacturers. The group "Compliance Alliance" police contractors conducting regular audits and will identify firms wage or otherwise violate the provisions of the Fair Labor Standards Act.[5]

The Clinton Administration's voluntary Model Business Principles, published in May, 1995, are relevant to this discussion. The principles encourage all businesses to adopt and implement voluntary codes of conduct for doing business around the world and suggest appropriate code coverage. A copy of the Guidelines is found in Appendix A.

AMERICAN ATTENTION DRIFTS TOWARD OTHER COUNTRIES

Neil Kearney, General Secretary of the International Textile, Garment and Leather Workers' Federation, describes the garment work place as follows:

> The reality today is that most of the 30 million jobs in the fashion industry around the world are low paid, often based in export processing zones where worker rights are usually suppressed. Wages are frequently below the subsistence level and falling in real terms. . . . Management by terror is the norm in many countries. Workers are routinely shoved, beaten, kicked, even when pregnant. Attempts to unionize are met with the utmost brutality, sometimes with murder.[6]

Once the American public considered its own conditions, it looked to other countries to see how labor was treated there. Following Reich's slap on the hand to American manufacturers, media attention turned toward the conditions in third world countries and toward American responsibility for or involvement in those conditions. In 1970, there were 7,000 multinational companies in the world. Today, there are more than 35,000.[7] The topic of conditions in those multinationals was destined for afternoon talk shows once it was announced that television personality Kathie Lee Gifford endorsed a line of clothing that had been made for Wal-Mart in Honduran sweatshops. These operations employed underage and pregnant women for more than twenty-hour days at $.31 per hour. The conditions were extremely hot and no worker was allowed to speak during the entire day.

The situation was brought to the attention of the press by Charles Kernaghan, director of the National Labor Committee, based in New York City. Kernaghan informed Gifford, and the press, of the conditions in the plant and asked her to respond. Gifford's immediate response was to immediately break off her relationship with the company.[8] Unfortunately, this is not what is always best for the exploited workers. Instead, Kernaghan impressed upon her the need to remain involved and to use her position and reputation to encourage a change in the conditions at the plants.

These arguments may remind the reader of those waged several years ago regarding divestment from South Africa. Proponents of investment argued that the only way to effect change would be to remain actively involved in the operations of the South African business community. Others argued that no ethical company should pour money into a country where apartheid conditions were allowed to exist. The same arguments can and have been made about conducting business in third world countries, and Gifford found herself right in the middle of them.

THE EL SALVADORAN LABOR ENVIRONMENT

El Salvador is a country that has been ravaged by internal conflicts culminating in a civil war that lasted for many years. In 1992, with the advent of peace, the country sought to rebuild what it had lost during wartime and is now considered one of the fastest growing economies in Latin America.[9] The objective of the El Salvadorans involved in the rebuilding process was to help the poor to overcome the conditions of poverty, dependence and oppression that they had experienced during the conflict. While the objectives of private investors may be different, all seem to share a common interest in social stability and development. Economist Louis Emmerij notes that the leading cause of social unrest is "the lack of sufficient and renumerative employment opportunities, bad living conditions and the lack of perspective and hope."[10]

In developing countries like El Salvador, long term strategies for improving a poor household's ability to generate disposable income on a sustained basis must consider if households have the skills, education and know-how to allow them to operate in the market. These strategies include support for training and education, access to markets and access to technology and credit. A large part of the labor problem in the *maquiladores* is the lack of agreement between the workers and management as to the minimum level of productivity expected per day, the level of compensation for a worker who achieves that level, and who should assume the burden of training in order to increase productivity.

Yet, low wages are the prime magnet for multinational firms coming to El Salvador. In 1990, a glossy full-color advertisement appeared in a major American apparel trade magazine showing a woman at a sewing machine and proclaiming, "Rosa Martinez produces apparel for U.S. markets on her sewing machine in El Salvador. *You* can hire her for 57 cents an hour." One year later, the same ad announced that Rosa's salary had gone down—"*You* can hire her for 33 cents an hour."[11] It appears that the publicists felt that Rosa's salary originally looked too high, in the eyes of the market players.

Critical to understanding these conflicts is an understanding of the Salvadoran culture itself. Salvadoran workers are not exempt from the consequences of their history. When they enter the work place. In addition, as a result of the repressive conditions in El Salvador during the war, the society suffers from a general lack of candor and a tendency on the part of individuals to protect themselves by not telling the truth.[12] But this quality is different than the deception that occurs in dealings. In this situation, it serves as a means of self-protection in a culture that offers little else. Moreover, the government does not protect individual and business interests, thereby allowing cartels to develop, flourish and continue.

The author of this case had the opportunity to travel to El Salvador in 1996 in order to observe a class in financial administration at an El Salvadoran university. During the course of a quiz in the class, the professor had reason to leave the classroom for a moment. Upon his return, he found that the students were now collaborating on the answers to the quiz. During the discussion that later ensued regarding the students' actions, the students articulated a need to help each other to succeed. They felt that they should bind together in order to help them all to move forward. If this meant helping a colleague who did not have time to study because he had to work to support his family, in addition to attending school, that seemed acceptable, if not necessary and ethical.[13]

During that same course, the graduate students (most, if not all, of whom worked full time in professional positions) were asked to identify the principal barriers to trust in Salvadoran business relationships, and the means by which those barriers could be broken down. Students responded as follows (translated from Spanish):

One barrier is that the big businesses are formed at the level of families and friends that form a close nucleus, prohibiting others from entering.

The government does not enact laws to guarantee business interests and growth without the intervention of stronger, "bully" businesses.

There is a failure of information—only certain people have access to the most important, business-related information. There is no requirement that business share information, even at a level that would mimic the American SEC requirements.

Create legal mechanisms that sanction companies violating the rules. These sanctions *do not* exist. Companies use illicit means to take advantage of their competitors and employing the same means is the only way to compete.

The period since the war has seen an increase in vandalism at an individual and corporate level, making it difficult to carry on a business.[14]

Consider the expectation of conflict in this scenario recounted by Fr. David Blanchard, Pastor of the Our Lady of Lourdes Church in Calle Real Epiphany Cooperative Association:

> In February of 1994, the cooperative had a serious labor conflict. The women became quite adept at sewing lab coats. But in February 1994, when the only contract available was for sewing hospital bathrobes, a serious labor conflict arose. Unfortunately, the women who were elected by their peers to negotiate with the contractor made some serious errors in judgment when they calculated the time required to sew this item.
>
> At the time, some women were earning 80 colones daily (twice the minimum wage). Most were making 50 colones. Only a few apprentices were making less than the minimum wage.
>
> With the transition to sewing bathrobes, production, and therefore income, was cut in half. Six of the highest wage earners subsequently staged a sit-down strike at their machines, claiming that they were being oppressed.
>
>> Father Blanchard asked, "Who negotiated your contract?"
>> "Our representatives," they said.
>> "Who elected your representatives?"
>> "We did."
>> "Who will suffer if this work is not completed?"
>> "We will."
>
> These women had entered this project with no prior skills. They had received high-quality and expensive technical, legal and social training. They were all self-employed, but when their wages plunged, they felt oppressed, frustrated and angry, and ended up leaving the cooperative. . . . Some of these women will continue to suffer in poverty. It is certain that they are victims. But they are the victims of hundreds of years of oppression and not of the immediate circumstances sewing hospital bathrobes. They responded to the problems created by the lack of education and their lack of abilities by generating conflict.[15]

Blanchard remarks that Salvadoran industrialists and managers are even more strident in generating conflict in the work place. For instance, consider the case of the Mandarin factory and many other similar plants throughout El Salvador.

THE MANDARIN PLANT AND ITS LABOR CONDITIONS

The San Salvador Mandarin International plant was established in order to assemble goods to be shipped to the U.S. under contract with major U.S. retailers such as The Gap and Eddie Bauer. The plant was built in the San Marcos Free Trade Zone, a zone owned by the former Salvadoran Army Colonel Mario Guerrero and created with money from the Bush Administration's U.S. Agency for International Development (USAID). David Wang, the Taiwanese owner of the plant, subsequently hired Guerrero as its personnel manager. In addition, the company also hired ex-military, plain-clothed armed guards as security for the plant.[16] Factories in El Salvador, as in the U.S., need protection for workers, for personal property and for real property.

While personnel managers are not security guards, such appointments have become commonplace with Salvadoran industrialists precisely because they expect conflict in the work place. However, in many situations, their personnel managers generate the conditions of conflict and attempt to control the conflict through the same methods employed during wartime.[17] For example, Colonel Guerrero himself told the workers at one point, "I have no problem, but perhaps you do; either the union will behave, leave, or people will die."[18]

While The Gap was one of the first companies to have a code of conduct for overseas suppliers (along with Reebok), this strategy might not be effective in the El Salvadoran business environment. Charles Kernaghan, Director of the National Labor Committee in Support of Democracy and Human Rights in El Salvador (NLC), believed that a preexisting code of conduct was practically useless and stated the following in an interview with *Business Ethics Magazine* in June, 1996:

> Consider the history of El Salvador's military, which specialized in the killing of nuns and priests and trade unionists. It is laughable to think that these same people will carry out a company's code of conduct. And there were no legal avenues to challenge any violation because the ministry of labor there is so ill-funded and ill-trained. So you can't depend on the laws. And the women were afraid to speak out.[19]

The following is a summary of events leading to the current situation between the Gap and the Mandarin plant, written by Charles Kernaghan, the Director of the National Labor Committee in Support of Democracy and Human Rights in El Salvador (NLC), a coalition of groups with shared interests in workers' rights.

WOMEN MAQUILADORA WORKERS UNDER ATTACK IN EL SALVADOR AT A PLANT PRODUCING FOR J.C. PENNEY, THE GAP, EDDIE BAUER, AND DAYTON-HUDSON[20]

In late January 1995, the women at Mandarin organized a union—the first union ever established in a free trade zone in El Salvador. At the time, the Salvadoran government and the Maquiladora Association pointed to Mandarin as living proof that workers rights and unions are respected in El Salvador. Reality proved otherwise.

Mandarin International immediately lashed out at the new union, at first locking out the workers and then illegally firing over 150 union members. The company hired two dozen ex-military plain-clothed; armed "security guards." The women workers were told their union will have to disappear one way or another, or "blood will flow."

Groups of five workers at a time are now being brought before their supervisors and told to renounce the union or be fired. Union leaders are followed around the plant by company security guards. At work, the women are forbidden to speak to one another. Colonel Guerrero himself has told workers at the San Marcos zone, "I have no problem, but perhaps you do; . . . either the union will behave, leave, or people may die."

These women want their union and they are struggling to keep it alive, but they are afraid. Along with the threats, the company is now systematically firing—a few each week—every union member and sympathizer. They cannot hold out much longer. They are appealing for solidarity.

The Salvadoran Ministry of Labor, which could be fining Mandarin $5,700 a day for violating the Labor Code, has done nothing to reinstate the fired workers or demilitarize the plant.

Mandarin produces clothing for J.C. Penney, GAP, Eddie Bauer and Dayton-Hudson. These companies have codes of conduct, which are supposed to govern their offshore operations, but the workers at Mandarin had never heard of or seen any of these codes. No codes of conduct are posted in the San Marcos free trade zone.

Conditions at Mandarin/Why the Workers Are Struggling for a Union

For eight hours of work at Mandarin, an employee earns $4.51 for the day, or 56 cents an hour. This comes to $24.79 for the regular 44-hour work week. However, overtime at Mandarin is obligatory, and if you do not stay for extra shifts whenever they demand it, even if it is at the last minute, you are fired the next day. A typical week includes at least eight hours of obligatory overtime.

Conveniently for itself, Mandarin pays the workers in cash in envelopes which do not list regular hours worked or overtime hours, or at what premium it was paid. This makes it almost impossible for the young workers to keep track of whether they are receiving proper pay.

The Mandarin plant is hot and the workers complain of constant respiratory problems caused by dust and lint. There is no purified drinking water, and what comes out of the tap is contaminated and has caused illnesses. The bathrooms are locked and you have to ask permission to use them—limited to twice a day—or you are "written up" and fired after three such sanctions.

Talking is prohibited during working hours. The women say the piece-rate quota for the day is very high, making the work pace relentless. The supervisors scream at the workers to go faster. The women told us of being hit, pushed, shoved or having had the garment they were working on thrown in their face by angry supervisors.

The workers say that if you are sick, the company still refuses to grant permission for you to visit the Social Security health clinic during working hours. Nor does Mandarin pay sick days. There is no child care center, which is a critical issue for the women, most of whom are mothers.

Working under these conditions you earn $107.45 a month, $1,397 for the entire year, if you are paid your Christmas bonus. These wages provide only 18.1 percent of the cost of living for the average family of four.

The women say that even by scrimping and eating very cheaply just to stay alive, meaning going without meat, fish and often milk, food for a small family of two or three people still costs over 1,000 colones a month, or $114.29, which is more than they earn. Rent for three small basic rooms costs around $57 a month, which they cannot afford. There are other basic expenses as well. Round-trip bus transportation to and from work can cost over $6.00 a week. Tuition for primary school costs $8.00 a month. For a maquiladora worker to eat a simple breakfast and lunch at work costs approximately $2.50 a day. The wages of the maquila workers cannot possibly meet their expenses. Many of the Mandarin workers are forced to live in tin shacks, without water and often lacking electricity in marginal communities on vacant land, along roadsides or polluted river banks. Asked if they had a T.V., a radio, or a refrigerator, the workers laughed. They could not afford those things, we were told. All the Mandarin workers can afford to purchase is used clothes shipped in from the U.S.

It is a myth on the part of the multinationals and their maquiladora contractors that the cost of living in El Salvador is so much less than in the United States, that 56 cents an hour is really not a bad wage. In El Salvador a "Whirlpool" washer costs $422.26, which is equal to 17 weeks worth of wages for a maquiladora worker. A refrigerator costs $467.35, or 19 weeks worth of wages. A queen-sized bed costs $177.85 on sale, or more than seven weeks of wages. A maquiladora worker would have to work three and a quarter hours to afford a quarter-pound cheeseburger, which costs $1.82. A two pound box of Pillsbury pancake mix costs $2.67, or nearly five hours of wages.

We asked mothers, now that they are working in the maquiladoras, if their children were better off. They told us no, that with their wages they simply could not afford the right food for their children. In Honduras and the Dominican Republic there is growing evidence that malnutrition is rising among the children of maquiladora workers.

How the Maquiladora System Works

Mandarin sews women's 3/4 sleeve T-shirts for the GAP, which had $3.6 billion in sales last year and made over $300 million in profits. The GAP T-shirts made at Mandarin sell for $20 each in the U.S.

A production line of 40 workers at Mandarin produces 1,500 GAP T-shirts a day. These T-shirts sell for $30,000 in the U.S. ($20 × 1,500). The 40 Mandarin workers who make these 1,500 T-shirts earn, collectively, $180.23 for the day (40 × $4.50/day wages). This means that the Mandarin workers earn .6 percent, or just a little more than one-half of one percent of the sales price of the GAP shirt they make. What happens to the other 99.4 percent?

Under the U.S. government's Caribbean Basin Initiative trade and aid benefits, maquiladora exports from El Salvador to the U.S. grew by an amazing 3800 percent between 1985 and 1994, increasing from $10.2 million to $398 million. The number of maquiladora workers producing for the U.S. market increased 14-fold, from 3,500 to 50,000. At the same time, the real wages of the maquiladora workers were slashed 53 percent—to the current 56 cents an hour or $4.50 a day, which provides only 18 percent of a family's basic needs.

This is what trade benefits look like from the perspective of the maquiladora worker on the ground. This is what happens when worker rights are divorced from trade and denied in reality. From the perspective of the GAP however, it means the system is working fine.

Mandarin and Its Young Workers

What kind of a company is Mandarin? Child labor came into focus as an issue toward the end of 1994, following the release of a U.S. Labor Department study and a Senate

Hearing, where the National Labor Committee showed a short film documenting child labor in Honduran maquiladoras producing for the U.S. In February 1995, afraid it might get caught, Mandarin summarily fired at least 100 minors between 14 and 17 years old who had been illegally hired. In El Salvador, minors can work only with special authorization from the Labor Ministry, and even then they cannot work more than seven hours a day. Mandarin, of course, worked the minors like everyone else, including forcing them to work overtime. Given that the average work week was 52 hours at Mandarin, this means that the minors were illegally forced to work 17 hours a week more than they should have by law. (7 hours × 5 days = 35; 52 − 35 = 17).

Mandarin, J.C. Penney, the Gap, Eddie Bauer and Dayton-Hudson have the responsibility to pay these fired minors back wages in the form of overtime payments to compensate them for the 17 hours a week they were forced to work illegally.

It is also interesting to note the absence of the Salvadoran Labor Ministry here as well. Even when it comes to monitoring and protecting child labor, the Ministry is nowhere to be found. It would be worthwhile to ask to see the Ministry's records on Mandarin.

There Are No Labor Rights in El Salvador

Any attempt to organize in the booming maquiladora sector in El Salvador must be clandestine. The mere mention of a union, even the suspicion of interest, will get you fired.

Between 1992 and 1994, maquiladora exports from El Salvador to the U.S. leapt nearly 2.5-fold, growing from $166 million to $398 million. The number of maquiladora plants soared 73 percent from 120 in April 1992, employing 30,000, to 208 assembly companies by December 1994, employing 50,000. The most recent figures show that the surge is continuing. A comparison of January and February 1994 with the same two months of this year shows maquiladora exports from El Salvador to the U.S. increasing 60 percent—a growth rate faster than any other country in the region.

During this same boom period over the last three years, the International Labor Organization (ILO) estimates that at least 1,000 workers have been illegally fired in El Salvador for trying to organize in the maquilas. In a devastating report on El Salvador released at the end of April 1995, the ILO concludes: ". . . to speak of union freedoms and the right of unionization in the maquiladora enterprises is impossible, quite simply because such rights do not exist . . ." This comes on top of an April 6 ILO condemnation of El Salvador for permitting systematic and grave abuses of worker rights, including assassinations, beatings, arrests, and illegal firings for union activity.

The history of worker rights violations at Mandarin fits the above to a "t."

A History of Repression at Mandarin

In November 1993, the maquiladora workers at Mandarin formed a local union. The minute the company was notified that the Ministry of Labor had granted legal status to a union at its plant, management illegally fired 100 workers, including the entire leadership of the new union. When the workers fought this, the Ministry of Labor said it could not help, and that they would have to turn to the courts (where such a case would drag out for at least two years). Mandarin then told the fired workers point blank to accept the firings, take your severance pay and clear out, or else you will be blacklisted and never again work in the maquila.

This fits in with what we were told in August 1992, during a National Labor Committee/60 Minutes investigation in El Salvador. Posing as potential investors, we met with John Sullivan, who directed USAID's private sector program in El Salvador during the Bush Administration. Sullivan told us we would not have to worry about unions in the free trade zones, since zone management used a computerized blacklist to prevent the unions from penetrating the zones.

Sullivan also told us that we could make a lot of money in El Salvador, where there were world class wages, about 40 cents an hour. If we put our workers on piece-rate and raised the production quota we could make even more money. Further, Sullivan encouraged us to fire our workers every year—keeping them on a year to year contract—rather than allow severance benefits to build up. Lastly, the USAID official suggested we form a Solidarista Association—a phony company union—which would help increase our security from disturbances. As we shall see, Mandarin did all these things.

Repression at Mandarin Worsens

Facing such repression, it was not until January 1995 that the workers at Mandarin were able to reorganize their union—the Union of Workers of the Mandarin International Company (SETMI). The union was organized by the Democratic Workers Central (CTD), which maintains fraternal relations with the AFL-CIO. When the Ministry of Labor granted SETMI legal status, it became the first union ever recognized in a free trade zone in El Salvador.

The Minister of Labor told union leaders that he would see to it that the union was accepted without delay by the Mandarin company. This was a time of considerable pressure on labor ministries across Central America and the Caribbean to demonstrate concrete advances in the respect for worker rights. In October 1994, the National Labor Committee was able to delay U.S. Congressional approval of $160 million a year in increased tariff benefits to maquila companies across the region until worker rights conditions improved.

However, despite promises from the Labor Minister, when the company was notified on February 7 that a legal union had been established at Mandarin, it responded by locking out all 850 workers the next day.

Mandarin representatives said that they would rather fire all of the workers than accept a union. The workers refused to leave the industrial park and spent that day and night camped out in front of the factory. On the following morning, February 9, one of the San Marcos Free Trade Zone administrators, Ernesto Aguilar, and several security guards attacked and beat a number of the women. Aguilar punched one woman in the face several times until she was bleeding badly.

An emergency commission was formed to mediate a resolution to the crisis, made up of National Assembly deputies, United Nations delegates, representatives of the Human Rights Ombudsman's Office, several Labor Ministry officials—including Inspector General Doctor Guillermo Palma Duran—as well as union officials and Mandarin management. At 6 P.M., February 9, an agreement was reached, and signed, by all of the participants.

Mandarin committed itself in writing to end the lock-out, to strictly comply with the Salvadoran Labor Code from this point forward, to recognize the union, and to continue negotiations to reach a collective contract. The company also stated that there would be no reprisals against union members.

Between the day Mandarin signed the agreement, along with officials from the

Labor Ministry, and today, Mandarin has illegally fired over 150 union members, in a systematic campaign to destroy the union and spread fear among the workers. The agreement Mandarin signed was not worth the paper it was written on.

The Ministry of Labor could be fining Mandarin $5,700 a day for violating the country's labor code, but for lack of power or will, nothing has been done.

Colonel Guerrero has responded to the workers' attempt to organize to defend their basic rights by "militarizing" his San Marcos Free Trade Zone. Colonel Guerrero hired ex-military people both as zone administrators and armed security guards. One of his administrators, Colonel Amaya, told the women at Mandarin that every single union affiliate at the plant will be fired until the union disappears, which is exactly what is happening. As has already been pointed out, over 150 union members have already been illegally fired, including the entire union leadership—something which is clearly prohibited by the Salvadoran Labor Code.

Five at a time, workers are being brought into management's offices and told to renounce the union or be fired.

Mandarin has brought in nearly two dozen ex-military to act either as plain-clothed, armed security guards, or to pose as mechanics so that they can spy on the workers. Armed guards are posted at all four Mandarin entrances. Whenever union leaders must move about the plant, armed company security guards follow them. If workers are seen speaking to a union leader, the guards immediately intervene. During working hours, the workers are not allowed to speak to each other.

Colonel Amaya, along with the security guards, have told the women workers that "blood will run" if the union does not leave Mandarin and the San Marcos Zone.

The union leaders fear that even their homes are at times under surveillance. On April 25, Mandarin's Chief of Production, Liou Shean Jyh, along with his bodyguard and two other company staff, went to the home of union leader Alonso Gil Moreno. When he refused to let them enter his home, they pushed the door open. Their message was simple: renounce the union. They also offered him a bribe.

Mandarin was worried that despite the systematic repression and threats, the union continued to grow. Even under these conditions, 300 workers had signed up to affiliate to the union. It was clear, that if it were not for the fear of losing one's job, the overwhelming majority of the 850 workers would side with the union. The union was asking for a secret ballot to determine support for their union.

Mandarin's response has been to step up the pace of the firings, and to demand that workers join Mandarin's Solidarista Association, or lose their job.

The union was about to be destroyed.

The Workers Fight Back

The U.S. State Department's latest "Country Reports on Human Rights Practices for 1994" (released in February 1995) observes that in El Salvador's maquiladora sector there are both documented cases of the illegal firing of union organizers and of physical abuse being used in the maquiladoras. In the face of these abuses, the State Department concludes: "[Salvadoran] Government actions against violations have been ineffective, in part because of an inefficient legal system and in part because of fear of losing the factories to other countries." Nor can the workers turn to the Ministry of Labor for protection. According to the State Department report: "The Ministry [of Labor] has very limited powers to enforce compliance, and has suffered cutbacks in resources to carry out certification and inspection duties, which curb its effectiveness."

The ILO report, mentioned earlier, found the Labor Ministry to be so underfunded and its staff so poorly paid that, "this precarious situation in terms of human and financial resources is the best guarantee that not even legally recognized labor rights in the area of union freedom are applied in the companies."

As of Monday, May 15, Mandarin had fired around 100 union members. Every day more unionists were being systematically dismissed. Mandarin was picking up the pace in its campaign to wipe out the shrinking union.

On Monday, May 15, at 9:30 A.M., the union called a work stoppage to protest the mass of illegal firings. As the union leaders stood up to announce the work stoppage, company goons moved in and attacked the union leaders. At one point seven company guards were punching and kicking Dolores Ochoa. They broke her leg. Marta Rivas and Esmeralda Hernandez were also beaten. Elisio Castro Perez, General Secretary of the SETMI union, was beaten and detained for several hours by company security guards.

Once again, Mandarin responded by locking out all 850 employees, and firing 50 more union members, including the union's entire leadership. Another commission was formed and another agreement was reached with the company. At 8 P.M. Monday evening, Mandarin committed itself to reopen the plant the next morning and to reinstate all of the fired workers.

As in the past, this agreement turned out to be worthless. When the fired workers showed up on Tuesday morning, May 16, the armed guards refused to let them enter the plant. When the union protested, the guards again roughed up the women.

At this moment, the union workers and their supporters—a majority of workers—have stopped working and left the plant to stand in solidarity with their fired sisters and brothers.

The workers are desperate and they are asking for our solidarity.

The Workers' Demands

The fired workers want their jobs back and they want their union and they want their security guaranteed. They specifically seek:

1. The immediate reinstatement, with back pay, of all fired workers;
2. The demilitarization of the Mandarin plant and the San Marcos Free Trade Zone, which means removing the armed security guards;
3. End completely the firings, the repression, the threats being directed against union affiliates and their supporters;
4. Mandarin's strict compliance with the Labor Code, including the union's right to organize free of company reprisals;
5. That Mandarin negotiate in good faith a collective contract with the SETMI union.

As North Americans became more and more aware of the working conditions in El Salvador, they began to take action against the retailers. On August 16, 1995, more than one hundred workers from UNITE (Union of Needles Trades and Industrial & Textile Employees) demonstrated in front of a Gap outlet store in downtown Toronto in protest of the working conditions at Gap suppliers. At the same time, thousands of miles South of Toronto, Guerrero claimed that "the working conditions here are good for us and good for the Salvadoran workers, but bad for those seeking to keep jobs in the United States . . . [Without the jobs in the maquilas,] young women would have few other work options apart from prostitution or crime."[21] The story becomes further blurred, however, when Guerrero's comments are compared with an earlier statement by Mandarin owner David Wang in connection with the wages paid to Mandarin workers: "If you really ask me, this is not fair."[22]

> "Workers wages make up less than 1% of the retail cost of GAP shirts. Is it any wonder that the company made $310 million in 1994, and paid its CEO Donald Fisher $2 million plus stock options?"[23]

> From Gap Sourcing Principles & Guidelines: "Workers are free to join associations of their own choosing. Factories must not interfere with workers who wish to lawfully and peacefully associate, organize or bargain collectively. The decision whether or not to do so should be made solely by the workers."[24]

Based on claims of a violation of its sourcing principles and in an effort to ameliorate the situation, the Gap decided to discontinue its relationship with the Mandarin (following in the footsteps of other previous Mandarin contractors such as Eddie Bauer, Liz Claiborne, J. Crew and Casual Corner); however, this action prompted strong cries of concern from labor activists. Contrary to the intentions of the Gap, this resolution was viewed as irresponsible and lacking in accountability.[25] Those concerned with the rights of workers in El Salvador contested the Gap's decision, claiming that this would be the worst possible solution to the problems in a country where 60% of the labor force is unemployed.[26] As a result of other pullouts, the Mandarin has had to cut its work force from 1,300 to 300, and 32 other maquilas have already shut down.[27] "Instead of acting responsibly and seeing that conditions are improved at Mandarin, the Gap is trying to wash its hands and to shift production to other maquilas in other countries with equally bad conditions."[28]

The Gap's original perspective is not without its supporters. Business executive and now Secretary of State for Economic Affairs, Joan Spero, explains, "A world community that respects democracy and human rights will provide a more hospitable climate for American trade and commerce. . . . Repression fosters instability in the long run and puts investment at greater risk of expropriation and loss."[29] Consider as well the following comments of John Duerden, former President of Reebok:

> As a public company, we have an ethical responsibility to build value for Reebok's shareholders—but not at all possible costs. What we seek is harmony between the profit-maximizing demands of our free-market system and the legitimate needs of our shareholders, and the needs and aspirations of the larger world community in which we are all citizens."[30]

"A Victory for All of Us Who Are Determined to Eliminate Sweatshops at Home and Abroad"[31]

The situation took a drastic turn in December 1995 when Reverend Paul Smith called a meeting between Gap Senior Vice President for Sourcing, Stan Raggio, Gap sourcing guidelines director, Dottie Hatcher, Gap consultant James Lukaszewski, Reverend David Dyson of the Interfaith Center for Social Responsibility and Charles Kernaghan (NLC). The Gap was feeling pressure from all sides. On the one hand, labor, religious, consumer, solidarity, children's and women's groups were arguing for dramatic changes in working conditions. On the other hand, the National Retailers' Federation contested the complaints and encouraged the Gap to ignore the demonstrations.

The Gap responded to the consumers, issuing a letter stating that it is "committed to ensuring fair and honest treatment of the people who make [its] garments in over 40 countries worldwide,"[32] and, in the words of the NLC, "took a major step forward in accepting direct responsibility for how and under what conditions the products it sells are made."[33] As a result of the meeting, the Gap agreed to implement an independent monitoring system in El Salvador, using the Human Rights Ombudsperson in El Salvador to monitor factories' compliance with its labor guidelines, as long as the Mandarin agreed to rehire the fired union activists.

The NLC and others saw this decision by the Gap as a benchmark against which all other multinational retailers will be measured. Says Kernaghan, "The message is clear: If you make it, you are responsible."[34] Not everyone agrees with Kernaghan's assessment. Larry Martin of the American Apparel Manufacturer's Association believes otherwise: "They've [labor] given us a black eye that most of us don't deserve. Most of us monitor contractors we use here and offshore."[35] One might understand Martin's concerns for the rest of American retailers when one considers the comments of U.S. Labor Secretary Robert Reich, "This raises the question for other big retailers who haven't moved in this direction—why not?"[36]

The Monitoring Process Begins

The Gap's reputation and image since the December 15, 1995, meeting has been rehabilitated in connection with workers' rights.[37] In fact, the response was almost instantaneous. On December 22, 1995, the Department of Labor added the Gap to its list of "good guy" businesses (the "Fair Labor Fashion Trendsetter List") that have pledged an attempt to avoid selling products manufactured in sweatshops.[38] The Gap consulted with Aaron Cramer, Director of the Business and Human Rights Program at California's Business for Social Responsibility (an association of over 800 firms for clearinghouse and consulting purposes). Cramer contacted several individuals in El Salvador to discuss the most effective means by which to establish the independent monitoring system at the Mandarin. One of these individuals was Father David Blanchard, Pastor of Our Lady of Lourdes in the Calle Real Epiphany Cooperative Association and Father Esteban Alliete, Pastor of Santiago in Ciudad Delagdo Vicariate for Human Development. Their evaluation of human rights monitoring in El Salvador follows:

THE MONITORING OF HUMAN RIGHTS IN THE MARKETPLACE: THE CASE OF EL SALVADOR

Your letter of February 5, 1996 asks to define independent monitoring.

First, the monitoring of human rights must be assumed by Salvadoran organizations. This is important because of the characteristics of organized labor, traditions of work and work codes that are unique to El Salvador. For example, in the United

States, unions choose to support one or another (and sometimes both) political parties in an election. They do this to maximize their interests. In El Salvador, the relationship of political parties to unions is often the reverse. Political parties establish and control unions as a means to expand their power as base.

Understanding the union's role in a labor dispute thus demands understanding the political culture that surrounds the conflict. Therefore, those who monitor the labor conflict in El Salvador must be independent of both the union, the political allies of that union and management. But they must be close enough to this situation to interpret accurately the possible sources and manifestations of the conflict.

The best agency to do this in El Salvador is the government Procurator for Human Rights. The Procurator for Human Rights guarantees that government offices function in ways that respect human rights. The Procurator is responsible for the supervision of the ministry of labor, which must assure compliance with work codes. It provides vigilance over the ministry of justice which must prosecute violations. It monitors the role of the security forces.

Should additional verification be required, the Vicariate for Human Development of the Archdiocese of San Salvador and the Human Rights Office of the University of Central America (IDUCA) both enjoy an international reputation for fairness and objectivity. The Vicariate for Human Development of the Archdiocese includes the social secretariat and CARITAS, both of which have promoted productive enterprises, and of course, Tutela Legal. In addition to its legal staff, IDUCA also has access to economists, academics in the faculty of management and business administration and other important intellectual resources.

Not to focus the monitoring process in local agencies such as these seriously undermines reconstruction efforts in El Salvador. These agencies have earned their right to speak out for justice. The vicariate for Human Development and IDUCA have paid for this right with the blood of faithful colleagues. The Procurator's office for Human Rights was created as a result of the 1992 peace accords. Its integrity is unblemished and it deserves a chance to take its place in the forum for human rights.

You ask how the effectiveness of the monitoring process should be measured. There are two measurable criteria.

First, as Lic. Maria Julia Hernandez has pointed out, each factory should minimally be made to follow the law. This includes the right to organize. Cases of violations should be prosecuted. The number of cases prosecuted and the results of these cases should be published.

Secondly, over the long term, the work force will become more qualified and more productive. When the minimal legal requirements are respected, a stronger work force has greater possibility to negotiate the value of its labor collectively and individually. The result will be seen in greater productivity, profits and an increased standard of living for the work force.

How can an Independent monitoring process be established in a cost-effective manner? It would certainly reduce costs greatly if monitoring is concentrated in Salvadoran institutions. Perhaps the interfaith Center on Corporate Responsibility and the National Labor Committee can collaborate asking the private foundations and donors who support your efforts to contribute to the Procurator for Human Rights, Tutela Legal and the IDUCA. Eventually, such monitoring will have to receive its support from local sources—workers, unions and corporations.

You ask how independent monitors should present their findings. Honestly individual cases should not be presented as representing a pattern. When patterns exist, they should be clearly presented. Also, all parties should attempt to de-personalize the way cases are presented and strive for objectivity. Where real cases of suffering and abuse exist, these should be treated immediately. Suffering should not be exploited to achieve a public relations victory.

Your question, "how should we gain input from concerned organizations in Central America?", suggests that the independent monitoring is something that should be done from outside, with data obtained from local organizations. Our response is that local organizations should gather the data; they should analyze this data and present their findings to organizations such as yours for dissemination.

Monitoring began and problems ensued. An impasse was reached in March 1996, followed by a Resolution Declaration regarding the rehiring of union activists at the plant. The Resolution also included a commitment of the signatories to

1. Peace and harmony among workers;
2. The maintenance of the existent peace between workers and management;
3. Insofar as possible, a promise to aggressively contact and encourage clothing retailers and manufacturers to direct orders to Mandarin International to help demonstrate that agreement and independent monitoring can and will work.[39]

By April, 1996, the Mandarin plant was in serious trouble. David Wang, owner of the plant, informed the monitoring team at an April 18 meeting that there was an 80% chance that the plant would have to be closed by May, 1996. Wang claimed that only a miracle would keep the plant from closing. Fr. Blanchard responded, "I personally believe in miracles, but they are nothing to base a business on."[40] The problem at the Mandarin plant was not much different than at any other manufacturing plant: contracts. The Mandarin was not going to be able to stay afloat without additional contracts. Its renewed contract with the Gap was simply insufficient alone to satisfy the financial needs of the plant. Because Wang believed the closing was imminent, he refused to provide the monitoring team with the information it required to conduct its responsibilities.

At the same time, the Gap hired two Central American Sourcing Compliance Officers "whose sole responsibility [was] to ensure that Gap contractors operated in full compliance with local laws and [its] Code of Vendor Conduct."

Moreover, the Salvadoran Minister of Labor established a government commission to review conditions in the free trade zone and indicated that foreigners would no longer be permitted to monitor the implementation of work codes in El Salvador.[41] This begs the question of why The Gap doesn't simply allow the El Salvadoran government to monitor the work conditions of the plant? Father Blanchard offers the following response:

We must consider what are the global consequences for disbanding this effort after less than one month in existence.

For example, recently we have learned that the Commerce Department of the United States has informed the international fishing industry that it will not allow the importation of shrimp that are caught with nets that also snare turtles. All fisherman who use nets, and who wish to sell their produce in the United States must use turtle-free nets. What is more, the industry must allow independent monitoring by outside agencies.

Salvadoran law permits the use of turtle-snaring nets. The United States has no authority to control the Salvadoran shrimp industry (one of the largest sources of external revenue for the Government of El Salvador). It has complete authority to determine the conditions under which shrimp may be imported into the United States.

The question remains: why not simply rely on the government of El Salvador to supervise compliance, especially given the importance of the shrimping industry in this country.

The answer lies in norms for the modernization of government and general guidelines for development being promulgated by the World Bank, the Inter American Development Bank and other loaning agencies. Governments that contribute to international loaning agencies insist on down-scaling government and allowing compliance to be monitored by the private sector in alliance with independent monitoring groups. In this scheme, Congress passes the law defining the kinds of nets that are required in the shrimp industry; people concerned about the welfare of turtles contribute to organizations like the International Wildlife Fund to guarantee that these laws are enforced; organizations like the International Wildlife Fund in turn collaborate with the fishing industry to guarantee that the norms are followed. When all is said and done, if nobody cares about the welfare of turtles, the laws are not passed and compliance never takes place.

What is good for turtles is also good for human beings.[42]

The Story Continues

Not only do these events continue to occur in El Salvador in connection with the Mandarin plant and others in the Free Trade Zone, but these same issues are also prevalent elsewhere throughout the world, as is evidenced by these comments made by Douglass Cassel, Director of the International Human Rights Law Institute, before the Chicago Council of Foreign Relations.

Shell in Nigeria

A hands-off stance was adopted by Shell Oil last year when Nigeria executed author and environmental activist Ken Saro-wiwa. For years Saro-Wiwa had led an activist group of the Ogoni ethnic minority in the Niger River Delta. The Ogoni claimed that Shell drilling and pipelines had polluted their waters and poisoned their lands, ruining not only their environment but their livelihoods, which depended on fishing and farming.

And, they claimed, they did not benefit from this exploitation of their land. Although Shell says it has supported dozens of community projects and recently boosted its budget for environmental improvements to over $100 million, the Ogoni say that most of the oil money that stayed in Nigeria went into the pockets of corrupt military officers.

In the early 1990's members of Saro-Wiwa's group allegedly sabotaged Shell's equipment, to the point where Shell ceased operations in Ogoniland in 1993. Still, to preserve its investment, Shell called upon—who else?—the local authorities.

Now in normal circumstances, summoning the gendarmes to protect one's property would seem to be the proper thing to do. In Nigeria, however, it is akin to calling in the Mafia. Nigeria is ruled by a corrupt, repressive, military regime, currently headed by General Sani Abacha. Its most recent election resulted in the imprisonment of the civilian winner.

When Shell called, the colonels responded predictably: By allegedly razing thirty Ogoni villages, killing more than 2,000 ogoni and displacing some 80,000.

But even this did not suffice to quell the unrest. So the regime had Mr. Saro-Wiwa and several other activists arrested, jailed and prosecuted on trumped-up murder charges. British Prime Minister John Major later called the trial "fraudulent." At its conclusion last October, Saro-Wiwa and his co-accused were sentenced to death.

As the trial unfolded and its unfairness became apparent, international protests mounted. Yet Shell kept mum. When the death sentence was announced, protests poured in from the United Nations Human Rights Commission, the United States and British governments, South African Nelson Mandela, Amnesty International and countless others.

But not from Shell, whose joint venture with Nigeria's state oil company supplies more than half the revenue for General Abacha's regime. "It is not for a commercial organization," the company explained, "to interfere with the legal processes of a sovereign state such as Nigeria."

Only after the General's Military Council confirmed the death sentences did Shell's Chairman send a last-minute letter "requesting clemency on humanitarian grounds." But this gesture was too little, too late: A few days later, Ken Saro-Wiwa and his colleagues were hanged.

Before the dirt on Saro-wiwa's grave could settle, Shell announced that it would go ahead with a $4 billion joint venture natural gas plant in Nigeria. Its partner: General Abacha's state oil company.

The Sullivan Principles

Still, during the 70's and 80's, there was one striking experiment in corporate codes of conduct for human rights: The Sullivan Principles for South Africa. Developed by Reverend Leon Sullivan, a General Motors Board member, these principles were initially adopted in 1977 by twelve U.S. firms, including GM. By 1986 some 200 of the 260 U.S. corporations doing business in South Africa had adopted the Sullivan Principles.

By adopting the Sullivan Principles, these firms adopted unprecedented, far-reaching commitments to corporate social responsibility toward human rights violations—albeit limited to a single country, and spurred by a desire to deflect growing call for divestment from that country.

Sullivan firms committed themselves not only to racially nondiscriminatory employment, but also to pay fair wages well above the minimum cost of living; to provide managerial training programs for Blacks and other non-whites; to provide them supportive services for housing, health care, transportation and recreation; and to use their corporate influence to help end apartheid in South Africa. And each firm's performance was subject to outside audit and public reports by A.D. Little.

Might events in Nigeria have turned out differently, had Shell undertaken similar commitments for the Ogoni?

Far-reaching as they were, however, the Sullivan Principles failed both in their ostensible goal—to bring down apartheid—and in their tactical goal—to offer a publicly palatable alternative to divestment from South Africa. By 1977 even Reverend Sullivan pronounced his principles a failure and disassociated himself from their further use. When apartheid ultimately did fall in South Africa, it was not because of the Sullivan Principles.

Northern Ireland: The MacBride Principles

In the mid-80's a similar experiment, called the MacBride Principles, was initiated for Northern Ireland. Their purpose differs from the Sullivan Principles: they aim not to deflect divestment (for which there has been no serious support), but instead to secure equal treatment for Catholic workers in Protestant-majority Northern Ireland. And their content is more limited, focusing on non-discrimination, without mandating higher wages and social services.

MacBride firms do, however, make one unusual commitment with potential applications elsewhere: To make reasonable, good faith efforts to protect the personal safety of their Catholic workers not only at the work place, but while travelling to and from work.

As of February 1995, 32 of the 80 publicly traded U.S. firms operating in Northern Ireland had signed on to the MacBride Principles. Sixteen states, including Illinois, and more than 40 cities, including Chicago, have passed MacBride Principles laws.[43]

Another highly publicized case of substandard working conditions involves the Nikomas Gemilang factory in Serang, Indonesia (where 1.2 million pairs of Nike shoes—more than a third of its products—are constructed each month), where the resolution has not come so quickly as with The Gap. In Serang, workers faint from exhaustion, humiliation of the workers is commonplace and, in contrast to Nike spokesperson Michael Jordan's multi-multi-million dollar salary, the workers earn $2.23 per day. One labor activist comments, "From the Outside it looks like heaven but for workers on the inside, it's hell."[44] In fact, only one worker interviewed at the Nikomas factory had even heard of Nike's Code of Conduct.[45] New York Times columnist Bob Herbert claims that the problem is that Nike overlooks atrocities such as the government-sponsored murder of thousands of innocent civilians "if there is a large enough labor force willing to work for next to nothing."[46]

In response to questions concerning his role as Nike spokesperson, Michael Jordan said, "It is up to Nike to do what they can to make sure that everything is correctly done. I don't know the complete situation. Why should I? I'm trying to do my job. Hopefully, Nike will do the right thing."[47] On the other hand, consumers are concerned. Herbert reported in another New York Times article that a woman from New York wrote the paper to state that she "simply cannot sit back and watch my two children frolic in their vacation surf knowing that other children suffer to enable my kids to have cute bathing suits."[48]

Other companies are well known for their intolerance of inhumane conditions. Levi Straus and Timberland received accolades for their 1993 decision to discontinue operations in China as a result of that country's stance on human rights. Reebok, as well, refused to operate in China under its martial law conditions following the Tian An Men square massacre in 1990. In 1992, Sears, Roebuck and Co. refused to import products produced by prison or other involuntary labor in China.[49] Recently, Talbots, K-Mart and J.C. Penney have introduced compliance programs specifically implementing monitoring procedures for suppliers.[50] Talbots' policy requires that a supplier must *actively* work to prevent sweatshop abuses if that supplier wants to do business with Talbots.[51]

Multimillion dollar globalized firms have the opportunity to make a difference in the countries in which they conduct business. That difference may be for the worse if they are seen to condone the poor labor conditions and treatment of workers in those countries, or may be for the better if they use their financial leverage to force a change in the conditions. But what is the responsibility of a foreign firm? If the Gap's costs increase as a result of its activities in El Salvador, are its customers willing to pay the price? If Nike's shoes cost more at the store, will its sales go down? The ultimate question of responsibility appears to be on the shoulders of every person with a dollar to spend.

Notes

1. Dept. of Labor, "No Sweat Initiative: Fact Sheet," http://www.dol.gov/dol/esa/public/forum/fact.htm.
2. Susan Chandler, "Look Who's Sweating now," *Business Week,* Oct. 16, 1995, pp. 96, 98. [In March, 1996, 72 Thai workers at the El Monte sweatshop were awarded more than $1 million in back wages in connection with the scandal. George White, "Sweatshop, Workers to Receive $1 Million," *L.A. Times,* Mar. 8, 1996, p. B1.]
3. Id. The study also found that 73% of the garment makers had improper payroll records, 68% did not pay appropriate overtime wages, and 51% paid less than the minimum wage. Id. at 98.
4. Id. at 96. Self-inspection may also be necessitated by the drop in the number of inspectors assigned by the Labor Department to investigate wage and hour law violations. Since 1989, that number has fallen from almost 1000 to less than 800. Id. at 98; Andrea Adelson, "Look Who's Minding the Shop," *New York Times,* May 4, 1996, p. 17.
5. Stuart Silverstein, "Self-Regulatory Group to Police Clothes Makers' Work Conditions," *L.A. Times,* June 20, 1995, p. D1.
6. http://www.dol/gov/dol/opa/public.forum/kearney.txt.
7. Douglass Cassel, "Human Rights Violations: What's a Poor Multinational To Do?" remarks before the Chicago Council on Foreign Relations, Feb. 7, 1996, p. 10.
8. "Gifford Counters Sweatshop Charges," May 2, 1996, p. 40 (Reuters).
9. Michael McGuire, "Lost in the Junkyard of Abandoned U.S. Policy," *Chicago Tribune* (April 7, 1996) sec. 2, p. 1, 4.
10. Louis Emmerij, *Social Tensions and Social Reform: Toward Balanced Economic, Financial and Social Policies in Latin America* (Washington, DC: Social Agenda Policy Group, Inter-American Development Bank, 1995) p. 7, *cited in* letter from Fr. David Blanchard, Pastor, O.L. Lourdes in Calle Real Epiphany Cooperative Assn. to Aaron Cramer, Director, Business and Human Rights Program, Business for Social Responsibility, February 6, 1996, p. 2.
11. Bob Herbert, "Sweatshop Beneficiaries," *New York Times,* July 24, 1995, p. A13.
12. Letter from Fr. David Blanchard, Pastor, O.L. Lourdes in Calle Real Epiphany Cooperative Assn. to Aaron Cramer, Director, Business and Human Rights Program, Business for Social Responsibility, February 6, 1996, p. 8, citing research by Fr. Ignacio Martin-Baro, a social psychologist and one of the six Jesuit priests slain in November 1989 at the University of Central America in El Salvador.

    The war has additional effects on the people of El Salvador, even if they were not alive at the time of the recent conflicts. For example, one American student recorded in his journal, "9/3/95: One of the little children handed me an old bullet that he must have found. I imagine there must be many bullets out there in the field. I just wanted the day to be over, for me and for this little boy." Student manuscripts, in possession of the author.
13. First-hand experience of the author, February, 1996.
14. Student Manuscripts, in possession of the author (June 1996).
15. Letter from Fr. David Blanchard, Pastor, O.L. Lourdes in Calle Real Epiphany Cooperative Assn. to Aaron Cramer, Director, Business and Human Rights Program, Business for Social Responsibility, February 6, 1996, p. 5.
16. Terry Kelly, "The GAP: Brutality Behind the Facade," part of *World History Archives* located at http://neal.ctstateu.edu/history/world.history/archives/canada/canada002.html, p. 1 (1995).
17. Letter from Fr. David Blanchard, Pastor, O.L. Lourdes in Calle Real Epiphany Cooperative Assn. to Aaron Cramer, Director, Business and Human Rights Program, Business for Social Responsibility, February 6, 1996, p. 6.
18. Terry Kelly, "The GAP: Brutality Behind the Facade," part of *World History Archives* located at http://neal.ctstateu.edu/history/world.history/archives/canada/canada002.html, p. 2 (1995).
19. Mary Scott, "Going After The Gap," *Business Ethics Magazine* (May/June 1996) p. 20.
20. Charles Kernaghan, *Urgent Action Alert* (June 3, 1995) http://www.miyazakimic.ac.jp/classes/compoliss/ElSalvadorlabor.html.

21. Letta Taylor, "Salvadoran Clothing Factory Accused of Worker Abuse," *Roanoke Times and World News* (Dec. 31, 1995) p. D4.
22. Bob Herbert, "Not A Living Wage," *New York Times,* Oct. 9, 1995, p. A17.
23. Terry Kelly, "The GAP: Brutality Behind the Facade," part of *World History Archives* located at http://neal.ctstateu.edu/history/world.history/archives/canada/canada002.html, p. 2 (1995).
24. Gap, Inc., *Code of Vendor Conduct,* section VIII, 1996. See also Christian Task Force on Central America, "Urgent Action El Salvador," http://www/grannyg.ba.ca/CTFCA/act1295a.html (Nov. 29, 1995) p. 1.
25. Letta Taylor, "Salvadoran Clothing Factory Accused of Worker Abuse," *Roanoke Times and World News* (Dec. 31, 1995) p. D4; Joanna Ramey, "Worker Rights Groups Slam Gap for Ending El Salvador Contract," *Women's Wear Daily,* Nov. 30, 1995.
26. Letta Taylor, "Salvadoran Clothing Factory Accused of Worker Abuse," *Roanoke Times and World News* (Dec. 31, 1995) p. D4.
27. Letta Taylor, "Salvadoran Clothing Factory Accused of Worker Abuse," *Roanoke Times and World News* (Dec. 31, 1995) p. D4.
28. Christian Task Force on Central America, "Urgent Action El Salvador," http://www/grannyg.bc.ca/CTFCA/act1295a.html (Nov. 29, 1995) p. 2.
29. Douglass Cassel, "Human Rights Violations: What's a Poor Multinational To Do?" remarks before the Chicago Council on Foreign Relations, Feb. 7, 1996, p. 9.
30. Douglass Cassel, "Human Rights Violations: What's a Poor Multinational To Do?" remarks before the Chicago Council on Foreign Relations, Feb. 7, 1996, p. 9.
31. Words of Jay Mazur, UNITE President, in National Labor Committee, "Gap Victory," http://www.alfea.it/coordns/work/industria/gap-victory.html (Feb. 1996).
32. Christian Task Force on Central America, "Urgent Action El Salvador," http://www/grannyg/bc.ca/CTFCA/act1295a.html (Nov. 29, 1995).
33. National Labor Committee, "Gap Agrees to Independent Monitoring Setting New Standard for the Entire Industry," http://www.alfea.it/coordns/work/industria/gap.agrees.html.
34. Industrial Workers of the World, "Unions Win Victory in Gap Battle," *The Industrial Worker,* http://fletcher.iww.org/~iw/feb/stories/gap.html (February, 1995). See also, Mary Scott, "Going After The Gap," *Business Ethics Magazine* (May/June 1996) pp. 18–20 ["What the Gap has done is historic. It will be a good pilot project to see if third party monitoring works," said Conrad McKerron, social research director of Progressive Asset Management.]
35. Paula Green, "The Gap Signs Accord on Conduct Code with U.S. Labor Group," *The News-Times,* http://www.newstimes.com/archives/dec2295/bzf.htm (12/22/95), p. 2.
36. United Auto Workers, "The Gap Agrees to Improve Conditions in Overseas Plants," *Frontlines,* http://www.uaw.org/solidarity/9601/frontlinesjan96.html (January 1996) p. 1.
37. See e.g., Paula Green, "The Gap Signs Accord on Conduct Code with U.S. Labor Group," *The News-Times,* http://www.newstimes.com/archives/dec2295/bzf.htm (12/22/95); Mary Scott, "Going After The Gap," *Business Ethics Magazine* (May/June 1996) pp. 18–20.
38. Stuart Silverstein, "Labor Department Adds Gap Inc. to 'Good Guy' Retailer List," *L.A. Times,* Dec. 22, 1995, p. D2.
39. Resolution Declaration, March 22, 1996, signed by: David Wang (Mandarin International), Hector Bernabe Recinos (Centra), David Blanchard (Archdiocese of San Salvador), Maria Julia Hernandez (Tutela Legal del Archdiocese), Benjamin Cuellar (Univ. of Central America), Lucia Alvarado Portan (Mandarin International Workers Assn.), and Eliseo Castro Perez (for former SETMI union leaders).
40. Memo from Fr. David Blanchard to Mark Annerm Coordinator, Independent Monitoring Team, April 19, 1996, p. 1.
41. Memo from Fr. David Blanchard to Mark Annerm Coordinator, Independent Monitoring Team, April 19, 1996, p. 4.
42. Memo from Fr. David Blanchard to Mark Annerm Coordinator, Independent Monitoring Team, April 19, 1996, pp. 5–6.
43. Douglass Cassel, "Human Rights Violations: What's a Poor Multinational To Do?" remarks before the Chicago Council on Foreign Relations, Feb. 7, 1996.
44. Mark L. Clifford, "Pangs of Conscience: Sweatshops Haunt U.S. Consumers," *Business Week* (July 29, 1996) p. 46.
45. Id. at p. 47.
46. Bob Herbert, "Nike's Bad Neighborhood," *New York Times,* June 14, 1996, p. A15.
47. Bob Herbert, "Nike's Pyramid Scheme," *New York Times,* June 10, 1996, p. A19.
48. Bob Herbert, "Buying Clothes without Exploiting Children," *New York Times,* August 4, 1995, p. A27.

49. Douglass Cassel, "The Gap: Getting Serious about Sweatshops," broadcast on *World View*, WBEZ, 91.5FM (Jan. 3, 1996) p. 3.
50. Office of Public Affairs, U.S. Dept. of Labor, "Reich Applauds Significant Steps taken by Retailers to Combat Worker Abuses in the U.S. Garment Industry," press release, June 17, 1996.
51. Id.

APPENDIX A: MODEL BUSINESS PRINCIPLES, U.S. DEPT. OF COMMERCE

The following statement of Model Business Principles and subsequent procedures were released by the U.S. Dept. of Commerce recently and should be viewed as voluntary guidelines for U.S. businesses. For more information, please see the *New York Times,* May 27, 1995, p. 17.

Recognizing the positive role of U.S. business in upholding and promoting adherence to universal standards of human rights, the Administration encourages all businesses to adopt and implement voluntary codes of conduct for doing business around the world that cover at least the following areas:

1. Provision of a safe and healthy work place.
2. Fair employment practices, including avoidance of child and forced labor and avoidance of discrimination based on race, gender, national origin or religious beliefs; and respect for the right of association and the right to organize and bargain collectively.
3. Responsible environmental protection and environmental practices.
4. Compliance with U.S. and local laws promoting good business practices, including laws prohibiting illicit payments and ensuring fair competition.
5. Maintenance, through leadership at all levels, of a corporate culture that respects free expression consistent with legitimate business concerns, and does not condone political coercion in the work place; that encourages good corporate citizenship and makes a positive contribution to the communities in which the company operates; and where ethical conduct is recognized, valued and exemplified by all employees.

In adopting voluntary codes of conduct that reflect these principles, U.S. companies should serve as models, encouraging similar behavior by their partners, suppliers, and subcontractors.

Adoption of codes of conduct reflecting these principles is voluntary. Companies are encouraged to develop their own codes of conduct appropriate to their particular circumstances. Many companies already apply statements or codes that incorporate these principles. Companies should find appropriate means to inform their shareholders and the public of actions undertaken in connection with these principles. Nothing in the principles is intended to require a company to act in violation of host country or U.S. law. This statement of principles is not intended for legislation.

Model Business Principles: Procedures

When President Clinton announced his decision to renew China's most-favored-nation (MFN) status last year, he also announced a commitment to work with the business community to develop a voluntary statement of business principles relating to corporate conduct abroad. The President made clear that U.S. business can and does play a positive and important role promoting the openness of societies, respect for individual rights, the promotion of free markets and prosperity, environmental protection and the setting of high standards for business practices generally.

The Administration today is offering an update on our efforts to follow-through on the President's commitment to promote the Model Business Principles and best practices among U.S. companies. The Principles already have gained the support of some U.S. companies. A process is ongoing to elicit additional support for these Principles and to continue to examine issues related to them.

The elements of this process are as follows:

1. *Voluntary Statement of Business Principles.* The Administration, in extensive consultations with business and labor leaders and members of the Non-Governmental Organization (NGO) community, developed these model principles, which were reported widely in the press earlier this spring. A copy is attached. This model statement is to be used by companies as a reference point in framing their own codes of conduct. It is based on a wide variety of similar sets of principles U.S. companies and business organizations already have put into global practice. The Administration encourages all businesses everywhere to support the model principles. (Copies of the model statement are available by calling the U.S. Department of Commerce Trade Information Center, 1-800-USA-TRADE.)

2. *Efforts By U.S. Business.* As part of the ongoing effort, U.S. businesses will engage in the following activities:

• Conferences on Best Practices Issues

In conjunction with Business for Social Responsibility, a non-profit business organization dedicated to promoting laudable corporate practices, and/or other appropriate organizations, the Administration will work to encourage conferences concerning issues relating to the practices contained in the Model Business Principles. Such conferences can provide a forum for information-sharing on new approaches for the evolving global context in which best practices are implemented. (For further information on Business for Social Responsibility, contact Bob Dunn, President, (415) 865-2500.)

• Best Practices Information Clearinghouse and Support Services

One or more non-profits will work with the U.S. business community to develop a clearinghouse of information regarding business practices globally. The clearinghouse will establish a library of codes of conduct adopted by U.S. and international companies and organizations, to be catalogued and made available to companies seeking to develop their own codes. The clearinghouse would be available to provide advice to companies seeking to develop or improve their codes, advice based on the accumulated experience of other companies. Business for Social Responsibility (described above) is highly respected and is one resource that businesses and NGOs alike can turn to for information on best business practices.

3. *Efforts by the U.S. Government.* The U.S. Government also will undertake a number of activities to generate support for the Model Business Principles:

• Promote Multilateral Adoption of Best Practices

The Administration has begun and will continue its effort to seek multilateral support for the Model Business Principles. Senior U.S. Government officials already have met with U.S. company officials and U.S. organizations operating abroad as well as with foreign corporate officials to seek support for the Principles. For example, the American Chambers of Commerce in the Asia Pacific recently adopted a resolution by which their members agreed to work with their local counterparts in the countries in which they operate to seek development of similar best practices among their members. The United States also will present the Model Business Principles at the Organization for Economic Cooperation and Development (OECD) and the International Labor Organization (ILO) as part of these organizations' ongoing behavior. Therefore, on an annual basis, the Administration will offer a series of awards to companies for specific activities that reflect best practices in the areas covered by the Model Business Principles. The awards will be granted pursuant to applications by interested companies. NGOs and private citizens will be encouraged to call attention to activities they believe are worthy of consideration. (For further information on the Best Practices Awards Program, contact Melinda Yee, U.S. Department of Commerce, (202) 482-1051.)

- Presidential-Business Discussions

  The President's Export Council (PEC), a high-level advisory group of Chief Executive Officers, provides a forum for the President to meet regularly with U.S. business leaders to discuss issues relating to U.S. industries' exports and operations abroad.

For Further general information about the Model Business Principles, please contact Jill Schuker (U.S. Commerce Department, (202) 482-5151), or David Ruth (U.S. Department of State, (202) 647-1625).

Study Questions

1. To what extent do the competitive forces that make third world production attractive rely on rules regarding property, risk–reward relationships, and information? What are the ethical and legal aspects of these latter three economic conditions?

2. To what extent can international organizations affect this problem? What would De George, Werhane, and Frederick say, for example?

3. Should consumers in first world markets care about how their goods are produced? If so, at what point do production conditions become bad enough to warrant consumer action?

CASE: Two Roads to China: Nice, and Not So Nice
David E. Sanger

Seattle—AFTER this month, in an extraordinary example of corporate diplomacy, the Boeing Company will airlift its entire board to China. Ostensibly, the directors will simply be holding their regular bimonthly meeting there, while touring sites like the vast construction hangars in Xian where, with Boeing's help, tens of thousands of workers are trying to transform China into a world-class aerospace power.

But the real purpose of the China tour is to deepen Boeing's ties to a small clutch of Chinese leaders who are by turns the aircraft maker's best customers and worst torturers. Just as oil companies have paved the way for Middle Eastern kings and emirs in America, Boeing is working harder than ever to impress the Chinese, intervening to defuse the cycle of recriminations between Beijing and Washington that has already begun to poison Boeing's hold on China's civilian aerospace market.

The company is looking for ways to offer China more aerospace technology. It is stepping up its role as Beijing's de facto lobbyist on Capitol Hill, even helping produce videos to soften China's public image in the American heartland. At times, it is reaching well beyond trade issues: Just the other day, a Boeing executive warned Chinese leaders that with Congress inflamed over Beijing's behavior, it would be foolish to go forward with a nuclear weapons test in northwestern China.

"We have credibility with the Chinese, and we try to use it toward good ends," said Philip M. Condit, Boeing's president and chief executive.

Just across Lake Washington, the Microsoft Corporation has developed a different approach—one that is often far more confrontational. William H. Gates, Microsoft's chairman, was in Washington 10 days ago to denounce China's failure to live up to its agreement to close the factories that produce billions of dollars of counterfeit versions of American software, music and videos. And just days away from Washington's June 17 deadline for China to close the pirate factories or face more than $2 billion in sanctions against Chinese goods, Microsoft lawyers are literally leading Chinese police to the pirates' lairs, insisting on raids.

But to Microsoft, business is business, and its stranglehold on something the Chinese desperately need—an understanding of the software that will make or break China's huge investment in the personal computer industry—allows it to stay clear of superpower diplomacy. "Nuclear weapons tests?" laughed Charles Stevens, its vice president for the Far East, when asked whether he too is providing China's leadership with advice. "We do Windows, not foreign policy."

The divergent approaches to dealing with China at Boeing and Microsoft—conciliatory versus confrontational—are a reminder that the Clinton Administration isn't the only one floundering to find a consistent and effective China policy. So is American business. Rarely have so many industries, with so many interests at stake, been so divided about how best to handle a country with so much market potential and so much political volatility. And those divisions have come to the surface more starkly than ever now that the Administration is threatening sanctions even as it presses Congress to renew most-favored-nation status for China.

So far, neither Boeing's nor Microsoft's tactics can be called an overwhelming success. Boeing has spent 25 years developing a nuanced corporate foreign policy toward China, yet it has been roughed up twice by the country in the last two months: to strike back at Washington, Beijing has handed Boeing's European competitors a major aircraft order and then given them a big share in a long-term effort by China to build its own 100-seat airliner.

Mr. Condit, whose executive team is considered the most China-savvy in corporate America, winces a bit over how China has treated its corporate ambassador in recent months. "We are the designated hostage," he sighed the other day.

And Microsoft executives, despite impressive sales gains in the last year, fear that China's reluctance to curb rampant software piracy and its inclination to exert Government control over the Internet could keep its business there tied down for years.

BOEING: A LONG FRIENDSHIP YET 2 SLAPS IN THE FACE

Boeing's diplomatic dance with China goes back 25 years, but it's not getting any easier.

When President Richard M. Nixon visited Beijing in 1972, he used the Boeing 707 as one of his lures to open relations. It made little difference that China had no commercial air service at the time. Within weeks, the Chinese ordered 10 planes, making Boeing the first company with a serious toehold in what has become the world's greatest emerging market.

Boeing quickly became China's most valuable lobbyist. It flexed its muscles at the Export-Import Bank, which only a few years ago overcame its moniker as "the Boeing Bank," to get low-cost, American-backed loans for Chinese airlines. Every year it took up China's cause in the most-favored-nation debate, reminding Congress that denying trade benefits to China would cost hundreds of thousands of jobs in the United States. Now it is championing China's effort to become a member of the World Trade Organization, an uphill battle because China refuses many of the market-opening commitments required of the other members.

Boeing's dedication to China is understandable: China is the world's most promising air market. In 1994, the company's best year there, sales hit $1.25 billion, more than 10 percent of its foreign sales and 25 percent of its commercial sales that year in the United States. Last year, a rough year for Boeing because of a big strike, the figure dropped to $721 million, but China still accounted for 1 of every 10 planes Boeing made.

The relationship is far deeper than just sales. What the Chinese want is technology, and they know how to use their leverage to get it. The results are visible on the floor of Boeing's huge assembly hangar in Renton, just south of Seattle. Every few weeks the giant Xian Aircraft Company, whose factory outside the famed walled city of Xian also produces China's military aircraft, ships Boeing a fully completed tail section and rear stabilizer for the Boeing 737. Half of all the tail sections produced for the 737 are now Chinese made; the other half are produced in Wichita, Kan.

"The Chinese are incredibly good at producing whatever we ask them to produce," Obrad Cvetovich, Boeing's vice president for quality and process management, said the other day as a giant overhead crane lifted the latest Chinese-made tail section onto Boeing 737 No. 2803. "They have an insatiable thirst for technology, and they pick it up and apply it right away." Dismissing complaints about quality from Boeing's unions, which went on strike last year partly because of China's growing role in producing the planes, Mr. Cvetovich said, "We haven't had any problems." As if on cue, it took only 12 minutes for the crane operators and mechanics to line up the Chinese-made tail section, slip it seamlessly onto the rear of the plane and bolt it into place.

What is happening in Renton is, in many ways, the future for all high-technology companies swarming into China. Volkswagen and Motorola and McDonnell Douglas have all begun building high-tech plants in China, and for reasons that have nothing to do with cheap labor. It is in return for market access. Whether it is worth the cost is a raging debate in American industry. It has paid off for Motorola, but McDonnell Douglas has been consistently disappointed, with small returns on its huge investments.

"We don't do it to save money," said Lawrence W. Clarkson, Boeing's senior vice president for planning and international development. "We do it for the business. By the time you are done training, doing the quality control and shipping the parts back here, it doesn't save a thing."

And there is a constant debate within Boeing over just how to satisfy China's thirst for technology without giving away the secret recipe of aircraft integration, producing a complete, airworthy plane.

"Obviously, you don't tell someone everything you know," Mr. Condit said. "But we've learned that you can't play a defensive game. Technology moves in a lot of channels rapidly. And the trick is to give something away just as you are developing something better."

Until recently, this policy of teaching China the magic of building airplanes while helping it out in Washington has made Boeing an indispensable corporate partner. But in the last year, Boeing learned it was not as indispensable as it had hoped.

Twice in the last two months China has dealt devastating blows to the aircraft maker. In April, Li Peng, China's Prime Minister, diverted a $1.5 billion aircraft order, widely expected to go Boeing's way, to Airbus Industrie, the European consortium. Then, in case anyone in Washington missed the point, Chinese officials made clear that Boeing would probably be frozen out of China's big new venture to build a fleet of 100-seat jetliners. The 30 percent Western stake in the project—on which billions of dollars in future revenue probably ride—would go instead to a consortium of European nations that don't lecture China about human rights, don't threaten sanctions for the piracy of music, videos and software and don't send their warships patrolling the Taiwan Straits.

Mr. Clarkson, a large, jovial man with remarkable contacts in China, has been traveling to Beijing for two years to lobby for a 20 to 30 percent equity share in the project. His eagerness was understandable. China can make and cancel orders for individual aircraft, depending on the political temperature of the moment. But if Boeing could become the technological linchpin of China's project, it would become virtually impossible for China to switch partners midstream. And until relations with Washington began going down the tubes this winter, Boeing clearly had the advantage: China's big airlines knew Boeing's technology intimately and wanted more of it.

"There's no doubt we are being punished," concluded Ronald B. Woodard, president of Boeing Commercial Airplane Group. It seemed as if China was making good on a warning one of its vice premiers gave Mr. Clarkson a year ago. "He said, 'Because your Government constantly chooses to kick us and harass us, many, many business opportunities that should go to the U.S. have gone elsewhere.'"

But Boeing remains optimistic that it can reverse the tide. Some say the 100-seat airplane deal may yet land on Boeing Field, especially if dealing with a number of European nations simultaneously turns into a morass. (Others were not entirely unhappy to lose the deal; Boeing would have had a 30 percent stake but virtually all of the responsibility for producing an airworthy plane.) And in the meantime, Boeing continues to do much of China's political spade work in the United States.

It has teamed up with Motorola, Allied Signal, Caterpillar and American International Group, which sells insurance in China, to create the China Normalization Initiative, an effort to buff China's image. It has produced a video that is a remarkably dewy-eyed depiction of China—no repression of dissidents, no sales of automatic weapons to gangs in Los Angeles, no nuclear proliferation, but plenty of Chinese enjoying American goods.

"This constant cycle of arguments has polarized the relationship," Mr. Clarkson said. That, of course, is exactly the message Beijing wants Boeing to send back to Washington—that the price of trying to impose America's will on China will be to cut off access to the greatest emerging market of them all.

MICROSOFT: THE IMPORTANCE OF BEING IMPORTANT

Microsoft doesn't make gauzy films about China and doesn't go to bat for the Chinese on Capitol Hill. It doesn't need to—at least so far. In a country of power relationships, it controls access to the personal computer software technology China most needs. And Chinese leaders know that, at least for now, there is no alternative source, no Airbus of the software world that China can use to whip Microsoft in line.

As a result, Microsoft can afford to take a hard line on software piracy. Its revenues in China are still tiny—roughly $20 million last year for a company with sales of nearly $6 billion. Its greatest competition is the pirates that hold 98 percent of China's software market, selling counterfeit copies of programs and compilation disks that combine thousands of dollars in software onto a single CD-ROM that sells for a few dollars. (In the United States, the percentage of illegally copied software sold to computer users is roughly 35 percent; In Europe around 50 percent.)

"This whole argument is about our longterm future in China, and China's long-term chances of developing a viable software industry," said William H. Neukom, Microsoft's general counsel. "We're an intellectual property company; it's where all of the value of our company rests. Our business requires a set of laws and culture that protects that."

So these days, Microsoft is spending half its time trying to build a legitimate software industry in China and the other half trying to rip apart an illegal one. It has stitched together partnerships with more than 20 fledgling Chinese software houses, which help produce local versions of Microsoft programs and then often turn out spinoff applications of their own. Through those connections, Microsoft executives try to convince provincial officials, local tycoons and Government bureaucrats that ending piracy is in their own economic interest.

"We tell them that letting people profit from legitimate programs is the only way to create an incentive for innovation," Mr. Neukom said. "And we tell them that we don't have a monopoly on Innovation—someday soon those battalions of Chinese software engineers will be turning out programs that they will want to protect."

Sounds nice, but it is a tough argument to make in the grimy industrial towns of Guangdong, the hotbed of piracy in southern China, where copying American software is the path to riches for the military, relatives of provincial officials and leaders of organized crime. So when it's not evangelizing, Microsoft has become the enforcer.

It was Microsoft, for example, that was behind the raid in late April on the Jin Die Science and Technology Development Company in Guilin, known as one of the most skilled producers of counterfelt Microsoft programs. An informant passed his wealth of knowledge about the plant to a Microsoft agent in the area. His report reached the office of Valerie Colbourn, a lawyer for the software maker in Hong Kong. With the help of other lawyers, Ms. Colbourn—operating through a consortium of American software concerns—persuaded the local office of the Administration of Industry and Commerce to move in.

Microsoft had spent months working its way into the good graces of the industry and commerce office. "The fellow in charge is someone we've worked with a lot and who has a good grasp of the problem," Ms. Colbourn said Inst week. "If we went to a different officer on a different day, maybe we would have gotten nothing."

After an all-night standoff with the plant manager, the authorities finally gained access to the storeroom and uncovered a cache of 5,700 CD-ROM's, mostly Microsoft titles. The plant has since been closed, but Ms. Colbourn has few illusions that it is out of business. The equipment is still there, and so is the profit motive.

"If there is an agreement in the next few weeks or not," she said, "we're still going to be fighting this battle for a long time."

But by bringing the power of China's central Government to bear on the pirates, some China experts fear, Microsoft may be creating a precedent that will come to haunt it. Chinese authorities are already threatening to limit access to the Internet, fearing it will end Beijing's control over news and dissenting views. There is a growing fear that China will use its obligations to control software piracy as an excuse to crack down on the Internet. As Boeing already knows, in China a collision between politics and business is never far away.

Study Questions

1. Compare and contrast the approaches of Microsoft and Boeing in ethical, economic, and legal terms at the corporate, market, national, and international levels.

2. How are Microsoft and Boeing trying to shape the institutional infrastructure of business?

3. How would Friedman, Cochran, and Freeman evaluate the actions of Microsoft and Boeing? Who has the best view? Explain.

Norman Bowie

The Moral Obligations of Multinational Corporations

Now that business ethics is a fashionable topic, it is only natural that the behavior of multinational corporations should come under scrutiny. Indeed, in the past few decades multinationals have allegedly violated a number of fundamental moral obligations. Some of these violations have received great attention in the press.

Lockheed violated an obligation against bribery. Nestle violated an obligation not to harm consumers when it aggressively and deceptively marketed infant formula to uneducated poor women in Third World countries. Union Carbide violated either an obligation to provide a safe environment or to properly supervise its Indian employees.

Other violations have received less attention. After the Environmental Protection Agency prohibited the use of the pesticide DBCP, the American Vanguard Corporation continued to manufacture and export the product in Third World countries. U.S. cigarette companies are now aggressively marketing their products abroad. Such actions have been criticized because they seem to treat the safety of foreigners as less important than the safety of U.S. citizens. Other charges involve the violation of the autonomy of sovereign governments. Companies such as Firestone and United Fruit have been accused of making countries dependent on one crop, while Union Miniere and ITT were accused of attempting to overthrow governments.[1]

The charges of immoral conduct constitute a startling array of cases where multinationals are alleged to have failed to live up to their moral obligations. However, the charges are of several distinct types. Some have also been brought against purely domestic U.S. firms—for example, issues involving a safe working environment or safe products. Other charges are unique to multinationals—the charge that a multinational values the safety of a foreigner less than the safety of a home country resident. Still others are charges that companies try to justify behavior in other countries that is clearly wrong in the United States, for example, the bribing of government officials.

In this essay, I will focus on the question of whether U.S. multinationals should follow the moral rules of the United States or the moral rules of the host countries (the countries where the U.S. multinationals do business). A popular way of raising this issue is to ask whether U.S. multinationals should follow the advice "When in Rome, do as the Romans do." In discussing that issue I will argue that U.S. multinationals would be morally required to follow that advice if the theory of ethical relativism were true. On the other hand, if ethical universalism is true, there will be times when the advice would be morally inappropriate. In a later section, I will argue that ethical relativism is morally suspect. Finally, I will argue that the ethics of the market

provide some universal moral norms for the conduct of multinationals. Before turning to these questions, however, I will show briefly that many of the traditional topics discussed under the rubric of the obligations of multinationals fall under standard issues of business ethics.

OBLIGATIONS OF MULTINATIONALS THAT APPLY TO ANY BUSINESS

As Milton Friedman and his followers constantly remind us, the purpose of a corporation is to make money for the stockholders—some say to maximize profits for the stockholders. According to this view, multinationals have the same fundamental purpose as national corporations. However, in recent years, Friedman's theory has been severely criticized. On what moral grounds can the interests of the stockholders be given priority over all the other stakeholders?[2] For a variety of reasons, business ethicists are nearly unanimous in saying that no such moral grounds can be given. Hence, business executives have moral obligations to all their stakeholders. Assuming that Friedman's critics are correct, what follows concerning the obligations of multinationals?

Can the multinationals pursue profit at the expense of the other corporate stakeholders? No; the multinational firm, just like the national firm, is obligated to consider all its stakeholders. In that respect there is nothing distinctive about the moral obligations of a multinational firm. However, fulfilling its obligations is much more complicated than for a national firm. A multinational usually has many more stakeholders. It has all the classes of stakeholders a U.S. company has but multiplied by the number of countries in which the company operates.[3]

It also may be more difficult for the multinational to take the morally correct action. For example, one of the appealing features of a multinational is that it can move resources from one country to another in order to maximize profits. Resources are moved in order to take advantage of more favorable labor rates, tax laws, or currency rates. Of course, the pursuit of such tactics makes it more difficult to honor the obligation to consider the interests of all stakeholders. Nonetheless, the increased difficulty does not change the nature of the obligation; multinationals, like nationals, are required to consider the interests of all corporate stakeholders.

Should a multinational close a U.S. plant and open a plant in Mexico in order to take advantage of cheap labor? That question is no different in principle from this one: Should a national firm close a plant in Michigan and open a plant in South Carolina in order to take advantage of the more favorable labor climate in South Carolina? The same moral considerations that yield a decision in the latter case yield a similar decision in the former. (Only if the interests of Mexican workers were less morally significant than were the interests of U.S. workers could any differentiation be made.)

These examples can be generalized to apply to any attempt by a multinational to take advantage of discrepancies between the home country and the host country in order to pursue a profit. Any attempt to do so without considering the interests of all the stakeholders is immoral. National firms and multinational firms share the same basic obligations. If I am right here, there is nothing distinctive about the many problems faced by multinationals, and much of the discussion of the obligations of multinationals can be carried on within the framework of traditional business ethics.

DISTINCTIVE OBLIGATIONS

Certain obligations of multinationals do become distinctive where the morality of the host country (any country where the multinational has subsidiaries) differs from or contradicts the morality of the home country (the country where the multinational was legally created). The multinational faces a modern version of the "When in Rome, should you do as the Romans do?" question. That question is the focus of this essay.

On occasion, the "when in Rome" question has an easy answer. In many situations the answer to the question is yes. When in Rome a multinational is obligated to do as the Romans do. Because the circumstances Romans face are different from the circumstances Texans face, it is often appropriate to follow Roman moral judgments because it is entirely possible that Romans and Texans use the same moral principles, but apply those principles differently.

This analysis also works the other way. Just because a certain kind of behavior is right in the United States does not mean that it is right somewhere else. Selling infant formula in the United States is morally permissible in most circumstances, but, I would argue, it is not morally permissible in most circumstances to sell infant formula in Third World countries. U.S. water is safe to drink.

Many moral dilemmas disappear when the factual circumstances that differentiate two cultures are taken into account. It is important to note, however, that this judgment is made because we believe that the divergent practices conform to some general moral principle. The makers of infant formula can sell their product in an advanced country but not in a Third World country because the guiding principle is that we cannot impose avoidable harm on an innocent third party. Selling infant formula in underdeveloped countries would often violate that common fundamental principle; selling the formula in developed countries usually would not.

This situation should be contrasted with cases where the home and the host country have different *moral* principles. Consider different moral principles for the testing of new drugs. Both countries face the following dilemma. If there are fairly lax standards, the drug may have very bad side effects, and if it is introduced too quickly, then many persons who take the drug are likely to be harmed—perhaps fatally. On the other hand, if a country has very strict standards and a long testing period, the number of harmful side effect cases will be less, but a number of people who could have benefited from benign drugs will have perished because they did not survive the long testing period. Where is the trade-off between saving victims of a disease and protecting persons from possible harmful side effects? To bring this problem home, consider a proposed cure for cancer or for AIDS. Two different countries could set different safety standards such that plausible moral arguments could be made for each. In such cases, it is morally permissible to sell a drug abroad that could not yet be sold in the United States.

If all cases were like this one, it would always be morally permissible to do as the Romans do. But alas, all cases are not like this one. Suppose a country totally ignores the problem of side effects and has no safety standards at all. That country "solves" the trade-off problem by ignoring the interests of those who might develop side effects. Wouldn't that country be wrong, and wouldn't a multinational be obligated not to market a drug in that country even if the country permitted it?

If the example seems farfetched, consider countries that are so desperately poor or corrupt that they will permit companies to manufacture and market products that are known to be dangerous. This is precisely the charge that was made against American Vanguard when it exported the pesticide DBCP. Aren't multinationals obligated to stay out even if they are permitted?

That question leads directly to the question of whether multinationals always should do in Rome as the Romans do. To sort through that issue, Figure 1 may be useful. Thus far, I have focused on I and IIA. The remainder of the essay considers the range of ethical problems found in IIB.

In IIB4, the multinational has an obligation to follow the moral principles of the host country because on the issue at hand those of the host country are justified while those of the home country are not. Although Americans may believe that there are few such obligations because their moral principles are far more likely to be justified, it is not hard to think of a contrary case. Suppose it is a moral obligation in a host country that no corporation fire someone without due cause. In other words, in the host country employment at will is morally forbidden. Although I shall not argue for it here, I think the employment-at-will doctrine cannot stand up to moral scrutiny. Hence, in this case, multinationals are obligated to follow the moral principle of the host country. Except for economic reasons (falling demand for one's product), a multinational is morally obligated not to fire an employee without just cause.

In IIB3, if the moral principles with respect to a given issue are not justified, then the multinational is under no moral obligation to follow them (except in the weak sense where the multinational is under a legal obligation and hence under a moral obligation to obey the law). Actually, IIB3 can be further subdivided into cases where the moral principles are not justified and where the moral principles cannot be justified. Theocratic states with moral principles based on revelation but not in contradiction with rationally justified moral principles are examples of the former. When the "moral" principles based on revelation are in contradiction with rationally justified moral principles, we have an example of the latter. In this latter case, a multinational is obligated not to follow the moral principles of the host country. In these cases, when in Rome, multinationals are not to do as the Romans do.

In Case IIB2, multinationals may do in Rome as the Romans do. In this case, the moral principles of the host country are justified.

Finally, in case IIB1, the multinational is obligated not to follow the moral principles of the host country. In these cases, the principles of the host country are contrary to the canons of ethics.

In summary, then, U.S. multinationals are obligated to do as the Romans do in IIB4, are permitted to do as the Romans do in IIB2 and in IIB3 where the moral principles of the Romans are consistent with what morality would justify. U.S. multinationals are obligated not to do as the Romans do in IIB1 and IIB3 where the moral principles of the Romans are inconsistent with what morality would justify.

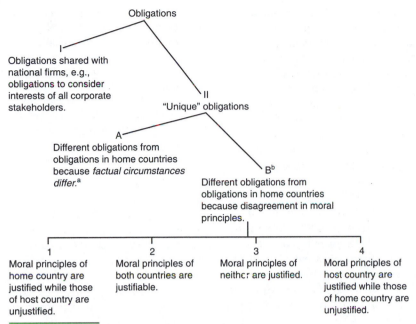

Figure 1   Obligations of multinationals.

[a]In my view, different obligations still conform to universal principles.
[b]It is assumed that the different moral principles referred to here and below refer to the same moral issue. It is also stipulated that "unjustified" in IIB1 and IIB4 means that the unjustified principles are in conflict with the canons of justification in ethics.

Notice, however, that the entire analysis assumes there is some means of justifying ethical principles independent of the fact that a society believes they are justified. Otherwise, for example, I could not say that the moral principles of a home country are not justified while those of the host country are. But who is to say whether the moral principles of a country are justified or when they run counter to universal morality. Besides, perhaps there is no universal morality. What then?

RELATIVISM

Cultural relativism is the doctrine that what is right or wrong, good or bad, depends on one's culture. If the Irish consider abortion to be morally wrong, abortion is morally wrong in Ireland. If the Swedes do not consider abortion to be morally wrong, then abortion *is not* morally wrong in Sweden. There is no uni-versal principle to which the Swedes and the Irish can appeal that determines whether abortion really is wrong or not.

If a person is a cultural relativist, then the implications for our discussion may seem quite clear. A corporation has an obligation to follow the moral principles of the host country. When one is in Rome, one is obligated to do as the Romans do. On our chart, IIB1, IIB3, and IIB4 have no referents. There are no members of those classes just as there are no members of the class of unicorns.

The officers and managers of many multinationals often speak and act as if cultural relativism were true. Who are we, they argue, to impose our moral standards on the rest of the world? For example, the U.S. Foreign Corrupt Practices Act, which prohibits the payment of unrecorded bribes to foreign governments or officials, has come under intense attack. After all, if the payment of bribes is morally acceptable in country X, why should we impose our moral views about bribery on that country. Besides if U.S. multinationals do not bribe, German and Japanese multinationals will—or so the argument goes. Former president Jimmy Carter's attempt to include a country's record on violating or not violating fundamental human rights when making foreign policy decisions came under the same kind of criticism. Who is the United States to impose its moral values on others?

This relativistic way of thinking has always been prominent in the thinking of many social scientists. After all, discoveries by anthropologists, sociologists, and psychologists have documented the diversity of moral beliefs and punctured some of the pseudo-justifications that had been given for the superiority of white Western male ways of thinking. Philosophers, by and large, welcomed the corrections to prejudicial moral thinking, but, nonetheless, found the doctrine of cultural relativism seriously flawed.

Recently, however, the situation in philosophy has taken a surprising turn. A number of prominent philosophers have either seemed to embrace cultural relativism or have been forced by the "critics" to admit that their own philosophical positions may be consistent with it. Three examples should make the point.

In 1971, John Rawls published his monumental work *A Theory of Justice.* In that work, Rawls intended to develop a procedure (the original position) that would provide principles for a just society. Although these principles might be implemented in different ways by different societies, Rawls seemed to think that any just society would conform to these principles. In part, Rawls held this view because he believed the original position provided a universal justification for the principles of justice the original position produced. Early critics charged that the assumptions behind the original position were individualistic, liberal, Western, and democratic. The original position was biased in favor of individualistic Western democracies; it did not provide a universal method of justification. In a 1985 article in *Philosophy and Public Affairs,* Rawls admitted that his critics were right.

In particular justice as fairness is framed to apply to what I call the basic structure of a modern constitutional democracy. . . . Whether justice as fairness can be extended to a general political conception for different kinds of societies existing under different historical and social conditions or whether it can be extended to a general moral conception . . . are altogether separate questions. I avoid prejudging these larger questions one way or the other.[4]

Another highly influential book in ethics. Alasdair MacIntyre's *After Virtue,* argued that the recent emphasis by ethicists on utilitarianism and deontology was seriously skewed. MacIntyre argued that a full moral theory must give a central place to the virtues. His own account was rich in description of the place of virtue in various societies. . . . However, MacIntyre's critics pointed out that what was considered a virtue in one society was frequently not considered a virtue in another—indeed one culture's virtue might be another culture's vice. MacIntyre now concedes that his earlier attempts to avoid these relativistic implications have largely failed.[5]

In theory, a cultural relativist could have two responses to CEOs of multinationals who wanted to know whether their personnel should behave, when in Rome, as the Romans do. Given that the morality of one culture cannot be shown to be superior to the morality of another, the personnel should follow the moral principles of the host country. Such an attitude of tolerance is the traditional response of most relativists.

But another response is possible. Even though the morality of one culture cannot objectively be shown to be superior to the morality of another, rather than embrace tolerance, once could simply assert the superiority of one's own culture. This is the approach taken by Richard Rorty, who has written extensively on the pretensions to objectivity in philosophy. In his 1984 article "Solidarity or Objectivity," he points out that the objectivist tries to create a dilemma for any subjectivist position. The dilemma is that either we attach a special privilege to our own community, or we pretend an impossible tolerance for every other group. I have been arguing that we pragmatists should grasp the ethnocentric horn of this dilemma. We should say that we must, in practice, privilege our own group, even though there can be no noncircular justification for doing so. . . . We Western liberal intellectuals should accept the fact that we have to start from where we are, and that this means that there are lots of views which we simply cannot take seriously.[6]

But how would Rorty's quotation strike the CEO of a U.S. multinational? In this case, the personnel of a multinational should *not* follow the moral principles of the host country unless they are consistent with U.S. principles. But what would this mean in terms of business practice? Given that in U.S. culture, the capitalist Friedmanite principle—maximize profits!—is the cultural norm, a U.S. multinational with a plant in South Africa would not refuse to follow the rules of apartheid or pull out. It would locate in South Africa and conform to local custom so long as it could make a profit.

Although I argued earlier that the classical view of profit maximization is seriously flawed, I did not do so from Rorty's ethnocentric position. I assumed an objective universal moral standpoint, as have those who have criticized the classical view. If Rorty's theory is correct, there is no transcultural objective perspective; because the classical view is a central principle in U.S. business and legal culture, I assume Rorty would have to accept it.

Hence, whether we are cultural relativists or ethnocentrists, some disconcerting implications seem to follow.

1. A corporation has no obligation to follow the Sullivan principles[7] in South Africa.

2. A corporation that wants to do business with the Arabs has no moral obligation to refuse participation in a boycott against Israel as a condition for doing business with the Arabs.

3. A corporation has no obligation to refrain from doing business with a state that is in systematic violation of human rights.

If these implications do follow, there seems to be something wrong with the position that entails them. Even Ronald Reagan has forbidden U.S. firms from doing business with Libya. Some set of criteria is needed for indicating when multinationals are permitted to follow the moral principles of the host country and when multinationals are forbidden to follow host-country principles. What is also needed are some principles that tell U.S. multinationals when they have an obligation to refrain from doing business either *with* a foreign (host) government or *in* a host country. However, unless cultural relativism is false, these principles will never be forthcoming.

THE ADEQUACY OF CULTURAL RELATIVISM

Although our primary concern is the obligations of multinationals, some considerations of the adequacy of cultural relativism must be made before we can speak meaningfully about the obligations of multinationals. As a starting point, I adopt a strategy used by Derek Parfit to undermine the doctrine of prudentialism.[8] Consider a continuum with three positions:

Individual Relativism	Cultural Relativism	Universalism

Individual relativism is the view that what is right or wrong, good or bad, depends on the feelings or attitudes of the individual. If an individual believes abortion is wrong, then abortion is wrong for that individual. If another individual believes abortion is not wrong, then abortion is not wrong for that individual. There is no valid cultural norm that will tell us which individual is objectively right.

The strategy is to show that any argument the cultural relativist uses against universalism can also be used by the individual relativist against cultural relativism. Similarly, any argument the cultural relativist uses against the individual relativist can be used by the universalist against the cultural relativist. As Parfit would say, the cultural relativist is constantly fighting a war on two fronts.

In this discussion, one example of this strategy will have to suffice. First, against an individual relativist, a cultural relativist would often argue that if individual relativism were the prevailing view, a stable society would be impossible. Arguments from Thomas Hobbes or decision theory would prove the point. If individual relativism were the prevailing norm, life would be "nasty, brutish, and short."

But in the present world, any arguments that appeal to social stability will have to be applied universally. In the atomic age and in an age where terrorism is an acceptable form of political activity, the stability problems that afflict individual relativism equally afflict cultural relativism. If the necessity for social stability is a good argument for a cultural relativist to use against an individual relativist, it is an equally good argument for a universalist to use against a cultural relativist.

This brief argument has not refuted relativism. It has only shown that if the stability argument works for the cultural relativist against the individual relativist, the argument also works for the universalist against the cultural relativist. Moreover, to accept the argument this far is only to show that some universal moral norms are required for stable relationships. The argument itself does not provide those universal moral norms. Multinational CEOs are likely to accept the argument thus far, however, because multinationals need a stable international environment if they are to make a profit in the long run. As any adviser for any multinational will verify, one of the chief factors affecting an investment decision in a foreign country is the political stability both of that individual country and of the region surrounding it. An unstable country or region is highly inimical to the conduct of international business.

THE MORAL MINIMUM FOR SOCIETY

Thus far we have established that multinational business requires stability and that commonly accepted moral rules are necessary for stability. But what specifically are these moral rules? To answer that question I will appeal to conceptual arguments that will assist in providing answers.

One argument that is especially effective against the charge of moral imperialism develops the point that some universal standards of conduct already have been accepted by all parties. Despite appearances to the contrary, a great deal of morality has already been internationalized either explicitly through treaty, through membership in the U.N., or implicitly through language and conduct. . . .

Note the following: The word *democracy* or *democratic* has become an honorific term. Nearly all national states claim they are democracies—people's democracies, worker democracies, but democracies nonetheless. The August 4, 1986, *Newsweek* carried a story about repression and the denial of civil rights in Chile. The president of Chile responded to his critics by calling his dictatorship a "democratic government with authority." I have yet to come across a state that brags it is not a democracy and has no intention of being one. (Some nations do indicate they do not want to be a democracy like the United States.) Hence, there is no moral imperialism involved in saying that host countries should be democracies. The controversy involves the question, What must a government be like to be properly characterized as a democracy?

A notion of shared values can be of assistance here as well. There is a whole range of behavior, such as torture, murder of the innocent, and racism, that nearly all agree is wrong. A nation-state accused of torture does not respond by saying that a condemnation of torture is just a matter of subjective morality. The state's leaders do not respond by saying, "We think torture is right, but you do not." Rather, the standard response is to deny that any torture took place. If the evidence of torture is too strong, a finger will be pointed either at the victim or at the morally outraged country. "They do it, too." In this case the guilt is spread to all. Even the Nazis denied that genocide took place. What is important is that *no* state replies there is nothing wrong with genocide or torture. Hence, the head of a multinational need have no fear of cultural imperialism when she or he takes a stand in favor of democracy and against torture and genocide.

This conceptual argument is buttressed by another. Suppose an anthropologist discovers a large populated South Pacific island. How many tribes are on the island? Part of the answer to that question will be determined by observing if such acts as killing and murder are permitted and if they are permitted, against whom are they permitted? If they are not permitted, that counts as evidence that there is only one tribe. If people on the northern half of the island permit stealing directed against southerners but do not permit northerners to steal from one another, that provides evidence that there are at least two tribes. What often distinguishes one society from another is the fact that society A does not permit murder, lying, and stealing against members of A—society A could not permit that and still be a society—but society A does permit that kind of behavior against society B. What this strategy shows is that one of the criteria for having a society is that there be a shared morality among the individuals that make up the society.

What follows from this is that there are certain basic rules that must be followed in each society—for example, do not lie; do not commit murder. There is a moral minimum in the sense that if these specific moral rules are not generally followed, then there will not be a society at all. These moral rules are universal, but they are not practiced universally. That is, members of society A agree that they should not lie to each other, but they think it is okay to lie to the members of other societies. Such moral rules are not relative; they simply are not practiced universally.

However, multinational corporations are obligated to follow these moral rules. Because the multinational is practicing business in the society and because these moral norms are necessary for the existence of the society, the multinational has an obligation to support those norms. Otherwise, multinationals would be in the position of benefiting from doing business with the society while at the same time engaging in activity that undermines the society. Such conduct would be unjust.

THE MORALITY OF THE MARKETPLACE

Given that the norms constituting a moral minimum are likely to be few in number, it can be argued that the argument thus far has achieved something—that is, multinationals are obligated to follow the moral norms required for the existence of a society. But the argument has not achieved very much—that is, most issues surrounding multinationals do not involve alleged violations of these norms. Perhaps a stronger argument can be found by making explicit the morality of the marketplace. That there is an implicit morality of the market is a point that is often ignored by most economists and many businesspersons.

Although economists and businesspersons assume that people are basically self-interested, they must also assume that persons involved in business transactions will honor their contracts. In most economic exchanges, the transfer of product for money is not simultaneous. You deliver and I pay or vice versa. As the economist Kenneth Boulding put it: "without an integrative framework, exchange itself cannot develop, because exchange, even in its most primitive forms, involves trust and credibility."[9]

Philosophers would recognize an implicit Kantianism in Boulding's remarks. Kant tried to show that a contemplated action would be immoral if a world in which the contemplated act was universally practiced was self-defeating. For example, lying and cheating would fail Kant's tests. Kant's point is implicitly recognized by the business community when corporate officials despair of the immoral practices of corporations and denounce executives engaging in shady practices as undermining the business enterprise itself.

Consider what John Rawls says about contracts:

> Such ventures are often hard to initiate and to maintain. This is especially evident in the case of covenants, that is, in those instances where one person is to perform before the other. For this person may believe that the second party will not do his part, and therefore the scheme never gets going. . . . Now in these situations there may be no way of assuring the party who is to perform first except by giving him a promise, that is, by putting oneself under an obligation to carry through later. Only in this way can the scheme be made secure so that both can gain from the benefits of their cooperation.[10]

Rawls's remarks apply to all contracts. Hence, if the moral norms of a host country permitted practices that undermined contracts, a multinational ought not to follow them. Business practice based on such norms could not pass Kant's test.

In fact, one can push Kant's analysis and contend that business practice generally requires the adoption of a minimum standard of justice. In the United States, a person who participates in business practice and engages in the practice of giving bribes or kickbacks is behaving unjustly. Why? Because the person is receiving the benefits of the rules against such activities without supporting the rules personally. This is an example of what John Rawls calls freeloading. A freeloader is one who accepts the benefits without paying any of the costs.

> In everyday life an individual, if he is so inclined, can sometimes win even greater benefits for himself by taking advantage of the cooperative efforts of others. Sufficiently many persons may be doing their share so that when special circumstances allow him not to contribute (perhaps his omission will not be found out), he gets the best of both worlds.

> . . . We cannot preserve a sense of justice and all that this implies while at the same time holding ourselves ready to act unjustly should doing so promise some personal advantage.[11]

This argument does not show that if bribery really is an accepted moral practice in country X, that moral practice is wrong. What it does show is that practices in country X that permit freeloading are wrong and if bribery can be construed as freeloading, then it is wrong. In most countries I think it can be shown that bribery is freeloading, but I shall not make that argument here.

The implications of this analysis for multinationals are broad and important. If activities that are permitted in other countries violate the morality of the marketplace—for example, undermine contracts or involve freeloading on the rules of the market—they nonetheless are morally prohibited to multinationals that operate there. Such multinationals are obligated to follow the moral norms of the market. Contrary behavior is inconsistent and ultimately self-defeating.

Our analysis here has rather startling implications. If the moral norms of a host country are in violation of the moral norms of the marketplace, then the multinational is obligated to follow the norms of the marketplace. Systematic violation of marketplace norms would be self-defeating. Moreover, whenever a multinational establishes businesses in a number of different countries, the multinational provides something approaching a universal morality—the morality of the marketplace itself. If Romans are to do business with the Japanese, then whether in Rome or Tokyo, there is a morality to which members of the business community in both Rome and Tokyo must subscribe—even if the Japanese and Romans differ on other issues of morality.

THE DEFENSE OF MARKETPLACE MORALITY

Up to this point I have argued that multinationals are obligated to follow the moral minimum and the morality of the marketplace. But what justifies the morality of the marketplace? Unless the marketplace morality can be justified, I am stuck in Rorty's ethnocentrism. I can start only where I am, and there are simply a lot of views I cannot take seriously. If a CEO of a U.S. multinational should adopt such an ethnocentric position, she or he would be accused of cultural imperialism. The claim of objectivity remains the central issue for determining the obligations of multinationals.

One possible argument is that capitalism supports democratic institutions. For example, Milton Friedman argues in *Capitalism and Freedom* that capitalism institutionally promotes political freedom.

> Economic arrangements play a dual role in the promotion of a free society. On the one hand freedom in economic arrangements . . . is an end in itself. In the second place economic freedom is also an indispensable means toward the achievement of political freedom. . . .
>
> No one who buys bread knows whether the wheat from which it is made was grown by a Communist or a Republican, by a constitutionalist or a Fascist, or for that matter by a Negro or a white. This illustrates how an impersonal market separates economic activities from political views and protects men from being discriminated against in their economic activities for reasons that are irrelevant to their productivity—whether these reasons are associated with their views or their color.[12]

Friedman also points out that freedom of speech is more meaningful so long as alternative opportunities for employment exist. However, these alternatives are impossible if the government owns and operates the means of production. In a private diversified economic community someone has a better chance to publish views that are contrary to the views of a given editor, the government, or even a majority of the public. Usually one can find some audience that is interested.

Moreover, even publishers who disagree might still publish. Fear of competition often overcomes the distaste for certain ideas.

Indeed, one of the arguments for morally permitting multinationals to operate in non-democratic countries is an extension of Friedman's point. Capitalism is allegedly a catalyst for democratic reform. If capitalism promotes democracy, then a moral argument can be made to justify capitalist investment in repressive regimes because investment will serve the moral end of making the government less repressive. This is precisely the argument that many have used to justify U.S. investment in South Africa. Indeed, the South African situation can serve as an interesting case study. The point of the Sullivan principles is to provide moral guidelines so that a company may be morally justified in having plants in South Africa without becoming part of the system of exploitation. The Sullivan principles also prevent profit-seeking corporations from morally justifying immoral behavior. No company can passively do as the South Africans do and then claim that its presence will bring about a more democratic, less racist regime. After all, if it is plausible to argue that capitalism can help create a democracy, it seems equally plausible to argue that a totalitarian regime may corrupt capitalism. The Sullivan principles help keep multinationals with South African facilities morally honest.

Moreover, the morality of the Sullivan principles depends on an empirical claim that profit-seeking corporations behaving in accordance with marketplace morality and acknowledging universally recognized human rights will in fact help transform totalitarian or repressive regimes into more democratic, more humane regimes. If that transformation does not take place within a reasonable amount of time, the moral justification for having facilities in that country disappears. Leon Sullivan recognized that point when he set May 31, 1987, as the deadline for reform of the South African government. When that reform was not forthcoming, he insisted that U.S. companies suspend operations in South Africa. . . .

What about the issue of human rights? Can multinationals ignore that question? No, they cannot. Part of what it means to be a democracy is that respect be shown for fundamental human rights. The only justification for a multinational's doing business with a regime that violates human rights is the claim that in so doing, the country's human rights record will improve. Again, business activity under that justification will have to be judged on results.

Even if the "contribution to democracy argument" is not convincing, there is another argument on behalf of the morality of the marketplace. On the assumption that a multinational business agreement is a voluntary exchange, the morality of the marketplace is voluntarily accepted. Economic prosperity seems to be highly desired by all countries. Given that multinational business is a device for achieving prosperity, participating countries voluntarily accept the morality of the market.

CONCLUSION

I have argued that on occasion multinationals have obligations that would require them *not* to do in Rome as the Romans do—for example, in those cases where Roman practice is in violation of marketplace morality. I have also provided arguments on behalf of marketplace morality, although those arguments require that businesses have obligations to pull out of oppressive countries if there is little hope of reform.

But the appeal to the morality of the marketplace has an added benefit. What often is forgotten by business is that the market is not a morally neutral, well-oiled machine; rather, it is embedded in morality and depends upon the acceptance of morality for its success. Ultimately, the obligations of multinationals, whether in Rome, Tokyo, or Washington, are the obligations required by the market. If corporations live up to those obligations, and if capitalism really could advance the cause of democracy and human rights throughout the world, then the morally responsible multinational could be a force for social justice.

However, I regret to say that I am discussing a goal and a hope rather than a reality.

Notes

I wish to thank Steven Luper-Foy for his helpful comments on an earlier version of this essay.

1. See "There's No Love Lost Between Multinational Companies and the Third World," *Business and Society Review* (Autumn 1974).
2. For the purpose of this discussion, a stakeholder is a member of a group without whose support the organization would cease to exist. The traditional list of stakeholders includes stockholders, employees, customers, suppliers, lenders, and the local community where plants or facilities are located.
3. Of course, one large U.S. company with 10 plants in 10 different states has more classes of stakeholders than 1 U.S. company with 1 U.S. plant and 1 foreign subsidiary.
4. John Rawls, "Justice as Fairness: Political Not Metaphysical," *Philosophy and Public Affairs* 14, no. 3 (Summer 1985):224–226. Also see John Rawls, *A Theory of Justice* (Cambridge, Mass.: Harvard University Press, 1971).
5. The most explicit charge of relativism is made by Robert Wachbroit, "A Genealogy of Virtues," *Yale Law Journal* 92, no. 3 (January 1983): 476–564. For Alasdair MacIntyre's discussion, see "Postscript to the Second Edition" in *After Virtue*, 2nd ed. (Notre Dame: University of Notre Dame, 1984) and his Eastern Division American Philosophical Association Presidential Address, "Relativism, Power and Philosophy" in *Proceedings and Addresses of the American Philosophical Association* 59, no. 1 (September 1985):5–22. Also see Michael Walzer, *Spheres of Justice* (New York: Basic Books, 1983).
6. Richard Rorty, "Solidarity or Objectivity," in *Post-Analytic Philosophy*, John Rajchman and Cornel West, eds. (New York: Columbia University Press, 1985), pp. 12–13.
7. The Sullivan code affirms the following principles: (1) that there be nonsegregation of the races in all eating, comfort, and work facilities; (2) that equal and fair employment practices be instituted for all employees; (3) that all employees doing equal or comparable work for the same period of time receive equal pay; (4) that training programs be developed and implemented that will prepare substantial numbers of blacks and other nonwhites for supervisory, administrative, technical, and clerical jobs; (5) that the number of blacks and other nonwhites in management and supervisory positions be increased; and (6) that the quality of employees' lives outside the work environment be improved—this includes housing, transportation, schooling, recreation, and health facilities.

8. See Derek Parfit, *Reasons and Persons* (New York: Oxford University Press, 1986), pp. 126–127.

9. Kenneth E. Boulding, "The Basis of Value Judgments in Economics," in *Human Values and Economic Policy,* Sidney Hook, ed. (New York: New York University Press, 1967), p. 68.

10. John Rawls, *A Theory of Justice* (Cambridge, Mass.: Harvard University Press, 1971), p. 569.

11. *Ibid.,* p. 497.

12. Milton Friedman, *Capitalism and Freedom* (Chicago: University of Chicago Press, 1962), pp. 8, 21.

Study Questions

1. Bowie argues that the *general* ethical obligations of domestic and international business are the same. Is this consistent with De George's and Werhane's view on this topic?

2. How does Bowie connect the growth of international economic standards with ethical principles such as fairness and ethical rules such as truthtelling?

3. How do Bowie's arguments fit with the data as Frederick (Chapter 7) sees it?

4. Does Bowie's article rely on ethics, economics, and law being integrated in an institutional framework?

Index